South-West France

Julia Wilkinson
John

LONELY PLANET PUBLICATIONS
Melbourne • Oakland • London • Paris

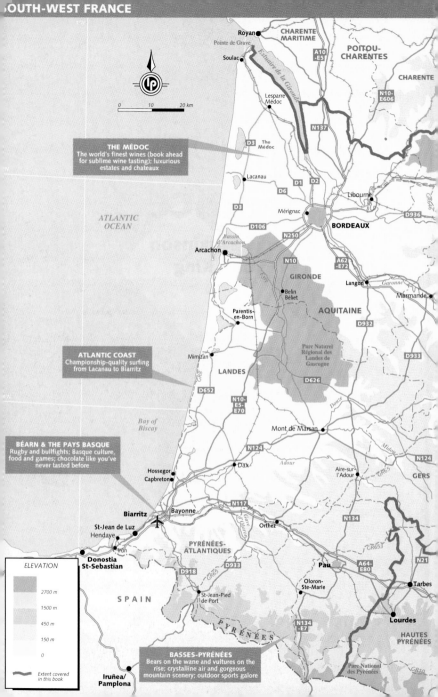

SOUTH-WEST FRANCE

THE MÉDOC
The world's finest wines (book ahead for sublime wine tasting); luxurious estates and chateaux

ATLANTIC COAST
Championship-quality surfing from Lacanau to Biarritz

BÉARN & THE PAYS BASQUE
Rugby and bullfights; Basque culture, food and games; chocolate like you've never tasted before

BASSES-PYRÉNÉES
Bears on the wane and vultures on the rise; crystalline air and gorgeous mountain scenery; outdoor sports galore

ATLANTIC OCEAN

Bay of Biscay

SPAIN

PYRÉNÉES

ELEVATION

	2700 m
	1500 m
	450 m
	150 m
	0

Extent covered in this book

0   10   20 km

CHARENTE MARITIME
POITOU-CHARENTES
CHARENTE

Royan
Pointe de Grave
Soulac
Estuaire de la Gironde
Lesparre-Médoc

The Médoc
Lacanau
Mérignac
BORDEAUX
Libourne
Langon
Marmande

GIRONDE
AQUITAINE

Arcachon
Bassin d'Arcachon
Belin-Béliet
Parentis-en-Born
Mimizan
LANDES
Pare Naturel Régional des Landes de Gascogne

Mont de Marsan
Aire-sur-l'Adour
GERS
Dax
Adour

Hossegor
Capbreton
Biarritz
Bayonne
St-Jean de Luz
Hendaye
Irún
Orthez
Pau
Oloron-Ste-Marie
Donostia St-Sebastian
PYRÉNÉES-ATLANTIQUES
St-Jean-Pied-de-Port
Tarbes
Lourdes
HAUTES-PYRÉNÉES
Pare National des Pyrénées

Iruñea/Pamplona

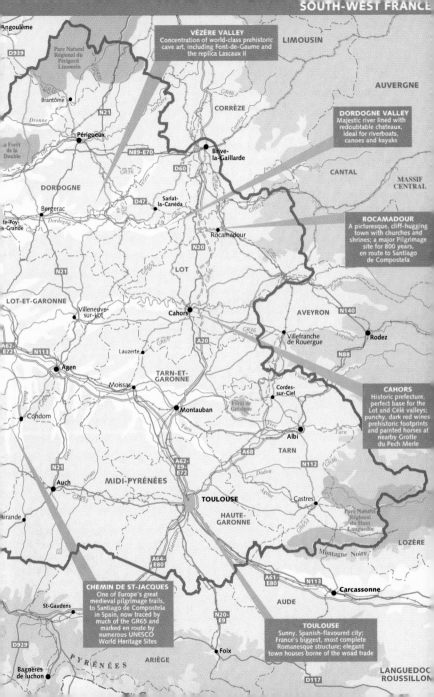

South-West France
1st edition – April 2000

Published by
Lonely Planet Publications Pty Ltd A.C.N. 005 607 983
192 Burwood Rd, Hawthorn, Victoria 3122, Australia

Lonely Planet Offices
Australia PO Box 617, Hawthorn, Victoria 3122
USA 150 Linden St, Oakland, CA 94607
UK 10a Spring Place, London NW5 3BH
France 1 rue du Dahomey, 75011 Paris

Photographs
All of the images in this guide are available for licensing from
Lonely Planet Images.
email: lpi@lonelyplanet.com.au

Front cover photograph
Terraced vineyards, Grilly Bernard (Tony Stone Images)

ISBN 0 86442 794 8

**Although the authors
and Lonely Planet try
to make the informa-
tion as accurate as
possible, we accept
no responsibility for
any loss, injury or
inconvenience sus-
tained by anyone
using this book.**

Contents – Text

Contents – Maps

MAP LEGEND – SEE BACK PAGE

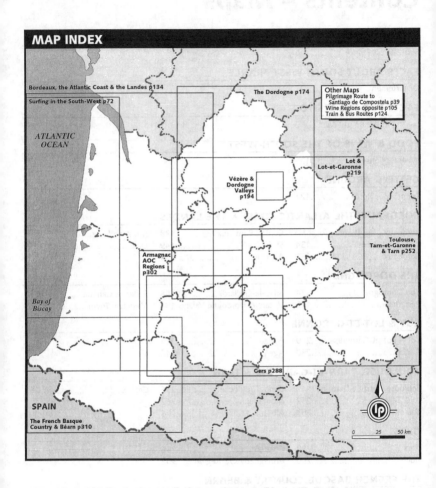

MAP INDEX

Bordeaux, the Atlantic Coast & the Landes p134

Surfing in the South-West p72

The Dordogne p174

Other Maps
Pilgrimage Route to
   Santiago de Compostela p39
Wine Regions opposite p105
Train & Bus Routes p124

ATLANTIC
OCEAN

Vézère &
Dordogne
Valleys
p194

Lot &
Lot-et-Garonne
p219

Toulouse,
Tarn-et-Garonne
& Tarn p252

Armagnac
AOC
Regions
p302

Bay of
Biscay

Gers p288

SPAIN

The French Basque
Country & Béarn p310

0   25   50 km

The Authors

Julia Wilkinson

Julia was first introduced to South-West France over 30 years ago, when her parents invested their hearts and savings in a tiny cottage in Périgord Noir. She has since been back almost every year (apart from the time she spent in Hong Kong as a freelance travel writer and photographer), more recently with husband John. While the cottage has seen some changes (no more sleeping on the floor or washing from a bucket), much about the place remains the same: the slow rural lifestyle, the gargantuan Périgordian meals at friends' houses and the meadows where she once ran wild and where her own two children now play. After long spells on the road – authoring Lonely Planet's *Lisbon*, co-authoring *Portugal* and contributing to *Western Europe* and *Mediterranean Europe*, among other things – there is always the reward of a return to this magical corner of South-West France.

John King

John grew up in the USA, and in earlier 'incarnations' has been a university physics teacher and an environmental consultant. In a rash moment in 1984 he headed off to China, where he ended up living for half a year. He and Julia met in Lhasa, and after surviving a three-month journey across China and Pakistan they decided anything was possible. John took up travel writing with the 1st edition of Lonely Planet's *Karakoram Highway*. He is also co-author of Lonely Planet's *Russia, Ukraine & Belarus*, *Pakistan*, *Central Asia*, *Czech & Slovak Republics*, *Prague* and – with Julia – *Portugal* and co-contributor to *Western Europe* and *Mediterranean Europe*.

From the Authors

We owe a great deal to the authors and updaters of Lonely Planet's *France* whose text in many areas forms the basis of this book. We are also indebted to staff at Lonely Planet's London office – especially Paul Bloomfield, Claire Hornshaw and Sara Yorke – for their extreme patience and formidably sharp eyes.

Julia would like to thank Gillian Green at the London office of Maison de la France, the French tourism organisation; Cécile Lambert of the Comité Régional du Tourisme d'Aquitaine; Martine Bouchet of the Comité Départemental du Tourisme du Lot; Annie Bersars of the Sarlat Office de Tourisme; and William Ballue of the Agence de Développement Économique de Bordeaux et de la Gironde.

For patience and extraordinary help, John especially thanks Catherine Tierce (Toulouse Office de Tourisme), Patricia Henrion-Hyde (Comité Départemental du Tourisme du Tarn), Christiane Bonnat (Agence de Tourisme du Pays Basque) and Marilys Caza-ubieilh (Comité Départemental du Tourisme des Landes). Other tourism officials who made a big difference are Christian Rivière (Albi), Hélène Barrere and Christelle Chirumberro (Bayonne), Christian Mercurol (Béarn), Pierre Tuchi and staff (Pau) and Marie-Hélène Hugon (Gers).

Thanks to Bruno Julia of Surf Trip and Antony Colas of YEP for generous help on the subject of surfing, and to Alain Bonhomme for his Toulouse tips. Charles Gerbet (Parc National des Pyrénées) introduced us to his brainchild, the Falaise au Vautours reserve, and Anne Fournier (Montauban Bureau d'Information Jeunesse) told us how to talk French to computers.

Peter Mills and Charles Page at Rail Europe, and Paul Gowen at the RAC, gave their usual excellent assistance. For patient help with airfares we thank Lonely Planet's Imogen Franks (London), Caroline Guilleminot (Paris) and Leonie Mugavin (Melbourne).

Dedication

We'd like to dedicate this book to our parents/parents-in-law, Darrell and Jo Wilkinson, who first gave us the chance to fall in love with Périgord Noir; and to our long-time friends in the village near our family cottage, who continue to make this corner of France a special place.

This Book

This book grew out of the relevant chapters of Lonely Planet's *France* guide. *South-West France* was researched and written by John King and Julia Wilkinson.

From the Publisher

This 1st edition of *South-West France* was edited and proofed in Lonely Planet's London office by Claire Hornshaw, with invaluable help from Anna Jacomb-Hood; Sam Trafford helped with the indexing. Claudia Martin helped to check the maps and assisted with last-minute layout corrections, as did Christine Stroyan. Sara Yorke coordinated the design and cartography, assisted by Adam McCrow and Ed Pickard. Sara designed the cover and Jim Miller created the back-cover map. Illustrations were drawn by Nicky Caven, Lisa Borg and Martin Harris, and Lonely Planet Images provided the photographs. Quentin Frayne compiled the Language chapter. Many thanks to John and Julia for their patience and quick responses during the course of this project.

Foreword

ABOUT LONELY PLANET GUIDEBOOKS

The story begins with a classic travel adventure: Tony and Maureen Wheeler's 1972 journey across Europe and Asia to Australia. Useful information about the overland trail did not exist at that time, so Tony and Maureen published the first Lonely Planet guidebook to meet a growing need.

From a kitchen table, then from a tiny office in Melbourne (Australia), Lonely Planet has become the largest independent travel publisher in the world, an international company with offices in Melbourne, Oakland (USA), London (UK) and Paris (France).

Today Lonely Planet guidebooks cover the globe. There is an ever-growing list of books and there's information in a variety of forms and media. Some things haven't changed. The main aim is still to help make it possible for adventurous travellers to get out there – to explore and better understand the world.

At Lonely Planet we believe travellers can make a positive contribution to the countries they visit – if they respect their host communities and spend their money wisely. Since 1986 a percentage of the income from each book has been donated to aid projects and human rights campaigns.

Updates Lonely Planet thoroughly updates each guidebook as often as possible. This usually means there are around two years between editions, although for more unusual or more stable destinations the gap can be longer. Check the imprint page (following the colour map at the beginning of the book) for publication dates.

Between editions up-to-date information is available in two free newsletters – the paper *Planet Talk* and email *Comet* (to subscribe, contact any Lonely Planet office) – and on our Web site at www.lonelyplanet.com. The *Upgrades* section of the Web site covers a number of important and volatile destinations and is regularly updated by Lonely Planet authors. *Scoop* covers news and current affairs relevant to travellers. And, lastly, the *Thorn Tree* bulletin board and *Postcards* section of the site carry unverified, but fascinating, reports from travellers.

Correspondence The process of creating new editions begins with the letters, postcards and emails received from travellers. This correspondence often includes suggestions, criticisms and comments about the current editions. Interesting excerpts are immediately passed on via newsletters and the Web site, and everything goes to our authors to be verified when they're researching on the road. We're keen to get more feedback from organisations or individuals who represent communities visited by travellers.

> Lonely Planet gathers information for everyone who's curious about the planet – and especially for those who explore it first-hand. Through guidebooks, phrasebooks, activity guides, maps, literature, newsletters, image library, TV series and Web site we act as an information exchange for a worldwide community of travellers.

Research Authors aim to gather sufficient practical information to enable travellers to make informed choices and to make the mechanics of a journey run smoothly. They also research historical and cultural background to help enrich the travel experience and allow travellers to understand and respond appropriately to cultural and environmental issues.

Authors don't stay in every hotel because that would mean spending a couple of months in each medium-sized city and, no, they don't eat at every restaurant because that would mean stretching belts beyond capacity. They do visit hotels and restaurants to check standards and prices, but feedback based on readers' direct experiences can be very helpful.

Many of our authors work undercover, others aren't so secretive. None of them accept freebies in exchange for positive write-ups. And none of our guidebooks contain any advertising.

Production Authors submit their raw manuscripts and maps to offices in Australia, USA, UK or France. Editors and cartographers – all experienced travellers themselves – then begin the process of assembling the pieces. When the book finally hits the shops some things are already out of date, we start getting feedback from readers, and the process begins again ...

WARNING & REQUEST

Things change – prices go up, schedules change, good places go bad and bad places go bankrupt – nothing stays the same. So, if you find things better or worse, recently opened or long since closed, please tell us and help make the next edition even more accurate and useful. We genuinely value all the feedback we receive. Julie Young coordinates a well-travelled team that reads and acknowledges every letter, postcard and email and ensures that every morsel of information finds its way to the appropriate authors, editors and cartographers for verification.

Everyone who writes to us will find their name in the next edition of the appropriate guidebook. They will also receive the latest issue of *Planet Talk*, our quarterly printed newsletter, or *Comet*, our monthly email newsletter. Subscriptions to both newsletters are free. The very best contributions will be rewarded with a free guidebook.

Excerpts from your correspondence may appear in new editions of Lonely Planet guidebooks, the Lonely Planet Web site, *Planet Talk* or *Comet*, so please let us know if you *don't* want your letter published or your name acknowledged.

Send all correspondence to the Lonely Planet office closest to you:

Australia: PO Box 617, Hawthorn, Victoria 3122
UK: 10A Spring Place, London NW5 3BH
USA: 150 Linden St, Oakland CA 94607
France: 1 rue du Dahomey, Paris 75011

Or email us at: talk2us@lonelyplanet.com.au

For news, views and updates see our Web site: www.lonelyplanet.com

HOW TO USE A LONELY PLANET GUIDEBOOK

The best way to use a Lonely Planet guidebook is any way you choose. At Lonely Planet we believe the most memorable travel experiences are often those that are unexpected, and the finest discoveries are those you make yourself. Guidebooks are not intended to be used as if they provide a detailed set of infallible instructions!

Contents All Lonely Planet guidebooks follow roughly the same format. The Facts about the Destination chapter or section gives background information ranging from history to weather. Facts for the Visitor gives practical information on issues like visas and health. Getting There & Away gives a brief starting point for re-searching travel to and from the destination. Getting Around gives an overview of the transport options when you arrive.

The peculiar demands of each destination determine how sub-sequent chapters are broken up, but some things remain constant. We always start with background, then proceed to sights, places to stay, places to eat, entertainment, getting there and away, and getting around information – in that order.

Heading Hierarchy Lonely Planet headings are used in a strict hierarchical structure that can be visualised as a set of Russian dolls. Each heading (and its following text) is encompassed by any preceding heading that is higher on the hierarchical ladder.

Entry Points We do not assume guidebooks will be read from beginning to end, but that people will dip into them. The trad-itional entry points are the list of contents and the index. In addition, however, some books have a complete list of maps and an index map illustrating map coverage.

There may also be a colour map that shows highlights. These highlights are dealt with in greater detail in the Facts for the Visitor chapter, along with planning questions and suggested itin-eraries. Each chapter covering a geographical region usually begins with a locator map and another list of highlights. Once you find something of interest in a list of highlights, turn to the index.

Maps Maps play a crucial role in Lonely Planet guidebooks and include a huge amount of information. A legend is printed on the back page. We seek to have complete consistency between maps and text, and to have every important place in the text captured on a map. Map key numbers usually start in the top left corner.

Although inclusion in a guidebook usually implies a recommen-dation we cannot list every good place. Exclusion does not necessarily imply criticism. In fact there are a number of reasons why we might exclude a place – sometimes it is simply inappropriate to encourage an influx of travellers.

Introduction

Imagine you were heading to South-West France for a holiday 700 years ago. Bad timing: you would have been in the thick of the Hundred Years' War between England and France, one of Europe's longest-running wars over control of the rich lands of Aquitaine (and other areas in the north). Castles and chateaux changed hands almost daily and revolutionary new *bastides* (fortified towns) were being built everywhere. Even if you had delayed your visit by a couple of centuries, you would have found warfare, this time between Catholics and Protestants, resulting in widespread destruction. But go back a few millennia – 15,000 years or so – and you would step into one of the world's finest art galleries: caves decorated with fantastic carvings and paintings of bison, mammoth and deer.

It's prehistoric cave art like this which has given South-West France much of its fame. But the legacy of those turbulent medieval days – the restored chateaux and bastides – makes an impressive backdrop to what has become one of the most tranquil and unspoilt corners of France. For since the 16th century, nothing much has matched the drama of those days. Indeed, time now moves so slowly that pre-Revolutionary place names are still preferred to the modern départemental ones – Périgord instead of Dordogne, Gascony for the Gers, Pays Basque and Béarn rather than Pyrénées-Atlantiques. The medieval *langue d'oc* (Occitan) language is spoken alongside French in many places. Modern-day Gascons still live off the reputations of their swashbuckling ancestors. Rural parts of the French Basque country

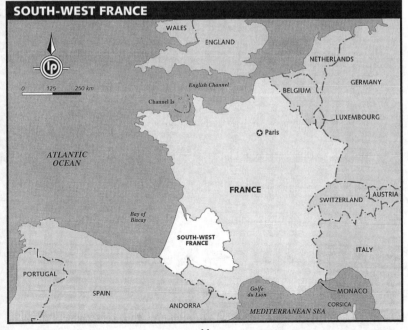

SOUTH-WEST FRANCE

WALES
ENGLAND
NETHERLANDS
GERMANY
English Channel
BELGIUM
Channel Is
LUXEMBOURG
○ Paris
0   125   250 km
ATLANTIC
OCEAN
FRANCE
AUSTRIA
SWITZERLAND
Bay of
Biscay
SOUTH-WEST
FRANCE
ITALY
PORTUGAL
SPAIN
Golfe
du Lion
MONACO
ANDORRA
CORSICA
MEDITERRANEAN SEA

and Béarn still look (and the locals still live) as they must have centuries ago.

This slow touch of time has given the people of the south-west a chance to relish life, particularly when it comes to food. In this gourmand heartland, the cuisine is both rich (no more so than *foie gras* and *confit d'oie*) and simple, distinguished by truffles, cep mushrooms, nuts and fruit. The quality wines of the Bordeaux region are the world's finest and hundreds of other vineyards produce top-class vintages. You're unlikely to move very far or fast on this kind of culinary trail.

Public transport helps you adjust to the pace, with limited services to remote areas. You're better off on foot, bike (the Lot département alone has some 3000km of signposted paths), or canoe. Many trails follow the pilgrimage routes to Spain's Santiago de Compostela, from whose 13th-century heyday have come dozens of ecclesiastical monuments (33 in South-West France are now UNESCO World Heritage Sites). The Atlantic coast offers different distractions: 250km of sandy beaches and world-class surfing. Or you can drift down the region's waterways in a houseboat.

Of course it's not all rural calm; Bordeaux and Toulouse are the region's largest, liveliest cities, high-tech industrial and aeronautical centres. But the soul of South-West France is rooted in the countryside – where the calendar is marked by truffle and foie gras markets, the gathering of grapes, tobacco or maize, or simply the chance to share some home-made eau de vie. It's a lifestyle that epitomises *la France profonde*. The tranquillity masks the sad reality of depopulation, with many villages struggling to survive. But tourism is bringing new revenues and, provided it doesn't abuse the hospitality on offer, may help keep this richly endowed corner of France on its slow, special way for many more centuries yet.

Facts about South-West France

HISTORY
Early Inhabitants

In no other region of the world is there such rich evidence of early human habitation and artistic skill as in South-West France. The best known artefacts are the cave paintings of Lascaux (near Montignac), created some 16,000 years ago, but Lower Palaeolithic (Old Stone Age) *Homo erectus* was probably hunting in the western Pyrénées some 450,000 years ago.

The Neanderthals of the Middle Palaeolithic period took the stage 150,000 years ago, only to disappear without a trace 35,000 years ago. Though thuggish in appearance – short and stocky with jutting jawbones and elongated heads – they were cleverer than *Homo erectus*, producing sophisticated tools and often burying their dead with special rituals. Their so-called Mousterian culture got its name from a site at Le Moustier in Périgord where a skeleton and flint implements were found in 1909.

But the real talent belonged to the *Homo sapiens sapiens* Cro-Magnon people, similar to us in appearance – tall and upright with long limbs and nimble hands – who flourished from the Upper Palaeolithic to the Neolithic (New Stone Age) periods, roughly 35,000 to 6000 years ago. They employed their hunting skills to kill reindeer, bison, horse and mammoth, and their artistic skills to produce some of the world's finest cave art, in the area around the Cro-Magnon cave shelter, near Les Eyzies de Tayac in Périgord, where three skeletons were found in 1868.

So prolific were the Cro-Magnons that several distinct subcultures have been defined. The early Périgordian and Aurignacian cultures – the latter named after Aurignac in the Haute-Garonne, where early discoveries were made – produced bone and horn tools, stone implements and wooden spears, as well as shell and bead necklaces. Most exciting: the first-known cave decorations: tiny, fleshy female figurines (most notably the so-called *Vénus à la Corne*, 'Venus with a Horn'), tracings in black or red of their own hands (as at Le Pech Merle in the Lot) and rudimentary animal sketches. Though Périgord has the lion's share of these sites, other works have been found in the Landes, the Gers and the Pyrénées.

The people of the Cro-Magnon Solutrean culture (from about 20,000 to 15,000 BC, named after the village in Central France where the early finds were made), well represented in the Dordogne, focussed more on tools than art, producing slim flint blades, stone and wood weapons, and the world's first sewing needles, complete with eyes.

This was a period of intense cold – the end of the last Ice Age – and the Cro-Magnons increasingly retreated to caves and rock shelters, plentiful in Périgord's Vézère Valley. Here, during the period of the so-called Magdalenian Culture (named after discoveries at La Madeleine near Les Eyzies de Tayac), roughly 15,000 to 9000 BC, they produced their finest art, crafting superb bone-and-ivory implements, and carving, engraving or painting increasingly realistic animal and hunting scenes. In addition to the superb friezes at Lascaux there are other startling creations in caves around Les Eyzies de Tayac and throughout the Pyrénées. See the boxed text 'The Painted Caves of the South-West' under Painting in Arts later in this chapter for more details of these extraordinary cave paintings. For more on Lascaux itself, see the Dordogne chapter.

The Cro-Magnons also enjoyed music and dance, performed fertility rituals and other ceremonies, and had fairly complex social patterns. However, with the climatic warming that forced reindeer herds northwards in search of lichen, the nomadic Cro-Magnon hunter-artists drifted after them and the area's cave art came to an end.

After the undistinguished Mesolithic

(Middle Stone Age) period came the Neolithic period, about 6000 to 3000 years ago. The warming climate saw the rise of farming (crops included wheat, barley, peas, beans and lentils), stock rearing and trading, and a more sedentary life. The most notable development in style was the appearance of decorated earthenware pottery. Most intriguing was the construction of megaliths – dolmens, tumuli, menhirs and stone circles – which still dot the area, especially the Lot, the Dordogne and the western Pyrénées. This was Europe's first real civilisation, with a sophisticated culture (including evidence of extraordinary astronomical knowledge) and a well-organised, probably matriarchal, society.

Another leap came with the metalworking cultures. By 2500 BC, descendants of Indo-European tribes from the Aegean were making copper tools and weapons on both sides of the Alps, with the Artenac people establishing a foothold around Bordeaux. Waves of newcomers included a tribe the Romans called the Aquitanii, who appeared around the 7th century BC. More significant were the Celts.

Celts & Romans

The Celts spread across modern-day France (known in Roman times as Gaul) and by 600 BC were trading with the Greeks along Neolithic trade routes; one of these, among Europe's oldest trading roads, ran from the Atlantic to the Mediterranean via Pau near the Spanish border. Settlements were generally either hilltop fortifications or larger *oppida* (defensive towns) with political, economic and religious functions. The Celts (or Gauls, as they came to be called) were known for their metalwork, and archaeological evidence from the Gironde area suggests there was a thriving handicraft industry producing everything from knives and axes to bracelets and bridle-bits.

It wasn't long before the Gauls came into conflict with the Romans who, by the 2nd century BC, had put their military toe in at Tolosa (Toulouse) and begun edging northwards. In 56 BC Burdigala (Bordeaux) was captured by Julius Caesar's colleague Crassus. Four years later the Gauls, under Vercingétorix, were finally defeated by Caesar himself at a still-disputed location in the Lot or Périgord. Many Gauls, such as the Vascone tribe, fled across the Pyrénées where they continued to put up stiff military and cultural resistance – just as their successors, the Basques, do today.

In AD 16 the Romans created the new province of Aquitania, spanning almost the entire south-west from the Loire River to the Pyrénées. Roman *nouveaux riches* took their pick of the land, introducing new crops such as walnuts, chestnuts and wine grapes. They built spa resorts (for example at Dax) and lavish villas such as the one excavated at Séviac in the Gers. Flourishing centres included Tolosa, Burdigala, Vesunna (Périgueux) and Divona Cadurcorum (Cahors). Early in the 4th century AD, Christianity arrived.

These deceptively prosperous times (the heavily-taxed poor, no better than slaves, just got poorer) came to an end soon afterwards. Germanic tribes, the Franks and the Alemanni, were already sweeping in from the east and by the early 5th century the more powerful Vandals and Visigoths arrived, snapping the already-weakened Roman rule. In 507 the Franks got the upper hand, chasing the Visigoths into Spain (where they chased many hapless Vascones back across the Pyrénées: Gascony is thought to derive from their name).

The Merovingians & Carolingians

The Christianised Franks adopted important elements of Gallo-Roman civilisation but lacked the Romans' authoritarian skills: the old land owning and religious elites gradually tightened their grip. Cahors, especially, flourished during this time thanks to its influential bishops.

At the turn of the 7th century, the Frankish Merovingian dynasty founded duchies of Aquitaine and the Vascones (Gascony), to keep a lid on this poor and potentially rebellious area. However, the Moors proved more of a problem, sweeping across the Pyrénées and seizing Bordeaux in the early

Take That, Roland

The earliest surviving work of French literature, the 11th-century *Chanson de Roland* (Song of Roland), is an epic ballad recounting the death of the larger-than-life knight, ambushed in the Pyrénées in 778 on the way back from his uncle Charlemagne's campaign against the Moors in Spain. Numerous local legends mirror this tale and the Pyrénées abound in natural landmarks said to have been made by Roland's sword Durandal, his foot, or whatever. Little real historical information is available on the man but what there is suggests that the ambush was laid by angry Basques. The ballad's substitution of Muslims as the villains may have been simply a battle cry for the Crusades, which kicked off at about the same time.

700s. Charles Martel (a member of the powerful Frankish Pepin family who increasingly took control from the Merovingian dynasty through their position as mayors of the palace) headed off Muslim rule of France by defeating the Moors at Poitiers in 732. Martel and his descendants (the Carolingian dynasty) brought the rebellious duchies into line. His ambitious grandson, Charlemagne, considerably expanded the boundaries of the Frankish empire and mollified the Duchy of Aquitaine by giving it the title of kingdom.

In the 9th century ferocious Vikings (also called Norsemen or Normans) began raiding the western coast, sacking Bordeaux in 848 and Bayonne in 862, and penetrating inland as far as Toulouse. By the time they were pushed back to what is now Normandy in 982, the south-west was fragmenting into independent feudal states. The Vascones south of the Pyrénées had already founded their own little kingdom of Navarre, and in the 10th century the baronies of Périgord (Mareuil, Bourdeilles, Beynac and Biron) were established. As the millennium dawned, the feudal states had spawned a patchwork of prosperous towns.

The Middle Ages

The most notable development at the start of the Middle Ages was the appearance of *bastides*, fortified new towns built by rich feudal lords anxious to protect their fiefdoms (see the boxed text 'Bastides' under Architecture in Arts later in this chapter). The increasingly powerful Church also began to express its power in mortar and stone: fabulous churches and abbeys in Romanesque style appeared all over the region, often funded by the Cistercian order or by local lords – especially the powerful counts of Toulouse and dukes of Aquitaine. By the 12th century, abbeys such as those at Chancelade and Cadouin (Dordogne) were among Europe's greatest.

In a parallel artistic vein, the region's many post-Roman dialects – collectively known as *Langue d'Oc* (the term refers to the area south of the Loire River also known as Occitan) – appeared for the first time in poetry, notably troubadour poetry (for more information see Literature under Arts later in this chapter), serving as a cultural and political focus for the so-called Occitan people.

It was the granddaughter of one of the finest troubadour poets (Guillaume IX, duke of Aquitaine) who was to turn the region on its historical head. As the sole heir to Aquitaine's vast lands and wealth, the beautiful and strong-willed Eleanor of was hot property on the royal marriage market, good enough for the king of France himself. But 15 years of marriage to the lacklustre Louis VII ended in annulment in 1152 and with hardly a fare-thee-well Eleanor married Henry Plantagenet, count of Anjou.

When Henry became king of England, Eleanor's dowry of Aquitaine and Gascony – a third of France – fell under English rule. The sting in the arrangement was that Henry, as duke of Aquitaine (or Guyenne as it was called by the English) had to pay homage to the king of France. The subsequent rivalry between France and England for control of Aquitaine and the vast English territories elsewhere in France (including Anjou, Lorraine and Normandy) would last for three centuries.

England vs France

The petty battles to consolidate English rule, often instigated by Eleanor's son, Richard the Lion-Heart (see the boxed text), were background noise to an otherwise orderly, well-liked English administration.

But in the 13th century the Albigensian Crusade (see the boxed text in the Albi section of the Toulouse chapter) was launched to subjugate the wealthy and independent-minded counts of Toulouse on the pretext of evicting Cathar heretics from Toulouse, Albi and the Languedoc. Simon de Montfort led a famously cruel campaign against Count Raymond VI of Toulouse (see the boxed text 'Simon de Montfort'), leading to Raymond's surrender in 1229.

French power was now uncomfortably close to the Plantagenet English rulers in Aquitaine, and the two sparred with increasing ferocity. In 1337 outright war – the start of what came to be called the Hundred Years' War – became inevitable when Philippe VI ordered the confiscation of Aquitaine on the pretext that Edward III had defaulted in his feudal service. Battles soon raged, with bastides and castles changing sides from one year to the next.

At first the English had the upper hand, winning at Crécy in 1346 and at Poitiers in

Richard the Lion-Heart

Richard Coeur de Lion is one of Aquitaine's most colourful historical characters. He was regarded as a hero as a result of his prowess in the Third Crusade (twice leading his forces to within a few miles of Jerusalem), as well as being a talented troubadour, and was probably gay. He was also an unreconstructed cad, with 'little or no filial piety, foresight, or sense of responsibility', as one historian put it.

Born in 1157 to Henry II and Eleanor of Aquitaine, he was given the duchy of Aquitaine when he was 11 and officially crowned duke four years later. At 16 he joined forces with his equally unfilial brothers (and his mother) in a revolt against his father. He later submitted, turning his attention instead to bullying the barons of Aquitaine. So obnoxious was his money-grabbing harassment that in 1183 the whole region rose up against him, enlisting the help of Richard's older brother Henry, the 'Young King'. To put a stop to the conflict, Henry II himself came to Richard's defence, though the Young King's sudden death ended the fighting.

It wasn't the end of father versus son: Richard was now heir to the English throne (and to all England's French possessions). Refusing his father's request to give Aquitaine to his younger brother, he sought the support of the young Philippe II of France and in 1189 joined forces with him to defeat Henry once and for all. The elderly, weakened king died later that year and Richard inherited the English throne.

Obsessed with recapturing Jerusalem, he plundered his late father's treasury and set sail to lead the Third Crusade. His military exploits, his quarrels with French, German and English crusaders and his subsequent captivity on his way home were the stuff of legend.

Greed and arrogance did him in at the age of 42. Back in France in 1199 (he spent only six months of his 'reign' in England and reputedly couldn't even speak English), he learned of a hoard of treasure hidden by the viscount of Limoges in his castle at Châlus. Richard besieged the castle and during the fighting his armour was pierced by an arrow from a new type of long-range cross-bow.

He was, ironically, buried beside his parents in the abbey of Fontevrault. Or rather, his body was buried there; his entrails were interred in Châlus and his heart in Rouen. As for the archer who killed him, he was flayed alive.

Simon de Montfort

The name of the Englishman Simon de Montfort heads the roll call of ruthless fighters in the medieval south-west. After earning his stripes in overseas crusades, he was asked in 1209 to lead a domestic one against the Cathars or Albigenses (see the boxed text 'The Albigensian Crusade' in the Albi section of the Toulouse chapter) and, while he was at it, to bring low the counts of Toulouse. Within a short time he had taken Béziers and Carcassonne, earning a reputation for merciless sieges and slaughters.

Raymond VI, count of Toulouse, called for help from his brother-in-law, King Pedro of Aragon, but was defeated by Montfort at Muret, near Toulouse, in 1213. In 1215 the Church declared that Raymond's lands should go to Montfort, who began styling himself count of Toulouse. Two years later Raymond's son instigated an uprising in Provence and, while Montfort was away, Raymond VI retook Toulouse. In besieging the city, Montfort was killed by a rock – lobbed, it's said, by a local woman.

NICKY CAVEN

Simon de Montfort was a major player in the Albigensian Crusade

The sons of Raymond and Montfort continued the struggle for another 16 years before the younger Montfort ceded his claim to the southern lands to Louis VIII, who then embarked on a more blatant 'crusade'. In 1229, Raymond VII finally surrendered.

1356 – the latter under the infamous Black Prince, Edward III's eldest son, who heaped insult on injury by capturing the French king, Jean II. As part of Jean's ransom, Aquitaine was officially ceded to the English crown in 1360. After some confused negotiations, the Black Prince installed himself as Aquitaine's new duke.

In 1370 France wrested back control of Aquitaine and a series of truces began. But the 15th century dawned with a new round of claims from the English. In 1415 Henry V defeated the French at Agincourt and five years later was recognised as king of France.

It took the legendary Joan of Arc (Jeanne d'Arc) to rally the French behind Charles VII: by 1450 Bergerac had fallen to the French, followed by the rest of Aquitaine and Bordeaux itself in 1451. The final battle of the Hundred Years' War was fought at Castillon-la-Bataille (near St-Émilion) two years later. The English had been booted out of Aquitaine forever (well, at least until the tourists arrived).

Repression & Religious Persecution

The 16th century ushered in a new wave of warfare, thanks to the spread of Protestantism and the radical ideas of Luther and Calvin. The south-west – already disgruntled by repressive French rule – embraced the new ideas with enthusiasm. Protestant communities first emerged in the 1530s in Agen and Béarn and by 1560 conflicts were erupting like brush fires: a massacre of Protestants in Cahors (which, like Périgueux, was a staunch supporter of the Catholic League, a national anti-Huguenot movement), expulsion of Protestants from Toulouse in 1562, and increasingly bloodthirsty attacks as towns took sides. Bergerac, Ste-Foy-la-Grande, Figeac and Montauban emerged as fiercely Protestant, supported by the bigoted Jeanne d'Albret of Navarre, the tiny Gascon kingdom that encompassed Béarn.

By 1562 the Wars of Religion had pitted the Huguenots (French Protestants) firmly against the Catholic League and Catholic monarchists, with atrocities – culminating in the St Bartholomew's Day Massacre of 3000 Huguenots in Paris in 1572 – committed all over the land. In the south-west, Cahors suffered a particularly nasty Protestant attack in 1580, but this brutal war brought desecration and suffering to every sphere of life elsewhere too. The most visible result was severe damage to churches and other religious icons, but feuds between families, villages and regions left scars that would last for decades or longer.

Protestantism, and its power in the south-west, took the spotlight in 1584 when Jeanne d'Albret's Huguenot son, Henri, inherited the French throne as Henri IV. Only after years of suspicious assassinations was his throne secure. Even then, Catholic Parisians remained hostile. After diplomatically converting to Catholicism in 1593, Henri issued the Edict of Nantes in 1598, mandating religious tolerance and an end to the Wars of Religion.

Revolts & Revolution

This was hardly the end of conflict. *Croquants* – disgruntled peasants of Périgord and Quercy – had revolted against high rents and taxes in the mid-1590s and did so again in 1637. Louis XIII and his ruthless minister, Cardinal Richelieu, were intent on forcing absolute obedience to the monarchy: Béarn's independence was quashed in 1620, and the Croquant movement and other civil disturbances were crushed.

While the king's soldiers made life a misery for peasants – billeting themselves wherever they wished, pillaging and raping when it suited them – these were good times for the nobility, who ploughed high rents into many a splendid new chateau. Toulouse found wealth from the manufacture of le *pastel* (dyer's woad) and from markets opened up by the new Canal du Midi (see the boxed text 'Les Canaux des Deux Mers' under Boats in the Getting Around chapter). Bordeaux augmented healthy wine revenues with a disreputable slave trade with the Americas.

When Louis XIV, Le Roi Soleil (the Sun King), came on the scene in 1643 assisted by another powerful cardinal, Mazarin, the drive for absolute monarchy went into high gear. A series of urban revolts, sparked in Paris in 1648 and known as Les Frondes (after the word for a sling), spread across the land and Mazarin was temporarily forced to flee for his life. One by one these uprisings were quashed, with Bordeaux the last of the Frondes' cities to submit, in 1653. In 1660 the young Louis took a year-long tour of his lands before his gala marriage to the Spanish princess Maria Teresa (Marie Thérèse) in St-Jean de Luz.

In 1685 the king earned the everlasting hatred of Protestants by revoking the Edict of Nantes. Brutal persecution drove many Huguenots to follow thousands of poor Aquitainians into exile in North America or Germany. Only the fiercely monarchist Basques were allowed a measure of independence, while the south-western provinces were largely ruled by *intendants* (governors) from Paris. Some, like the Marquis de Tourny, who instigated major town planning projects in Bordeaux and Périgueux, made lasting contributions; others were bitterly resented.

As the 18th century progressed, new economic and social circumstances rendered the *ancien regime* (old order) dangerously out of step with the needs of the country. The regime was further weakened by the anti-establishment and anticlerical ideas of the Enlightenment. In the rural south-west, general unrest over rising prices, falling wages and a booming population (in Quercy it rose by 70% between 1700 and 1786) helped pave the way for the collapse of the regime in 1789, when the urban masses of Paris took to the streets and launched the Revolution.

Among the Revolution's first victims

were the so-called Girondins, a faction of moderate republican deputies from Bordeaux, representatives of the upper mercantile class, who lost power to the radical Jacobins. But after the Reign of Terror had finally wound down in 1794 (with the loss of some 17,000 heads), it was the Girondins' brand of moderation which won the day.

Napoleon & the Dawn of the Republics

Meanwhile, a dashing young Corsican general named Napoleon Bonaparte was winning glorious successes in a military campaign against Austria. On his return to an unstable Paris in 1799 he assumed power. By 1804 he had himself crowned Emperor of the French and launched a series of wars against his European neighbours to consolidate and legitimise his authority. He also instituted a number of important reforms including a reorganisation of the judicial system and the promulgation of a new legal code, the Code Napoleon (or civil code) which forms the basis of the French legal system to this day. A Périgordian from Domme, Jacques de Maleville, was one of its authors.

Among Napoleon's most loyal fans were the people of Périgord and the Lot, who sent thousands of their young men (including several who became high-ranking generals) to join his *Grande Armée*. Many met their end in Napoleon's disastrous Russian campaign of 1812; two years later the allied armies forced Napoleon to abdicate. Though he returned briefly for a 'Hundred Days' of power, his fate was sealed when his forces were defeated by the English under the Duke of Wellington at Waterloo in 1815.

After the excitements of war (en route from Spain to battle with Napoleon, Wellington besieged Bayonne and got a warm welcome in Toulouse), the south-west sank into obscurity and poverty. Bordeaux, which had suffered from the allies' blockade and the abolition of the slave trade, plunged to an all-time low. In Paris, republics came and went; in 1851 Napoleon's nephew, Louis Napoleon, took advantage of the instability to lead a coup d'etat and proclaim himself Emperor Napoleon III, ushering in the Second Empire.

During this period, France enjoyed significant economic growth and even the south-west claimed Napoleon III's attention: his major achievement here was to transform the once-desolate Landes – a region of marshy swamps, encroaching sand and poor soil – into Europe's largest pine forest. He and his Spanish wife, Eugénie, spent holidays in Biarritz and the Basque region, turning them into popular resorts. Thermal spas followed suit, with Pau a favourite among English visitors.

The tourism trade became an essential new revenue-earner, especially vital after a phylloxera epidemic in 1868 nearly wiped out the region's entire wine production, a body blow to an area already struggling to survive. Despite the arrival of the railway in the 1850s, young men left in their thousands to seek their fortunes elsewhere. Village populations dwindled with alarming speed. With the onset of the World Wars, the decline quickened.

The World Wars

Like his uncle, Napoleon III led his Empire to its end after a series of inadvisable wars. In 1870 the Prussians inflicted a humiliating defeat on the French, forcing the government to negotiate an armistice and hold elections.

After a rocky start, the Third Republic launched into an era known as the *belle époque* (beautiful age), with the introduction of Art Nouveau architecture, a whole field of 'isms' from impressionism onwards and advances in science and engineering. In the south-west, Bordeaux picked itself up, boosted by a brief reign as the nation's capital in 1870 (twice more, in times of war, it was to serve as a temporary capital, in 1914 and 1940). But when France entered WWI – eager to reclaim Alsace and Lorraine which had been lost to Germany in 1871 – the south-west suffered terribly, each village losing at least a third of its young men to the war.

After WW1 there followed a brief respite, during which Paris became a centre of the avant-garde and the south-west made its own artistic contributions with the discovery, in 1940, of the Lascaux cave and other prehistoric sites (archaeological interest in the area had been sparked off by the 1868 discovery of Cro-Magnon remains).

The country was soon engulfed in conflict once again; within a year of declaring war on Germany in 1939, France had fallen. Bordeaux was the scene of the armistice with Hitler in June 1940.

The Germans divided France into a directly occupied zone (the north and the entire Atlantic coast) and a puppet state based in the spa town of Vichy. For four years and two months the south-west, like the rest of France, dealt with the Occupation in various ways. Some residents collaborated, helping to round up groups persecuted by the Germans. Many did nothing. A small minority joined the underground *Résistance*, gathering intelligence for the Allies, helping airmen that had been shot down and publishing anti-German leaflets. Many in the Basque region smuggled escapees into Spain and Allied agents into France; indeed Spaniards, half a million of whom had fled to South-West France after Franco's onslaught on the Spanish Basque country in 1937, constituted a large proportion of the area's Résistance.

Almost every town and village has its memorial to those who died before and during the Occupation. Several suffered particularly horrific attacks, especially at the end of the war when the Germans launched a wave of attacks in retaliation against the Résistance, increasingly effective from its hideaways in the caves and *causses* (limestone plateaus) of Quercy and Périgord. In Tulle in June 1944, 99 residents were hanged; over a hundred more were deported and never seen again. In Rouffignac the only part of the town that escaped a mass torching in March 1944 was the church.

Liberation of the south-west came in August 1944. A former Résistance fighter, Jacques Chaban-Delmas, became deputy and later mayor of Bordeaux, rejuvenating the city with urban-renewal projects. Less worthy post-war administrators included a

former general secretary of Gironde, Maurice Papon, appointed *préfet* (prefect) of the Landes in 1945 and later a chief of police in Paris and a minister in Giscard d'Estaing's government. In 1983 it was revealed that Papon had been a Nazi collaborator, he was finally tried and found guilty in Bordeaux in April 1998. The delay in the meting out of justice indicates all too clearly how much trouble many French people still have in coming to terms with WWII skeletons in their cupboards.

Post-War Revival

After the German capitulation, Général Charles de Gaulle, who had set up a French government-in-exile in London, returned to head a provisional government, resigning within months in a failed gamble to provoke a popular outcry for his return. The Fourth Republic saw 26 different governments.

After an unsuccessful attempt to quash a nationalist uprising in Algeria (whose population included over a million French settlers), civil war seemed to loom and de Gaulle was indeed called back as president. He drafted a new constitution, launching the Fifth Republic in 1958 and establishing a strong, stable executive with a powerful presidential role.

Troubles in Algeria escalated in 1961 and in 1962 de Gaulle gave Algeria its independence. Some 750,000 *pieds noirs* (literally 'black feet', as Algerian-born French are known in France) flooded into the country. The south-west hosted many of them, and their continued presence – along with descendants of refugees from the Spanish Civil War – gives the area a distinctive diversity.

Economically, the area's biggest post-war boom has been in Toulouse, which has become the base for Aérospatiale, Airbus and the French space agency, and a lively rival to Bordeaux, which regained some of the limelight by hosting several World Cup matches in 1998.

And what of the rural hinterland? The ongoing exodus of the young and the depopulation of villages has been offset slightly by the arrival of thousands of foreign settlers, from the Netherlands, Germany and particularly

England, who since the 1960s have established holiday homes in abandoned farmhouses and run-down chateaux. Indeed, tourism is today's lifeblood for many regions, especially the Dordogne.

With the election in 1981 of the Socialist François Mitterand, several measures affected the region, in particular a decentralisation programme which created the *régions* (administrative regions) of Aquitaine and Midi-Pyrénées, providing the first steps away from centuries of heavy-handed Parisian control. Rather less welcome was the appointment of the unpopular former prime minister Alain Juppé as mayor of Bordeaux (his 1995–7 tenure as prime minister was marked by widespread hostility to his pension reforms and economic austerity measures). He has since won approval for his dynamic approach and has been careful not to jeopardise his chances of a return to the Paris hot seat.

Meanwhile, the current right-wing Gaullist president, Jacques Chirac (in power since 1995), tries to hold together a precarious coalition government of Socialists, Communists and Greens, led by the Socialist prime minister, Lionel Jospin.

GEOGRAPHY

The area covered by this guide, roughly 65,700 sq km (about 12% of France's land area), spans what is known as the Aquitaine Basin (Bassin Aquitaine), embraced to the north by valley-crossed limestone plateaus, to the north-east by the foothills of the Massif Central and to the south by the Pyrénées (for more information see the following Geology section). An extraordinary diversity of landscapes is to be found here.

Some 230km of fine, sandy Atlantic coastline (known as La Côte d'Argent, or The Silver Coast) stretches arrow-straight from Pointe de Grave (100km north of Bordeaux) almost to the Spanish border. Here is Europe's longest, highest sand dune belt, surmounted by the 114m-high Dune du Pilat and broken only by the Bassin d'Arcachon, a 250 sq km inland sea. Southwards and inland lies the 14,000 sq km plain of the Landes, a mix of dunes, marshland and

A Muddle of Names

In Roman times, Aquitania was a vast area extending as far north as the Loire and east to the Massif Central. The kingdom of Aquitaine declared by Charlemagne corresponded to the modern départements of Gironde, most of Lot-et-Garonne, the Dordogne, Lot and Aveyron, and acquired the alias Guyenne or Guienne around the time the English arrived (because, say some, the Anglo-Saxons couldn't pronounce 'Aquitaine').

When Henry II married Eleanor of Aquitaine, her dowry also included Gascony (roughly corresponding to the modern départements of Gers and Landes). By this time, though reference was still made to 'Aquitaine', it no longer existed as a political entity: its various provinces – which changed hands continually during the Hundred Years' War – included Poitou (the area west of Poitiers), Guyenne, Gascony and several smaller provinces.

Aquitaine has been revived as one of France's 22 *régions*, made up of the Dordogne, Gironde, Landes, Lot-et-Garonne and Pyrénées-Atlantiques départements.

Other historical names that still pop up are Quercy (during the Middle Ages a part of Guyenne, and corresponding to modern-day Lot and most of Tarn-et-Garonne), Languedoc (east of the Garonne, including Toulouse, Armagnac (stretching from the Pyrénées, including Béarn, to Agen) and Périgord (synonymous with the modern département of the Dordogne).

nearly a million hectares of pine and oak plantations (established in the 19th century to hold back the encroaching sand), Europe's largest cultivated forest.

Behind the Landes' dunes lies a mosaic of lakes and lagoons, whose often-turbulent outlets to the sea provide locations for some of the south-west's finest watersports. The lakes themselves, from Étang d'Hourtin-Carcans (at 16km, France's longest lake) in the north to Étang d'Orx in the south, offer calmer activities and havens for wildlife.

Inland, one of France's five major rivers – the 575km-long Garonne – rises in the Pyrénées and shapes 56,000 sq km of the south-west before emptying into the Atlantic at Europe's largest estuary, the Estuaire de la Gironde. Garonne's tributaries include some of the country's loveliest waterways: the Dordogne, Lot and Tarn. Others are the Vézère, Dronne and Isle (all in the *département* – administrative division – of the Dordogne), Aveyron (in Tarn-et-Garonne), Grande Leyre (in Gironde; called the Eyre or Leyre in lower reaches), Gers and Baïse (in the Gers). Little wonder the Romans called this Aquitania (land of waters).

The region's other major river, the Adour, also rises in the Pyrénées, crossing the southern Landes to the sea at Bayonne. Its major branches – the Nive, Oloron and Pau – drain the Pyrénées-Atlantiques département. An artificial waterway that has become part of the landscape is the body comprising the Canal du Midi and Canal Latéral à la Garonne (see the boxed text 'Les Canaux des Deux Mers' under Boats in the Getting Around chapter).

GEOLOGY

Of the mighty 450km Pyrénées range defining the France-Spain border, this book covers only the western arm, the Basses-Pyrénées, sheltering Béarn and the Basque lands. This part of the range, scored by picturesque and fertile valleys, rises highest at Pic du Midi d'Ossau (2884m), near the border south of Pau.

Equally dramatic formations are revealed in the Lot's causses – monumental, 1000m-high limestone plateaus separating lush, deeply cut gorges. The causses host splendid clifftop villages, such as Rocamadour, and hide a network of caves and subterranean waterways quite at odds with the almost semi-desert conditions on the surface. A spectacular example of the latter is the Gouffre de Padirac (in the Causse de Gramat, near Cahors) where a navigable river flows 103m below ground level.

Lining the wide, looping valleys of the rivers Vézère and Dordogne in Périgord are hard, cave-riddled limestone cliffs which have given shelter since prehistoric times. Towards Brive-la-Gaillarde, these ridges peter out in a depression of sandstone and schist.

CLIMATE

Like most of France, the south-west has a temperate, Atlantic-influenced climate. Rainfall is below the countrywide average, owing to the influence of the Massif Central, and summers are warmer and often punctuated by dramatic thunderstorms. The hottest months are July and August, with average daytime temperatures of about 25°C.

Winter temperatures drop to around 10°C in December and January; chill winds make this season particularly harsh on the high

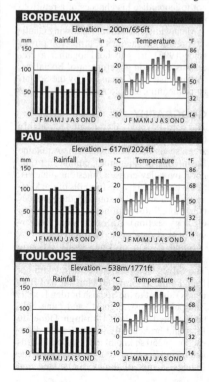

plateaus. There's enough snow for skiers from December to March or April in the Basses-Pyrénées, though weather in the foothills is quite mild – indeed, Pau is famed for its year-round mild climate.

The mountains see as much as 1000mm of rain each year, compared with Toulouse's 656mm. Elsewhere in the south-west the heaviest rains usually occur in spring and late autumn, with fog and frost common in Périgord in spring. In November 1999 the country's worst floods of the century (following a year's worth of rain in just 24 hours) affected the Tarn and neighbouring coastal départements, and resulted in some 22 deaths.

ECOLOGY & ENVIRONMENT

The south-west is loved by the French and foreigners alike for its rural charm and tranquillity, unspoilt villages and traditional farming lifestyle – 'la France profonde', to quote the late President Mitterand. But the tranquillity masks a mounting worry: France's rural depopulation has reached such a level that in the next decade an estimated 1500 villages and 200,000 farms will be left to rot. In Périgord alone, the number of farmers has dwindled in 20 years from 104,000 to 32,000. The exodus started in the 19th century and was exacerbated by war (WWI alone took 1.5 million French lives), industrialisation and the appeal of city life.

To forestall this social 'desertification' the government, in October 1998, introduced legislation aimed at preserving rural communities and encouraging farmers to be more responsible for the environment – in effect making them guardians of la France profonde – in return for subsidies. But in reality it's not agriculture but tourism which is now the future for many départements in the south-west, particularly the Dordogne The benefits are obvious: many deserted farms have been bought and lovingly restored by foreigners; new ferme-auberges (farm restaurants) and tables d'hôtes (meals in private houses) provide income for small family farms; and the summer tourist invasion guarantees a healthy revenue for many

service providers. The downside is also clear: pollution (from traffic on the roads and watersports on the coast and rivers), damage to the limestone cliffs, caves and prehistoric cave paintings of Périgord, and small-town resources stretched to their limit. For information on how to avoid adding to this problem, see Responsible Tourism in the Facts for the Visitor chapter.

Toulouse, France's fastest-growing city after Grenoble, saw a 20% population spurt in the 1960s and, as the country's aerospace capital, faces an increasing industrial pollution problem. Supporting industries are also growing there. Bordeaux is another major industrial centre. Small-town industry plays its part: a paper factory at Condat-le-Lardin (near Brive-la-Gaillarde) dirties the Vézère River, and the stink from another at Mimizan (near Arcachon) drifts to nearby coastal resorts. A fight is raging over plans for a 30,000 tonnes-per-year toxic waste incinerator at Graulhet, south-west of Albi.

Nuclear power stations loom over the landscape at Blaye (40km north of Bordeaux on the Gironde estuary) and Golfech (50km up the Garonne from Agen). Another energy project that has its own environmental risks is the country's largest oilfield, near the coast at Parentis-en-Born (Landes).

One of France's hottest environmental controversies surrounds the E7, a proposed four-lane highway up Béarn's beautiful Vallée d'Aspe, threatening its fragile lifestyle and France's last community of bears (see Endangered Species in Flora & Fauna later in this chapter).

A growing network of environmental organisations keep watch on trouble spots, including:

Agir pour l'Environment
   (email ape@globenet.org)
Association pour la Sauvegarde et l'Avenir
   de la Dordogne
   (☎ 05 53 22 03 35) Sarlat
Greenpeace
   (☎ 01 53 43 85 85, fax 01 42 66 56 04,
   email greenpeace.france@diala.greenpeace.org)
   21 rue Godot de Mauroy, 75009 Paris
   Web site: www.greenpeace.org

La Ligue pour la Protection des Oiseaux
(League for the Protection of Birds)
(☎/fax 05 56 91 33 81)
Maison de la Nature, 3 rue de Tauzia,
33800 Bordeaux
Head office:
(☎ 05 46 82 12 34, fax 05 46 83 95 86,
email lpo-birdlife@a2i-micro.fr)
La Corderie Royale, BP 263,
17305 Rochefort-sur-Mer
Les Amis de la Terre (Friends of the Earth –
France)
(☎ 05 53 08 55 45,
email amiterre@micronet.fr)
2 chemin de Maisonneuve, 24000 Périgueux
Protection de la Vallée de la Vézère,
La Tempeyre, 24290 Valajoulx
Verts Aquitaine
(email vertscra@aol.com)
Verts Dordogne
(email vertsdordogne@wanadoo.fr)

The bimonthly French-language magazine
Dordogne Nature (22FF) lists other local
organisations and features the latest environmental news.

FLORA & FAUNA
Flora
Wildflowers – especially springtime orchids – thrive in the meadows and alluvial
plains of Périgord, devoted largely to cattle
grazing, tobacco and maize, walnut and
chestnut plantations and geese farms. Look
for early purple orchid, white and narrow
leafed helleborines, greater butterfly, bee
and lady orchids. Holm oaks flourish, especially in Périgord Noir.

The sparse soil of the limestone plateaus
(see the Geology section earlier in this
chapter) supports only stunted oak and
maple, and occasional juniper shrubs and
lavender. Forest plantations are mainly of
beech, oak, spruce and pine; maritime pine,
cork oak, ilex, hibiscus and black cypress
dominate the vast Landes forest. Along
many riverbanks, poplars and willows are
common (poplars were traditionally planted
for a daughter's dowry). The forests' treasure of wild mushrooms is highly prized
by locals. For more information on finding
and enjoying this local delicacy see the
special Food & Wine section.

Fauna
Thanks largely to a regional passion for *la
chasse* – the hunt (see Treatment of Animals under Society & Conduct later in this
chapter) – there's little left in the wild. During the hunting season (mid-July to end of
March) anything that moves is fair game. In
many forests and meadows, where you'd
expect the occasional deer, rabbit or bird,
you may be lucky to spot a hedgehog or
fieldmouse. Only the network of caves is
safe, home to millions of bats, beetles and
millipedes.

One animal on the increase is the *sanglier* (wild boar). Culls of 350,000 in 1998
and a similar number in 1997 have hardly
dented an estimated nine-fold increase over
the last 25 years. Reasons may include de-
liberate re-stocking to keep hunters happy
and falling numbers of hunters with the
general rural exodus.

Animals and birds escape the hunters in
three major regional parks (see National &
Regional Parks later in this section): the
Parc National des Pyrénées hosts vultures
and wild bear as well as thousands of
lizards, and the Parc Naturel Régional du
Haut Languedoc is home to many mouflon
(wild mountain sheep). The Parc Naturel
Régional des Landes de Gascogne includes
the marshy saltwater and freshwater Parc
Ornithologique du Teich, a major nesting
ground and stopover for migratory birds.
Over 280 different species have been identified here, including 13 species of duck and
a host of breeding species including purple heron, bittern, spotted crake and Savi's
warbler. Migrants include white and black
storks, night heron, osprey, common crane
and several species of tern. Even the mute
swan has returned.

The lakes along the Côte d'Argent (especially the Étang de Cousseau) are havens
for birdlife and waterfowl (as well as deer,
genets, terrapins and the rarely seen otter).
Birds of prey in the dark forests of Périgord
Noir and along the Dordogne include black
kite, goshawk and short-toed eagle. Other
birds in the area include nightingale, melo-
dious warbler, red-backed shrike, middle
spotted woodpecker and crag martin.

For guided bird-watching tours and other information, contact Maison de la Nature du Bassin d'Arcachon (see Parc Ornithologique du Teich in the Bordeaux, the Atlantic Coast & the Landes chapter) or La Ligue pour la Protection des Oiseaux (for contact details see Ecology & Environment earlier in this chapter).

Endangered Species

Otters, which were once abundant in the south-west, have fallen victim to trappers. The Pyrenean ibex and several species of bats are endangered. A quarter of fish species are also in trouble. The brown bear – 300 of whom roamed the Pyrénées in the 1930s – has fallen in number to fewer than 15. A proposed highway through the Vallée d'Aspe (see Ecology & Environment earlier in this chapter) could finish them off.

Some animals have returned from the edge of extinction thanks to re-introduction programmes, including one at a private reserve called La Falaise au Vautours in Béarn's Vallée d'Ossau. Alpine dwellers such as the chamois (a mountain antelope) and the bouquetin (a type of ibex) were widely hunted until the founding of the Pyrénées and other national parks.

In the French Basque country (Pays Basque) a unique, tiny horse, the *pottok*, was rescued by l'Association Nationale du Pottok (ANAP) and the Pyrénées-Atlantiques département (which organised a forum discussing the horse in 1996).

LISA BORG

Barely there: tourism has taken its toll and the Pyrénéan bear could be facing extinction.

Standing from just 1.15m to 1.32m tall, the pottok is invaluable not only in the wild where it keeps shrubs and undergrowth at bay but also in riding schools where it's a perfect choice for children. After years of agricultural cross-breeding, a programme (Pottok 2000) is underway to establish a core of purebreds.

National & Regional Parks

Within the region covered by this book lie part of a national park, a regional natural park and parts of two others. For further information on the regional parks contact the Fédération des Parcs Naturels Régionaux de France (☎ 01 44 90 86 20, fax 01 45 22 70 78, email info@parcs-naturels-regionaux.tm.fr), 4 rue de Stockholm, 75008 Paris. Web site: www.parcs-naturels-regionaux.tm.fr/.

Parc National des Pyrénées This 457 sq km park, created in 1967, stretches across the Hautes-Pyrénées for about 100km along the Franco-Spanish border, eastwards from Béarn's Vallée d'Aspe. It's bordered by a 2060 sq km buffer zone where controlled development is permitted. Roughly 40% of the park is within the scope of this book, in the Pyrénées-Atlantiques département. On the Spanish side is the 150 sq km Parque Nacional de Ordesa y Monte Perdido.

The main park office (☎ 05 62 44 36 60, fax 05 62 44 36 70) is at 59 rte de Pau, 65000 Tarbes, in the Hautes-Pyrénées département. There are plans to open a park office at Laruns in the Vallée d'Ossau by 2000.

Parc Naturel Régional des Landes de Gascogne This 2620 sq km park, centred on Le Parc Ornithologique du Teich in the Leyre valley (see Parc Ornithologique du Teich in the Bordeaux, the Atlantic Coast & the Landes chapter), was founded in 1970 to protect the area's valuable pine forests, marshlands and birdlife. The flat terrain and well-marked trails make this an attractive destination for cyclists. Other points of interest are the three sites of the Ecomusée de la Grande Lande: an open-air ethnological museum at Marquèze, a resin workshop in Luxey and a museum of religious heritage and popular beliefs at Moustey (see the Bordeaux, the Atlantic Coast & the Landes chapter).

Park headquarters (☎ 05 56 88 06 06, fax 05 56 88 12 72) are at Place d'Eglise, Belin-Béliet, 30km south-east of Arcachon. For information on species, and on guided visits by canoe, kayak or foot, head for Maison de la Nature du Bassin d'Arcachon (☎ 05 56 22 80 93, fax 05 56 22 69 43) in Le Teich.

Parc Naturel Régional du Haut-Languedoc Founded in 1973 to protect the natural beauty of this isolated and economically deprived region, the heavily forested, 2606 sq km park straddles the border between the Tarn and Hérault départements (the latter in the Languedoc-Roussillon région). Highlights on the Tarn side include the Montagne Noire range south of Castres, home to mouflon and several species of eagle, and the bizarre granite outcrops of the Sidobre, north-east of Castres.

The park office (☎ 04 67 97 38 22, fax 04 67 97 38 18) is at 13 rue du Cloître, 34220 St-Pons de Thomieres (Hérault).

Parc Naturel Régional du Périgord-Limousin Overlapping the départements of the Dordogne and Haute-Vienne (the latter in the Limousin région), this 1800 sq km park was only founded in 1998. Its many lakes host a rich variety of birdlife, mammals including deer, otters and bats, and numerous species of orchids. Park headquarters (☎ 05 53 60 34 65, fax 05 53 60 39 13, email perilim.perigord@wanadoo.fr) are at 24300 Abjat-sur-Bandiat (Dordogne).

GOVERNMENT & POLITICS

France is divided into 22 régions, each subdivided into départements. This book covers all of the Aquitaine région, most départements of the Midi-Pyrénées région and a corner of Limousin's Corrèze département. Though pre-Revolution regional names are still often used (see the boxed text 'A Muddle of Names' under Geography earlier in this chapter) each département's two-digit code is the official last

What's Your Number?

These are the official codes for the départements that feature in this book. They appear as the first two digits of each département's postcodes, and as the last two numbers on all its automobile number-plates. If the last three digits of a town's postcode are zeros it indicates that this is a préfecture.

région	département	code
Aquitaine	Dordogne	24
	Gironde	33
	Landes	40
	Lot-et-Garonne	47
	Pyrénées-Atlantiques	64
Midi-Pyrénées	Gers	32
	Haute-Garonne	31
	Lot	46
	Tarn	81
	Tarn-et-Garonne	82
Limousin	Corrèze	19

word; see the boxed text 'What's Your Number?' for details.

Each région has an elected regional council *(conseil régional)* with limited powers, based at its capital (Bordeaux for Aquitaine, Toulouse for Midi-Pyrénées, Limoges for Limousin). The main town of each département is a prefecture *(préfecture)*, seat of the regional council and of the government's representative, the prefect *(préfet)*. Each département is split into smaller districts *(arrondissements)* – whose main towns are sub-prefectures *(sous-préfecture)* – themselves divided into parishes *(cantons)* and smaller *communes* (villages), the basic administrative unit of local government. Each commune is presided over by a mayor *(maire)* based in a town hall *(mairie* or *hôtel de ville)*.

Traditionally, the south-west (particularly the Dordogne) harbours some of France's most fiercely leftist political sympathisers. In all three régions covered by this book, March 1998 elections installed left-wing governments and gave a resounding vote of confidence to Lionel Jospin's Socialist-led coalition government (awkwardly cohabiting with a right-wing president, Jacques Chirac).

But with Jospin's popularity on a downward slide (exacerbated by strikes, continued unemployment and economic turbulence) the Right's hopes are high; even the former Gaullist prime minister, Alain Juppé, who led the Right to defeat in June 1997, has won points as the dynamic mayor of Bordeaux. Toulouse's popular centrist mayor, Dominique Baudis, has held power since 1983.

ECONOMY

The tranquil, heavily rural
some unexpected economic st
all the fact that this is Euro
aerospace region, with all branches of the aeronautics industry represented and annual sales of US$3.3 billion.

While Bordeaux is a European centre for components testing, a world leader in rocket motors and France's largest exporter of auto parts and equipment (Ford recently invested 15 billion francs in a new production line in Gironde), it's rival Toulouse which captures the aeronautics limelight: four Aérospatiale

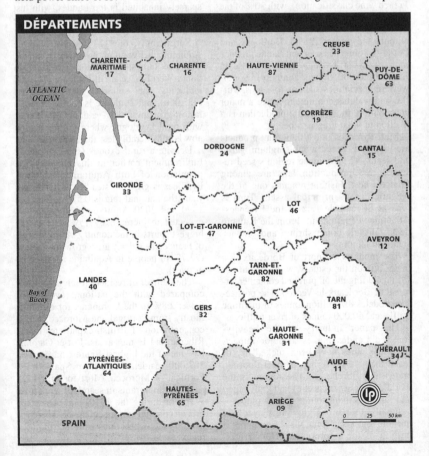

DÉPARTEMENTS

...ctories – responsible for Concorde, Airbus and ATR (regional transport planes) – make this Europe's aeronautics capital. Also here is the National Space Center which is behind the development of the Ariane rocket, and cutting-edge satellite imaging.

Of course agriculture plays a major role in the economy too. Aquitaine contributes more to the national agriculture economy than any other region (10.6%), with 8.8% of its workforce in agriculture, almost twice the national average. Aquitaine is the world's leading producer of vins d'appellation d'origine contrôlée (AOC; the highest French wine classification), with 30% of the country's output. It's also the leading European producer of maize (84% of France's output) and prunes (83%). Dordogne and Lot-et-Garonne départements alone produce more strawberries than anywhere else in Europe (20,000 tonnes annually). South-western specialities such as foie gras, truffles and walnuts continue to make a major contribution, though truffle production is a fraction of what it used to be.

Midi-Pyrénées' most important products are yarn and carded wool, sorghum, garlic and seeds. The Toulouse region's seed research and production labs are among France's best. Fishing remains one of the Atlantic coast's principal assets. Tuna is tops at St-Jean de Luz in the Pyrénées-Atlantique département. From the Estuaire de la Gironde come shrimp and prawns, shad and lamprey.

The modernised port of Bordeaux is a major hub on the estuary, with six harbour sites including the oil port and container terminal of Bordeaux-le-Verdon. The port accommodates 8.7 million tonnes of maritime traffic and 60,000 tonnes of river traffic.

The paper industry of the heavily-forested Landes makes a major impact. After the pines have been sucked dry of resin, they are made into parquet flooring, crates and fibreboard. The region is the world's leading producer of laid kraft paper, and Europe's main source of fluff pulp.

Finally, tourism is growing player. Six million tourists a year visit Aquitaine, a million of them foreigners. Not surprisingly, the service industry is the region's biggest employer (69% of the workforce, compared with 16% in industry) and set to grow steadily as agriculture declines.

POPULATION & PEOPLE

South-West France is home to about 4.3 million people (a small percentage of the 60m national population), 2.9 million of them in Aquitaine. The greatest population density – 129 per sq km – is in Gironde, though overall density is just 70 per sq km in Aquitaine and 55 per sq km in Midi-Pyrénées (the national average is 108 per sq km). Most sparsely inhabited is the Landes, with just 35 people per sq km. Even the Dordogne seems relatively empty at 43 per sq km.

Surprisingly, though, two out of three Aquitainians live in an urban environment. The two largest urban concentrations in South-West France are in Toulouse (741,000 including the suburbs) and Bordeaux (733,000), and Toulouse is one of France's fastest-growing cities – a dramatic contrast with rural Dordogne where the population now is considerably less than 150 years ago.

Despite a rural exodus (see Ecology & Environment earlier in this chapter), the population of both Aquitaine and Midi-Pyrénées is growing steadily at 0.53% per year (the national rate is 0.57%). Between 1990 and 2020 Aquitaine's population is expected to increase by 15%, one of the biggest spurts in the country. As in the rest of France, the elderly are a growing fraction (23.7% of people in Aquitaine are aged 60 or over).

The number of resident foreigners is low compared with the national average of 6.3%: 2.8% in the Dordogne, for example, mostly from Portugal and Morocco, with a concentration of British expatriates in the Ribérac and Eymet areas. Lot-et-Garonne has one of the highest figures: 5.5% of its 307,000 residents hail from Spain, Italy, Portugal or Morocco. Most foreigners arrived as immigrants in search of work after WWI, or during the 1950s and 60s as the French colonial empire collapsed. There appear to be few problems with racism in the region.

ARTS
Literature
Medieval The most famous literary era in South-West France was also the earliest: between the 11th and 13th centuries a new form of lyric poetry emerged from the feudal courts of Aquitaine, expressed in song by troubadours. These poet-musicians invented melodies in the native Langue d'Oc (*tobar* means 'find' in Occitan) rather than in Latin, the literary language of the Middle Ages. They created new rhythms and poetic forms, mostly songs lamenting unrequited love and accompanied on the lute. The earliest known troubadour was Guillaume IX (1071–1127), duke of Aquitaine.

Encouraged by royal patronage (Eleanor of Aquitaine, granddaughter of Guillaume IX, was a leading light), troubadours continued to write of chivalry and courtly love right into the 13th century when the Albigensian Crusade wreaked havoc on the region's nobility. But the troubadours' legacy remained: the new poetic forms spread to northern France, Germany, Italy and the Iberian peninsula, and influenced medieval secular music and many later poets, including the 20th-century American Ezra Pound.

16th Century Pierre de Bourdeilles (pseudonym Brantôme), born in 1540 to a baron of Bourdeilles, was a courtier and lascivious soldier of fortune who, rather ironically, became Abbot of Brantôme. After a fall from his horse in the 1580s put a stop to his martial wanderings, he retired to the abbey and wrote two works, *Les vies des hommes illustres et grands capitaines* (Lives of illustrious men and great commanders) and the spicier *Les vies des dames galantes* (Lives of the courtesans). The latter brought him fame, though many consider his enthusiastic descriptions of war and bravery superior.

The region's best known writer had a different attitude to life: Michel Eyquem de Montaigne (1533–92) was born (and died) at Château de Montaigne near St-Émilion, son of a Catholic father (and mayor of Bordeaux) and Jewish mother. A brilliant student, he was brought up speaking only Latin until he was six and was then educated by a French-speaking Scottish humanist, George Buchanan. He practised law in Bordeaux until he was 39 when, disgusted by the hypocrisy of it all and the cruelty of the Wars of Religion, he retired to the family chateau and started to write *essaies* – literally 'attempts' – a new genre which was to be his literary legacy. But Montaigne's philosophy of life was even more revolutionary: the true aim of life, he proclaimed, was

> not to win, or to write books, or to gain battles and lands, but to live orderly and tranquilly. To live properly is our great and glorious masterpiece.

He put his philosophy into practice as mayor of Bordeaux, valiantly trying to reconcile Protestants and Catholics.

The Troubadours of the Dordogne

No wonder Henry Miller called the Dordogne 'the cradle of the poets'. It was here that some of the finest troubadour poets flourished in the 12th century – notably Arnaut Daniel (Ribérac), Elias Carels (Sarlat), Arnaut de Mareuil (Mareuil), Girault de Borneil (Excideuil) and Bertrand de Born (Hautefort).

Not all specialised in love: Bertrand de Born was notorious for bloodthirsty songs of war and biting satirical ballads (called *sirventès*) which made him as many enemies as fans. Indeed, he almost lost his life when a furious King Henry II accused him of provoking his eldest son, Henry (known as the 'Young King') into battle against his brother (Richard the Lion-Heart) and King Henry himself. It was de Born's own moving lament for the Young King (who died during the conflict) that led Henry II to pardon him.

Montaigne's greatest friend, Étienne de la Boétie, born in Sarlat in 1530, was a skilful counsellor in the Bordeaux regional court of law *(parlement)*, and a writer of sonnets; however, he's most famous for his impassioned *Contr'un* (literally 'Against One' better known as 'A Discourse on Voluntary Servitude'), a remarkable treatise on liberty he wrote at the age of 18 and which later influenced Jean-Jacques Rousseau. The essay's argument – that the sycophants and supporters of a tyrant are as evil and guilty as the tyrant himself – was nothing short of subversive at that time. Montaigne's moving 'Essay on Friendship', written when Boétie died at the tragically early age of 32, now tends to overshadow Boétie's work.

17th & 18th Centuries Another gently tolerant humanist followed in Montaigne's footsteps: François de Salignac de la Mothe-Fénelon (1651–1715), the 13th child of an aristocratic family (with their own chateau west of Souillac), trained as a priest and in 1689 became tutor to Louis XIV's dull grandson, the duke of Burgundy. Some years earlier Fénelon had inherited the priory-deanery of Carennac from his uncle and it was there, tradition has it, that he wrote *Télémaque*, an educational allegory for the duke about truth and virtue, based on the legends of Odysseus and his son Telemachus. Though the novel led to nothing but trouble for him it eventually received due praise and was reprinted over 180 times.

Baron Charles Louis de Montesquieu (1689–1755) was, like Montaigne, an intellectual who found peace and inspiration in the countryside of his birth, at Château de la Brède near Bordeaux. Vine-grower, magistrate and eventually deputy president of the Bordeaux court of law (a post he later sold to fund his social activities in Paris), and member of the Académie Française (a prestigious learned society founded in 1634), this liberal political philosopher and writer became best-known for his seminal *L'esprit des lois* (The spirit of the law; 1748), a masterpiece of political theory. In his day he became equally famous for satirical works such as *Lettres persanes* (Persian letters), mocking Parisian civilisation, social classes and the reign of Louis XIV. He also wrote a travelogue of his journey through Europe, an anthology of French songs, Latin poems and an essay on the English constitution.

19th & 20th Centuries The story of a peasant, written by a humble citizen of Périgord, is perhaps the region's most relevant work of literature. Eugène Le Roy was the son of the steward of Château de Hautefort. After a Paris education, funded by the baron of Hautefort, he joined the finance department and became a tax-collector in Montignac. A passionate republican, concerned about the hard life of his fellow Périgourdins, he briefly lost his job because of his views. By the time he took up his pen, religious tolerance and equality were declining under a new wave of ultra-royalists, powerful clergy and nobility. Published in 1899, his *Jacquou le Croquant* – recalling the Croquant peasant rebels of the 15th and 16th centuries – tells the bitter tale of a young peasant boy struggling against injustice and fighting for revenge. What makes this and Le Roy's other novels still so popular in Périgord is his lovingly detailed portrait of the region; here is a true local who knew the ways of the people and was fluent in the *patois* or local dialect which colours the text.

No literary work since then has shown such an attachment to the area, though several outstanding writers emerged during this time: André Herzog (1885–1967) lived in Périgord after WWI and wrote enthusiastically about the region under the pen-name André Maurois, though it's his novels and biographies of the English for which he's best known. François Mauriac (1885–1970), born and brought up in Bordeaux until his early 20s when he left for Paris, won the 1952 Nobel prize for Literature. He had little affection for his home town, although the Atlantic coast features in his novel *Thérèse Desqueyroux*.

As for *Cyrano de Bergerac* – Edmond Rostand's sad and successful 1897 verse play about a large-nosed swordsman and poet – it has little to do with the town of Bergerac. Even his real, 17th-century namesake, one Savinien de Cyrano de Bergerac, is believed to have spent only a few nights in Bergerac.

Architecture

Prehistoric France's earliest monuments are stone megaliths erected in Neolithic times (from about 4000 to 2400 BC), ranging from simple menhirs (huge standing stones) to dolmens (several vertical stones topped by a horizontal slab). Although mainly found in northern France, there are several striking examples in the south-west, especially the Lot (tumuli and dolmens have been found near Gramat, Cajarc and Puy l'Evêque). The Pierre de Grimann near Sabres is the Landes' most famous dolmen, while the Dolmen du Blanc, south of Beaumont in the Dordogne, is still an eerily impressive sight.

Gallo-Roman South-West France's richest Gallo-Roman remains are in the two main oppida of the time: Vesunna (now Périgueux), elegant capital of the Gallic Petrocorii tribe, and Burdigala (Bordeaux), capital of Aquitania.

Remains at Vesunna include stones from its amphitheatre, part of a defensive wall and a tower from a temple dedicated to the goddess of the city. Nearby are vestiges of a Roman town house. Périgueux's Musée du Périgord displays Vesunna's best artefacts. In Bordeaux (which still has two main Gallo-Roman roads, rue Ste-Catherine and rue de la Porte Dijeaux), the most impressive Roman site is the Palais Gallien, the ruins of a huge 3rd-century amphitheatre. The Musée d'Aquitaine has a superb collection of mosaics, steles and amphora, decorated ceramics and some striking statues. Another noteworthy site is the remains of a 4th-century Roman aristocrat's luxurious country home, at Séviac near Montréal (Gers).

There's no agreement on the location of Uxellodunum, the Gauls' last hold-out before their defeat by Caesar. The strongest claim is for Puy d'Issolud, a high plateau near Martel (Lot), where you can make out traces of the earthworks which once made it the strongest oppidum in the region.

Romanesque A religious and economic revival in the 11th century saw much fine construction in the Romanesque style, so-called because of the adoption of features such as vaulting and round arches from Gallo-Roman architecture. Romanesque buildings typically have heavy walls, few windows and a simplicity of ornamentation bordering on the austere.

Christianity had been fostered in Périgord in the 9th century by Charlemagne who supported the Benedictines' new monasteries (such as at Sarlat and Brantôme). In the 11th to 13th centuries such religious orders flourished, building churches and abbeys throughout the region, for example at Belvès, Périgueux, Moissac and St-Sever (Benedictine); Cadouin (Cistercian); Sergeac (Knights Templar); St-Cyprien, St-Amand de Coly and St-Jean de Côle (Augustinian). The surging popularity of the pilgrimage to Santiago de Compostela – and the financial benefits from catering to the thousands of pilgrims – generated many grand Romanesque projects, notably Toulouse's Basilique St-Sernin, Europe's largest Romanesque church.

Certain features make Périgordian Romanesque distinctive, particularly the use of a Byzantine dome for the vaulting. Believed to be an influence brought back from the crusades, it can be seen on over 60 churches in the region and is particularly impressive in Périgueux's Cathédrale St-Front (with five domes over a Greek-cross plan) and Souillac's Église Ste-Marie. Many churches in northern Périgord are built of golden-hued sandstone and roofed with slabs of the region's limestone. One of the finest of these is at St-Léon-sur-Vézère, with a perfect harmony of radiating chapels, arcade bell tower and domed transept.

Elsewhere in the south-west, for example at Martel and Moissac, the Languedoc school of sculpture inspired flamboyant sculptural decorations (see Sculpture later in this section). In a reflection of the uncertainty of the times, several churches (notably St-Amand de Coly in the Dordogne) are more fortress than church, exhibiting Romanesque austerity at its most extreme.

The region's best secular Romanesque architecture is represented by parts of various castles, notably Beynac and Biron, Bourdeilles and Castelnaud. The most impressive feudal fortress, the Château de Castelnau-Bretenoux, has a fortified Romanesque keep.

Gothic In the 12th to 15th centuries the south-west continued to develop its own architectural styles, notably the so-called Southern Gothic. In churches this was distinguished by a single wide nave with no transept, catering to a post-Albigensian

Bastides

In the disorderly Middle Ages, living and working in the countryside was a hazardous affair – especially in South-West France. The first *bastides* (from the Occitan *bastida*, meaning a group of buildings) appeared in the mid-13th century in the Albi and Toulouse areas, probably a response to the uncertainties of the Albigensian Crusade and the urge for orderly settlements which could provide a steady income for local lords.

Within 150 years over 300 of these rigidly-planned, fortified new towns had appeared all over the south-west, many valued as much for their military significance as their economic importance. Indeed, one of their leading proponents, Edward I of England, built bastides such as Beaumont and Monpazier specifically to counter the threat from the French versions. Bastides were fought over and changed hands frequently during the Hundred Years' War.

Bastides all followed a square or rectangular grid pattern, with unusually wide streets (for carts) criss-crossed by narrow pedestrian streets leading out to the fields. In the centre was a market square, often with a timber-roofed *halle* (market hall), surrounded by covered, arcaded passageways *(cornières)* for shops. There were strictly designated plots for houses and others for gardens, with allotments outside the town for further cultivation. The whole unit was enclosed within defensive walls, with the church often fortified as well (as at Montauban) though no longer necessarily the focal point of the settlement.

To entice villagers to live in these newfangled towns – whose style emphasised an unprecedented openness to trade – residents were offered certain privileges including protection in times of attack and exemption from military service. A town charter allowing regular market fairs was a major financial attraction. In return, new arrivals had to build their houses – one plot per family – within a set time and pay their taxes to a bailiff who also dispensed justice. In some places, such as Libourne, settlers were recruited by force but in most cases bastides flourished naturally.

Though some bastides were obliterated in the Hundred Years' War and the Wars of Religion, or decimated by plague or famine in the 14th century, many survive to this day, either grown into cities (Villeneuve-sur-Lot, Libourne, Montauban) or retaining their beautifully simple design (Domme, Monpazier, Monflanquin, the unusual circular Fourcès). The region has several museums devoted to the bastide era, including the Musée des Bastides at Monflanquin (covered in the Lot chapter) and Labastide d'Armagnac (covered in the Gers chapter).

Purpose-built, fortified rural towns from an earlier era included 11th and 12th century *sauvetés* or *sauveterres* (sanctuary-towns, usually founded by ecclesiastical officials) and *castelnaus* (villages that grew up around the chateaux of local lords). These terms often still appear in modern place names, such as Sauveterre de Béarn. The city of Pau started life as a castelnau.

trend of preaching to vast congregations, including pilgrims en route to Santiago de Compostela.

The only outstanding Northern Gothic monument in the region is Bayonne's Cathédrale Ste-Marie, with typical radiating chapels and a long spacious nave. The more common Languedoc (or Toulouse) style favoured the use of brick and was also distinguished by a wide *clocher-mur* (literally 'bell-wall') on the façade, most impressively on Toulouse's Basilique St-Sernin. Toulouse's Cathédrale St-Étienne has a more unusual rectangular belfry-keep that combines Southern and Northern styles, while Albi's massive Cathédrale Ste-Cécile is one of the south-west's best representatives of Southern Gothic with its single nave, dark and huge, and buttresses sheltering a dozen chapels.

Several striking Gothic monuments from the 15th century are in Bordeaux, including the Basilique St-Michel's hexagonal belfry (Tour St Michel), the arched and turreted Porte de la Grosse-Cloche gateway and the Porte Cailhau triumphal arch. The region also has many castles with Gothic features and decorated town houses such as Figeac's Hôtel de la Monnaie and Martel's Hôtel de la Raymondie.

Cahors' Pont Valentré, built in the mid-14th century, is the most striking example of the region's military architecture, while the most outstanding secular architecture from this era is the bastides (see the boxed text) that first appeared in the 13th century.

Renaissance The Renaissance, which started in Italy in the early 15th century, aimed for a rebirth of classical Greek and Roman culture. It had its first impact on France at the end of the 15th century following a series of invasions of Italy by Charles VII. In the 500 years following the end of the Hundred Years' War, the south-west embraced the new style enthusiastically.

The most striking examples of civil Renaissance architecture are the beautiful mansions built by the wealthy textile and woad merchants of Toulouse and Albi in the mid-15th to mid-16th centuries – for example Albi's Hôtel de Reynès and Toulouse's Hôtel d'Assézat, among many in those cities. In the Dordogne, similar Renaissance flourishes are best seen in town houses in Périgueux's former merchants' district near Cathédrale St-Front. Examples in Sarlat include the Hôtel de Malleville and the Maison de la Boétie. Other sites with Renaissance touches include the graceful 16th-century chateaux of Montal and Puyguilhem, typical of chateaux of the Loire.

Various Dordogne fortresses also incorporate Renaissance features, notably the Château de Biron with its striking Renaissance chapel. An ecclesiastical Renaissance masterpiece is the stained glass and the carved oak choir stalls of Auch's Cathédrale Ste-Marie.

Baroque & Classical During the baroque period, from the end of the 16th century to the late 18th century, painting, sculpture and classical architecture were integrated in structures and interiors of great subtlety, refinement and elegance. In the south-west, architects followed Parisian models, introducing few original touches. Bordeaux, which underwent major urban redevelopment in the 18th century, has some of the finest work from this era, including the Église Notre Dame.

Classical architecture, reflecting the Louis XVI style inspired by the art of antiquity, is best represented in the region by Bordeaux's 18th-century Grand Théâtre, one of France's finest classical buildings. Along the city's quayside and in place du Parlement are several outstanding, recently restored 18th-century buildings including the Palais de la Bourse (Stock Exchange) and Hôtel de Sèze. Among the region's chateaux, Hautefort best exemplifies the classical style, merging harmoniously with Renaissance features, while in the Basque country churches are distinguished by their massive, gabled or tiered belfries.

19th & 20th Century Neoclassical architecture, which remained in vogue from about 1740 to the early 19th century, had roots in a renewed interest in classical forms: many of the Gironde wine country's *chartreuses* (small chateaux) reflect this style. The 19th-century popularity of seaside resorts like Arcachon, Cap Ferret, Biarritz and Hendaye led to an outburst of more whimsical luxury villas, casinos and spas, copying styles from almost every era and European country – medieval, Renaissance and Gothic, Spanish, Swiss and English. It was in this region, too (especially in Biarritz and Dax) that the Art Deco movement was taken up most enthusiastically, in casinos and private houses.

Many ecclesiastical projects of the late 19th century were restorations – often controversial – of ancient monuments. Paul Abadie's Second Empire-style restoration (more a complete rebuilding, lasting almost 50 years) of the once-Romanesque Cathédrale St-Front in Périgueux still arouses passionate indignation. Contemporary projects like Bordeaux's Cité Mondiale business centre and the concrete glass-and-steel Meriadeck District administrative centre have also failed to win general approval.

Vernacular Architecture Traditional domestic architecture is very distinctive in the south-west, depending on local materials, climate and agricultural demands. On the limestone plateaus of the Lot, for example, the white limestone houses have thick walls to protect against the wind and an outer staircase leading directly to the first floor. In the valleys of the Lot, houses often feature towers and a *cave* (an underground cellar) traditionally used for cattle and nowadays mostly used for storing wine and produce. In the Dordogne (especially Périgord Noir) the golden limestone houses have steeply pitched roofs covered with *lauzes* (limestone slabs), whereas typical houses in the Toulouse and Albi areas are nearly always made of brick and traditionally plastered with pink stucco, their gently sloping roofs covered in brick tiles.

Throughout the region you'll come across charming *pigeonniers* (dovecotes), often free-standing, some resting on stone columns. Originally used as much for collecting droppings (a valuable manure) as for housing the pigeons themselves, they were also a status symbol: landowners had to buy the right to keep pigeons.

More mysterious are small, round, drystone huts called *bories*, *cabanes* or *gariottes*, usually tucked away in isolated fields. They're believed to have been used for storage (as they still are today) but no-one knows quite when they first appeared.

Painting

Prehistoric Perhaps South-West France's finest and most unique contributions to the arts are the extraordinary prehistoric paintings – discovered in the 20th century – in the limestone caves of the Dordogne and the Lot. See the boxed text 'The Painted Caves of the South-West' for more information.

Medieval & Later Frescoes and murals are the most remarkable artworks of this period, notably in Cahors Cathédrale St-Étienne, whose west dome is covered with frescoes from the 14th century. Many of the region's small Romanesque churches have fine frescoes, some only discovered in the 20th century (such as the splendid 15th-century frescoes at Allemans du Dropt near Duras) 15th-century France might have become a meeting ground for the rich artistic traditions of Italy and Flanders, but the Hundred Years' War got in the way. In the following century, the Wars of Religion further hampered the development of French painting. Most French Renaissance painters copied Italian models with little passion or inspiration.

19th Century Two big names stand out in this century – Henri de Toulouse-Lautrec and Jean Dominique Auguste Ingres. They couldn't have been more different. Ingres was born in 1780 in Montauban, the son of a painter and musician. From an early age he produced perfectly executed portraits and huge neoclassical works, many of them commissioned by Napoleon. Criticised first for his sensual nudes and later for what was seen as an over-meticulous, stuffy approach, it's his skill as a draughtsman and his intimate, daring portraits which are particularly recognised today.

The Painted Caves of the South-West

There are more prehistoric decorated caves in South-West France than anywhere else in the world: over a hundred of them, mostly concentrated in the Vézère and Lot valleys. The extraordinary paintings of horses, buffalo, bison and mammoth found in these caves – most famously in Lascaux (Montignac), Font de Gaume (Les Eyzies), Pech Merle (Cabrerets), Rouffignac and Cougnac (Gourdon) – date from between 35,000 and 10,000 BC and were discovered only in the early and mid-20th century.

At first, they were thought to be fakes but, with the discovery in 1895 of the Grotte de la Mouthe (Les Eyzies) which contained not only paintings and engravings but also a prehistoric lantern, sceptics were forced to accept that Upper Palaeolithic *Homo sapiens sapiens* – particularly Cro-Magnons of the Magdalenian period (15,000 to 9000 BC) – had indeed produced these subtle and beautiful works, full of symbolism and three-dimensional effects.

Just why this area is so blessed with prehistoric art and why the Cro-Magnons retreated into these dark recesses and tunnels to paint (they never lived in these galleries) is open to debate: the area's many limestone shelters and caves were certainly ideal sites (and preserved the art for millennia afterwards). Perhaps, too, increasing pressure on resources in this Late Ice Age landscape (a surge in population growth leading to more intensive hunting by smaller groups of hunters) made these people look towards more ritual and creative approaches to finding food. Certainly much of the most striking cave art is about hunting animals.

However, since only about 15% of the works depict wounded animals, many art historians argue that these paintings must have had other purposes than hunting magic – perhaps to initiate children into adulthood (prehistoric adolescent footprints are still visible in Pech Merle) or as models for human social groups centred around pregnant woman (there are many pregnant horses and bison to be seen). Perhaps the work helped forge alliances between far-flung tribes when they met for ceremonial gatherings (hundreds of ornaments discovered near Les Eyzies suggest such meetings). Was it a way to record stories and beliefs about man and nature? Or, dare one say, was it simply for the pleasure of painting?

Theories abound, but there's no question about the breathtaking impact of the art itself, especially when seen *in situ* (as at Pech Merle and Font de Gaume, among the few painted caves still open to the public). The paintings are coloured red, brown or yellow (from ochres of iron oxide) or black (from manganese dioxide). These natural pigments were probably applied by the dim light of oil lamps with fingers, feathers or brushes, or even blown through a tube, as suggested by the early handprints at Pech Merle. Most impressive is the way the natural contours of the rock are often used to depict the shape of an animal – a protruding belly or sweeping hump, or the length of a mammoth's tusk. Several paintings, perhaps produced thousands of years apart, may overlap. Many combine engraving with painting.

With good reason, the finest of all the area's grottoes is the most famous one: the 'Hall of Bulls' at Lascaux (now partly recreated in the replica Lascaux II), where four huge bulls rampage through a fantastic frieze of horses, stags, ox and deer. This, said Henri Breuil, the local priest and art historian who discovered many of the caves, is 'the Sistine Chapel of prehistoric art' (for more information on the Lascaux caves see under Montignac in the Dordogne chapter).

Toulouse-Lautrec was born in Albi in 1864, to a French count and his German wife. He moved to Paris when he was 18 and flung himself with such enthusiasm into the city's debauched low life that by the age of 37 he was dead, of alcoholism and syphilis. He was already famous by then for his lithographs and posters depicting bars and nightclubs.

His hometown never featured in his work, though he often visited Arcachon (where he had a seaside villa and shocked the neighbours by swimming naked in the sea) and the nearby family home, the Château de Malromé, where he died in 1901.

Both home towns have good museums dedicated to the work of their prodigal sons – the Musée Toulouse-Lautrec in Albi and the Musée Ingres in Montauban.

20th Century French painting in the 20th century has been characterised by a bewildering diversity of styles such as fauvism and cubism, expressionism and surrealism. While the south-west produced no stars in these genres (though André Lothe produced good cubist-figurative works), it was home to a leading painter-turned-tapestry maker, Jean Lurçat. Appointed head designer of the famous but flagging Aubusson tapestry factory in 1939, he discovered the Lot as a Résistance fighter and settled in St Céré in 1945. There he designed his extraordinary cartoons, woven into tapestries at Aubusson, distinguished by brilliant colours, an abstract world of birds and animals and especially his leitmotiv, the cockerel.

The region has several good museums of 20th-century and contemporary art, notably Bordeaux's Musée d'Art Contemporain and the north wing of the city's Musée des Beaux-Arts, the Maison des Arts Georges Pompidou in Cajarc and the Musée Despiau-Wlérick in Mont de Marsan (for more information on this see the following Sculpture section).

Sculpture

At the end of the 11th century, sculptors began to decorate the portals, capitals, altars and fonts of Romanesque churches, illustrating Bible stories, moral tales and the lives of the saints for the illiterate. The most outstanding examples are found in Moissac and Toulouse, centres of Romanesque sculpture which came to influence the whole region. The richly decorated tympana, cloisters and doorway of Moissac's abbey and Toulouse's Basilique St-Sernin gave birth to other work, notably in churches at Carennac, Martel, Beaulieu-sur-Dordogne and Cahors

in the Lot. Striking, too, is the 12th-century portal of Souillac's Église Ste-Marie, especially its famously stylised figure of the prophet Isaiah, so alive it looks as if he's dancing. A fine collection of the works of the Toulouse school is displayed in Toulouse's Musée des Augustins.

As well as adorning churches, sculpture in the following centuries was commissioned for the tombs of the nobility (this can be seen at Montpezat de Quercy's Collégiale St-Martin and the church at Espagnac Ste-Eulalie) and for life-sized representations of biblical scenes (as in the cloisters of Carennac's Église St-Pierre).

The Renaissance era is best exemplified by the delicate reliefs on the facade of the Château de Montal and on its fantastic stairway. The elaborately decorated doorways of the Hôtel d'Assézat in Toulouse reflect the revival of interest in stone sculpture on secular buildings at this time.

The region's two leading sculptors of the 19th and 20th centuries were students of Rodin: Émile Antoine Bourdelle (1861–1929), from Montauban, produced similarly powerful busts and figures, and Charles Despiau (1874–1946), from Mont de Marsan, was a leading figure in the era's revival of interest in sculpture and created a more original style, especially in his nudes and female busts. Robert Wlérik (1882–1944), also from Mont de Marsan, became famous for his work on the equestrian statue of Maréchal Foch in Paris. The Musée Despiau-Wlérick in Mont de Marsan is the only one in France devoted to modern figurative sculpture and displays works by over a hundred artists.

Another unusual museum, Musée Zadkine in the remote village of Les Arques (between Gourdon and Puy l'Evêque in the Lot) houses works by the Cubist sculptor, Ossip Zadkine, who lived here in the 1930s.

SOCIETY & CONDUCT
Traditional Culture

Throughout the region, passion for football and rugby are eroding support for the traditional games of *pelote* and *boules* (see the Spectator Sports section in the Facts for the

Visitor chapter), with every village cafe adorned with the local teams' trophies and announcements.

In the French Basque country and the Landes there's still considerable support for their unique versions of bullfighting (the *corrida* and *les courses landaises*; see Spectator Sports). The stilt-walking shepherds of the Landes (see the boxed text 'On Your Stilts' in the Bordeaux, the Atlantic Coast & the Landes chapter) are long gone, but some 20 folklore groups keep the practice alive, many appearing at festivals where the region's *bandas* (traditional brass bands) also perform.

Many rural traditions quietly continue everywhere, including celebratory dinners (invariably for the menfolk) at the end of the fruit and grape harvests and of the hunting season. During the winter truffle and foie gras season, markets are at their traditional best.

Do's & Don'ts

To generalise somewhat rashly, the Garonne River is the Mason-Dixon Line of social conduct, with more reserve to the north and more gusto to the south. Influenced perhaps by centuries of English rule, the folk of Périgord and Quercy – no-one would dream of identifying themselves by modern département names like Dordogne and Lot – exhibit almost courtly politeness and hospitality. South of the Garonne there's considerable pride in being a real 'Gascon' – honest, brave, down-to-earth, with a passionate *joie de vivre*. The Basques have an even stronger cultural identity, manifest in their own language, traditions and lingering desire for independence.

Some historical understanding is an important prerequisite to correct small-talk in South-West France. Everyone laughs about how the English are conquering Aquitaine for a second time by buying up old farmhouses as holiday homes, but the loss of land (both in the Middle Ages and now) can be a sensitive issue. Among the elderly you will still find considerable emotion about WWII: this was, after all, one of the strongest bastions of the Résistance and the

scene of many Nazi atrocities at the war's end.

But talk about food and wine and you're on safe ground everywhere in this gourmand heartland. You may find wine connoisseurs a little stuffy in Bordeaux but there's no snobbery in the hinterland, where the locals often finish their soup by splashing in some house red wine, a practice known as *chabrol*. If you're invited to aperitifs in a local home, you'll be pressed to drink – and drink and drink. They'll think you're a great Gascon if you polish off a bottle of their home-made *vin de noix* (nut wine). If you're lucky enough to be invited to a Périgordian home for dinner, fast beforehand if you want to get through the dozen courses. A suitable gift for such occasions is a bunch of flowers (but not chrysanthemums, which are only brought to cemeteries).

Women should expect lots of kisses on greeting country folk – as many as four quick pecks (not lingering, slurpy kisses) may be exchanged among family or friends, starting with the right cheek. In cities (especially Anglophile Bordeaux) two is the norm. Men – or women if they are strangers – nearly always exchange handshakes, though it's cool for young women to exchange kisses even with strangers. Little kids always give – and get – kisses.

Even if you're not on kissing terms, it's essential to greet all and sundry with a *Bonjour, monsieur/madame/mademoiselle*. French people are delightfully cordial to one another and will typically acknowledge everyone at large with a *bonjour* or a *'m'sieur/m'dame'* when walking into a shop or cafe, and with a *merci, monsieur..., au revoir* when leaving. Both *s'il vous plait* and *merci* (please and thank you) should be used liberally if you want to give a good impression of your foreign manners.

Treatment of Animals

Hunting Traditions in the south-west are among the strongest in the country, with *la chasse* (the hunt) considered a right of the common man entrenched since the Revolution. Out of the country's 1.5 million hunters, Gironde boasts the largest number of any département – over 60,000 – many of whom head to the forests and woodlands with their dogs the moment the season opens at the end of July.

Others lie in wait in specially-constructed hides for migratory birds to pass overhead: especially popular are *tourterelle* (turtle doves) which are illegally hunted from early May. Box and clap nets are used throughout Aquitaine to catch skylarks and wood-pigeons, and an estimated 50,000 ortolan buntings and some 350,000 chaffinches and bramblings are illegally trapped each year in the region. Despite a 1979 EU directive to protect wild birds in member states, France has yet to make the directive's provisions part of French law. As a result, environmentalists have in the past rented entire mountain passes on birds' flight paths in order to keep hunters away.

Unfortunately, the hunting lobby is strong; there's even a new political party, Chasse Pech Nature Tradition, which supports hunting practices. In February 1998 some 150,000 hunters joined a Paris demonstration against an EU directive which limits the wildfowl hunting season, protects endangered habitats and restricts access to private land. Five months later the government actually extended the hunting season (from 14 July to 28 February), up to two months longer than in the rest of the EU.

This period affects 24 migratory species of rare or declining status. The European Commission is seeking to fine France for contravention of the EU directive. Anti-hunting campaigns are also active throughout France, chiefly by La Ligue pour la Protection des Oiseaux (LPO; see Flora & Fauna earlier in this chapter for contact details). The south-west's major anti-hunting body is Rassemblement des Opposants à la Chasse (ROC; ☎ 05 53 03 24 55).

Foie Gras The issue of *le gavage* – the force-feeding of geese to make foie gras – also rouses strong feelings, though mostly among foreign visitors horrified at the sight of a funnel being thrust down a goose's neck. However, foie gras is one of the region's major income-earners and unlikely to be banned on the basis of foreign sensitivities.

Geese are force-fed on boiled maize or corn three times daily for three weeks to increase the quality and size of their livers to a massive 1.3kg. Ducks are also subjected to the practice. Battery farming is used in many cases, though the best foie gras comes from free-range geese. See the special Food & Wine section for more background information.

Bullfighting Spanish-style bullfighting is at its most popular in the Landes and the Gers, where fights take place regularly during the July to September season. There appear to be few protesters or anti-bullfighting movements, though the gentler bull-running competition called les courses landaises attracts a sizeable following too. See Spectator Sports in the Facts for the Visitor chapter for more details.

RELIGION
Some 80% of French people identify themselves as Catholic but, though most have been baptised, relatively few attend church. This is certainly true in the south-west, where you'll invariably find only the elderly attending mass in village churches.

There's also a strong Protestant following here, especially in Béarn, where the first of France's Protestant communities appeared in the 1530s, encouraged by its staunchly Protestant ruler, Jeanne d'Albret. The 1598 Edict of Nantes decreeing religious tolerance put an official end to the Wars of Religion which had torn the region apart, but Catholic-Protestant hostilities still simmered and, when the Edict was revoked in 1685, some 300,000 Protestants fled France, founding major communities in the UK and South Africa.

Nationally some 1.8% of French people are Protestant. Orthez, a former capital of Béarn, has an unusually high 10%, while the populations of some isolated villages of the Ossau and Aspe valleys are as much as 50% Protestant. The French refer to a Protestant church as a *temple*, and Protestants are apt to be offended if you call their church an *église*.

The Pilgrims of St-Jacques

It all began two thousand years ago, when King Herod beheaded James the Great, making him the first apostle to be martyred for his beliefs. A legend grew that he had been buried on the coast of Galicia in north-western Spain. As luck would have it, his tomb was 'discovered' in the early 9th century just when the flagging Christian forces of Spain needed some 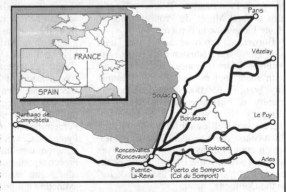 help against the Moors; St James (Santiago in Spanish) proved his worth by appearing on a white horse at the battle of Clavijo in 844, helping to defeat the Moors.

A church was built on the site of his tomb, the town of Compostela grew around it and within a few years the first pilgrims arrived at this *campus stelae in finis terrae* (field of stars at the world's end). By the Middle Ages, the trickle had turned into a flood of two million visitors per year.

In France the *Jacquets*, as the pilgrims were called (from Jacques, the French name for James), used a network of routes – four main ones and various branches like the coastal route from Soulac – which converged at Pyrénéan passes including Roncevaux and Col du Somport. The journey evolved into a series of mini-pilgrimages taking weeks or months, with detours to other shrines en route.

New churches were built to cater to (and skim money from) the passing faithful and hospices and hostels were established by the Benedictine monks of Cluny, the Knights Templars and the Hospitallers of St John. In the 12th century the first-ever tourist guide appeared, the *Codex Calixtinus*, written in Latin by a French monk to clue pilgrims in on the best holy spots and hostels, and on avoiding the 'barbarous Basques.' It was, of course, a best seller.

Thanks to the Wars of Religion and to the more ambitious ideals of the Renaissance, the popularity of the pilgrimage began to wane by the 17th century, but today its popularity is again on the rise, with tens of thousands making it over the Pyrénées to Santiago de Compostela each year. UNESCO has designated the whole route a World Heritage Site, with 69 monuments currently listed, of which 50 are in France and 33 within the scope of this book. Tourist boards now market the routes (Aquitaine has the lion's share) and walkers' topoguides exist for each section of the route.

For further information, contact the Association de Coópération Inter-Régionale 'Les Chemins de St-Jacques de Compostelle' (☎ 05 61 25 57 31, fax 05 61 25 59 33), 42 rue des Saules, 31400 Toulouse, or the Association Régionale des Amis de St-Jacques en Aquitaine (☎ 05 56 89 11 78), Prieuré de Cayac, 257-A cours du Général de Gaulle, 33170 Gradignan. Among many outfits organising walks along the route is La Pèlerine (☎ 04 66 69 60 87, fax 04 66 69 60 90, email pelerine.randonnee@wanadoo.fr), Romagnac F, 43580 St-Vénérand.

See the French Basque Country & Béarn chapter for details about Orthez's good Musée du Protestantisme Béarnais. There is also a small Musée du Protestantisme en Haute-Languedoc in Ferrières (Tarn).

Bordeaux, Toulouse and some larger towns have small Muslim and Jewish communities. Islam is France's second religion, with about four million adherents nationally. France's 650,000-strong Jewish community is Europe's largest. Above the Périgord Noir village of St-Léon-sur-Vézère is a well-established Tibetan Buddhist centre (with resident Tibetan monks) which attracts many visitors and has even hosted a visit by the Dalai Lama (see the boxed text 'Meditation on the Côte de Jor' in the Dordogne chapter).

LANGUAGE

French is one of the great languages of the world; a language of society, culture and diplomacy. Being able to speak some French will broaden your travel experience and ensure you are treated with great appreciation. It is the mother tongue of about 75 million people around the world. The total number of French speakers, including those who use it as a second language, is estimated as more than 200 million. For more information about the French language, some useful words and phrases and a food glossary, see the Language chapter later in this book.

Pride and perseverance have ensured the survival of local dialects in the region of South-West France (although it is unlikely you will hear anything but standard French being spoken).

Dialects of South-West France

The origins of the Basque language (Euskara) are still shrouded in mystery. Some scholars believe it to be related to languages from the Caucasus, others link it to languages from Africa, and still others highlight similarities with languages from Asia (Japanese for example). Despite the successive invasions of the Gauls and the Romans, Basque has managed to survive to the present day and is still spoken by about one million people in France and Spain. The French Basque Country is north of the Pyrénées. Centuries of neglect and marginalisation, combined with two centuries of French republicanism and 40 years of Spanish fascism, pushed Basque to the brink of extinction but pride in the language has resulted in its preservation. There is now a television station in France that broadcasts entirely in Basque.

The generic term of 'Occitan' refers to the variety of dialects that are spoken over a large territory in the south of France, spreading from the area north of Bordeaux to the region south of Grenoble, and even extending partially into northern Italy. As the language of the troubadours, Occitan enjoyed great literary prestige during the Middle Ages. However, economic and religious imperialism from the north resulted in the Parisian dialect being imposed in administrative spheres. Occitan has no standard and so reference is often made to the individual varieties: Provençal, Gascon, Limousin, Languedocien and so on. Recent estimates suggest there are around eight million speakers, of which two million still use the language every day.

Facts for the Visitor

PLANNING
When to Go
Mid-season, during spring (April to June) and autumn (September to October), is the best time to visit the south-west. During the high season (July and August, and sometimes June and September too) – especially in the Dordogne and at the Atlantic resorts – temperatures soar, rooms are scarce or wildly overpriced, bus services dwindle, roads are choked and local markets are awash with tour groups. But these months are also the best for water sports, beaches, high-elevation trekking and festivals (see Public Holidays & Special Events later in this chapter) – and a few sights, restaurants, shops, tourist offices and camp sites are only open at this time.

Spring brings cool to mild temperatures, a landscape bursting with wild flowers, and mid-season rates for accommodation, but beware the weekends of Easter and Pentecost (the seventh Sunday after Easter) when it's high season again. In autumn, the grape harvest *(vendange)* and walnut-gathering make a fascinating backdrop to forays into the Médoc wine area and the Dordogne – but be prepared for dramatic thunderstorms in late September. Cool spring and autumn are the best low-elevation walking and cycling seasons. The climate in Pau seems to stay mild even in winter.

Winter is when skiers head to the Pyrénées and truffle-lovers go to markets in the Dordogne and Lot. In January a great many hotels, restaurants and cultural sights close down altogether. During school holidays, at Christmas and New Year, in February and March, crowds (and room prices) again mushroom.

On Sundays and public holidays during the year, many small towns seem to shut down completely, which can leave you gasping for a coffee and a baguette – though *boulangeries* (bakeries) often open on Sunday morning (and close all day Monday).

Maps
Quality regional maps are widely available outside France. Many bookstores stock locally relevant regional maps, and you can also find a wide selection in the FNAC stores in Bordeaux, Toulouse and Pau. Town maps are easily found on arrival, at tourist offices, bigger newsagents (often called Maison de la Presse), bookshops and some newspaper kiosks.

Road Maps Michelin does the best road maps. Its red-jacketed *Southern France* (No 919) map covers the whole region at a glance, at 1:1,000,000 (1cm = 10km). More detailed and useful for drivers is the yellow 1:200,000 (1cm = 2km) series; seven maps (Nos 71, 75, 78, 79, 82, 83 and 85) cover the area of this book. Some other handy Michelin maps include *Aquitaine* (No 234, 1:200,000) and *Dordogne* (No 4024, 1:150,000).

Tourist Maps The best topographic maps are published by the Institut Géographique National (IGN). They're sold in better bookshops (and FNAC stores), and also through IGN's French-language Web site at www.ign.fr/.

Hikers will like IGN's 1:25,000 (1cm = 250m) Séries bleue maps (46FF); in many tourist zones these are being replaced with the TOP 25 series (58FF) which contain more information, for example on trails and sport facilities. Nature trails and fishing, walking and bathing spots feature on the 1:50,000 (1cm = 500m) Séries plein-air maps. Covering a wider area and more suitable for cyclists are the 1:100,000 (1cm = 1km) Séries verte maps or their tourist versions in the TOP 100 series (both 29FF). A good map in the 1:250,000 (1cm = 2.5km) TOP 250 series (29FF) is No 110, *Bordelais-Périgord*.

Other publishers start with these maps and add details. Didier-Richard publishes excellent 1:50,000 trail maps in its Tracés

Highlights

Some things you just shouldn't miss in the south-west – a visit to a prehistoric painted cave, for instance, and a splurge on some of the region's fantastic food. Here are a few more recommendations:

Prehistoric Art

Gaze in wonder at the 15,000- to 20,000-year-old paintings and carvings at Font de Gaume (Les Eyzies), Pech Merle (Cabrerets) and Cougnac (Gourdon). The replica Lascaux II cave is well worth a visit, too (book ahead in high season).

Romanesque Art

Track down wonderful Romanesque carved stone in Toulouse's Basilique St-Sernin, Souillac's Abbaye Ste-Marie (especially its 'dancing' statue of Isaiah), Cahors' Cathédrale St-Étienne, Moissac's Abbaye St-Pierre, the Cathédrale Notre Dame at Lescar (Pau) and Abbaye-Église St-Sever near Mont de Marsan.

Outdoor Activities

See the region from a different point of view: canoe, kayak or raft the Dordogne or the Lot, pedal the well-marked bike trails of Gironde or the Landes, or ride a horse almost anywhere. Surfers will find some of Europe's best beaches on the Aquitaine coast, especially at Lacanau, Biscarrosse, Hossegor and Anglet. The Basses-Pyrénées (Béarn) offer high-elevation treks, parasailing, fishing, white-water rafting, skiing and more.

Bastides

Discover the charming atmosphere of these orderly, medieval 'new towns' – at their best at Monpazier, Monflanquin, Villeréal, Domme, Montauban and Cordes-sur-Ciel.

---

grand-air series for 71FF each. Hikers may also like the 98FF Guide Franck maps with short walks around specific areas (for example Bergerac, Périgueux and Sarlat in the Circuits Pedestres Périgord series). Families with young children should look for the *Les sentiers d'Emilie en...* series, suggesting gentle walks in specific areas.

A handsome series of big IGN département maps from 1:100,000 to 1:140,000 (29FF) are crammed with topographic detail, roads, political boundaries, town plans and a town index. Similar ones in IGN's découvertes régionales series (35FF) include *Aquitaine* (1:250,000), *Dordogne* (1:125,000), *Midi-Pyrénées* (1:275,000) and *Pyrénées-Atlantiques* (1:125,000).

Several 1:1,000,000 IGN maps (29FF) are useful for overall planning: *France – Grand Randonnée* (No 903) shows long-

distance GR trails; *France – VTT & randonnées cyclos* (No 906) indicates dozens of rural bicycle tours; *France – canöe-kayak et sports d'eau vive* (No 905) is useful for water-sports enthusiasts.

City Maps Free tourist-office *plans* (street maps) range from superb to useless. Michelin's *Guide rouge* series (see Guidebooks under Books later in this chapter) have maps for larger cities, towns and resorts showing one-way streets and numbered town entry points; these are coordinated with Michelin's yellow-jacketed 1:200,000 road maps.

Blay-Foldex publishes *plans-guides* city map/guides for Agen, Albi, Arcachon, Bayonne, Bordeaux, Brive-la-Gaillarde, Cahors, Montauban, Pau, Périgueux and Toulouse, costing from 20FF to 30FF.

Highlights

Chateaux & Fortresses
Take your pick of beautiful chateaux – notably the Renaissance marvels of Montal and Puyguilhem – and hugely fortified hilltop castles disputed by the French and English in the Hundred Years' War, such as Beynac-et-Cazenac and Biron. Château de Hautefort and the redoubtable Château de Castelnaud are very impressive, too.

Museums
Bordeaux's Musée d'Aquitaine gives a great overview of the region's treasures from all ages; Auch's Musée des Jacobins is one of France's best provincial museums; and Bayonne's Musée Bonnat is a treasure-trove of 19th-century artwork. Maison des Arts Georges Pompidou (Cajarc) is a surprising contemporary art gallery in the back of beyond. For modern figurative sculpture the Musée Despiau-Wlérick (Mont de Marsan) is the only one of its kind in France.

Views & Landscapes
Marvel at nature's work at Dune du Pilat (Arcachon), Gouffre de Padirac (Padirac) or the Cirque de Lescun in the Vallée d'Aspe (Pyrénées). Have your camera ready at the hilltop sites of Albi, Rocamadour, St-Cirq Lapopie and the beautiful old towns of Sarlat-la-Canéda, Martel and Carennac. Dream away the hours in the serene Célé and Vézère valleys.

Regional Food
You haven't discovered the south-west until you've tasted an *omelette aux truffes* (truffle omelette), *pâté de foie gras* (foie gras pâté), *magret confit de canard* (fillet of duck preserved in its own fat, cooked until crisp), prunes from Agen (the world's best) and chocolate from Bayonne. Pick up local walnuts (or walnut cake or oil), honey, strawberries and goat's cheese at weekly markets throughout the region.

What to Bring
Bring as little as possible: forgotten items can be picked up practically anywhere in the region. If you'll be on the move a lot, or even just humping everything between hotels and stations, a backpack is the way to carry it. An internal-frame pack whose straps can be zipped inside can be made to resemble a nylon suitcase; some have exterior pouches that zip off to become daypacks.

Hostellers must provide their own towel and soap. Bedding is almost always provided or available for hire, though you might want to have your own sheet bag. You'll sleep easier with your own padlock on the storage locker that's often provided by hostels.

Other items to consider are a torch (flashlight), an adapter plug (for electrical appliances such as an immersion heater for preparing tea), a universal bath/sink plug (a plastic film canister sometimes works), a few clothes pegs and premoistened towelettes. Essential items for surviving the July and August sun are a water bottle, sunglasses, a sun hat, suncream (including sunblock) and after-sun lotion (in case you burn). Among other uses, a big cotton handkerchief can be soaked in fountains and used to cool off. Bring a warm sweater in spring or autumn and a small collapsible umbrella in any season.

RESPONSIBLE TOURISM
The summertime tourist invasion of the south-west brings environmental and social stress: narrow rural roads are clogged with cars and tour buses, pretty villages lack the infrastructure to cope with the invasion, and

locals may hardly get a look-in at popular markets and summer festivals.

You can reduce your own impact by travelling by train, bike (on your own or on small group tours) or even on foot, instead of in a car. You can do even better – and keep your own stress level down – by lingering longer in a smaller number of places, and by visiting during the low or midseason when everything is less fraught and your francs are more appreciated. Staying in *camping à la ferme* (camping on the farm), or *chambres d'hôte* (B&Bs) rather than mainstream hotels gives locals a bigger share of what you spend (for more information on accommodation see Accommodation later in this chapter). So does buying *produits du terroir* (local, home-made produce) straight from the farm or small town market rather than the supermarket or tourist shop.

When exploring the Vézère and Lot valleys and their prehistoric cave sites, remember that it's illegal in many areas to dig for fossils, flints or other artefacts: the locals have been doing it for decades, of course, but then it's their land.

TOURIST OFFICES
Local Tourist Offices
Every city, town and village seems to have an *office de tourisme* (a tourist office run by some unit of local government) or *syndicat d'initiative* (a tourist office run by an association of local merchants). Both are excellent resources and can almost always provide a map and information on accommodation possibilities. Some offices provide additional services such as making local hotel reservations or exchanging foreign currency.

The south-west has two regional tourist offices: the Comité Régional du Tourisme d'Aquitaine (☎ 05 56 01 70 00, fax 05 56 01 70 07, email tourisme@cr-aquitaine.fr), Cité Mondiale, 23 Parvis des Chatrons, 3307 Bordeaux, and the Comité Régional du Tourisme de Midi-Pyrénées (☎ 05 61 13 55 55, fax 05 61 47 17 16, email crt.midi-pyrenees@wanadoo.fr) at 54 blvd de l'Embouchure, BP 2166-31022, Toulouse.

For on-the-spot inquiries you'll find the *comité départemental du tourisme* (CDT; départemental tourist bureau) more useful. The Pyrénées-Atlantiques département has two separate offices at this level, referred to as *agences*, for the French Basque country (Pays Basque) and for Béarn. Operating independently, but usually in association with almost every départemental office, is a leisure-booking organisation known as Les Services Loisirs Accueil, which can organise and book independent or group activities, courses, tours, meals, accommodation and more. Each tourist office can provide contact details.

Agence Touristique du Béarn
 (☎ 05 59 30 01 30, fax 05 59 84 10 13)
 Maison du Tourisme, 22ter rue JJ de Monaix, F-64000 Pau
Agence de Tourisme du Pays Basque
 (☎ 05 59 46 46 64, fax 05 59 46 46 60, email pbasque@wanadoo.fr)
 1 rue Donzac, BP 811, 64108 Bayonne
CDT Corrèze
 (☎ 05 55 29 98 78, fax 05 55 29 98 79)
 quai Baluze, 19000 Tulle
CDT Dordogne
 (☎ 05 53 35 50 24, fax 05 53 09 51 41)
 25 rue du Président Wilson, 24000 Périgueux
CDT Gers
 (☎ 05 62 05 95 95, fax 05 62 05 02 16, email cdtdugers@wanadoo.fr)
 7 rue Diderot, BP 106, 32002 Auch
CDT Gironde
 (☎ 05 56 52 61 40, fax 05 56 81 09 99)
 21 cours de l'Intendance, F-33000 Bordeaux
CDT Landes
 (☎ 05 58 06 89 89, fax 05 58 06 90 90)
 22 rue Victor Hugo, BP 407, F-40012 Mont de Marsan
CDT Lot
 (☎ 05 65 35 07 09, fax 05 65 23 92 76, email le-lot@wanadoo.fr)
 107 quai Cavaignac, BP 7, 46001 Cahors
CDT Lot-et-Garonne
 (☎ 05 53 66 14 14, fax 05 53 68 25 42)
 4 rue André Chénier, BP 158, F-47005 Agen
CDT Tarn
 (☎ 05 63 77 32 10, fax 05 63 77 32 32, email cdt_du_tarn@wanadoo.fr)
 Moulins Albigeois, BP 225, 81006 Albi
CDT Tarn-et-Garonne
 (☎ 05 63 63 31 40, fax 05 63 66 80 36)
 place Maréchal Foch, 82000 Montauban

French Tourist Offices Abroad

Information on the south-west is also available from French government tourist offices abroad:

Australia
(☎ 02-9231 5244, fax 9221 8682,
email frencht@ozemail.com.au)
25 Bligh St, 22nd floor, Sydney,
NSW 2000

Belgium
(☎ 0902 88 025, fax 02-502 0410,
email maisondelafrance@pophost.eunct.be)
21 ave de la Toison d'Or, 1050 Brussels

Canada
(☎ 514-288 4264, fax 845 4868,
email mfrance@mtl.net)
1981 McGill College Ave, Suite 490,
Montreal, Que H3A 2W9

Germany
(☎ 069-758 021, fax 745 556,
email maison_de_la_France@tonline.de)
Westendstrasse 47, D-60325 Frankfurt
(☎ 030-218 2064, fax 214 1238)
Keithstrasse 2–4, D-10787 Berlin

Ireland
(☎ 01-703 4046, fax 874 7324)
35 Lower Abbey St, Dublin 1

Italy
(☎ 166 116 216, fax 02 5848 6222,
email entf@enter.it)
Via Larga 7, 20122 Milan

Netherlands
(☎ 0900 112 2332, fax 020-620 3339,
email fra_vvv@euronet.nl)
Prinsengracht 670, 1017 KX Amsterdam

South Africa
(☎ 011-880 8062, fax 880 7722,
email mdfsa@frenchdoor.co.za)
Oxford Manor, 1st floor, 196 Oxford Rd,
Illovo 2196

Spain
(☎ 91-541 8808, fax 541 2412,
email maisondelafrance@mad.sericom.es)
Alcalá 63, 28014 Madrid

Switzerland
(☎ 01-211 3085, fax 212 1644),
Löwenstrasse 59, 8023 Zürich
(☎ 022-732 8610; fax 731 5873)
2 Rue Thalberg, 1201 Geneva

UK
(☎ 0891 244 123, fax 020-7493 6594,
email piccadilly@mdlf.demon.co.uk)
178 Piccadilly, London W1V 0AL

USA
(☎ 212-838 7800, fax 838 7855,
email info@francetourism.com)
444 Madison Ave, 16th floor, New York,
NY 10022-6903
(☎ 312-751 7800, fax 337 6339)
676 North Michigan Ave, Chicago,
IL 60611-2819
(☎ 310-271 6665, fax 276 2835,
email fgtola@juno.com)
9454 Wiltshire Blvd, Suite 715, Beverly
Hills, CA 90212-2967

VISAS & DOCUMENTS

Passport

The law requires that everyone in France, including tourists, must carry identification at all times. For foreign visitors this means a passport or national ID card. Your passport must be valid for three months beyond the date of your departure from France.

Visas

Tourist Visa France is one of the 15 countries that have signed the Schengen Convention, an agreement whereby all EU member countries (except the UK and Ireland) plus Iceland and Norway have agreed to abolish checks at common borders by the end of 2000. The other EU countries are Austria, Belgium, Denmark, Finland, Germany, Greece, Italy, Luxembourg, the Netherlands, Portugal, Spain and Sweden. Legal residents of one Schengen country do not require a visa for another Schengen country. Citizens of the UK and Ireland are also exempt from visa requirements for Schengen countries. In addition, nationals of a number of other countries, including Canada, Japan, New Zealand and Switzerland, do not require visas for tourist visits of up to 90 days to any Schengen country.

In practice, however, it is not recommended to travel without a passport as signatories reserve the right to implement both temporary and more permanent border controls (your passport is also necessary as a form of ID in France; see the previous passport section for details). The French government have chosen to exercise this right and passport control at its borders with Belgium and Luxembourg are still in place (the differing drug laws made France nervous about removing border controls).

Individual Schengen countries may also

impose additional restrictions on certain nationalities. It is, therefore, worth checking visa regulations with the consulate of each country you plan to visit. For up-to-the-minute information call the EU information office in Brussels on 03-22 295 1780.

The standard tourist visa issued by French consulates is the Schengen visa. To obtain a visa you must present your passport, air or other tickets in and out of France, proof of finances and possibly accommodation, two passport-size photos and the visa fee in cash. A 30 day tourist visa generally costs around US$31 and a three month single/multiple-entry visa US$37/44. Visas are usually issued on the spot.

Rules for obtaining Schengen visas have been tightened and it's now mandatory that you apply in your country of residence. You can apply for no more than two Schengen visas in any 12 month period and they are not renewable inside France. If you are going to visit more than one Schengen country you are supposed to apply for the visa at a consulate of your main destination country or, if you have no main destination, the first country you intend to visit. It's worth applying early for your visa, especially in the busy summer months.

Tourist visas cannot be extended except in emergencies (such as medical problems). If you have an urgent problem you should first consult your own nearest consular office in France or call the nearest *préfecture* (see Carte de Séjour below).

Long-Stay, Student or Au Pair Visa
If you'd like to work or study in France, or stay for over three months, apply for the appropriate *séjour* (long-stay) visa. Unless you're an EU citizen, it's difficult to get a visa allowing you to work in France, although student-visa holders can apply for permission to work part time (ask at your place of study). For any long-stay visa, begin the paperwork in your home country several months before you plan to leave.

Carte de Séjour If you're issued with a visa valid for six months or more, you'll probably have to apply for a *carte de séjour* (residence permit) within eight days of arrival in France. You'll need it to work legally. Getting it is almost automatic for EU nationals and almost impossible for anyone else except full-time students. Ask at your place of study or at the local prefecture *(préfecture)*, subprefecture *(sous-préfecture)*, city or town hall *(mairie* or *hôtel de Ville)*, or *commissariat* (police station).

The prefectures in Bordeaux (☎ 05 56 90 60 60, esplanade Charles de Gaulle), Périgueux (☎ 05 53 02 24 24, 2 rue Paul Courrier), Pau (☎ 05 59 98 24 24, 2 rue du Maréchal Joffre), Agen (☎ 05 53 77 60 47, place Verdun), Mont de Marsan (☎ 05 58 06 58 06, 26 rue Victor Hugo), Cahors (☎ 05 65 23 11 73, Cité Bessières) and Toulouse (☎ 05 34 45 34 45, 31 rue de Metz) have special visa sections which also handle cartes de séjour.

Travel Insurance
Travel insurance covers you for basic medical expenses, of luggage theft or loss (vital if you intend visiting the coast in the high season) and cancellation or delays in your travel arrangements. Cover depends on your policy and sometimes on what type of airline ticket you have. It's sensible to buy travel insurance as early as possible; if you buy it the week before you fly, you may find, for example, that you're not covered for flight delays caused by industrial action.

Driving Licence & Permits
Driving licences from EU countries are valid in France. So are many non-European licences, but it's still a good idea to bring an International Driving Permit (IDP). This is a multilingual translation of the details on your local licence; it's not valid unless accompanied by the original. An IDP can be obtained for a small fee from your local automobile association – take a passport photo and a valid licence.

Hostels Card
A Hostelling International (HI) card is only necessary at official *auberges de jeunesse* (youth hostels). You can buy one at most official French hostels for 70/100FF if you're

under/over 26 years old. One-night membership (where available) costs 19FF and a family card is 100FF.

Student, Youth, Teachers & Journalists' Cards

The International Student Identity Card (ISIC) and Teacher's Card (ITIC) can pay for themselves through half-price admissions, discounted air and ferry tickets, and cheap meals in student cafeterias. Valid for a year, the cards are available from student unions, youth-oriented travel agencies such as USIT Campus, STA Travel, Council Travel and Travel CUTS for around UK£6, and from French travel agencies such as Accueil des Jeunes en France (AJF) for 60FF.

If you're under 26 but not a student you can apply for a Euro under 26 or Go25 card, available from the same sources and for about the same price as an ISIC card.

A *Carte Jeunes* is available to anyone under 26 who has been in France for at least six months. It gets you discounts on things like air tickets, car rental, sports events, concerts and films. In France, details are available from ☎ 08 03 00 12 26. Qualifying young people can pick one up at AJF and other student travel agencies, a card valid for one year costs 120FF.

Seniors' Cards

The Rail Europe Senior Card gives discounts of around 30% on international train tickets for women over 60 and men over 65. It is available from Rail Europe (see Train under Continental Europe in the Getting There & Away chapter) for UK£5. You must first have a local seniors' railcard; in the UK this is called a Senior Railcard and costs UK£18 at mainline train stations. SNCF issues a *Carte Senior* to those aged over 60, good for reductions of between 20 and 50% on domestic train tickets. A Carte Senior valid for up to four train tickets costs 140FF; one valid for a year and unlimited tickets costs 285FF.

Discounts are also available for people aged over 60 at most museums, galleries and public theatres.

Camping Card International (CCI)

The CCI is a campers' ID that guarantees insurance coverage for any damage you may cause, and many camping grounds offer a small discount if you sign in with one. CCIs are issued by automobile associations, camping federations and, sometimes, on the spot at camping grounds. In the UK, the RAC issues them to its members for UK£4.

Copies

All important documents (passport data page and visa page, credit cards, travel insurance policy, air/bus/train tickets and driving licence) should be photocopied before you leave home. Leave one copy with someone at home and keep another with you, separate from the originals.

It's also a good idea to store details of your vital travel documents in Lonely Planet's free online Travel Vault in case you lose the photocopies or can't be bothered with them. Your password-protected Travel Vault is accessible online anywhere in the world – create it at www.ekno.lonelyplanet.com.

EMBASSIES & CONSULATES
French Embassies & Consulates

France's diplomatic and consular representatives abroad include:

Australia
  Embassy:
  (☎ 02-6216 0100, fax 6273 3193)
  6 Perth Ave, Yarralumla, ACT 2600
  Consulates:
  (☎ 03-9820 0944/0921, fax 9820 9363)
  492 St Kilda Rd, Level 4, Melbourne, Vic 3004
  (☎ 02-9262 5779, fax 9283 1210)
  St Martin's Tower, 20th floor, 31 Market St, Sydney, NSW 2000
Belgium
  Embassy:
  (☎ 02-548 8711, fax 513 6871)
  65 rue Ducale, 1000 Brussels
  Consulate:
  (☎ 02-229 8500, fax 229 8510)
  12A place de Louvain, 1000 Brussels
Canada
  Embassy:
  (☎ 613-789 1795, fax 562 3704)
  42 Sussex Drive, Ottawa, Ont K1M 2C9

Consulates:
(☎ 514-878 4385, fax 878 3981)
1 Place Ville Marie, 26th floor, Montreal,
Que H3B 4S3
(☎ 416-925 8041, fax 925 3076)
130 Bloor St West, Suite 400, Toronto,
Ont M5S 1N5

Germany
Embassy:
(☎ 0228-955 6000, fax 955 6055)
An der Marienkapelle 3, 53179 Bonn
Consulates:
(☎ 030-885 90243, fax 885 5295)
Kurfürstendamm 211, 10719 Berlin
(☎ 089-419 4110, fax 089-419 41141)
Mohlstrasse 5, 81675 Munich

Ireland
(☎ 01-260 1666, fax 283 0178)
36 Ailesbury Rd, Ballsbridge, Dublin 4

Italy
Embassy:
(☎ 06 68 60 11, fax 68 60 13 60)
Piazza Farnese 67, 00186 Rome
Consulate:
(☎ 06 68 80 64 37, fax 68 60 12 60)
Via Giulia 251, 00186 Rome

Netherlands
Embassy:
(☎ 070-312 5800, fax 312 5854)
Smidsplein 1, 2514BT The Hague
Consulate:
(☎ 020-624 8346, fax 626 0841)
Vijzelgracht 2, 1000 HA Amsterdam

New Zealand
(☎ 04-472 0200, fax 472 5887)
1-3 Willeston St, Wellington

Spain
Embassy:
(☎ 91-435 5560, fax 435 6655)
Calle de Salustiano Olozaga 9, 28001 Madrid
Consulates:
(☎ 91-319 7188, fax 308 6273)
Calle Marques de la Enseñada 10,
28004 Madrid
(☎ 93-317 8150, fax 412 4282)
Ronda Universitat 22, 08007 Barcelona

Switzerland
Embassy:
(☎ 031-359 2111, fax 352 2191)
Schosshaldenstrasse 46, 3006 Bern
Consulates:
(☎ 022-311 3441, fax 310 8339)
11 rue Imbert Galloix, 1205 Geneva
(☎ 01-268 8585, fax 268 8500)
Muhlebachstrasse 7, 8008 Zurich

UK
Embassy:
(☎ 020-7201 1000, fax 7201 1004)

58 Knightsbridge, London SW1X 7JT
Web site www.embafrance.org.uk
Consulate:
(☎ 020-7838 2000, fax 7838 2001)
21 Cromwell Rd, London SW7 2DQ
Visa section:
(☎ 020-7838 2051, fax 7838 2001)
6A Cromwell Place, London SW7 2EW
(☎ 0891 887 733 for general information on
visa requirements)

USA
Embassy & Consulate:
(embassy ☎ 202-944 6000, fax 944 6166;
consulate ☎ 202-944 6195, fax 944 6148;
direct fax for visa section 202-944 6212)
4101 Reservoir Rd NW, Washington,
DC 20007
Consulates:
(☎ 212-606 3688, fax 606 3620)
934 Fifth Ave, New York, NY 10021
(☎ 415-397 4330, fax 433 8357)
540 Bush St, San Francisco, CA 94108;
Other consulates are in Atlanta, Boston,
Chicago, Houston, Los Angeles, Miami and
New Orleans.

Embassies & Consulates in South-West France

It's important to realise what your own embassy – the embassy of the country of which you are a citizen – can and can't do to help you if you get into trouble.

Generally speaking, your embassy won't be much help in emergencies if the trouble you're in is your own fault. Remember that you are bound by the laws of the country you are in. Your embassy will not lend a sympathetic ear if you end up in jail after committing a crime locally, irrespective of whether such actions are legal in your home country.

In genuine emergencies you might get some assistance, but only if other channels have been exhausted. For example, if you need to get home urgently, a free ticket is exceedingly unlikely – the embassy would expect you to have insurance. If you have all your money and documents stolen, it might assist with getting a new passport, but a loan for onward travel is absolutely out of the question.

Some embassies used to keep letters for travellers or, in some cases, there would be a small reading room with newspapers from back home but these days the mail holding service has usually been stopped altogether and even newspapers tend to be out of date.

All foreign embassies are in Paris, but many countries have consulates in Bordeaux, Toulouse, Pau or Bayonne:

Algeria
(☎ 05 56 99 03 36)
41 rue F Despagent, Bordeaux
(☎ 05 61 62 97 07)
23 rue Arnaud-Vidal, Toulouse

Belgium
(☎ 05 56 52 29 49)
12 cours Balguerie Stuttenberg, Bordeaux
(☎ 05 61 52 67 93)
3 rue Mage, Toulouse

Canada
(☎ 05 61 99 30 16)
30 blvd de Strasbourg, Toulouse

Germany
(☎ 05 56 17 12 22, fax 56 42 32 65)
377 blvd Président Wilson, Bordeaux
(☎ 05 61 52 35 56)
24 rue de Metz, Toulouse

Holland
(☎ 05 61 13 64 94)
4th floor, 54 bis rue d'Alsace-Lorraine, Toulouse

Italy
(☎ 05 34 45 48 48)
13 rue Alsace Lorraine, Toulouse

Portugal
(☎ 05 56 00 68 20)
11 rue H Rodel, Bordeaux
(☎ 05 61 80 43 45)
22 ave Camille Pujol, Toulouse
(☎ 05 59 25 55 97)
6 rue Jacques Lafitte, Bayonne

Spain
(☎ 05 56 52 80 20, fax 56 81 88 43)
1 rue Notre Dame, Bordeaux
(☎ 05 61 52 05 50)
16 rue Ste-Anne, Toulouse
(☎ 05 59 59 03 91)
Résidence du Parc, 4 blvd du BAB, Bayonne
(☎ 05 59 27 32 40)
place Royale, Pau

Switzerland
(☎ 05 56 52 18 65)
14 cours Xavier Arnozan, Bordeaux
(☎ 05 61 40 45 33)
36 allées Jean Jaurés, Toulouse

Toulouse
(☎ 05 61 63 61 61)
19 allées Jean Jaurès, Toulouse

UK
(☎ 05 57 22 21 10, fax 56 08 33 12)
353 blvd Président Wilson, Bordeaux
(☎ 05 61 15 02 02)
20 chemin de Laporte, Toulouse

The nearest USA consulate (☎ 04 91 54 92 00) is at 12 blvd Paul Peytral, Marseille.

CUSTOMS

The usual allowances apply to duty-free goods purchased at airports or on ferries outside the EU: tobacco (200 cigarettes, 50 cigars or 250g of loose tobacco), alcohol (1L of strong liquor or 2L of less than 22% alcohol by volume; 2L of wine), coffee (500g or 200g of extracts) and perfume (50g of perfume and 0.25L of toilet water).

Do not confuse these with duty-paid items (including alcohol and tobacco) bought at normal shops and supermarkets in another EU country and brought into France, where certain goods might be more expensive. In this case the allowances are very generous: 800 cigarettes, 200 cigars or 1kg of loose tobacco; 10L of spirits (more than 22% alcohol by volume), 20L of fortified wine or aperitif, 90L of wine or 110L of beer.

Americans on the way home, take note: USA customs' regulations ban the import of edibles (including nuts, fruit and non-pasteurised cheeses) and plant products.

MONEY
Currency

The French franc (FF) remains the national currency until January 2002 when it will be exchanged for the euro (€). The franc ceases to be legal tender on July 2002. See the boxed text 'Euroland' for more details.

One franc is divided into 100 centimes. French coins come in denominations of 5, 10, 20 and 50 centimes (0.5FF) and 1, 2, 5, 10 and 20FF; the two highest denominations have silvery centres and brass edges. French franc banknotes come in denominations of 20FF (with a picture of Claude Debussy), 50FF (Antoine de St-Exupéry, creator of the Little Prince), 100FF (Paul Cézanne), 200FF (Gustave Eiffel) and 500FF (Marie and Pierre Curie).

Euroland

Since 1 January 1999 the franc and the euro – Europe's new currency for 11 of the European Union (EU) countries – have both been legal tender in France, with a fixed exchange rate. Euro coins and banknotes are scheduled to be issued in January 2002 but you can already get billed in euros and opt to pay in euros by credit card. Essentially, if there's no hard cash involved, you can deal in euros. Travellers should check bills carefully to make sure that any conversion has been calculated correctly.

The whole idea behind this note-less and coin-less period is to let euro-fearing punters limber up arithmetically. The most confusing period will probably be January to July 2002 when there will be two sets of notes and coins. But on 1 July 2002, the franc and 10 other currencies will go into the dustbin of history.

The euro should actually make a traveller's life easier. Euro coins (in denominations of one, two, five, 10, 20 and 50 cents, and €1 and €2) and notes (€5, €10, €20, €50, €100, €200 and €500) will be usable in all of Euroland's countries (Austria, Belgium, France, Finland, Germany, Ireland, Italy, Luxembourg, the Netherlands, Portugal and Spain) and in any other country that accepts euros. So, you won't need to change money between these countries, and banks won't be able to profit by buying money from you at one rate and selling it back at another, as they do now. Each participating state can decorate the reverse of its euro coins with its own designs.

You can log on to the euro Web site at www.europa.eu.int/euro/html/entry.html/. The Lonely Planet Web site (www.lonelyplanet.com) has a link to a currency converter and up-to-date news on the integration process.

Exchange Rates

country	unit	euro	FF
Australia	A$1	0.63	4.15
Canada	C$1	0.67	4.41
euro	€1	—	6.56
Germany	DM1	0.51	3.35
Japan	¥100	0.96	6.31
New Zealand	NZ$1	0.49	3.23
Spain	100 ptas	0.60	3.94
United Kingdom	UK£1	1.61	10.54
United States	US$1	0.99	6.52

Exchanging Money

Cash Cash is not a safe way to carry money; banks tend to pay more for travellers cheques than for cash, to make the cost of buying them worthwhile. But it's smart to carry a small stash of cash (the equivalent of around US$100) for emergencies. Bring low-denomination notes: fear of counterfeits makes many banks and others reluctant to accept US$100 notes.

Travellers Cheques & Eurocheques

Most banks charge a commission to exchange travellers cheques, typically 20FF or more per transaction, or a percentage fee for large sums; the post office charges 30FF. American Express offices charge nothing for their own cheques, but 3% (minimum 40FF) for other brands. The whole business goes more smoothly if you have cheques denoted in francs.

Eurocheques, available if you have a European bank account, are guaranteed up to a certain limit. When cashing them you must show your signed Eurocheque card. Many hotels and merchants refuse to accept Eurocheques because of the relatively large commissions.

Lost or Stolen Travellers Cheques If your American Express travellers cheques are lost or stolen in France, call toll-free ☎ 08 00 90 86 00. Reimbursement can be made at American Express offices in Bordeaux (☎ 05 56 00 63 33, fax 05 56 00 63 39,

14 cours d'Intendance) or Biarritz (☎ 05 59 24 19 22, Havas Tourisme, 8 place Clemenceau). If you lose your Thomas Cook travellers cheques, call toll-free ☎ 08 00 90 83 30. They will tell you the nearest bank where you can get a refund.

ATMs In French, automated teller machines (ATMs) are *distributeurs automatiques de billets* (DABs) or *points d'argent*. ATM cards can give you direct access to your cash reserves back home at a superior exchange rate. Although French banks limit the size of a transaction (typically between 600 and 1800FF), only your home bank charges commission (typically about 1.5%). Most ATMs are linked to the international Cirrus and Maestro networks. If you remember your PIN code as a string of letters, translate it back into numbers, as keyboards may not show letters.

Credit Cards This is the cheapest way to pay for things and to get cash advances. Visa (Carte Bleue) is the most widely accepted, followed by MasterCard (Access or Eurocard). American Express cards are not very useful except at upmarket establishments but they do allow you to get cash at certain ATMs and at American Express offices.

Taking along two different credit cards (stashed in different wallets) is safer than taking one, as it may be impossible to replace a lost Visa or MasterCard until you get home (American Express and Diners Club International offer on-the-spot replacement cards).

Lost or Stolen Cards If your Visa card is lost or stolen, call Carte Bleue (☎ 02 54 42 12 12) to freeze the account; to replace the card you must deal with the issuer. Report a lost MasterCard, Access or Eurocard to Eurocard France (☎ 01 45 67 53 53) and, if you can, to the issuer. For cards from the USA, call ☎ 1 314 275 6690.

If your American Express card is lost or stolen, call ☎ 01 47 77 70 00 or ☎ 01 47 77 72 00, both staffed 24 hours. In an emergency, American Express card holders from the USA can call a US number collect ☎ 202 783 7474 or 202 677 2442. Replacements can be arranged at any American Express office (see Lost or Stolen Travellers Cheques earlier).

Report a lost Diners Club card on ☎ 01 47 62 75 75.

International Transfers Telegraphic transfers are not very expensive but can be quite slow. It's quicker and easier to have money wired via American Express (at a cost of US$50 for US$1000). Western Union's Money Transfer system (☎ 01 43 54 46 12) and Thomas Cook's MoneyGram service (☎ 08 00 90 83 30) are popular.

Exchange Bureaus In Bordeaux and Toulouse, *bureaux de change* are faster, open longer and usually give better rates than the banks, but shop around. For relatively small transactions, even exchange places with less than optimal rates may leave you with more francs in your pocket.

Costs

The worst time to come if you want to save money is the high season – July and August – when prices for accommodation soar; some places even insist on you taking *demi-pension* (half-board) during this period. But off-season, if you stay in camp sites, hostels or budget hotels and have picnics rather than dining out, it's possible to get by for about US$30 a day per person (US$40 in July and August). An occasional meal out (see the following Tipping and Bargaining) may add another US$5 to the weekly budget.

Travelling with someone else immediately cuts costs: few hotels in the region offer single rooms, and those that do charge only marginally less than, or sometimes the same as for a double. Triples and quads (often with only two beds) are the cheapest per person and can offer an amazing price/comfort ratio.

You can cut costs by how you eat and drink, too: hearty picnics of baguette and cheese are a pauper's banquet. Carrying a water bottle instead of forking out between

15FF and 25FF for a canned drink is another money saver. In restaurants, go for the *menu du jour*, guaranteed to stuff you and to cost less than dining à la carte. *Menus* at lunchtime are often cheaper than in the evening. When it comes to drinks, ask for *une carafe d'eau* instead of bottled water, and order the house wine instead of beer.

Discounts Museums, cinemas, the SNCF, ferry companies and other institutions offer a range of price breaks to people aged under 25 or 26, to ISIC or other card-holders, and to those aged over 60 or 65 (for information on discount cards see the Visa & Documents section earlier in this chapter). Look for the words *demi-tarif* (half-price) or *tarif réduit* (reduced price) and ask if you qualify. Those aged under 18 get an even wider range of discounts, including free or reduced entry to most museums.

Look out for freebies too – for example entry to Bordeaux museums is free on the first Sunday of the month. Throughout the region, numerous galleries, palaces, museums, gardens and other historic or cultural places which usually demand an entrance fee are free on the third weekend in September during France's *Journées du Patrimoine* (Days of Patrimony, privately-owned mansions and monuments are open to the public).

Tipping & Bargaining

French law requires that restaurant, cafe and hotel bills include a service charge (usually 10 to 15%), so a *pourboire* (tip) is neither necessary nor expected. However, most people – dire service apart – usually leave a few francs in restaurants. Taxi drivers appreciate a few francs, and the normal tip for service station attendants who do your windows and check your tyres is around 5FF; for lavatory attendants it's a few centimes.

Little bargaining goes on in the region's markets.

Taxes & Refunds

France's Value Added Tax (*taxe sur la valeur ajoutée*; TVA) is 20.6% on most goods except food, medicine and books, for which it's 5.5%; it reaches 33% on such items as watches, cameras and video cassettes. Prices are rarely given without TVA.

If you are not an EU resident, you can get a refund of most of the TVA provided you're over 15, you'll be spending less than six months in France, you purchase goods worth at least 1200FF (tax included, not more than 10 of the same item) at a single shop, and the shop offers *vente en détaxe* (duty-free sales), usually indicated by a sign on the door or at the till.

Present your passport at the time of purchase and ask for a *bordereau de détaxe* (export sales invoice). Some shops refund 14% of the purchase price rather than the full 17.1% you are entitled to, in order to cover the time and expense of the refund procedure. When you leave France or another EU country, ensure that customs officials validate all three pages of the bordereau; the green sheet is your receipt. You'll receive a transfer of funds in your home country.

If you're flying out of Bordeaux or Toulouse airport, certain stores can arrange for you to receive your refund as you're leaving the country, but you must make such arrangements at the time of purchase. When you arrive at the airport, customs will validate your bordereau and tell you which customs refund window exchange bureau (*douane de détaxe*) to go to for your refund.

POST & COMMUNICATIONS
Post

Postal service in France is fast (next-day delivery for most domestic letters), reliable, bureaucratic and expensive. Post offices are signposted *La Poste*; older branches may be marked with the letters PTT (Postes, Télégraphes, Téléphones). To mail things, go to a postal window marked *toutes opérations*.

Postal Rates Domestic letters up to 20g cost 3FF. From France, by *service ordinaire*, postcards and letters up to 20g cost 3FF within the EU, 3.80FF to most of the rest of Europe, 3.90FF to Africa, 4.40FF to the USA, Canada and the Middle East,

4.90FF to Asia, and 5.20FF to Australasia. Aerogrammes *(enveloppes prétimbrées)* cost 5FF for delivery to all destinations. France's worldwide express mail delivery service, Chronopost, costs a fortune.

Sending parcels overseas is costly since nearly everything international now goes by air; keep your parcel under 2kg for the cheapest *service économique* rates (taking around 10 days). Sample prices include 49FF within the EU, 67FF to the USA and Canada, and 114FF to Australasia. A sea-mail service is available for books (called *livre/brochure*), though you won't always be told about it; delivery takes about a month, and up to 5kg costs 54FF to the UK, 90FF to the USA or Australia.

You can pay with a credit card at bigger post offices.

Sending & Receiving Mail Most shops which sell postcards sell *timbres* (stamps) too. Stamps bought from coin-operated machines inside post offices come out as an uninspiring, blue-coloured sticker.

When addressing mail to a French destination, do it the French way: write the *nom de famille* (surname or family name) in capital letters first, followed by the *prénom* (first name) in lower case. Insert a comma after the street number and don't capitalise 'rue', 'ave' or 'blvd'. Cedex after the city or town name just means mail sent to that address is collected at the post office rather than delivered to the door.

A poste restante service is available at all post offices.

Telephone
Emergency The following emergency numbers are toll-free everywhere:

SAMU medical treatment/ambulance	☎ 15
Police	☎ 7
Fire Brigade	☎ 18
Rape Crisis Hotline	☎ 08 00 05 95 95

France has one of the world's most sophisticated and modern telecommunications systems. Most public telephones require a *télécarte* (phonecard, costing 49FF or 87.50FF), sold at post offices, *tabacs* (tobacconists), supermarket checkout counters and SNCF ticket windows.

If you can follow instructions in French, choose the better-value Omnicom cards: try *l'Économique France* for calls within France or *L'Économique Carte Monde* for overseas calls. They cost 50FF or 100FF and are available at many tobacconists.

Calling South-West France From Abroad Lonely Planet's eKno Communication Card (see the insert at the back of this book) is aimed specifically at independent travellers and provides budget international calls, a range of messaging services, free email and travel information – for local calls, you're usually better off with a local card. You can join online at www.ekno .lonelyplanet.com, or by phone from South-West France by dialling ☎ 1 213 927 0101. Once you have joined, to use eKno from France, dial ☎ 0 800 91 20 66.

Check the eKno Web site for joining and access numbers from other countries and updates on super budget local access numbers and new features.

French telephone numbers all have 10 digits. To call anywhere in the south-west from abroad, dial your country's international access code, followed by 33 (France's country code) and the 10 digit number, dropping the first 0. To call abroad from France, dial ☎ 00 (France's international access code), followed by the country code, area code (dropping the initial zero if there is one) and local number.

Collect Calls & Inquiries To make a reverse-charge (collect) call *(en PCV)* or a person-to-person call *(avec préavis)*, dial ☎ 00-33, then the country code of the place you're calling (dial 11 instead of 1 for the USA and Canada). If you're using a public phone, you must insert a télécarte or, in the case of public coin telephones, a 1FF coin, to place operator-assisted calls through the international operator.

To find out a country code *(indicatif pays)*, call directory enquiries (☎ 12). To find out a subscriber's telephone number abroad, call international directory enquiries (☎ 00-3312 plus the relevant country code). In public phones, you can access this service without paying; from private phones it costs 7.30FF per inquiry.

International Rates The cheapest time to call home is during reduced tariff periods – generally on weekday evenings from 9.30 pm to 8 am, weekends and public holidays.

The rate for a phone call to Europe is 2.47FF to 4.45FF per minute (reduced tariffs 1.98FF to 3.46FF, Carte Monde 1.42FF). Calls to the USA and Canada cost 2.97FF per minute (reduced tariff 2.35FF, Carte Monde 1.42FF), while Australia, New Zealand, Japan, Hong Kong or Singapore cost 6.55FF per minute (reduced tariff 5.20FF, Carte Monde 2.90FF). Calls to elsewhere in Asia, non-Francophone Africa and South America cost from 6.55FF to 9.77FF per minute (reduced tariffs 5.20FF to 7.79FF, Carte Monde 4.55FF).

Domestic Tariffs Local calls are quite cheap. The regular, 1.39FF per minute *tarif rouge* applies from 8 am to 12.30 pm Monday to Saturday and from 1.30 to 6 pm Monday to Friday. The 1.02FF *tarif blanc* applies from 12.30 to 1.30 pm Monday to Saturday and from 6 to 9.30 pm Monday to Friday. The 0.56FF *tarif bleu nuit* applies from 10.30 pm to 6 am; at other times the 0.74FF *tarif bleu* applies.

Numbers starting with 08 36 are more expensive than other domestic calls: those starting 08 36 67 are billed at 1.49FF per minute; those starting 08 36 64/5 cost a flat 3.71FF, irrespective of duration. Avoid 08 36 70 numbers which command an 8.91FF connection fee as well as the 2.23FF per minute charge.

A 10 digit number which starts with 06 indicates a mobile phone, expensive to call.

Toll-Free Numbers Two digit emergency numbers (see Emergency under Telephone earlier in this section), Country Direct numbers and toll-free numbers (*numéros verts* literally, 'green numbers' – which have 10 digits and start 0 800), can be dialled from public phones without a télécarte or coins.

Minitel

Minitel is a telephone-connected, computerised information service – which is expensive to use and is being given a good run for its money by the Internet. Numbers all consist of four digits (for example 3611, 3614, 3615 etc) and a string of letters. We have not included Minitel addresses in this book except those that may represent an especially cheap or easy route, or the only one.

However, France Telecom has an electronic directory which you can access in some post offices. 3611 is the prefix for general address and telephone inquiries. 3615 SNCF and 3615 TER provide train information.

Fax

Virtually all town post offices can send and receive domestic and international faxes (*télécopies* or *téléfaxes*), telexes and telegrams. It costs about 20FF to send a one page fax.

Email & Internet Access

Among the handiest places from which to access the Internet are the many state-funded youth resource centres called Bureaux d'Information Jeunesse (BIJ) or, in Toulouse and Bordeaux, Centres Régionaux d'Information Jeunesse (CRIJ). Online fees vary; for example it's free in Toulouse's CRIJ but costs 20FF per hour at many BIJs. If you have a Web-based email account like Hotmail, you're all set. If not, some will let you send a message or two via their own email server, though they're not enthusiastic about your receiving mail there. These facilities are intended for the use of young French people, so please don't overuse or misuse them.

The number of cybercafes in the region is small but growing. Most are in university towns like Bordeaux, Toulouse, Agen, Bayonne and Mont de Marsan. France Telecom has started opening public access points

Internet en Français

If you surf the Web in France, you may have to do it in French. Following is a bit of useful French cyber-speak:

aide	help
cancel or *annuler*	cancel
coller	paste
copier	copy
couper	cut
edition	edit
fermer	close
fichier	file
ouvrir	open
précédent	back/preceding
quitter or *abandon*	exit
signet	bookmark
suivant	forward/next
vue	view

(they are open in Bordeaux and Toulouse) where you can send/receive email and surf the Web via Telecom's own server, Wanadoo, and pay for it with a telecard. The French postal service has begun installing Internet terminals in about a thousand larger post offices across the country (including Toulouse), with payment by special magnetic cards (50FF per hour initially and 30FF per hour upon 'recharge' of the card).

All such resources are noted under Post & Communications for each town.

If you've got your own laptop and modem, and an account with a server which has local access points in France, you should be able to log on from your hotel room for the cost of a local or long-distance call. You'll need an *adapteur* between your telephone plug and the standard T-shaped French receptacle. You can pick these up at a local electronics shop or you could check out a Web-based dealer like Magellan's (www.magellans.com) or Konexx (www.konexx.com). If the telephone is hard-wired into the wall, ask if you can plug directly into the hotel's fax line. Many of the mid-range places are now quite savvy about the Internet.

You're best off with buying a reputable 'global' modem before you leave home, or buy a local PC-card modem if you're spending an extended time abroad.

Before French email addresses (whose French accents can, in general, safely be ignored), you often see *mél*, short for *message électronique*.

INTERNET RESOURCES

The World Wide Web is a rich resource for travellers. You can research your trip, hunt down bargain air fares, book hotels, check on weather conditions or chat with locals and other travellers about the best places to visit (or avoid!).

A good place to start your Web explorations than the Lonely Planet Web site (www.lonelyplanet.com). Here you'll find succinct summaries on travelling to most places on earth, postcards from other travellers and the Thorn Tree bulletin board, where you can ask questions before you go or dispense advice when you get back. You can also find travel news and updates to many of our most popular guidebooks, and the subWWWay section links you to the most useful travel resources elsewhere on the Web.

In addition to Web sites noted elsewhere in this book, one that is worth checking out is www.franceguide.com, the French- and English-language site of Maison de la France, the French national tourism board, with background information on the south-west, events, activities, accommodation, transport, package tours and more.

BOOKS

As a general rule books are published in different editions by different publishers in different countries. Therefore it is possible for a book to be a hardcover rarity in one country while it's readily available in paperback in another. Fortunately, bookshops and libraries search by title or author, so your local bookshop or library is best able to advise you on the availability of the books recommended here. The following list is limited to works still in print and generally available in paperback.

Lonely Planet

Lonely Planet publishes guides to *France*, *Western Europe* and *Mediterranean Europe* which include chapters covering South-West France. It also publishes a handy *French phrasebook*. Watch out for Lonely Planet's *Walking in France*, due out in May 2000, for an overview of walking options all over the country.

Guidebooks

Michelin produces a guide rating France's great restaurants with one, two or three stars. The *Guide Gault Millau France* (175FF), also published annually, awards up to four *toques rouges* (red chefs' caps) to restaurants who offer exceptionally creative cuisine, and *toques blanches* (white chefs' caps) to those with good modern or traditional cuisine. Gault Millau is said to be quicker at picking up-and-coming restaurants than the Guide Rouge. An English edition is available.

Larger travel bookshops carry hundreds of titles on virtually every aspect of South-West France. *The Way of Saint James (GR65)* from Cicerone Walking Guides takes walkers along this famous *grande randonnée* trail across the Lot, Tarn-et-Garonne, Gers and Pyrénées-Atlantiques *départements*.

Travel

Freda White's *Three Rivers of France: Dordogne, Lot, Tarn* (1962) is a much-admired classic; although its details are often out-of-date, the perceptive comments and knowledge of the area remain unbeatable. *Down the Dordogne* (1991) by Michael Brown recounts the author's often-amusing adventures as he follows the river on foot (and at times by canoe and bike) from its source to Bordeaux.

An out-of-print book worth looking for is *A Guide to the Dordogne* by James Bentley, with fascinating background information on regional history, cuisine, art and literature, and a gazetteer of even the tiniest hamlets.

History & Politics

The Hundred Years' War (1988) by Christopher Allmand is a comparative study of how people in England and France coped with this long-running war. Desmond Seward's book of the same name is a fascinating account by an historian who clearly knows his stuff. A third work with the same title (1992) by travel-writer Robin Neillands is an easier read, geared for travellers, and tilts the bias towards the French for a change.

Eleanor of Aquitaine (1992) by Marion Meade is a colourful and engrossing account of the life of this powerful woman. *The Albigensian Crusade* by Jonathan Sumption examines the background to the 13th-century repression of Catharism which set the seal on the future of Toulouse and Languedoc.

Vichy France and the Resistance (1985) by Harry R Kedward is a well-recognised classic about this period. *Das Reich: The March of the 2nd SS Panzer Division through France* (awaiting reprint) by Max Hastings chillingly follows the movements of a German armoured division through the Dordogne in 1944.

Art & Architecture

The Cambridge Illustrated History of Prehistoric Art (1998) by Paul Bahn is a beautifully illustrated, worldwide survey which gives generous treatment to the cave carvings and paintings of South-West France. *The Shamans of Prehistory: Trance & Magic in the Painted Caves* (1998) by Jean Clottes, a rock-art expert, will get the goat of many art historians with its argument that the region's Cro-Magnon cave art is the work of shamans; nicely provocative. *The Cave of Lascaux: The Final Photographs* (1987) is pricey but lavishly illustrated by Mario Ruspoli. Patricia Lauber's *Painters of the Caves* (1998) is aimed at nine to 12-year-olds and describes how the cave painters lived, ate and painted, it is illustrated with photos and computer-generated images.

Jean-Auguste-Dominique Ingres (1990) by Robert Rosenblum is a biography of the enigmatic painter and son of Montauban. *Ingres in Fashion: Representations of Dress & Appearance in Ingres's Images of Women* (1999) by Aileen Ribeiro, the head of dress at London's Courtauld Institute of Art, is a revelation of social and fashionable mores in mid-19th-century France as depicted in Ingres's detailed portraits. *Toulouse-Lautrec: A Life* (1994) by Julia Frey is a scholarly but sympathetic appraisal of the artist, based on previously unavailable family papers.

Food & Wine

Life & Food in the Dordogne (1986) by James Bentley offers all you need to know about how and why this region became so famous for its cuisine, with recipes, personal anecdotes (Bentley lived in the area for years) and historical snippets. *The Cooking of Southwest France* (1983) by Paula Wolfert brings to life the people and food of the region in a highly acclaimed collection of recipes. Jeanne Strang's *Goose Fat and Garlic* (1993) is another classic on the subject.

A Taste of Périgord (1991) by Helen Raimes paints an evocative picture of local life while providing over 200 recipes, many (in true local style) requiring only simple, inexpensive ingredients. *Dordogne Gastronomique* (1994) by Vicky Jones is a richly-photographed tome with some great recipes and absorbing cultural detail. Paul Strang's *Take 5000 Eggs* (1997) mixes recipes with an encyclopaedic guide to the region's markets.

The most comprehensive guide to Bordeaux wines is David Peppercorn's *The Wines of Bordeaux* (1982), detailing not only the famous vineyards but the local brews which become our favourite *vins de table* (table wines). Paul Strang is here again with *Wines of South-West France* (1994), a thorough guide to the region's 200-plus wineries, plus generous insights on their history and personalities.

General

The Most Beautiful Villages of the Dordogne (1996) is a lavish coffee-table book with text by James Bentley and photographs by Hugh Palmer. *Pétanque – The French Game of Boules* by Garth Freeman may give you a rolling start in case you stumble on this gentle, ancient and well-loved game.

The White Company is a gripping historical novel by Sir Arthur Conan Doyle recounting the adventures of an English monk who learns about the age of chivalry, battle and bravado in Sir Nigel's White Company in France during the Hundred Years' War – a great read for kids and adults alike. Two other books aimed at children are: Julianna Simor Lees' *Périgord Summer*, on Aquitaine and its past, featuring notable figures such as Eleanor of Aquitaine; and *Signs of Life* (1995) by Jean Ferris, weaving prehistory with modern life, in a tale of how a young girl comes to grips with her sister's death during a family visit to Lascaux.

NEWSPAPERS & MAGAZINES

The major regional daily newspapers are *Sud Ouest* in Aquitaine and *La Depêche du Midi* in the Midi-Pyrénées, each with various regional editions or inserts. Regional weeklies include *La Semaine du Pays Basque* and *La République des Pyrénées*. *The News* (12FF) is a monthly English-language newspaper 'for residents and lovers of France', published from Périgueux with features, tips and columns of interest to expats.

International daily newspapers such as the *Guardian* and the *Times*, the *International Herald Tribune*, the *Washington Post* and *USA Today* are widely available in Bordeaux, Toulouse and other tourist centres. Foreign magazines like the *Economist* are usually only available in big towns.

RADIO & TV

If you've got a short-wave radio you can pick up a mix of BBC World Service and BBC for Europe at 12095 kHz; other bands are at 17640 kHz during the day and at 3955, 6195 and 9410 kHz in the morning and evening. BBC Radio 4 broadcasts at 198 kHz long wave. The Voice of America (VOA) is on short-wave at 7170, 9535, 9680, 9760, 9770, 11805, 15135, 15255,

15410 and 15580 kHz, and intermittently on AM at 1197 kHz.

Toulouse has its very own TV channel, TLT Télé-Toulouse, with exclusively local programming. The local radio station, Sud-Radio, is on 819 kHz AM and 101.4 MHz FM.

For Occitan-language broadcasts (plus some Portuguese, Spanish, German, English and Italian), tune into Radio Occitanie at 98.3 or 99 MHz FM, daily from 6 am to midnight. Radio France Toulouse also broadcasts in Occitan on 945 kHz AM, at noon on Saturday.

VIDEO SYSTEMS

Unlike the rest of Western Europe and Australia which use PAL, and the USA and Canada which both use NTSC, France uses SECAM. Non-SECAM TVs won't work in France nor can French videotapes be played on video recorders and TVs that lack a SECAM capability.

PHOTOGRAPHY & VIDEO

Colour-print and slide *(diapositive)* film are widely available in supermarkets, photo shops and FNAC stores, as are replacement video cartridges for your camcorder (but see the preceding section for imformation on compatibility).

In bright summer sun, avoid snapping at midday when glare is strongest. Photography is rarely forbidden, except in museums, art galleries and some churches. Snapshots of military installations might get you into trouble. When photographing people, ask permission; if your French isn't good enough, smile and point at your camera and they'll get the picture – as you probably will.

TIME

French time is GMT/UTC plus one hour, except during daylight-saving time (from the last Sunday in March to the last Sunday in October) when it is GMT/UTC plus two hours. The UK and France are always one hour apart – when it's 6 pm in London, it's 7 pm in Bordeaux. New York is six hours behind France.

France uses the 24-hour clock so time is written like this: 15h30 (ie, 3.30 pm).

ELECTRICITY

France runs on 220V, 50Hz AC. Old-style wall sockets take two round pins. Newer sockets accept fatter prongs and have a protruding earth (ground) pin. Many old-style sockets are recessed so the newer round plugs cannot be used in them; to avoid getting stuck with an up-to-date appliance in an out-of-date hotel, it might be worth carrying an adapter.

WEIGHTS & MEASURES

France uses the metric system. When writing numbers with four or more digits, the French use full stops (periods) or spaces (as opposed to commas): one million is 1.000.000 or 1 000 000. The decimals place is indicated with a comma, so English 1.75 becomes French 1,75.

LAUNDRY

Doing laundry on the road is a straightforward affair. Most towns have a *laverie libre-service* (unstaffed, self-service laundrette), often open 24 hours; they are noted in the individual chapters. They're not cheap, usually charging around 20FF for a 7kg load (plus 2/5FF for five/12 minutes of drying).

TOILETS

Public toilets, signposted *toilettes* or WC are frustratingly few and far between, though you can usually find a free one in the town hall or the market hall, open even when the rest of the building isn't. Expect to pay from 2FF to 5FF for a wad of toilet paper at staffed toilets. Some places – usually in car parks and public squares – have coin-operated, self-flushing toilet booths which cost 2FF to enter: highly disconcerting contraptions should the automatic mechanism fail when you inside.

The easiest option is often just to use the facilities in a cafe or restaurant – preferably after ordering a drink or snack, though most proprietors aren't fussed if you don't. Ask, *est-ce que je peux utiliser les toilettes, s'il vous plaît?*

Bashful males be warned: some toilets are semi-mixed; the urinals and washbasins are in a common area through which all and sundry pass to get to the closed toilet stalls. Older establishments often sport *toilettes à la turque*, squat loos with high-pressure flushing mechanisms that can soak your shoes if you're not quick.

Few public toilets, except at airports and newer bus and train stations, are wheelchair-accessible.

Bidets

A bidet is a porcelain fixture that looks like a shallow toilet with a pop-up stopper. Originally conceived to improve the personal hygiene of aristocratic women, its primary purpose is for washing the genitals and anal area, though its uses have expanded to include everything from hand-washing laundry to soaking your feet.

HEALTH

The south-west is a healthy place. Your main risks are sunburn, foot blisters, insect bites and an upset stomach from eating and drinking too much.

Predeparture Planning

Immunisations Innoculations are not required to travel to France. A few routine vaccinations are recommended whether you're travelling or not: polio (usually administered during childhood), tetanus and diphtheria (usually administered together during childhood, with a booster shot every 10 years), and sometimes measles. All vaccinations should be recorded on an International Health Certificate, available from your doctor or government health department.

Health Insurance Citizens of EU countries are covered for emergency medical treatment throughout the EU on presentation of an E111 certificate, though charges are likely for medications, dental work and secondary examinations including x-rays and laboratory tests. Ask about the E111 at your national health service or travel agent at least a few weeks before you go. In the

Medical Kit Check List

Following is a list of items you should consider including in your medical kit – consult your pharmacist for brands available in yourcountry.

- ☐ **Aspirin** or **paracetamol** (acetaminophen in the USA) – for pain or fever
- ☐ **Antihistamine** – for allergies, eg hay fever; to ease the itch from insect bites or stings; and to prevent motion sickness
- ☐ **Antibiotics** – consider including these if you're travelling well off the beaten track; see your doctor, as they must be prescribed, and carry the prescription with you
- ☐ **Loperamide** or **diphenoxylate** –'blockers' for diarrhoea; **prochlorperazine** or **metaclopramide** for nausea and vomiting
- ☐ **Rehydration mixture** – to prevent dehydration, eg due to severe diarrhoea; particularly important when travelling with children
- ☐ **Insect repellent, sunscreen, lip balm** and **eye drops**
- ☐ **Calamine lotion, sting relief spray** or **aloe vera** – to ease irritation from sunburn and insect bites or stings
- ☐ **Antifungal cream** or **powder** – for fungal skin infections and thrush
- ☐ **Antiseptic** (such as povidone-iodine) – for cuts and grazes
- ☐ **Bandages, Band-Aids (plasters)** and other wound dressings
- ☐ **Scissors, tweezers** and a **thermometer** (note that mercury thermometers are prohibited by airlines)
- ☐ **Cold** and **flu tablets, throat lozenges** and **nasal decongestant**

UK you can get the forms at the post office. Claims must be submitted to a local *caisse primaire d'assurance-maladie* (sickness insurance office) before you leave France.

Most travel insurance policies also include medical coverage. For important suggestions about travel insurance, see Visas & Documents earlier in this chapter.

Other Preparations Ensure you're basically healthy before you start travelling. If you are going on a long trip make sure your teeth are OK. If you wear glasses take a spare pair and your prescription. If you require a particular medication take an adequate supply, as it may not be available locally. Take part of the packaging showing the generic name, rather than the brand, which will make getting replacements easier (and cheaper). It's a good idea to have a legible prescription or letter from your doctor to show that you legally use the medication, to avoid any problems.

Medical Treatment in France

Major hospitals are indicated on the maps in this book, and their addresses and phone numbers are mentioned in the text. Tourist offices and hotels can put you onto a reliable doctor or dentist.

Public Health System Anyone (including foreigners) who is sick can receive treatment in the *service des urgences* (casualty ward or emergency room) of any public hospital. Hospitals try to have people who speak English in casualty wards, but it's not always the case. If necessary, the hospital will call in an interpreter. It's a good idea to request a copy of any diagnosis – in English, if possible – for your doctor back home.

Treatment for illness or injury in a public hospital costs less in France than in many other western countries: a consultation costs about 170FF (more on Sunday, public holidays and at night). Blood tests and other procedures each have a standard fee. Full hospitalisation costs from 3000FF a day. Hospitals usually ask that visitors from abroad settle accounts immediately after receiving treatment.

Dental Care Most major hospitals offer emergency dental services.

Pharmacies French pharmacies are usually marked by a green cross, the neon components of which are lit when it's open. *Pharmacien(ne)s* (pharmacists) can often suggest treatments for minor ailments.

If you are prescribed a medication, make sure you understand the dosage, how often and when you should take it. Ask for a copy of the *ordonnance* (prescription) for your records. During the mushroom-picking season (autumn), pharmacies act as a mushroom-identifying service (see Poisonous Mushrooms under Dangers & Annoyances later in this chapter).

Pharmacies coordinate their closures so that a town isn't left without a place to buy medication. Details on the nearest *pharmacie de garde* (pharmacy on weekend and night duty) are posted on all pharmacy doors. There are 24-hour pharmacies in Bordeaux and Toulouse.

Emergency

SAMU When you ring ☎ 15, the 24-hour dispatchers of the Service d'Aide Médicale d'Urgence (SAMU; Emergency Medical Aid Service) will take down details of your problem and send out a private ambulance with a driver (250–300FF) or, if necessary, a mobile intensive care unit. For less serious problems, SAMU can dispatch a doctor for a house call. If you prefer to be taken to a particular hospital, mention this to the ambulance crew, as the usual procedure is to take you to the nearest one. You must pay cash at the time, although in emergency cases (those requiring intensive care units), billing is taken care of later.

Basic Rules

Everyday Health Normal body temperature is 37°C (98.6°F); more than 2°C (4°F) higher indicates a high fever. The normal adult pulse rate is 60–100 beats per minute (children 80–100, babies 100–140). As a general rule the pulse increases about 20 beats per minute for each 1°C (2°F) rise in fever. Respiration (breathing) rate is also an indicator of illness. Count the number of breaths per minute: between 12 and 20 is normal for adults and older children (up to 30 for younger children, 40 for babies). People with a high fever or serious respiratory illness breathe more quickly than normal. More than 40 shallow breaths a minute may indicate pneumonia.

Water Tap water all over France is safe to drink. But fountain water isn't always *eau potable* (drinkable). Look for the signs.

It's very easy to not drink enough liquids, particularly in summer on hot days or at high altitude. Don't rely on thirst to indicate when you should drink. Not needing to urinate or very dark-yellow urine is a danger sign. Carrying your own water bottle is a good idea.

In rural areas, beware of natural sources of water. A burbling stream may appear crystal clear, but it's inadvisable to drink untreated water unless you're at the source and can see it coming out of the rocks.

The simplest way of purifying water is to boil it thoroughly. At high altitude water boils at a lower temperature, so germs are less likely to be killed. Boil it for longer in these environments.

Environmental Hazards

Fungal Infections Fungal infections occur more commonly in hot weather and are usually found on the scalp, between the toes or fingers, in the groin and on the body (ringworm). You get ringworm (which is a fungal infection, not a worm) from infected animals or other people. Moisture encourages these infections.

To prevent fungal infections wear loose, comfortable clothes, avoid artificial fibres, wash frequently and dry carefully. If you do get an infection, wash the infected area at least daily with a disinfectant or medicated soap and water, and rinse and dry well. Apply an antifungal cream or powder like Tolnifate (Tinaderm). Try to expose the infected area to air or sunlight as much as possible; wash all towels and underwear in hot water, change them often and let them dry in the sun.

Heat Exhaustion Dehydration and salt deficiency can cause heat exhaustion. Take time to acclimatise to the high temperatures, drink sufficient liquids and do not do anything too physically demanding.

Salt deficiency is characterised by fatigue, lethargy, headaches, giddiness and muscle cramps; salt tablets may help, but adding extra salt to your food is better.

Prickly Heat This is an itchy rash caused by excessive perspiration trapped under the skin. It usually strikes people who have just arrived in a hot climate. Keeping cool, bathing often, drying the skin and using a mild talcum or prickly heat powder or resorting to air-conditioning may help.

Sunburn You can get sunburnt surprisingly quickly, even through cloud. Use a sunscreen, hat, and barrier cream for your nose and lips. Calamine lotion or Stingose are good for mild sunburn. Protect your eyes with good quality sunglasses, particularly if you will be spending time near water, sand or snow.

Hay Fever Hay fever sufferers should be aware that the pollen count is especially high in May and June.

Infectious Diseases

Diarrhoea Simple things like a change of water, food or climate can all cause a mild bout of diarrhoea, but a few rushed toilet trips with no other symptoms is not indicative of a major problem.

Dehydration is the main danger with any diarrhoea, particularly in children or the elderly, as it can occur quickly. Fluid replacement (at least equal to the volume being lost) is most important. Weak black tea with a little sugar, soda water, or soft drinks allowed to go flat and diluted 50% with clean water are all good. Keep drinking small amounts often. Stick to a bland diet as you recover.

Hepatitis There are almost 300 million carriers of Hepatitis B in the world. It is spread through contact with infected blood, blood products or body fluids, for example through sexual contact, unsterilised needles and blood transfusions, or contact with blood via small breaks in the skin. Other risk situations include having a shave, tattoo, or having your body pierced with contaminated equipment. You should seek medical advice, but there is not much you can do apart from resting, drinking lots of fluids and eating lightly.

AIDS & HIV The Human Immunodeficiency Virus (VIH in French), develops into AIDS, Acquired Immune Deficiency Syndrome (SIDA in French), which is a fatal disease. HIV is a major problem in many countries. Any exposure to blood, blood products or body fluids may put an individual at risk. The disease is often transmitted through sexual contact or dirty needles – vaccinations, acupuncture, tattooing and body piercing can be as dangerous as intravenous drug use. HIV/AIDS can also be spread through infected blood transfusions; some developing countries cannot afford to screen blood used for transfusions.

If you do need an injection, ask to see the syringe unwrapped in front of you, or take a needle and syringe pack with you.

Fear of infection with HIV should never preclude treatment for serious medical conditions.

AIDS & HIV Information For information on free and anonymous HIV-testing centres *(centres de dépistage)* in France, ring the 24-hour SIDA Info Service toll-free (☎ 0 800 84 08 00).

AIDES (Association de Prévention, Information, Lutte contre le SIDA) is a national organisation that works for the prevention of AIDS and assists AIDS sufferers. Regional centres are AIDES Midi-Pyrénées (☎ 05 61 77 04 88, fax 05 61 42 99 58), 36 ave Lombez, Toulouse; and AIDES Aquitaine (☎ 05 56 24 33 33, fax 05 56 98 93 10), 173 bis rue Judaïque, Bordeaux (open from 2 to 7 pm Monday to Friday or telephone calls from 9 am to 7 pm). Another AIDS information and awareness centre in Bordeaux is ACT-UP (☎ 05 57 85 96 48), 112 rue Ste-Cathérine.

Sexually Transmitted Diseases Gonorrhoea, herpes and syphilis are among these diseases; sores, blisters or rashes around the genitals, discharges or pain when urinating are common symptoms. In some STDs, such as wart virus or chlamydia, symptoms may be less marked or not observed at all, especially in women. Syphilis symptoms eventually disappear completely but the disease continues and can cause severe problems in later years.

While abstinence from sexual contact is the only 100% effective prevention, using condoms is also effective. The treatment of gonorrhoea and syphilis is with antibiotics. The different sexually transmitted diseases each require specific antibiotics. There is no cure for herpes or AIDS.

Condoms All pharmacies carry *préservatifs* (condoms) and many have 24-hour automatic condom dispensers outside the door. Some brasseries, discotheques and WCs in cafes and petrol stations are also equipped with condom machines. Condoms that conform to French government standards are marked with the letters NF *(norme française)* in black on a white oval inside a red and blue rectangle.

Cuts, Bites & Stings

Rabies This is a potentially fatal viral infection found in many countries. Animals can be infected and it is their saliva that carries the virus. Any bite, scratch or even lick from a warm-blooded, furry animal should be cleaned immediately and thoroughly. Medical help should be sought promptly to receive a course of injections to prevent the onset of symptoms and death.

Insect Bites & Stings Bee and wasp stings are usually painful rather than dangerous. However, in people who are allergic to them severe breathing difficulties may occur and they may require urgent medical care. Calamine lotion or Stingose spray will give relief, and ice packs will reduce the pain and swelling.

Leeches & Ticks Check all over your body if you have been walking through a potentially tick-infested area, as ticks can cause skin infections and other more serious diseases. If a tick is found attached, press down around the tick's head with tweezers, grab the head and gently pull upwards. Avoid pulling the rear of the body as this may squeeze the tick's gut contents through the attached mouth parts into the skin, increasing the risk of infection and disease. Smearing chemicals on the tick will not make it let go and is not recommended.

Women's Health

Sexually transmitted diseases are a major cause of vaginal problems. Symptoms include a smelly discharge, painful intercourse and sometimes a burning sensation when urinating. Sexual partners must also be treated. Medical attention should be sought and remember in addition to these diseases HIV or hepatitis B may also be acquired during exposure.

Antibiotic use, sweating, synthetic underwear and contraceptive pills can lead to fungal vaginal infections when travelling in hot climates. Maintaining good personal hygiene, loose-fitting clothes and cotton underwear will help to prevent them.

Fungal infections, characterised by a rash, itch and discharge, can be treated with a vinegar or lemon juice douche, or with yoghurt. Nystatin, miconazole or clotrimazole pessaries or vaginal cream are the usual treatment.

WOMEN TRAVELLERS

Some French men have clearly given little thought to the concept of *harcèlement sexuel* (sexual harassment), and still believe that leering at a passing woman is paying her a compliment. Women need not walk round the region in fear, however. Suave stares are about as adventurous as most French men get, with women rarely being physically assaulted on the street or touched up in bars at night. Still, as in any country, the best way to avoid trouble is to be conscious of your surroundings, avoid going to bars and clubs alone at night and be aware of potentially dangerous situations: deserted streets, lonely beaches or dark corners of large train stations in cities such as Toulouse and Bordeaux.

Of course, it's not just French men that women travellers have to concern themselves with. While solo women travellers attract little unwanted attention in the rural south-west, it can be a different ball game at some of the popular Atlantic coastal resorts which attract macho personalities of all nationalities. Again, common sense is your best guide to avoiding unwanted attention here.

Topless sunbathing is not generally interpreted as deliberately provocative.

Organisations

In Bordeaux, the Centre d'Information sur les Droits de la Femme (☎ 05 56 44 30 30), 5 rue Jean-Jacques Rousseau, is the leading women's information and advice centre. Although geared to assist local women with family or marital problems it can also offer practical support and information (such as contacts for creches and baby-sitters), job assistance and general advice to women.

Its equivalent in Périgueux, the Centre d'Information et de Documentation des Femmes et des Familles de la Dordogne (CIDFF; ☎ 05 53 35 90 90), 15 rue Kléber, is active in women's rights and sheltering women in need. SOS Femmes Dordogne (☎ 05 53 35 03 03, fax 05 53 35 31 21), 120 blvd du Petit-Change, also provides a state-funded centre in Périgueux for victims of violence or women in need.

The national rape-crisis hotline is on ☎ 0 800 05 95 95.

GAY & LESBIAN TRAVELLERS

France is one of Europe's most liberal countries when it comes to homosexuality, in part because of the long French tradition of public tolerance towards people who have chosen not to live by conventional social codes. In October 1999 the government passed a controversial bill (known as the Civil Solidarity Pact) giving legal and fiscal rights (such as tax and property rights) to unmarried couples including homosexuals.

The south-west doesn't have a very prominent gay scene – the biggest communities are in Toulouse and Bordeaux. The lesbian scene is even less public than its gay counterpart and is centred mainly around women's cafes and bars.

There are several publications giving a good overview of the scene in (and beyond) the south-west; the free publication entitled 'Gay Friendly France: Liberté,

Egalité, Diversité'; the guide can be ordered from Gay Friendly France, French Government Tourist Office, PO Box 386 Bohemia, NY 11716, USA, email info@ francetourism.com. The *Guide Gai Pied*, a French- and English-language annual guide (79FF) to France with lists of gay-friendly cafes, bars, shops and gay organisations including those in Toulouse and Bordeaux. Their Web site is at www.gaipied.fr. At bookstores or newsstands in major towns and cities you should be able to pick up national gay publications (published monthly) such as *Gay*, *3 Keller* and *Lesbia*.

There are also several Web sites geared specifically for gay and lesbian travellers which are worth checking before starting your trip:

www.lonelyplanet.com.au/thorntree/gay/topics
    The site provides up-to-date advice from recent visitors on where to go and what to see.
www.outandabout.com
    The Web spin-off from the gay travel magazine *Out and About*, with updated information on the gay scene in various cities plus a handy calendar of gay events around the world.
www.guidemag.com/travel
    A site offering tips on gay-friendly hotels, bars and nightclubs.
www.nyu.edu/pages/sls/travel/gltravel
    This site lists everything from nightclubs and bookstores to gay community centres.

Organisations

In addition to the following there are also AIDS-awareness and help groups in Toulouse and Bordeaux – see the Health section earlier in this chapter.

Collectif pour un Centre Gai et Lesbian Bordeaux
    (☎/fax 05 56 81 73 14, ☎ 05 56 01 12 03)
    BP 230, 33012 Bordeaux Cedex. A leading organisation involved in many social activities, it also publishes its own journal; at the time of writing it was about to open a centre in Bordeaux.
CRIPS Aquitaine
    (☎ 05 57 57 18 80, fax 05 57 57 18 82)
    Université de Bordeaux II, 3ter place de la Victoire. Aquitaine's centre for regional news and AIDS awareness, this organisation is open from 9 am to 6 pm Monday to Thursday.

Gais et Lesbiennes en Marche
    (☎ 05 60 99 02 48, fax 05 61 62 29 49)
    9 rue Jacques-Laffitte, Toulouse. Defends the right of gays and takes part in many gay events, notably the 6 June Gay Pride march.
Le Centre Gai et Lesbien de Toulouse
    (☎ 05 61 62 30 62)
    4 rue de Belfort. The main drop-in gay centre in Toulouse and home to other gay associations; it is open from 5 to 8 pm Monday to Friday and from 3 to 8 pm at weekends.
Lesbian & Gay Pride Bordeaux
    (☎ 05 56 87 97 34)
    Organises the Gay Pride march in Bordeaux on 6 June.
Rassemblement des Gays Libéraux
    (☎ 05 56 01 29 47)
    Offers legal advice and does gay-rights lobbying; it publishes a monthly newsletter and takes telephone calls from 10 am to 1 pm on Monday, Tuesday and Friday.

DISABLED TRAVELLERS

The region is not user-friendly for *handicapés* (disabled people): kerb ramps are few and far between, older public facilities and budget hotels lack lifts, and the cliff-hugging hilltop villages of the Lot and Dordogne are a nightmare to navigate in a wheelchair. As for the prehistoric caves for which the region is so famous, you can practically forget those.

But all is not lost. Many two- or three-starred hotels are equipped with lifts; Michelin's *Guide Rouge* indicates hotels with lifts and facilities for disabled people, while the *Gîtes Accessibles aux Personnes Handicapées* (60FF from Gîtes de France) lists regional *gîtes ruraux* and chambres d'hôte with disabled access (for more information see Accommodation later in this chapter).

For a general overview of the facilities available to the disabled, pick up *European Holidays and Travel Abroad: A Guide for Disabled People*, published by the Royal Association for Disability & Rehabilitation (RADAR; ☎ 020-7250 3222), 12 City Forum, 250 City Rd, London EC1V 8AF. The Association des Paralysés de France (☎ 01 40 78 69 00), a Paris-based, national organisation, also has details of wheelchair-friendly accommodation in the region.

In recent years, the SNCF has made efforts to make its trains more accessible. Wheelchair travellers (*fauteuil roulant*) are welcome on TGV and regular trains provided they make a reservation by phone or at a train station at least a few hours before departure. Details are available in SNCF's booklet, *Guide du Voyageur à Mobilité Réduite*. You can also contact SNCF Accessibilité on toll-free ☎ 0 800 15 47 53.

Toulouse and Bordeaux airports both have wheelchair access and offer assistance to wheelchair travellers (such as allocated parking spaces at the terminal); make sure you tell the airline in advance of your requirements and they will make arrangements to help you onboard.

SENIOR TRAVELLERS

Senior citizens (those in what the French call *le troisème âge*, the third age) are entitled to discounts, for example on public transport and museum admission charges, provided they show proof of their age. In some cases an official-looking card or pass might move things along (see Seniors' Cards under Visas & Documents earlier in this chapter).

At mainline train stations, SOS Voyageurs (Toulouse ☎ 05 61 62 27 30, Bordeaux ☎ 05 56 92 24 31) – a voluntary group usually run by retirees – offers help to elderly train travellers.

TRAVEL WITH CHILDREN

Successful travel with young children requires planning and effort. Don't overdo things; trying to see too much can cause problems. Include the kids in the trip planning. Balance a day traipsing round Romanesque churches or bastides with time canoeing on the river, swimming at a *base de loisir* (leisure complex) or an outing to a theme park; for more information see under Activities later in this chapter.

Many towns (such as Rocamadour, Domme, St-Émilion, Lacanau, Périgueux) cater to kids (and foot-weary mums and dads) with 'Le Petit Train Touristique' electric trains which trundle round the town and can perk up a day's sightseeing. If these are a hit, look out for other special train rides in

---

Tops for Kids

Here are some suggestions to keep the kids happy. Details can be found under the relevant town listings.

Amusement & Theme Parks
Walibi Parc d'Attractions (Agen); Prehisto Parc (Tursac); Le Thot (Thonac); Village du Bournat (Le Bugue) and Musée en Plein Air du Quercy (Cabrerets).

Historic Sights, Caves & Great Museums
Cité de l'Espace (Space Park museum and planetarium), Toulouse; Croiseur Le Colbert (navy cruiser), Bordeaux; bastide museum with touch-screen audio-visuals, Monflanquin; guided visit to awesome fort, Beynac-et-Cazenac; Château de Biron (spooky recreated torture chamber); Rouffignac cave (with mini train ride), Rouffignac; Gouffre de Padirac (eye-opening cave adventure deep, deep down), near Rocamadour.

Outdoor Thrills & Spills
Biking on miles of signposted trails along the Atlantic Coast and inland (see the Bordeaux. the Atlantic Coast & the Landes chapter); canoeing and kayaking along the Dordogne and Lot (see those chapters); horse-riding practically everywhere; the massive Dune de Pilat (see the Bordeaux, the Atlantic Coast & the Landes chapter).

Fun Train Rides
Steam train from Martel (Lot) and the coastal ride from Ponte de Grave to Soulac (Atlantic Coast); cog-wheel railway up La Rhune Mountain (French Basque country); century-old train from Sabres to Marquèze (the Landes); Le Petit Train d'Artouste in the Vallée d'Ossau (Béarn).

---

the region (see the boxed text 'Tops for Kids'). If you're into hiking, the *Les Sentiers d'Emilie en...* series of walking guides offers easy route suggestions suitable for families.

Nature-loving kids might enjoy Les Fermes des Découverte (Discovery Farms), in the Bienvenue à la Ferme (Welcome to the Farm) programme; see the boxed text of the same name under Accommodation later in this chapter. If the kids are itching to have their own rural holiday, *sans parents*, check out the Gîtes de France (see under Accommodation later in this chapter) range of rural Gîtes d'Enfants, with organised excursions and activities for four to 13 year-olds, or the L'Accueil Toboggan programme for children aged under 7 in the Midi-Pyrénées (contact the Comité Régional de Midi-Pyrénées – see under Tourist Offices earlier in this chapter – for details).

Getting around the region is easiest if you hire a car. Most car-rental firms have children's safety seats for hire at a nominal cost; book in advance. The same goes for highchairs and cots (cribs); they're standard in most restaurants and hotels but numbers are limited. The choice of baby food, infant formulas, soy and cow's milk, disposable nappies (diapers) and the like is as great in French supermarkets as it is back home, but beware of opening hours. Run out of nappies on Saturday afternoon and you face a long and messy weekend.

Eating out can be a nightmare if you choose an upmarket restaurant: French children are trained from an early age to sit still and cope with the dozens of courses their parents enjoy at a painstakingly leisurely pace. Foreign tourists can be just as child-intolerant. So save your nerves and choose an outdoor cafe or restaurant where the kids can flick bread across the table without the maitre d' glaring. Some readers have recommended the restaurants in huge shopping malls like Carrefour and Mammouth (on the outskirts of larger towns and usually open daily including Sunday).

Our kids found rural *fermes auberges* and *tables d'hôtes*, and many small village restaurants, far more fun, especially when there were hens, pigs, dogs or cats to play with once the first course has been gulped down (leaving mum and dad to enjoy the other ten courses and wine in relative peace).

Most tourist offices have a list of *gardes d'enfants* (baby-sitting services) and creches. Or check out local Bureaux d'Information Jeunesse (details in local listings) which have noticeboards listing similar services. Lonely Planet's *Travel with Children* is another good source of general information.

DANGERS & ANNOYANCES

For emergency numbers see under Telephones in the Post & Communications section earlier in this chapter.

Theft

The south-west is a pretty safe place. The biggest problem for tourists is theft *(vol)*, especially from easily identifiable rental cars. Other common problems are pickpocketing and bag-snatching (not just handbags but daypacks), particularly in crowded train stations, cinemas, rush-hour public buses and even tourist offices. Keep an eye on your bags and always keep your money, credit cards, tickets, passport, driving licence and other important documents in a belt or pouch worn inside your clothes. Keep enough money for the day in a separate wallet.

If you leave your bags at a left-luggage office or luggage locker at a train station, treat the claim chit or locker code like cash. Daypack snatchers have taken stolen chits to the train station and claimed the rest of their victims' belongings.

Theft from hotel rooms is less common but it's still unwise to leave your valuables in your room. In hostels, lock non-valuables in the locker provided and take everything

---

Cops

There are of two kinds of law enforcers in France. *Gendarmes* – the ones with the traditional pill-box hats – are quasi-military police under the Ministry of Defence and typically the only law enforcers in the countryside. Their headquarters is called a *gendarmerie*. *Police*, who wear soft caps and come under the umbrella of the Ministry of the Interior, are found only in the cities and larger towns, at the *commissariat de police*.

With the possible exceptions of Toulouse or Bordeaux you will find few of either who can speak much English. In a medical emergency you'll have better luck at a hospital, since doctors are required to study English.

valuable with you. Upmarket hotels have *coffres* (safes).

The Hunt

Throughout the south-west, gun-toting French people are on the move during the hunting season (end of July to March), making hiking a potentially hazardous activity, especially if you wander into areas signposted *chasseurs* or *chasse gardé* (although some hunters illegally sneak into *chasse interdite* areas too), and especially if you're dressed in anything that might remind a near-sighted hunter of a deer or wild boar. Accidents do happen (some 50 French hunters die each year after being shot by other hunters) so beware of wandering into remote forests or woodland areas.

Poisonous Mushrooms

Wild-mushroom picking is a passion in the south-west. Pick by all means but don't eat anything until it has been positively identified. Most pharmacies offer a mushroom-identifying service. In the Bordeaux region there's a hotline (☎ 05 56 96 40 80) for advice on what to do if you suspect mushroom poisoning.

Coastal Dangers

There are strong undertows and currents along the Atlantic coast. If sleeping on a beach, always ensure you are above the high-tide mark. Between Biscarosse-Plage and Mimizan-Plage the Centre d'Essai des Landes is a missile testing area and strictly off-limits.

Smoke

Serious non smokers should consider holidaying in another country – or at least sticking to outdoor dining areas. Many French people smoke like Vesuvius, and even in the region's very few no-smoking restaurants some still cheerfully light up.

LEGAL MATTERS

The police are allowed to search anyone at any time, regardless of whether there is an obvious reason to do so.

As elsewhere in the EU, laws are tough when it comes to drink-driving. The acceptable blood-alcohol limit is 0.05%, with drivers who exceed this amount facing fines of up to 30,000FF and even jail terms. Licences can be immediately suspended.

Importing or exporting drugs can lead to a jail sentence of between 10 and 30 years. The fine for possession of drugs for personal use can be as high as 500,000FF. If you litter, you risk a 1000FF fine.

BUSINESS HOURS

Museums and shops (but not cinemas, restaurants or boulangeries) are closed on public holidays. On Sunday, a boulangerie is usually about all that is open (morning only) and public transport services are less frequent. In villages, many shops (including the boulangerie) close for a long lunch between 2 and 4 pm. Hotels, restaurants, cinemas, cultural institutions and shops usually choose a few weeks or more in winter for their *congé annuel* (annual closure). For information on high/low seasons see 'When to go' under Planning earlier in this chapter. The majority of shops open at about 9 or 10 am. Commercial banks are generally open from 8 or 9 am to sometime between 11.30 am and 1 pm, and from 1.30 or 2 pm to 4.30 or 5 pm Monday to Friday. Many banks in towns with Saturday markets open on Saturday and then close on Monday.

PUBLIC HOLIDAYS & SPECIAL EVENTS

French National Holidays

The following *jours fériés* (public holidays) are observed throughout France and are often a cue for festivities to spill into the streets.

1 January
    New Year's Day (*Jour de l'An*)
Late March/April
    Easter Sunday (*Pâques*)
    Easter Monday (*lundi de Pâques*)
1 May
    May Day (*Fête du Travail*)
8 May
    Victoire 1945
    In celebration of the Allied victory in Europe that ended WWII.

May
Ascension Thursday (L'Ascension)
A national holiday celebrated on the 40th day after Easter.
Mid-May to mid-June
Pentecost/Whit Sunday (Pentecôte)
A national holiday celebrated on the seventh Sunday after Easter.
Whit Monday (lundi de Pentecôte)
14 July
Bastille Day/National Day (Fête Nationale)
15 August
Assumption Day (L'Assomption)
1 November
All Saints' Day (La Toussaint)
11 November
Remembrance Day (L'onze novembre)
In celebration of the armistice of WWI.
25 December
Christmas (Noël)

Those holidays celebrated with greatest gusto are Bastille Day and May Day; on the latter, many people (especially kids) sell muguets (lilies of the valley), which are said to bring good luck.

When a holiday falls on a Tuesday or a Thursday you'll probably find them linked to the nearest weekend to make a four-day break: the doors of banks are a good place to look for announcements of upcoming long weekends.

The following are not public holidays in France: Shrove Tuesday (Mardi Gras; the day before the first day of Lent); Maundy (or Holy) Thursday (jeudi saint) and Good Friday (vendredi saint) just before Easter; and Boxing Day (26 December).

Regional Festivals

The south-west offers a feast of festivals, with dozens of annual musical (especially jazz and folk), medieval and Basque traditional events, plus, of course, any excuse to celebrate the region's most beloved pastime – food. Régional and most départemental tourist offices have information on local celebrations.

January
Foire aux Pottoks
A two-day opportunity to see the famous wild horse (pottok) of the French Basque country, held in Espelette.

Jazz Bonanza

South-West France loves its jazz. During the summer you can find jazz festivals everywhere. Here are some of the best:

July

Festival de Jazz
Held for two days at the start of the month in Oloron-Ste-Marie (Béarn).

Jazz à Moissac
Held in Early July in Moissac.

Jazz à Montauban
10 days from mid-July in Montauban.

Souillac en Jazz
Four days in mid-July, featuring some big European names, in Souillac.

Jazz aux Remparts
Held over five days, on the ramparts of Bayonne old town.

Jazz et Vin
Marriage of jazz and gastronomy in Pauillac.

Festival de Jazz d'Albi
Held in the Last week of July in Albi.

August

Jazz au Marciac
10 days in mid-August, featuring international names, free concerts and street performances, in Marciac (near Auch).

February
Carnaval
A major event on the religious calendar with festivities all over France during the last few days before Lent (about six weeks before Easter). There are particularly joyous celebrations in Albi, with folk groups, bands and processions.

Fête des Boeufs Gras
A promenade of fattened cows reliving a medieval custom, held around 11 February in Bazas.

Salon du Chocolat
Gorge on the region's best chocolate during this two-day fair during early February in Biarritz.

March
Fête Bi Harriz Lau Xori
A celebration of the Basque country and language in a series of lectures, music and dance performances in the last week of the month in Biarritz.

Foire Internationale
Big trade fair with accompanying music, dance and other events, held in Toulouse.

April

Fête de Flamenco
A fortnight's flamenco jamboree held in early April in St-Palais (French Basque country).

Weekend Portes Ouvertes dans les Châteaux du Médoc
A weekend in early April when everyone from small producers to *grands crus classés* (classified as producing superior quality wine) opens their cellars and fermenting rooms to let you discover the latest vintages (Médoc region).

May

Festival 'Alors...Chante!'
A celebration of French song lasting five-days in Montauban.

Festival International de 'Bandas y Penas'
Two days of music, street performances, marching bands, processions and high jinks celebrating the folk traditions of Gascony; held in early May in Condom.

Fête de St-Sicaire
A traditional fair held on 1 May, complete with food stalls and fairground, in Brantôme.

Fête des Corridas
Bullfight fever over Pentecost weekend in Vic Fezensac.

Fête Médiévale
Two days of medieval costumes, music and dance. Held in late May in Puy l'Evêque.

Foie Gras Expo
A national competition in cooking and preserving foie gras, held in Dax.

Foire aux Foie Gras
A foie gras market in Thiviers.

Foire International de Bordeaux
The biggest trade fair in the region with art and craft exhibits, music and dance. Held in mid-May.

Formula 3000 Grand Prix
A high gear event over Pentecost weekend in Pau.

La Fête des Fromages
Held on Pentecost (White Sunday) in honour of Rocamadour's famous *fromage de chèvre* (goat cheese) and other cheeses.

June

Auch 'n' Blues
Big names in blues perform for four days at the end of the month in Auch.

Festival de Pau
A festival of drama, dance and music, held from mid-June to mid-July in Pau.

Festival de Théâtre d'Enfants
A four-day children's drama festival held in early June in Toulouse.

Fête de St-Jean
Festivities include fireworks and bonfires on 22 June in various towns, especially Bazas.

Fête du Vin
A hugely popular three-day wine festival, held in late July on Bordeaux's river bank.

Printemps de Cahors
A three-week celebration of visual arts and photography, with night-time shows and projections on buildings, held from mid-June to early July in Cahors' old town.

July

Festival d'art Flamenco
A five-day celebration of flamenco music and dance held in early July in Mont de Marsan.

Festival de Blues
A popular blues event running for four days in mid-July in Cahors.

Festival de Country Music
A week of performances by exponents of the genre from Texas to Gascony, held in mid-July in Mirande.

Festival du Folklore
A fortnight of folk festivities held from late July to early August in even numbered years (alternate years in Jaca, across the border in Spain) in Oloron-Ste-Marie (Béarn).

La Félibrée

On the first Sunday in July, in a village in Périgord (a different village hosts the event each year), Occitan language, music and traditions are brought back to life. Everyone dresses in traditional costume (embroidered shawls and long skirts for the women, black waistcoats and felt hats for the men) for a day of singing old *Langue d'Oc* (the local dialect) songs – accompanied by instruments such as the hurdy-gurdy – dancing and feasting, processions and parades.

The Félibrée society was founded by a group of poets and writers in the mid-19th century in reaction against the central government's attempts to suppress regional cultures and is still a driving force in keeping Occitan traditions alive.

Festival du Folklore
Also called the *Festival de Montignac* this is a week-long celebration of international folk music and dance, held during late July in Montignac.

Festival du Haut Quercy
Three weeks of sacred music, choral and instrumental works, in Martel and Rocamadour.

Festival du Périgord Noir
A celebrated series of classical concerts held in churches (especially St-Léon-sur-Vézère) and chateaus from mid-July to late August.

Festival du Quercy Blanc
A mostly music festival, held from late July to mid-August in Cahors and nearby towns.

Festival International de Folklore
A gathering of traditional singers and dancers from as far afield as Poland and Tahiti, held in Biarritz.

Festival International du Ciel et de l'Espace
A week-long festival on the theme of astronomy and the links between man and the stars, held in Fleurance.

Festival Goya
No, not Goya paintings but Latin and North African music, dance, theatre, even rock, rap and street performances, held over two weeks in late July in Castres.

Festival Lyrique de St-Cér
Two weeks of concerts and opera performances, from late July to mid-August.

Festival Musiques et Paroles en Ribéracois
World music, classical and jazz performances, from mid-July to mid-Augus in Ribérac.

Festival Tempo Latino
Salsa and other South American sounds feature in this festival held over the last weekend of July in Vic-Fezensac and nearby villages.

Fête de la Madeleine
A lively festival held in several towns, especially Duras and Mont de Marsan, over the third weekend in July.

Fête de la Transhumance
A traditional three-day pastoral festival when shepherds in the Vallée d'Ossau lead their flocks to new pastures, celebrated by fetes and activities in villages en route.

Fêtes du Grand Fauconnier
A two-day medieval fair, with traditional markets, costumes and parades, held mid-July in Cordes.

Foire d'Oie
A goose fair held at the end of the month in odd-numbered years in Rouffignac.

Garonne Festival
Concerts, drama and other events celebrating the Garonne River, in the first fortnight in July in Toulouse.

Musiques en Périgord
Music from classical and folk to rock and blues (plus street performances), held from late July to early August, mostly centred around Le Bugue and Les Eyzies.

August
Fêtes de Bayonne
A week of Basque music, bullfights, a float parade and rugby matches starting on the first Wednesday of the month in Bayonne.

Festival de Force Basque
One of the largest displays of Basque manpower (*la force Basque*) including rock-lifting and tug-of-war. Held in mid-August in St-Palais (near Bayonne); similar events take place throughout the region during July and August.

Festival du Mime Automate
Souillac's famous automaton museum is the focus for this weekend festival which also features street performances.

Festival International du Mime Mimos Contemporain
A huge international nine-day mime festival with outdoor performances, held in Périgueux.

Fête du Pain et du Moulin
A celebration of traditional flour-grinding and bread-baking, held in Lautrec.

Fête du Vin
A wine fair in the appropriately named town of Buzet (near Nérac), 7–8 August.

Grande Semaine de Pélote Basque
Pélote fever in the second week of August in villages throughout the French Basque country.

Musique en Côte Basque
A three-week musical menu from late July to early September, held mainly in St-Jean de Luz.

September
Festival des Cineet Cultures d'Amérique Latine
A one-week festival of Latin American film and culture, held from late September to early October in Biarritz.

Fête de la bonne vie
A gastronomic splurge on the second or third Sunday of the month in Cordes.

Fête des Montgolfiades
A two-day hot-air balloon fiesta held at the end of the month in Rocamadour.

Fête du Sel
A festival in celebration of salt. It's held for four days in early September in the salt town of Salies de Béarn.

Jurade de St-Émilion
A proclamation on the third Sunday of the month of the beginning of the wine harvest by

the Wine Brotherhood of St-Émilion; processions and solemn Mass.

Les Mondinas
A three-day celebration of contemporary Occitan language and culture, held in early September in Toulouse.

Sinfonia en Périgord
A major baroque music event, with weekend performances of choral-plus-instrumental works held in the Abbaye de Chancelade, Cathédrale de Périgueux and the medieval Château de Bourdeilles.

October

Cinéspana
A festival of Spanish cinema held during the last two weeks of the month in Toulouse.

Course Landaise
A contest to find the best bullfighter in this local (and bloodless) version of the *corrida*; culmination of the season's bullfight series in Dax.

Danse en Tarn-et-Garonne
A festival combining traditional and contemporary dance in Montauban.

Festival Européen des Cerfs-Volants
European kite festival: exhibition and trade fair, featuring demonstrations and just plain fun; held in late October in Hossegor.

Fête du Piment
A day's pimento festival where they like things hot – Espelette (French Basque country).

November

Concours International de Rayonnement du Cirque d'Avenir
An international festival of circus arts in Auch.

Festival du Film
Held during early November in Sarlat.

Fête de Ste-Cathérine
A religious-based festival with agricultural and gastronomic fairs all over the region. Held 20–21 November.

Journées de la Danse Traditionelle en Midi-Pyrénées
Concerts, ballet and courses on the theme of Occitan traditional dance, held during La Toussaint every other year in Toulouse.

December

Marchés de Gras
Foie gras markets with fattened duck and geese and foie gras products are held in villages and towns throughout the region.

ACTIVITIES

South-West France offers an array of outdoor pursuits to please the most adventur-ous tastes. On the Atlantic coast you may surf, swim, scuba dive or pamper yourself with a fortnight of thalassotherapy. You can climb the canyons of the Basses-Pyrénées, jump off them with a paraglider, fly over them in a hot-air balloon or, in winter, ski down some of them. You can pilot a houseboat on, or drop a fishing line into, a network of canals and calm rivers, or kayak, raft or go canyoning down the frisky streams of the Béarn and the Tarn. The limestone of Périgord is honeycombed with caves to explore. And you can walk, ride a bike or gallop all over the place.

Most départemental tourist offices and many municipal ones in South-West France publish their own *guide loisirs* (leisure guide) booklets, listing things to do and local outfits who will help you do them. Les Services Loisirs Accueil, a leisure services organisation with branches in each département (see Tourist Offices earlier in this chapter), also has details of activities and courses. Numerous travel agencies run thematic tours built around cycling, walking and other activities; for contact details see Organised Tours in the Getting There & Away chapter.

Surfing

The coast of Gironde, the Landes and the French Basque country is dotted with prime surfing beaches, many of them championship quality (see the boxed text 'Surfing in the South-West' on the next page). Surfing first arrived here in the 1950s and the first World Surfing Championships to be held in Europe took place in 1968 at Anglet on the Basque coast.

Surfing is a year-round activity, though conditions tend to be best (and crowds minimal) during September and October. Aquitaine's tidal variations are extreme, with miserable conditions often turning brilliant an hour later. Those who don't fancy stand-up surfing can plunge in with a bodyboard. The top spots, or adjacent towns, have surf schools, surf shops, places for gear rental *(locations)*, and a brisk social scene. Surf schools cater for every level.

You can rent a surfboard for between

Surfing in the South-West

No two surfers agree on the best swells, but a good starting point would be the beaches that have consistently served as past world surfing championship venues – such as Lacanau in Gironde, Anglet in the French Basque Country and Biscarrosse and Hossegor in the Landes.

Following is a rundown of Aquitaine's better surfing beaches. Those which have been preferred venues for national or world championship in the past are shown by (*). Those with spots suitable for novices are shown by (+). Those with dubious water quality are shown by (=). Be aware that each beach may consist of several spots (surfing locations) of varying quality. Note that many of these spots have no lifeguards.

Gironde

Le Verdon	Verdon-sur-Mer
Soulac	Soulac-sur-Mer+
	l'Amélie
Montalivet	Le Gurp
	Montalivet-les-Bains
Hourtin	Le Pin Sec
	Hourtin Plage*
Carcans	Carcans Plage*
Lacanau	Lacanau Océan*
Lège	Le Porge*
	La Jenny
	Le Grand Crohot
Cap-Ferret	Le Truc Vert
	Le Petit Train
	Cap Ferret*
	Le Petit Nice

Landes

Biscarrosse	La Salie+=
	La Limite
	Biscarrosse Plage*
Mimizan	Mimizan Plage*=
Lit-et-Mixe	Lespécier
	Contis Plage
	Cap de l'Homy
St-Girons	St-Girons Plage
Vieux-Boucau	Moliets Plage*
	Messanges Sud
	Vieux Boucau*

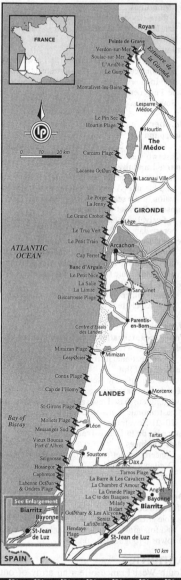

Surfing in the South-West

Seignosse	Seignosse*
Hossegor	Hossegor*
Capbreton	Capbreton*=
Labenne	Labenne Océan
	Ondres Plage
Boucau	Tarnos Plage=

French Basque Country
Anglet	La Barre*
	Les Cavaliers,
	Plages d'Anglet
	Sables d'Or
	VVF
	La Chambre d'Amour
Biarritz	La Grande Plage*
	La Côte des Basques
	Milady
Bidart	Bidart
Guéthary	Guéthary*
	Les Alcyons
	Senix
	Lafiténia
St-Jean de Luz	Erromardie
	Ste-Barbe
	Ciboure
	Socoa
Hendaye	Hendaye-Plage+=

MARTIN HARRIS

Beginner or pro, the Atlantic coast offers some of the best surfing in Europe.

More Information
For surf conditions (in French), contact Swell Line (☎ 08 36 68 40 64). Those with Internet access can see live video footage of the waves at Lacanau, Hossegor or Anglet at www.swell-line.com/. For information on surf clubs and competition dates, contact the Fédération Française du Surf (☎ 05 58 43 55 88, fax 05 58 43 60 57), 30 impasse Digue Nord, BP 28, 40150 Hossegor.

The Stormrider Guide: Europe, a handsome atlas of European surfing, has 80 pages of maps and information on the Aquitaine coast. It's sold for 230FF in surf shops, travel book-shops and FNAC superstores, or for UK£25 from its UK publisher, Low Pressure (☎/fax 020-7792 3134) at 23 Kensington Park Rd, London W11.

Surf Etiquette
Surfers may look like seaborne anarchists, but they have their own unwritten safety rules; among them:
- On the way out, stay clear of anyone on a wave and *never* let go of your board.
- Hanging around where waves break puts you and others at risk.
- When there are many people on a wave, priority goes to the first on the peak or, if that's not clear, to the first surfer to stand or the first bodyboarder to go.
- Don't surf between blue flags, which mark swimmers-only zones.

75FF and 150FF per day, or a bodyboard for less. Individual surfing lessons cost from 120FF to 300FF per hour. A cheaper option is a group course; a five half-day course costs from 1500FF to 2500FF. The youth hostels at Anglet and Biarritz offer course-plus-accommodation packages: a week in high season with half-board costs about 1780FF.

Cycling

The French take their cycling seriously; whole parts of the country – including the Pyrénées in South-West France – almost grind to a halt during the annual Tour de France (see Spectator Sports later in this chapter).

Pedalling South-West France is tremendously popular, both by road bicycle *(vélo)* and by mountain bike *(vélo tout-terrain;* VTT). The richly picturesque back roads of the Dordogne and the easy coastal trails of the Landes are big favourites with visitors. So are the foothills of the Pyrénées, including the Basque country; except in the Haut-Béarn, there are few killer hills.

You can hire bicycles in most larger towns for around 80FF a day. VTTs are permitted on some GR trails (see Walking), but take care not to startle hikers. VTTs are forbidden off-road in the Parc National des Pyrénées. A *piste cyclable* is a cycling path.

Many local cycling clubs organise tours that are open to visitors; look for their announcements in tourist offices or, just ahead of the events, on roadside signs. Many tourist offices sell itineraries (some in English) compiled by these clubs, and each département publishes its own French-language guide to cyclable trails. Didier-Richard publishes *Les guides VTT*, a series of cyclists' topoguides (in French). Another resource on trips and facilities in France is the Fédération Française de Cyclotourisme (☎ 01 44 16 88 88) in Paris.

For information on road rules, cycling organisations, bicycle transport and rental, see the Bicycle section of the Getting Around chapter. See Organised Tours in the Getting There & Away chapter for bicycle tours. Places that rent bikes are noted under Getting Around in each city or town listing.

Walking

South-West France is criss-crossed by walking trails. No permits are needed for hiking, though there are restrictions on where you can camp, especially in the Parc National des Pyrénées.

The best-known trails are *sentiers de grande randonnée*, long-distance footpaths whose names begin with 'GR', marked by red and white stripes on everything from trees and rocks to walls and posts. The GR6 crosses the Dordogne from west to east, while the GR36 threads together the Dordogne, Lot and Tarn départements. The popular GR10 spans the Pyrénées from the Mediterranean to the Atlantic, and the GR8 runs down the Aquitaine coast. The GR65 and its branches take in many of the pilgrim routes to Santiago de Compostela (see the boxed text 'The Pilgrims of St-Jacques' under Religion in the Facts about South-West France chapter) across the Lot, Tarn-et-Garonne, Gers and the French Basque country.

Most of the *grandes randonnées de pays* (GRP), marked yellow and red, are loop trails designed for a close, multi-day look at one area. Shorter day-hike trails are *sentiers de pettiest randonnées* (PR) or *sentiers de pays*; many of these are circular too.

The Way of Saint James, from Cicerone Walking Guides, is a detailed, two-part, English-language guide to the famous GR65. The Fédération Française de Randonnée Pédestre (FFRP) publishes French-language 'topoguides' on GR, GRP and PR trails. Check out their Web site at www.ffrp.asso.fr/. Local topoguides are also available, with information on trail conditions, flora, fauna, villages, camp sites, accommodation and other general information. Larger bookshops and tourist offices often stock some of these. Lonely Planet's own *Walking in France* will be published in July 2000.

For further information on maps, see Planning earlier in this chapter. For information on *refuges, gîtes d'étape* and other overnight accommodation for hikers, see Accommodation later in this chapter. If the weather looks dodgy, contact Météo Consult (☎ 08 36 70 12 34). Alternatively contact Minitel 3617 METPLUS for local forecasts, or check out its Web site at www.meteoconsult.fr/an/index.html.

Sailing & Windsurfing

Sailing (voile) and windsurfing (planche à voile) are popular wherever there's water and a breeze. The big coastal lakes and basins of Gironde and the Landes (Hourtin Carcans, Lacanau, Arcachon, Cazaux, Sanguinet, Biscarosse Parentis, Aureilhan, Léon, Soustons and Hossegor) are especially good, and it's easy to rent gear and take lessons.

Scuba Diving & Snorkelling

The Atlantic coast and its inshore lakes and basins (see Sailing & Windsurfing) offer attractive opportunities for diving (plongée). A big favourite is the Bassin d'Arcachon. Shops and clubs where you can hire equipment or take a diving course are listed in the relevant regional chapters.

Swimming

The Atlantic coast abounds in fine, sandy beaches; good places to start are those listed in the boxed text 'Surfing in the South-West' under Surfing. In France, any beach not signposted as private is open to the public.

Topless bathing for women is pretty normal in France; if others are doing it, you can assume it's OK. The Atlantic coast is also well-endowed with nude beaches, some of them associated with naturist camp sites.

River & White-Water Sports

In summer, local agencies organise serene canoe and kayak trips on every river of any size in South-West France, complete with drop-off and pick-up services.

For serious white-water (eau vive) junkies, these and other outfits also run day and multi-day kayak and raft trips on frisky streams like the lower Aveyron (along the border between the Tarn-et-Garonne and Tarn départements), the Ossau, Oloron and Pau in Béarn, and the Nive in the French Basque country. We note such outfits in the regional chapters. The

Fédération Française de Canoë-Kayak (☎ 01 45 11 08 50, fax 01 48 86 13 25), 87 Quai de la Marne, 94340 Joinville le Pont, Paris, has information on canoeing and kayaking clubs around the country.

Hydrospeed is white-water rafting without the raft: participants are only equipped with a sturdy individual board, wetsuit and helmet. Canyoning tackles all the challenges offered by a river canyon: trekking, swimming, abseiling and rock climbing. A few agencies, as noted in the regional chapters, offer programmes for visitors in these high-adrenalin activities.

Parasailing

Parasailing or paragliding (parapente) is popular all over France. All you have to do is hurl yourself down a mountain on a sunny day, dragging a rectangular parachute behind you. As it opens and catches thermal currents, the parachute lifts you up in the air like an aircraft wing. With favourable thermals you can circle peacefully for hours, enjoying breathtaking views. Conditions are best in the Pyrénées; among schools of parasailing there are two at Accous in the Vallée d'Aspe, and one north of St-Jean Pied de Port at Irissary. A baptême en parapente (tandem introductory flight) costs between 250FF and 500FF.

Other ways to ride the thermals are gliding and hang-gliding (vol à voile). For information on gliding clubs in France, contact the Paris-based Fédération Française de Vol à Voile (☎ 01 45 44 04 78, fax 01 45 44 71 93). Add a motor and you have a microlight (ULM, for ultraléger motorisé). At numerous microlight schools in the region, a baptême en ULM costs around 200FF.

Rock Climbing

In Béarn alone there are at least half a dozen small, reputable companies who can teach you rock climbing (escalade) and show you where to do it in the Basses-Pyrénées, for around 145FF to 160FF per half-day or from 250FF to 280FF per day. Many also organise nature-study, walking, caving, canyoning, and combination trips. The

Vézère valley of the Dordogne has a few similar outfits, usually those offering canoe and kayak trips too.

Caving

The scientific study of caves, *spéléologie*, was pioneered by a Frenchman named Édouard-André Martel late in the 19th century. The word also refers to the sport of exploring caves, which has adapted many of the skills of divers and rock climbers. In return for the weird and breathtaking places they wriggle into, serious 'spelunkers' must get accustomed to long periods in cold, wet, dark and very cramped places. Claustrophobes need not apply. The limestone grottoes of the Dordogne are a spelunker's dream and many of the same companies who run treks and climbing expeditions will take you underground for similar prices. The Basses-Pyrénées are also full of explorable caves.

Horse Riding

Horse riding *(équitation)* is a popular pastime everywhere. Look for roadside signs almost anywhere for directions to *centres hippiques* (equestrian centres) offering *promenades à cheval* (horseback rides). We list many in each regional chapter. Typical rates are from 75FF to 100FF per hour or 150FF to 250FF per half-day; many places also have ponies for children at lower rates, and some organise thematic and multiday trips. Note that a few places are reservation-only and that some are open only in July and August. Some GR and GRP trails (see Walking earlier in this section for details) are open to horses.

Canal Boating

One of the calmest ways to see the south-west is to pilot a houseboat on a leisurely cruise along its hundreds of kilometres of canals and navigable rivers, whose often tree-lined channels pass through some of Europe's loveliest countryside. The continent's oldest functioning canal system is the Canal du Midi, which with the Canal Latéral à la Garonne provides a continuous route between the Atlantic and the Mediter-

ranean. Branching from this are navigable stretches of the Garonne, Baïse, Lot and Tarn. See under Boat in the Getting Around chapter for more on how to hire your own.

Fishing

Angling *(pêche)* in France requires not only a licence *(carte de pêche)* but familiarity with seasons, sizes, catch limits and other regulations that vary between régions, between streams and between species. Licences, issued by local fishing associations (but often valid for other areas), are sold in tackle shops. Cheaper tourist licences, good for short summer periods, are also available. Most tourist offices and tackle shops have details on regulations and on local fishing organisations.

The south-west's best fishing areas are the Bassin d'Arachon and nearby lakes (Gironde), the French Basque country and Béarn . Gironde tourist board's *Nature randonnée et loisirs* brochure lists relevant sites. For information on camp sites and other accommodation tailored to anglers in the French Basque country and Béarn, contact the Association Dedu Tourisme Pêche des Pyrénées-Atlantiques (☎ 05 59 39 98 00, fax 05 59 39 43 97) in Oloron.

Skiing & Snowboarding

South-West France's few ski resorts are in the Basses-Pyrénées. With wetter, heavier snow than in the Alps, and less of it, these resorts are best suited to beginners and intermediates. The ski season generally lasts from December to March or April, with the best conditions in January and February. The slopes get crowded during the February and March school holidays.

The biggest downhill skiing *(ski de piste* or *ski alpin)* resort is at Gourette in the Vallée d'Ossau. Up the valley is another at Artouste-Fabrèges, with a big snowboarding centre. In the Vallée de Barétous is Arette la Pierre St-Martin, good for beginners and kids. At the head of the Vallée d'Aspe is the fairly basic Le Somport cross-country skiing *(ski de fond)* area.

The cheapest way to ski in France is with a pre-booked package deal. A resort association called Ski France, 61 Blvd Haussmann, 75008 Paris, publishes an annual resort directory, *France: The Largest Ski Domain in the World*. This is also available at overseas offices of Maison de la France (see Tourist Offices earlier in this chapter). Its Web site is at www.skifrance.fr.

Bird-Watching

The great near-shore lakes and basins of Gironde and the Landes offer an unparalleled look at migratory and resident waterbirds. You can pay visits year-round to the Parc Ornithologique du Teich on the Bassin d'Arcachon in Gironde. Important *réserve naturelles* (nature reserves) which can be visited at certain times of the year in the Landes are Marais d'Orx (Labenne), Étang Noir (Seignosse) and Courant d'Huchet (Léon). *Where to Watch Birds in France* (1989), a spotters' guide written by the French League for the Protection of Birds, includes maps and marked itineraries cross-referenced to the text.

Golf

The continent's first golf club was founded in Pau in 1856 by five Scottish aristocrats, and France's finest old golf courses are all in the south-west. Details about these and others (there are some 50 in Aquitaine alone) are listed in a free booklet called *Golf in France*, available from overseas offices of Maison de la France (see Tourist Offices earlier in this chapter). Or contact the Fédération Française de Golf (☎ 01 41 49 77 00, fax 01 41 49 77 01), 68 rue Anatole France, 92309 Levallois-Peret, Paris. A Web site called *Golf in France* at www.ecs.net has information on golf tours in the region.

Naturism

The region's many *naturiste* (nudist) centres – all family-oriented – are listed in a brochure called *Naturism in France*, available at most tourist offices. On the Atlantic coast there are three in Gironde and one in the Landes; inland, the Dordogne has five, the Gers and Haute-Garonne two each, and the Lot-et-Garonne and Lot one each. They range from small rural camp sites to holiday villages complete with cinemas, tennis courts and shops. Most are open from April to October, some year-round.

Visitors must have an International Naturist Federation (INF) *passeport naturiste*, available at many naturist holiday centres, or a membership card from a naturist club. The Fédération Française de Naturisme (☎ 01 47 64 32 82, fax 01 47 64 32 63), 65 rue de Tocqueville, 75017 Paris, is a good source of further information.

Spas & Thalassotherapy

For over a century, the French have been keen fans of *thermalisme* (water cures), for which visitors with ailments ranging from rheumatism to serious internal disorders flock to hot-spring resorts. Once the domain of the wealthy, spa centres now offer fitness packages aimed at a broad range of income and age. Most of the region's spas, numbering about a dozen, are in south-western Landes and in the Basses-Pyrénées. A major centre for information on thermalism is at Dax.

A salty variant is *thalassothérapie*, based on the curative properties of sea water and a marine climate. Overseas offices of Maison de la France (see Tourist Offices earlier in this chapter) have a free booklet, *Thalassotherapy in France*, which has information on treatments and centres. There are four major centres on the Basque coast. A six-day programme (the minimum recommended) for two, with accommodation and half-board, ranges from 1720FF to 1980FF per day.

Leisure Complexes

Many towns with limited history or architecture to offer visitors have climbed aboard the leisure bandwagon, building their own vast leisure complexes *(bases de loisirs)* centred on artificial lakes or just a wide place in the nearest river. With canoes swimming pools, windsurfers, water slides, pedal-boats and dry-land sports facilities, courses and lots of programmes for young people, they can be great outlets if you're travelling with energetic kids.

COURSES

A great souvenir of South-West France that won't take up any space in your luggage is a skill you can take home with you. Of course an obvious subject is French, but in this heartland of fine food and fine wines, how about cookery or wine-tasting? Bear in mind that these courses are taught in French, unless stated otherwise. Multiday courses include accommodation and full board, unless otherwise noted. Tourist offices will tell you about other local offerings too. The French word for a course of study is *stage*.

Language

Of course there's no better place to learn French than in France and a formal course – anything from an intensive two weeks to three months or more – is a good way to cement what you're learning out on the street.

Overseas offices of Maison de la France (see Tourist Offices earlier in this chapter) have lots of information on studying French in France. Another good source is one of the many Bureaux d'Information Jeunesse in bigger towns of the region (see the boxed text 'Bureaux d'Information Jeunesse' in Work later in this chapter). Following are some reliable private schools with a choice of courses for foreigners; most can either provide, or help you find, accommodation too:

Academie Aquitaine de Français
(☎/fax 05 56 44 54 05,
email cheneook@ctanet.fr)
44 Allées de Tourny, Bordeaux
Individual or small group tuition, flexible hours (30 hours, 2900FF).
Alliance Française de Bordeaux
(☎/fax 05 56 79 32 80, email alliance
.bordeaux@alliance-ordeaux.org)
38 rue Ferrère, 33000 Bordeaux
Web site: www.alliance-bordeaux.org
Intensive courses lasting one month (60 hours, 3000FF) or two weeks (30 hours, 1500FF, accommodation extra) during the summer, plus other courses during the rest of the year.
Alliance Française de Toulouse
(☎ 05 61 23 41 24, fax 05 61 23 05 51, email infos@alliance-toulouse.org)

9 place du Capitole, 31000 Toulouse
Web site: www.alliance-toulouse.org
Summer intensive four-week courses at all levels (65 hours, 2500FF, accommodation extra); other courses during the rest of the year.
Bordeaux Language Studies
(☎ 05 56 51 00 76, fax 05 56 51 76 15, email bls@imaginet.fr)
Web site: www.bls-bordeaux.com
1 cours Georges Clemenceau, Bordeaux
Small two- to three-week group courses at various levels, for example two weeks (15 hours per week, 2700FF) or French for business (25 hours per week, 4550FF).
Centre d'Ètudes de Langues
(☎ 05 59 46 58 00, fax 05 59 46 59 73, email ccf@bayonne.cci.fr)
Centre Consulaire de Formation, 50-51 allées Marines, BP 215, 64102 Bayonne, Pyrénées-Atlantiques
Month-long introductory courses (5 hours per week, 600FF).
Institut d'Études Françaises pour Étudiants Étrangers
(☎ 05 59 92 32 22, fax 05 59 92 32 65)
Faculté des Lettres, Université de Pau et des Pays de l'Adour, ave du Doyen Poplawski, BP 1160, 64013 Pau, Béarn, Pyrénées-Atlantiques
General and tailored courses (15 hours per week for a minimum of four weeks during the summer, 3300FF; 20 hours per week for a minimum of 11 weeks, 4900FF, year-round).
Juliette Freyche, Bel Air
(☎ 05 65 40 92 82, fax 05 65 40 98 80)
46120 Le Bouyssou, Dordogne
Normal and intensive group courses, also more specialised courses such as French for cooking, fine arts and sports.
Service Loisirs Accueil Dordogne
(☎ 05 53 35 50 24, fax 05 53 09 51 41)
25 rue du Président Wilson, 24009 Périgueux, Dordogne
Week-long courses at all levels (4200FF).

A number of agencies offer youth-oriented summer language programmes (ranging from a week to an academic year) plus accommodation and board at youth centres, university residences or homes. Those with options in South-West France include the following:

ACTE International
(☎ 01 43 42 48 84, fax 01 43 41 51 17, email acte_int@club-internet.fr)
39 rue du Sahel, 75012 Paris

APM Option Vacances
   (☎ 01 53 24 90 90, fax 01 53 24 90 91,
   email apmovj@aol.com)
   13 rue Ste-Cécile, 75009 Paris
Association Contacts
   (☎ 02 47 20 20 57, fax 02 47 20 68 92)
   3 rue du Maréchal Foch, 37000 Tours
BEC Séjours Linguistiques
   (☎ 01 42 60 35 57, fax 01 42 60 36 55)
   5 rue Richepanse, 75008 Paris
Séjours Internationaux Linguistiques et Culturels
   (SILC; UK ☎ 01623-660 333, fax 660 555,
   email rod@silcuk.freeserve.co.uk)
   PO Box 5562, Mansfield, Nottinghamshire,
   NG21 0GN, UK

Cookery

Why not learn to prepare your own magret
de canard, or get acquainted with the mysterious truffle? Prices for all the multiday
courses include accommodation and full
board, except as indicated.

Association des Logis de France des Landes, CCI
   293, ave Foch, 40000 Mont de Marsan, Landes
   Three- to seven-day courses covering Nouvelle Cuisine.
Actour 47
   (☎ 05 53 66 14 14, fax 05 53 68 25 42)
   4 rue André Chénier, 47008 Agen, Lot-et-
   Garonne
   Weekend courses in cuisine de canard.
Chef André Daguin, Hotel de France
   (☎ 05 62 61 71 71, fax 05 62 61 71 81)
   2 place de la Liberation, 32003 Auch, Gers
   Three-day courses in the cuisine of Gascony
   including foie gras and confit de canard (run
   between October and April) cost 2850FF;
   longer courses are also available.
Ferme Esponda Buru
   (☎/fax 05 59 28 55 89)
   64560 Ste Éngrace, Pyrénées-Atlantiques
   Courses in preparing confit de canard et de
   porc (three days) and making honey (five
   days).
Hôtel de la Reine Jeanne
   (☎ 05 59 67 00 76, fax 05 59 69 09 63)
   44 rue de Bourg Vieux, 64300 Orthez, Béarn,
   Pyrénées-Atlantiques
   A three-day course that focuses on foie gras.
La Borderie
   (☎ 05 53 51 00 24, fax 05 53 23 60 25) 24120
   Chavagnac, Dordogne
   This school runs weekend and one- and two-
   week courses in the cuisine of Périgord.
Le Tourisme Basque
   (☎ 05 59 26 23 87, fax 05 59 26 18 82)

100 rue Gambetta, 64500 St-Jean de Luz,
   Pyrénées-Atlantiques
   Four-day courses in Basque cuisine.
Les Hôteliers du Sud Adour
   (☎ 05 58 05 44 62, fax 05 58 73 13 48)
   Three- to seven-day courses covering Nouvelle Cuisine.
Office du Tourisme de Sarlat
   (☎ 05 53 31 45 45, fax 05 53 59 19 44,
   email 0t24.sarlat@perigord.tm.fr)
   place de la Liberté, BP 114, 24203 Sarlat,
   Dordogne
   Information on a range of courses including:
   foie gras (three days, from 1100FF to 1435FF,
   longer courses also available), cuisine of the
   Périgord Noir (three days, 1790FF) and truffles (two days, 900FF; weekend courses also
   available).
Madame Echilley
   (☎ 05 53 22 06 89)
   Monpazier, Dordogne
   One-day Gourmandises de Confiture (jam-
   making) course with lunch and a visit to
   Monpazier (500FF, minimum four people,
   year-round).
Mme Mireille Pinatel
   (☎ 05 65 22 90 42, fax 05 65 24 91 05)
   La Grande de Marcillac, 46800 St-Cyprien,
   Dordogne
   Week-long winter courses in Quercy cuisine
   (2400FF), weekend courses in truffles or foie
   gras (880FF).
Palmagri
   (☎ 05 56 65 40 81, 05 56 65 48 78)
   76 rte de Grignols, 33124 Auros, Gironde
   One-day and weekend courses in the cuisine of
   Gironde.
Restaurant Pavillon de St-Agnan
   (☎ 05 53 51 38 91, fax 05 53 51 61 75),
   near Hautefort, Dordogne
   Weekend courses in the cuisine of Périgord
   (1050FF).
Service Loisirs Accueil Dordogne
   (☎ 05 53 35 50 24, fax 05 53 09 51 41)
   25 rue du Président Wilson, 24009 Périgueux,
   Dordogne
   Information on a range of courses including:
   cuisine of Périgord (winter weekends, between
   1200FF and 1500FF, longer courses also available), truffles (winter weekends, 1500FF), cuisine du canard (winter weekends, from 800FF
   to 1300FF), and mushrooms (between 895FF
   and 1300FF).

The exhaustive listings in Shaw Guide's
online annual *Guide to Cooking Schools*
(www.shawguides.com) include schools in

the Dordogne and the French Basque country. For information on a combined cycling-and-cooking tour of the Bordeaux area, see Organised Tours in the Getting There & Away chapter.

Oenology & Wine Tasting

The following private institutions, tourist offices and chateaux will walk you through the minefield of subjectivity that is wine-tasting, and help you to appreciate the best (and avoid the worst) of the region's wines.

Actour 47
(☎ 05 53 66 14 14, fax 05 53 68 25 42)
4 rue André Chénier, 47008 Agen,
Lot-et-Garonne
Weekend courses.
Bordeaux Quintessence
(☎ 05 56 35 83 93, fax 05 56 35 86 50)
23 rue des Houx, 33320 le Taillan Médoc,
Gironde
Two- to five-day courses, available in English.
Château Loudenne
(☎ 05 56 73 17 80, fax 05 56 09 02 87) 33340
St Yzans de Médoc, Gironde
Two- to five-day courses, available in English.
l'École du Bordeaux
(☎ 05 56 59 24 24, fax 05 56 59 01 89)
Château de Cordeillon Bages, rte des Châteaux, 33250 Pauillac, Gironde
One- to five-day courses, available in English.
l'École du Vin, Conseil Interprofessionel du Vin
de Bordeaux (CIVB)
(☎ 05 56 00 22 66, fax 05 56 00 22 82, email
ecole@vins-bordeaux.fr)
Web site: www.vins-bordeaux.fr
3 cours du 30 Juillet, 33075 Bordeaux
An introduction to Bordeaux wines, courses
are available in English (120FF, two hours on
selected evenings, year-round; 1900FF for
weekend intensive courses; from 2000FF to
2500FF for three-day intensive courses,
1200FF to 1600FF for students).
Espace Maucaillou
(☎ 05 56 58 01 23, fax 05 56 58 00 88)
33480 Moulis en Médoc, Gironde
Three-day courses, available in English.
Maison des Vins, CIVRB
(☎ 05 53 63 57 57, fax 05 53 63 01 30,
email vin.civrb@wanadoo.fr)
2 place du Docteur Cayla, 24100 Bergerac,
Dordogne
Courses held during the summer.
Maison du Tourisme de la Gironde
(☎ 05 56 52 61 40, fax 05 56 81 09 99)

21 cours de l'Intendance, 33000 Bordeaux
Information on weekend courses.
Réveil Papiles
(☎ 05 56 92 89 79, fax 05 56 92 89 05)
9 rue des Menuts, 33000 Bordeaux
Day and evening courses available.
Service Loisirs Accueil Dordogne
(☎ 05 53 35 50 24, fax 05 53 09 51 41)
25 rue du Président Wilson, 24009 Périgueux,
Dordogne
Information on weekend courses.

Fine Arts

In tourist office brochures or just on signs by the roadside, *atelier* indicates workshops or studios where the artists will show you what they do and how they do it, in the hope that you'll buy some of it. At a few of these, such as the ones noted here, you may be able to arrange classes. Where details in the following list are not specific, it indicates that the artist may tailor the length and content of a class to your interests.

Aletta Baker van der Have
(☎/fax 05 53 28 59 69)
Hôtel de Gèrard, 3 rue Fènelon, 24200 Sarlat,
Dordogne
Teaching the art of glass-making, for adults or
children.
Art en Périgord
(☎/fax 05 53 29 75 02)
Pech d'Ambirou, 24200 Sarlat, Dordogne
Course focusing on drawing, painting and interior design.
Atelier Créac
(☎ 05 63 41 82 66)
Le Cambou, 81800 Mézens, Tarn
Courses in wood and stone sculpture and
weaving (week-long and weekend courses,
year-round).
Atelier du Chemin Vert
(☎ 05 63 75 03 58, fax 05 63 75 29 67)
81470 Lacroisille, Tarn
Courses focusing on watercolour, oil painting,
drawing, sculpture, casting and jewellery,
held in a restored Occitan farmhouse; English
is spoken (one- or two-week summer courses).
Atelier Greschny
(☎ 05 63 55 14 82 or 05 63 45 40 69)
La Maurinié, 81430 Marsal, Tarn
Courses in enamelling, icons and Byzantine-
style art run by the family of late artist Nico-
las Greschny.
Clémentine et Emmanuel Alexia
(☎ 05 65 10 87 87)

La Claveyrie, 46400 Frayssinhes, Dordogne
Ten-day courses in the art of making stained-glass windows.

Destination Salies
(☎ 05 59 38 00 33, fax 05 59 38 02 95), rue des Bains, 64270 Salies de Béarn, Béarn, Pyrénées-Atlantiques
Courses in watercolour, oil painting, drawing (three days and nights from 855FF).

Hélène and Francis Pratt, Painting School of Montmiral
(☎ 05 63 33 13 11)
rue de la Porte Neuve, 81140 Castelnau de Montmiral, Tarn
Summer painting courses with visiting artists (15-day courses).

Léo Amery Vitrail
(☎ 05 65 37 40 07, fax 05 65 37 44 56) 46600 Martel, Dordogne
Five-day courses in the art of making stained-glass windows (2500FF).

Service Loisirs Accueil Dordogne
(☎ 05 53 35 50 24, fax 05 53 09 51 41) 25 rue du Président Wilson, 24009 Périgueux, Dordogne
Courses in making stained-glass windows (weekend courses, 2355FF); woodworking, furniture-making, restoration (four-day summer courses, 2200FF); painting (six days during July and August, 2000FF).

Suzanne Legallou
(☎ 05 59 82 61 20)
rte de Marie Blanque, 64260 Bilhères, Vallée d'Ossau, Béarn, Pyrénées-Atlantiques
Courses in ceramics.

Outdoor Activities

For information on classes in outdoor sports including surfing, caving, climbing, parasailing and riding, see Activities earlier in this chapter. For details of companies, see regional or individual town listings.

Other Courses

From May to September, the Rucher École (☎ 05 53 22 40 35) in Beaumont en Périgord, Dordogne, offers a one-week course in bee-keeping for 1700FF, including accommodation and meals.

WORK

To work legally here you need a residence permit known as a carte de séjour (see Visas & Documents earlier in this chapter). Getting one is almost automatic for EU nationals but almost impossible for anyone else except full-time students. Non-EU nationals must also get a work permit (autorisation de travail) before arriving in France.

The government does seem to tolerate undocumented workers helping out with some agricultural work, especially during harvests, though you get no workplace insurance protection in case of an accident, either to you or involving you. The national minimum wage for nonprofessionals is about 40FF an hour, although employers willing to hire in the black are also apt to ignore minimum wage laws.

Tourist offices may direct you to départemental Chambres d'Agriculture, to growers' cooperatives, or to the nearest office of the Agence National pour l'Emploi (ANPE; France's national employment service, who have a Web site at www.anpe.fr). A more accessible source of help with temporary jobs are the ubiquitous BIJs in most sizeable towns. We have identified these in individual town listings. For more on what these centres have to offer, see the boxed text 'Bureaux d'Information Jeunesse'.

Over half of all French students take temporary jobs in July and August, so the competition is fierce at this time.

Agricultural Work

Important items on the south-west's harvest calendar include apples (September), asparagus (March to June), cherries (June), maize (July to mid-August) and tobacco (late August and September). Many farmers prefer hiring people who know at least a bit of French.

Vendange The south-west's annual vendange happens largely in September, with southern varieties ripening in October or even later. The starting date in any given area changes from year to year, and is normally announced by the préfecture no more than a week before picking starts. Once started, it lasts just a couple of weeks. Food is usually supplied but accommodation is often not.

Work opportunities are shrinking as more and more vendanges are done by machine,

Bureaux d'Information Jeunesse

Centres, Bureaux and Points d'Information Jeunesse form a dense, countrywide network of state-funded resource offices with a wide range of information for young people on education, professional training, jobs, housing, health, sports, travel, events, discounts and more.

Bureaux d'Information Jeunesse (BIJ) – sometimes signposted Maison de Jeune – are mainly located in départemental capitals, while smaller towns may have only a one-room Point d'Information Jeunesse (PIJ). Each régional capital – Bordeaux and Toulouse in the case of South-West France – has a big Centre Régional d'Information Jeunesse (CRIJ) with additional facilities such as a library and a budget travel agency. CRIJs and most BIJs also offer Internet access, at a modest online rate, and some have limited free email services.

Foreign visitors are usually welcome to use the services of these offices. Those who speak some French may also find them good places to meet local young people. We have included details under individual town listings. The régional centres (CRIJ) for South-West France are:

Centre Régional d'Information Jeunesse Aquitaine
　(☎ 05 56 56 00 56, fax 05 56 52 83 21)
　125 cours Alsace-Lorraine and 5 rue Duffour-Dubergier,
　33000 Bordeaux (Minitel 3615 TOPCIJA)
Centre Régional d'Information Jeunesse Toulouse Midi-Pyrénées
　(☎ 05 61 21 20 20, fax 05 61 27 28 29, email bdienot@crij.mipnet.fr)
　17 rue de Metz, 31000 Toulouse (Minitel 3615 CIJ)

though mechanical picking is disdained by the most prestigious chateaux. The most effective way of getting vendange work is to approach the various *domaines* (wine-producing estates) directly, from early May onwards. Tourist offices have lists of producers, as do the Maisons des Vins (see the Food & Wine section for contact details).

Building Restoration

Here's a different and worthy summer job: help in the restoration of old buildings and monuments. Besides mixing concrete and carrying hods, you'll also learn about the finer aspects of the craft. The work is unpaid, but food and lodging are free. Contact Companions Bâtisseurs (☎ 05 6372 59 64), 2 rue Claude Bertholet, 81000 Castres (Tarn-et-Garonne).

Au Pairing

Under the au pair system, single people aged between 18 and about 27 who are studying in France can live with a French family and receive lodging, full board and a bit of pocket money in exchange for childcare, light housework and perhaps teaching English to the children. Most families want native English speakers, but may also insist on some knowledge of French. The minimum commitment ranges from two to six months.

EU residents can easily arrange for an au pair job after arriving in France. Non-EU applicants must apply for an au pair visa before leaving home.

Beach Hawking & Busking

Selling goods and services on the beach is one way to make a few francs, but you'll have to sell a lot of ice cream to make a living. If you play an instrument or have some other talent in the performing arts, you could try busking, for example as a street musician, actor, juggler or pavement artist. Check with other street artists to avoid hassles – with the police, music-hating shop owners, and other buskers.

Ski Resorts

The ski resorts in the Basses-Pyrénées offer few work opportunities; if you contact a resort months in advance you might find some work in a hotel or restaurant.

ACCOMMODATION

Accommodation in the region gets expensive in summer, but with some foresight you can almost always find something to suit your budget. Municipal tourist offices usually maintain lists of accommodation that cover a wide price range and will help you find (and sometimes book) a place, though they scrupulously avoid making recommendations.

Most prices are seasonal. Many places give discounts for longer stays, but you usually need to ask. We use the following price categories for an establishment's most basic double with toilet and shower/bath: budget (to about 200FF); mid-range (from 200FF to 400FF); top end (over 400FF). Unless noted, prices quoted are for peak season, and include taxes and service charges.

Advance reservations eliminate the headache of a hotel search and are especially useful if you're arriving late in the day. A simple call ahead, on the day (or even the morning) before you arrive, is often enough. Budget places are generally full by midday in summer, but they are rarely booked days or weeks ahead as with top-end accommodation.

Camping

South-West France has hundreds of camp sites, many beautifully set on river banks, lakeshores, beaches or mountain sides. Most close for at least a few months in winter and some are open only in summer. Many are far from the major sights, so campers without their own wheels must do some commuting. North American visitors should be ready for a more cheek-by-jowl style of camping than they're used to at home. Camping outside designated sites is illegal, though it's tolerated in some places (but never in a national park).

Camp sites are rated with a system of one to four stars based on facilities and amenities. Separate tariffs are usually charged per person, per tent or caravan, per car or motorcycle, and for electricity. Some places offer a *forfait* (package) rate for two people plus car and tent or caravan. Children up to about age 12 enjoy big discounts. In this

---

Oops

Mind your French, campers: an *aire naturelle* is a primitive farm camp site; an *aire naturiste* is a nudist camp.

---

book we quote sample high season prices per adult, per tent and per car.

Some camp sites are part of big, well-advertised municipal leisure complexes (*bases de loisirs*), complete with kids' activities, artificial lakes, water slides, windsurfing, swimming pools and more. Some hostels (see Hostels later in this section) will let you pitch a tent in the garden. Most camping à la ferme is coordinated by Gîtes de France or Clévacances (see the following Chambres d'Hôte & Self-Catering Accommodation section for contact details).

If you'll be doing lots of car camping, a good investment is the *Guide officiel* of the Fédération Française de Camping et de Caravaning, which lists just about every site in the country. Michelin's multilingual *Camping & Caravanning* includes around one-third of them, in more detail. Both cost about 80FF. Free booklets published annually by Aquitaine and Midi-Pyrénées Comités Régionaux de Tourisme list most camp sites in each région (see Tourist Offices earlier in this chapter for contact details).

For information on the Camping Card International see under Visas & Documents earlier in this chapter.

Chambres d'Hôtes & Self-Catering Accommodation

Several types of rural accommodation – often in charming, traditional-style houses with gardens – are suitable for travellers with their own transport. A chambre d'hôte is essentially a B&B: a room in a private home, rented by the night, with breakfast always included in the price. Prices for a double room start at about 200FF per night. An evening meal may be available for an extra charge.

The most popular self-catering accommodation is a *gîte rural*, a private farm or farm building, which has been restored as

euro currency converter 10FF = €1.52

furnished, self-catering holiday lodgings with kitchenette and bathroom. Weekly prices start at about 1200FF in June and September or 2000FF in July and August. *Meublé* (furnished accommodation) and *meublé de tourisme* are other common terms for self-catering places. It's essential to book these places well ahead in peak season. Local tourist offices have listings.

Most chambres d'hôte and gîtes ruraux – and many gîtes d'étape (see the following section) and camp sites – are represented by Gîtes de France (☎ 01 49 70 75 75, fax 01 42 81 28 53, email info@gites-de-france .fr), 59 rue St-Lazare, 75439 Paris Cedex 09. Check out their Web site at www.gites-de-france.fr. A smaller outfit dealing in self-catering properties is Clévacances (☎ 05 61 13 55 66, fax 05 61 13 55 94), 54 blvd de l'Embouchure, BP 2166, 31022 Toulouse. Départemental branches publish annual listings, complete with photos. Listings and addresses are available from local tourist offices. You can book through the branch

---

Bienvenue à la Ferme

Bienvenue à la Ferme (literally 'welcome to the farm') is a network of chartered farms offering a convenient taste of rural life for tourists. Look for the sunflower logo in départemental tourism brochures and elsewhere. Little English is spoken. Programmes, which must normally be booked in advance (this can be done through the nearest tourist office), include:

Fermes de Séjour farm accommodation, meals and activities
Campings en Ferme d'Accueil camping on the farm
Fermes Auberges farm restaurants
Goûters à la Ferme afternoon teas from farm produce
Produits de la Ferme sales of farm produce
Fermes de Découverte small-group farm tours
Fermes Équestres horse riding and other programmes

---

offices or directly with property owners. A useful Web site listing both chambres d'hôte and self-catering places is at www.frenchconnections.co.uk/.

For a programe of farm-based accommodation and other offerings that overlap with this, see the boxed text 'Bienvenue à la Ferme'. Gîtes d'Enfants is a Gîtes de France programme of one-week stays on vetted farms, with full board and activities for groups of children aged from four to 10 or six to 13.

Refuges & Gîtes d'Étape

Gîtes d'étape and refuges offer basic, dormitory-style options for hikers, horse-riders and mountaineers.

Refuges are simple mountain shelters run by park authorities or private organisations. They're usually marked on hiking maps and are often accessible only on foot. They're equipped with bunks, mattresses and blankets, but not sheets (these are sometimes available to rent). Nightly rates are from 50FF to 90FF per person and meals are usually available for about 80FF to 100FF. Most are staffed only in summer but may be partly open but unstaffed in winter. For more information, visit a tourist office near where you'll be hiking. If you'll be in the Basses-Pyrénées, look for *Hébergement en Montagne*, published by Éditions Randonnées Pyrénéennes and available in many bookshops.

Gîtes d'étape, usually better equipped and more comfortable than refuges, tend to be located in towns or villages. They cost around 70FF per person and are listed in *Gîtes d'Étape et de Séjour* (70FF), published annually by Gîtes de France. Note that some gîtes d'étape accommodate only pilgrims.

Homestays

Students, young people and tourists can stay with French families under an arrangement called *hébergement chez l'habitant* or *hôtes payants* (literally, 'paying guests'), under which you rent a room and have limited access to the family's kitchen and telephone. Rates for a single room with breakfast start at about 3000FF per month, 1200FF per week or 130FF per day.

Most language schools (see Courses earlier in this chapter) arrange homestays for their students. Hundreds of agencies in the USA and Europe arrange homestay accommodation in France; for a list, contact any overseas French tourist office (for contact details see Tourist Offices earlier in this chapter).

Hostels

France's official youth hostels – called auberges de jeunesse – all belong to one of three associations: the Fédération Unie des Auberges de Jeunesse (FUAJ), the Ligue Française pour les Auberges de la Jeunesse (LFAJ) or the Union des Centres de Rencontres Internationales de France (UCRIF).

Expect to pay from 40FF to 90FF a night for a bunk in a single-sex dormitory in high season. This does not include a (sometimes optional) continental breakfast costing from 15FF to 20FF. FUAJ and LFAJ affiliates require Hostelling International or similar cards (see Visas & Documents earlier in this chapter). They also require that you either bring a sleeping sheet or rent one for between 15FF and 20FF per stay. Most don't accept telephone reservations so get there early, especially in July and August. Be aware that smaller places may have a curfew.

In university towns you may also find *foyers*, student dormitories converted for use by travellers during summer holidays. In certain towns, co-ed dormitories called *foyers de jeunes travailleurs* are available for young workers and may accept short-term guests when they have space.

Club Léo Lagrange is a loose network of international youth centres, a few of which have dorm-style accommodation available to walk-in visitors, at around 50FF per bed, and simple meals by arrangement. There is no central governing body and you cannot book ahead.

Most auberges de jeunesse as well as some hostels and foyers have kitchen facilities of one sort or another.

Hotels

Hotels are rated on a system of one to four stars, based on quantifiable criteria such as the size of the entry hall, rather than on the quality of service or cleanliness, so a one-star establishment may be more pleasant than some two or three-star places. The prices tend to reflect these intangibles better than the ratings do.

Most hotels in the mid-range and above have TVs and telephones. Breakfast is rarely included in room prices; expect an extra 25FF to 40FF (up to 100FF at top-end places) for that. Breakfast at a nearby cafe will be cheaper and usually more pleasant. Some places in very touristy areas insist that you take breakfast or demi-pension (breakfast and either lunch or dinner).

Rather than a pillow (oreiller), beds in many lower-end places have only a sausage-shaped bolster called a *traversin*.

Budget Allow between 150FF and 200FF per night for a double with a washbasin (and often a bidet), with shared toilet and shower. A shower down the hall (referred to throughout this book as a hall shower) is sometimes free but often costs from 10FF to 25FF a go. Most budget hotels will not offer you the cheapest option right off the bat; but if you ask, they may well have something cheaper for example on the top floor, or in poorer condition). The majority also have pricier rooms with toilet and shower or bath. Most demand pre-payment; check out the room before parting with any cash. Prices stay the same year-round.

Many budget hotels have no singles, only rooms with a double bed (un grand lit) costing the same for one or two guests. There may be a considerable jump in price if you want twin beds (lits séparés or lits jumeaux). Those with genuine singles usually charge at least 70% of the price of a double.

Thin-walled, unatmospheric but clean and dependable chain hotels in urban outskirts are good value for those passing through by car. Chains include Formule 1, which charges 140FF for a three-bed room with shared shower and toilet (150FF in

July and August); their English-language Web site at www.hotelweb.fr was under construction at the time of writing. Première Classe (www.premiereclasse.com/) and B&B (www.hotel-bb.com/) also have rooms with attached shower and toilet.

Mid-Range Some 350 hotels in South-West France – many of them family-run – belong to Logis de France, an organisation whose affiliates must meet strict standards of service and amenities. They generally offer very good value. The Fédération Nationale des Logis de France (☎ 01 45 84 70 00, fax 01 45 83 59 66), 83 ave d'Italie, 75013 Paris, issues a detailed annual guide (95FF) to all of them. Check out their Web site at www.logis.de france.fr.

Expect to pay between 200FF and 400FF for a room. Mid-range hotels usually have seasonal prices. For information on high/low season see When to Go under Planning earlier in this chapter.

FOOD

The south-west is made for foodies. Périgord, particularly, boasts among its specialities such luxuries as truffles and foie gras (liver of goose or duck). Though you may not be able to splash out on a truffle omelette every day, you can pick up other regional produce like walnuts, strawberries and goat's cheese from the markets.

Even serious gourmands may find a Périgord meal too much to handle every day. Goose fat and walnut oil are basic to many regional recipes, making traditional meals sumptuous, filling affairs. A 'simple' family meal might feature home-made *pâté de canard* (duck pâté) or foie gras, topped with a slice of truffle, and followed by confit de canard. Even potatoes become delicacies as *pommes de terre sarladaises*: sizzling in goose fat, mixed with *cèpe* (cep) mushroom pieces, garlic and parsley.

Meals of the Day

Breakfast If you're accustomed to a big fry-up at breakfast you're in for a shock. The traditional *petit déjeuner* is microscopic, usually a croissant or bread, some-times with butter and jam, washed down with *café au lait* (coffee with lots of hot milk), strong black coffee or hot chocolate. Hotel breakfasts may include fruit juice and more.

Lunch & Dinner Lunch *(déjeuner)* is the main meal of the day. It starts at noon and can last until 2.30 or 3 pm. Restaurants (but not brasseries; see the following Types of Eateries section) close from 3 to 7 pm and serve dinner *(dîner)* from 7.30 to around 10 pm. Most restaurants close on Sunday.

Traditional lunch and dinner fare are similar: starter *(entrée)*, main course *(plat principal)*, salad, cheese and/or dessert. Bread is usually free and freely available. Drinks *(boissons)* cost extra unless the *menu* says *boisson comprise*. If it says *vin compris* you'll probably get a small *pichet* (jug) of plain *vin de table*. The waiter will ask if you want to finish with coffee, which usually costs extra.

If you go the whole hog, this is the order in which courses are served:

Apéritif – pre-dinner drink plus nibbles
Entrée – first course or starter; one or more
Plat principal – main course
Légumes – vegetables or potatoes, sometimes with the main course
Salade – usually just lettuce and dressing
Fromage – cheese
Dessert
Fruit
Café
Digestif – after-dinner drink such as Armagnac or brandy

Menus & Menus

In French, *le menu* is a list of the dishes comprising a single complete meal. What English speakers think of as a 'menu,' ie a folder or book listing all of a restaurant's available meals and dishes, is *la carte*. Throughout this book, *menu* is italicised whenever it is used in the French sense.

Types of Eateries

Restaurants & Brasseries Lots of restaurants offer excellent French meals for between 150FF and 200FF – Michelin's Guide rouge is full of them – but good, inexpensive restaurants are rare. Some of the best are attached to mid-range hotels (almost all hotel restaurants are open to non-residents). Another option for quick, hearty meals is the loose chain of Les Routiers (truckers' restaurants) which are usually found on the outskirts of towns and cities, and along major roads. The annual Guide des Relais Routiers (120FF), available in major bookshops, lists every one.

But the best choice for inexpensive dining at any time of day is a brasserie. While restaurants often specialise in one type of food (for example regional, traditional, North African, Vietnamese) and open only for lunch and dinner, brasseries (which often look like cafes) serve a wider selection of standard fare, more cheaply and in a more casual atmosphere.

Restaurant or brasserie lunch *menus* start at around 60FF. At 40 to 50FF, the dish of the day *(plat du jour)* is the best budget choice. Evening *menus* (especially in restaurants) cost from 70FF to 400FF per person.

Cafes & Bars The cafe is an integral part of French society; in the rural south-west the village cafe may double as bar, meeting place and bistro. Most can serve up a sandwich (half a baguette filled with cheese, ham or pâté) or croque-monsieur (toasted cheese and ham sandwich) for 20FF to 25FF. An urban cafe on a grand boulevard charges more than a place on a quiet side street; and all charge according to where you choose to have your drink: standing at the counter (comptoir, the cheapest option), sitting at a table indoors (salle) or outside (terrasse), the most expensive. But once you've ordered you can stay as long as you like, with no pressure to order anything more. The price of drinks usually goes up at night, after about 8 pm.

Keeping Costs & Stress Down

France can be hard work at mealtimes, because of the language barrier (and food names which are obscure even if you're fluent), widespread Sunday and/or Monday closures and generally quite high prices. Many travellers end up living on picnics, snacks and take-aways, but it doesn't have to be this way:

- Choose brasseries, not restaurants: they're usually cheaper, quicker, more casual, open longer and serve bigger helpings.
- Get good value for money with the cheapest lunchtime *menu* or *menu du jour*, or a *formule* (choose any two courses from starter, main course and dessert), or even just the *plat du jour* (dish of the day) with no accompaniments, and eat lightly in the evening when things cost more; avoid ordering à la carte (selecting courses individually).
- Arrive punctually at opening time to avoid long waits and to get that *plat du jour* before it runs out (and to escape before the place fills with cigarette smoke).
- Order tap water *(de l'eau du robinet)*, not expensive bottled mineral water *(l'eau de source)*; or a *pichet* of house wine, usually cheaper than beer.
- Skip dessert, which is usually pricey.
- Look for a *menu enfant* for children under 12.
- Vegetarians can assemble a meal by ordering one or more side dishes.

You will nearly always find a *carte* (menu) posted outside so you can check it all out before committing yourself.

Feasts on the Farm

It was the Dordogne département that first invented the *ferme auberge* idea: a simple, rustic restaurant on a farm where visitors can dine on home-cooked regional dishes made mostly from ingredients produced on the farm. Struggling farmers make extra money and tourists can enjoy genuine local cuisine.

Today there are more than 90 such places in the Dordogne, and dozens in other départements. They're listed (with prices) in *Bienvenue à la Ferme* brochures available at tourist offices; these also list farms where you can buy produce, or even stay the night (see the boxed text under Accommodation).

Note that most fermes auberges need advance notice to prepare a meal. *Menus* are rarely posted outside; indeed there may not be any *menu* at all, just whatever's on the stove. A few serve tourist-geared fare at tourist prices; on the other hand, you might dine like a king for next-to-nothing.

At busy or touristy cafes you may be asked to pay *l'addition* (the bill) when your drink arrives, but in most places you'll spend ages catching the waiter's attention so you can leave.

Salons de Thé & Creperies Salons de thé (tearooms) are trendy, somewhat pricey establishments serving quiches, salads, pies and pastries in addition to tea and coffee. Creperies, found everywhere and especially in tourist spots, specialise, of course, in crepes – either ultra-thin pancakes with a sweet or savoury filling, or thicker, usually savoury versions called galettes, made with buckwheat flour.

Vegetarian You're in the wrong part of France for gourmet vegetarian fare: this is after all the land of foie gras. But it's also the land of truffles and wild mushrooms, asparagus and strawberries, walnuts and goat cheese: you can pick up a cornucopia of veggie fare at the markets, and order salads (usually generous) or vegetarian entrées at restaurants. Creperies invariably have vegetarian options. If you eat fish, there's nearly always a good choice in restaurants. Dedicated vegetarian restaurants, and even vegetarian menus, are rare.

Ethnic Restaurants Toulouse, Bordeaux and Agen have many restaurants and stalls selling North African couscous and lamb kebabs, and Chinese, Indian and Vietnamese restaurants. Even in rural markets you're likely to find a range of Oriental specialities, Indian-inspired samosas and Italian-influenced paellas.

Self-Catering

If the cuisine of the south-west wasn't so tempting you could easily get by on daily gourmet picnics: it's easy to shop for delicious fresh bread, pastries, cheese, fruit, vegetables and prepared dishes from supermarkets, speciality shops or weekly markets. Just don't leave it till Sunday afternoon or Monday when many food shops close.

A boulangerie or *dépôt de pain* (breadseller) is the essential first stop: in addition to the traditional *baguette* (long, thin loaf) and fatter, softer *pain*, you'll find *pain complet* (wholemeal), *pain de campagne* (country loaf) and *pain de seigle* (rye bread). Eat your baguette the same day or it will turn to stone; the other loaves keep longer. Many boulangeries also sell cakes and pastries; if not, find a *pâtisserie* for *pain au chocolat* (chocolate croissant), *pain aux raisins* (spiral pastry filled with sultanas), *tarte aux fruits* (fruit tart) or *canelé* (Bordeaux's own custard pastry).

Speciality shops, not supermarkets, sell the best and ripest produce. Cheese is best from a *fromagerie* where you can *goûter* (taste) those you don't know or ask for recommendations. Shop for sliced cold meat, pâté, seafood salads, olives and spicy sausage at a *charcuterie* (delicatessen); you can always get just a few *tranches* (slices) of meat or *un petit bout* (small chunk) of sausage, or enough *pour une/deux person-nes*. A *traiteur* sells ready-to-eat dishes. If there's a *marché couvert* (covered market, often known as *les halles* and open up to six days a week) you'll probably find such speciality shops all here. Anything else you need is probably at the local *épicerie* (grocery store) or *alimentation générale* (general food shop); though generally pricier than supermarkets, they're central, accessible and often open on days when other shops close.

Markets

Marchés en plein air (outdoor markets) are one of the great pleasures of South-West France. Quite apart from the produce, they're a fantastic social rendezvous for everyone, from elderly farmers who only venture into town for this event to itinerant artisans selling trinkets and jewellery.

Every town of any size has a weekly market, and many have two; we note many in the text. Here you'll find the freshest local fruit and vegetables (look for strawberries and asparagus in spring and summer and walnuts, mushrooms and truffles in winter), home-made jams and honey, goat's cheese, walnut cake and oil, and pâté de foie gras. Local wines are on display (free tastings usually available), and local arts and crafts

on sale. There's usually produce from other regions, too – olives and fish, mussels and oysters, garlic and herbs – and ready-to-eat roast chickens, seafood paellas and Vietnamese spring rolls.

There's no bargaining. Weighing is by hand scales, or not at all. Get there early (around 8 am) for the buzz and the best choice; by midday everyone starts packing up or drifting into cafes for a beer, wine or eau de vie.

DRINKS

Alcohol consumption in France has dropped 20% since WWII, but the trend hasn't reached the south-west yet. Thanks to the major wine-growing regions of Bordeaux, Bergerac and Cahors, wine is not just a mealtime accompaniment but an anytime-at-all tipple. So too are home-made brews such as *vin de noix* (walnut wine) and *eau de vie* (see Alcoholic Drinks later in this section).

Nonalcoholic Drinks

Tap water in the south-west is safe to drink. Water in public fountains or streams often isn't drinkable, indicated by signs saying *eau non potable* (not drinking water). In restaurants, ask for *de l'eau* or *de l'eau du robinet* (tap water) or you'll get pricey *eau*

Best of the Dordogne Markets

The Dordogne is famous throughout France for the quality and variety of its market produce and the markets' picturesque settings. Here are some of the best:

Sarlat-la-Canéda (Saturday) The prettiest setting, the most packed with tourists, but worth the crowds and traffic jams: fruit (especially strawberries), vegetables, foie gras, *charcuterie* (products made with pork), honey, wines and walnut bread; in winter, truffles, wild mushrooms, walnuts and foie gras. Stake out a cafe table overlooking place de la Liberté and watch it unfold, or come on Wednesday for a smaller version.

Périgueux & Bergerac (Wednesday and Saturday) Hearty regional markets catering to locals, backed by imposing churches. Bergerac has good local wines; Périgueux has great fruit, vegetables and cheeses (and truffles from mid-November to mid-February).

Ribérac & Brantôme (Friday) Brantôme is pretty – embraced by the Dronne river – rather than plentiful, but has lots of truffles from December to February; Ribérac has all you'll need for a gourmet *pique-nique* (picnic), and from October to December it has a Wednesday market that specialises in walnuts.

de source (mineral water) which comes *plate* (flat) or *gazeuse* (fizzy).

Canned or bottled soft drinks are expensive (up to 20FF in cafes). A cheaper option is a *sirop* (syrup) served with water or soda – *cassis* (blackberry), *grenadine* (pomegranate), *menthe* (mint) or *citron* (lemon). The most expensive choice is *citron* or *orange pressé* – freshly squeezed lemon or orange with iced water and sugar. For a refreshing alternative, try a *panaché* (shandy). If you want ice cubes *(des glaçons)* in your drink, you'll probably have to ask for them.

Coffee costs about 7FF to 10FF a cup. Unless you specify otherwise, you get a small, strong, black expresso. If you need a bigger punch, ask for *un grand café* (double espresso). Milky versions include *un café crème* (espresso with steamed milk) and *un café au lait* (hot milk with a dash of coffee).

Thé (tea) and *chocolat chaud* (hot chocolate) are widely available. Our kids like the cold chocolate bottled drink called *Cacolac*. *Tisane* – herbal tea (sometimes known as an *infusion*) – is also popular, especially mint, *camomille* (camomile) or *tilleul* (lime).

Alcoholic Drinks

Wine See the special Food & Wine section.

Aperitifs & Digestifs You may get offered an aperitif at any time of the day, not just before a meal. Popular with men is *pastis* (also referred to by brand names such as Pernod and Ricard), a 90% proof aniseed drink that turns cloudy when mixed with water. Women are usually offered milder drinks such as sweet port, *kir* (white wine or vin de Cahors sweetened with cassis), *fenelon* (walnut liqueur with cassis and red wine) or *pineau* (cognac and grape juice).

The south-west's home-grown, dry and pungent digestif, Armagnac (see the boxed text under Le Pays d'Armagnac in the Gers chapter) is made from distilled white wine and often used to put a punch in regional sauces. *Floc de Gascogne*, made from Armagnac mixed with selected red or white wines, is like a sweet port and is served chilled as an apéritif. The Basque country has its own potent herbal liqueur called *izarra*.

Although *eaux de vie* (literally, 'waters of life' – fiery brandies distilled from local fruits) are theoretically digestifs, they pop up as apéritifs too, especially if made by the patron himself. Popular versions are *eau de vie de prune* (plum brandy) and *eau de vie de framboise* (raspberry brandy) – irresistible and deceptively potent.

Beer Beer is usually either Alsatian, or imported from Belgium or Germany. In cafes and pubs it's cheaper *à la pression* (on draught) than *en bouteille* (by the bottle) – just ask for *une pression* to get a *demi* (about 330mL) for between 12FF and 16FF. Prices may rise as the night wears on.

ENTERTAINMENT

Local tourist offices are the best source of information about what's on. Many of them publish their own monthly or seasonal listings of events. Several regional newspapers also carry comprehensive cinema, theatre and festival listings.

FNAC superstores are a good source for tickets for everything from opera to rock concerts. Most have a booking and ticket desk with a calendar of upcoming events. There are FNAC's with ticket desks in Bordeaux, Toulouse and Pau.

Music

Every city and many towns lay on at least one music festival each year (see Public Holidays & Special Events earlier in this chapter), some internationally known. The contemporary music scene is dominated by jazz (see the boxed text 'Jazz Bonanza' in Public Holidays & Special Events earlier in this chapter) and the sounds of Cuba, Brazil and Africa. The *chansons* (songs) of Edith Piaf, Georges Brassens and Belgian-born Jacques Brel have never gone out of style. On the classical side, Toulouse has its own well-regarded symphony orchestra and a national chamber orchestra, Bordeaux boasts national and municipal orchestras and an opera company, and many smaller towns have their own orchestras.

One of the simplest but most appealing musical manifestations we came across is the monthly Baïona Kantus, essentially a public Basque singalong, in Bayonne (with others in smaller towns of the French Basque country).

Bars, Discos & Clubs

Most départemental capitals have at least one or two cheerful bars with live or recorded blues, country, folk or rock music. Discos *(discothèques)* and clubs *(boîte du nuit)*, once rare beyond the urban confines of Bordeaux, Bayonne and Toulouse and the anything-goes summer communities of the Atlantic coast, are popping up in smaller towns. Most don't hit their stride until at least midnight. Music (live or recorded) ranges from jazz to Latino to techno.

Tenue correcte exigée means 'appropriate dress required'. Muscled *videurs* (bouncers) keep out undesirables, which can range from unaccompanied men who aren't dressed right to members of certain minority groups. All are careful to filter out people who are drunk.

Cinema

You can see foreign films in their original language (with French subtitles) in selected cinemas in most bigger towns. Look for the letters v.o *(version originale*, non dubbed) or v.o.s.t *(version originale sous-titrée*, with subtitles) on cinema billboards. v.f *(version française)* means the film has been dubbed into French. Count on paying 40FF to 50FF for a first-run film. Most French cinemas offer discounts to young people, students and people aged over 60, except at weekends. Many also give discounts to everyone on Wednesday.

SPECTATOR SPORTS

The people of the south-west take their spectator sports seriously, although they and their northern cousins don't share the same priorities. Bullfighting stirs passions in the Landes, Gers and the French Basque country, along with a bloodless variant called *les courses landaises* (see Courses

Landaises later in this section). The most popular contact sport is not football but rugby. The gentlest of pastimes – to play or to watch – is *pétanque* (boules). And only in or near the Basque country will you find the unique menu of games and competitions known as *jeux Basques.*

FNAC superstores are a good source of rugby and football tickets.

Bullfighting

Corrida first appeared in France around 1850, though a debate still rages about whether the first venue was in Bayonne in the French Basque country, or at Vic-Fézensac in the Gers. Other towns where the sport is big today include Mont de Marsan and Dax in the Landes, and Estang in the Gers.

A bull, bred to be aggressive, matches wits with a team of French or Spanish toreros – banderilleros with small harpoons,

---

Cruel?

Those who cannot help but see the *corrida* (bullfight), and even the *courses landaises* (bull run), as cruel sports can contact the following organisations for information and suggested action:

People for the Ethical Treatment of Animals (PETA)
Britain: (☎ 020-7388 4922, fax 7388 4925) PO Box 3169, London NW1 2JF
USA: (☎ 757-622-PETA, fax 622-1078) 501 Front St, Norfolk, VA 23510
World Society for the Protection of Animals (WSPA)
Britain: (☎ 020-7793 0540, fax 7793 0208, email wspahq@gn.apc.org) 2 Langley Lane, London SW8 1TJ
USA: (☎ 617-522-7000, fax 522-7077, email wspa@world.std.com) PO Box 190, Boston, MA 02130
Canada: (☎ 416-369-0044 fax 369-0147, email 102232.3627@compuserve.com) 44 Victoria St, suite 1310, Toronto, Ont M5C 1Y2

---

mounted picadors with lances, and the matador, dressed like a flamenco dancer and armed with a sword, whose skill is measured by his cool pivots with the cape and the final swiftness of the kill. The spectacle is colourful and bloody, and the bull dies a drawn-out death, though there is as yet little debate about animal rights here (see the boxed text 'Cruel?' on the previous page). South-westerners regard the corrida as a passionate celebration of tradition, without making apologies to anyone.

The main season for corridas is from July through the first week in September. Major tournaments are held about half a dozen times each summer, with tickets selling for as little as 80FF and as much as 450FF, depending on whether your seat is *soleil* (in the sun), *ombre et soleil* (mixed shade and sun) or *ombre* (in the shade). Advance reservations are usually necessary; ask at the nearest tourist office.

Courses Landaises

Prior to some corridas (see the preceding Bullfighting section), the bulls were run through the streets to the arena and some daring villagers would run along with the bulls. This grew into a 'sport' in its own right and some towns in the far south-west still include a running of the bulls (or cows) in their annual festivals.

Laws in the 19th century required these to be confined and the modern result is *les courses landaises*, in which participants face cows – the Landes' own black, long-horned, ill-tempered variety – in an arena. Cattle ranches field teams of six *écarteurs* (dodgers) who goad the cows into charging and then dodge artfully or even jump over them. A jury awards points to each individual and/or team. To an outsider it may look like clowning around, but aficionados regard it as a sport of danger and grace.

Cycling

The Tour de France is the world's most prestigious bicycle race. For three weeks each July, 189 of the world's top cyclists (in 21 teams of nine) take on a 3000km-plus route. The route changes each year, but always includes five or six days in the Alps and the Pyrénées, and always finishes down the Champs-Élysées in Paris.

Each daily stage is timed and the winner is the rider with the lowest accumulated time. Three special jerseys are awarded and re-awarded each day: the yellow one for race leader, the green one for points leader and the red polka dot one for the 'king of the mountains'. To win one, especially the yellow jersey, even for a day is certain to make headlines back home for that rider.

The 1999 Tour was won by American Lance Armstrong, the first winner in 15 years to take four stages, the first in a decade to take both the mountain and time-trial stages, and the first ever to average more than 40 km/h. Most amazing of all, Armstrong had only just bounced back from severe testicular cancer.

Brightly-clothed riders – many no doubt with their sights on the Tour de France – hurtle along the back roads of the south-west year-round, especially in summer. Visit the organiser's Web site at www .letour.fr for information on the current or upcoming Tour.

Rugby

Rugby has been played with enthusiasm in France since 1900, nowhere more so than in the south, where the sport generally eclipses football in popularity.

Rugby union (15s) is most common. Favourite teams include Toulouse (who are Castres, Bayonne, Biarritz, Bordeaux, Brive-la-Gaillarde, Montauban, Mont de Marsan, Pau and Périgueux. Rugby league (13s), less popular in France on the whole, also has a loyal following here.

Rugby enthusiasts can stay abreast of these and other teams at the Web site midol.compuserve.com. The finals of the Championnat de France de Rugby take place in late May and early June.

Football

France's love affair with football (soccer) got a big boost when it hosted and won the 1998 World Cup, beating the reigning champions and tournament favourite,

Brazil, by three goals to one in a one-sided final, thanks to two goals from Zinedine Zidane and one from Emmanuel Petit. Millions of elated supporters celebrated on the streets of Paris and other cities. Ironically, the 1995 Bosman decision – allowing any European club to field any number of European players – has resulted in an exodus of French players (including Zidane and Petit) to clubs outside the country, where they're better paid.

South-West France's biggest football club is Girondins de Bourdeaux, although even here rugby (see the preceding section) has a bigger following. Two other regional clubs in good standing are at Toulouse and Brive-la-Gaillarde.

Pétanque

France's most popular traditional games – especially popular in the south – are pétanque and the similar, though more formal, boules. Both are usually played by village men on a rough gravel or sandy pitch known as a *boulodrome*, scratched out on any handy patch of flat, shady ground. Some towns have purpose-built boulodromes. The favoured time is the cool of late afternoon and spectators are always welcome.

The object is to throw your boules (solid metal balls) as close as possible to the small coloured ball thrown at the start (see the boxed text 'Feet Tied & Bowled Out'). Despite its humble appearance, pétanque is a serious sport. Since their inception in 1959, the Pétanque Open World Championships have been won 19 times by France. There have been separate pétanque world championships for women and juniors since 1987.

Basque Sports

You know you're in the land of the Basque people when every town centre has a fronton, an outdoor concrete court with one tall, rounded wall, where any and all play variants of the traditional game of *pilota* (in local dialect; *la pélote Basque* in French). Pairs or teams of players volley with a small, rubber- or leather-covered ball

---

Feet Tied & Bowled Out

Despite *pétanque's* seemingly informal nature, its rules are precise and inviolable.

Two to six people, divided into two teams, can play. Each player has three solid metal boules (two if there are six players), weighing between 650g and 800g and stamped with the hallmark of a licensed boule maker. The game revolves around the *cochonnet* (jack), a small wooden ball 25mm to 35mm in diameter. Each team takes it in turn to aim a boule at this marker, the idea being to land the boule as close as possible to it. The team with the closest boule wins the round; points are allocated by totting up how many boules the winner's team has closest to the marker (one point for each boule). The first to notch up 13 wins the match.

The team throwing the cochonnet (initially decided by a coin toss) has to throw it from within a small circle, 30cm to 50cm in diameter, scratched on the ground. It must be hurled 6m to 10m away. Each player aiming a boule must likewise stand in this circle, *pieds tanques* (literally 'feet tied'), with both feet firmly on the ground. At the end of a round, a new circle is drawn round the cochonnet, determining the spot where the next round will start.

Underarm throwing is compulsory. Beyond that, players can choose to roll the boule along the ground (this is called *pointer*, 'to point'), or hurl it high in the air in the hope of it landing bang on top of an opponent's boule, sending it flying out of position. This flamboyant tactic (called *tirer*, 'to shoot') can turn an entire game around in a matter of seconds.

Throughout matches, boules are lovingly polished with a soft white cloth. Players unable to stoop to pick up their boules can lift them up with a magnet attached to a piece of string.

Nicola Williams

---

against the wall, smacking it with their bare hands or with wooden racquets.

Less familiar are the extraordinary displays of male muscle-power known as *indar jokotak* (local dialect; *la force Basque* in French) at certain festivals – not unlike the Scottish Highland Games.

For more on these and other Basque games see the French Basque Country and Béarn chapter. For information on tournaments and games (and lessons), see the local listings in that chapter.

SHOPPING

Every town of any size has a weekly open-air market *(marché en plein air)* – and regular big *brocante* (second-hand goods) and speciality markets.

Not surprisingly, most products worth taking home are of the edible or drinkable variety. Refer to the special Food & Wine section for details on what's local and what's good.

Pâté de foie gras, as well as confits (conserves) of goose, duck and pork liver, are available almost everywhere. Keep an eye out, even on the remotest roads, for *produits de la ferme* signs. Fresh *truffes* (truffles) are very expensive (up to 3000FF per kilogram) and only available in the winter months, at major truffle markets such as Périgueux or Ribérac. But you can easily find truffles preserved in Armagnac or tinned in truffle juice at souvenir and speciality food shops everywhere. Preserved truffles travel well and last a long time. You can also find pâté de foie gras flavoured with truffles for about 100FF per 140g.

Other worthy farm products to be found in certain areas include local cheeses – especially the *fromage de brebis* or ewe's cheese of the Pyrénées, aggressively marketed under the Ossau-Iraty label at dozens of roadside farms, fromageries and cooperatives in the French Basque Country and Béarn chapter. Also from the Basque country comes popular *jambon de Bayonne* (Bayonne ham), the best of which bears the Ibaïona label. Tourist offices have lists of reliable local sellers, many of them part of the Bienvenue à la Ferme programe.

Nut-lovers will love the Dordogne's walnut products – walnut oil goes for around 35FF for a 35cl bottle (though it only lasts a few months), and local markets have walnut cakes galore.

And of course there's wine, in enough varieties to make your head spin. Don't overlook very drinkable but less well-known wines such as the reds of Pécharmant, Madiran and Irouléguy, and the whites of Montravel and Jurançon (see the special section on Food & Wine for more details). Other drinkables for which the south-west is known are the Armagnac of Gascony (Landes and Gers) and its mellower apéritif derivative, *floc d'armagnac*. Izarra, the Basque Country's own potent herbal liqueur, is sold all over France.

Non-consumables worth considering include locally made embroidery (almost everywhere); Basque linen – serviettes, tablecloths, curtains, pillowcases, quilts – and cotton products; and espadrilles (fibre-soled cotton shoes in every style) for next to nothing. If you have a bit of money to spend, be the only one on your block with a *makhila*, that splendid Basque aristocrat of walking sticks, each handmade to order.

Non-EU residents may be able to get a rebate on some of France's 20.6% value-added tax; see Taxes & Refunds under Money in this chapter. American visitors take note: USA customs' regulations forbid the import of all edibles (including non-pasteurised cheeses, nuts and fruit) and plant products.

FOOD & WINE
OF THE
SOUTH-WEST

SALLY DILLON

FOOD

SALLY DILLON

The cuisines of Périgord, Gascony (the Gers and the Landes) and the French Basque country (Pays Basque) are among the richest and most diverse in the French culinary lexicon – *le cuisine du terroir* (country cooking) at its best. While the French Basque country is a land apart, with a cuisine that's the spiciest in the land, Gascony and Périgord head the list of regional cuisines with an influence stretching nationwide. For this is the land of truffles *(truffes)* and foie gras, luxuries that have made gourmands swoon for centuries: 'Heaven', exclaimed Reverend Sydney Smith, 'is eating pâté de foie gras to the sound of trumpets.'

Lest you assume that all the following richness is bad for you, remember that heart disease is famously low here: despite eating more animal fat than anyone else in the industrialised world, Gascons have the longest life expectancy in France.

For information on cookery and wine-tasting courses see Courses in the Facts for the Visitor chapter.

Périgord & Gascony

Many of us feel squeamish rather than passionate about eating the livers of force-fed fowl but there's no escaping the fact that the goose is central to the region's cuisine. In addition to foie gras, the goose contributes a supply of rich cooking fat. *Confit d'oie* is perhaps the region's most traditional dish: goose legs and wings slowly cooked in their own fat and preserved in jars or earthenware pots, a pre-refrigerator technique also suitable for duck *(confit de canard)* and pork *(enchaud* or *enchaud périgourdin)*. You may also find goose roasted, boiled or stuffed with chestnuts *(châtaignes)* or plums *(prunes)*.

The duck has its own prominence as steak-like *magret*, lightly roasted or grilled duck breast. Beef dishes are rare apart from *tourne-dos*, a fillet in a foie gras and truffle sauce. You may come across game dishes like *pâté de sanglier* (boar pâté), *de marcassin* (young boar) or *de faisan* (pheasant). Freshwater fish are popular, especially trout stuffed with foie gras or cooked with truffles – grilled, marinated or cooked in ashes. Other common fish and seafood treats are crayfish, shard, salmon and sturgeon.

If this all sounds too rich, there's the lightness of walnut oil in unique salad dressings. Walnuts themselves are also used in salads (such as *salade landaise*), cakes and tarts.

Although Périgourdine specialities dominate, Gascony contributes its own favourites – notably *cassoulet*, a dish of confit de canard (or d'oie), sausages and haricot beans, and *agneau de causse*, lamb from Quercy's limestone plateaus, roasted with garlic. Sausages feature a lot: *boudin blanc* (soft chicken and veal sausage), *saucisse de Toulouse* (a fat pork

Previous page: Bordeaux is famous for its *canelés*, small pastries named after their copper baking moulds.

Inset: Statue of Bacchus, the Greek god of wine.

sausage) and *andouillettes* (chitterling sausages). The prunes of Agen appear in several pork dishes, usually with a dose of wine, while a delicious veal dish, *bresolles*, comprises slices of veal baked in a mould with shallots and white wine, layered with minced ham and herbs. *Alicuit* is a traditional favourite, a humble ragout of poultry giblets and vegetables. In the Lot you might come across an old peasant dish – *miques* – maize flour dumplings added to a chicken stock.

Vegetarians may relish two of the region's finest and most essential ingredients – truffles and ceps *(cèpes)* – but they won't come cheap. Truffles are edible subterranean fungi, snuffled out by trained dogs or pigs (see the boxed text 'Truffles'). Ceps – *cèpe bordelais (Boletus edulis)* and the cheaper, less tasty *cèpe de pins (Boletus pinicola)* – are round-capped, fleshy mushrooms which emerge in autumn. These are gathered from early September to November, both for personal consumption and to sell (the profitable cep has become a controversial source of untaxed income, with villagers literally coming to blows over their right to scour the forests). Both kinds are used liberally in omelettes and stews, fried lightly in goose fat or *à la Périgourdine* (with bacon, herbs and grape juice), grilled with garlic and served with ham or, as in Sarlat, cooked in *verjus*, the acidic juice of unripe grapes (used since medieval times as a vinegar substitute). Out-of-season tinned or dried ceps are often cooked with finely chopped onion and garlic in goose fat, then simmered in cream. Other mushrooms that may feature in local dishes during the autumn are the highly prized chanterelle *(Cantharellus cibarius)*, orange *girolles* (chanterelles), black *trompettes de mort* (horn of plenty) and spongy *morilles* (yellow morel; *Morchella esculenta*).

One ingredient that doesn't feature much here is cheese. The region's only well-known cheeses are *cabecou de Rocamadour*, made from sheep's milk in spring and goats' milk in summer, and the French Basque country's similar *fromage de brebis*. Among blue cheeses worth trying are *bleu de Quercy* from Figeac and Gourdon, similar to the soft and

---

Potatoes, Sarlat-Style

Pommes de Terre Sarladaises

Serves 4

  1kg potatoes
  2–3 tablespoons goose fat (or butter)
  1 tablespoon finely chopped truffles (or cep mushrooms)
  salt and pepper

Slice the peeled potatoes, and wash and dry them. Heat the fat in a large frying pan, then add the potatoes, salt and pepper. Fry quickly for two minutes, reduce the heat and add the truffles, cooking until the potatoes are ready (don't wait till they're mushy).

Truffles

Truffles (Truffes; Tuber melanosporum) are edible black subterranean fungi that grow on the roots of certain oak and hazelnut trees. Known as 'the black diamond of French cuisine' for their fabulous aroma and flavour, they're notoriously difficult to grow, favouring certain soils and humidity levels, and only appearing at least 10 years after the trees have been planted. They can vary from pea- to fist-sized.

LISA BORG

They're also fiendishly difficult to find. Traditionally, sows were used to snuffle them out between November and March – apparently truffles smell like male pigs – but, since the sows tended to eat them on the spot, more trainable dogs have now become the truffle-hunter's friend. Many rabassaïres (truffle hunters) look for a telltale patch of scorched-looking earth, with a certain kind of bronze-coloured midge hovering above. Some use divining sticks.

Two centuries ago truffles were so numerous that Christmas turkeys might be stuffed with up to 5kg of them. Even at the turn of the 20th century over 1000 tonnes were harvested. During WWI truffle orchards were neglected and, despite all attempts to revive production, France is lucky to get 50 tonnes per year now (6 tonnes from the Dordogne département).

Consequently they're pricey. A 100g specimen might fetch 3000FF per kilogram at winter markets such as those at Périgueux, Sarlat or Montignac. They're graded from extra (top quality) to deuxième choix (second choice) and they're sold whole, as truffes en morceaux (truffle pieces) or as pelures (truffle skins, for flavouring). Also useful for flavouring is jus de truffes (truffle juice).

Truffle fraud is common: white Italian truffles have been stained with walnut dye and passed off as the real thing. Chinese truffles have begun flooding the market at a quarter of the price of French ones and artificial truffle flavouring has become the norm in many restaurants. However, there's no mistaking the real thing, renowned for its distinctive aroma.

Truffles are at their best when eaten fresh and only keep for about a week. After eating one with a glass of good wine, said the famous French chef Brillat-Savarin, 'a man becomes more lovable, a woman more loving'. They're traditionally added to many sauces and dishes, and to foie gras and pâté, and are delicious sliced thinly into omelettes and salads. They can be preserved in Madeira or Armagnac, with some loss of flavour.

To find out more, check out the Ecomusée de la Truffe in Sorges (see the boxed text in the Dordogne chapter).

Truffle Omelette

Omelette aux Truffes

Serves 4

   8 eggs
   1–2 small truffles (about 75g when diced)
   1½ tablespoons of goose fat (or butter)
   salt, pepper
   small glass of Monbazillac (optional)

Before you start, put the truffles and eggs in an airtight plastic container or sealed bag for several hours – an old Périgord housewives' trick that supposedly imbues the eggs with the truffle aroma (keep them together for a week, they say, and the eggs will be so aromatic you won't even need to use the truffle).

Beat the eggs, adding a dash of salt and pepper. Chop the truffles finely and cook slowly in half the fat (and Monbazillac) until the liquid has evaporated (don't include the juice if the truffles come from a tin – you can add that just before serving). Heat the remaining fat in a large frying pan until it's very hot, add the eggs and truffles and cook until set (use a smaller pan for individual omelettes).

Ideally (so says another old custom) you should eat your truffle omelette with a serviette draped over your head, to capture the full truffle aroma.

savoury *bleu d'Auvergne*, and *bleu des Causses*, similar to Roquefort.

The Dordogne and Lot produce more walnuts than anywhere else in France, and *tartes aux noix* (nut tarts) feature on the best *menus*. Chestnut gateaux are yummy too, and chestnut puree features in many desserts. The region's abundant fruit – prunes, plums, quinces, cherries and pears – ensures excellent *tartes aux fruits* (fruit tarts); prune *tourtières* are paper-thin, flaky-pastry tarts. Strawberries reign supreme: the Dordogne produces more than any other *département* in France. The best months are May and June but you can now find them almost year-round. Local varieties include long, super-sweet *garriguettes* and perfumed *marats des bois*, like tiny wild strawberries.

Local fruit often crowns a meal as a *digestif*, apricots or cherries in armagnac or a fiery *eau de vie de prune*. If you've got this far and can still stand up, congratulations: a full-scale Périgord-Gascon meal is quite a challenge.

Foie Gras The enlarged, fatty liver of a goose or duck is known as foie gras. Geese are migrating birds in the wild, with an instinct to stuff themselves after the autumn moulting season to survive the long flight south. The ancient Egyptians were the first to take advantage of this

Shopping for Foie Gras

With so many varieties of foie gras on the market and so many shops selling it, it's easy to make a very expensive mistake. Read the small print: some livers are actually imported from Hungary or Poland. Priciest is *foie gras d'oie* (goose liver) but *foie gras de canard* (duck liver) is cheaper and – many say – just as tasty. Expect to pay at least 135FF for 200g of best-quality *mi-cuit* foie gras d'oie, 95FF for a 140g tin of *pâté de foie gras* or 80FF for a 200g tin of *bloc de foie gras d'oie*. The best buys are often at small town markets or direct from small producers and farms.

bloc 100% de foie gras – from the processed livers of more than one bird (goose or duck)

délice de foie gras or *mousse 25% foie gras* – contains about 25% foie gras; the mousse is a puree, with the other 75% comprising various ingredients, from eggs to pork meat

foie gras au torchon – brandy-steeped livers rolled around truffles and poached in wine

foie gras entier – all or part of a single liver (goose or duck), cooked and preserved in jars *(bocal)* or tins *(boîte de conserve)*

parfait de foie gras – about 75% foie gras, the rest pork pâté

pâté de foie gras or *pâté périgourdin* – about 50% foie gras and 50% pork pâté or pork meat, often flavoured with truffles

mi-cuit – literally 'half-cooked', must therefore be kept chilled

---

tendency, force-feeding domestic geese to enlarge their tasty livers. The Romans fed theirs with figs and by the 16th century the French were doing it with corn.

A foie gras 'industry' took off in the 1820s and is now a major income-earner for farmers (and factories) in the south-west. Young geese and ducks destined for *gavage* (force-feeding) are allowed to range freely for between three and five months, fed with grain and alfalfa to expand the digestive system. At the end of that time they're moved to a smaller enclosure and force-fed three times daily for around four weeks (three for ducks) with ground meal and then corn. It's usually done by hand with a simple funnel, though electric-powered force-feeders may be used. Proponents point to the birds' lack of distress, even claiming that they sometimes jostle to be first in the queue.

The process triples or even quadruples the weight of the birds' livers to between 700g and 900g for a goose and between 400g and 500g for a duck. Livers produced by small farmers are usually sold fresh at weekly *marchés du gras* (literally 'fat markets'), common in the south-west from November to May.

Aficionados say goose liver is best served raw and chilled, with a glass of sweet Monbazillac. Next-best is *mi-cuit* (half-cooked), served with lemon, salt and pepper, verjus, white grapes and toast. Most of us will have to settle for pâté. See the boxed text 'Shopping for Foie Gras' for a guide to the options.

The Atlantic Coast & the Gironde

This area's most famous culinary contribution is probably sauce *à la bordelaise* – a thick wine-based sauce with parsley, shallots and bone-marrow (or sometimes ceps), best with grilled steak *(entrecôte à la bordelaise)* or lamb *(agneau à la bordelaise)*. Even traditional soups here favour meat: *gabure* is so thick with meat and cabbage you're supposed to spread it on bread. If you see *palombe* on a menu, think twice: these wood pigeons are caught in their thousands while migrating through the region in October. Hunters like them *en salmis* (in a casserole or ragout) or roasted and flambeed in armagnac.

Easier on the conscience are seafood and fish, which of course feature strongly in coastal areas, with *huîtres* (oysters) from Arcachon heading the list. In Bordeaux they're often served with small sausages called *crépinettes*. Popular shellfish include mussels (served in a garlic or curry sauce), cockles and clams. *Moules marinière* are mussels cooked in their own juice with onions. Ugly, eel-like lampreys are big favourites, as are elvers from the Gironde estuary – grilled or *à la ravigote* (in a highly-seasoned white sauce) – crayfish, and tiny cuttlefish in a casserole.

More mainstream fish, also caught in the estuary, include shad,

Right: Oysters are sold still wet from the ocean around Arcachon

salmon and sturgeon. Shad is tasty when stuffed with sorrel, marinated in white wine and grilled.

Dessert specialities include peaches and plums from the Garonne Valley (prunes steeped in armagnac are also popular) and crepes flambeed in armagnac. When you're in St-Émilion, don't miss the macaroons; in Bordeaux, look for the small pastries called *canelé*.

French Basque Country

The food here is among France's spiciest, suffused with the deep-red chillies hanging out to dry everywhere in summer. One of the region's favourite pepper dishes is *piperade* – a mixture of green peppers, tomatoes, garlic and whipped eggs.

The Basque country likes its meat, too: popular dishes include *axoa* (chopped veal with peppers) and *gigot* (roast leg of lamb). You might also be offered *sanglier* (wild boar). Salty *jambon de Bayonne* (Bayonne ham) is famous (and pricey), although most actually comes from around Orthez; its cheaper Spanish cousin *jamón serrano* is far more common in *menus*. Also special to the region are *loukinkos* (miniature garlic sausages) and *tripotcha* (a mutton pudding or blood sausage not unlike a small black pudding). If that doesn't take your fancy there's the ubiquitous *poulet basquaise*, a tasty chicken stew full of peppers, tomatoes, mushrooms and wine.

There are some delicious and distinctive soups too, often as thick as stews. Try the fish soup called *ttoro*, which includes a host of different fish such as scampi, hake, monkfish and conger eel. *Elzeckaria* soup is mostly vegetable, while *gabure* includes *trebuc* (preserved goose), *camot* (ham shank) and *coustoun* (pork ribs). Among fish dishes, *koskera* (hake) is popular, as are tuna and scallop, cuttlefish and baby eel.

For dessert there's the obligatory *gateau basque*, an almond cake often served with cherry sauce and, from Bayonne, some of the best chocolate in France.

Piperade

Serves 2

    4 eggs, lightly beaten
    500g tomatoes (chopped)
    2 green peppers (chopped)
    2 onions (chopped)
    2 cloves garlic
    1 tablespoon olive oil

Cook the onions in the oil over a low heat for 10 minutes, then add the finely chopped or crushed garlic, the tomatoes and peppers. Season with salt and pepper and cook gently for another 15 minutes. Now pour the beaten eggs into the pan and stir until cooked.

WINE

The south-west produces some of the world's finest wines – notably from Bordeaux – as well as a host of other less august but eminently drinkable ones, principally from Bergerac, Monbazillac, Cahors and Jurançon (south of Pau).

Grapes have been grown in the region since the Romans introduced wine-making to Gaul. In the Middle Ages, important vineyards developed around monasteries. Large-scale wine production later moved closer to ports, chiefly Bordeaux, for export.

In 1863 a kind of aphid known as phylloxera was accidentally brought to Europe from the USA. It ate through the roots of Europe's grapevines, destroying around 10,000 sq km of vineyards in France alone. It looked as if European wine production was doomed until phylloxera-resistant root stocks were brought from California and older varieties were grafted onto them.

Wine-making is a complicated chemical process but ultimately the quality of the wine depends on four factors: the type(s) of grape used, the climate, the soil – and the art of the wine-maker. Some viticulturists have honed their skills to such a degree that their wine is known as *grand cru* (literally, 'great growth'). Such wine produced in a year of optimum climatic conditions becomes a *millésime* (vintage). Grands crus are aged first in small oak barrels and then in bottles, sometimes for 20 years or more, before they develop their full taste and aroma. These are the memorable (and pricey) bottles that wine experts talk about with such passion.

Wine Lexicon

appellation d'origine contrôlée (AOC) – good to superb wines which have met stringent government regulations governing where, how and under what conditions the grapes are grown and the wine fermented and bottled

chai – local term for a winery/cellar

cuvée – a limited vintage

dégustation – the fine art of tasting wine

domaine – a wine producing estate

grand cru – wine of recognised superior quality; literally 'great growth'

producteur – a wine producer or grower, also known as a *vigneron*

vendange – grape harvest

vignoble – vineyard

vin délimité de qualité supérieure (VDQS) – good wine from a specific place or region

vin de pays – literally, 'country wine', of reasonable quality and generally drinkable

vin de table – table wine also known as *vin ordinaire*

vintage – the year or growing season in which a wine was produced

The south-west boasts over 80 separate *vins d'appellation d'origine contrôlée* (AOCs – wines with the highest French wine classification), at least 57 of them in the Bordeaux area. Following is a rundown of the better-known varieties. Refer to the map opposite page 97 for general locations.

Les Vignobles Bordela

France's most famous region for fine wines is Bordeaux. Wines from here have enjoyed a favourable reputation since Roman times. Britons (who call the reds claret) have hungered for them since the mid-12th century, when King Henry II tried to gain favour with the citizens of Bordeaux by allowing them, among other concessions, tax-free trade with England. As a result, Bordeaux wines were the cheapest imported wines and the demand for them has never abated. The wines have since gained a world-wide reputation.

Bordeaux has an ideal climate and soil for producing fine wine. Its proximity to the Atlantic protects the vines from frost and excessive heat while the forests of the Landes provide a natural windbreak. The vineyards, covering 113,000 hectares, stretch beside the Gironde estuary, between the Dordogne and Garonne Rivers and to the north of Libourne. They contain over 8000 wine-producing chateaux (or estates). These typically produce around one-quarter of France's total AOC wine (650 million bottles a year), classified into 57 different appellations.

Some 82% of Bordeaux wines are reds and rosés, often described as well-balanced, a quality achieved by blending several grape varieties. The grapes predominantly used are Merlot, Cabernet Sauvignon and Cabernet Franc. The whites are produced from Sauvignon, Sémillon and Muscadelle grape varieties. Many areas produce both whites and reds.

The many appellations are often divided into seven 'families':

Bordeaux Supérieur and **Bordeaux** fruity wines produced all over the area, labelled Supérieur if they have good ageing potential.

Côtes include widely produced Côtes de Bordeaux which can be enjoyed young, and soft, full-bodied reds and whites of Côtes de Bourg, Côtes and Premières Côtes de Blaye.

Médoc and **Graves** are produced from gravelly soil (hence the name Graves), ideal for slightly spicy red Graves and the world-famous fruity, ruby-red Médoc wines; the latter often need time to bring out their full potential.

Rosé, Clairet, Crémant and **Fine** are speciality wines: Bordeaux Rosé and the slightly fuller-bodied Clairet are rosés, best enjoyed chilled and young; Crémant, a sparkling wine, ranges from dry to sweet; Fine de Bordeaux is a brandy made from white grapes.

St-Émilion, Pomerol and **Fronsac** are deep-red, rich wines; the lesser-known Pomerol has an outstanding bouquet, and Fronsac wines have a slightly spicy flavour.

Vins Blancs Moelleux et Liquoreux are sweet white wines best enjoyed with dessert; the most famous is Sauternes.

Vins Blanc Secs are popular, dry white wines, offering excellent value for money, especially crisp Graves and fruity Entre-Deux-Mers.

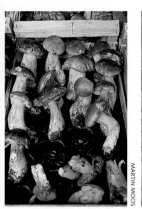

A matter of pride for the locals and a delight for visitors, the gastronomic treats abundant in South-West France are renowned worldwide.

WINE REGIONS OF SOUTH-WEST FRANCE

Bordeaux:
1. Médoc
2. Haut Médoc
3. Côtes & Premières Côtes de Blaye
4. Côtes de Bourg
5. Bordeaux & Bordeaux Supérieur
6. St-Emilion, Pomerol & Fronsac
7. Côtes & Premières Côtes de Bordeaux
8. Ste-Foy-Bordeaux
9. Entre-Deux-Mers
10. Graves
11. Sauternes

Bergerac:
1. Montravel
2. Bergerac, Côtes de Bergerac
3. Rosette
4. Pécharmant
5. Monbazillac
6. Saussignac
7. Côtes de Duras

Others:
Béarn
Buzet
Cahors
Côtes du Brulhois
Côtes de St-Mont
Côtes du Frontonnais
Gaillac
Irouléguy
Jurançon
Madiran & Pacherenc du Vic-Bilh
Tursan

Les Vignobles du Sud-Ouest Other wines of the south-west took longer to be acknowledged: with vineyards farther from the port of Bordeaux (in the past, wine could only be shipped slowly by *gabarre* – flat-bottomed boat – to the port), it was harder to export the wines to wine-hungry countries such as England. Nowadays Bergerac, Pécharmant, Cahors, Côtes de Duras, Buzet and the sweet white Monbazillac are familiar names.

Bergerac, produced largely from Sauvignon grapes, comes in a dozen AOCs, both red and white. The reds can be drunk young and have a firm, fruity bouquet. The whites are dry and go well with seafood. Also included are sweeter Côtes de Bergerac Moelleux and Côtes de Montravel. Pécharmant reds are strong and full-bodied, best appreciated when they've matured.

Monbazillac is the area's supreme sweet white wine; a cheaper alternative to the Sauternes of Bordeaux, it is golden, syrupy and very alcoholic, and an excellent accompaniment to foie gras or dessert. It's best drunk after a minimum of three years but can keep for up to 30 years.

Cahors wines, made largely from Cot Noir grapes to the west of Cahors, are deep red or almost black in colour, with a full-bodied, tannic flavour which becomes velvety with age. Cahors wines from the chalky causse need up to 15 years to mature (look for the *vieux* – aged – label), while wines produced from the Lot valley can be enjoyed after a year or so.

Distinctive reds which are good value and increasingly popular are the **Côtes de Duras**, **Buzet** (near Nérac) and neighbouring **Côtes du Brulhois**. Lesser-known reds worth trying include those from **Gaillac** on the banks of the Tarn and the tannic **Madiran & Pacherenc du Vic Bilh**, **Côtes de St-Mont** and **Tursan** (north-east of Pau).

A mild climate and the protection of the mountains have enabled the grapes of **Béarn** and **Jurançon** to ripen right into November. The Jurançon whites, produced south-west of Pau, come in both dry and sweet dessert varieties. Jurançon Sec has a rich, exotic bouquet – fruity when young and almondy when mature – while sweet Jurançon Moelleux, best drunk when it's been matured for 15 to 25 years, is lighter than many other sweet wines, with a distinctive aroma of fruit and honey. The Béarn AOC vineyards produce red, white and rosé wines.

Also popular are the wines of Irouléguy, in the Pyrénéan highlands near the Spanish border, ranging from full-bodied reds to fresh rosés.

Information on Vineyards & Tours The following centres can provide maps of the vineyard regions, details of chateaux open to the public, organised tours and wine-tasting courses:

Béarn & Jurançon
  Cave des Producteurs
  (☎ 05 59 21 57 03, fax 05 59 21 72 06)
  53 ave Henri IV, 6429 Gan

Cave Cooperation des Vins d'Irouléguy
(☎ 05 59 37 41 33)
64430 St-Étienne-de-Baïgorry
Bergerac
CIVRB
(☎ 05 53 63 57 57 fax 05 53 63 01 30, email vin.civrb@wanadoo.fr)
1 rue des Recollets, 24100 Bergerac
Bordeaux
Conseil Interprofessionel du Vin de Bordeaux
(CIVB; ☎ 05 56 00 22 66, fax 05 56 00 22 82,
email civb@vins-bordeaux.fr)
La Maison du Vin de Bordeaux, 1 cours du 30 Juillet,
33075 Bordeaux
This organisation represents all the region's winegrowers and shippers.
The Bordeaux tourist office (for contact details see Bordeaux in the
Bordeaux, the Atlantic Coast & the Landes chapter) also runs summer
tours, including tasting, to several different vineyards.
Web site: www.vins-bordeaux.fr
Cahors
l'Union Interprofessionnelle du Vin de Cahors
(☎ 05 65 23 22 24)
430 ave Jean Jaurès, 46000 Cahors
Médoc
Maison du Tourisme et du Vin du Pauillac
(☎ 05 56 59 03 08, fax 05 56 59 23 38)
33250 Pauillac
St-Émilion
Maison du Vin de St-Émilion
(☎ 05 57 55 50 55)
place Pierre Meyrat, BP 52 33330 St-Émilion

Wine Tasting Wine tasting is an art and a tradition. The wine is
poured into a small, shallow cup called a *taste-vin*. Tasters use a rich
vocabulary to describe wines: wine can be nervous, elegant, fleshy,
supple or round and taste of vanilla, strawberry, cherry, cinnamon and
even cigars and cedar.

Caves (wine cellars) and *chais* (a local word for wineries) provide an
opportunity to purchase wine straight from the vigneron. Often you'll
be offered a *dégustation* (tasting), with the wine poured straight from
enormous wood barrels or sparkling stainless steel vats (you don't have
to spit it out). It's usually free, but you won't be popular if you sample
several vintages and then leave without buying anything. Cellars often
require that you buy in bulk *(en vrac)* – a 5L minimum is common in
some places. Be careful not to indulge in too many dégustations if
you're driving: Bordeaux wines, in particular, are very alcoholic.

See Courses in the Facts for the Visitor chapter for details of various
wine-tasting courses, lasting from one hour to several days.

Study, Swirl, Sniff, Sip & Swallow

Wine tasting is a complex process, taking years to fully appreciate (and usually requiring an extensive vocabulary of adjectives, the more obscure the better). Here's our guide to help you bluff your way through.

1. **Colour** Look through the wine towards a source of light. Then tilt the glass slightly and look through it towards a pale background. What you're looking for is clarity and colour. Clarity is obvious (no good wines have particles floating around in them) but colour is more complex. A deep colour indicates a strong wine. The colour can also reveal the types of grapes used as well as the wine's age (in red wines a blue hue indicates youth, whereas an orange hue indicates age).

2. **Smell** Swirl the wine around and smell it in one inhalation. The agitation will release the wine's full bouquet. Close your eyes and concentrate: what do you smell? There are 11 main groups of smells associated with wine, ranging from fruits to plants, herbs and spices – and even toast.

3. **Taste** Take a sip, swill it around in your mouth and then (here's the tough part) draw in some air to bring out the flavour. Our taste-buds can identify four sensations: bitter, acidic, salty and sweet. After doing this, swallow the wine. A fine wine should leave an aftertaste.

Getting There & Away

Note that this chapter includes not only international connections but also domestic transport to and from South-West France. For information on transport between regional towns and cities, see the Getting Around chapter.

AIR

Quoted fares are approximate discounted, economy, return fares during the peak air-travel season, based on advertised rates at the time of writing. Use them as a guide only. None constitutes a recommendation for any airline. Except as noted, only direct flights are mentioned here.

Airports & Airlines

South-West France's two most important airports aren't in South-West France at all, but in Paris: Roissy Charles de Gaulle and Orly, served by most major international carriers. Although some airports in South-West France bill themselves as international hubs, most long-haul flights still require a change of plane in Paris or another European capital such as London or Brussels. On domestic routes from Paris to South-West France, Air France (the national airline) is the leading carrier, followed by Air Liberté.

The south-west's two main airports are at Toulouse and Bordeaux. Together they have direct connections with over three dozen cities around France, Europe and North Africa. At Agen, Bergerac, Brive-la-Gaillarde and Périgueux there are smaller regional airports with direct connections to Paris and elsewhere in the region covered by this book but close enough to be useful gateways are at Carcassonne, 70km south-east of Toulouse, and at Tarbes-Ossun-Lourdes, 70km south-west of Auch.

Some of the smaller airports now provide international connections, for example Ryanair flies to London to Biarritz and Carcassonne.

Airline Booking Numbers

Air Afrique
(Bordeaux ☎ 05 56 81 58 71)
Air Algerie
(Toulouse ☎ 05 61 21 80 30)
Air France
(☎ 08 02 80 28 02)
Air Liberté
(☎ 08 03 80 58 05)
Air Littoral
(☎ 08 03 83 48 34)
British Airways
(☎ 08 02 80 29 02)
Crossair
(☎ 08 02 30 04 00)
Flandre Air
(see Air Liberté)
Jersey European Airways
(☎ 08 45 84 51 11)
KLM
(Paris ☎ 01 44 56 18 18,
Toulouse ☎ 05 61 15 79 00)
Lufthansa Airlines
(☎ 08 01 63 38 38)
Régional Airlines
(☎ 08 03 00 52 00)
Royal Air Maroc
(Bordeaux ☎ 05 56 52 49 50,
Toulouse ☎ 05 34 45 22 90)
Ryanair
(airport information ☎ 05 59 43 83 83,
Carcassonne ☎ 04 68 71 96 65;
no Biarritz office at time of writing,)
Sabena/Swissair
(Bordeaux ☎ 08 02 30 04 00)
Tunis Air
(Bordeaux ☎ 05 56 44 05 22,
Toulouse ☎ 05 61 62 99 70)

Buying Tickets

A plane ticket will probably be the most expensive item in your budget. Shop around and start early as some cheap tickets must be purchased months in advance. Check travel ads in major newspapers, too. Some travel agencies just handle tours, while a full-service agency can arrange everything from tours and tickets to car rental and hotel bookings. If all you want is a cheap flight, you need an agency that specialises in finding low air fares.

You may decide that it's worth paying a bit more for the security of a high-profile, experienced travel agency. Most offer the best deals to students and travellers aged under 26 but they're open to all. Their local details are given in the following sections.

You're safest if an agency is a member of the International Air Transport Association (IATA) or a national association such as the American Society of Travel Agents (ASTA), the Association of British Travel Agents (ABTA) or the Australian Federation of Travel Agents (AFTA). If you've bought your ticket from a member agency which then goes bust, the association guarantees a refund or an alternative. Member agencies must also have professional indemnity insurance, which serves as a secondary safety net. The agencies mentioned above are all members of their national travel agent association.

Competition from no-frills carriers such as Ryanair (see The UK & Ireland later in this section for more details) has forced many established airlines to offer conditional, limited availability cheap fares. Typically these must be booked at least two weeks in advance, involve staying a Saturday night and cannot be changed or refunded.

Travellers with Special Needs

If you have special requirements – you're on crutches, vegetarian, terrified of flying – let the airline know when you book, again when you reconfirm, and again when you check in. It may even be worth ringing round the airlines before you book.

With advance warning most international airports can provide escorts from check-in to the plane, and most have ramps, lifts, accessible toilets and telephones. Aircraft toilets, on the other hand, present problems for wheelchair travellers, who should discuss this early on with the airline and/or their doctor.

Flying with Children In general, children under two travel for 10% of the standard fare (or free, on some airlines), as long as they don't occupy a seat. They don't get any baggage allowance. Bassinets or 'skycots' – for children weighing up to about 10kg – can usually be provided by the airline if requested in advance. Children aged between two and 12 can usually occupy a seat for half to two-thirds of the full fare, and do get a baggage allowance. Pushchairs (strollers) can often be taken as extra hand luggage.

Airport Taxes

Airport taxes – imposed by both the country you are departing from and the country you are flying to – are added to the price of your airline ticket when you buy it. At the time of writing, the airport tax for domestic flights to/from Paris was 85FF. Taxes are included in fares quoted here.

Other Parts of France

The variation in French domestic air fares is astonishing, depending on who you are, when you book and when you decide to travel, among other things. Travellers aged over 60, families and couples are entitled to some discounts. Youth/student fares (with no restrictions or advance booking requirements) are often available to under 26s and student card-holders. Generally speaking, unless you're eligible for one of these, it's cheaper to take the train.

Paris branches of reliable youth-oriented travel agencies include: Accueil des Jeunes en France (AJF; ☎ 01 42 77 87 80), Council Travel (☎ 01 44 55 55 44), with a Web site at www.counciltravel.com, OTU Voyages (☎ 01 44 41 38 50), Voyages Wasteels (☎ 01 43 62 30 00) with a Web site at www.voyages-wasteels.fr. and usit CONNECT (☎ 01 42 34 56 90), with a Web site at www.campustravel.com. Outside France, Air France representatives sell tickets for many domestic flights.

From Paris (mainly Orly), Air France and Air Liberté together have nearly three dozen flights a day to Toulouse and nearly two dozen to Bordeaux. Air Liberté and/or its subsidiary Flandre Air have daily or almost-daily direct connections from Paris Orly to Agen, Bergerac, Brive-la-Gaillarde and Périgueux. Air France flies almost daily from

Air Travel Glossary

Baggage Allowance This will be written on your ticket and usually includes one 20kg item to go in the hold, plus one item of hand luggage.

Bucket Shops These are unbonded travel agencies specialising in discounted airline tickets.

Bumped Just because you have a confirmed seat doesn't mean you're going to get on the plane (see Overbooking).

Cancellation Penalties If you have to cancel or change a discounted ticket, there are often heavy penalties involved; insurance can sometimes be taken out against these penalties. Some airlines impose penalties on regular tickets as well, particularly against 'no-show' passengers.

Check-In Airlines ask you to check in a certain time ahead of the flight departure (usually one to two hours on international flights). If you fail to check in on time and the flight is overbooked, the airline can cancel your booking and give your seat to somebody else.

Confirmation Having a ticket written out with the flight and date you want doesn't mean you have a seat until the agent has checked with the airline that your status is 'OK' or confirmed. Meanwhile you could just be 'on request'.

Courier Fares Businesses often need to send urgent documents or freight securely and quickly. Courier companies hire people to accompany the package through customs and, in return, offer a discount ticket which is sometimes a phenomenal bargain. In effect, what the companies do is ship their freight as your luggage on regular commercial flights. This is a legitimate operation, but there are two shortcomings – the short turnaround time of the ticket (usually not longer than a month) and the limitation on your luggage allowance. You may have to surrender all your allowance and take only carry-on luggage.

Full Fares Airlines traditionally offer 1st class (coded F), business class (coded J) and economy class (coded Y) tickets. These days there are so many promotional and discounted fares available that few passengers pay full economy fare.

ITX An ITX, or 'independent inclusive tour excursion', is often available on tickets to popular holiday destinations. Officially it's a package deal combined with hotel accommodation, but many agents will sell you one of these for the flight only and give you phoney hotel vouchers in the unlikely event that you're challenged at the airport.

Lost Tickets If you lose your airline ticket an airline will usually treat it like a travellers cheque and, after inquiries, issue you with another one. Legally, however, an airline is entitled to treat it like cash and if you lose it then it's gone forever. Take good care of your tickets.

MCO An MCO, or 'miscellaneous charge order', is a voucher that looks like an airline ticket but carries no destination or date. It can be exchanged through any International Association of Travel Agents (IATA) airline for a ticket on a specific flight. It's a useful alternative to an onward ticket in those countries that demand one, and is more flexible than an ordinary ticket if you're unsure of your route.

No-Shows No-shows are passengers who fail to show up for their flight. Full-fare passengers who fail to turn up are sometimes entitled to travel on a later flight. The rest are penalised (see Cancellation Penalties).

On Request This is an unconfirmed booking for a flight.

Air Travel Glossary

Onward Tickets An entry requirement for many countries is that you have a ticket out of the country. If you're unsure of your next move, the easiest solution is to buy the cheapest onward ticket to a neighbouring country or a ticket from a reliable airline which can later be refunded if you do not use it.

Open Jaw Tickets These are return tickets where you fly out to one place but return from another. If available, this can save you backtracking to your arrival point.

Overbooking Airlines hate to fly empty seats and since every flight has some passengers who fail to show up, airlines often book more passengers than they have seats. Usually excess passengers make up for the no-shows, but occasionally somebody gets 'bumped' onto the next available flight. Guess who it is most likely to be? The passengers who check in late.

Point-to-Point Tickets These are discount tickets that can be bought on some routes in return for passengers waiving their rights to a stopover.

Promotional Fares These are officially discounted fares, available from travel agencies or direct from the airline.

Reconfirmation If you don't reconfirm your flight at least 72 hours prior to departure, the airline may delete your name from the passenger list. Ring to find out if your airline requires reconfirmation.

Restrictions Discounted tickets often have various restrictions on them – such as needing to be paid for in advance and incurring a penalty to be altered. Others are restrictions on the minimum and maximum period you must be away, such as a minimum of 14 days or a maximum of one year.

Round-the-World Tickets RTW tickets give you a limited period (usually a year) in which to circumnavigate the globe. You can go anywhere the carrying airlines go, as long as you don't backtrack. The number of stopovers or total number of separate flights is decided before you set off and they usually cost a bit more than a basic return flight.

Stand-by This is a discounted ticket where you only fly if there is a seat free at the last moment. Stand-by fares are usually available only on domestic routes.

Transferred Tickets Airline tickets cannot be transferred from one person to another. Travellers sometimes try to sell the return half of their ticket, but officials can ask you to prove that you are the person named on the ticket. This is less likely to happen on domestic flights, but on an international flight tickets are compared with passports.

Travel Agencies Travel agencies vary widely and you should choose one that suits your needs. Some simply handle tours, while full-service agencies handle everything from tours and tickets to car rental and hotel bookings. If all you want is a ticket at the lowest possible price, then go to an agency specialising in discounted fares.

Travel Periods Ticket prices vary with the time of year. There is a low (off-peak) season and a high (peak) season, and often a low-shoulder season and a high-shoulder season as well. Usually the fare depends on your outward flight – if you depart in the high season and return in the low season, you pay the high-season fare.

Paris to Castres. Another option from Orly is the daily flight to Tarbes-Ossun-Lourdes.

Sample adult/youth return fares from Paris at the time of writing were about 630/420FF to Toulouse, 630/360FF to Bordeaux, 840/600FF to Périgueux and 900/690FF to Biarritz.

To Toulouse and Bordeaux there are daily or almost-daily flights from Annecy, Avignon, Clermont-Ferrand, Dijon, Lille, Lyons, Marseilles, Metz-Nancy, Nantes, Nice, Perpignan, Reims, Rennes, Strasbourg, St-Étienne, and Toulon, plus flights to Carcassonne–Toulouse, Montpellier–Bordeaux and Mulhouse–Toulouse. Other links include Nice–Biarritz, Lyons and Rodez to Castres, Nantes and Clermont-Ferrand to Pau.

Continental Europe

The only direct scheduled flights to South-West France from elsewhere in Continental Europe are to Toulouse and Bordeaux. Cities with daily or almost-daily connections to Toulouse include Amsterdam, Basle, Brussels, Geneva, Madrid, Milan, Munich and Venice, with less frequent links from Dusseldorf and Zurich. Daily or almost-daily connections to Bordeaux include Barcelona, Basle, Brussels, Geneva, Madrid, Munich and Rome, with less frequent links from Bilbao and Lisbon.

Two sources of cheap air fares in Germany are STA Travel (☎ 069-9790 7113) at Leipziger Strasse 17a, Frankfurt, with over two dozen branches and a useful Web site at www.sta-travel.com, and SRS Studenten Reise (☎ 030-283 3094) in Berlin. In Amsterdam, try NBBS Reizen (☎ 020-620 50 71) at Schilphoweg 101, 2300 AJ Leiden. In Belgium try Connections (☎ 550 01 00), Rue Midi 19, Brussels. In Spain try Barcelo Viajs (☎ 91 559 18 19) at Princesa 3, Madrid 28228. In Portugal try Wasteels (☎ 886 97 93) Mados Caminhosde, Ferno 90, 1100 Lisbon.

Sample return fares from various European centres at the time of writing include:

To Toulouse:
 Amsterdam f558, Madrid 35,400 ptas, Milan L679,000

To Bordeaux:
 Brussels f8290, Lisbon 66,400$00, Munich DM358

The UK & Ireland

Cheap fares appear in the Saturday *Independent* and *Sunday Times* travel sections and, in London, in *Time Out*, the *Evening Standard* and *TNT* (a free magazine that is available from bins outside underground stations).

The UK's best known bargain-ticket agencies are STA (☎ 020-7361 6161), with a Web site at www.sta-travel.co.uk, Trailfinders (☎ 020-7937 5400), with a Web site at www .trailfinder.com, usit CAMPUS (☎ 020-7730 3402), with a Web site at www.campustravel.com, and Travel CUTS (☎ 020-7637 3161), with a Web site at www.travelcuts.com. All have branches throughout London and the UK.

In Ireland, reliable sources for bargain air fares include usit NOW (☎ 01-602 1600), with a Web site at www.usitcampus.co.uk and Trailfinders (☎ 01-677 7888), see above for Web site address. Both are based in Dublin.

Dublin-based Ryanair (☎ 0870 156 9569 in the UK, ☎ 01-609 7800 in Ireland) operates daily flights from London Stansted to Biarritz and Carcassonne. At the time of writing, its promotional fares to Biarritz were around UK£50 return, while the fare to Carcassonne was around UK£100. A flight from Dublin to Stansted costs around IR£25. Its Web site is at www.ryanair.ie. At the time of writing, Ryanair was the only no-frills airline flying direct to South-West France.

British Airways (BA; ☎ 0845 722 2111) has three direct flights daily to both Toulouse and Bordeaux from London Gatwick, and three to Toulouse from London Heathrow. Typical discounted fares for either destination at the time of writing were about UK£160. Jersey European Airways (☎ 0870 567 6676) was also offering a restricted fare of about UK£160 on its daily-except-Saturday flights to Toulouse from Birmingham (with connections from Belfast, Glasgow and Exeter).

Via Paris An alternative from the UK is to fly via Paris. Air France (08450 845111) offered a Saturday-night-away flight from Dublin to Paris for around IR£200 return. KLM uk (☎ 0870 507 4074) was flying daily from London Stansted to Paris for as little as UK£49 return. BA offered a Saturday-night-away flight for UK£95 return, subject to availability. BA's unrestricted London–Paris youth fares were as low as UK£188. For connecting flights from Paris to South-West France, see Other Parts of France earlier in this chapter.

The USA & Canada

On Sunday the *Los Angeles Times*, *San Francisco Examiner*, *Chicago Tribune*, *New York Times*, Toronto *Globe & Mail* and *Vancouver Sun* have big travel sections with lots of travel agent ads.

Council Travel (toll-free ☎ 800 226 8624) has a useful Web site at www.counciltravel.com. STA Travel (toll-free ☎ 800 777 0112/781 4040), with a Web site at www.sta-travel.com, is also worth checking out. Both companies are reliable sources of cheap tickets in the USA and both have offices all over the country. Nouvelles Frontières also has offices in New York and Los Angeles and a Web site at www. newfrontiers.com. The best bargain-ticket agency in Canada is Travel CUTS (☎ 888-838 2887) with some 50 offices. There is no toll-free number but their excellent Web site is at www.travelcuts.com.

Although there are no direct flights from North America to South-West France, there are plenty via Paris, London and other European centres. You can fly from New York to Paris for about US$800 return; equivalent fares from the west coast are US$100 to US$300 higher. A flight from Toronto to Paris costs around $600.

Australia & New Zealand

Saturday's travel sections in the *Sydney Morning Herald* and the Melbourne *Age* have many ads for cheap fares to Europe.

One of Australasia's best discount-air fare shops is Flight Centre (☎ 03-9650 2899), 19 Bourke St, Melbourne. STA

Travel has offices in Sydney (1255) and Auckland (☎ 09-3 Web site is at www.sta-trave agencies have branch offices ....wide. Trailfinders has branches in Sydney (☎ 02-9247 7666), Brisbane (☎ 07-3229 0887) and Cairns (☎ 07-4041 1199), and a Web site at www.trailfinder.com.

The cheapest fares to Europe are usually routed through Asia. Shop around, as airlines like Thai Airways International (THAI), Malaysia Airlines, Qantas Airways and Singapore Airlines have frequent promotional fares. At the time of writing, low/high-season return fares to Paris started at about A$1430/1870 from Melbourne or Sydney, or NZ$2015/2415 from Auckland.

LAND
Other Parts of France

Bus Forget about trying to get a bus from Paris to South-West France. French transport policy is heavily lopsided in favour of the state-owned rail system, and inter-regional bus services are very limited. Take the train.

Train France's excellent rail network, run by the state-owned SNCF (Société Nationale des Chemins de Fer), reaches almost every part of the country. The network is very Paris-centred, with the most important lines radiating from the capital like the spokes of a wheel. While this makes for some tedious rail travel between towns on different 'spokes,' it means that getting almost anywhere from Paris is fast and easy.

SNCF's pride and joy is the world-famous TGV (pronounced 'teh-zheh-veh'), short for *train à grande vitesse* (high-speed train). Thanks to the TGV, travel between some cities can be faster and easier by rail than by air, especially when the time and hassle of airport transport is taken into account.

South-West France is served by the TGV Atlantique service, which runs from Paris to Bordeaux (with a branch via Agen and Montauban to Toulouse), Facture (with a branch to Arcachon), Dax (with a branch via Pau to Tarbes), and via Bayonne to the

Spanish border at Irún/Hendaye. At the time of writing there were 24 daily direct TGV services in each direction from Paris to Bordeaux, seven to Bayonne and four to Toulouse.

SNCF calls its slower, cheaper, non-TGV services Corail. Some of these use TGV *grandes lignes* (main lines). Other towns in the region are linked to these lines by *trains express régionaux* or TER (regional express trains) – slower and less frequent than mainline trains. Many towns not on the SNCF network are linked with nearby railheads by SNCF or TER buses.

TGV Atlantique services depart from Paris' Gare Montparnasse, while all other services to South-West France use Gare d'Austerlitz. New track around Paris links the Atlantique line directly with the two other domestic TGV lines, TGV Nord and TGV Sud-Est (as well as with Roissy Charles de Gaulle airport).

Information Most larger stations have both ticket windows and information/booking offices. Here you can pick up SNCF's free, pocket-size timetables. These can be daunting, with complex footnotes indicating the days on which each train runs. Some may *circule* (run) only on certain days or dates, or *tous les jours sauf* (every day except) Saturday, Sunday and/or *fêtes* (holidays). In the end you may be better off asking at the information office.

Services, Reservations & Tickets Most trains, including TGVs, have 1st- and 2nd-class sections. In this book we quote 2nd-class fares, which on non-TGV trains work out at about 50FF to 70FF per 100km for

long trips, or 70FF to 100FF per 100km for short hops (compare this with autoroute tolls and petrol, each costing about 40FF to 50FF per 100km). Travel in 1st class costs 50% more than 2nd class. Return tickets cost double the single-ticket price. Children aged under four travel free; those aged between 4 and 11 travel half-price.

A 25FF reservation fee is mandatory for TGV travel and on certain other popular trains during holiday periods, and is handy on other services. Most overnight trains have *couchettes* (sleeping berths; six/four per 2nd/1st class compartment), for which you must make a reservation and pay a 105FF fee.

Reservations can be made up to two months in advance at major travel agencies, by toll-free telephone (☎ 08 36 35 35 35 in French, ☎ 08 36 35 35 39 in English), online at SNCF's Web site (www.sncf.com), at any SNCF ticket office or at one of the automatic ticket vending machines in every station. Note that SNCF won't post tickets outside France. Tickets bought on board are pricey.

Tickets can be paid for with a credit card or, in stations, with cash. Ticket vending machines are of two kinds: touch-screen *billetteries automatiques* issue all types of tickets and accept cash or credit cards; *billetteries régionales* sell only regional tickets and accept only coins. A ticket bought with cash can be reimbursed for cash, so keep yours in a safe place.

You risk an on-the-spot fine if you fail to validate your ticket before boarding: time-stamp it in one of the orange *composteurs* (ticket punching machines) at the platform entrance.

Rail Route Information

destination	TGV time (hours)	TGV fare (FF)	corail time	corail fare (FF)
Bayonne	4½	420	6½	395
Bordeaux	3	345	4½	321
Brive-la-Gaillarde	N/A	N/A	4	288
Toulouse	5	440	6½	371

See the boxed text 'Rail Route Information' for some sample TGV and Corail 2nd-class, one-way, full-price fares and best journey times from Paris.

SNCF Discounts & Passes Discounted fares (about 25% reduction) automatically apply to: travellers aged from 12 to 25; one to four adults travelling with a child under 12 years old; seniors aged over 60, two people travelling on a return journey together; or anyone taking a return journey of at least 200km and spending a Saturday night away. Other discounts are also available. A one-year travel pass gives between 25 and 50% discounts: Carte 12–25 for travellers aged 12 to 25 (270FF), Carte Enfant Plus for one to four adults travelling with a child under 12 years old (350FF) or Carte Sénior for travellers aged over 60 (285FF).

Rail Passes The **Euro Domino Pass** (Freedom Pass in the UK) can be used for three to eight consecutive days of 2nd-class travel within a specified month, in one of 29 participating countries, you're eligible for this if you have been resident in Europe for at least six months. They're available from major train stations in most European countries. Euro Domino Pass has adult versions costing from UK£119 to UK£239 and under-26 versions for UK£99 to UK£189.

The **France Railpass** entitles people who are not residents of France to unlimited travel on the SNCF system for three to nine days over the course of a month. In 2nd class, the three-day version costs US$175 (US$140 each for two people travelling together); each additional day of travel costs US$30. There is also a cheaper youth version.

You can get these and other European passes from SNCF subsidiary Rail Europe (☎ 0870 5848 848) in London at 179 Piccadilly and at Victoria Train Station. Contact Rail Europe in the USA at toll-free ☎ 800 438 7245 or 800 4 EURAIL, fax 800 432-1FAX; or in Canada at toll-free ☎ 800 361-RAIL, fax 905 602-4198. The Rail Europe Web site is at www.raileurope.com/.

Even with one of these passes you must pay for seat and couchette reservations, and all supplements on express trains.

Left Luggage Most larger SNCF stations have both a *consigne manuelle* (left-luggage office) where you pay by the day (around 30FF per bag) and a 72-hour computerised *consigne automatique*. Make sure you note their closing hours!

Auto Train Under the SNCF Auto Train scheme you can load your car or motorcycle on the train at certain stations and on certain days. Among routes to South-West France where this is possible are: between Paris, Calais or Lille and Biarritz, Bordeaux, Brive-la-Gaillarde or Toulouse; between Metz or Strasbourg and Biarritz or Bordeaux; Lyons–Bordeaux; Marseilles–Bordeaux; Nantes–Toulouse; and Nice–Toulouse.

The cost depends on the starting point, destination, date and vehicle size. A small car taken from Paris to Bordeaux in high/low season would cost 750/450FF and a motorcycle 450/250FF. Cars are loaded on the train one hour before departure and unloaded 30 minutes after arrival.

Car & Motorcycle The first rule for motoring down to South-West France is: avoid it in July and August if you can, or prepare yourself for massive congestion, everywhere. This is when most of France seems to go on holiday.

The main motorway from Paris (via Orléans, Tours and Poitiers) to Bordeaux and

Bis

You will often see signs for autoroute exits marked *bis* on an orange panel. This stands for *bison futé* and indicates alternative routes which avoid areas prone to peak-period congestion. An annually updated, free map of bis routes is published by the French government; contact your local automobile organisation or Maison de la France (see Tourist Offices in the Facts for the Visitor chapter) for a copy.

euro currency converter 10FF = €1.52

the Spanish border at Hendaye has the European designation E5. To the French, it's the A10 to Bordeaux, the N10 through most of the Landes, and the A63 from Dax to the border. An alternative and less congested route into the Dordogne from Poitiers is the Bis route (see the boxed text 'Bis') E62/N147 to Bellac, D675 to Rochechouart, D901 to Châlus and N21 to Périgueux.

The main motorway south (via Limoges) to Toulouse branches at Orléans as the E9. Its French names are the A71 to Vierzon, the A20 to Brive-la-Gaillarde, a mixture of A20 and N20 from there via Cahors to Montauban, and the A62 to Toulouse. An alternative Bis route from Limoges is the D704/D15 to Châlus, N21 to Périgueux, D710 to Fumel and the D102, D2 and D927 to Montauban and the A20/N20 to Toulouse.

Approximate road distances, average travelling times and selected automobile

Roads & Tolls in France

There are four types of intercity road in France. **Autoroutes**, whose alphanumeric names begin with A, are multilane motorways, usually toll roads, often with *aires de repos* (rest areas) with restaurants and pricey petrol stations. **Routes nationales**, whose names begin with N (or RN on older maps and signs), are main highways; newer ones are wide and well marked. **Routes départmentales**, designated by D, are secondary and tertiary local roads. **Routes communales** are minor rural roads whose names sometimes begin with C. Many major highways also have European designations, beginning with E.

Most stretches of autoroute are subject to road tolls to the tune of 40FF to 50FF per 100km. Some segments have toll plazas every few dozen kilometres, at or soon after your entry onto the autoroute, with machines that issue a ticket, which you hand over at a *péage* (toll booth) when you exit. You can pay in French francs or by credit card.

Help Along the Way

Tune into Autoroute FM 107.7 MHz for traffic reports in English, broadcast every 30 minutes at peak times. For information on autoroute tolls, itineraries and conditions call Autoroutel on ☎ 08 36 68 09 79. Plan your Itinerary (☎ 01 47 05 90 01) will advise on where to go and how to get there.

tolls to Bordeaux and Toulouse from major towns elsewhere in France include the following (for routes linking Channel ferry ports, see The UK under Sea in this chapter; for information on regional arteries, see the Getting Around chapter):

route	distance (km)	time (hours)	toll (FF)
Calais–Bordeaux	819	8	364
Paris–Bordeaux	581	5½	258
Nantes–Bordeaux	320	3	112
Paris–Toulouse	697	7	350
Lyons–Toulouse	535	5	221
Marseilles–Toulouse	407	4	—

Hitching See the Getting Around chapter for advice about hitching and details of Allostop, a company that acts as a intermediary between hitchhikers and drivers.

Continental Europe

Bus Several companies include South-West France in their European routes.

Eurolines Eurolines (☎ 08 36 69 52 52, fax 01 49 72 51 61, email info@eurolines.fr), an association of companies that forms Eur-ope's largest international bus network, links cities all over Western and Central Europe, Scandinavia and Morocco.

Buses are slower and less comfortable than trains, but cheaper, especially if you qualify for a 10 to 20% discount for those aged under 26 or 60 and over, or 30 to 40% discounts for children aged from four to 12. During the summer it's a good idea to make reservations a few days in advance.

Eurolines' main offices in South-West France are at or near the main bus stations in Bordeaux (☎ 05 56 92 50 42), Bayonne (☎ 05 59 59 19 33) and Toulouse (☎ 05 61 26 40 04). The other Eurolines stops in South-West France are at Agen, Brive-la-Gaillarde, Cahors, Dax, Montauban, Pau, Souillac and Toulouse.

Among Eurolines affiliates around Europe are those in Amsterdam (☎ 020-560 87 87), Barcelona (☎ 93-490 4000), Berlin (☎ 030-86 0960), Brussels (☎ 02-203 0707), Madrid (☎ 91-528 1105), Rome (☎ 06 44 23 39 28) and Vienna (☎ 01-712 0435).

Following are some sample adult/youth one-way fares; return fares are about 15% lower than two one-ways.

Brussels to Bordeaux or Toulouse: f140/120
Valencia to Bayonne: 10,500 ptas
Barcelona to Toulouse: 5300 ptas
Bilbao to St-Jean de Luz, Bayonne or Toulouse:
    5600 ptas

For more information check out the Web site at www.eurolines.com/.

Intercars Intercars (www.intercars.fr) operates buses between towns in southern and Central Europe. Its main hub in South-West France is at the central bus station in Toulouse (☎ 05 61 58 14 53); other offices are in Bordeaux and St-Jean de Luz, and buses also stop in Orthez, Pau and Tarbes. Some destinations and sample one-way fares from Toulouse include Madrid (305FF), Porto (500FF) and Berlin (730FF). Discounts of up to 15% for those aged under 26 or 60 and over, and up to 50% for those aged from two to 12, are available.

Busabout UK-based Busabout (☎ 020-7950 1661, fax 7950 1662, email info@busabout.co.uk), runs coaches around several loops covering a wide variety of destinations in Western and Central Europe, Scandinavia and Morocco. Its Web site is at www.busabout.com/. Two loops that include France go to northern Europe and to Spain and Portugal. A Busabout Pass – valid for 15 or 21 days, for one, two or three

months, or for an unlimited period – lets you get on and off whenever you choose, at designated pick-up points. Pick-up points are often convenient to youth hostels and camp sites. Busabout operates year-round, with services at each pick-up point every two or three days.

Passes are sold through major youth-travel agencies. At the time of writing a one/two/three month pass costs UK£425/595/755 (UK£325/485/595 for youth or student card-holders).

Train Paris abounds with connections from all over Europe. Other major border stations in France are in Lille, Metz, Strasbourg, Mulhouse, Lyons and Nice. Bordeaux has links, with a change at Irún/Hendaye, from Spain and Portugal: for example three times a day from Madrid (9½ hours; 13,000 ptas). Toulouse has links, with a change at Nice, from Italy: for example twice daily from Milan (12½ hours; L200,000). A couchette costs about 4300 ptas or L50,000 extra.

You can book tickets and get information from Rail Europe up to two months ahead. Visit their Web site at www.raileurope.com. In Germany, contact Rail Europe Deutschland (☎ 069-9758 4641). In Belgium, try Rail Europe Benelux (☎ 02-534 4531). Direct bookings with SNCF (☎ 08 36 35 35 35 in French, ☎ 08 36 35 35 39 in English) are possible, but SNCF won't post tickets outside France. For more on SNCF see Train under Other Parts of France earlier in this chapter.

If you intend to do a lot of train travel, consider purchasing the *Thomas Cook European Timetable*, updated monthly with a complete listing of schedules, plus information on reservations and supplements. Single issues cost about UK£11, available from Thomas Cook Publishing (☎ 01733-503571, fax 503596, email publishing-sales@thomascook.com) in the UK.

Auto Train Auto Train (see Train in the earlier Other Parts of France section) permits the transport of cars by passenger train between certain European stations. International links to South-West France include

Germany (Cologne, Frankfurt, Hamburg or Hanover to Bordeaux), Belgium (Brussels or Liège to Biarritz, Bordeaux, Brive-la-Gaillarde or Toulouse) and the Netherlands (Bois le Duc to Biarritz, Bordeaux, Brive-la-Gaillarde or Toulouse).

SNCF offices in France have Auto Train information, as do Rail Europe offices. For most international journeys you should book Auto Train at least two months in advance.

The UK

Bus Eurolines has direct, year-round bus services, two to four times weekly, from London's Victoria Coach Station, via the Dover–Calais Channel crossing. Adult/youth one-way fares during the peak season (July and August) at the time of writing included Paris (UK£44/39), Bordeaux, Périgueux, Bergerac or Agen (UK£99/89), or Toulouse, Bayonne, Pau or Montauban (UK£116/99). Non-peak fares are around 10% less. Bookings can be made with Eurolines UK (☎ 0870 5143 219 or ☎ 01582-404511, fax 400694), through their Web site at www.eurolines.co.uk or at any National Express office.

For Busabout services from London, see Continental Europe in this chapter. If you're beginning your journey in London, Busabout charges an extra UK£15 for the Channel crossing.

Train The cheapest rail route from the UK to South-West France is from London to Paris on a 'rail–sea–rail' ticket (crossing the Channel by ferry, hovercraft or SeaCat), with a change of trains in Paris (and stations too, by metro from Gare du Nord to Gare d'Austerlitz) for the journey south by Corail train (see Train in the preceding Other Parts of France section). Connex South Eastern (☎ 0870 603 0405) handles this London–Paris route and sells tickets for the onward journey too. At the time of writing a full 2nd class, adult/youth return fare was UK£114/99 for London–Bordeaux.

Eurostar, the much-heralded passenger service through the Channel Tunnel, takes just three hours from London (Waterloo) to Paris. There is no direct Eurostar service to South-West France, but you can take Eurostar to Lille and transfer to a direct TGV to Bordeaux (eight hours from London) or Toulouse (11½ hours). Full fares can be more than twice those for rail-sea-rail, but certain nonrefundable, nonexchangeable Eurostar tickets can be good value: a 2nd-class London to Bordeaux adult ticket costs UK£119 (book at least a week ahead and stay a Saturday night). The under-26 fare of UK£109 is nonrefundable but otherwise unrestricted.

In the UK, both Eurostar and non-Eurostar tickets are available from travel agents, many mainline train stations and SNCF-owned Rail Europe. For Eurostar information only, you can contact Eurostar UK (☎ 0870 5186 186) or visit its Web site at www.eurostar.com/. In France, contact SNCF (☎ 08 36 35 35 39 in English) or visit its Web site at www.sncf.com/.

Car & Motorcycle High-speed shuttle trains of Euro-tunnel(☎ 0870 5353 535, ☎ 01303-288680 for bicycle bookings in the UK; ☎ 03 21 00 61 00 in France) take cars, motorcycles, bicycles and coaches through the Channel Tunnel from Folkestone to Coquelles, 5km south-west of Calais. The service (formerly known as Le Shuttle) runs 24 hours with up to four departures an hour at peak periods. Passport and customs controls are cleared before boarding. During the 35-minute trip, passengers can sit in their cars or walk around the train. The Eurotunnel Web site is at www.eurotunnel.com/.

A regular one-way fare for a car plus all its passengers ranges from about UK£90 (winter) to UK£150 (mid-July to early September). While tickets are sold on an as-available basis at check-in, they're best bought at least a day in advance and many promotional deals are only available in advance. The return fare for a bicycle plus its rider is UK£15.

Auto Train services (see Train under Other Parts of France earlier in this chapter) are available only within Continental Europe. The only UK-connected French port where this service is available is Calais.

SEA

Although no direct international ferries serve South-West France, there are many options from the UK and Ireland to northern France, from where you can drive south, and several from the UK to northern Spain, not far from Bayonne and the French Basque country (Pays Basque).

Fares are wildly seasonal, with some winter tickets costing less than half as much as in high season (and each company has its own complex definition of high season). Three- or five-day excursion return fares cost about the same as regular one-way tickets. Return fares generally cost less than two one-way tickets. Children aged four to 14 or 15 travel for half to two-thirds of an adult fare. Most crossings also have higher fares for lounge seats and cabins.

Following are the main ferry companies:

Brittany Ferries
(France ☎ 08 03 82 88 28, UK ☎ 0870 536 0360, Cork ☎ 021-277 801, Santander ☎ 942-36 06 11)
Web site: www.brittany-ferries.com

Condor Ferries
(St-Malo ☎ 02 99 20 03 00, Weymouth ☎ 01305-761551, Poole ☎ 01202-207207)
Web site: www.condorferries.co.uk

Hoverspeed
(France ☎ 08 00 90 17 77, UK 0870 524 0241)
Web site: www.hoverspeed.co.uk

Irish Ferries
(Cherbourg ☎ 02 33 23 44 44, Roscoff ☎ 02 98 61 17 17, UK ☎ 0870 517 1717, Rosslare ☎ 053-33158)
Web site: www.irishferries.ie

P&O Portsmouth
(France ☎ 08 03 01 30 13, UK ☎ 0870 600 3300, Bilbao ☎ 94 423 4477)
Web site: www.poportsmouth.com

P&O Stena Line
(France ☎ 08 03 01 30 13, UK ☎ 0870 600 0612)
Web site: www.postena.com

SeaFrance
(Calais ☎ 03 21 34 55 00, Dover ☎ 0870 571 1711)
Web site: www.seafrance.co.uk

The sample prices given here are for standard, weekday, high-season, one-way tickets for a car plus driver and one passenger; for a motorcycle plus driver and passenger; for a bicycle plus rider; and for a pedestrian. Also suggested are road routes linking the ports with South-West France.

The UK

The shortest ferry crossings from the UK to France are Dover–Calais and Folkestone–Boulogne. Longer crossings include Poole to Cherbourg and St-Malo; Newhaven–Dieppe; Portsmouth to Le Havre, Ouistreham (Caen), Cherbourg and St-Malo; Weymouth to St-Malo; and Plymouth to Roscoff.

Although rail passes are not valid for UK–France ferry travel, some discounts are available for students and young people.

Via Far Northern France Dover–Calais and Folkestone–Boulogne are very competitive routes, with frequent cheap promotional fares if you book well in advance.

SeaFrance and P&O Stena together run about 45 ferries daily from Dover to Calais (1½ hours). SeaFrance charges UK£149/80/15/15; P&O Stena's more frequent, slightly faster ferries cost a bit more. Dover–Calais on Hoverspeed's hovercraft (UK£115/65/25/25, 20 daily) takes 35 minutes; more sea-worthy SeaCat catamarans take 50 minutes. Hoverspeed SeaCats also make the 55-minute Folkestone–Boulogne crossing (UK£105/59/25/25, four daily).

For drivers, the big drawback of these crossings is the lack of a straightforward route around Paris on your way to the south-west. The best you can do is the A16 and A28 to Rouen, and the N154 via Evreux and Chartres to the E5/A10 past Orléans.

Via Normandy The UK's southern ports have numerous links with Dieppe, Le Havre, Ouistreham (Caen) and Cherbourg.

In 1999 P&O Stena announced the closure of its Newhaven–Dieppe service, the longest-running of all UK–France ferries. Hoverspeed's SuperSeaCats make the two-hour crossing three times daily (UK£124/65/25/25).

P&O Portsmouth makes its six-hour trip (eight hours overnight) from Portsmouth to

Le Havre (UK£147/60/37/32) three times daily. Its five-hour Portsmouth–Cherbourg connection (5½ to seven hours overnight) goes six times daily and costs the same. Both run less frequently between October and March.

Brittany Ferries makes a four-hour Poole–Cherbourg crossing (UK£147/58/32/32) once or twice daily. Its six-hour Portsmouth–Ouistreham connection goes two or three times daily between March and September, less often during the rest of the year, and costs the same. Students get 10% off fares paid in francs.

By car from Dieppe, make your way to Rouen and see the suggestions in the previous Via Far Northern France section. From Le Havre, Ouistreham or Cherbourg the most direct route southwards is from Caen on the N158 and N138 via Le Mans to Tours.

Via Brittany Services to St-Malo and Roscoff in Brittany run much less frequently than those across the Straits of Dover, especially in winter.

Ferries to St-Malo include Brittany Ferries from Portsmouth (UK£169/67/36/36), a nine-hour daily crossing (less frequent from early November to early March). Students get a 10% discount on fares paid in francs. From May to mid-October, Condor Ferries has daily catamarans to St-Malo via Guernsey and Jersey from Weymouth (UK£163/78/26/26, five hours) and from Poole (same fares, 5½ to 6½ hours).

From mid-March to mid-November, the Plymouth–Roscoff route (six hours) is served by one to three Brittany Ferries a day (UK£155/62/33/33); during the rest of the year there is only one a week. Students get a 10% discount on fares paid in francs.

By car, make your way to Rennes (on the N137 from St-Malo or the E50/N12 from Roscoff), and from there on the A83 to the A10 at Niort.

Via Spain For a minimum of driving between the UK and South-West France, several ferry services via northern Spain are worth considering.

P&O Portsmouth runs twice-weekly ferries from Portsmouth to Bilbao (UK£370/160/100/90, 29 to 35 hours), which is just 150km west of Bayonne. From mid-March to mid-November, Brittany Ferries has twice-weekly services from Plymouth to Santander (UK£338/144/80/80, 24 hours), which is about 250km west of Bayonne. During the winter, except in January and early February, ferries sail from Poole or Portsmouth (about 31 hours). Students are eligible for a 10% discount on fares paid in francs.

The fastest route by car from Santander and Bilbao to Bayonne is via autoroutes E70/A8 and E5/A63.

Ireland

Irish Ferries links Rosslare with Roscoff (15 hours; summer only) and Cherbourg (17 hours) every other day from April to August and two or three times a week during the rest of the year (IR£120/75/45/45). Eurailpass-holders get a 50% discount if they book ahead. From April to early October, Brittany Ferries has one weekly ferry linking Cork and Roscoff (IR£356/214/97/78, 14 hours).

RIVER & CANAL

The best-known inland water route into South-West France is the beautiful Canal du Midi, running north-west to Toulouse from the Bassin de Thau (Thau Basin) on the Mediterranean coast. At Toulouse the Canal du Midi meets the Canal Latéral à la Garonne, which parallels the Garonne River to within about 50km of Bordeaux. This canal system, plus the lower Garonne and the Gironde Estuary, comprises a 360km navigable waterway all the way from the Mediterranean to the Atlantic. Linked directly to it are navigable stretches of the Garonne, Dordogne, Lot, Baïse and Tarn rivers.

See under Boat in the Getting Around chapter for details about self-navigated holidays on the water, and the boxed text 'Les Canaux des Deux Mers' in that chapter for background information on the region's canals.

ORGANISED TOURS

Following are details of some reliable tour operators offering special-interest or made-to-order tours to South-West France. For organised activity programmes, see Activities in the Facts for the Visitor chapter.

A good listing of the UK's most interesting specialist tour operators is the free *AITO Directory of Real Holidays*, an annual index of member companies of the Association of Independent Tour Operators. It's available from AITO (☎ 020-8744 9280, fax 8744 3187).

Cycling Tours

Cycling is perhaps the finest way to explore South-West France and there are lots of outfits offering appealing ways to do it.

The UK's biggest cycling organisation, is the Cyclists' Touring Club (CTC; ☎ 01483-417217, fax 426994, email cycling@ctc.org.uk). Among good-value, not-for-profit tours run by and for CTC members are several to South-West France. These and scores of commercial bicycle holiday outfits are listed in CTC's *Cycle Holiday Guide* magazine. See Cycling Organisations under Cycling in the Getting Around chapter for more about the CTC.

Other UK based companies include Alternative Travel Group (☎ 01865-315678, fax 315697, email info@alternative-travel.co.uk) and Sherpa Expeditions (☎ 020-8577 2717, fax 8572 9788), offering self-guided, inn-to-inn tours of the Dordogne. Belle France (☎ 01797-223777, fax 223666) runs several eight- to 12-night guided Dordogne tours. Bike Tours (☎ 01225-310859, fax 480132, email biketours@aol.com) takes you from Bordeaux via the Landes and Gers on a mostly-camping tour to Barcelona.

True to its name, Susi Madron's Cycling for Softies (☎ 0161-248 8282, fax 248 5140, email susimadron@its.itsnet.co.uk) runs no-worries trips in the Dordogne and elsewhere. Another UK operator offering trips to the region is Headwater Holidays (☎ 01606-813333, fax 813334, email info@headwater.com), represented in Australia by Peregrine (☎ 03-9663 8611).

Blue Marble Travel (☎ 973-326 9533, fax 326 8939) from the US runs a four-week trans-Iberian tour (South-West France, northern Spain and northern Portugal), plus shorter trips in the Dordogne and in the French and Spanish Basque country. Canada-based Butterfield & Robinson (toll-free ☎ 800 678 1147, fax 416-864 0541) offers several biking tours with deluxe accommodation in Aquitaine. Backroads (toll-free ☎ 800 462 2848, fax 510-527 1444, email goactive@backroads.com) runs week-long inn-to-inn and camping trips in the Dordogne, the Lot and the French Basque country.

See also Cycling in the Getting Around chapter for more information on cycling in South-West France.

Walking Tours

The UK has many walking specialists with good small-group packages. Pyrenees Adventures (☎/fax 01433-621498, email rick@pyradv.demon.co.uk) runs escorted tours in the hilly Basque country from its base near St-Jean Pied de Port. Similar walks in the Lot are offered by Andrew Brock Travel (☎ 01572-821330, fax 821072, email abrock3650@aol.com). For a week-long guided boating, cycling, walking and camping tour of the Dordogne, contact Explore Worldwide (☎ 01252-319448, fax 343170, email info@explore.co.uk).

Many operators organising cycling tours (see the preceding Cycling Tours section) also run walking tours to the same places. Sherpa Expeditions offers flexible, self-guided walks in the Dordogne, Gers and Tarn. Alternative Travel Group offers similar, well-researched tours (guided or self-guided) to the Dordogne and the Basque country. Headwater Holidays offers several eight- or nine-day guided walks in the Dordogne, Lot and Tarn valleys. Belle France runs a week-long, fixed-base walk round the Lot valley east of Cahors.

Other Specialist Tours

UK-based Winetrails (☎ 01306-712111, fax 713504, email sales@winetrails.co.uk) samples the wines of Bordeaux in three gentle ways: escorted walks, escorted cycling tours and go-anytime, unguided wine tours. Arblaster & Clarke Wine Tours (☎ 01730-893344, fax 892888) offers wine tours in the Bordeaux region and elsewhere.

Martin Randall Travel (☎ 020-8742 3355, fax 8742 7766, email info@martinrandall .co.uk) arranges high-quality, one-week art and architecture tours.

USA-based International Kitchen (toll-free ☎ 800 945 8606, ☎ 847-295 5363, fax 295 0945, email info@intl-kitchen.com) runs a six-day, cycling-and-cooking tour of the Bordeaux area from a B&B in St-Quentin de Baron, outside Bordeaux.

Family-Oriented Programmes
Canvas Holidays (☎ 08709-022022, fax 01383 620075) and Eurocamp (☎ 01606-787878, email enquiries@eurocamp.co.uk) offer kid-friendly camping holidays, using their tents or caravans, at deluxe camp sites all over South-West France. Eurocamp affiliates can also help with sites and bookings for those with their own tents or caravans. A UK tour operator offering adventure packages aimed at families and children is Pyrenees Adventures (see Walking Tours earlier in this chapter).

Self-Drive, Self-Catering & Short Breaks
Perhaps you'd just like to chill out for a week in a rural farmhouse or a restored chateau. One of the first UK operators to arrange cottage holidays, VFB Holidays (☎ 01242-240336, fax 570340) has a wide choice of places in every département covered in this book, and also offers longer trips.

Among other UK agencies who can set up self-drive, rail-drive and fly-drive holidays are Chez Nous (☎ 01484-684075, fax 685852, email cheznous@cnts.demon

.co.uk), Drive France (☎ 08700-771771, fax 780191, email holidays@indiv-travellers .com), French Collection (☎ 01202-666400, fax 441114), Inghams Just France (☎ 020-8780 4488) and Vintage Travel (☎ 01954-261431, fax 260819, email holidays@ vintagetravel.co.uk).

Several of the UK–France ferry operators have set up their own bargain-holiday agencies, including Brittany Ferries Holidays (☎ 0870 5360 360) and SeaFrance's European Life (☎ 0870 242 4455). Other UK tour operators with packages to South-West France include The Magic of France (☎ 020-8741 0208, fax 8748 3732) and Cresta Holidays (☎ 0870 333 3303).

The France Holiday Store (www.fr-holidaystore.co.uk) is a one-stop online shop for holidays from the UK to France – everything from Eurostar deals to package breaks, property searches and online bookings.

Warning
The information in this chapter is particularly vulnerable to change: prices for international travel are volatile, routes are introduced and cancelled, schedules change, special deals come and go, and rules and visa requirements are amended. Airlines and governments seem to take perverse pleasure in making price structures and regulations complicated. Check directly with the airline or a travel agent to make sure you understand how a fare works. In addition, the travel industry is highly competitive and there are many lurks and perks.

The upshot is that you should get opinions, quotes and advice from as many airlines and travel agents as possible before you part with your cash. The details given in this chapter should be regarded as pointers and are not a substitute for your own careful, up-to-date research.

Getting Around

This is not as easy as you might think, thanks to a national transport policy biased in favour of the state-owned rail system and to the compartmentalisation of bus transport by région and département.

None of the eight airports in South-West France with scheduled services has regular direct links with any of the others.

Domestic bus links between the Aquitaine and Midi-Pyrénées régions are scarce; from Toulouse, for example, it's easier to find a bus to Spain than to Bayonne. Bus routes within each région are département-centred, with inter-département services doled out to specific companies or associations. Eurolines and its privately owned long-haul competitors are limited to international routes.

Regional express train (TER) services are slower and less frequent than those of SNCF (Société Nationale des Chemins de Fer), the main Paris–Bordeaux, Paris–Toulouse and Bordeaux–Toulouse lines, but the network runs just as efficiently. Trains are generally the way to go if you don't have the dosh for a car or the stamina to ride a bike.

Note that this chapter deals only with transport within South-West France. For connections to/from the Other Parts of France, see the Getting There & Away chapter.

BUS

Buses are useful for short-distance travel within départements – especially in the Gers and eastern Landes where there are no railway lines – and they're fairly frequent between main towns. Away from these towns, services can shrink to almost nothing, especially at the weekend, and even more acutely when schools are on holiday (see the boxed text 'School Holidays'). Without a car you'll find it hard to visit more than one or two of those pretty perched villages in a day.

Autocars (regional buses) are operated

School Holidays

Rural bus services thin out when there are no students to carry. This means not only during July, August and the first week of September but typically a week around All Saints' Day (late October or early November), two weeks for Christmas and New Year, two weeks for 'February holidays' (February to early March; dates vary with locality) and two weeks during the month after Easter (late March or April; dates vary with locality). Bus timetables indicate which are school-term-only services, and many have a *calendrier scolaire* at the back.

by a muddle of different companies, most with an office at the bus station of each town they serve. One company may sell tickets for all the companies operating from the same station. Over the years, SNCF has replaced certain unprofitable railway lines with bus services; unlike privately operated buses, these are free if you happen to have a rail pass.

Timetables change from year to year, and many local tourist offices have surprisingly little information on bus services, except for those to the nearest market town. In small villages you may get the best information from the cafe or hotel nearest the bus stop.

TRAIN

For detailed information on SNCF services, tickets and discounts, see Train under Other Parts of France in the Getting There & Away chapter.

If you'll be doing a lot of rail travel you can buy a SNCF book called *Indicateur Horaires: Ville à Ville*, with point-to-point timetables for just about any major journey. It costs 60FF at Hachette newsagent kiosks in bigger stations. The Aquitaine

TRAIN & BUS ROUTES

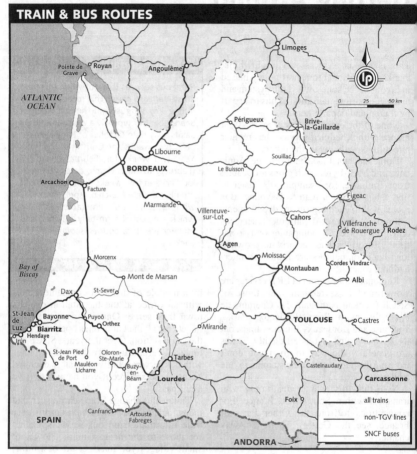

and Midi-Pyrénées regional governments each publish a free *Guide Régional des Transports*, with detailed SNCF bus and interregional rail schedules. They're available from large tourist offices throughout the region.

Reservations are unnecessary on most regional trains, though if you plan to travel on a main route like Toulouse–Bordeaux in high season, it's wise to buy your ticket at least a few days in advance. Reservations can be made through travel agencies, by toll-free telephone (☎ 08 36 35 35 35 in French, ☎ 08 36 35 35 39 in English), at any

SNCF ticketing office or at one of the automatic ticket vending machines in every station. Tickets are valid for two months from the date of purchase.

Following are some 2nd-class, one-way fares and average journey durations. Fares and distances quoted are TGV/non-TGV (TGV fares all include the mandatory 25FF reservation fee): Bordeaux–Bayonne (168/133FF, 199km, 1½/2¼ hours), Toulouse–Bayonne (non-TGV only; 213FF, 323km, 3¾ hours), Toulouse–Bordeaux (198/183FF, 257km, 2¼/2½ hours), Toulouse–Brive-la-Gaillarde (non-TGV only; 141FF, 214km,

Little Trains

Several narrow-gauge trains ply short lines in Aquitaine in the warm months. A century-old locomotive pulls equally old carriages up from Sabres to the Ecomusée de la Grande Lande at Marquèze, in the Landes. A 4km–long cog-wheel railway ascends La Rhune mountain, south-east of St-Jean de Luz in the French Basque country. From Artouste-Fabrèges in the Vallée d'Ossau (Béarn) the Petit Train d'Artouste – once used to transport dam workers – runs for 10km offering views across the Basses-Pyrénées. See those sections in the French Basque Country & Béarn chapter for more on seasons, timetables and fares.

3½ hours), Bordeaux–Brive-la-Gaillarde (non-TGV only; 135FF, 203km, 2½ hours).

CAR & MOTORCYCLE

Unless you're cycling, a car or motorcycle is the key to discovering the many parts of South-West France where public transport hardly goes. If you stay off the autoroutes, petrol costs (40FF to 50FF per 100km) are lower than train fares (50FF to 100FF per 100km), though of course this neglects added costs such as insurance, maintenance, and wear and tear.

A car also gives you cheaper accommodation options (camp sites, hostels and hotels on city outskirts) or at least more interesting ones (restored farmhouses and chateaux, for example). Even renting a car for a couple of days will change the way you see this region.

Drivers should refer to Other Parts of France – Car & Motorcycle in the Land section of the Getting There & Away chapter for information on how to get to South-West France from elsewhere in the country.

The fastest arteries across the region are the E72/A62 (the Autoroute des Deux Mers, alongside the Canal Latéral) between Bordeaux and Toulouse, and the E80/A64 between Bayonne and Toulouse. When it's

completed (scheduled to be early 2002), the E9/A20 between Brive-la-Gaillarde and Toulouse will be similarly fast; until then, drivers are shunted on and off the scenic but congested N20. The E5–E70 (variously A10, N10 or A63) runs arrow-straight across the Landes between Bordeaux and Bayonne.

But you're here to see the place, not cross it. If you're not in a hurry, get off the autoroutes and even the lorry-choked N roads. Michelin and other road maps indicate many scenic routes (green shading), though of course everybody else has one of these maps too. Obscure, rambling D roads will show you more gentle landscapes and faraway places than we could possibly fit into this book.

Documents & Equipment

By French law, all drivers must carry a national ID card or passport; a valid *permis de conduire* (driving licence); car ownership papers, known as *carte grise* (grey card); and proof of insurance, known as *carte verte* (green card). If you're stopped by the police and don't have one or more of these, you are liable for a 900FF on-the-spot fine. Keep photocopies of all of them in a safe place. Never leave your car ownership or insurance papers in the vehicle.

A reflective warning triangle, to be used in the event of breakdown, must be carried in the car. Recommended accessories are a first-aid kit, a spare bulb kit and a fire extinguisher. A right-hand drive vehicle brought to France from the UK or Ireland must have deflectors fixed to the headlights to avoid dazzling oncoming traffic.

Road Rules

In France, as throughout continental Europe, people drive on the right and overtake on the left. Note that, unless otherwise indicated, you must give way to cars coming from the right (see the boxed text '*Priorité à Droite*' on the next page). North American drivers should also remember that turning right on a red light is illegal in France.

Unless otherwise signposted, there is a speed limit of 50km/h in all areas designated

Priorité à Droite

For overseas visitors, the most confusing – and dangerous – traffic law in France is the 'priority on the right' rule, under which any car entering an intersection from a road on your right (and that includes those entering main roads from smaller ones) has right-of-way over you. French drivers tend to take full advantage of this and pull boldly into intersections or on to main roads.

This is a recipe for pandemonium at roundabouts (traffic circles). Fortunately priorité à droite has been suspended at most roundabouts, so that cars already on the roundabout have right of way. This is indicated by signs on approach roads reading *vous n'avez pas la priorité* (you do not have right of way) or *cédez le passage* (give way) or with a roundabout symbol (a circle made of three curved arrows). But pay attention, because in a few areas the old protocol still exists (for example in the centre of Auch).

Priorité à droite is also suspended on major highways and other *routes à caractère prioritaire* (priority roads), marked by a yellow diamond with a black diamond in the middle. Such signs appear every few kilometres and at intersections. Priorité à droite is reinstated if you see the same sign with a diagonal bar through it.

as built up, no matter how rural they may look. On intercity roads, you must slow to 50km/h the moment you pass a white sign with a red border bearing a place name in black or blue letters. This limit remains in force until you arrive at the other edge of town, where you'll pass an identical sign with a red diagonal bar across the name.

Outside built-up areas, speed limits are:

90km/h (80km/h if it's raining) on undivided N and D highways.
110km/h (100km/h if it's raining) on dual carriageways (divided highways) or short sections of highway with a divider strip.

130km/h (110km/h in the rain, 60km/h in icy conditions) on autoroutes.

Speed limits are generally not posted unless they deviate from these. If you drive as slow as the speed limit, count on having lots of cars coming to within a few metres of your rear bumper and overtaking at the first opportunity.

Oncoming drivers who flash their lights at you are probably indicating that there are gendarmes ahead, keeping an eye on the traffic, and that you'd better watch your speed.

Motorcycle riders and passengers are required to wear crash helmets.

Road Signs

On signs showing the way to towns, parts of towns or highways, *toutes directions* (all directions) or *autres directions* (other directions) indicates the route to anything not listed on the sign.

Sens unique means 'one way'. If you come to a *route barrée* (closed road), you'll usually also find a yellow panel with instructions for a *déviation* (detour). *Sauf riverains* on a no-entry sign means 'except residents'. *Verglas fréquent* means 'frequent road ice'. Road signs containing the word *rappel* (remember) mean you should already know what the sign is telling you (such as the speed limit).

Alcohol

French law is very tough on drunk drivers. To catch drivers whose blood-alcohol concentration is over 0.05%, the police sometimes conduct random breathalyser tests. Fines range from 500FF to 8000FF and licences can be suspended.

Petrol

At the time of writing, *essence* (petrol or gasoline), also called *carburant* (fuel), was a bit cheaper in France than in the UK, but a lot more expensive than in Australia or North America. In mid-1999, 95-octane *sans plomb* (unleaded) petrol cost around 6.10FF per litre (US$3.70 per US gallon). *Gazole* (diesel fuel) was 4.40FF per litre

(US$2.70 per US gallon). Prices may fluctuate by as much as 20% depending on where you go; fuel is cheapest at petrol stations on city outskirts and those at supermarkets.

Petrol stations stay open 24 hours along motorways and other major roads. *Le plein, s'il vous plaît* means 'fill it up, please'.

Parking

Parking, whether you are in a big city or a touristy village, may be your single biggest headache. In city centres, the best bet is to park the car and walk or take public transport.

For street parking, the old *disque bleu* honour system is still in use in many towns: where a time-limited space is outlined in blue, you set a small cardboard disk to your time of arrival and leave it on the dashboard. Should you come across such *zones bleu*, you can buy a disque bleu (which isn't necessarily blue) at any *tabac* (tobacconist). Increasingly, street parking is metered, as indicated by *payant* on a sign or painted on the road: you feed a meter or buy a ticket from the nearest *horodateur* machine and leave that on the dashboard, at least at certain hours. Typical rates are 5FF to 10FF per hour.

Most big cities have public car parks (often underground), which are signposted with a white 'P' on a blue background. Many of the touristy hilltop villages keep cars out by requiring visitors to park in sprawling, purpose-built car parks down below.

'No parking' is *defense de stationner*; 'parking this side only' is *côte de stationnement*. No-parking areas may be indicated by stanchions or short fences at the kerb.

Repairs

If your car is *en panne* (broken down), you'll have to find a garage that handles your *marque* (make of car). There are Peugeot, Renault and Citroën garages all over the place but if you have a non-French car you may have trouble finding someone to service it in remote areas. Michelin's *Guide Rouge* lists garages at the end of each town entry.

Accidents

If you're involved in a minor accident with no injuries, the easiest way for drivers to

Road Distances (km)

	Agen	Albi	Auch	Bayonne	Bordeaux	Cahors	Mont de Marsan	Montauban	Pau	Périgueux	Toulouse
Agen	---										
Albi	157	---									
Auch	74	151	---								
Bayonne	206	376	220	---							
Bordeaux	142	287	207	190	---						
Cahors	88	108	137	312	218	---					
Mont de Marsan	110	266	108	98	131	197	---				
Montauban	75	72	85	346	204	60	183	---			
Pau	163	277	120	112	200	309	85	247	---		
Périgueux	139	235	213	303	127	127	201	178	266	---	
Toulouse	119	75	77	295	248	116	184	55	192	256	---

sort things out with their insurance companies is to fill out a Constat Aimable d'Accident Automobile (jointly agreed accident report), known in English as a European Accident Statement. This is usually included in the documents you get with a rental car. Make sure the report includes any details that will help you prove that the accident was not your fault.

If problems crop up, it's usually not hard to find a police officer. To alert the police, dial ☎ 17.

Rental

Although multinational agencies like Hertz, Avis, Budget and Europcar are absurdly expensive for on-the-spot rental, their prepaid promotional rates can be a fraction of walk-in rates. Fly-drive deals are also worth looking into. For on-the-spot rental, domestic firms like Rent-a-Car Système and Century, and some youth travel agencies, have the best rates. The largest French car hire company is ADA (☎ 08 36 68 40 02), with offices in many bigger towns. Companies are noted in the Getting There & Away section for individual cities; major firms also have desks at Bordeaux and Toulouse airports. Make a reservation at least a few days in advance in summer.

Most firms require the driver to be aged over 21 (or in some cases 23) and to have had a driving licence for at least one year. The packet of documents you get on hiring a car should include a 24-hour number to call in case of a breakdown or accident. Check how many 'free' kilometres are included; *kilométrage illimité* (unlimited mileage) means you can drive to your heart's content.

Insurance *Assurance* (insurance) for damage or injury to other people is mandatory, but collision-damage waivers vary from company to company. Policies offered by smaller companies may leave you liable for a deductible (excess) cost (*franchise*) of up to 8000FF. If you're in an accident where you're at fault, or if the car is damaged and the guilty party is unknown, or if the car is stolen, this is the amount for which you're liable before the collision-damage policy kicks in. Check the small print when you shop around.

Rates At the time of writing, an Opel Corsa from Avis in the UK, including unlimited mileage and a collision-damage excess of 2000FF, costs about UK£135 per week if you pay in advance. A similar deal from Europcar was about UK£100 per week, or 1200FF (UK£120) if paid in France. The cost to hire a small car for a week (maximum distance 1000km), with 3000/6000FF accident/theft excess, was 1099FF from Rent-a-Car Système.

All the major rental companies accept payment by credit card. All insist on a *caution* (deposit); for this, some ask you to leave a signed credit card slip without a sum written in. If this makes you uncomfortable, ask them to make out separate slips for the rental and for the deposit, and see that the latter is destroyed when you return the car.

Motorcycle

South-West France is gorgeous for motorcycle touring, with good roads and stunning scenery. Be sure your wet-weather gear is up to scratch in spring and autumn. Riders and passengers must wear helmets; those caught bareheaded can be fined and have their bike confiscated. Bikes of over 125cc must have headlights on during the day. No special licence is required to ride a motorcycle of less than 50cc.

To rent a *scooter* or *moto* (motorcycle) you must leave a deposit of several thousand francs, which you forfeit – up to the value of the damage – if you're in an accident and it's your fault. Since insurance companies won't cover theft, you'll also lose the deposit if the bike is stolen. Most places accept deposits made by credit card, travellers cheque or Eurocheque.

BICYCLE

If you've got the stamina, you couldn't ask for a better way to see South-West France up close than by bicycle. A network of old inland D roads, with relatively light traffic, are the ideal vantage point for viewing its

Getting seriously cheesy at St-Céré market, Lot

A local gourmet, Dordogne

Geese are farmed to produce foie gras.

Sunflowers are one of the region's cash crops.

JULIA WILKINSON

JULIA WILKINSON

SALLY DILLON

JULIA WILKINSON

JOHN KING

This array of windows exemplifies the variety in architectural styles to be found throughout South-West France.

rural landscapes (one pitfall: they rarely have proper shoulders). Périgord, in particular, attracts legions of pedal-pushers, and beside the Canal du Midi and Canal Latéral runs one of Europe's longest unbroken bicycle paths. Probably because so many French people ride bikes themselves, you're also more likely to be treated with real warmth (and admiration) if you roll up on a bicycle.

By law your bicycle must have two functioning brakes, a bell, a red reflector on the back and yellow reflectors on the pedals. After sunset, and when visibility is poor, you must turn on a white light in front and a red one at the rear. When being overtaken by a car or truck, cyclists are required to ride in single file.

Never leave your bike locked up outside overnight if you want to see it again. You can leave bikes in train station left-luggage offices for around 35FF a day.

Cycling Organisations

The volunteer-run Fédération Française de Cyclotourisme (☎ 01 44 16 88 88, fax 01 44 16 88 99), 8 rue Jean-Marie Jégo, Paris, provides a liaison among France's cycling clubs, and will send you a free packet of general information in English. It also sells touring itineraries, cycling maps and topoguides for cyclists, and organises bicycle trips that are open to visitors.

For its members, the Cyclists' Touring Club in the UK (CTC; ☎ 01483-417217, fax 426994, email cycling@ctc.org.uk) publishes a useful, free booklet on cycling in France, plus touring notes for some 70 routes around the country, including in the Dordogne and Vézère valleys, the Bordeaux area, Gironde, the Landes, the Gers, Tarn Gorges, Canal du Midi, the Pyrénées and the French Basque country (Pays Basque). The CTC also offers tips on bikes, spares, insurance and other general information; they also sell maps, topoguides and other publications by mail order. For more information on the CTC have a look at their Web site at www.ctc.org.uk/.

European Bike Express (☎ 01642-251440) facilitates independent cycling

holidays by transporting cyclists and their bikes by bus and trailer from the UK to places all over France.

See Activities in the Facts for the Visitor chapter for more cycling information. Organised Tours in the Getting There & Away chapter contains information on bicycle tours.

Transporting a Bicycle

Bicycles are rarely allowed on local or intercity buses.

On a few trains, bikes can be taken free of charge, but only if they're either folded up or packed, with wheels removed, in special covers (available from cycle shops) measuring no more than 120 by 90cm. You're responsible for loading and unloading them. Services where this is allowed are indicated in timetables by a little bicycle symbol by the train number.

You can also send a boxed bicycle as checked baggage between any two stations big enough to have a baggage office, for 195FF, or door to door for 295FF. It may take three or four days. For information call SNCF on ☎ 08 03 84 58 45.

To take your bike with you on an aircraft, you can either take it apart and pack it in a bike box, or wheel it to the check-in desk, where it will be treated as baggage. Check all this (and weight limits) with the airline well in advance.

See The UK, under Sea in the Getting There & Away chapter, for information about taking a bicycle on cross-channel ferries.

Rental

Most sizeable towns and many resorts have at least one shop that hires out *vélos tout-terrains* (VTTs; mountain bikes) for between 60FF and 100FF per day, or cheaper touring bikes. Most places require a deposit (1000FF to 2000FF), which you forfeit if the bike is damaged or stolen. In general, deposits can be made in cash, with travellers cheques or by credit card (though a passport will often suffice). Rental outlets are listed in the Getting Around sections of city and town listings.

HITCHING

Hitching is never entirely safe in any country in the world and travellers who decide to hitch should understand that they are taking a small but potentially serious risk. On the other hand, if you speak some French, thumbing affords opportunities to meet local people from all walks of life and pick up the occasional tip on what to see. So we offer the following advice.

A woman hitching on her own faces a definite risk; two women hitching together are somewhat safer. Two men together may have a harder time getting picked up than a man travelling alone. The best (and safest) combination is a man and a woman. Never get in the car with someone about whom you are the least bit uneasy. Keep your belongings with you on the seat.

To maximise your chances of being picked up, stand where it's easy for drivers to stop; orient your backpack so it looks as small as possible to oncoming drivers; look cheerful, presentable and nonthreatening, and make eye contact with drivers. It also helps to hold up a sign with your destination followed by the letters *s.v.p.* (*s'il vous plaît*, meaning 'please').

Paris-based Allostop (☎ 01 53 20 42 42 within Paris, ☎ 01 53 20 42 43/44 from outside Paris, email allostop@ecritel.fr) puts people looking for rides in touch with drivers. Each passenger pays a per-kilometre fee to the driver, in addition to a subscription fee to Allostop that depends on the length of the journey. Allostop has branches in Bordeaux (☎ 05 57 95 91 11) and Toulouse (☎ 05 61 21 20 20) and a French-only Web site at www.ecritel.fr/allostop. Brittany-based Association Pouce (☎ 02 99 31 97 95, email allopouce@infonie.fr) has similar rates but no subscription fee. Its French-only Web site is at www.pouce.com.

Drivers and hitchhikers also advertise for one another under *Trajets* (Journeys) in the regional *Sud-Ouest* newspaper.

BOAT

A relaxing way to see South-West France from a unique vantage point is to rent a houseboat or cabin-cruiser and tootle along the region's many canals and rivers. You can tie up at a marina, a village or in the middle of nowhere, unload your bicycle and go exploring or shopping, and at the end of the day your boat is your hotel. Anyone aged over 18 can pilot a river boat without a licence. Learning the ropes, and the rules of the river, will only take about half an hour.

With the completion (probably in summer 2002) of locks and canals making the Lot navigable from Villeneuve-sur-Lot to St-Cirq Lapopie, a continuously navigable 350km network of canals and rivers will span the Gers, the Lot, Lot-et-Garonne and Tarn-et-Garonne départements. These waterways include the Canal du Midi, the Canal Latéral à la Garonne (Castets-en-Dorthe to Toulouse), the Baïse (below Valence-sur-Baïse), the Lot (below St-Cirq-Lapopie) and the Tarn (below Montauban). Other major rivers with navigable stretches include the Garonne, Dordogne and Adour, and the Gironde Estuary.

France's biggest river tourism agency is the Crown Blue Line, with offices for Aquitaine (☎ 05 53 89 50 80, fax 05 53 89 51 13) in Le Mas d'Agenais and for the Canal du Midi (☎ 04 68 94 52 72, fax 04 68 94 52 73) in Castelnaudary. Two local houseboat-rental firms with more modest options are Locaboat Plaisance (☎ 05 53 66 00 74, fax 05 53 68 26 23, email locaboat@locaboat.com) at Agen with a Web site at www.locaboat.com, and Aquitaine Navigation (☎ 05 53 84 72 50, fax 05 53 84 03 33, email aquinav@aquitaine-navigation .com) at Buzet-sur-Baïse, with a Web site at www.aquitaine-navigation.com.

From the UK you can book a boat holiday with Crown Blue through Crown Travel (☎ 01603-630513, fax 664298, email crownhols@ dial.pipex.com), or one with Locaboat Plaisance through Andrew Brock Travel (☎ 01572-821330, fax 821072, email abrock3650@aol.com).

The tourist cruising season lasts from Easter to November, but to get a boat in July and August, when many waterways are as crowded as the Champs-Elysées, you must

Les Canaux des Deux Mers

The Romans were the first of many to study the idea of a canal across southern France between the Mediterranean and the Atlantic, a low-anxiety alternative to the 5000km sea journey via the Straits of Gibraltar. The stumbling block was always the Seuil de Naurouze (Naurouze Sill) watershed, a 190m-high ridge along the boundary between today's Midi-Pyrénées and Languedoc-Rousillon régions: how to get a canal over it and how to keep it filled with water?

The solution, suggested by a wealthy Languedoc tax collector and amateur scientist named Pierre-Paul Riquet (1604–80), attracted the support of Colbert, Louis XIV's chief minister. Riquet proposed to collect water from the streams of the Montagne Noire, store it in the Seuil de Naurouze and spill it down both sides of the watershed. He backed up the idea with detailed calculations on feasibility and economic potential (for example, for the transport of grain from Toulouse to the markets of the Languedoc).

In 1666 Louis XIV gave his official blessing to what would be the century's biggest-ever engineering project, to stretch 241km from the Bassin de Thau to Toulouse. The Canal du Midi was 14 years in the building. Riquet, who was granted hereditary control over the canal and who sank his life savings into its construction, died exhausted and penniless with just 4km left to build. Riquet's two sons carried on and the canal was inaugurated in May 1681.

The canal, built with commerce in mind, got off to a roaring start. Cargo and passenger traffic volumes shot up in the following decades. Riquet's descendants did well from the canal's tolls and in return maintained a smoothly functioning system.

It was not until 1776 that the little Brienne Canal got round the shallows at Toulouse, thus linking the Canal du Midi directly with the Garonne. Nevertheless all goods going beyond Toulouse had to be shifted to river boats and navigation down the Garonne was at the mercy of low summer flows and often-violent flooding.

Sébastien de Vauban, the king's redoubtable commissioner for fortifications, was employed to tackle many residual design problems. It was he who understood that the sea-to-sea crossing needed something better than the fickle Garonne, and urged the construction of a canal *latéral à la Garonne* (parallel to the Garonne), so that canal boats could make the entire journey. Less inspired, but equally amazing, the Canal Latéral was inaugurated in 1856, linked to the Canal du Midi at Toulouse's Port de l'Embouchure, completing Riquet's dream.

And only just in time: with the arrival of the railway, tonnage on the canal soon began to decline. Despite a state buy-out of the canal in 1898 and the abolition of all tolls, the slide continued. Today, cargo traffic has vanished: the Canal du Midi's locks cannot accommodate boats longer than about 30m. Passenger traffic, on the other hand, has recovered with the advent of canal-boat tourism, and the cool, tree-shaded canals have become fine venues for walking, cycling and boat trips.

This is Europe's oldest functioning canal system, with little brick bridges, tiny tunnels, handsome aqueducts and oval locks that often come in cascades, to hoist boats up and down the flanks of the Montagne Noire. It's an achievement of extraordinary harmony, imagination and breadth, and in 1996 the two canals were together designated a UNESCO World Heritage Site.

reserve months ahead. Boats typically accommodate two to 12 passengers and are hired out on a weekly basis, though there are some short breaks on offer. Weekly prices for a two-person boat in low/high season start at around 4000/6500FF; Crown

euro currency converter 10FF = €1.52

Travel's UK rates start at about UK£600/900. A security deposit of between 3000FF and 6000FF is normally required.

Many more local outfits hire boats by the hour, day or evening, and others offer short guided cruises. These are noted in listings for individual towns.

LOCAL TRANSPORT

Getting around towns in South-West France is straightforward, thanks to good public transport systems. Toulouse is the only city with a metro. Details of routes, fares and tourist passes are available at tourist offices and local bus company information counters; see the Getting Around sections for individual cities and towns.

Taxis are generally expensive. Most towns have a taxi rank in front of the train station. Fares are about 13.50FF flag fall plus 3.50FF per kilometre for daytime travel and 5FF per kilometre at night, on Sunday and on holidays (including the price of a return trip if you go somewhere where a return passenger is not assured). Sitting still or creeping along in traffic at less than about 20km/h is calculated by time (75FF per hour) rather than distance. There may be a 5FF surcharge to get picked up at a train station or airport and a fee of 6FF per bag.

Bordeaux, the Atlantic Coast & the Landes

Bordeaux, capital of the Aquitaine région, is the south-west's second-largest city after Toulouse, and the centre of a world-renowned wine-growing area. With an international airport and excellent transport links it's a natural jumping-off point for the region. But don't hurry away: Bordeaux itself has much to offer, as does the nearby medieval town of St-Émilion and the popular resort of Arcachon. Then there are 230km of Atlantic coastline – the so-called Côte d'Argent (Silver Coast) – where you can surf or just work on your tan. Inland are a million hectares of pine plantations, Europe's largest cultivated forest, threaded with bike trails and dotted with lakes. If all this makes you tired, you can soak your bones in one of southern Landes' many thermal spas.

Bordeaux

postcode 33000 • pop 733,000 (city centre 215,000) • elevation 7m

Bordeaux is known for its neoclassical architecture, wide avenues and well-tended public squares and parks, which give the city a certain 18th-century grandeur. Too many grimy façades suggest that there have been better days, but excellent museums and restaurants, ethnic diversity – including size-able Spanish, Portuguese and North African communities – and a lively university population (with some 60,000 students) make it a great place to hang out for a few days.

History

Inhabited from the 4th century BC, Bordeaux – then called Burdigala – was seized in 56 BC by the Romans, who made this flourishing port the capital of Aquitainia. Pillaged by the Vikings in AD 848, it revived under a dynasty of dukes all named

Highlights

- Enjoy Bordeaux's excellent museums, lively nightlife and great seafood
- Gamble in Arcachon's casino or climb Europe's largest dune
- Taste the world's finest wines on a tour around The Médoc's sumptious chateaux
- Surf at championship sites or cycle along miles of pine-forested trails along the Atlantic Coast
- Spot some of Europe's rarest and most beautiful birds or take a trip by sea kayak in Parc Ornithologique du Teich
- Check out some of France's finest modern sculpture in Mont de Marsan

entrecôte à la bordelaise – grilled steak in a thick wine sauce

canelé pastries from Bordeaux – small, soft-centred custard cakes

macaroons from St-Émilion – soft cookies made from egg whites, almond powder and sugar

BORDEAUX

BORDEAUX, THE ATLANTIC COAST & THE LANDES

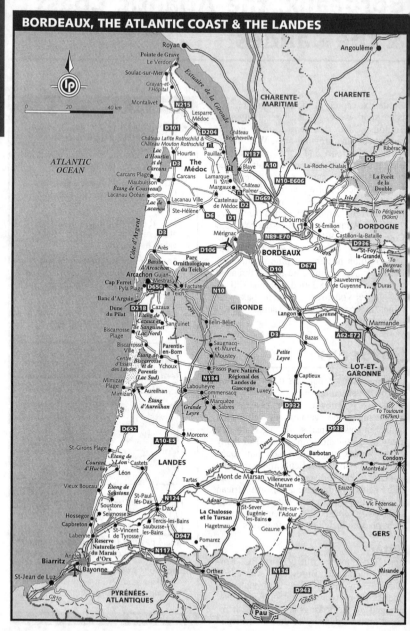

Guillaume, the most famous being Guillaume IX, early troubadour and grandfather of Eleanor of Aquitaine.

With Eleanor's 1152 marriage to Henry Plantagenet, Bordeaux became English 'territory' and remained so for 301 years. The city did well under the English, who grew fond of the region's red wine – which they called claret – granting wine-growers tax and other privileges. No wonder the Bordelais resisted when the French retook the city in 1453.

Commerce slumped with the loss of the English wine trade. From 1648 to 1653 the city joined in the series of urban revolts known as Les Frondes, with Bordeaux's the last to be quelled. By the 18th century the city had found new wealth from the trade in slaves and in sugar, and the centre was rebuilt by several enthusiastic royal governors, notably Claude Boucher and the Marquis de Tourny.

Bordeaux took a triple blow in the 19th century with the end of the slave trade in 1815, a slump in the sugar trade, and the 1878 destruction of its vines by phylloxera. Shame and occupation arrived with WWII: Bordeaux was the scene of the 1940 armistice with Hitler.

However, Bordeaux served briefly as the capital of France on three occasions when the country was on the verge of defeat: during the Franco-Prussian War of 1870–71; at the beginning of WWI (1914); and for two weeks in 1940, just before the Vichy government was proclaimed.

Today, with a vigorous aeronautical industry and a revived wine trade (the city's top economic activity is the marketing and export of fine wines), Bordeaux is on the

Eleanor of Aquitaine

It was thanks to the beautiful and wealthy Eleanor of Aquitaine that France – and particularly the south-west – was rocked by the Hundred Years' War. Born in 1122 to Guillaume X, duke of Aquitaine, she was his only heir, and in 1137 her considerable wealth (including one of the largest domains in France) became part of the French crown when she married Louis VII.

Although she bore him two daughters and influenced him greatly, Eleanor never much fancied the dull Louis who for his part was so annoyed by her flirtatious behaviour during the Second Crusade that he annulled the marriage in 1152. The ink had hardly dried on the paper when 30-something Eleanor (who still had possession of Aquitaine) found her true love: 19-year-old Henry Plantagenet, duke of Normandy and count of Anjou. In 1154 he became King Henry II of England, thereby bringing vast areas of French land under the control of the English Crown and sparking off centuries of rivalry between the French and English.

Eleanor's sons were a lousy lot (see the boxed text on her favourite, 'Richard the Lion-Heart', in the History section of the Facts about South-West France chapter). Her support of their revolt against their father – support probably borne of fury at her husband's infidelities – cost her her freedom for many years: Henry had her imprisoned in England and it was only on his death in 1189 that she returned to Aquitaine, to act as Richard's administrator while he was engaged in the Third Crusade.

In addition to managerial prowess, Eleanor also had enormous cultural and social influence. A whole new chivalric attitude towards women was promoted at her brilliant court in Poitiers, where the novel idea that men belonged to women was celebrated in troubadour poetry.

After a jaunt across the Pyrénées at the age of 80 to fetch her granddaughter Blanche from the court at Castile for marriage to the son of the French king, she retired to her castle on the isle of Oléron. She died in 1204 at the abbey-church of Fontevrault, eulogised by the nuns as a queen 'who surpassed almost all the queens of the world'.

rise again. In 1995 ex-prime minister Alain Juppé took over as mayor from the ageing Jacques Chaban-Delmas, who had 'reigned' for 48 years. Juppé, from Mont de Marsan, has injected new life into the city with a flurry of urban projects.

Orientation

The city centre lies between place Gambetta and the wide Garonne River. The train station, Gare St-Jean, is in a seedy area 3km south-east of the centre. Cours de la Marne stretches from the Gare St-Jean to place de la Victoire, itself linked to place de la Comédie by the 1.1km-long rue Ste-Catherine pedestrian mall.

Information

Tourist Offices The tourist office (☎ 05 56 00 66 00, fax 05 56 00 66 01, email otb@bordeaux-tourisme.com), 12 cours du 30 Juillet, is open from 9 am to 8 pm daily (to 7 pm on Sunday) from June to September; it's open to 7 pm Monday to Saturday and from 9.45 am to 4.30 pm on Sunday during the rest of the year. Check out its free bimonthly *Bordeaux Tourisme* magazine, detailing tours and current events. The free Bordeaux Découverte card provides discounts at some restaurants and for follow-up visits to many museums; versions are available which also include unlimited bus travel for one day (23.50FF) or three days (54.50FF).

A branch tourist office at Gare St-Jean (☎ 05 56 91 64 70) is open from 9 am to noon and 1 to 7 pm daily (from 10 am and to 6 pm Sunday) June to September; from 9 am to noon and 1 to 6 pm daily except Sunday during the rest of the year. An airport branch (☎ 05 56 34 50 50) is open from 5 am to 11 pm daily. Offices covering a wider area include La Maison du Tourisme de la Gironde (☎ 05 56 52 61 40, fax 05 56 81 09 99), 21 cours de l'Intendance, and La Maison des Pyrénées (☎ 05 56 44 05 65, fax 05 56 52 37 29), 6 rue Vital Carles.

Useful monthly or bimonthly what's-on booklets on sale at newsagents include *Spectaculaire 33*, *Bordeaux Plus* (including a list of restaurants open on Sundays) and *L'Essentiel* (which also covers the Gironde).

Maison du Vin de Bordeaux For maps and information on wine-tasting courses visit the Maison du Vin de Bordeaux (☎ 05 56 00 22 66, fax 05 56 00 22 82, email ecole@vins-bordeaux.fr) 3 cours du 30 Juillet, open weekdays from 8.30 am to 6 pm (and Saturday from 9 am to 4 pm between June and mid-October).

CIJA The Centre d'Information Jeunesse d'Aquitaine (☎ 05 56 56 00 56, fax 05 56 52 83 21), 5 rue Duffour Dubergier and around the corner at 125 cours d'Alsace et Lorraine, is Bordeaux's central youth information centre. It has a library full of data on work and education, and can help you find jobs, discounts, lifts and accommodation. At the cours d'Alsace branch is a youth travel agency. Both are open from 9 am to 6 pm on weekdays.

Money Numerous banks on cours de l'Intendance, rue de l'Esprit des Lois and cours du Chapeau Rouge are open on weekdays, with a few open Saturday morning. American Express (☎ 05 56 00 63 33, fax 05 56 00 63 39), 14 cours de l'Intendance, is open to from 8.45 am to noon and 1.30 to 6 pm on weekdays.

Post The main post office is at 52 rue Georges Bonnac. Branch offices include place St-Projet (on rue Ste-Catherine) and 29 Allées de Tourny. All are open until at least 6 pm on weekdays and until noon on Saturday.

Email & Internet Access Aquitaine Europe Communication (☎ 05 56 01 76 76) at the Cité Mondiale, 23 Parvis des Chartrons, offers one hour's free internet access per person per day. It's open from 2 to 6 pm Monday to Friday.

France Telecom's Esp@ce Internet (☎ 08 00 35 23 19), at the corner of rue Judaïque and rue du Château d'Eau, open from noon to 7 pm Monday to Saturday, charges 30FF per hour of online time (students 20FF).

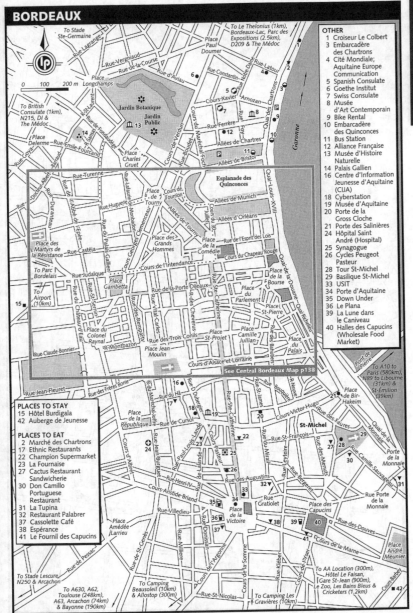

BORDEAUX

To Le Thelonius (1km),
Bordeaux-Lac, Parc des
Expositions (2.5km),
D209 & The Médoc

To Stade
Ste-Germaine

To British
Consulate (1km),
N215, DI &
The Médoc

To Parc
Bordelais

To
Airport
(10km)

To Stade Lescure,
N250 & Arcachon

To A630, A62,
Toulouse (248km),
A63, Arcachon (74km)
& Bayonne (190km)

To Camping
Beausoleil (10km)
& Allostop (300m)

To Camping Les
Gravières (10km)

To AA Location (300m),
Hôtel Le Faisan,
Gare St-Jean (900m),
Le Zoo, Les Bains Bleus &
Cricketers (1.2km)

To A10 to
Paris (580km),
N89 to Libourne
(31km) &
St-Emilion
(39km)

Jardin Botanique

Jardin
Public

Esplanade des
Quinc:onces

St-Michel

See Central Bordeaux Map p138

OTHER
1 Croiseur Le Colbert
3 Embarcadère
   des Chartrons
4 Cité Mondiale;
   Aquitaine Europe
   Communication
5 Spanish Consulate
6 Goethe Institut
7 Swiss Consulate
8 Musée
   d'Art Contemporain
9 Bike Rental
10 Embarcadère
   des Quinconces
11 Bus Station
12 Alliance Française
13 Musée d'Histoire
   Naturelle
14 Palais Gallien
16 Centre d'Information
   Jeunesse d'Aquitaine
   (CIJA)
17 Cyberstation
19 Musée d'Aquitaine
20 Porte de la
   Gross Cloche
21 Porte des Salinières
24 Hôpital Saint
   André (Hospital)
25 Synagogue
26 Cycles Peugeot
   Pasteur
28 Tour St-Michel
29 Basilique St-Michel
33 USIT
34 Porte d'Aquitaine
35 Down Under
36 Le Plana
39 La Lune dans
   le Caniveau
40 Halles des Capucins
   (Wholesale Food
   Market)

PLACES TO STAY
15 Hôtel Burdigala
42 Auberge de Jeunesse

PLACES TO EAT
2 Marché des Chartrons
17 Ethnic Restaurants
22 Champion Supermarket
23 La Fournaise
27 Cactus Restaurant
   Sandwicherie
30 Don Camillo
   Portuguese
   Restaurant
31 La Tupina
32 Restaurant Palabrer
37 Cassolette Café
38 Espérance
41 Le Fournil des Capucins

CENTRAL BORDEAUX

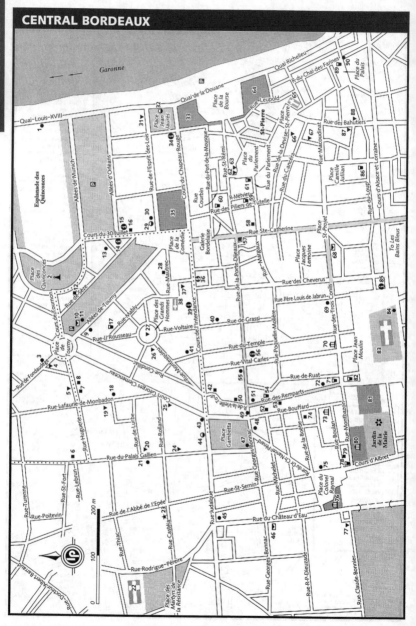

CENTRAL BORDEAUX

PLACES TO STAY
6   Hôtel Dauphin
7   Hôtel Studio
8   Hôtel Touring
12 Hôtel Royal Médoc
16 Hôtel des 4 Soeurs
28 Hôtel Blayais
42 Hôtel de la Tour Intendance
50 Hôtel d'Amboise
52 Hôtel Bristol
53 Hôtel de Lyon
57 Hôtel de la Presse
58 Quality Hôtel Ste-Catherine
74 Hôtel La Boëtie
79 Hôtel Boulan

PLACES TO EAT
4   Fromagerie Antonin
5   Restaurant Baud et Millet
19 Le Flambeau
20 Cassolette Café
24 Restaurant Agadir
25 La Crêperie
26 Bar-Brasserie des Grands Hommes
27 Marché des Grands Hommes; Food Market
31 Jean Ramet
37 La Chanterelle
62 Café de la Place
63 Chez Édouard
66 Saveur Latine Restaurant
67 Didier Gélineau

77 Auchan Supermarket; Centre Commercial Mériadeck
87 Au Clair de Lune
88 Le Médiéval

OTHER
1   Bike Rental
2   Monument aux Girondins
3   Espace Laverie (Laundrette)
9   Air France
10 Post Office
11 Nouvelles Frontières
13 Bordeaux Magnum
14 Maison du Vin de Bordeaux
15 Tourist Office; Vinothèque
17 La Factory
18 Lavarie Lincoln (Laundrette)
21 Lavarie Lincoln (Laundrette)
22 Basilique St-Seurin
23 Hôtel de Police
29 Buses for Airport
30 Air France
32 Urban Bus Station
33 Bourse du Commerce
34 CGFTE Bus Information Kiosk
35 Grand Théâtre
36 American Express
38 Église Notre Dame
39 La Maison du Tourisme de la Gironde
40 Théâtre Femina
41 Cinéma Trianon
43 Bordeaux Language Studies
44 Buses for Airport

45 Esp@ce Internet
46 Post Office
47 CGFTE Kiosk
48 Virgin Megastore
49 Porte Dijeaux
51 Bouquets de Chocolats de Bayonne
54 Le Moyen Age
55 Librairie Mollat
56 La Maison des Pyrénées
59 Calle Ocho
60 Bodega Bodega
61 XO Café
64 Hôtel des Douanes
65 Église St Pierre
68 Post Office
69 FNAC
70 Centre National Jean Moulin
71 Seven Café
72 Occitane
73 Musée des Arts Décoratifs
75 Bradley's Bookshop
76 Galerie des Beaux-Arts
78 Connemara
80 Musée des Beaux-Arts
81 Hôtel de Ville
82 BHV
83 Cathédrale St-André
84 Tour Pey-Berland
85 Centre d'Information Jeunesse d'Aquitaine (CIJA)
86 L'Aztecal
89 La Reine Carotte
90 Porte Cailhau

Cyberstation (☎ 05 56 01 15 15, email info@cyberstation.fr), 23 cours Pasteur, is open from 11 am to 2 am daily (from 2 pm to midnight on Sunday) and charges 25/40FF for 30/60 minutes (30FF per hour from noon to 2 pm and 7 to 9 pm).

Travel Agencies Nouvelles Frontières (☎ 05 56 79 65 85, fax 05 56 79 06 87), 31 allées de Tourny, offers a wide range of special air fare promotions. Usit CONNECT (☎ 05 56 33 89 90, fax 05 56 33 89 91, email usitconnect@usit.ie), 284 rue Ste-Catherine, sells ISIC cards and cheap air fares. CIJA (see earlier in this Information section) also has an efficient travel agency.

Bookshops Bordeaux's biggest bookshop is Librairie Mollat (☎ 05 56 56 40 40),

15 rue Vital Carles, stocking books on Bordeaux and the region, plus CDs and cassettes. It's open from 9.15 am to 7 pm Monday to Saturday. Bradley's Bookshop (☎ 05 56 52 10 57), 8 cours d'Albret, sells a wide selection of English-language books. It's open from 9.30 am to 12.30 pm and 2 to 7 pm (closed Monday morning and Sunday).

Cultural Centres The library at the Goethe Institut (☎ 05 56 48 42 60, fax 05 56 48 42 66, email goetbxp@easynet.fr), 35 cours de Verdun, is open from 2 to 6.30 pm Monday and Friday and from 9 am to noon and 2 to 8 pm Tuesday to Thursday (to 6.30 pm on Wednesday).

Laundry Three laundrettes open daily are Espace Laverie, 5 rue de Fondaudège (from

7 am to 8 pm), Lavarie Lincoln at 31 rue de Palais Gallien (from 8 am to 8 pm), and another on rue Lafaurie de Monbadon (from 7 am to 9 pm).

Medical Services & Emergency Hôpital Saint André (☎ 05 56 79 56 79 ext 43230), 1 rue Jean Burguet, is open 24 hours. The Hôtel de Police (police station; 05 56 99 77 77) is at 29 rue Castéja; other police stations are at place de la Victoire (☎ 05 56 94 27 64) and Gare St-Jean (☎ 05 56 91 34 88).

Walking Tour

The landscaped **Jardin Public** along cours de Verdun, established in 1755, includes a meticulously catalogued **Jardin Botanique** (☎ 05 56 52 18 77), founded in 1629; it's open from 8 am to 6 pm (7 pm in summer). Nearby, off rue de Fondaudège, is the city's most impressive Roman site, the **Palais Gallien**, the ruins of a 3rd-century amphitheatre. From here head south, joining rue du Palais Gallien. Turn left into rue Huguerie and walk straight along until you come to the vast **Esplanade des Quinconces**. This was once the site of the fortress-like Chateau Trompette, built in 1691 but demolished less than a century later to create this dull square (see the boxed text 'Monument aux Girondins').

From the southern side of the Esplanade walk south down cours du 30 Juillet. An architectural highlight on the place de la

---

Monument aux Girondins

By far the most interesting thing in place des Quinconces is the exuberant 1902 Monument aux Girondins, dedicated to a group of moderate National Assembly deputies executed for trying to moderate the French Revolution. The entire ensemble was dismantled by the Nazis for its 52 tonnes of bronze, but the train carrying it away was bombed by the Résistance. It wasn't until 1983, when Bordeaux's mayor, Jacques Chaban-Delmas, needed a few votes, that restoration was completed.

Comédie is the neoclassical **Grand Théâtre**, designed by Parisian architect Victor Louis in the 1770s, with a Corinthian colonnade decorated with 12 figures of the Muses and Graces outside, and some fantastic decor inside. The nearby, lifeless **riverside area** is the focus of an ambitious redevelopment scheme by architect Dominique Perrault, who plans to transform both banks of the river into 30 hectares of parkland and promenades.

The **St-Pierre district** to the south-east, once a separate walled quarter and later a medieval merchants' enclave, is now the heart of a lively ethnic restaurant and cafe district with some fine 18th-century *hôtels particuliers* (town houses), for example in place St-Pierre.

The main shopping area is westwards along **cours de l'Intendance**, pedestrianised **rue de la Porte Dijeaux**, and especially **rue Ste-Catherine**, chock-a-block with fashion shops, cafes and department stores. The latter two streets were once major Gallo-Roman thoroughfares. **Galerie Bordelaise**, an ornate 19th-century shopping arcade, is at the intersection of rue de la Porte Dijeaux and rue Ste-Catherine. Nowadays **place Gambetta** is a lively centre with lots of cafes and bar-brasseries, but during the Reign of Terror after the Revolution a guillotine severed 300 counter-Revolutionary heads here.

Museums

The outstanding **Musée d'Aquitaine** (Museum of Aquitaine; ☎ 05 56 01 51 00), 20 cours Pasteur, presents 25,000 years of history and ethnography. Exceptional artefacts include several prehistoric stone carvings of women and a collection of Gallo-Roman steles, statues and ceramics. A booklet (available in English for a 10FF deposit) explains the exhibits; signs are minimal.

The collection of the **Musée des Beaux-Arts** (Fine Arts Museum; ☎ 05 56 10 16 93), 20 cours d'Albret, in two wings of the 1770s Hôtel de Ville, includes 17th-century Flemish, Dutch and Italian paintings. Around the block at place du Colonel Raynal, an annexe called the **Galerie des Beaux-Arts** (☎ 05 56 96 51 60) hosts short-term exhibitions. The nearby **Musée des**

Arts Décoratifs (Museum of Decorative Arts; ☎ 05 56 00 72 50), 39 rue Bouffard, specialises in faïence, porcelain, silverwork, glasswork, furniture and the like.

Entrepôts Lainé, built in 1824 as a warehouse for exotic products of France's colonies, now houses the **Musée d'Art Contemporain** (Museum of Contemporary Art; ☎ 05 56 00 81 50); the entrance is opposite 16 rue Ferrère. The **Musée d'Histoire Naturelle** (Natural History Museum; ☎ 05 56 48 26 37) is on the south-western edge of the nearby Jardin Public.

The **Centre National Jean Moulin** (Jean Moulin Documentation Centre; ☎ 05 56 79 66 00), facing the northern side of Cathédrale St-André, has exhibits on France during WWII. **Croiseur Le Colbert** (☎ 05 56 44 96 11), a French navy missile cruiser decommissioned in 1991, is now permanently docked at quai des Chartrons. You can explore it from 10 am to 6 pm daily (to 7 pm at weekends; closed Monday from October to March) for 42FF (31FF for children aged five to 16; reduced charges also for families, students and seniors).

Cathédrale St-André

In 1137, the future King Louis VII married Eleanor of Aquitaine in this cathedral, recently made a UNESCO World Heritage Site along with the Basiliques de St-Seurin and St-Michel, all important sites on the pilgrimage route to Santiago de Compostela (see the boxed text 'The Pilgrims of St-Jacques' under Religion in the Facts about South-West France chapter). The exterior wall of the nave dates from 1096, most of the rest from the 13th and 14th centuries. The interior can be visited from 10 am noon and 2 to 5 pm daily except Monday (10 am to 6 pm daily between June and September).

The 15th-century belfry, the **Tour Pey-Berland**, behind the choir, is open from 10 am to 6.30 pm daily between June and October, and from 10 am to 12.30 pm and 2 to 5.30 pm daily except Monday during the rest of the year; admission costs 25FF.

Basilique St-Seurin

One of Bordeaux's oldest sacred sites, the place des Martyrs de la Résistance where the Basilique St-Seurin now stands was once the site of a Gallo-Roman cemetery and church. The basilica dates from the 11th century, with many later additions, notably from the 18th and 19th centuries. Look at the 11th- to 14th-century carvings on and above the central door and the 7th-century sarcophagus (now the altar) in the chapel of St-Étienne. Under the crypt is a 4th-century **Paleo-Christian site**, open from 3 to 7 pm daily from mid-June to mid-September; admission costs 10FF.

Basilique St-Michel

This Gothic basilica, finished in the mid-16th century, took 200 years to build. Check out the chapels for fine sculptures, paintings and carved altarpieces. The separate belfry, the 114m-high, late-15th-century **Tour St-Michel**, is the tallest tower in the region. You can climb to a 47m-high look-out point between 3 and 7 pm daily from mid-June to mid-September (10FF). Now at the heart of a vibrant Portuguese-North African quarter, it also overlooks a fantastic flea market (see Shopping later in this section).

Porte de la Grosse Cloche & Porte Cailhau

The 15th-century Grosse Cloche (Big Bell) clock-tower-cum-gateway spans the ancient road to Compostela, rue St-James. It was restored in the 19th century and has recently been spruced up again.

On the edge of the St-Pierre district, on place du Palais, Porte Cailhau is the city's other ornate 15th-century gateway. Its historical displays can be seen from 3 to 7 pm daily from mid-June to mid-September for 10FF. The top floor has a great view.

Place de la Bourse

This square boasts the city's finest ensemble of 18th-century architecture. On the northern side is the Palais de la Bourse (now housing the Chambre de Commerce or Chamber of Commerce), to the south the Hôtel des Douanes (customs house). At the centre is La Fontaine des Trois Grâces, representing Queen Victoria, Empress Eugénie and the Queen of Spain.

Synagogue

The architecture of this synagogue (☎ 05 56 91 79 39) on rue du Grand Rabbin Joseph Cohen is a mix of Sephardic and Byzantine styles. Inaugurated in 1882, it was ripped apart and turned into a prison by the Nazis but painstakingly rebuilt after the war. Visits are possible from 5 to 6 or 6.30 pm Monday to Thursday; ring the bell marked *gardien* at 213 rue Ste-Catherine.

Activities for Children

Pick up the free quarterly *Clubs & Comptines* from the tourist office, with details of events, facilities and courses for kids around Bordeaux. In the city centre, the Jardin Public (take bus No 7 or 8 from place Gambetta) and Parc Bordelais (about 2km north-west of the centre; take bus No 17 or 18 from place Jean Jaurès) have playgrounds. A good adventure-style playground and a carousel are on the quai des Chartrons near Croiseur Le Colbert; a larger carousel is opposite the tourist office.

What's Free

On the first Sunday of every month, all the museums offer free admission. Also on this day you can rent bikes for free (see Bicycle under Getting Around later in this section).

Organised Tours

The tourist office runs a wide range of guided tours, including good two-hour **walking tours** of the city centre, with French and English commentary, at 10 am daily (40FF; students and seniors 35FF).

River cruises from Embarcadère des Quinconces include daily ones from 11 am to 6.30 pm with a lunch stop (130FF or 185FF with meal) and dinner cruises from 9 pm to midnight (200FF); contact Alienor (☎ 05 56 51 27 90) for details. Le Burdigala – La Maison du Fleuve (☎ 05 56 20 06 40) run occasional evening wine-tasting cruises (230FF). Ville de Bordeaux (☎/fax 05 56 52 88 88) run slightly cheaper daytime cruises starting at 80FF.

Special Events

A major event is the Foire Internationale de Bordeaux (☎ 08 36 69 61 62), an international trade fair in May featuring 10 days of music, drama and other events at the Parc des Expositions, Bordeaux-Lac.

In June there's the Gay Pride festival (☎ 05 56 01 12 03) and in even-numbered years the Fête du Vin (Wine Fair; ☎ 05 56 00 66 00), a three-day event with stalls and wine-tasting at place de la Bourse and elsewhere. The new Fête du Fleuve (River Celebration; (☎ 05 56 00 66 00) promises to enliven the city's quaysides for four days in late June. For information in English ask at the tourist office.

In October, the Fête du Vin Nouveau et de la Brocante (☎ 05 56 81 50 25) celebrates *vin nouveau* (still-fermenting white wine, traditionally enjoyed with hot chestnuts). It's organised by *brocante* (bric-a-brac) shops on rue Notre Dame where the festival takes place.

For exact dates, contact the tourist office.

Places to Stay – Budget

Bordeaux has lots of reasonably priced hotels. You're better off *not* staying in the seedy area around Gare St-Jean.

Camping At *Camping Beausoleil* (☎ 05 56 89 17 66, 371 cours du Général de Gaulle), about 10km south-west of the city centre in Gradignan, *forfait* (fixed price deal covering two people) rates are 66FF or 85FF with a car. Take bus G from place de la Victoire towards Gradignan Beausoleil and get off at the last stop. The camp site is open year-round.

Camping Les Gravières (☎ 05 56 87 00 36, place de Courréjean) is 10km south-east of the city in Villenave d'Ornon and charges 19/22/ 16FF per adult/tent/car. Take bus B from place de la Victoire towards Courréjean and get off at the terminus. Les Gravières is also open year-round.

Hostels The *Auberge de Jeunesse* (☎ 05 56 91 59 51, fax 05 56 94 02 98, 22 cours Barbey) charges 62FF (72FF without a Hostelling International card) per bed in segregated dorms. Curfew is 11 pm except by prior arrangement. Reception is staffed from 8 to 10 am and 3 to 11 pm, but bags can be dropped off any time except between noon and 2 pm.

At the time of writing, the hostel was closed for renovations and is unlikely to re-open before 2001.

Hotels Plain but good value, the *Hôtel de Lyon* (☎ 05 56 81 34 38, fax 05 56 52 92 82, 31 rue des Remparts) is just south-east of place Gambetta, where buses from the airport and Gare St-Jean stop. Doubles/twins/triples with toilet and shower cost 135/160/180FF; breakfast costs 18FF. Its sister hotel with the same rates is *Hôtel d'Amboise* (☎ 05 56 81 62 67, fax 05 56 52 92 82, 22 rue de la Vieille Tour).

The quiet *Hôtel Boulan* (☎/fax 05 56 52 23 62, 28 rue Boulan) has modest doubles without/with shower for 110/140FF; hall showers cost 10FF. At *Hôtel La Boëtie* (☎ 05 56 81 76 68, fax 05 56 81 24 72, 4 rue de la Boëtie), plain, modern doubles/triples with toilet and shower start at 160/180FF. *Hôtel Blayais* (☎ 05 56 48 17 87, fax 05 56 52 47 57, 17 rue Mautrec) has big simple singles/doubles with shower and toilet costing 190/220FF.

North of the city centre (take bus No 7 or 8 from Gare St-Jean) is a clutch of cheapies, the best of them being the friendly

Hôtel Touring (☎ 05 56 81 56 73, 16 rue Huguerie), where spotless doubles without/ with toilet and shower cost 140/220FF; hall showers cost 15FF and breakfast is 26FF.

Hôtel Studio (☎ 05 56 48 00 14, fax 05 56 81 25 71, email studio@hotel-bordeaux .com, 26 rue Huguerie) is the headquarters of Bordeaux's cheap-hotel empire: the family owns three other places nearby. Charmless, small but serviceable singles/doubles with flimsy shower, toilet, mini-fridge and cable TV start at 98/120FF; rooms for between three and five people cost from 180FF to 250FF.

Places to Stay – Mid-Range

Good value in this range is *Hôtel Dauphin* (☎ 05 56 52 24 62, fax 05 56 01 10 91, 82 rue du Palais Gallien), where bright, high-ceilinged singles/doubles/triples with toilet and shower cost 179/189/209FF; breakfast is 25FF.

At the central *Hôtel Bristol* (☎ 05 56 81 85 01, fax 05 56 51 24 06, email bristol@ hotel-bordeaux.com, 2 rue Bouffard) cheerful doubles/triples with bathroom, toilet and minibar start at 210/280FF. Comfortable, soundproofed rooms at *Hôtel Royal Médoc* (☎ 05 56 81 72 42, fax 05 56 51 74 98, 3 rue de Sèze) cost 250/310FF for doubles/triples with bathroom.

Friendly, well-run *Hôtel de la Tour Intendance* (☎ 05 56 81 46 27, fax 05 56 81 60 90, 1416 rue de la Vieille Tour) has functional rooms with toilet and shower starting at 250/370FF; off-street parking costs 40FF.

At *Hôtel des 4 Soeurs* (☎ 05 57 81 19 20, fax 05 56 01 04 28, 6 cours du 30 Juillet), by the tourist office, immaculate singles/ doubles with mini-bar, TV and telephone start at 240/350FF (330/400FF with bath). Doubles/twins/triples with bigger beds at *Hôtel de la Presse* (☎ 05 56 48 53 88, fax 05 56 01 05 82, 68 rue de la Porte Dijeaux) start at 390/440/480FF or 465/480/520FF with bath; breakfast costs 40FF.

Facing Gare St-Jean, *Hôtel Le Faisan* (☎ 05 56 91 54 52, fax 05 56 92 93 83, 28 rue Charles Domercq) has pleasant doubles/triples with shower, toilet and TV for 270/330FF.

Places to Stay – Top End

A modest and central choice is *Quality Hôtel Ste-Catherine* (☎ 05 56 81 95 12, fax 05 56 44 50 51, email quality.bordeaux@ wanadoo.fr, 27 rue du Parlement Ste-Catherine) where smallish doubles with TV, air-con and tartan carpets cost 430/600FF with shower/bath; a buffet breakfast is 70FF and off-street parking is available.

The five-star *Hôtel Burdigala* (☎ 05 56 90 16 16, fax 05 56 93 15 06, email burdigala@burdigala.com, 115 rue Georges Bonnac), in a renovated 18th-century building, offers all the frills (including Internet access in the rooms). You won't get much change from 1000FF for a double.

Places to Eat

Those on a strict budget will find cheap *cafes* and take-away *sandwich* and *kebab bars* at the southern end of rue Ste-Catherine, along rue du Palais Gallien and in the ethnic districts of St-Michel and St-Pierre.

Restaurants – Budget & Mid-Range
French The *Cassolette Café* (☎ 05 56 92 94 96, 20 place de la Victoire) offers great value in family-style French food: small/large *cassolettes* (plates) cost 12/ 36FF. It's open for lunch and dinner daily except Sunday. A central branch (☎ 05 56 51 17 09, 26 rue du Palais Gallien) is open on Sunday night but closed Saturday and Sunday lunchtimes.

The very popular *Chez Édouard* (☎ 05 56 81 48 87, 16 place du Parlement), open daily, offers French bistro-style meat and fish dishes, with *menus* starting at 69FF and a 57FF lunchtime *express menu*. Its neighbour, the unpretentious *Café de la Place* (☎ 05 56 48 12 85), is slightly cheaper.

La Chanterelle (☎ 05 56 81 75 43, 3 rue de Martignac) serves moderately priced traditional French and regional cuisine, with lunch *menus* starting at 69FF and a 120FF evening *menu*; it's closed on Wednesday night and Sunday. Dishes at *Bar-Brasserie des Grands Hommes* (☎ 05 56 81 18 26, 10 place des Grands Hommes), by the shopping mall of the same name, start at 60FF.

Restaurant Baud et Millet (☎ 05 56 79 05 77, 19 rue Huguerie), open from 9 am to midnight (closed Sunday), serves cheese-based, mostly vegetarian cuisine, including an all-you-can-eat 110FF buffet and *menus* starting at 140FF. This area has several other tempting restaurants including *Le Flambeau* (☎ 05 56 44 31 03, 29 rue Lafaurie de Monbadon), open until 11 pm daily. It offers 50FF kangaroo-meat kebabs plus good-value midday *menus express* starting at 45FF. *La Crêperie* (☎ 05 56 48 54 47, 23 cours George Clemenceau) is open from noon to midnight daily serving delicious *galettes* (wheat pancakes, with plenty of vegetarian choices) and crepes, and even has a no-smoking area.

Restaurants – Top End French
Classic French and Bordelais cuisine is served at *Jean Ramet* (☎ 05 56 44 12 51, 7 place Jean Jaurès) amid mirrors, white tablecloths and sparkling tableware. Lunch/dinner *menus* start at 160/260FF. It's closed Saturday lunchtime and Sunday.

La Tupina (☎ 05 56 91 56 37, 6–8 rue porte de la Monnaie) has simple decor and lavish *menus*: 100FF for lunch or 250FF for the evening *menu de saison* (seasonally changing *menus*). It's open until 2 am daily (book ahead for the 180FF Sunday lunch).

Didier Gélineau (☎ 05 56 52 84 25, 26 rue du Pas St-Georges) has a modern setting and cuisine with fantastic, seasonally changing lunch/dinner *menus* de saison starting at 120/150FF. The desserts are out of this world. It's closed Saturday lunchtime and Sunday.

Restaurants – Other
At *La Fournaise* (☎ 05 56 91 04 71, 23 rue de Lalande) the speciality is the cuisine of Réunion Island, which has strong Indian, Chinese, Basque and Breton elements. *Menus* start at 55/ 75FF (weekday lunch/dinner). It's closed Sunday and Monday.

Restaurant Palabrer (☎ 05 56 92 77 32, 9 rue Gratiolet) serves simple, tasty African food at a modest 39FF per dish, from 7.30 pm to 2 am Tuesday to Saturday. At *Restaurant Agadir* (☎ 05 56 52 28 04, 14 rue du Palais Gallien) Moroccan couscous and *tajines* (spicy North African stews) cost from 70FF to 90FF and lunch/dinner *menus* start at 60/100FF.

In the Portuguese and North African St-Michel district, try the 52FF lunch *menu* at *Don Camillo Portuguese Restaurant (☎ 05 56 91 31 50, 7 rue Camille Sauvageau)*, or kefta (kebab with minced meat, onion and parsley) or doner kebab for less than 20FF at the *Cactus Restaurant Sandwicherie (1 rue Gaspard Philippe)*.

An even richer culinary pot is the St-Pierre district. *Au Clair de Lune (☎ 05 56 81 09 18, rue des Bahutiers)* serves Berber (North African) specialities daily except Tuesday. *Le Médiéval (☎ 05 56 48 22 81, 42 rue des Bahutiers)* offers Lebanese dishes daily except Sunday. For Tex-Mex delights, head for *Saveur Latine Restaurant (☎ 05 56 51 02 75, 3 rue de la Devise)* where lunch/dinner *menus* start at 45/69FF. It's closed Sunday lunchtime.

Near the Musée d'Aquitaine on rue du Hâ are *restaurants* serving Vietnamese, Indian, Lebanese and other cuisines. A selection of *Chinese restaurants* are along rue St-Rémi, a block north of place du Parlement.

Self-Catering The upmarket food stalls in the basement of the *Marché des Grands Hommes (place des Grands Hommes)* open from 7 am to 7.30 pm Monday to Saturday. The Sunday-only *Marché des Chartrons*, beside Croiseur Le Colbert, sells seafood and superb pre-prepared food (with places to sit and consume them) as well as general produce.

The city's best cheese shop, *Fromagerie Antonin (6 rue de Fondaudège)* is open from 8.30 am to 12.45 pm and 4 to 7.30 pm (closed Monday morning and Sunday, and on Saturday afternoon in July and August). *Le Fournil des Capucins (62–64 cours de la Marne)* is a 24-hour boulangerie. *Espérance (10 cours de la Marne)*, a grocery shop, is open daily until midnight (2 am on Thursday, Friday and Saturday nights).

Two supermarkets open into the evening (closed all day Sunday) are *Auchan*, in the Centre Commercial Mériadeck off rue du Château d'Eau, and *Champion*, 190 rue Ste-Catherine.

Entertainment

Bordeaux bops at night; details on venues and events appear in the *Clubs & Concerts* brochure, free from the tourist office and CIJA, and in other what's-on periodicals (see Information earlier in this section). Student nightlife centres around place de la Victoire.

Buy tickets for concerts and sporting events at the Virgin Megastore (☎ 05 56 56 05 55), 17 place Gambetta, open until 8 pm (midnight on Friday and Saturday, 7 pm on Sunday), and at FNAC (see Shopping later in this section), open Monday to Saturday to 7 pm.

Cinemas Nondubbed films are often screened at *Cinéma Trianon (☎ 05 56 44 35 17, 6 rue Franklin)*, also known as Centre Jean Vigo. Most cinema tickets cost about 34FF (27FF on Wednesday).

Classical Music The 18th-century *Grand Théâtre (☎ 05 56 48 58 54, place de la Comédie)* stages operas, ballets and concerts. The ticket office, which also handles ticketing for plays, dance performances and variety shows at *Théâtre Femina (rue de Grassi)*, is open from 11 am to 6 pm Monday to Saturday.

Bars Except as noted, the following bars stay open until 2 am, and are closed on Sundays. The *Down Under (☎ 05 56 94 52 48, 104 cours Aristide Briand)*, run by an ex-Aucklander, serves up Foster's and twice-monthly theme parties. *Calle Ocho (☎ 05 56 48 08 68, 24 rue des Piliers de Tutelle)* offers Cuban cigars costing from 25FF to 100FF and seductive mixed drinks. The popular tapas bar *Bodega Bodega (☎ 05 56 01 24 24, 4 rue des Piliers de Tutelle)* is open from noon to 3.15 pm and 7 pm to 2 am (closed for lunch on Sunday and holidays). The *Connemara (☎ 05 56 52 82 57, 18 cours d'Albret)* has big screen football, darts, pool, regular live Irish music and a restaurant serving Irish and English grub. It's open from midday (from 6 pm on Sunday).

Clubs & Live Music South-east of the city centre, *Le Zoo (☎ 05 56 85 71 85, 48 quai* *de Paludate)* attracts a young crowd with techno, dance and house tracks, from 11 pm to 5 am on Thursday, Friday and Saturday nights, for 20FF. *Les Bains Bleus (☎ 05 56 85 71 85, 1418 rue de Commerce)* attracts older clubbers on the same nights, from midnight to 6 am; admission costs 50FF including a drink. For hardcore punk, reggae and ska – live about twice a month – try *La Lune dans le Caniveau (☎ 05 56 31 95 92, 39 place des Capucins)*, open from 11 pm to 5 am Wednesday to Saturday. Admission is free except for some concerts.

Cricketers (☎ 05 56 49 69 56, 72 quai de Paludate) features live, sometimes big-name blues two or three times a week (from 40FF to 80FF). It's open from 6 pm to 5 am daily. *Le Plana (☎ 05 56 91 73 23, 22 place de la Victoire)*, hugely popular with students, has live jazz at 10 pm every Sunday, and pop and funk at 10.30 pm on most Mondays and Tuesdays; it's open to 2 am daily. Another jazz venue, *Le Thelonius (☎ 05 56 11 00 50, 18 rue Bourbon)*, warms up at about 10 pm most nights. It's north of the city: take bus No 8 from place Gambetta to the end of the line.

XO Café (☎ 05 56 01 12 43, 11 rue du Parlement Ste-Catherine) is a DJ bar featuring everything from 70s to hip hop and soul, open from 6 pm to 2 am Tuesday to Saturday. *L'Aztecal (☎ 05 56 44 50 18, 61 rue Pas St-Georges)* plays salsa, latino, soul and motown from 11 pm to 5 am.

Gay & Lesbian Venues Mellow *Le Moyen Age (☎ 05 56 44 12 87, 8 rue des Remparts)*, one of France's oldest gay bars, is open from 10 pm to 2 am (closed Tuesday). *BHV (☎ 05 56 44 05 08, 4 rue de l'Hôtel de Ville)* is open from 11.30 am daily (6 pm on weekends) to 2 am, with a transvestites' night every few Sundays at 11 pm.

La Factory (☎ 05 56 01 10 11, 28 rue Mably) is a mainly gay disco, open from midnight to 5 am daily, with a 50FF cover charge on Friday and Saturday. *Seven Café (☎ 05 56 48 13 79, 73 rue des Trois Conils)* is open from 6 pm to 2 am daily, and its basement disco kicks off on Saturday and Sunday morning after La Factory closes, until noon or 1 pm.

La Reine Carotte (☎ 05 56 01 26 68, 32 rue du Chai des Farines) is a lesbian bar open on Friday and Saturday nights.

Spectator Sports

Bordeaux's football team, Girondins de Bordeaux, is the region's best, with (almost) championship-quality playing. Catch them at Stade Lescure on place Johnston, southwest of town. Rugby enthusiasts will find Stade Bordelais UC playing at Stade Ste-Germaine, rue Ferdinand de Lesseps. For ticket outlets, see Entertainment.

Shopping

Bordeaux wine in all price ranges is on sale at several speciality shops near the tourist office, including Bordeaux Magnum (☎ 05 56 48 00 06), 3 rue Gobineau, and Vinothèque (☎ 05 56 52 32 05), 8 cours du 30 Juillet. Speciality shops on rue des Remparts include Occitane at No 68, selling deluxe Périgord groceries, and Bouquets de Chocolats de Bayonne at No 6.

For low-brow antiques and junk, go to the flea market by Basilique St-Michel, which is active from 8 am to 5 pm Tuesday to Friday and from 8 am to 1 pm on Sunday – especially the second Sunday of March, June, September and December. The tourist office has a list of other markets.

For CDs, cassettes, CD-ROMs and computer gear go to FNAC (☎ 05 56 00 21 30), in Centre St-Christoly, 17 rue Père Louis de Jabrun.

Getting There & Away

Air Bordeaux's international airport (☎ 05 56 34 50 50) is 10km west of the centre at Mérignac.

Air France and Air Liberté together operate nearly two dozen flights a day to Bordeaux from Paris (mainly Orly airport). There are also daily or almost-daily flights from at least 17 other French cities, and from Barcelona, Basel, Brussels, Geneva, Madrid, Munich and Rome. British Airways flies three times a day from London Gatwick.

Air France (☎ 05 56 00 40 40 or toll-free ☎ 0 802 802 802) has offices at 29 rue de l'Esprit des Lois and 44 allées de Tourny. Other airlines are represented only at the airport. See the Getting There & Away chapter for details, and for booking numbers.

Bus The main bus station, with connections around Gironde and into nearby départements, is on Esplanade des Quinconces. Citram Aquitaine (☎ 05 56 43 68 67, 05 56 43 68 44) runs most buses. The information kiosk (☎ 05 56 43 68 43) is open from 7 to 8.30 am (from 6 am on Monday) and 1 to 8.30 pm weekdays, 9 am to 12.30 pm and 5 to 8.30 pm on Saturday, and 8.30 to 10.30 am and 5 to 8.30 pm on Sunday.

Several bus companies run infrequent services to the Landes and Côte d'Argent destinations from Gare St-Jean: RDTL (☎ 05 58 56 80 80) has one per weekday to Mont de Marsan; Rapides de la Côte d'Argent (☎ 05 58 09 10 89) goes to Biscarrosse, and Cars Ouest Aquitaine (☎ 05 56 70 12 13) runs to Lacanau. For details of buses to the Médoc and St-Émilion see Getting There & Away for those towns later in this chapter.

Eurolines (☎ 05 56 92 50 42), facing Gare St-Jean at 32 rue Charles Domercq, is open from 9 am to noon and 2 to 7 pm Monday to Saturday. You can also buy Eurolines tickets at CIJA (see Information earlier in this section).

Train The train station, Gare St-Jean (☎ 08 36 35 35 35), is about 3km south-east of the city centre, and is served by bus Nos 7 and 8. The SNCF information office at Gate 14 is open from 9 am to 7 pm (closed Sunday and holidays). The left-luggage office at Gate 54 is open from 8 am to 12.15 pm and 1.30 to 8 pm daily, and lockers are available from 7 am to 10.30 pm (to 8.30 pm Saturday; from 9 am Sunday).

Regional destinations served by multiple daily direct trains include Bayonne (133FF), Bergerac (78FF), Brive-la-Gaillarde (135FF, most changing at Périgueux), Sarlat (118FF) and Toulouse (163FF). For information on getting to the Médoc, St-Émilion and Arcachon, see Getting There & Away for those towns later in this chapter. Paris is served by Corail (to Gare d'Austerlitz; 295FF) and TGV (Gare Montparnasse; 345FF).

Car Major car rental agencies, represented at the airport and Gare St-Jean, include Europcar (☎ 05 56 34 05 79), Budget (☎ 05 56 47 84 22), Hertz (☎ 05 56 34 59 59) and the cheaper French company ADA (☎ 05 56 31 21 11). Another car rental agency AA Location (☎ 05 56 92 84 78) is at 185 cours de la Marne.

Getting Around
To/From the Airport (☎ 05 56 34 50 50) shuttles between Gare St-Jean, bus stops opposite the Grand Théâtre (29 rue de l'Esprit des Lois) and place Gambetta, and the airport every 30/45 minutes on weekdays/weekends from 5.30 am until 9.30 pm (last departure from the airport at 10.45 pm). The trip takes around 30 minutes and costs 35FF one-way (people under 26 and seniors 27FF). Inbound, the bus stops wherever you want; no announcements are made, so get a city map from the airport's tourist office. For a taxi to the airport (around 150FF), call ☎ 05 56 97 11 27.

Bus Bordeaux's urban bus network, Compagnie Génerale Français des Transports d'Enterprise (CGFTE; ☎ 05 57 57 88 88) has information kiosks at Gare St-Jean, place Gambetta (4 rue Georges Bonnac) and place Jean Jaurès. They, and sometimes *tabacs* (tobacconists), can provide an easy-to-use *Plan Poche* (pocket route map).

Single tickets sold on board cost 7.50FF and no transfers are allowed. With tickets from a prepaid carnet of 10 (54.50FF), available at tabacs and CGFTE kiosks, you can transfer up to three times; you must time-stamp the ticket each time you board and you may be asked to show the numbered *talon* (coupon) that comes with the carnet.

A version of the Bordeaux Découverte card, sold at the tourist office, allows unlimited bus travel for one day (23.50FF) or three days (54.50FF). Time-stamp it only the first time you use it.

euro currency converter 10FF = €1.52

Some time in 2002 the first three lines (22km) of a new Tramway system will open, serving the city centre and suburban area and linking both sides of the Garonne river.

Car Street parking is scarce in the centre. Some, but not all, meters allow you to pay at night for parking the next morning. Daytime meter rates are around 3FF for 30 minutes. The cheapest car park (8FF per hour, 41FF for 12 hours, free overnight) is opposite place de la Bourse. Pricier, shadier car parks are north of allées d'Orléans and allées de Bristol. Sogeparc 24-hour underground car parks (such as at allées de Tourny) charge 10FF per hour (5FF from 8pm to 8am).

Taxi To order a taxi call ☎ 05 56 91 47 05 (place de la Victoire), available 24 hours.

Bicycle Bordeaux has some 15km of *pistes cyclables* (bike lanes) running north along the riverside from quai Louis XVIII to Bordeaux-Lac. Bord'Eaux Velos Loisirs (☎ 06 81 83 23 03) rents bikes and *voiturettes* for children from the Quinconces quay at 20FF per hour (50FF per day) or 20FF for the children's enclosed circuit. It's open from 10 am to 8 pm daily June to September; from 1 to 6 pm at other times.

Cycles Peugeot Pasteur (☎ 05 56 92 68 20), 42 cours Pasteur, rents *vélos tout-terrains* (VTTs; mountain bikes) for 70/250FF per day/week. It's closed on Sunday and, in July and August, on Monday morning and Saturday afternoon. On the first Sunday of every month, bikes are available for free by the Monument aux Girondins for use on a traffic-free route to place Gambetta and back.

Around Bordeaux

ST-ÉMILION
postcode 33330 • pop 3000 • elevation 106m
This medieval village 39km east of Bordeaux found fame when Émilion, a miracle-working Benedictine monk from Brittany, lived in a cave here from 750 to 767. A monastery founded on the site became a stop on one of the medieval pilgrimage routes to Santiago de Compostela.

Today St-Émilion is best known for its full-bodied, deep-red wines. These and the town's picturesque location above the Dordogne River attract ever more eager tourists and accommodation is expensive. Visit early in the morning to see the town at its best.

Orientation & Information
Rue Guadet (the D122) is the main commercial street. From place du Marché a steep lane climbs to the tourist office (☎ 05 57 55 28 28, fax 05 57 55 28 29, email st-emilion.tourisme@wanadoo.fr) at place des Créneaux. It's open from 9.30 am to 12.30 pm and 1.45 to 6 pm daily (to 6.30 pm from April to November). Hours are from 9.30 am to 8 pm in July and August.

The Maison du Vin (☎ 05 57 55 50 55), around the corner on place Pierre Meyrat, has the low-down on local vintages. It stocks the 50FF *Wine Buyers' Guide – St-Émilion*, and also sells wine. It's open from 10 am to 12.30 pm and 2.30 to 6 pm Monday to Saturday and from 9.30 am to 12.30 pm and 2 to 6.30 pm on Sunday during the summer (from 9.30 am to 7 pm daily in August).

Banks include Caisse d'Épargne on rue Guadet and Crédit Agricole (with ATM) on rue des Girondins. The post office on rue Guadet can also exchange foreign currency.

Town Tour
The most interesting sites can be visited only on the tourist office's 45-minute guided tour (every 45 minutes from 10 to 11.30 am and 2 to 5 pm or later). Two or three a day are in English. The tour costs 33FF (students 20FF, children aged 12 to 18 years 16FF).

The 13th-century **Chapelle de la Trinité**, with original frescoes, is just above **Grotte de l'Ermitage**, the saint's famous cave. The **Catacombs**, first used for burials in the 9th century, came to light in the 1950s when a villager attempted to enlarge his wine cellar. In fact the town sits atop some 200 caves but archaeologists can't excavate them for fear the buildings above might collapse.

The astounding **Église Monolithe**, carved out of solid limestone over the 9th to the 12th centuries, measures 20m by 38m with an 11m-high ceiling. None of the original frescoes have survived but a few hauntingly simple bas-reliefs remain. Scaffolding has been erected in the middle of the church to keep the roof from collapsing due to the weight of the **bell tower** directly above.

The tower, a Gothic spire on a Romanesque base, dating from the 12th to 15th centuries, offers a grand view of the village for 6FF. The entrance is on place des Créneaux and it's open the same hours as the tourist office.

Other Things to See

The former **Collégiale** (collegiate church), now a parish church, has a narrow Romanesque nave (12th century) and a spacious, almost square, choir (14th to 16th centuries). The church's 14th-century cloister, **Cloître de l'Église Collégiale**, is accessible via the tourist office.

The **Cloître des Cordeliers**, a ruined monastery on rue des Cordeliers, is open

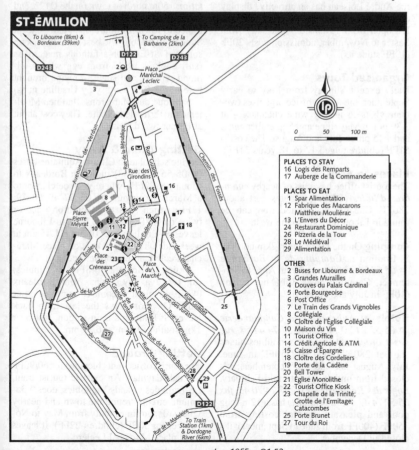

ST-ÉMILION

PLACES TO STAY
16 Logis des Remparts
17 Auberge de la Commanderie

PLACES TO EAT
1 Spar Alimentation
12 Fabrique des Macarons Matthieu Mouliérac
13 L'Envers du Décor
24 Restaurant Dominique
26 Pizzeria de la Tour
28 Le Médiéval
29 Alimentation

OTHER
2 Buses for Libourne & Bordeaux
3 Grandes Murailles
4 Douves du Palais Cardinal
5 Porte Bourgeoise
6 Post Office
7 Le Train des Grands Vignobles
8 Collégiale
9 Cloître de l'Église Collégiale
10 Maison du Vin
11 Tourist Office
14 Crédit Agricole & ATM
15 Caisse d'Épargne
18 Cloître des Cordeliers
19 Porte de la Cadène
20 Bell Tower
21 Église Monolithe
22 Tourist Office Kiosk
23 Chapelle de la Trinité; Grotte de l'Ermitage; Catacombes
25 Porte Brunet
27 Tour du Roi

year-round free of charge. The eponymous winery that has shared the site for over a century makes sparkling wine; free tours of its cellars take place at 3, 4, 5 and 6 pm daily.

More fine views are available from the 13th-century **Tour du Roi** (King's Tower), open from 10.30 am to 12.45 pm and 2.15 to at least 6.45 pm daily from about May to October, and mainly in the afternoon only during the rest of the year. Admission costs 6FF.

The Musée de la Poterie des Hospices de la Madelaine (☎ 05 57 55 51 65) at 21 rue André Loiseau has an attractive display of ancient iron and ceramic pots and jugs. It's open from 10 am to 7 pm daily from Easter to November, admission costs 20FF (10FF students).

Organised Tours

Daily except Sunday from May to early September, the tourist office organises two-hour visits to nearby wine chateaux – at 3.30 pm in May, June and September and 2 and 4.15 pm in July and August. The cost is 51FF (children aged 12 to 18 years 31FF).

Places to Stay

The tourist office has a list of nearby *chambres d'hôtes* (B&Bs); doubles cost about 280FF. Cheaper accommodation can be found in Libourne, 8km to the west.

Camping On the D122 about 2km north of St-Émilion is *Camping de la Barbanne* (☎ 05 57 24 75 80); open from April to September. Camping costs 36FF per person (40FF in July and August).

Hotels At *Auberge de la Commanderie* (☎ 05 57 24 70 19, fax 05 57 74 44 53, rue des Cordeliers), spacious doubles/quads start at 280/480FF (380/550FF in June, July, August and most of September); it's closed from mid-January to mid-February. *Logis des Remparts* (☎ 05 57 24 70 43, fax 05 57 74 47 44, rue Guadet) has a 12m-long pool and pleasant doubles costing from 350FF (400FF from June to September); it's closed in December.

Places to Eat

Restaurant Dominique (☎ 05 57 24 71 00, rue de la Petite Fontaine) serves regional specialities and *menus* from 68FF. *L'Envers du Décor* (☎ 05 57 74 48 31, rue du Clocher) offers excellent 60FF *plats du jour,* vintage wine by the glass and a nice garden; it's closed on Sunday evening. *Le Médiéval* (☎ 05 57 24 72 37, place de la Porte Bouqueyre) serves generous 45FF *plats du jour* and *menus* from 78FF. *Pizzeria de la Tour* (☎ 05 57 24 68 91, rue de la Grande Fontaine) serves crepes and pizza.

There are two groceries, a *Spar Alimentation* 150m north of town on the D122, and a smaller *Alimentation* at the southern entrance to town. Both are open daily except Sunday afternoon. The best place to pick up some of St-Émilion's famous macaroons (soft cookies made from egg whites, almond powder and sugar, a recipe brought here in the 17th century by Ursuline nuns) is Fabrique des Marcarons Matthieu Mouliérac on Tertre de la Tente. They cost about 30FF per two dozen.

Getting There & Away

During school term Citram Aquitaine buses (☎ 05 56 43 68 43) run from Bordeaux to Libourne (32FF), where you can change to a Marchesseau bus (☎ 05 57 40 60 79; 11FF) which runs to St-Émilion once or twice daily. The last bus back to Libourne leaves St-Émilion at 5.10 pm (11.45 am at weekends). The bus stop is on place Maréchal Leclerc at the northern edge of town.

Trains to Bergerac (48FF, 50 minutes) run twice a day, trains from Bordeaux (43FF, 40 minutes) come two or three times daily. On most days the last train back leaves St-Émilion's train station, just over 1km south of town, at 6.30 pm.

Getting Around

The tourist office rents bicycles for 60/90FF per half-day/day. An electric tourist train, Le Train des Grands Vignobles, does a 35-minute circuit around the town and nearby vineyards ten times daily from May to November for 30FF (children 22FF). It leaves from place Maréchal Leclerc.

THE MÉDOC

North-west of Bordeaux, along the shore of the Gironde Estuary, lie some of Bordeaux's most celebrated vineyards, those of Haut Médoc, Margaux and neighbouring *appellations* (wine-producing areas).

Information

Those who have an interest in wine should visit the Maison du Tourisme et du Vin (☎ 05 56 59 03 08, fax 05 56 29 23 38, email tourismeetvindepauillac@wanadoo .fr) in Pauillac. It's open from 9.30 am to 12.30 pm and 2 to 6.30 pm daily (until 6 pm November to June; 9 am to 7 pm from July to mid-September). It offers information and wine-tasting courses, sells some 300 different wines at chateaux prices and can make appointments (for 25FF) to visit specific *chais* (wine cellars). The annual *Médoc Guide Découverte* map-brochure, available here and at other tourist offices, has details on chateaux that welcome visitors.

Vineyards & Chateaux

The gravelly soil of the Médoc's rolling hills nurtures meticulously tended grape vines (mainly Cabernet Sauvignon) that produce some of the world's most sought-after red wines. The rose bushes at the end of each row are like canaries in coal mines: more susceptible to disease (especially mildew) than the vines, they tell the grower when treatment is necessary. The most beautiful part of the wine-growing area is along the D2 and D204 north of Pauillac.

Wine-Tasting à Pied

An unusual way to see the Médoc is by running in the Marathon des Châteaux du Médoc (☎ 05 56 59 17 20, fax 05 56 59 62 38, email medocmar@aol.com). Held in early September (you'd need to book in January), it's limited to 7500 participants, most of whom are in costume and invariably fall for the charms of the wines en route: real Médoc runners are in it for the fun as much as for the run.

Illustrious growers in the Pauillac appellation that welcome visitors – though by appointment only – include **Château Lafite Rothschild** (☎ 05 56 73 18 18), open weekdays but closed August to November and **Château Mouton Rothschild** (☎ 05 56 73 21 29), open daily from June to November and weekdays only during the rest of the year, for 20FF. Nearby in the St-Julien appellation, **Château Beychevelle** (☎ 05 56 73 20 70) is open on weekdays year-round, plus Saturday in July and August. About 20km to the south, in Margaux, you can visit **Château Margaux** (☎ 05 57 88 83 83) on weekdays. No reservations are necessary for **Château Palmer** (☎ 05 57 88 72 72), on the D2 in Issan, 3km south of Margaux, open daily from April to October, weekdays only during the rest of the year.

Visiting hours for most chateaux are around 9.30 to 11 am and 2 to 6 pm. The better-known ones are marked on Michelin's yellow road maps.

Getting There & Away

Pauillac is about an hour north of Bordeaux, by train (54FF, six daily on weekdays, two to four at weekends) or Citram Aquitaine bus (48FF). Bikes can be carried on most weekday trains, or the Maison du Tourisme et du Vin rents them for 50/70FF per half/full day. A 5FF map shows six signposted routes around the area suitable for walkers or cyclists.

The Atlantic Coast

The fine-sand beaches of the Côte d'Argent, backed by dunes, lagoons and the vast pine forest of the Landes, stretch for 230km from Pointe de Grave to Biarritz. This is the perfect family destination, with 200km of easy bicycle trails, quiet lakes (including 16km-long Lac d'Hourtin et de Carcans, France's longest lake), well-equipped camp sites and holiday villages – and an army of summer visitors. But it's chic and sporty, too, thanks to some of Europe's finest surfing and to scores of places to sail, kayak, ride a horse, hike, climb or golf. For details, check out *Gironde – Terres du Bordeaux, Terre d'Aventures*, a brochure available at most tourist offices.

SOULAC-SUR-MER
postcode 33780 • pop 2800

This lively summer resort, 9km south of Pointe de Grave, seems an unlikely religious site but its Romanesque basilica – twice buried by the sands – was once the first stop for pilgrims sailing from England to Santiago de Compostela (see the boxed text 'The Pilgrims of St-Jacques' under Religion in the Facts about South-West France chapter).

Orientation & Information
The commercial axis is pedestrianised rue de la Plage, perpendicular to the beach. The tourist office (☎ 05 56 09 86 61, fax 05 56 73 63 76) at No 68 is open from 9 am to 12.30 pm and 2 to 5.30 pm daily (except Sunday afternoon); and from 9 am to 7 pm daily in July and August. Bus and ferry schedules are posted in the window. Nearby there's a branch of Crédit Agricole bank with ATMs. The post office, which also exchanges currency and is open until noon on Saturday, is one street north on rue du Maréchal d'Ornano.

Basilique de Notre Dame de la Fin des Terres
One of many Santiago de Compostela sites recently added to the UNESCO World Heritage list is this Romanesque Benedictine abbey with a dramatic name (Our Lady at the End of the Earth). Inside are some finely carved capitals, including one dedicated to Ste Veronica, said to have brought Christianity to the region. Admission is free.

Activities
The swells and the wide, safe beach here are good for bodyboarders and novice surfers. For courses or equipment hire during July and August, contact CAP 33 (☎ 05 56 09 82 99) from 10 am to noon and 3.30 to 5.30 pm at the Centre Culturel, rue du RP Brottier, a block inland from the seafront and just south of rue de la Plage.

Places to Stay
Without prior reservation, accommodation is nonexistent in July and August.

Camping Of nearly a dozen nearby sites, four are close to the beach at L'Amélie, 5km to the south. *Camping Mussonville* (☎ 05 56 09 73 40, route de Bordeaux), 700m south-east of Soulac, charges 66FF forfait; caravans cost from 1300FF/week.

Euronat (☎ 05 56 09 33 33, fax 05 56 09 30 27, email info@euronat.fr), 10km south of Soulac near Grayan et l'Hôpital, is one of two huge, well-equipped naturist camp sites in the area, with 1.5km of beachfront. High-season forfait rates with a tent/caravan are 121/187FF. Weekly rates for a bungalow sleeping two/five are 2400/3270FF (1085/1400FF outside July and August). For more on naturism in the region, see Activities in the Facts for the Visitor chapter.

Hotels At *Hôtel de la Gare* (☎/fax 05 56 09 85 60), opposite Soulac's train station, modern rooms start at 170FF (hall showers are free). Two Logis de France inns nearer the centre are *Hôtel La Dame de Coeur* (☎ 05 56 09 80 80, fax 05 56 09 97 47, 103 rue de la Plage), where plain doubles/triples cost 250/280FF and *Hôtel L'Hacienda* (☎ 05 56 09 81 34, fax 05 56 73 65 57, 4 ave Perier de Larsan), 150m south of the church, where doubles cost 320FF (290FF half board).

Places to Eat
Between rue de la Plage's many pizzeria-creperies are several seafood restaurants, including *Le Pavillion de la Mer* (☎ 05 56 09 80 82), where the *menu du pêcheur* (fisherman's menu) costs 90FF. *Le Nautilus* (*Esplanade des Girondins)* has *raclette* (melted cheese with cold cuts and pickles) for 95FF and pizzas from 45FF. Friendly, seafront *Le California* (☎ 05 56 73 65 43) serves generous portions of Tex-Mex food and 60FF paellas, but watch the drinks bill. The restaurant at *Hôtel L'Hacienda* (see Places to Stay) has a 60FF weekday lunch *menu*.

Opposite the tourist office is a *covered food market*, open until 1 pm daily.

Getting There & Away

Bus & Train Soulac's bus stand is near the basilica, and the train station is 700m south of town. The trip from Bordeaux takes 1¾ hours by train (82 FF; change at Lesparre Médoc) or SNCF bus (82FF, two to five daily), or two hours by Citram Aquitaine bus (75FF, three to five daily). From Pointè de Grave, two to four daily buses run to Soulac (11FF) and Bordeaux (87/75FF for SNCF/Citram, 2¼ hours).

Ferry Soulac is linked with Royan, across the estuary, by a car ferry (☎ 05 56 09 60 84; 25 minutes, six to 17 daily) from Le Verdon, 2km south of Pointe de Grave. Fares are 17/123/17/8FF per person/car/ motorcycle/bicycle. The service runs until 7 am (6.30 am July and August; 8 am winter weekends) to 8.30 pm (9.30 pm from Royan), or until 6.30 pm (7.15 pm from Royan) outside July and August. Another ferry crossing (☎ 05 57 42 04 49) is 70km to the south, between Lamarque and Blaye. The trip costs 17/164/17/8FF

Getting Around

Bikes are available to hire from Ericycles (☎ 05 56 73 62 89), near the tourist office at 5 rue Cardinal Donnet.

A little tourist train, called PGVS or Le Petit Train (☎ 05 56 09 61 78), does a one hour, Pointe de Grave–Le Verdon–Soulac circuit twice daily in July and August (weekends only from April to July) for 25FF (children 20FF).

LACANAU

postcode 33680 • pop 2500 • elevation 20m
This little resort, with some of the finest surfing in the south-west, hosts 120,000 World Surfing Championship spectators at the Lacanau Pro in late August. Even in July you'll share Lacanau with about 80,000 visitors, so book your accommodation in advance. Don't worry if you've forgotten your board: equipment rental outfits are everywhere.

Orientation

As with many Aquitaine coastal towns there are two Lacanaus: inland Lacanau Ville (or Lacanau Médoc, or just Lacanau), on Lac de Lacanau, and the livelier, coastal Lacanau Océan, 13km to the west. There are four main beaches, from plage Nord, 800m north of the centre, to plage Super Sud, 1km south.

Information

Lacanau Océan's tourist office (☎ 05 56 03 21 01, fax 05 56 03 11 89, email lacanau@lacanau.com, place de l'Europe) is 400m east of seafront blvd de la Plage. It's open from 9 am to 7 pm daily in July and August, and from 9 am to noon and 1 to 6.30 pm the rest of the year (to 5.30 pm from October to April; closed Sunday afternoon from November to March). Ask for the free *Plan des Pistes Cyclables*, showing bike trails from Lacanau to Hourtin.

You can exchange money at the post office (opposite the tourist office) and at Crédit Agricole on ave Garnung (from the tourist office head seaward and turn left). Kanalo (☎ 05 56 03 17 31, email kanalo@ wanadoo.fr) on rue Charles Chaumet charges 60FF per hour for Internet access, from 9.30 am to 1 pm and 3.30 to 8 pm daily from mid-June to August, and from 9.30 am to 12.30 pm daily except Tuesday during the rest of the year.

Réserve Naturelle de l'Étang de Cousseau

This protected lake, between Lac d'Hourtin et de Carcans and Lac de Lacanau, is a haven for birds and other wildlife. Lacanau's tourist office runs free, weekly guided visits (usually Sunday) from July to September; call ☎ 05 56 91 33 65 for details.

Surfing, Bodyboarding & Windsurfing

Lacanau's surf clubs offer lessons (typically 170/800FF for two/five hours), courses (1400FF for five days) and surf camps with accommodation. Many cater to kids. July and August rates are about 10% higher.

Lacanau Surf Club
(☎ 05 56 26 38 84, fax 05 56 26 38 85)
Maison de la Glisse. On the seafront; this is the official organiser of the Lacanau Pro.

Les Dauphins
 (☎ 05 56 26 33 55)
 6 rue Boileau. This is a good place to take youngsters.
Bo & Co
 (☎ 05 56 26 33 99)
 5 ave Poincaré
Voile Lacanau Guyenne
 (☎ 05 56 03 05 11, fax 05 56 26 23 34)
 Club House de la Grande Escoure. On the western shore of Lac de Lacanau, this place offers combined surfing and windsurfing courses.
Sports-Ocean
 (☎ 05 56 03 02 57)
 plage du Moutchic. On the northern shore of Lac de Lacanau, windsurf rental here costs 60/200FF per hour/half-day.

Places to Stay

Of eight camp sites around Lacanau, closest to the sea is **Les Grands Pins** (*☎ 05 56 03 20 77, fax 05 57 70 03 89, email grands .pins@wanadoo.fr*), 350m from plage Nord, which costs from 130FF/150FF high/low season for two people. It's open from April to October.

Wave Trotters (*☎ 05 56 03 13 01, blvd de la Plage*) has dorm beds costing from 85FF to 120FF, two doubles costing from 150FF to 190FF and two kitchens.

Best value among the hotels are the Logis de France **L'Étoile d'Argent** (*☎ 05 56 03 21 07, place de l'Europe*), where doubles cost 400FF (closed December and January) and **Le Marian** (*☎ 05 56 03 21 02, fax 05 56 03 16 47, allées Pierre Ortal*), on the main road to the beach, where doubles/triples cost 440/520FF.

Doubles/triples at the seafront **Inter Hotel L'Oyat** (*☎ 05 56 03 11 11, fax 05 56 03 12 29*), open April to October, cost 590/ 710FF.

The tourist office has long lists of villas and studios for rent.

Places to Eat

If you're sick of pizza and crepes, try the 145FF Sunday lunchtime seafood buffet at **Chez L'Australien** (*allées Pierre Ortal*); fish, meat and pasta dishes cost from 45FF. Opposite the tourist office is **La Taverne de Neptune** (*☎ 05 56 03 21 33*) offering a 68FF midday *menu* (including wine). Nearby is a **Spar grocery**, closed Wednesday and Sunday afternoons.

Getting There & Away

Cars Ouest Aquitaine (☎ 05 56 70 17 27) run buses to/from Bordeaux via Lacanau Ville three times daily (64FF, 1¼ hours).

Getting Around

There are four bike rental outfits, including Locacycle (☎ 05 56 26 30 99), near the tourist office, where VTTs cost 30/45FF per half/full day.

ARCACHON

postcode 33120 • pop 13,700 • elevation 7m

Arcachon was popular with bourgeois Bordelais at the end of the 19th century, thanks to a casino, luxury seaside hotels and a new railway line. Today the attractions are seafood – especially *huîtres* (oysters) – a broad beach and the extraordinary Dune du Pilat (see Around Arcachon later in this section). The resort is well-served by trains and makes an easy day trip from Bordeaux

Orientation

Arcachon is on the southern shore of the Bassin d'Arcachon (Arcachon Basin), linked to the Atlantic by a 3km-wide channel west of town. Across the channel is the peninsula of Cap Ferret.

The town has two distinct quarters: the summertime, bayfront Ville d'Été and the sheltered, inland Ville d'Hiver to the south. Arcachon train station is 500m south of the beach.

Information

The tourist office (☎ 05 57 52 97 97, fax 05 57 52 97 77, email tourisme@ arcachon.com) on place Président Roosevelt is open from 9 am to 12.30 pm and 2 to 6 pm Monday to Saturday (9 am to 7 pm in July and August); it's also open from 9 am to1 pm on Sunday and holidays from April to September.

Currency exchange is available at Crédit Agricole next to 252 blvd de la Plage, several other banks around the *mairie* (town hall), and at the main post office at place Président Roosevelt.

The laundrette at the corner of blvd Général Leclerc and rue Molière is open from 7 am to 10 pm daily.

Central Arcachon

The liveliest part of the Ville d'Été is around the **Jetée Thiers** (Thiers pier).

The **Musée de la Maquette Marine** (☎ 05 57 52 00 03), 19 blvd Général Leclerc, exhibits an exquisite of 1:100 scale model ships, commissioned as prototypes. It's open from 2 to 6 pm at weekends from

Easter to September, and from 10 am to 12.30 pm and 3 to 7 pm daily in July and August. Admission costs 30FF (children aged four to 12 years 15FF).

The **Ville d'Hiver** dates from the start of the 20th century, when rich Bordelais came to amuse themselves or recover from tuberculosis. A lift near the southern end of rue du Maréchal de Lattre de Tassigny climbs to **Parc Mauresque**, where you can see a model of the ornate 19th-century Casino Mauresque, burnt to a cinder in 1977.

A verdant promenade runs west and south from plage d'Arcachon to **plage**

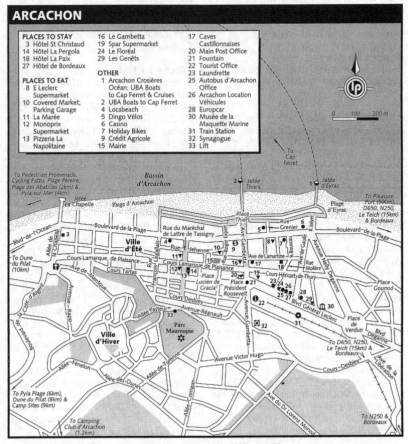

ARCACHON

PLACES TO STAY	16	Le Gambetta	17	Caves
3	Hôtel St Christaud	19	Spar Supermarket		Castillonnaises
14	Hôtel La Pergola	24	Le Floréal	20	Main Post Office
18	Hôtel La Paix	29	Les Genêts	21	Fountain
27	Hôtel de Bordeaux			22	Tourist Office
		OTHER	23	Laundrette
PLACES TO EAT	1	Arcachon Croisières	25	Autobus d'Arcachon
8	E Leclerc		Océan; UBA Boats		Office
	Supermarket		to Cap Ferret & Cruises	26	Arcachon Location
10	Covered Market;	2	UBA Boats to Cap Ferret		Véhicules
	Parking Garage	4	Locabeach	28	Europcar
11	La Marée	5	Dingo Vélos	30	Musée de la
12	Monoprix	6	Casino		Maquette Marine
	Supermarket	7	Holiday Bikes	31	Train Station
13	Pizzeria La	9	Crédit Agricole	32	Synagogue
	Napolitaine	15	Mairie	33	Lift

0   100   200 m

To Cap Ferret

Bassin d'Arcachon

Jetée Thiers

Jetée d'Eyrac

To Pedestrian Promenade,
Cycling Paths, Plage Péreire,
Plage des Abatilles (2km) &
Pyla-sur-Mer (4km)

Jetée La Chapelle

Plage d'Arcachon

Place Thiers

Plage d'Eyrac

To Pleasure Port (500m), D650, N250, Le Teich (15km) & Bordeaux

Blvd-de-l'Océan

Boulevard-de-la-Plage

Rue du Maréchal de Lattre de Tassigny

Rue Grenier

Boulevard-de-la-Plage

To Dune du Pilat (10km)

Allée de Chapelle

Ville d'Été

Rue Jehenne

Ave de Lamartine

Avenue Nelly Deganne

Cours Lamarque de Plaisance

Cours Tartas

Place Lucien de Gracia

Place Président Roosevelt

Rue Molière

Place Gounod

Cours Hévicart de Thury

Cap Pereire

Avenue Rapp

Avenue de Montque

Cours Desbiey

Blvd Général Leclerc

Place de Verdun

Côte d'Argent

Allée Pasteur

Avenue-Régnault

Parc Mauresque

Ville d'Hiver

Allée Fénelon

Allée-de-Turenne

Avenue-Victor-Hugo

Cours-Desbiey

To Pyla Plage (6km),
Dune du Pilat (8km) &
Camp Sites (9km)

Allée-des-Dunes

Allée Corrigan

Ave du Dr Lorenz Monod

To N250 & Bordeaux

To Camping Club d'Arcachon (1.2km)

To D650, N250, Le Teich (15km) & Bordeaux

THE ATLANTIC COAST

Péreire, **plage des Abatilles** and **Pyla-sur-Mer**. Cycle paths link Arcachon with Biscarrosse, 30km to the south, and towns around the bay.

Boat Excursions

Union des Bateliers Arcachonnais (UBA; ☎ 05 56 54 60 32) runs daily cruises around Île aux Oiseaux (Bird Island) in the bay at 3 pm (70FF; five times daily in July and August), from Jetée d'Eyrac. Arcachon Croisières Océan (☎ 05 56 54 36 70) runs similar excursions from April to October. At 11 am daily in July and August, and at weekends and by request in June, UBA goes to Banc d'Arguin (70FF), a sandbank off the Dune du Pilat. At very high tide UBA boats also sail up the Leyre River.

Places to Stay

In July and August, accommodation is scarce and many hotels require that you take half board.

Camping The nearest camp site, 1.2km south of town, is shady *Camping Club d'Arcachon* (☎ 05 56 83 24 15, fax 05 57 52 28 51, 1 allée de la Galaxie), with forfait rates of 110FF for up to three people (130FF in July and August). See the following Around Arcachon section for details of other options.

Hostels A small, idyllic *youth hostel* (☎ 05 56 60 64 62, 87 ave de Bordeaux) across the bay in Cap Ferret is open only in July and August and fills up fast. Beds cost from 31FF to 45FF and there's no restaurant.

Hotels – Budget The family-run *Hôtel La Paix* (☎ 05 56 83 05 65, 8 ave de Lamartine) is open from April to November. Doubles/triples/quads cost 167/220/277FF, and doubles with toilet and shower cost 190/212FF). Prices include breakfast and hall showers are free. From June to September, half board (320/436/575FF) is obligatory. Studio apartments are available year-round for 1000FF to 2900FF per week.

At *Hôtel St-Christaud* (☎/fax 05 56 83 38 53, 8 allée de la Chapelle), simple

doubles cost from 99FF to 145FF (129FF to 185FF with shower and toilet). Hall showers are free. Half board (100FF extra per person) is obligatory in July and August.

Hotels – Mid-Range At *Hôtel La Pergola* (☎ 05 56 83 07 89, fax 05 56 83 14 21, 40 cours Lamarque de Plaisance), modern doubles with shower and toilet cost 230FF (417FF in July and August), two with washbasin cost from 150FF to 250FF and studios are 1000FF to 2600FF per week. Breakfast is included.

Opposite the train station, *Hôtel de Bordeaux* (☎ 05 56 83 80 30, fax 05 56 83 69 02, 39 blvd Général Leclerc) has plain doubles/triples with shower and toilet for 200/360FF (300/420FF from mid-June to September).

Places to Eat

Several *bar-brasseries* offer good-value plats du jour with mounds of mussels for a bargain 45FF. *Le Gambetta* (☎ 05 57 52 29 69, 25 ave Gambetta) also has plats du jour costing 55FF and *Le Floréal* (☎ 05 56 83 48 44, 49 blvd Général Leclerc) offers a 38FF plat du jour and 75FF evening *menu*.

In summer the promenade between Jetée Thiers and Jetée d'Eyrac sprouts tourist *restaurants*, *pizzerias* and *creperies*. Rue du Maréchal de Lattre de Tassigny has several Chinese, Indian and Italian restaurants including *Pizzeria La Napolitaine* (☎ 05 57 52 20 50) at No 28, which serves a three-course 48FF *menu*. In summer, French *menus* at *Hôtel La Paix* (see Places to Stay) start at 59FF.

For excellent 99FF seafood *menus* try *Les Genêts* (☎ 05 56 83 40 28, 25 blvd Général Leclerc), closed on Sunday night and Monday or *La Marée* (☎ 05 56 83 24 05, 21 rue du Maréchal de Lattre de Tassigny), closed on Monday night and Tuesday.

The *covered market* (rue Roger Expert), beneath a parking garage, is open daily from 8 am to 1 pm. Supermarkets include *Spar* (57 blvd Général Leclerc), *E Leclerc* (224 blvd de la Plage) and *Monoprix* (46 cours Lamarque de Plaisance).

Caves Castillonnaises (*32 ave de Lamartine*) sells bottled and bulk wine, the latter for as little as 8FF per litre.

Getting There & Away

Some Bordeaux–Arcachon trains (52FF, 45 minutes; nine to 17 daily) meet Paris–Bordeaux TGVs. The last one back to Bordeaux leaves at 8 pm (9.50 pm on Sunday and holidays, 9 pm on other nights in July and August).

From June to September, UBA runs hourly ferries from Jetée Thiers and Jetée d'Eyrac to Cap Ferret (30/50FF one way/return). During the rest of the year there is at least one run (four in April, May and October) each Monday, Wednesday, Friday and Sunday from Jetée Thiers.

Getting Around

Car & Motorcycle There's unmetered parking south of the casino on ave de Gaulle and at the western end of blvd de la Plage.

Two car rental firms, open daily except Sunday, are Arcachon Location Véhicules (☎ 05 57 72 40 40), 43 blvd Général Leclerc, and Europcar (☎ 05 56 83 48 00), at No 35. Locabeach (☎ 05 56 83 39 64), 326 blvd de la Plage, and Holiday Bikes (☎ 05 56 22 45 15) at No 218, rent scooters from 160FF per half-day; larger motorbikes require deposits of between 4000FF and 9000FF, payable by credit card.

Bicycle From Easter to September, Dingo Vélos (☎ 05 56 83 44 09), rue Grenier, Locabeach and Holiday Bikes (see Car & Motorcycle) rent bikes/VTTs from 50/80FF per day. Dingo Vélos, open from 9.30 am to 7 pm daily (to midnight in July and August), also rents bikes for two to five riders.

AROUND ARCACHON
Dune du Pilat

The remarkable Dune du Pilat (or Dune de Pyla) is Europe's highest sand dune, some 114m high. It begins 8km south of Arcachon along the D218 and stretches for almost 3km. While the sea-facing side is gentle and dotted with grass, the inland side is steep enough to ski down. At the bottom, dead trees smothered by the dune as it moves relentlessly eastwards – at about 4.5m each year – poke out of the sand.

The view from the top is magnificent. To the west are the shoals at the mouth of the Bassin d'Arcachon and Cap Ferret. Eastwards, almost as far as the eye can see, stretch the dense pine forests of the Landes. The GR8 passes nearby.

Be careful while swimming in this area: powerful currents swirl around the small sandy bays, especially when the sea is rough.

Places to Stay On the inland side of the dune are five pine-shaded, pricey camp sites. One is *La Forêt* (☎ 05 56 22 73 28, *fax 05 56 22 70 50, email camping.foret@ hol.fr*), open from Easter to October; forfait costs 75FF.

Getting There & Away From June to September Autobus d'Arcachon (☎ 05 56 83 07 60) runs twice daily (19FF, four times in July and August) between Arcachon train station and the camp sites, and every 45 minutes to the Dune du Pilat parking lot (16FF). The rest of the year buses go only to Pyla Plage (Haïtza), 1km from the dune (11FF, five to seven times daily). The tourist office has timetables.

Parc Ornithologique du Teich

The Bassin d'Arcachon is a shallow, 250 sq km tidal bay. With just 20% underwater at low tide, it's ideal bird habitat and some 260 species, resident and migratory, visit each year. The Parc Ornithologique du Teich (☎ 05 56 22 80 93) at Le Teich, east of Arcachon, on the bay at the mouth of the Leyre (or L'Eyre) River, is an important centre for the preservation of endangered species and a fine place to see some of Europe's rarest and most beautiful birds such as the spoonbill, little egret, blue throat and black kite. The park is home to two dozen nesting pairs of storks, who take to the air at midday. Circuits of 2.5km and 6km take you to a series of camouflaged observation points. A longer circuit is set to open in 2000.

From August to October, waders and other migratory birds from Scandinavia and

Greenland pass through. May is a good time to observe species rarely seen farther north (such as in the UK). From late summer and throughout the winter, it's easiest to observe the birds at high tide when they're close to shore.

Information The park is open from 10 am to 6 pm daily (to 7 pm from mid-April to mid-September, to 10 pm in July and August) year-round. Admission costs 36FF (children aged five to 14 years 25FF). Binoculars can be rented and bird food bought there.

There's a tourist office (☎ 05 56 22 80 46, fax 05 57 70 31 70) opposite the post office in Le Teich, open from 10 am to 12.30 pm and 2 to 6.30 pm Monday to Friday (daily except Sunday afternoon in July and August).

Activities The **Sentier du Littoral** footpath passes the park, running 5km south-east to Lamothe along the forested banks of the Leyre, and 5km west to the oyster-fishing port of Gujan-Mestras.

Canoe and kayak trips run by the park's **Maison de la Nature du Bassin d'Arcachon** (☎ 05 56 22 80 93, fax 05 56 22 69 43) include guided sea kayak tours of the Leyre delta (100FF, three hours) and the Bassin d'Arcachon (200FF, all day) once or twice a month and, from June to September, unguided canoe trips on the Leyre (from 140FF to 200FF for up to two adults and two children). Book at least a couple of days ahead.

From mid-June to mid-September you can rent a bike or canoe, or ride a horse, at **Villetorte Loisirs** (☎ 05 56 22 66 80), 800m south-east of the park off rue de Port.

Places to Stay The nearest camp site is *Camping Ker Helen* (☎ *05 56 66 03 79, fax 05 56 66 51 59*), 2.2km to the west near Gujan-Mestras. Rates range from 18FF to 26FF per person and 35FF to 50FF per tent, depending on the season. It's open from March to November.

At *Hôtel Le Central* (☎/fax *05 56 22 65 64, 61 ave de la Côte d'Argent*), opposite

the church in Le Teich, doubles/triples with shower cost 170/200FF.

Getting There & Away The park is 15km east of Arcachon on the D650. Le Teich' train station, 1.2km south of the park, is on the line linking Bordeaux (44FF, 35 minutes) with Arcachon (16FF, 15 minutes) with at least 10 connections daily.

BISCARROSSE
postcode 40600 • pop 17,000 • elevation 26m
Biscarrosse, 30km south of Arcachon, is one of the Landes département's most popular resorts, thanks partly to its proximity to two lakes, étang de Cazaux et de Sanguinet (Lac Nord for short) and étang de Biscarrosse et de Parentis (or Lac Sud). It's not all postcard stuff – the town of Parentis en Born hosts France's largest oilfield and between Biscarrosse and Mimizan is the strictly-off-limits Centre d'Essais des Landes missile range – but the hordes of sea and lake visitors hardly notice.

Orientation & Information
Biscarrosse Ville (or Biscarrosse Bourg) has shops, banks and a museum, but the tourist office (☎ 05 58 78 20 96, fax 05 58 78 23 65, email biscarrosse@biscarrosse .com) is in Biscarrosse Plage, on the coast 10km to the west. It's on place de la Fontaine and open from 9 am to 12.30 pm and 2 to 6.30 pm weekdays and from 10 am to 12.30 pm and 3 to 6 pm at weekends (from 9 am to 10 pm daily in July and August). Pick up the 5FF regional map showing bike trails.

The main post office is in Biscarrosse Ville, 102 rue de la Poste. Cybercafé L'Estrela (☎ 05 58 78 74 86), 93 ave de la République (700m north of the church), is open from 10 am to 12.30 pm Monday, Wednesday and Saturday and from 4 pm to 1 am daily; Internet access costs 30/50FF per 30/60 minutes.

Musée Historique de l'Hydraviation
This little museum at 332 ave Louis Bréguet in Biscarrosse Ville exhibits full-size sea

planes and lots of aviation paraphernalia. Biscarrosse's big, sheltered lakes made it a centre of interwar seaplane development, with St-Exupéry and other pioneers flying from here. The museum (☎ 05 58 78 00 65) is open from 2 to 6 pm daily (3 to 7 pm from April to October, and 10 am to 7 pm in July and August) and admission costs 25FF (children aged 6 to 12 years 5FF).

Activities

Biscarrosse Plage has half a dozen surf clubs, including Monomoi (☎ 05 58 78 33 61) on the seafront at 372 blvd des Sables, open April to September. The tourist office has a full list. Bisca Nature Active (☎ 05 58 78 39 87, fax 05 58 78 23 65) at 55 place de la Fontaine offers everything from surfing and scuba-diving to canoeing and barefoot water-skiing, and can arrange off-season accommodation.

Port Maguide, on the south-western shore of Lac Nord, is the main centre for lake watersports. Contact Cyana (☎ 06 10 49 52 60) for scuba-diving and the Centre Nautique Biscarrosse Olympique (☎ 05 58 78 10 51) for courses in other watersports. L'Idylle Cafe (☎/fax 05 58 09 87 84) rents canoes and kayaks; the tourist office has a list of other centres.

For hikers and horse-riders, the GR8 meanders past both lakes.

Places to Stay

There are nine shady lakeside camp sites including *Camping Lou Galip* (☎ 05 58 09 81 81, fax 05 58 09 86 03), at Navarosse on Lac Nord, which charge 70FF forfait. Three beachfront sites include *Campéole Le Vivier* (☎ 05 58 78 25 76, fax 05 58 78 35 23, 681 rue du Tit), open May to September and charging 98FF forfait.

Surprisingly cheap considering its forest location near Lac Sud is *Hôtel en Chon* (☎ 05 58 78 13 52, fax 05 58 78 77 64, 233 chemin d'En Chon), where doubles start at 160FF. For a beach hotel with a pool, try *Les Jardins de L'Océan* (☎ 05 58 83 98 98, fax 05 58 78 32 03, 1068 ave de la Plage) where doubles cost from 200FF (400FF in July and August).

Getting There & Away

Les Rapides Côte d'Argent buses (☎ 05 58 09 10 89) make the 1¾ hour trip between Bordeaux Gare St-Jean and Biscarrosse Ville once a day (three times daily in July and August) for 55FF. In July and August, Autobus d'Arcachon (☎ 05 56 83 07 60) runs to/from Arcachon three to four times daily (37FF), and a twice-daily service links Biscarrosse (Plage and Ville) with Ychoux train station, on the Bordeaux–Dax line, 17km east of Biscarrosse Ville.

Getting Around

Three bike rental outfits include Cycles Evasion (☎ 05 58 78 33 63), opposite the tourist office in Biscarrosse Plage, where VTTs cost from 50/74FF per half/full day (children's bikes are also available) and scooters from 248FF per day.

HOSSEGOR & CAPBRETON
postcodes Hossegor 40150, Capbreton 40130
• pop 8000 • elevation 10m

These two villages astride a small pleasure port form a single resort, the busiest seaside destination between Arcachon and Biarritz. Several kilometres offshore is a 3km-deep undersea canyon, the Gouf de Capbreton, probably instrumental in producing the huge swells that have made the area a surfers' paradise.

Capbreton was a medieval whaling port when, for a time, the Adour River emptied into the sea here. In the early 20th century environmentally-conscious artists, writers and architects founded a lively community in what is now Hossegor. The 1930s saw the start of a property boom and the slow demise of the area's charm. Capbreton still has a fishing harbour but beyond its tiny square little has survived the bulldozer.

Orientation & Information

The two towns are separated – Hossegor north and Capbreton south – by the canal du Bourret and the marina. Just north of Hossegor is another popular resort and surfing centre at Seignosse.

The tourist office in Hossegor (☎ 05 58 41 79 00, fax 05 58 41 79 09, email hossegor.tourisme@wanadoo.fr) on ave de Paris is open from 9 am to 7 pm daily in July and August, and from 9 am to noon and 2 to6 pm (except Sunday) the rest of the year. Just about everything useful is within a few blocks including the post office, at least three which have exchange desks and ATMs, several bike-rental outfits (see Getting Around later in this section), surf shops and cheap eateries.

From the tourist office, walk west on ave Paul Lahary and ave de la Grande Dune about seven blocks to place des Landais, which faces the splendid central beach.

Surfing
Capbreton's swells tend to be smaller (and more polluted) than those at Hossegor and Seignosse. The best spots are to the north: Épi Nord and Gravière, within 0.5km of place des Landais; Culs Nuls, a further 1km up; and the Seignosse beaches of Estagnots, Bourdaines, Penon and Casernes. These include several regular world championship venues.

Good local surf schools include Surf Trip (☎ 05 58 41 91 06, fax 05 58 41 91 11), at 56 rue Maurice Martin (from the tourist office, cross the canal and turn left past the Sporting Casino), and Hossegor Surf Club (☎ 05 58 43 80 52) on impasse de la Digue Nord (place des Landais).

Lac Marin d'Hossegor
This 2km-long tidal lake, parallel to the seafront, has several beaches, warm salt water and tiny waves, making it ideal for children. At plage du Rey you can rent windsurfing and sailing gear or take lessons. With villas and pines all round, it's a nice place to ride a bike too.

Ecomusée de la Mer
This little museum (☎ 05 58 72 40 50) in Capbreton's municipal casino on ave Georges Pompidou is about the history of fishing along the Landes coast, with model ships, aquaria and marine fossils. It's open from 9.30 am to noon and 2.30 to 7 pm daily from June to August, from 2 to 6 pm daily in April, May and September, and

from 2 to 6 pm on Sunday and holidays during the rest of the year.

Étang Blanc & Étang Noir
These two lakes adjacent to Seignosse are home to over 400 plant species and a veritable encyclopedia of fish and migratory birds. The smaller Étang Noir (Black Lake) is classified as a Réserve Naturelle. Elevated walkways allow you to get a proper look. It's open daily except Sunday from April to October, with guided tours in July and August. Contact the reserve office (☎ 05 58 72 85 76) for details. Admission costs 10FF.

Other Attractions
Capbreton's **Estecade pier**, built in Napoleon II's time, offers a fine view of the coastline. Hossegor has an 18-hole **golf course** (☎ 05 58 43 56 99) whose clubhouse is a block south-east of the tourist office; Seignosse has one too.

Summer Events
The tourist office organises **street events** almost daily, from children's shows to dance and music concerts. You can see weekly **pélote Basque** matches at Sporting Casino (just across the canal from the tourist office): *grand chistéra* at the outdoor fronton at 9 pm every Monday, and high-speed *cesta punta* in the indoor court at 9 pm every Thursday. **Courses landaises** (see Spectator Sports in the Facts for the Visitor chapter) take place every Wednesday at 9.30 pm in the arena five blocks north-east of the tourist office.

Among big annual events here are a kite festival which is held in late April, the Landes surfing championships held in mid-May, and the big Hossegor Rip Curl Pro world surfing championships at the end of August.

Places to Stay
Camping Camp sites here tend to open from April or May to September or October. Hossegor's modest municipal *La Forêt* (☎ 05 58 43 75 92, 116 ave de Bordeaux) costs 24/24/7FF per adult/tent/car. Closer

The Tricolour, national flag of post-revolutionary France, flies over the Garonne River, Bordeaux.

Detail of an 11th-century church, Bordeaux

Fresco, Chapelle de la Trinité, St-Émilion

Making spectating a sport: cafe society watches the world go by in Lacanau Océan, Bordeaux.

to the lake is *Le Lac* (☎ *05 58 43 53 14, 480 rte des Lacs*), costing 99FF forfait or 26/29FF per adult/tent.

Just over the canal in Capbreton is the *Bel Air* (☎ *05 58 72 12 04*) costing 25/29FF per adult/tent. It is open year-round. At the other end of Capbreton, quiet *La Pointe* (☎ *05 58 72 14 98, ave des Biches*) costs 28/35/10FF per adult/tent/car, and *La Civelle* (☎ *05 58 72 15 11*) charges about 95FF forfait.

Close to Seignosse's plage des Estagnots is *Camping Municipal Hourn-Naou* (☎ *05 58 43 30 30, fax 05 58 41 64 21, ave des Tucs*), a bargain 48FF forfait or 25/29FF per adult/tent. Near plage des Casernes are *Campeole Les Oyats* (☎ *05 58 43 37 94, fax 05 58 43 23 29*) and *Les Chevreuils* (☎ *05 58 43 32 80, fax 05 58 90 10 49*), both charging about 100FF forfait.

Hotels Two hotels in Hossegor with good food and modest prices (doubles from 200FF to 250FF) are to be found a few blocks north of the tourist office: *Le Neptune* (☎ *05 58 43 51 09, fax 05 58 43 49 49, 1053 ave du TCF*) and *Le Rond Point* (☎ *05 58 43 53 11, fax 05 58 43 85 85, 866 ave du TCF*). More expensive but still good value is *Les Hélianthes* (☎ *05 58 43 52 19, fax 05 58 43 95 19, 156 ave Côte d'Argent*), about 600m from the tourist office (cross the canal and bear right), charging from 250FF to 400FF.

Apartments An option if you are intending to stay for a while is to rent your own flat. In August a furnished flat for four will cost from 3000FF to 5000FF per week, it will be cheaper during other times of the year. Ask at the tourist office or visit the Association des Propriétaires et Loueurs en Meublés (☎/fax 05 58 43 55 12), 56 ave des Écoles (four blocks north of the tourist office), open on weekdays from 10 am to noon.

Places to Eat

A surfers' favourite is the all-hours bar-restaurant *Le Rock-Food* (☎ *05 58 43 54 43, place des Landais*). In the same mould is *L'Orange-Bleue* (☎ *05 58 43 77 22, 28 ave Paul Lahary*), just west of the tourist office.

On the eastern side of the lake, *Dégustation du Lac* (☎ *05 58 43 54 95, 1830 ave du TCF*) offers pricey but delicious seafood platters from April to September. For a hit of Basque and Spanish food costing from 60FF to 120FF per *plat*, try *Amigo* (☎ *05 58 43 54 38, place des Landais*).

If you've busted your budget, the beach is lined with pizzerias and other cheap places where the 50FF *formule* (fixed price two course meal) should fill you up. And don't forget the *market*, just north of the tourist office: inside every morning and outside on Monday, Wednesday, Friday and Sunday mornings.

Getting There & Away

If you are coming from far away (for example Bordeaux or Paris), take the train to Dax or Bayonne, though some Corail services stop slightly nearer at St-Vincent de Tyrosse and Labenne. From any of these places catch an RDTL Dax–Bayonne bus, which runs two or three times daily (except Sunday) via Capbreton, Hossegor and Seignosse; Dax–Hossegor costs about 37FF. RDTL's daily (except Sunday) coastal service running to/from Bayonne stops at Capbreton and Hossegor every one to 1½ hours.

Getting Around

At least three outfits near the tourist office rent bicycles and scooters: Lannemajou (☎ 05 58 43 54 45) at 619 ave du TCF; Locavelo (☎ 05 58 43 73 54) at 60 ave Paul Lahary; and VTT Loisirs (☎ 05 58 41 91 81) on allée des Pins Tranquilles. By the sea, go to the Sunrise Bike Shop (☎ 05 58 43 92 90) at Point d'Or, just south of place des Landais.

RÉSERVE NATURELLE DU MARAIS D'ORX

Just inland of another surfing haven, at Labenne, is the Orx Marsh, for centuries a major nesting site for migratory birds. Napoleon III had the marsh drained but over the years nature has reclaimed it and the birds have started to return. In 1989 the Worldwide Fund for Nature and the private Conservatoire du Littoral bought 800 hectares of marshland and adjacent meadows and farmland, and established a nature reserve.

Summer is perhaps the least interesting time of year to visit. The most dramatic months are October and November, when birds in their thousands stop on their way south. Some thousand greylag geese and 1500 common teal stay for the winter, along with rare white-fronted geese. During the spring you can see breeding spoonbill, heron and little egret. Among four-legged denizens are some of Europe's last remaining mink.

Six hectares of the reserve are open to the public, via walkways, from 9 am to noon and 2 to 5 pm on weekdays (to 4 pm on Friday), and from 2 to 5 pm at the weekend. Admission is free, guided tours cost 20FF (children aged under 16 years 15FF) and binoculars can be rented at the small visitor centre. For further information contact Le Syndicat Mixte pour l'Aménagement et la Gestion du Marais d'Orx (☎ 05 59 45 42 46), Maison du Marais, Domain du Marais d'Orx, 40530 Labenne.

Places to Stay & Eat

Between Labenne and the coast are at least eight camp sites, including four with forfait rates under 110FF: *La Savane* (☎ 05 59 45 41 13), *Marina* (☎ 05 59 45 45 49), *Oceanic* (☎ 05 59 45 46 22) and *La Mer* (☎ 05 59 45 42 09).

Hotel-restaurants in Labenne include *Chez Léonie* (☎ 05 59 45 41 64, fax 05 59 45 78 30) and the *Européen* (☎ 05 59 45 41 49, fax 05 59 45 72 91), they both offer good food and doubles from 180FF to 240FF.

Getting There & Away

The visitor centre is just east of the A63 and N10 at Labenne. See Getting There & Away in the preceding Hossegor & Capbreton section for details of buses from there and from Dax and Bayonne.

The Landes

The Landes (literally 'moors') is France's second-largest département, a 14,000 sq km plain with 106km of coastline between Biscarrosse and Bayonne and some 600,000 hectares of forest, in the midst of which is the Parc Naturel Régional des Landes de Gascogne.

These natural attractions are supplemented by a string of lakes and lagoons, sheltered by the longest, highest strip of dunes in Europe. This great wall of sand once marched inland at up to 27m a year but in the 19th century the first plantations of maritime pine and oak, shrubs and grasses were established. It's now Europe's largest cultivated forest.

This many trees would be dull except for the lakes, coastal resorts and a network of bike trails (see the boxed text 'Biking the Coast'). Inland, you can explore the park on foot, ride a horse or hike (for example on 220km of the GR8), or canoe down the Leyre. South of Mont de Marsan by the fish-rich Adour River, the forests give way to Pyrénées foothills.

Farther south is the fertile Tursan and Chalosse area, famous for its foie gras, wines and thermal spas.

PARC NATUREL RÉGIONAL DES LANDES DE GASCOGNE

This 290,000 hectare regional park, established in 1970, stretches from the Bassin d'Arcachon to just north of Mont de Marsan

---

Biking the Coast

There are 200km of *pistes cyclables* – paved bike trails – along the Landes coast, most of them conveniently pine-shaded. Once sandy tracks used by resin tappers, they were paved by the Nazis in WWII. Dozens of bike hire outlets make it easy to go exploring. Pick up maps, complete with suggested circuits and bike outlets, from most Gironde and Landes tourist offices.

Ecomusée de la Grande Lande

The Parc Naturel Régional des Landes de Gascogne operates a three-part *ecomusée* (open-air museum) devoted to life in this unique landscape. There's an old resin-products workshop at Luxey, a museum of popular beliefs at Moustey and, best of the trio, a reconstructed 19th-century settlement at Marquèze (☎ 05 58 07 52 70, fax 05 58 07 56 85) which illustrates the finely-balanced web of interdependence between humans, animals and a fairly barren land 'before the trees came', and its collapse into a feudal monoculture afterward.

You can walk through the houses of shepherds, labourers and the resin-tappers who displaced them, and through fields, mills and kitchens where their work is again carried on in traditional ways. The museum is open from April to October, with a series of special events including sheep shearing in mid-May, millet threshing in late September and a week of traditional cooking in mid-October.

Adding to the atmosphere is the fact that you can only get there from the village of Sabres on a train with a century-old locomotive and coaches – the only surviving segment of a narrow-gauge line laid in 1880 to Labouheyre, in the days of the pine-resin trade. Trains depart daily from Sabres every 40 minutes: from 2 to 4 pm in April, May and October (with two to three additional services at weekends); from 10.10 am to 12.10 pm and 2 to 4.40 pm June to September (also at 5.20 pm in July and August). In high season the last train back is at 7 pm.

Tickets are 47/40/32FF for those over 25/19–25/6–18 years old and entitle you to a guided visit (in French) and an excellent guidebook (with text in other languages). A small tourist office at the station is open from 10 am to 12.30 pm and 1.30 to 6 pm daily from mid-June to mid-September.

Places to Stay & Eat About 400m south of the centre of Sabres on the D327 is the Logis de France *Auberge des Pins* (☎ 05 58 07 50 47, fax 05 58 07 56 74), a hotel-restaurant where doubles start at 200FF. Nearby is the comfortable *Camping du Peyricat* (☎ 05 58 07 51 88, fax 05 58 07 51 86), open from mid-June to mid-September for 50FF forfait or 16/16/13FF per adult/tent/car.

Getting There & Away Sabres is 35km north-west of Mont de Marsan on the N134. There's no public transport.

and encompasses the river valleys of the Leyre, Petite Leyre and Grand Leyre, the pine forests of the interior and the delta area famous for its Parc Ornithologique du Teich (see the Atlantic Coast section earlier in this chapter for details on the park). The best things about the park are its hiking and biking trails, its canoeing and kayaking facilities and a three-part open-air museum (see the boxed text above).

Information

The park's head office (☎ 05 56 88 06 06, fax 05 56 88 12 72) is at place de l'Église,

Belin-Béliet, though you'll find park information (mostly in French) in local tourist offices, the museum at Sabres or the Maison de la Nature du Bassin d'Arcachon (for details see Parc Ornithologique du Teich in the Atlantic Coast section earlier in this chapter).

Among useful park publications are the *Carte-guide des Découvertes* (a map showing bike trails) and *Le Parc vous guide*, both with contacts for horse-riding, biking, canoeing and other activities and the *Guide des Hébergements* which has accommodation listings.

THE LANDES

On Your Stilts

Before the marshland of the Landes was tamed by Napoleon III, local farmers and shepherds had a hard time moving around their fever-swamp. Someone in the 16th-century discovered that, on stilts (*tchanques* in Gascon, *échasses* in French), they could navigate the bogs and keep track of their flocks on this flat landscape. People even learned to dance with the things on.

Stilt-walking died out once the forest took hold, but some 20 folk groups keep the dancing alive at local festivals and summer tourist events, for example at Seignosse (at 9.30 pm on Tuesday during July and August) and Hossegor (at 9 pm on Monday from June to September).

If you'd like to try, contact Nouvelles Échasses (☎ 05 56 88 80 58) at Belin-Béliet, which organises stilt-walking courses and even stilt-rambles.

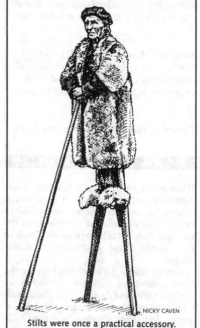

NICKY CAVEN

Stilts were once a practical accessory.

Activities

The park's main activity centres – for canoeing, sea and river kayaking, nature rambles, bird-watching, cycling, orienteering, rock-climbing, archery and multiactivity courses – are at Le Teich, the Centre d'Animation du Graoux (☎ 05 57 71 99 29, fax 05 57 71 99 20) at Belin-Béliet, and the Atelier Gîte de Saugnac et Muret (☎ 05 58 07 73 01). Other park activities include weekend discovery tours (on foot, bike, canoe, horse or donkey) and week-long hikes. Ask for the *Séjours au naturel* brochure.

Canoes and kayaks can be hired at various places along the Grande Leyre, including Graoux; the Base Nautique de Mexico (☎ 05 58 07 05 15) near Commensacq, open May to October; and the Base de Testarrouman at Pissos (☎ 05 58 08 91 58) and Base de Saugnac (☎ 05 58 07 73 01), both open year-round. All have camping facilities.

MONT DE MARSAN
postcode 40000 • pop 32,000
• elevation 27m

Mont de Marsan, prefecture (préfécture) of the Landes département, is best known as a base from which to visit the fine Romanesque monastery-church of St-Sever (see the following section). Its own pride and joy is France's only museum of modern figurative sculpture, and the compact town centre is dotted with arresting, life-size bronze nudes by two favourite sons, Charles Despiau and Robert Wlérick. The place has more spirit than charm, but a welcoming feel.

Orientation

Old Mont de Marsan straddles the confluence of the Douze and Midou Rivers which form the Midouze. From the train station, the centre is a 10 minute walk north via place Jean Jaurès, ave Sadi-Carnot and rue Léon Gambetta, and less than that from several of the long-distance bus stands.

Information

The tourist office (☎ 05 58 05 87 37, fax 05 58 05 87 36), 5 place du Général Leclerc, is open from 9 am to 12.30 pm and 1.30 to

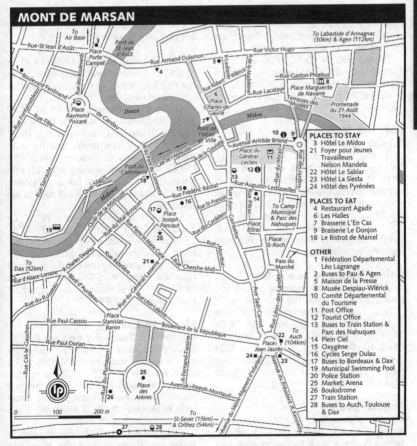

MONT DE MARSAN

PLACES TO STAY
3 Hôtel Le Midou
21 Foyer pour Jeunes Travailleurs Nelson Mandela
22 Hôtel Le Sablar
23 Hôtel La Siesta
24 Hôtel des Pyrénées

PLACES TO EAT
4 Restaurant Agadir
6 Les Halles
7 Brasserie L'En Cas
9 Brasserie Le Donjon
18 Le Bistrot de Marcel

OTHER
1 Fédération Départementale Léo Lagrange
2 Buses to Pau & Agen
5 Maison de la Presse
8 Musée Despiau-Wlérick
10 Comité Départemental du Tourisme
11 Post Office
12 Tourist Office
13 Buses to Train Station & Parc des Nahuques
14 Plein Ciel
15 Oxygène
16 Cycles Serge Dulau
17 Buses to Bordeaux & Dax
19 Municipal Swimming Pool
20 Police Station
25 Market; Arena
26 Bouldodrome
27 Train Station
28 Buses to Auch, Toulouse & Dax

6 pm Monday to Saturday (all day and to 6.30 pm from June to September). For information about the Landes in general, visit the Comité Départemental du Tourisme (☎ 05 58 06 89 89, fax 05 58 06 90 90), upstairs at 4 ave Aristide Briand.

Two good bookshops are Maison de la Presse at 3 rue Laubaner, open to 7 pm daily (until noon on Sunday) selling guidebooks, maps and foreign newspapers, and Plein Ciel, 65 rue Augustin Lesbazeilles.

Oxygène cybercafe (☎ 05 58 46 47 46, email oxygene@oxygene.fr), 32 rue Frédéric Bastiat, offers Internet access from 10 am to noon and 2 to 7 pm, Tuesday to Saturday.

Musée Despiau-Wlérick

This is the only French museum dedicated exclusively to early 20th-century sculpture. Some one hundred artists are represented, with the Art Deco period of the 1930s figuring strongly. Prominent are the works of two locals, Charles Despiau (1874–1946) and Robert Wlérick (1882–1944).

Despiau's lifesize bronze, marble and plaster figures look still and vulnerable, as if the models themselves were sitting there without their clothes. Upstairs, Wlérick's figures have more dash and muscle. Many works by contemporaries and followers are more statue than sculpture.

The museum (☎ 05 58 75 00 45), in the 14th-century Donjon Lacataye, 1 place Marguerite de Navarre, is open from 10 am to noon and 2 to 6 pm daily except Tuesday and holidays. Admission is free.

Parc des Nahuques

Take the children to this open-air wildlife park and walk among llama, wallaby, flamingo, emu and black swan. The park (☎ 05 58 75 94 38) is east of the town centre; take bus No 1 to the Nahuques stop. It's open from 9 am to noon and 2 to 6 pm on weekdays (to 7 pm in summer) and from 3 to 7 pm at weekends and on holidays. Admission is free. Nearby are tennis courts and a riding school.

Other Things to See & Do

A simple covered **boulodrome** (boules and pétanque court) is near the train station.

From June to September the Fédération départemental Léo Lagrange (☎ 05 58 06 36 00 or 05 58 06 90 91, fax 05 58 05 96 85) at the Maison des Associations, 2224 blvd Ferdinand de Candau, organises river trips by canoe or kayak down the sluggish Midouze to Tartas, a two hour jaunt.

Special Events

Mont de Marsan wakes up in mid-July for the big Fête de la Madeleine, with parades, fireworks, concerts, balls and sports events (including bullfights and courses landaises in the arena), and an airshow at the big air base north of town.

Places to Stay

Camping Plain, shady *Camp Municipal* (☎ 05 58 75 04 73, 341 ave de Villeneuve), beside the Parc des Nahuques (see the earlier Parc des Nahuques section), costs 10/5/4FF per adult/tent/car and is open year-round. Take bus No 1 to the Nahuques stop.

Hostels Staff at the *Foyer pour jeunes travailleurs Nelson Mandela* (☎ 05 58 06

83 84, 8 bis rue du Général Lasserre) say it's for French workers under 26 years old but may let you have a bed.

Hotels The plain *Hôtel Le Midou* (☎ 05 58 75 24 26; 5 place Porte Campet), close to the Pau bus stand, has six doubles/twins with shower for 130/180FF.

At *Hôtel des Pyrénées* (☎ 05 58 46 49 49, fax 05 58 06 43 57, 4 ave du 34ème Régiment d'Infanterie), a five-minute walk from both the town centre and the train station, comfortable doubles cost 120FF (200FF with shower, starting at 260FF with toilet). Its two-chimney Logis de France rating is probably for the good food in the restaurant.

A stone's throw away are *Hôtel Le Sablar* (☎ 05 58 75 21 11, fax 05 58 75 67 13, 3 place Jean Jaurès), where doubles/twins with shower and toilet cost 240/270FF, and there's a garden at the back; and *Hôtel La Siesta* (☎ 05 58 06 44 44, fax 05 58 06 09 30, 8 place Jean-Jaurès), where rooms cost 220/240FF.

Places to Eat

Our choice is *Brasserie l'En Cas* (☎ 05 58 75 17 58, 2 place Charles de Gaulle), by the covered market and the Midou, which offers a generous 50FF lunchtime *plat du jour*, plus salads and *assiettes* (regional savouries). Along the same lines is *Brasserie le Donjon* (☎ 05 58 46 09 09, 2 ave Aristide Briand), open daily.

There's a good-value hotel-restaurant at *Hôtel des Pyrénées* (see the preceding Places to Stay section), where *menus* start at 70FF. The 47FF lunch *formule* and 85FF dinner *menu* at *Le Bistrot de Marcel* (☎ 05 58 75 09 71, 1 rue du Pont du Commerce) are the town's best take on Landaise cooking; the restaurant is closed on Sunday and at lunchtime on Monday.

For a change, try the Moroccan dishes at little *Restaurant Agadir* (19 rue Armand Dulamon). Self-caterers will like the Saturday morning food market in the *covered market* (Les Halles) in pass du Marché; and the small daily *market* in place Charles de Gaulle.

Getting There & Away

Bus Long-distance operators include RDTL (☎ 05 58 05 66 00; stops at place Joseph Pancault), Massein (☎ 05 58 74 09 81; place Joseph Pancault), Rivière (Auch ☎ 05 62 05 46 24; train station), SNCF (☎ 05 58 75 22 89; train station), SERAG (☎ 05 58 75 22 89; train station) and Citram Pyrénées (Pau ☎ 05 59 27 22 22; place Raymond Poincaré).

For Dax (49FF, one to 1½ hours), RDTL and Massein together have one to three services daily except Sunday; SNCF has four to five daily. RDTL has one per weekday to Bordeaux (about 90FF, two hours). Citram Pyrénées runs daily services, except Sunday, to Pau (83FF, two hours). Rivière goes to Auch and Toulouse daily except Sunday, and SERAG to Agen (117FF) daily except Saturday. Tickets are bought on board the bus.

Train Mont de Marsan is linked daily with Bordeaux (107FF, 1½ hours) by two direct trains and several requiring a change at Morcenx, and with Bayonne (88FF, 2½ hours) by two or three a day daily with a change at Dax or Morcenx.

Getting Around

Bus From place Général Leclerc, useful local Transport Urbain Montois buses (☎ 05 58 05 66 00) include No 1 (from place Général Leclerc to the camp site and Parc des Nahuques, and No 2 to the train station. The fare is 5.60FF.

Bicycle Cycles Serge Dulau (☎ 05 58 75 28 60), 25 rue Frédéric Bastiat, rents VTTs for 60FF per day (summer only).

ST-SEVER

postcode 40500 • pop 4800 • elevation 100m
One of southern France's finest Romanesque buildings is the Benedictine abbey-church in this town 15km south of Mont de Marsan, on the northern edge of the hilly Tursan and Chalosse region.

Dedicated to St-Severus, who in the 5th century converted the Roman governor himself to Christianity, this was the most important monastery in Landes in medieval times.

Orientation & Information

The bus drops you at place de la République, from where it's a 400m walk northwest through place de Verdun to place du Tour du Sol. Here are the abbey-church and, opposite in an 18th-century town house, the tourist office (☎ 05 58 76 34 64, fax 05 58 76 43 70), open from 9.30 am to 1 pm and 2 to 6 pm Monday to Saturday and 10.30 am to 12.30 pm on Sunday in July and August; from 9.30 am to noon and 1.30 to 5.30 pm Monday to Saturday (to 4.30 pm Saturday) and 10.30 am to 12.30 pm Sunday the rest of the year.

Abbaye-Église St-Sever

The abbey-church was founded in 988 as part of an effort by Guillaume Sanche, Count of Gascony, to stake a political claim in the region. A major reconstruction under the abbacy of Grégoire de Montaner (1028–72) set a tone of artistic exuberance, and not only in its multichapel floor plan.

Let your eye climb the interior columns for a parade of carved stone capitals, high enough (or subtle enough) to have escaped the ravages of Huguenots, Revolutionaries and 19th-century restorers. The earliest look like foliage, with grinning animals here and there. Later highlights include The Feast of Herod, complete with dancing Salome, just inside the west door; a quartet of phoenix birds and a tiny, realistic human figure, across the nave from the Feast of Herod; and Daniel holding two lions by their tongues, between the middle and inner side-chapels on the southern side. Outside, the (otherwise 19th-century) northern portal bears a crumbling Romanesque tympanum.

The church is open from 8 am to noon and 2 to 6 pm daily; admission is free.

Musée des Jacobins

Upstairs in the gloomy remnants of a 13th-century Dominican cloister near the bus stop is the dusty little Musée des Jacobins, with old postcards, artefacts from an excavated Roman villa, and... The Hall of the

Apocalypse! Here is a series of facsimile pages of the *Apocalypse of St-Sever*, an extraordinary illuminated manuscript produced under Grégoire de Montaner and now in the Bibliothèque National in Paris. The museum is open from 3 to 6.30 pm daily except holidays; admission is free.

Morlanne

From the Abbaye-Église St-Sever, walk north-east up rue Lafayette, across the main road and then left up ave de Morlanne to a park on the site of the original Roman governor's palace. It's easy to see what attracted the Romans, and later the Counts of Gascony: St-Sever sits on a cornice of land historically known as the Cap de Gascogne (Cape of Gascony), with an impressive view north over the Adour to the forests of the Landes.

Places to Stay

The simple municipal *Camping Les Rives d'Adour* (☎ 05 58 76 04 60), on the Adour about 2km north-east of the centre, is open in July and August only, and costs 9.50/4.70/5.10FF per adult/tent/car.

Hôtel Lauqué (☎ 05 58 76 00 25, rue A Marrast), opposite the Musée des Jacobins, has a few doubles with shared shower and toilet for 110FF to 130FF. *Hôtel Alios* (☎ 05 58 76 44 00) in Bas Mauco, 3km north on the D933, has rooms with shower costing from 210FF. The tourist office has details of several rural *camp sites*, *chambres d'hôtes* and *gîtes* (cottages).

Places to Eat

The modest *Restaurant Le Touron* (☎ 05 58 76 03 04, rue de Touron), 200m north-west of the tourist office, has *menus* from 58FF. *La Table des Jacobins* (☎ 05 58 76 36 93, rue des Arceaux), behind Abbaye-Église St-Sever on place de Verdun, has a lunchtime *menu du jour* costing 55FF. *Menus* at the restaurant at *Hôtel Alios* (see Places to Stay) start at 80FF.

Getting There & Away

SNCF has buses from the train stations at Mont de Marsan (12FF; 15 minutes) and Dax (46FF; 50 minutes). Useful departures from Mont de Marsan are at 7.31 am and 2.20 pm, with 11.36 am and 5.12 and 8.14 pm departures from St-Sever. Leave from Dax at 10.47 am and head back at 2.34 or 6.38 pm.

DAX

postcode 40100 • pop 20,000 • elevation 9m

Dax is France's biggest thermal spa, in terms of visitor count and the sheer volume of hot water bubbling from the ground. These waters have been known since Roman times for their relief of rheumatic ailments, and Dax has also become a centre for special mud treatments (see the boxed text 'Ple-ease Don't Call it Mud'). The town itself has managed to stay free of the twee, cloying atmosphere of many smaller spas (see the boxed text 'Thermalisme in the Landes' later in this section).

Dax has a train station on the TGV Atlantique line where it branches to Bayonne and Pau. It's therefore a transport hub, a gateway west to the resorts of Hossegor, Capbreton and Seignosse, and east into Gascony.

Orientation & Information

The adjacent train and bus stations are nearer the satellite town of St-Paul-lès-Dax than to Dax. To reach the centre of Dax, climb ave de la Gare and turn left (south) for 1km along ave St-Vincent de Paul, across the Adour River to place Thiers.

Ple-ease Don't Call it Mud!

It's *le péloïde de Dax*, a greenish, noisome, mineral-rich paste prepared from silt harvested where thermal springs bubble along the banks of the Adour and fermented in the sun for several months. The formula is specific and a local quality-control body, the Régie Municipale des Boues – the Municipal Mud Agency, more or less – oversees those resorts where patients have their joints smeared with the stuff.

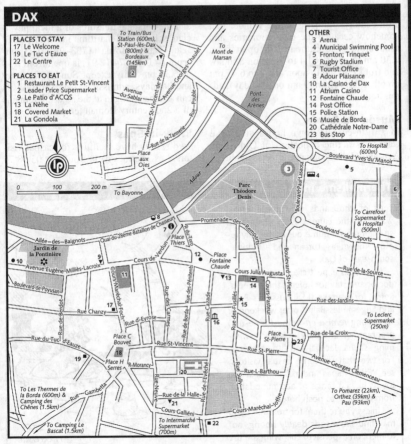

DAX

PLACES TO STAY
17 Le Welcome
19 Le Tuc d'Eauze
22 Le Centre

PLACES TO EAT
1 Restaurant Le Petit St-Vincent
2 Leader Price Supermarket
9 Le Patio d'ACQS
13 La Nèhe
18 Covered Market
21 La Gondola

OTHER
3 Arena
4 Municipal Swimming Pool
5 Fronton; Trinquet
6 Rugby Stadium
7 Tourist Office
8 Adour Plaisance
10 La Casino de Dax
11 Atrium Casino
12 Fontaine Chaude
14 Post Office
15 Police Station
16 Musée de Borda
20 Cathédrale Notre-Dame
23 Bus Stop

Here is the tourist office (☎ 05 58 56 86 86, fax 05 58 56 86 80, email tourisme .dax@wanadoo.fr), open from 9.30 am to 12.20 pm and 2 to 6 pm weekdays (6.30 pm from April to October, and daily without a lunch break in July and August). Pick up their good French-language booklet, *Dax en poche!*, which details activities, museums, food and other highlights around the Landes.

The police station (05 58 56 58 58) is on rue des Fusillés, behind the post office. The municipal hospital is east out along blvd Yves du Manoir or blvd des Sports.

Fontaine Chaude

This is the perfect symbol for the town: a perpetually steaming pool, built in 1818 and overflowing (through lion-headed spigots) with 64°C water from the biggest of the town's wells. It's fenced off, presumably to keep enthusiastic visitors from boiling themselves alive.

Cathédrale Notre Dame

This cross-breed of a cathedral is all flying buttresses and towers outside, gloomy baroque and classical inside. The best part is the interior portal in the north transept, depicting the Last Judgement – an amazing 13th-century southern Gothic wonder that somehow escaped the revolutionaries and renovators. The cathedral is open from 7.30 am to noon and 4 to 7 pm on Sunday, and from 7.15 am to noon and 2 to 6.45 pm on other days (from 9 am on Monday); admission is free.

Musée de Borda

In a 17th-century town house at 27 rue Cazade is a fine collection of Old Stone Age and Gallo-Roman artefacts, medieval sculpture, 18th- and 19th-century paintings, and the personal treasures of a local physician, scholar and maritime inventor named Jean-Charles Borda (1733–99). The museum (☎ 05 58 74 12 91) is open from 2.30 to 6.30 pm daily except Sunday, Tuesday and holidays; admission costs 15FF. Visits can also be arranged to the adjacent remains of a 2nd-century Roman temple.

Walk-in Spas

Two resorts have facilities for casual visitors. Les Thermes de la Borda (☎ 05 58 74

Thermalisme in the Landes

Tens of thousands take the thermal waters of the Landes every year. Small spa centres are numerous in the hilly region known as Tursan and Chalosse, south-east of Dax.

Most spas expect clients to consult a doctor and stay for at least three weeks. Some, for example at Saubusse-les-Bains and Eugénie-les-Bains, offer weekend or week-long *remise-en-forme* ('tone-up') programmes including massage, swimming, sauna, Jacuzzi and fitness rooms. For two that welcome casual visitors, see Walk-in Spas under Dax. Most spa towns have a range of accommodation from camping to posh hotels.

Unless you're there for treatment you may find spa resorts deadly boring, not to mention expensive. Following are the Landes' best:

NICKY CAVEN

Sweating and regretting: for those who find the gastronomic delights of the region difficult to resist

Dax 18 spas, year-round; see Dax
St-Paul-lès-Dax three spas, year-round; tourist office ☎ 05 58 91 60 01, fax 05 58 91 97 44
Eugénie-les-Bains one spa, February–December; spa ☎ 05 58 05 06 07, tourist office ☎ 05 58 51 13 16
Saubusse-les-Bains one spa, March–November; spa ☎ 05 58 57 40 00
Tercis-les-Bains one spa, mid-February to mid-December; spa ☎ 05 58 57 82 08

Elegant Eugénie-les-Bains is known as France's weight-loss capital, though it can't be easy: here is the *Hôtel La Maison Rose* (☎ 05 58 05 05 05), whose owner, Michel Guérard, is probably the south-west's most imaginative and celebrated chef. Take a double room with breakfast (from 400FF to 430FF), or blow your taste buds away: full-board costs from 1050FF to 1220FF.

86 13) is 1.5km west of the centre at 30 rue des Lazaristes (take bus No 4 from the covered market to the Lazaristes stop). Calicéa (☎ 05 58 90 66 00) is on Lac de Christus in St-Paul-lès-Dax (take bus No 1 north from place St-Pierre to the Frison stop). Both have pools, Jacuzzis, hot and cold fountains, saunas and more. Calicéa is open to 9 pm daily, and costs 55FF per two hours; Les Thermes de la Borda is open to 8 pm daily except Sunday, it costs 30/40FF per half/full hour.

Special Events
The **Faria de Dax**, held annually from 12 to 17 August, features bullfights, courses landaises, pélote Basque, brass bands and much more. Bullfights and lots of Latin music are part of the **Toros y Salsa** festival in September.

Places to Stay
Two camp sites, open from mid-March to October, are about 2km west of the centre. *Les Chênes* (☎ *05 58 90 05 53, fax 05 58 56 18 77, Bois de Boulogne*) charges 95FF forfait and has a swimming pool, restaurant and bar. *Le Bascat* (☎ *05 58 56 16 68, fax 05 58 56 20 56, rue de Jouandin*) costs 16/25/6FF per adult/tent/car. Take bus No 4 from the covered market, to the Bascat stop for Les Chênes and to the Jouandin stop for Le Bascat. St-Paul-lès-Dax also has several camp sites.

The town brims with top-end hotels for spa patients (the tourist office has a list of these and half a dozen rural chambres d'hôtes). Three plain, non-spa hotels offering doubles with shower and toilet from about 180FF are less than 500m south of the tourist office: *Le Centre* (☎ *05 58 74 07 02, 6 cours Maréchal Joffre*), *Le Tuc d'Eauze* (☎ *05 58 90 90 60, 9 rue du Tuc d'Eauze*) and *Le Welcome* (☎ *05 58 90 00 91, fax 05 58 74 03 34, cours Maréchal Foch*).

Places to Eat
Good value at the lower end is *Restaurant Le Petit St-Vincent* (☎ *05 58 56 97 92, 63 ave St-Vincent de Paul*), about 300m north of the river, where *menus* start at 55FF; it's closed on Sunday. A good hotel-restaurant is *Le Tuc d'Eauze* (see Places to Stay), with a 60FF lunch *menu* and 88FF *menu du chef* (chef's menu). *Le Borda* is a recommended spa-restaurant at Les Thermes de la Borda (see the earlier Walk-In Spas section).

Two cheerful brasseries with good salads and assiettes costing from 30FF to 50FF are *La Nèhe (cours Julia Augusta)* and *Le Patio d'ACQS (ave Eugène Milliès-Lacroix)*.

Dax seems to have a lot of pizzerias; one is *La Gondola (rue de la Halle)*, where most dishes cost around 50FF; it's closed on Wednesday evening and Sunday.

Do-it-yourselfers should visit the Saturday morning *covered market* at the marché couvert. There are also four *supermarkets* near the centre.

Entertainment
From June to September you can watch pélote Basque every Wednesday evening, at 5.30 pm at the fronton or 8 pm in the covered trinquet or jaï alaï, both of them near the rugby stadium on blvd Yves du Manoir. For scheduled rugby matches, ask at the tourist office.

Le Casino de Dax, at the western end of ave Eugène Milliès-Lacroix, is open from 3 pm daily with roulette, blackjack and floorshows. The Art-Deco Atrium Casino (1928) on cours de Verdun is not for gambling but for conventions.

Shopping
A big clothes market materialises at place St-Pierre and in front of the Cathédrale Notre Dame all day Saturday. The covered market hosts a big all-day flea market on the first Thursday of every month.

The Landes' biggest foie gras market is on Monday and Wednesday at Pomarez, 22km south-east of Dax, though it's busiest in November and December. Get there by 6 am to see it at its best.

Getting There & Away
Daily train connections to Dax station (☎ 05 58 56 80 80) include four from Mont de Marsan (58FF, 1¼ hours), eight from

Bayonne (48FF, 40 minutes) and five from Bordeaux (110FF, 1½ hours).

All long-distance buses use the stand by the train station, but many also stop at place St-Pierre. For Mont de Marsan (49FF, one to 1½ hours), RDTL/Massein have one to three services daily except Sunday; SNCF runs four to five daily. RDTL goes to Bayonne (46FF, 1½ to 2½ hours) two or three times daily except Sunday.

Getting Around

Infrequent Urbus buses will get you to/from the train station (No 1, every hour or two) and camp sites (No 4, five times a day). For a local taxi, call ☎ 05 58 74 71 53.

Bicycle rental outfits include Cycles Castets Arnaud (☎ 05 58 74 27 37) 13 cours Gallieni, and Localoisirs (book over the telephone and the bike will be delivered; ☎ 05 58 90 80 81).

The Dordogne

The Dordogne département, an area historically and still locally known as Périgord (after the name of the region's pre-Roman tribe, Petrocorii), is one of the cradles of human civilisation. The prehistoric remains of Neanderthal and Cro-Magnon people have been discovered throughout the region and quite a number of local caves – including the world-famous Lascaux – are adorned with extraordinary works of prehistoric art (see the Arts section in Facts about South-West France). In addition, Périgord's numerous hilltop chateaux and defensive *bastides* (fortified villages) testify to the bloody battles waged here during the Hundred Years' War when much of the area was in English hands.

To make the region's other attractions more accessible to visitors, Périgord has been divided into four areas and assigned colours according to their most prominent features. The fields and forests to the north are known as Périgord Vert (green). In the centre, the limestone area surrounding the capital, Périgueux, is known as Périgord Blanc (white). The wine-growing area of Périgord Pourpre (purple) lies to the south around Bergerac. Périgord Noir (black) encompasses the Vézère valley and the Dordogne River valley to the south, an area known for its dark oak and pine forests; between the two valleys lies the capital of Périgord Noir, the attractive medieval and Renaissance town of Sarlat-la-Canéda.

Thanks to all its natural and cultural attractions, tourism has become a major revenue earner for the region, accounting for over 22% of the département's annual income. Some two million tourists a year flock here; during the summer you may well encounter 60-seat coaches navigating back roads barely wide enough for two Twingos. But in winter, the region goes into deep hibernation and many hotels, restaurants and tourist sites close.

Included in this chapter are several places officially belonging to neighbouring Corrèze

Highlights

- Marvel at Lascaux II, the replica of one of the world's most famous prehistoric painted caves; then see more of the real thing – 12,000-year-old painted horses and mammoth, bison and deer – still in situ, at Font de Gaume in Les Eyzies de Tayac

- Canoe or kayak down the grand Dordogne River in the shadow of medieval fortresses and chateaux

- Meander through Sarlat-la-Canéda, a beautifully preserved medieval and Renaissance town, at its liveliest on Saturday market day

- Truffles – tasteless and dull? Or simply sublime? You'll never know until you've tasted these black subterranean tubers, at their best in Périgord, finest when fresh (from November to March) and delicious any time in an *omelette aux truffes*

- Discover the dreamy Dronne valley, north of Périgueux, and Fôret de la Double, south of Ribérac, rich with Romanesque churches

DORDOGNE

Périgueux ●
p177

Brive-la-Gaillarde ●
p188

Vézère & Dordogne Valleys p194

Sarlat-la-Canéda p204 ●
Medieval Town p205

pâté de foie gras – enlarged goose/duck liver

pommes de terre sarladaises – fried potatoes with truffles

gâteau aux noix – walnut cake

173

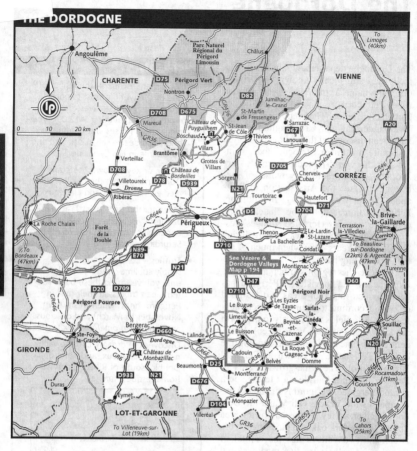

THE DORDOGNE

département: Brive-la-Gaillarde (an important transport hub), and Collonges-la-Rouge and Beaulieu-sur-Dordogne, both major attractions nearby.

Information

There are several useful brochures available at most tourist offices: *La Fête en Périgord* gives festival dates and opening times of everything from caves to chateaux plus courses and workshops; *Bienvenue à la Ferme* lists rural places to stay or eat or to buy farm produce. The département's Service de Reservation Loisirs Accueil (see Tourist Offices in the Périgueux section) publishes a brochure of accommodation, activity holidays and courses in the region; and Sarlat's *Loisirs et Curiosités* is packed with information on Périgord Noir (French only). The département's (French-only) Web site at www.perigord.tm.fr is also worth checking.

Want to walk through Périgord? Pick up Topo-Guide 321, *Traversée du Périgord,* full of tempting hikes, especially along the GR6 and GR36.

The département's main tourist office is in Périgueux (see Tourist Offices under Information in the Périgueux section).

Activities

Horse Riding There are dozens of horse-riding outfits (most with ponies for kids too); the average cost is between 75FF and 100FF per hour (60FF per hour for pony rides). Details are available from local tourist offices.

Canoe & Kayak Most canoe and kayak operators in the Vézère and Dordogne valleys are near the Dordogne River's La Roque Gageac and Cénac, or near Montignac on the Vézère. Costs, depending on the distance covered, range from about 25/40FF per person per hour in a canoe/kayak to around 110/130FF per day. Two- to seven-day trips (or longer) are also possible (roughly 230FF to 700FF per person, including tent). Remember to check whether the operator includes free transport and life-jackets. The following are mostly open from June to September and accept telephone reservations during the rest of the year.

Aventure Plein-Air
   (APA; ☎/fax 05 53 50 67 71)
   St-Léon-sur-Vézère
Canoë Copeyre
   (☎ 05 53 28 95 01)
   This company has a dozen centres in the area, including Beynac-et-Cazenac and Beaulieu-sur-Dordogne (☎ 05 55 91 27 25); there are special prices for family canoes.
Canoës des Courrèges
   (☎ 05 53 08 75 37, fax 05 53 03 98 02)
   Two kilometres south of Le Bugue off route du Buisson, this company offers trips on both the Vézère and Dordogne.
Canoë Dordogne
   (☎ 05 53 29 58 50, fax 05 53 29 38 92)
   La Roque Gageac
   This company offers good rates for four-person canoes.
Canoë-Kayak
   (☎ 05 53 50 19 26)
   Montignac
   This company offers trips along the Vézère to Thonac or La Roque St-Christophe.
Canoës-Loisirs
   (☎ 05 53 28 23 43)
   Vitrac
   This outfit is 2km east of La Roque Gageac.
Canoë-Raid
   (☎ 05 53 31 64 11, fax 05 53 29 58 09)
   This company has offices in both Siorac-en-Périgord and Cénac.

Randonnée Dordogne/Canoë Cénac
   (☎ 05 53 28 22 01, fax 05 53 28 53 00)
   Cénac
Randonnée Vézère
   (☎ 05 53 51 27 50)
   This company has three bases: Condat, Thonac and St-Léon-sur-Vézère.
Safaraid
   (☎ 05 65 30 74 47, fax 05 65 30 74 48)
   This is part of a major chain of canoe-kayak centres which can arrange trips on the Dordogne (one to 14 days) plus camp-site reservations and luggage transport.
   Web site: www.canoe-france.com

Rock-Climbing Several canoe operators can also arrange rock-climbing: APA, Canoë Dordogne and Randonnée Dordogne (see the Canoe & Kayak section). Costs are around 110FF per person for a half-day.

Organised Tours

The Service de Reservation Loisirs Accueil (see Tourist Offices under Information in the Périgueux section) can arrange everything from a gastronomic two-day tour of the region to a week's trundle in a deluxe gypsy caravan. Also on offer are organised trips on horseback, bike or foot, or on the Vézère or Dordogne rivers in a canoe or *gabarre* (the now-motorised 19th-century-style sailing boat once used to transport wine down to Bordeaux). Hike through the hills the easy way, with a donkey to carry the load: Association Arcâne (☎ 05 53 59 63 79), with a Web site at www.bourricot .com, can arrange an accommodating animal (for around 250FF per person per day).

Périgord Blanc

At the heart of the Dordogne, the focus of 'White' Périgord is the départemental capital, Périgueux, while its cultural highlight is the Château de Hautefort.

PÉRIGUEUX
postcode 24000 • pop 30,000
• elevation 106m
Périgueux, capital of Périgord and prefecture (*préfécture*) of the Dordogne département, is disappointingly dull, its only

THE DORDOGNE

highlights a restored medieval and Renaissance quarter (Puy St-Front) and the Musée du Périgord – one of France's best museums of prehistory. Founded over 2000 years ago on a hill bounded by a curve in the gentle Isle River, Périgueux (originally called Vesunna) flourished under Roman rule, only to be decimated by post-Roman invaders. It became the modest capital of Périgord in the 10th century but was soon eclipsed by its neighbour, the sanctuary and market town of Puy St-Front. The two finally united under the name of Périgueux in the 13th century.

Today the town is at its most appealing on the Wednesday and Saturday market days (from November to March truffles and foie gras are the market's main attractions).

Orientation

Puy St-Front, the old medieval and Renaissance city, is on the hillside between the Isle River (to the east) and blvd Michel Montaigne and place Bugeaud (to the west). On the other side of place Bugeaud is its historic rival, the largely residential Cité, centred around the ruins of a Roman amphitheatre. The train station is about 1km north-west of Puy St-Front.

Information

Tourist Offices The Maison du Tourisme, the town's tourist office (☎ 05 53 53 10 63, fax 05 53 09 02 50, email contact@ ville-perigueux.fr) at 26 place Francheville, next to Tour Mataguerre, is open from 9 am to 6 pm daily except Sunday. During July and August it's open from 9 am to 7 pm Monday to Friday and 10 am to 6 pm on Sunday and holidays. In summer, the municipality sets up an information kiosk on place André Maurois.

For general information about the Dordogne département (and the Service de Reservation Loisirs Accueil – see Organised Tours earlier in this chapter), head for the Comité Départemental du Tourisme's Espace Tourisme Périgord (☎ 05 53 35 50 24, fax 05 53 09 51 41, email dordogne .perigord.tourisme@wanadoo.fr) at 25 rue du Président Wilson. It's open from 9 am to

12.30 pm and 2 to 5.15 pm on weekdays (to 5 pm on Friday).

The Centre d'Information Jeunesse (☎ 05 53 53 52 81, email contact@ville-perigueux .fr), beside the Nouveau Théâtre de Périgueux, at 1 ave d'Aquitaine, has information on jobs, long-term lodging and youth-related activities. It's open from 8.30 am to noon and 2 to 6 pm on weekdays only.

Bookshops Regional guides and maps are available at the Maison de la Presse bookshop, 11 place Bugeaud.

Money & Post Several banks can be found on cours Michel Montaigne. The main post office, at 1 rue du 4 Septembre, also has exchange facilities and is open until noon on Saturday morning as well as on weekdays.

Laundry In Puy St-Front, La Lavandière, on place Hoche, opens from 8 am to 8 pm daily.

Near the train station, La Lavandière, at 18 rue des Mobiles de Coulm, is open daily from 8 am to 9 pm, as is its counterpart at 61 rue Gambetta (the latter is open until 8 pm on Saturday).

Medical Services & Emergency The Hôpital de Périgueux (hospital; ☎ 05 53 07 70 00) is at 80 ave Georges Pompidou, 1km north-east of the city centre. The Hôtel de Police (☎ 05 53 01 17 67), at 17 rue du 4 Septembre, is open 24 hours.

Puy St-Front

Established around the abbey of St-Front in the 6th century, Puy St-Front is Périgueux's most appealing neighbourhood for a relaxing stroll. On the site of the abbey stands the eye-catching **Cathédrale St-Front**, topped with five domes studded with bumps and many equally bumpy smaller domes. When seen against the evening sky it looks like something you might come across in Istanbul. But, by day, the sprawling structure, controversially 'restored' in the late 19th century by Abadie (who used similar designs in his later creation of Paris' Sacré

PÉRIGUEUX

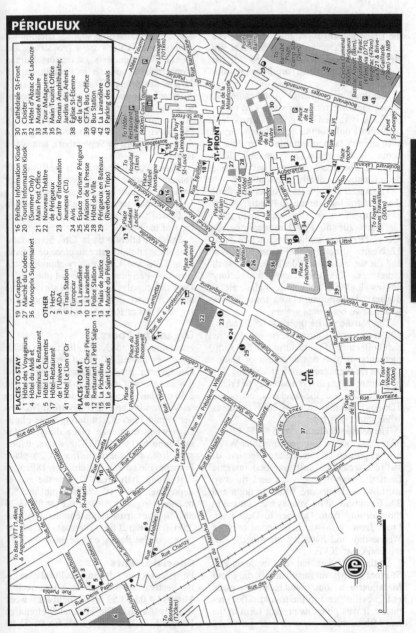

PLACES TO STAY
1 Hôtel des Voyageurs
4 Hôtel du Midi et
   Terminus & Restaurant
5 Hôtel Les Charentes
17 Hôtel-Restaurant
   de l'Univers
41 Hôtel Le Lion d'Or

PLACES TO EAT
8 Restaurant Chez Pierrot
12 Restaurant Le Petit Saigon
15 La Picholine
18 Le Saint Louis

19 La Grappa
27 Marché du Coderc
36 Monoprix Supermarket

OTHER
2 Hertz
3 ADA
6 Train Station
7 Europcar
9 La Lavandière
10 La Lavandière
11 Police Station
13 Palais de Justice
14 Musée du Périgord

16 Péribus Information Kiosk
20 Tourist Information Kiosk
   (Summer Only)
21 Main Post Office
22 Nouveau Théâtre
   de Périgueux
23 Centre d'Information
   Jeunesse (CIJ)
24 Avis
25 Espace Tourisme Périgord
26 Maison de la Presse
28 Hôtel de Ville
29 Périgueux en Bateaux
   (Riverboat Trips)

30 Cathédrale St-Front
31 Cloister
32 Hôtel d'Abzac de Ladouze
33 Musée Militaire
34 Tour Mataguerre
35 Main Tourist Office
37 Roman Amphitheatre;
   Jardins des Arènes
38 Église St-Étienne
   de la Cité
39 CFTA Bus Office
40 Bus Station
42 La Lavandière
43 Parking des Quais

euro currency converter 10FF = €1.52

Cœur), looks contrived and overwrought in the finest pseudo-Byzantine tradition. The carillon sounds the same hour chime as Big Ben (in London). The best views of the cathedral (and the town) are from pont des Barris.

The unadorned interior of the cathedral, whose entrance faces the south end of rue St-Front, is shaped like a Greek cross. It is noteworthy only for the spectacularly carved 17th-century baroque **retable** in the choir. It is open from 8 am to 12.30 pm and 2.30 to 7.30 pm. The eclectic cloister, next to place de la Clautre, is equally unexceptional.

The ancient cobblestone streets north of the cathedral include **rue du Plantier**. A few blocks to the west, the area's main thoroughfare, **rue du Puy Limogeanne**, has graceful Renaissance buildings at Nos 3 and 12. Nearby streets, including rue Éguillerie and rue de la Miséricorde, have more such structures. The 15th- and 16th-century houses along rue Aubergerie include **Hôtel d'Abzac de Ladouze**, across from No 19, with its two octagonal towers.

The **Musée du Périgord** (☎ 05 53 06 40 70), at 22 cours Tourny, is renowned for its rich collection of prehistoric tools and implements. It also has a wealth of Gallo-Roman artefacts from ancient Vesunna. It's open from 10 am to 6 pm Monday to Friday and 1 to 6 pm at the weekend (closed on Tuesday). Admission costs 20FF (students 10FF, under-18s free).

The **Musée Militaire** (☎ 05 53 53 47 36), 32 rue des Farges, founded right after WWI, has a particularly varied collection of swords, weapons, uniforms and insignia from the Napoleonic wars and the two world wars. Hours are 10 am to noon and 2 to 6 pm (closed on Sunday); it's closed in the morning from October to December. From January to April, it's open only on Wednesday and Saturday afternoons. Admission costs 20FF.

Of the 28 towers that once made up Puy St-Front's medieval fortifications, only **Tour Mataguerre**, a stout, round bastion on place Francheville (next to the tourist office) remains. It was given its present form in the late 15th century.

La Cité

The only remains of Vesunna – later known simply as La Cité – are a few stones and arches of Périgueux's 1st-century **Roman amphitheatre**, now set in a public garden **Jardins des Arènes**. The rest of the massive structure, designed to hold 30,000 spectators, was disassembled and carried off in the 3rd century to construct the city walls. It can be visited from 7.30 am to 6 pm (to 8 pm from April to September); admission is free.

Some 300m to the south is the 20m-high **Tour de Vésone**. Shaped like a gargantuan anklet, it's the only remaining section of a Gallo-Roman temple thought to have been dedicated to the goddess Vesunna, protectress of the town.

Église St-Étienne de la Cité, 50m southeast of the amphitheatre on place de la Cité, is an 11th- and 12th-century church which served as Périgueux's cathedral until 1669. Only two cupolas and two bays survived the devastation wrought by the Huguenots during the Wars of Religion (1562–98).

Organised Tours

From mid-June to October the tourist office organises guided 90-minute walks of the Cité Quarter at 10 am from Monday to Friday and tours of the Puy St-Front quarter at 2.30 pm daily except on Sunday (at 2.30 pm on Wednesday and Saturday from November to mid-June except during school holidays when they take place daily, as for mid-June to October). The walks, which start from the tourist office at 26 place Francheville cost 25FF (children 18FF).

Running daily from May to the end of September, from 10 am to 6 pm, are 50-minute *Périgueux en Bateaux* (☎ 05 53 24 58 80) river trips (with commentary) for 35FF (children 20FF). The boats leave from near pont des Barris, east of the cathedral.

Special Events

Périgueux's most dynamic cultural event is its Festival Internationale Mime Actuel Mimos (☎ 05 53 53 55 17) held for a week in early August. The Festival Sinfonia en Périgord (☎ 05 53 53 32 95, fax 05 53 03

78 77, email sinfonia@perigord.tm.fr) features highbrow classical concerts in the cathedral and nearby chateaux (for example Château de Bourdeilles) for two weeks in September.

Places to Stay

Camping & Hostels Situated about 2km south of the train station along Isle River, *Barnabé Plage* (☎ 05 53 53 41 45) camp site is open year-round. Prices are 16.50/16/10FF per adult/site/car. To get there, take the hourly bus No D from place Michel Montaigne to the rue des Bains stop (last bus at 6.20 pm; no service on Sunday).

The *Foyer des Jeunes Travailleurs* (☎ 05 53 06 81 40), also called Résidence Lakanal (and associated with the Hostelling International network) is just off blvd Lakanal, 600m south of the cathedral. A bed costs 73FF a night, including breakfast. Reception is staffed from 4 pm and it is open year-round. To get there, take bus No G from place Michel Montaigne to the Lakanal stop.

Hotels The pleasant *Hôtel de l'Univers* (☎ 05 53 53 34 79, 18 cours Michel Montaigne) has three small attic doubles for 180FF as well as other rooms, all with shower, starting at 220FF (280FF with bath and toilet). *Hôtel Le Lion d'Or* (☎ 05 53 53 49 03; fax 05 53 35 19 62) at 17 cours Fénelon offers ordinary doubles/triples with washbasin and bidet from 160/200FF (180/220FF with shower and toilet).

Among the budget hotels near the train station, *Hôtel des Voyageurs* (☎ 05 53 53 17 44, 26 rue Denis Papin) has doubles with cracked linoleum for only 80FF (100FF with shower). The amiable *Hôtel du Midi et Terminus* (☎ 05 53 53 41 06, fax 05 53 08 19 32, 18 rue Denis Papin) has doubles/triples from 145/215FF (215/255FF with shower and toilet). Hall showers are free. *Hôtel Les Charentes* (☎ 05 53 53 37 13, 16 rue Denis Papin) has doubles with shower costing 165FF (195FF with WC; 225FF for a twin). Reception (at the bar) is closed from 2 to 7 pm on Sunday.

Several notches higher is the welcoming

Ecomusée de la Truffe

To unravel the mysteries of truffles, a visit to the **Ecomusée de la Truffe** (☎ 05 53 05 90 11) is a must. The Maison de la Truffe and its nearby truffle path, which make up the ecomuseum, are in Sorges, 20km north-east of Périgueux. This village calls itself the capital of truffles (as do several other Dordogne towns!), thanks largely to its major truffle market held on the Sunday nearest 20 January.

The museum makes a heroic attempt at explaining why and where truffles grow (signs in English and French) and then encourages you to take a 3km promenade in fields across the road to see typical truffle terrain.

The museum is open the same hours as the adjacent tourist office, from 10 am to noon and 2 to 5 pm daily except Monday (from 9.30 am to 12.30 pm and 2.30 to 6.30 pm daily during July and August; guided visits during this period take place every Thursday at 3.30 pm). Admission costs 20FF (children 10FF).

And for those who want to taste the real thing, award-winning chef Pierre Core, a few steps down the road at **Auberge de la Truffe** (☎ 05 53 05 02 05) can whip up an *omelette aux truffes* for you for 120FF.

Logis de France *Hôtel-Restaurant du Périgord* (☎ 05 53 53 33 63, fax 05 53 08 19 74, 74 rue Victor Hugo) where doubles (with shower and WC) start at 230FF (300FF twin). It's on a busy main road so try to get a room facing the back garden.

Places to Eat

Restaurants In Puy St-Front, there are a number of eateries on rue Éguillerie and the streets that branch off it. *La Picholine* (☎ 05 53 53 86 91, 6 rue du Puy Limogeanne) specialises in cuisine Provençale and has a tempting midday *menu* for 60FF (closed on Sunday). The friendly bar-brasserie, *Le Saint Louis* (☎ 05 53 53 53 90, 26 rue Éguillerie),

THE DORDOGNE

serves tasty sandwiches, salads, pizzas, a good-value *plat du jour* for 37FF and evening *menus* from 55FF. It is open daily (except on Sunday) from October to Easter).

La Grappa (☎ 05 53 09 74 88, 13 place St-Silain) has outdoor tables in a pleasant shady area and serves pizzas from 35FF or *menus* from 85FF. *Hôtel de l'Univers*, with its vine-covered terrace, and *Hôtel-Restaurant du Périgord* (see Places to Stay) both have good *menus* from around 75FF.

A few hotels around the train station have *menus* starting at about 78FF – *Hôtel du Midi et Terminus* (see Places to Stay) is a favourite with locals. *Restaurant Chez Pierrot* (☎ 05 53 53 43 22, 78 rue Chanzy), has a hearty 50FF *menu* including 500ml of wine.

For Chinese or Vietnamese fare, try *Restaurant Le Petit Saïgon* (☎ 05 53 09 51 99, 1 place Général Leclerc) which has dishes from 45FF. It's closed on Sunday.

Self-Catering Near the cathedral, a *food market* is held on place de la Clautre on Wednesday and Saturday mornings. From mid-November to March an additional speciality market (*marché de gras*, literally 'market of fatty livers') takes place on the same day in nearby place St-Louis, selling not only foie gras but also truffles, wild mushrooms, walnuts, *confits* (conserves, typically of duck or goose) and other delicacies.

There are *food shops* and *traiteurs* (places with ready-made dishes) along rue du Puy Limogeanne; the *Marché du Coderc*, near the southern end, is open daily until about 1.30 pm. *Monoprix supermarket*, between place Bugeaud and place Francheville, is open from 8.30 am to 8 pm Monday to Saturday.

Getting There & Away

Air The Périgueux-Bassilac airport (☎ 05 53 02 79 70) is 8km east of the city. Flandre Air-Air Liberté (☎ 05 53 02 79 70, toll-free ☎ 08 03 80 58 05) has flights to Paris (Orly Sud) at least twice-daily on weekdays and once daily on Saturday and Sunday. Taxis to/from town cost around 70FF.

Périgord Market Days

You'll find traditional, open-air markets everywhere, every day of the week. Usually mornings only, they're the ideal places to find home-made or home-grown produce such as honey, goat's cheese, jam and cakes, wine, fruit and *confits* (preserves of duck or goose). In winter look for specialities such as foie gras, truffles, walnuts and ceps (*cèpes;* wild mushrooms). Ceps get their own special fair in Montpazier's place des Cornières every Thursday afternoon in September; truffles are available in the markets every Wednesday and Saturday in Périgueux between mid-November and March; and walnuts every Wednesday from October to December in Montignac and Ribérac, and every Friday in Brantôme.

Here are when the regular markets take place year-round:

Monday Les Eyzies de Tayac
Tuesday Le Bugue
Wednesday Périgueux, Hautefort, Montignac, Bergerac, Sarlat-la-Canéda, Ribérac
Thursday Monpazier, Domme
Friday Brantôme
Saturday Bergerac, Belvès, Beaumont, Le Bugue, Monpazier, Montignac, Périgueux, Sarlat-la-Canéda, Thiviers
Sunday St-Cyprien

Bus The bus station is on the southern side of place Francheville. Timetables are posted on the platforms (and are also available at the tourist office). The major carrier, CFTA (☎ 05 53 08 43 13), has an office (open from 8 am to noon and 2 to 6 pm weekdays only, to 5 pm on Friday) on the storey overlooking the waiting room at the terminal's western end. Other local carriers include Rey (☎ 05 53 07 27 22) and Laribière (☎ 05 53 05 30 07).

Except on Sunday and holidays, destinations served include Bergerac (40FF, 1½ hours, three daily), Brantôme (28FF, 40 minutes, one or two daily), Le Bugue (46FF, one hour, one daily during term-time), Ribérac (30.50FF, one hour, four daily) and Sarlat-la-Canéda (49.50FF, 1½ hours, one or two daily; only on Wednesday and Saturday in July and August) via the Vézère valley town of Montignac (34FF, one hour).

Train The information office (☎ 08 36 35 35 35) in the train station, near rue Denis Papin, is open from 9 am to 7.30 pm daily (closed on Sunday). It is connected to place Michel Montaigne by bus Nos A and C. You can leave luggage here for 20FF per 24 hours.

Destinations with direct services include Agen (112FF, 2½ hours, five daily); Bordeaux (98FF, 1½ hours, six to nine daily); Brive-la-Gaillarde (64FF, one hour, four daily) and Les Eyzies de Tayac (41FF, 30 minutes, two to four daily).

Service to Paris' Gare d'Austerlitz (274FF, 4½ hours) is via Limoges and to Toulouse (174FF, four hours) via Agen. To get to Sarlat (75FF), you have to change at Le Buisson or Libourne.

Car Near the train station are Europcar (☎ 05 53 08 15 72) at 7 rue Denis Papin; Hertz (☎ 05 53 53 88 88), place de la Gare; and ADA (☎ 05 53 53 17 70) on ave H Barbusse. Avis (☎ 05 53 53 39 02, fax 05 53 03 45 88) is at 18 rue du Président Wilson.

Getting Around

Péribus, the local bus company, has an information kiosk (☎ 05 53 53 30 37) on place Michel Montaigne, the main bus hub, where you can pick up timetables. It is open from 9 am to 12.15 pm and 2 to 5.45 pm, weekdays only.

Free car-parking is available at Parking des Quais. The central underground parks under place Michel Montaigne and place Francheville cost 4FF per hour (8FF for three to four hours). For a taxi call ☎ 05 53 09 09 09 or 05 53 53 70 47.

Cycles Cumenal (☎ 05 53 53 31 56), about 500m east of the city at 41 bis cours St-Georges, rents town/mountain bikes for 50/80FF per day or 170/250FF per week. It's open daily except on Sunday and Mon-

day. Base VTT (☎ 05 53 35 39 58) northwest of the city centre on route d'Angoulême, behind Salle Omnisports (take Péribus line No 7) rents mountain bikes for 50/80/150FF half-day/day/weekend. It's open from 9 am to 6 pm daily.

HAUTEFORT
postcode 24390 • pop 1050 • elevation 200m
Boasting the Dordogne's grandest chateau, this small hilltop village, 40km east of Périgueux, revolves around the tourism devoted to chateau visitors. There are some tempting walks in the nearby Auvézère valley.

Orientation & Information
The tourist office (☎ 05 53 50 40 27, email hautefort@fnotsi.net) has a splendid location in part of the 17th-century Ancien Hospice de Hautefort, on place de l'Église, at the top of the village. It's open from 10 am to noon and 2 to 6 pm daily, except on Tuesday, from 1 April to 30 June; from 10 am to 7 pm daily from July to October. At other times, call the town hall (☎ 05 53 50 40 20).

Available here are detailed trail maps for the immediate area, *Promenades et Randonnées Canton de Hautefort* (15FF), indicating 120km of signposted trails for walkers, horse-riders and mountain-bikers. Also in the building is the **Musée de la Médecine**, open the same hours as the tourist office (but afternoons only from April to June). Admission costs 25FF (under-12s 10FF).

Château de Hautefort
Visible for miles around, the strategically placed hilltop chateau (☎ 05 53 50 51 23), with its eye-catching domed towers, had several predecessors before its present 17th-century-style reincarnation. Its 12th-century version was the birthplace of the famously pugnacious troubadour, Bertrand de Born; in 1836, Eugène Le Roy (author of *Jacquou le Croquant*) was also born here, to a family working on the estate.

In the 20th century, the chateau was meticulously restored over a period of 39 years by the Bastard family but in 1968, the

euro currency converter 10FF = €1.52

THE DORDOGNE

year it was finished, the whole thing went up in flames. Undeterred, the family restored it all over again. Interior highlights include 17th-century paintings and tapestries and some fine chestnut timberwork. It's surrounded by immaculate gardens.

It's open from 10 am to noon and 2 to 6 pm daily from 28 March to 10 October; from 9.30 am to 7 pm between 11 July and 29 August, with the last visit at 6.30 pm; from 2 to 6 pm daily from 11 October to 1 November; and from 2 to 6 pm on Sunday only for the rest of the year (except during school holidays when it's open daily from 2 to 6 pm). It's closed entirely from mid-December to mid-January. The 45-minute guided visits cost 35FF (five to 13 year-olds 20FF).

Places to Stay & Eat
The nearest camp site is 3km to the south (off the D704) at the *Étang de Coucou* (☎ 05 53 50 46 55), a large lake with a bar-restaurant at one end. All-inclusive rates are 41FF per person. It's open from Easter to October. Some 7km to the west, at Tourtoirac, *Les Tourterelles* (☎ 05 53 51 11 17, fax 05 53 50 53 44) has a pool, a tennis court and horses to ride. Rates are 22/56FF per person/site.

Hôtel-Restaurant Le Médiéval (☎ 05 53 50 40 47, place de l'Eglise), near the tourist office, has basic doubles for 120FF with shower and *menus* from 60/75FF (midday/evening). At the foot of the chateau, *Auberge du Parc* (☎ 05 53 50 88 98, fax 05 53 51 61 72) has spiffier rooms for 200FF. The tourist office has details of *self-catering accommodation* in the area.

Getting There & Away
You'll need to stay a couple of nights if you're coming by bus: there's only one daily during the week, from Périgueux, at 5.25 pm, returning at 7.30 am the next day (1.10 pm on Wednesday). The bus stop is on place de l'Eglise, by the tourist office.

The nearest train station is at La Bachellerie (15km to the south) with infrequent connections to Brive-la-Gaillarde (33FF, 30 minutes; twice daily) and Périgueux (42FF,

40 minutes; twice daily). A taxi (☎ 05 53 50 44 64) between the train station and Hautefort costs around 80FF.

Périgord Vert

Stretching in a crescent shape across the north of the Dordogne département, Green Périgord receives less of the limelight than areas to the south, though it has a generous sprinkling of chateaux and attractive towns. Useful bases include Ribérac and Brantôme.

RIBÉRAC
postcode 24600 • pop 5000 • elevation 68m
There's not much to see in this drowsy little town in the heart of the Dronne valley – unless you come on a Friday when the biggest market in Périgord makes the place buzz – but it's a reasonable base for exploring the surrounding countryside by bike, or on foot or horseback. Two major attractions are the 50,000-hectare Forêt de la Double stretching to the south and west of town and the dozens of Romanesque churches in the area, several within easy walking and cycling distance.

Orientation & Information
Place National is the heart of town, where the Friday market is concentrated. Just to the west of here is place du Général de Gaulle, at the far end of which is the tourist office (☎ 05 53 90 03 10, fax 05 53 91 35 13). It's open from 9 am to noon and 1.30 to 6.30 pm Monday to Friday, 10 am to noon and 3 to 6 pm on Saturday from mid-April to late September (same weekday hours during the rest of the year but closed at the weekend). During July and August it's open on Sunday, too, from 9 am to noon.

An SNCF train ticket service (☎ 05 53 90 26 82) operates from the tourist office daily except on Wednesday and Saturday afternoon.

Activities
Walkers on the Romanesque churches' trail can find *Le circuit des églises à coupoles du Ribéracois* brochure at the tourist office, as

well as *Sentiers du Périgord* (60FF), a pack of *petits randonnées* (small walks from two to 20km). Other maps and books are available at the Maison de la Presse on place National.

The two nearest horse-riding centres are Madrix (☎ 05 53 90 03 53) a couple of kilometres to the north, at Villetoureix; and Le Centre Equestre de la Meyfrenie (☎ 05 53 91 69 38, fax 05 53 90 38 00), 12km to the north at Verteillac, just off the D708.

The municipal camp site (see Places to Stay & Eat) rents out canoes and kayaks from June to September.

Places to Stay & Eat
The municipal camp site *Camping de la Dronne* (☎ 05 53 90 50 08) is a couple of kilometres to the north (off the D708) on the banks of the Dronne River. It's open from June to mid-September and charges 11/11FF per person/site.

The unappealing *Hôtel de l'Univers* (☎ 05 53 90 04 38, fax 05 53 90 98 39, 2 ave de Verdun), across the road from the tourist office, has doubles at 160FF and a *menu du jour* at 60FF.

Offering a better ambience is *Hôtel de France* (☎ 05 53 90 00 61, fax 05 53 91 06 05, 3 rue Marc-Dufraisse), on the other side of the square, where doubles start at 225FF. The popular restaurant serves excellent regional fare; *menus* cost 80/100FF (weekday lunch/dinner).

Getting There & Away
The nearest train station is at Périgueux (32km to the east). CFTA (☎ 05 53 08 43 13) run buses four times daily Monday to Friday (once only on Saturday) to Périgueux (30.50FF; one hour). The bus stop is at Café du Palais near the tourist office (which has timetables).

Getting Around
Cycles Cumenal (☎ 05 53 90 33 23) at 35 rue du 26 mars (en route to the camp site), rents classic/mountain bikes at 50/80FF per day (170/250FF a week). You can drop the bike off at Cumenal's other shops in Périgueux or Sarlat. It's open from 9 am to noon and 2 to 7 pm daily except on Sunday, Monday and Thursday. From June to September, bikes can also be rented from the municipal camp site (see Places to Stay & Eat).

Car rental is available from Garage Peugeot (☎ 05 53 90 01 09).

BRANTÔME
postcode 24310 • pop 2100 • elevation 105m
One of the most attractive towns in Périgord Vert, Brantôme lies 22km north of Périgueux in a crook of the Dronne River. Famous for its extraordinary 11th-century abbey and picturesque setting on an island in the river, Brantôme has long been popular with expats and still tends to crawl with middle-aged Brits.

Orientation & Information
The abbey is tucked into a cliff-face on the north-western side of the river, connected to the island-town by several bridges. At its western end is a zig-zag bridge where the tourist office (☎/fax 05 53 05 80 52) is located, in a cute Renaissance pavilion beside the D78. It's open from 9 am to noon and 1.30 to 6 pm daily (closed Thursday

---

Brantôme's Saucy Abbot

The most notorious abbot in Brantôme's history – and one of French literature's wittiest story-tellers – was Pierre de Bourdeilles (1540–1614), who became the abbey's 'lay' or commendatory abbot in 1562. Hardly pious, he spent most of his life racing round Europe on various military or romantic adventures – though he did save his abbey from the Huguenots during the Wars of Religion after a tête-a-tête with their leader, a former military buddy. Finally grounded after a fall from his horse, Brantôme (as he came to be known) spent the rest of his life at the abbey writing saucy, spicy tales culled from his roving days (notably *Les vies des dames galantes*, Lives of Court Mistresses) which made his posthumous fame.

THE DORDOGNE

morning) from Easter to the end of October, it is open from 9 am to 1 pm and 2 to 7 pm daily during July and August. Winter hours are surprisingly whimsical for such a popular place, but you should at least get someone answering the telephone. At the other end of the zig-zag bridge is the Jardin des Moines, site of the May Fair (see Special Events).

L'Abbaye

The abbey (☎ 05 53 05 80 63), founded in the 8th century by Charlemagne to house the relics of St Sicaire, was rebuilt in the 11th century and became a major pilgrimage site. But the natural spring and surrounding caves of the cliff-site had attracted pagan worship long before. The monks initially lived in the caves and later used them as refuges at times of attack. They're still the most atmospheric and extraordinary part of the complex, especially the one decorated with a haunting 15th-century carving of the Last Judgement. The oldest and most interesting part of the abbey building – largely rebuilt in the 18th and 19th centuries and now housing the town hall – is the detached 11th-century gabled belltower.

The abbey is open from 10 am to 12.30 pm and 2 to 6 pm daily. Admission costs 20FF (seven to 18 year-olds 15FF). An English text is available to supplement fascinating explanatory boards at each cave.

Musée Rêve et Miniatures

This quaint little museum (☎ 05 53 35 29 00), at 8 rue Puyjoli (also called rue Meyjounissas, the road on the island-town opposite the abbey entrance), displays a collection of miniature interiors from different eras; not your trivial doll's house affair but a haven for serious miniaturists. It's open from 2 to 6 pm from April to June (closed on Friday); from 10.30 am to 6 pm during July and August; and from 2 to 5.30 pm between September and 11 November. Admission costs 25FF.

Activities

For trips along the Dronne River, contact Allo Canoës (☎ 05 53 06 31 85), 300m east

of the abbey; or Brantôme Canoë (☎ 05 53 05 77 24), 400m east of town, off the D78 (bikes available here, too). They operate daily from mid-May to mid-September (and on request out of season).

Special Events

Huge fairs have been held here every 1 May since the medieval pilgrimages of St-Sicaire. Other noteworthy market fairs include those devoted to the walnut harvest every Friday from November to mid-December.

Places to Stay

The friendly riverside *Camping Municipal* (☎ 05 53 05 75 24), off the D78, 1.2km east of town, charges 15/14FF per person/tent. It's open from 4 May to 30 September. The smaller, hilltop *Camping de Puynadal* (☎ 05 53 06 19 66, route de Périgueux), off the D939, 2.3km to the south, has an assortment of dogs, a small swimming pool and horses for hire. Rates are 13/14/8FF per person/tent/car; chalets from 700FF a week. It's open from 1 April to 30 September.

The road-noisy *Hôtel de la Poste* (☎ 05 53 05 78 55, 33 rue Gambetta) right in the centre of town, has doubles at 130FF (200FF with shower). Similar prices were available during our visit to the *Restaurant-Hôtel Bar Brasserie Versaveau Frères* (☎ 05 53 05 70 15, 8 place Charles de Gaulle), to the north of the river, though recent renovations may mean higher rates. A notch up is the nearby, ivy-clad *Hostellerie du Périgord Vert* (☎ 05 53 05 70 58, fax 05 53 46 71 18, route de Thiviers), a Logis de France hostelry where doubles cost from 255FF and *menus* from 95FF. The tourist office has details of *chambres d'hôte* and *gîtes* (B&Bs and cottages) in the area.

Places to Eat

The riverside *Bar du Marché* (☎ 05 53 05 80 49, 13 rue Victor Hugo), opposite the abbey entrance, has outdoor tables and a reasonable 65FF *menu*. The chic *La Petite Venise* (☎ 05 53 05 74 16), down an alley off 24 rue Puyjoli, has salads, *galettes* (wheat pancakes) and an outdoor dining area. It closes on Monday.

Au Fil de L'Eau (☎ 05 53 05 73 65, 21 quai Bertin) has a very pleasant riverside location opposite the Jardin des Moines and pricey but popular *menus* from 95FF (closed on Monday evening and on Tuesday). *Le Vieux Four* (☎ 05 53 05 73 65, 7 rue Pierre de Mareuil), almost opposite turning on the D78 that goes to Thiviers turning, is tucked into the rockface, giving it an ambience it calls *typique troglodyte* (literally 'typical cave dweller'). Their pizzas, cooked in a traditional oven, are the best in town, but service can be slow.

Getting There & Away

There's a CFTA bus two to four times daily, once on Sunday (28FF, 35 minutes) to/from Périgueux (to connect with the TGV trains to Paris).

AROUND BRANTÔME
Château de Bourdeilles

The tiny village of Bourdeilles, about 10km south-west of Brantôme, was once the seat of Périgord's oldest barony (the others are Mareuil, Beynac and Biron) and is now completely overshadowed by its chateau (☎ 05 53 03 73 36). There are two parts: a medieval section with a huge octagonal keep (built to keep the English out during the Hundred Years' War and still affording great views); and a 16th-century addition next door which was designed by Jacquette de Montbron (sister-in-law to Pierre de Brantôme; see the boxed text 'Brantôme's Saucy Abbot' in the Brantôme section) to impress a visiting Catherine de Medici (who, ironically, never turned up). The Renaissance features and furnishings are outstanding, notably the *salon doré* (gilded room), with its painted ceiling, and some bawdily carved food cabinets.

The chateau is open from 10 am to 12.30 pm and 1.30 to 7 pm daily except Tuesday from April to September. At other times it closes at 5.30 pm (closed entirely from 3 to 26 January). Admission costs 30FF (six to 12 year-olds 15FF). Visits may be guided if there are enough people; otherwise a detailed text in English, French or German is available.

Places to Stay & Eat Opposite Château de Bourdeilles, *Hôtel-Restaurant Les Tilleuls* (☎ 05 53 03 76 40) has basic doubles with shower costing 150FF and a daily midday *menu* for 60FF.

Around Villars

Grottes de Villars Situated 4km northeast of Villars (16km north-east of Brantôme), these grottoes (☎ 05 53 54 82 36) are more impressive for their stalactites and stalagmites than their cave art, but the 18,000-year-old blue horses and dusky image of a bison and so-called wizard (a rare painting of a human) are noteworthy. The grottoes are open from 2 to 6.30 pm daily from 14 April to 14 June and 15 September to 31 October, from 10 am to noon and 2 to 6.30 pm from 15 to 30 June and 1 to 14 September; and 10 am to 6.30 pm during July and August. Admission costs 38FF (children 25FF).

Château de Puyguilhem Set in dreamy countryside 1km north-west of Villars, this 16th-century chateau (☎ 05 53 35 50 10) is famous for its ornate stone carvings, both inside and out (more were lost during 18th-century renovations). The 90-minute guided tour of the rather barren interior can be taxing but reveals some fascinating details in the Renaissance tapestries and furnishings; a stone chimney carved with the Labours of Hercules is the *piece de resistance*.

It's open from 10 am to 7 pm daily during July and August; from 10 am to 12.30 pm and 1.30 to 7 pm daily except Monday from 1 April to 30 June and 1 September to 1 November (to 5.30 pm at other times except from 2 to 26 January when it closes entirely). Admission costs 30FF (children 15FF).

L'Abbaye de Boschaud Two kilometres north-west of Villars off a rural lane, this once-huge 12th-century Cistercian abbey now languishes in ruins in a field of crowing cockrels, its fine simple lines and pure Cistercian architecture still visible.

Places to Stay & Eat The simple *chambres d'hôte de Mme Marcelle* (☎ 05 53 54 80 76) in Villars costs around 180FF for a

THE DORDOGNE

double. The attractive *Le Relais de L'Ar-cherie* (☎ *05 53 54 88 64, fax 05 53 54 21 92*), on the Villars main road, has doubles from 190FF and *menus* from 80/100FF (midday/evening).

There's a *ferme de séjour* (☎ *05 53 54 82 86*), 4km east of Villars en route to St-Jean de Côle, where rooms cost 180FF (including breakfast) and *menus* 85FF.

St-Jean de Côle

Eight kilometres north-east of Villars (7km west of Thiviers) this is one of the prettiest villages in South-West France, with narrow lanes of tiled-roof houses and a broad main street beside the Côle River. Once a busy base for the Knights Templar crusaders, it's surprisingly uncommercialised. The 15th-century **Château de la Marthonie** in the village centre is open from 10.15 am to noon and 2 to 7 pm daily during July and August only. Admission costs 20FF. The well-equipped **tourist office** (☎ 05 53 62 14 15), by the chateau, is open from 10 am to 1 pm and 2.30 to 5.30 pm daily between April and November (to 7pm from July to September).

Places to Stay & Eat A farm camp site 5km to the north is *Camping en Ferme d'Accueil de Lage* (☎ *05 53 62 31 86, St-Martin de Fressengeas*). Rates are 10/25FF per person/site; meals are also available for between 60FF and 80FF. The riverside *Au Moulin de Feuyas* (☎ *05 53 55 03 99, St-Romain et St-Clement*) a few kilometres to the east, serves excellent meals from 80FF to 130FF and has space for a few campers at 12/10FF per person/tent; it's open from 16 March to 14 November.

In St-Jean de Côle itself, *Hôtel St-Jean* (☎ *05 53 52 23 20*) has doubles from 180FF (200FF with shower and WC) and weekday *menus* from 70FF. *Restaurant Les Templi-ers* (☎ *05 53 62 31 75*), by the tourist office, has outdoor tables and a 59FF *menu du jour*; its 75FF *menu* includes Périgord specialities such as *magret de canard* (lightly cooked steak-like breast of duck).

Getting There & Away The nearest train station is Thiviers (7km east of St-Jean de

Côle), which has connections to Périgueux (see Getting There & Away under Thiviers). A taxi from Thiviers (☎ 05 53 55 16 54) to St-Jean de Côle will cost around 60FF.

THIVIERS
postcode 24800 • pop 3500 • elevation 270m
This small market town 34km north-east of Périgueux calls itself the Foie Gras capital of Périgord: its winter foie gras markets (held every Saturday from mid-November to mid-March) are the oldest and most famous in the region and it even boasts a museum on the subject. Rather dull otherwise, it does have useful train connections, making it a handy base for exploring the hinterland.

Orientation & Information
From the train station, follow rue du General Lamy 600m south and you'll reach the town centre, place du Maréchal Foch, where you'll find the tourist office (☎/fax 05 53 55 12 50). It's open from 9 am to 12.15 pm and 2 to 6.15 pm Tuesday to Saturday from mid-May to mid-September; 10 am to noon and 3 to 6 pm during the rest of the year.

The train station is some 600m north of the town centre. A Maison de la Presse, selling maps, is behind the tourist office and there is a bank opposite.

Musée du Foie Gras
The museum diligently describes the production and history of foie gras. It is open the same hours as the adjacent tourist office (admission costs 10FF, children 7FF).

If you want to buy some of the stuff afterwards, you'll find several speciality shops along rue de la Tour (turn left and left again outside the museum) including Foie Gras Barby at No 9.

See the special section 'Food & Wine of the South-West' earlier in the book for more information about foie gras.

Places to Stay & Eat
The spacious *Le Repaire* camp site (☎/fax 05 53 52 69 75), 2.3km east of town, off the D707, has a small swimming pool and charges 20/25FF per person/tent (20/35FF during July and August) and 1600FF per

week for bungalows (2000FF in July and August).

Opposite the station, *Hôtel-Bar Restaurant des Voyageurs* (☎ 05 53 55 09 66, *rue Pierre-Sémard*) is a bit run-down, but you can't complain about the prices: doubles cost from 125FF (140FF with shower; 150FF twin). The popular restaurant serves a 60/85FF lunchtime/evening *menu*.

At Sarrazac, 10km to the north-east, *Laupilière ferme de séjour* (*☎/fax 05 53 62 52 57*) has rooms for 230FF (including breakfast) and evening meals for 80FF.

Getting There & Away

Thiviers station (☎ 05 53 55 00 21) is on the Bordeaux–Limoges line, with connections to Périgueux (38FF, 20–35 minutes) and Bordeaux (117FF, around two hours, some requiring a change at Périgueux) about a dozen times daily.

BRIVE-LA-GAILLARDE
postcode 19100 • pop 45,000
• elevation 142m

Although not in the Dordogne département, Brive-la-Gaillarde, a major rail junction 73km east of Périgueux, is a useful provisioning and accommodation base as well as a jumping-off point to the region. Situated on the left bank of the Corrèze River, Brive earned the moniker *la gaillarde* (the bold one) in 1356 as a reward for its martial gallantry. Nearby agricultural lands are known for their mild climate and *primeurs* (early-ripening vegetables and fruits). Brive's rugby team, Club Athlétique Brive Corrèze, have also put the place on the European rugby map with some recent international successes.

Orientation

Brive is centred around the heavily restored Église St-Martin on place Charles de Gaulle. Some 10 streets – many of them pedestrianised – radiate in all directions from the church and one of them, rue de l'Hôtel de Ville, becomes ave Jean Jaurès as it heads to the train station, 900m to the south-west. The tourist office and main bus hub are 400m north of the church on place du 14

Juillet, where there's also an eye-catching modern covered market, Marché Georges Brassens (also called Marché Couvert).

Information

Tourist Offices Housed in a 19th-century water tower in place du 14 Juillet, the tourist office (☎ 05 55 24 08 80; fax 05 55 24 58 24) is open from 9 am to noon and 2 to 6 pm Monday to Saturday (9am to 12.30 pm and 2 to 7 pm in July and August, when it's also open from 10 am to 1 pm on Sunday). During July and August they run 90-minute guided visits round the town, every Tuesday and Thursday at 10 am (25FF).

The Service Information Jeunesse (SIJ, ☎ 05 55 23 43 80, fax 05 55 17 07 66), at 12 place Jean-Marie Dauzier, has information on lodgings and youth-oriented events (including sports). It's open from 9 am to noon and 1.30 to 6 pm on weekdays.

Money There are banks along ave de Paris and blvd Géneral Koenig. Currency exchange is also available at the main post office near place Winston Churchill (known locally as place Thiers).

Post & Communication In addition to the main post office (see Money above), there's a smaller office at 28 blvd Anatole France, both are open until noon on Saturday as well as on weekdays. For Internet connections, Ax'ion (☎ 05 55 23 44 22), at 33 blvd Géneral Koenig, charges 13FF per 15 minutes (50FF/hour). It's open from 9 am to 7 pm Monday to Saturday.

Laundry The Lavarie at 39 rue Dubois is open from 6.30 am to 9.30 pm daily.

Medical Services & Emergency The Centre Hospitalier (hospital; ☎ 05 55 92 60 00) is at blvd Dr Verlhac about 1km north of the town centre. The main police station, Hôtel de Police (☎ 05 55 17 46 00), is at 4 blvd Anatole France.

Église St-Martin

This former monastery, dating from the 12th century but with 14th- to 19th-century

THE DORDOGNE

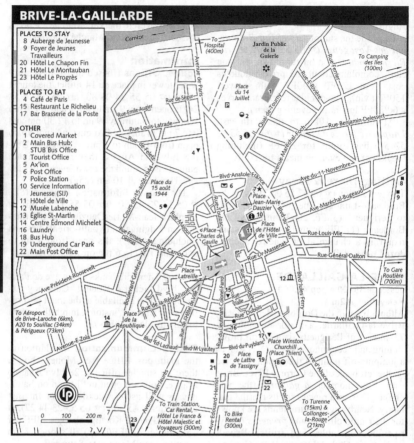

BRIVE-LA-GAILLARDE

PLACES TO STAY
 8 Auberge de Jeunesse
 9 Foyer de Jeunes
   Travailleurs
20 Hôtel Le Chapon Fin
21 Hôtel Le Montauban
23 Hôtel Le Progrès

PLACES TO EAT
 4 Café de Paris
15 Restaurant Le Richelieu
17 Bar Brasserie de la Poste

OTHER
 1 Covered Market
 2 Main Bus Hub;
   STUB Bus Office
 3 Tourist Office
 5 Ax'ion
 6 Post Office
 7 Police Station
10 Service Information
   Jeunesse (SIJ)
11 Hôtel de Ville
12 Musée Labenche
13 Église St-Martin
14 Centre Édmond Michelet
16 Laundry
18 Bus Hub
19 Underground Car Park
22 Main Post Office

additions and restorations, is at the very heart of the old town.

Built over the 5th-century tomb of St-Martin (a Spaniard who brought Christianity to ungrateful inhabitants who promptly massacred him), it has a Romanesque apse and choir and tall, cylindrical pillars of exceptional slenderness.

Musée Labenche

This well-arranged museum (☎ 05 55 24 19 05) at 26 bis blvd Jules Ferry, housed in the most outstanding of Brive's Renaissance mansions, covers archaeology, regional history and tapestries. It is open from 10 am to 6.30 pm between April and November (closed on Tuesday) and from 1.30 to 6 pm daily except on Tuesday for the rest of the year. Admission costs 27FF (children/seniors 13.50FF).

Centre Édmond Michelet

Housed in the family home of Édmond Michelet, a former minister under General de Gaulle who was interned at Dachau during WWII, this Centre National de la Résistance et de la Déportation (☎ 05 55 74 06 08) at 4 rue Champanatier has exhibits on the French Resistance during WWII and the deportations to Nazi concentration camps. Admission is free and it is open from 10 am to noon and 2 to 6 pm (closed on Sunday and holidays).

Places to Stay
The municipal riverside *Camping des Iles* (*π/fax 05 55 24 34 74, 13 blvd Michelet)*, about 400m north-east of town, charges 18/16FF per person/tent.

The modern *Auberge de Jeunesse (05 55 24 34 00, fax 05 55 84 82 80, 56 ave du Maréchal Bugeaud)* is in a pleasant little park about 700m east of town. A bed costs 48FF. Nearby, the *Foyer de Jeunes Travailleurs (π 05 55 17 40 00, fax 05 55 17 10 19, 32 rue Clément Ader)* also has rooms available if you're aged between 16 and 25 and in employment; be sure to call ahead for reservations. A dorm bed costs 80FF. To get to the Auberge de Jeunesse and the Foyer de Jeunes Travailleurs take the urban STUB bus No 5 from the train station to place du 14 Juillet, then change to a bus No 2 or No 4.

Near the train station, the cluster of cheap, basic and rather dreary hotels along ave Jean Jaurès includes *Hôtel Le France (π 05 55 74 08 13)*, at No 60, which has doubles costing 140FF; the *Hôtel Majestic et Voyageurs (π 05 55 24 10 20)*, at No 67, where basic doubles cost from 90FF (150FF with shower); and *Hôtel Le Progrès (π 05 55 24 04 52)*, at No 32 (reception closed on Sunday), which has doubles from 100FF (120FF with shower).

Two more upmarket Logis de France hotels in the town centre are *Hôtel Le Montauban (π 05 55 24 00 38, fax 05 55 84 80 30, 6 ave Édouard Herriot)*, where doubles cost from 230FF (250FF with bath; 240FF twin); and, opposite, the slightly pricier *Hôtel Le Chapon Fin (π 05 55 74 23 40, fax 05 55 23 42 52, 1 place de Lattre de Tassigny)*.

Places to Eat
There are several good-value bar-brasseries near the train station and also around place du 14 Juillet, including the trendy *Café de Paris (π 05 55 24 29 57, 11 ave de Paris)*

with 40FF *plats du jour* and a big-screen TV showing sports videos. It's closed on Sunday.

Bar Brasserie de la Poste (π 05 55 17 70 36, 33 rue Gambetta) is a lively, good-value place, open till 2 am daily except on Sunday. The modest *Restaurant Le Richelieu (π 05 55 24 47 98, 6 rue Vialle)* serves regional dishes from 33FF.

Getting There & Away
Air The tiny Aéroport de Brive-Laroche (π 05 55 86 88 36) is about 6km west of town. Air Liberté flies to Paris two to three times daily except Saturday. A taxi into town (there is no bus service) costs around 50FF.

Bus The Gare Routiére (bus station) is a kilometre east of town on ave Leo Lagrange but nearly all services stop at the town centre's bus hub on place du 14 Juillet. There's an urban bus service (STUB) information desk here (π 05 55 74 20 13) which can also answer queries about services to other destinations with the main regional bus company, CFTA (π 05 55 86 07 07). It's open from 8.15 am to noon and 2 to 6.15 pm from Monday to Saturday. Some services also go from place Winston Churchill.

Buses do not run on Sunday or holidays. Destinations served include Beaulieu-sur-Dordogne (34.50FF, two services daily during term-time), Collonges-la-Rouge (16.50FF, 30 minutes, four daily); Montignac (28FF, 1¼ hours, one daily in late afternoon); Sarlat-la-Canéda (42FF, 1¾ hours, one daily in the late afternoon); and Turenne (18.50FF, 20 minutes, one or two daily).

Train Brive is on the north–south line from Paris' Gare d'Austerlitz (268FF, four hours) to Toulouse (141FF, two or three hours), with stops including Limoges (78FF, one hour 10 minutes) and Cahors (79FF, 1¼ hours); and on the east–west line linking Bordeaux (135FF, 2½ hours) with Ussel, which passes through Périgueux (64FF, one hour) and continues east to Clermont-Ferrand. The station's information office (π 08 36 35 35 35) is open from 9 am to 6.30 pm (closed on Sunday and holidays).

THE DORDOGNE

If you're feeling rich and lazy you can take your car on the train all the way to Calais (see Train in the Getting There & Away chapter for details).

Getting Around

Opposite the train station on ave Jean Jaurès, Europcar (☎ 05 55 74 14 41), Hertz (☎ 05 55 24 26 75) and Avis (☎ 05 55 24 51 00) are at Nos 52, 54 and 56 respectively. Head for the well-signed, underground car park at place Winston Churchill for the cheapest parking (5FF per hour or 13FF for three hours).

Alain Brissard (☎ 05 55 23 04 40) at 40 ave Léon Blum rents bikes for 80/250FF per day/week (discounts for longer periods). He's open from 9 am to noon and 2 to 7 pm but closed on Sunday and for a week in August.

AROUND BRIVE-LA-GAILLARDE
Turenne
postcode 19500 • pop 740 • elevation 480m

Dubbed 'the small town with a great past', Turenne is named after the family of that name. The Turenne viscounts ruled their own territory for centuries – in other words it didn't come under the control of the French Crown – but in the 18th century, when they finally ran out of money, they sold out to the crown, bringing their independence to an end.

The village is dominated by its ruined hilltop chateau, perched on a rocky promontory. All that remains is **Caesar's Tower**, with stunning views, and a 13th-century red-stone **clock tower**. The chateau's opening times are posted on the tourist office window: it should be open from 10 am to noon and 2 to 6 pm daily from April to June; and from 10 am to 7 pm daily during July and August. Admission costs 16FF (seven to 18 year-olds 10FF).

The large **church** below the chateau dates from the 16th century and is in the form of a Greek cross. The rest of the village has steep, narrow streets and attractive, cream-coloured, stone houses with grey-slate turrets, including the imposing **Maison Tournadour**, near the church, once a salt warehouse.

Orientation & Information Turenne is 15km south of Brive, just off the D8. At the crossroads of the D8 and the steep rue du Commandant-Charollais is the helpful tourist office (☎ 05 55 85 94 38). Open from mid-April to mid-September it operates from 10 am to noon and 3 to 6 pm weekends only (closed on Saturday mornings in April), except during July and August when it's open daily. During the rest of the year, contact the town hall (☎ 05 55 85 91 15).

Among pamphlets worth picking up here are *Circuit roman en Quercy-Turenne* for a suggested tour of Romanesque churches in an area about 9km to the south; and *Randonnées en Vicomte de Turenne* (15FF) for walks in the immediate area.

Places to Stay & Eat The only hotel, *Restaurant-Hôtel Maison des Canoines* (☎ 05 55 85 93 43), is near the church and has just three stylish doubles that cost from 330FF and a popular *restaurant* with *menus* from 100FF (both closed from mid-November to February). The restaurant, with its tree-shaded terrace, is closed on Tuesday and Wednesday evenings (except during July and August).

Down on the main road you'll find humbler fare (sandwiches and crepes) at *Café Borie*. Turenne-Gare, the new town 2.8km to the south down the D8, also has some cheaper *restaurants*. The tourist office has details of *gîtes* and *chambres d'hote* nearby.

Getting There & Away
Cars Quercy Corrèze (☎ 05 65 38 71 90) run buses from Brive (18.50FF, 20 minutes) once or twice daily; train connections to Turenne-Gare (18FF) are infrequent.

Collonges-la-Rouge
postcode 19500 • pop 380 • elevation 280m

On a gently angled slope situated above a tributary of the Dordogne River, 18km south-east of Brive, the quaint narrow alleyways of 'Collonges the Red' (built entirely of bright red sandstone) squeeze between old, wisteria-covered houses topped with round turrets. Surrounded by lush greenery – and, in the spring, flowers of every colour

– the tiny hamlet is entirely devoted to tourism, with souvenir shops and craft displays on every corner. It gets horribly swamped in summer. But it can be a delightful place for a stroll, in part because after about three minutes you'll be out in the countryside.

Orientation & Information The tourist office (☎ 05 55 25 47 57), called Collonges Accueil, is in a wooden building in the car park alongside the D38 on the north-east edge of town. It is open from 2 to 5 pm Monday to Saturday mid-April to September but from 10.30 am to 12.30 pm and 2 to 7 pm daily during July and August. A local group, Les Amis de Collonges, organises guided tours of the village during high season (15FF); the tourist office has details.

Maison de la Sirène This charming 16th-century house (named after the decoration on the outside of a mermaid holding a comb and mirror) has been converted into a tiny two-room museum (☎ 05 55 25 42 48) showing old agricultural tools and household furnishings from the 19th century. It's open from 10 am to 12.30 pm and 3 to 6 pm at the weekend from April to September, but daily (and the same hours) during July and August; admission costs 10FF.

Church The partly Romanesque church, built between the 11th and the 15th century on the foundations of an 8th-century Benedictine priory, was once an important resting place on the pilgrimage route to Santiago de Compostela. In the late 16th century, local Protestants held prayers in the south nave and their Catholic neighbours prayed in the north nave, where a gilded wood retable erected in the 17th century still stands. Nearby, the ancient wood-and-slate roof of the **old covered market**, held up by stone columns, shelters an ancient baker's oven.

Castel de Vassinhac and Castel de Maussac These are the two most impressive manor houses in the village, the first (follow the lane east of the church) adorned with a mighty array of towers and turrets (its owner was a captain); and the second, to the north, a smaller, more homely affair with an elegant turret over its doorway.

Places to Stay The camp site *Le Moulin de la Valane* (☎ 05 55 25 41 59) is 700m to the south, off the D38 (adjacent to the municipal swimming pool). Open from May to October, *forfait* (fixed price deal covering two people) rates are 60FF for two.

The only hotel is the *Relais de Saint Jacques de Compostelle* (☎ 05 55 25 41 02, fax 05 55 84 08 51), in a partly medieval building in the centre of the village. Doubles with shower and toilet start at 310FF (one without shower costs 190FF). It is closed from mid-November to mid-March. *Auberge Le Prieuré* (see Places to Eat) has a beautifully furnished, romantic apartment for 450/600FF double/triple (including fridge and dining area).

The tourist office has details of *chambres d'hôte* in the area, including *La Vigne Grande* (☎ 05 55 25 39 20), 2.5km away, which has doubles/triples in renovated barns for 235/295FF.

Another alternative is to head 1.7km to the south, to Meyssac, where you'll find the Logis de France *Relais du Quercy* (☎ 05 55 25 40 31, fax 05 55 25 36 22) on the main road, which has doubles from 200FF (280FF with shower) and *menus* from 78FF.

Places to Eat The restaurant at *Relais de Saint Jacques de Compostelle* (see Places to Stay) has midday/evening *menus* of Périgord and Quercy-style dishes from 70/85FF. *Auberge Le Prieuré* (☎ 05 55 25 41 00, place de L'Église) has an attractive outdoor dining area by the church and *menus* from 80FF (closed on Wednesday except during July and August).

Cheaper fare is on offer at *Le Tourtou* (☎ 05 55 25 34 15), 100m downhill, which serves *tourtous* (a kind of *galette de Sarrazin*, or wheat pancake) and salads. It's open daily from April to September.

Getting There & Away Except on Sunday and holidays, Collonges is linked with Brive

THE DORDOGNE

by four buses daily (16.50FF; 30 minutes). The bus stop is near Collonges Accueil.

BEAULIEU-SUR-DORDOGNE
postcode 19120 • pop 1300
• elevation 140m

The verdant, aptly named town of Beaulieu (literally 'beautiful place'), 44km south-east of Brive, is one of the most attractive medieval villages along the upper Dordogne, famed for its majestic abbey-church. Nearby streets have picturesque houses that date from the 14th and 15th centuries.

There are some lovely spots for a stroll nearby, including the banks of the Dordogne. The GR480, a spur of the GR46, also passes by here. An English-language brochure of suggested walking trails is available at the tourist office.

Orientation & Information
Beaulieu has two main squares: place Marbot and place du Champ de Mars, on the south-west side of rue du Général de Gaulle (as the D940 is known in the town centre). The old city is between rue du Général de Gaulle and the river. Rue Rodolphe de Turenne begins across the street from place du Champ de Mars.

The tourist office (☎ 05 55 91 09 94), on place Marbot, is open from 9.30 am to 12.30 pm and 3 to 6 or 7 pm between April and mid-September, and from 10 am and 12.30 pm and 3 to 5.30 pm daily during the rest of the year.

The post office, also on place Marbot, is open until noon on Saturday as well as on weekdays and offers currency exchange.

Abbatiale
The Abbatiale is a 12th-century Romanesque abbey-church that was once a stop on the way to Santiago de Compostela. The southern portal's brilliant tympanum (circa 1130) illustrates the Last Judgement with vivid medieval scenes. Based on prophesies from the books of Daniel and the Apocalypse, the graphic figures include monsters devouring the heads and arms of the condemned and a seven-headed dragon from hell.

The treasury, open in summer (ask at the tourist office), has a 12th-century gilded Virgin and a 13th-century enamel reliquary.

Places to Stay
The shaded *Camping des Iles* (☎ 05 55 91 02 65), on an island sandwiched between two branches of the Dordogne, is open from May to September. Rates are 21.50/24FF per person/tent.

The delightful *Auberge de Jeunesse de la Riviera Limousine* (☎ 05 55 91 13 82, fax 05 55 91 26 06, place du Monturu), along the river by the Romanesque Chapelle des Penitents, occupies a 14th-century building. It has bunks for 41FF and a kitchen; and is open between April and October. The owner is a great hiker.

Best of the budget hotels is the *Hôtel L'Étape Fleurie* (☎ 05 55 91 11 04, place du Champ de Mars), which has bright, modern doubles costing from 150FF (220FF with shower and WC; 190FF twin). The recently renovated *Auberge Les Charmilles* (☎ 05 55 91 29 29, fax 05 55 91 29 30, 20 blvd Rodolphe de Turenne), right on the river, has smart doubles with shower and toilet from 310FF. During low season reception is closed on Sunday.

The Logis de France *Central Hôtel Fournié* (☎ 05 55 91 01 34, fax 05 55 91 23 57, 4 place du Champ de Mars), is open from mid-March to mid-November. It has doubles without shower for 180FF and larger doubles/triples/quads with shower and toilet from 260/300/320FF (320FF twin). The charming *Hôtel Le Turenne* (☎ 05 55 91 10 16, fax 05 55 91 22 42, 1 blvd Rodolphe de Turenne) has doubles/triples for 270/315FF.

Places to Eat
Good hotel restaurants (see Places to Stay) include the rustic *restaurant* in the Hôtel L'Étape Fleurie, where the midday/evening 78/98FF *menus* feature local specialities, and Hôtel Le Turenne, which has a 75FF lunchtime *menu* or a 95FF *menu du promeneur* (walker's *menu*).

Cheaper places on place du Champ de Mars include *Café Tabac Brasserie* (☎ 05

Nestling into the cliff, the stone houses of La Roque Gageac overlook the Dordogne River.

Spectacular views from Château de Castelnaud

The cliffs of La Roque St-Christophe, Dordogne

JULIA WILKINSON

St-Léon-sur-Vézère's Château la Salle ...

JULIA WILKINSON

... and Renaissance Château de Clérans

JULIA WILKINSON

Château de Losse, in the Vézère Valley, boasts 16th- and 17th-century tapestries and furniture.

55 91 18 34), which has salads and a midday *menu* for 65FF; and *Chez Didier* (☎ *05 55 91 10 04)* which serves crepes, pizzas and other cheap fare from noon to midnight daily in summer. Tucked in an alley behind the church is the chic little crepe and salad place, *Au Beau Lieu Breton* (☎ *05 55 91 20 46, rue du Presbytère)*.

On Wednesday and Saturday mornings, there's an open-air **market** next to the Abbatiale. There are two **grocery stores** on place Marbot, open daily except on Sunday afternoon. And in early May you can feast on strawberries galore during the town's Fête de la Fraise which usually features a 800kg strawberry cake!

Getting There & Away
Beaulieu is on the Brive to Argentat bus run (☎ 05 55 91 16 68): during term-time (except on Sunday and holidays), and during July and August, there are two buses daily to/from Brive (34.50FF). Schedules are posted at the bus shelter on place du Champ de Mars (opposite Hôtel L'Étape Fleurie) and outside the tourist office.

The nearest train station, Bretenoux-Biars (8km to the south), is on the Brive–Aurillac line, with twice-daily connections to Brive (42FF, 40 minutes).

Getting Around
Beaulieu Sports (☎ 05 55 91 13 87) at 21 rue du Général de Gaulle rents mountain bikes for 60/80/400FF a half-day/day/week. It is closed on Sunday afternoon.

Périgord Noir

This very popular region, encompassing the Vézère and Dordogne valleys, is dense with attractions dating from prehistoric to Renaissance times. Of the Vézère valley's 175 known prehistoric sites, the most famous ones (including the world-renowned cave paintings in Lascaux) are situated between Le Bugue (near where the Vézère joins the Dordogne) and Montignac, 25km to the north-east. Most are closed in winter – the best time to come is in spring or autumn,

when things are open but the crowds not overwhelming.

Public transport is very limited; if you don't have your own car, biking through the area is a pleasant alternative. Good bases include Le Bugue, Les Eyzies de Tayac, Montignac or the capital of Périgord Noir, Sarlat-la-Canéda (between the two valleys).

LE BUGUE
postcode 24260 • pop 2764 • elevation 63km
This small market town, 10km west of Les Eyzies de Tayac, has managed to retain something of its own character despite being surrounded by tourist sites and theme parks. As a base, it makes a pleasant alternative to staying in Les Eyzies.

Orientation & Information
The well-equipped tourist office (☎ 05 53 07 20 48, fax 05 53 54 92 30, email bugue@perigord.com), with a Web site at www.perigord.com/bugue, is 200m west of place de la Volaille, the centre of town where the market takes place (on Tuesday and Saturday) and where the D710 from Périgueux crosses the Vézère.

The office is open from 9.30 am to 12.30 pm and 2.30 to 6.30 pm daily from April to October (from 9 am to 1 pm and 3 to 7 pm daily during July and August; closed on Sunday and Monday from November to April). Currency exchange is available here and there is a SNCF train ticketing service (closed on Sunday except during July and August).

The post office is 80m north of the tourist office, on rue de la Boétie, and banks and shops are on the main rue de Paris running north of place de la Volaille.

Things to See
Some 600m east of the town centre, just off the D703 Les Eyzies road, the **Aquarium du Périgord Noir** (☎ 05 53 07 16 38) makes a change from prehistoric attractions. It is the largest privately owned aquarium in Europe and is open from 9 am to 7 pm daily between June and September (until midnight on Saturday during July and August) and from 10 am to 6 pm in April, May and September;

THE DORDOGNE

VÉZÈRE & DORDOGNE VALLEYS

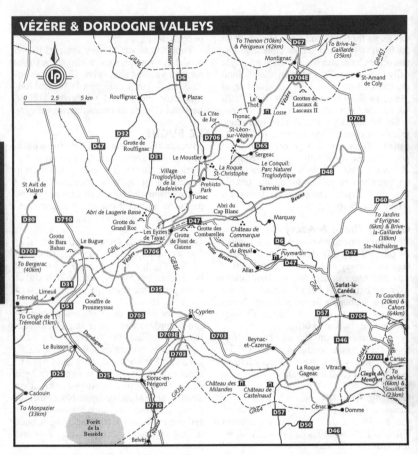

from 10 am to noon and 2 to 5 pm at other times. Admission to the aquarium costs 47FF (children 35FF).

The adjacent **Le Village du Bournat** (☎ 05 53 08 41 99) is a Périgordian theme park where you can watch farmers, bakers, carpenters and other artisans at work on traditional local crafts. There are funfair rides and restaurants, too. It's open from 10 am to 7 pm daily from May to October (to 5 pm for the rest of the year, closed in January). Admission costs 50FF (children 30FF).

See Prehistoric Sites later in this chapter for details of caves in the area.

Places to Stay & Eat

The camp site *Le Port* (☎ 05 53 07 24 60), 1km from town (follow the track past the aquarium), is open from mid-May to mid-September and charges 15/25/63FF per person/site/car or 70FF forfait for two. The municipal swimming pool is next door to the camp site.

Some 1.7km to the south, off the road to Le Buisson, *Le Rocher de La Granelle* (☎ 05 53 07 24 32) is a spacious riverside site open from April to October. Charges are 40FF per person or a forfait of 96FF for up to three people.

Hôtel de Paris (☎ 05 53 07 28 16, fax 05 53 04 20 89, 14 rue de Paris) offers good-value doubles/triples for 150/190FF (170/220FF with shower).

More upmarket is the Logis de France *Hôtel-Restaurant Le Cygne* (☎ 05 53 07 17 77, fax 05 53 03 93 74), a few steps from the tourist office, where you can find comfortable rooms with TV, shower and toilet from 250FF and restaurant *menus* from 88FF (from 100FF for dinner). The tourist office has details of many *chambres d'hôte* around town.

Le Trois As (☎ 05 53 08 41 57, 78 rue de Paris) is one of Le Bugue's best restaurants, with *menus* from 98FF. It's closed on Tuesday and Wednesday for lunch.

A good-value *Intermarché supermarket* is just across the bridge, on the road to Le Buisson.

Getting There & Away
The train station is 1km east of town, off the Les Eyzies road. Le Bugue is on the Paris (Gare d'Austerlitz, 287FF, 5¾ hours, one or two services daily) to Agen (81FF, 1¼ hours, two to three daily) line via Périgueux (46FF, 37 minutes, one or two daily). There are also connections to Bordeaux (105FF, via Le Buisson).

Getting Around
Garage Perusin (☎ 05 53 07 22 27), 1.5km north of town on the D710 route de Périgueux (look for the Avia petrol sign), rents mountain bikes for 60/360FF per day/week. It's open daily except Saturday afternoon and Sunday.

AROUND LE BUGUE
Limeuil
This charming little village, 6km downriver from Le Bugue, where the Vézère and Dordogne rivers meet, is surprisingly unspoilt despite its picturesque location. Climb up its steep streets to the municipal **parc Limeuil** (15FF; free for children aged under 12) a rambling, unkempt arboretum created in 1891. It's open from 2 to 6 pm on weekdays (11 am to 7 pm at the weekend) in June and September, 11 am to 8 pm

daily during July and August, 10 am to 6 pm at the weekend only during October and closed the rest of the year.

Places to Stay & Eat The hilltop *La Ferme des Poutiroux* camp site (☎ 05 53 63 31 62) 1.6km to the north of the village, is small and friendly (with a swimming pool) though without much shade. Rates are 20/18FF per person/tent and slightly less off-season.

At the top of Limeuil, *Hôtel-Restaurant Bon Accueil* (☎ 05 53 63 30 97, fax 05 53 73 33 85) has doubles with shower for 170FF; its restaurant is popular for its Périgordian cuisine, with *menus* from 75FF.

Getting There & Away The nearest train stations are at Le Bugue or Le Buisson (5km to the south, see Getting There & Away under Cadouin). For a taxi call ☎ 05 53 22 06 51.

Cadouin
postcode 24480 • pop 380 • elevation 246m
This tiny, sleepy village 9km south of Limeuil is entirely dominated by the astonishingly grand Cistercian **L'Abbaye de Cadouin** (☎ 05 53 63 36 28). Built in 1117 to house what was thought to be the cloth used to wrap the head of Christ (and which was later revealed to be of 11th-century Egyptian origin) it became a major pilgrimage site. It consists of a sturdy Romanesque church and a gorgeous Gothic cloister where carved stone faces peep out at every corner and the doorways are intricately carved.

The 15th- to 16th-century cloisters are open from 10 am to 12.30 pm and 1.30 to 5.30 pm daily except on Tuesday (from 10 am to 7 pm daily during July and August). It's closed in January. Admission costs 30FF (six to 12 year-olds 15FF). Opposite is a fine old **covered market**.

The other attraction in Cadouin is the **Musée du Vélocipède** (☎ 05 53 63 46 60) open from 10 am to 6 pm daily, which houses the world's largest collection of vintage bicycles including Penny Farthings. Admission costs 30FF (children 20FF).

THE DORDOGNE

The Dordogne River

The mighty Dordogne rises on the Puy de Sancy high in the Massif Central, flowing south-westwards and then due west for 472km – through five dams – to a point about 20km north of Bordeaux, where it joins the Garonne River to form the Gironde Estuary. The river, though fast and temperamental, was once a vital economic byway, with *gabarres* (flat-bottomed boats) taking wine and and oak to Bordeaux and *saliers* returning with salt from Libourne. Today, it's been harnessed and generates huge quantities of hydroelectric power.

Périgord Noir boasts some of the most scenic and famous stretches of the river, particularly the two huge loops known as Cingle de Trémolat (west of Limeuil) and Cingle de Montfort (east of Domme) and the stretch between Limeuil and Domme, with its fairytale chateaux and fortresses and meadows of tobacco, maize, walnut and poplars.

NICKY CAVEN

Flat-bottomed *gabarres* once plied the river.

Places to Stay & Eat The *Auberge de Jeunesse* (☎ 05 53 73 28 78, fax 05 53 73 28 79) is one of the region's most spectacularly located hostels, right inside the abbey complex. Beds cost 51FF a night (68FF with breakfast). It's closed mid-December to February.

Opposite the abbey, the charming *Hôtel-Restaurant d'Abbaye* (☎ 05 53 63 40 93, fax 05 53 61 72 08) has doubles (all with bath and WC) for 210FF; its restaurant (closed on Sunday) serves good regional fare with *menus* from 60FF. *Hôtel du Périgord* (☎ 05 53 61 24 97) just south of the abbey, has doubles with shower from 145FF (185FF half board).

Getting There & Away Le Buisson train station (where you can pick up connections to Les Eyzies and Périgueux) is 5km to the north-east.

For a taxi call ☎ 05 53 22 06 51.

LES EYZIES DE TAYAC

postcode 24620 • pop 850 • elevation 74m

Completely devoted to tourism, this dull town but immensely important prehistoric centre shelters under a huge cliff and an eye-catching (and misleadingly brutish) model of Cro-Magnon man (the place which gave its name to this line of *Homo sapiens sapiens* after a discovery of three of their skeletons in 1868 is just north of town). Les Eyzies' two museums are a good place to bone up on prehistory before visiting the valley's other sites.

Information

The tourist office (☎ 05 53 06 97 05; fax 05 53 06 90 79) is on Les Eyzies' main street, the D47, right below the most prominent part of the cliff. It's open from 9 am to noon and 2 to 6 pm Monday to Saturday and from 10 am to noon and 2 to 5 pm on Sunday; it closes at 5 pm on weekdays and all day on Saturday and Sunday from November to mid-March. It's open from 9 am to 8 pm daily in July and August (to 6 pm on Sunday).

IGN maps and topoguides are on sale at the Maison de la Presse opposite the tourist office.

Currency exchange is available at both the tourist office and post office (200m to the south).

Musée National de la Préhistoire

This absorbing National Museum of Prehistory (☎ 05 53 06 45 45), built into the cliff above the tourist office, provides a great introduction to the area's prehistoric human habitation. Its well-presented collection of artefacts can be visited from 9.30 am to noon and 2 to 5 pm daily except on Tuesday (to 6 pm from mid-March to mid-November); it's open until 7 pm daily and there's no midday closure in July and August (until 10 pm on Friday). Admission costs 22FF; youths and seniors, and everyone on Sunday, 15FF. An English book (28FF) about the museum is available at the ticket window.

Abri Pataud

About 250m north of the Musée National de la Préhistoire along the cliff face, this Cro-Magnon shelter, now a museum (☎ 05 53 06 92 46) was inhabited over a period of 15,000 years starting some 37,000 years ago; bones and other artefacts. The ibex carved into the ceiling is about 19,000 BC.

It is open daily except Monday. One-hour guided tours – the guides generally know some English – are offered from 10 am to 12.30 pm and 1.30 to 7 pm (to 5.30 pm from November to January and February to end of March; it's closed from 3 to 25 January). It's open 10 am to 7 pm daily during July and August. Admission costs 30FF (six to 12 year-olds 15FF).

Places to Stay & Eat

The small, hilltop *Camping à la Ferme Le Queylou* (☎ 05 53 06 94 71) is 2.5km west of Les Eyzies (3.1km from the train station;

pick-up is possible) off the D706. Sites cost 24FF per person including use of a fridge. The owners speak English and also rent out two cottages (for four to six people) from 750FF a week (1700FF in July and August).

Hôtel des Falaises (☎ 05 53 06 97 35), across the street from the Abri Pataud, has doubles with shower and toilet from 170FF (180FF twin). Opposite, rooms in the comfortable *Chambres d'hôte Madame Bauchet* (☎ 05 53 06 97 71) are similarly priced.

Across the square from the tourist office, *Auberge La Grignotière* (☎ 05 53 06 91 67), open from April to November, has doubles/triples from 190/220FF and restaurant *menus* from 58FF. Its neighbour, the Logis de France *Hôtel du Centre* (☎ 05 53 06 97 13; fax 05 53 06 91 63) has doubles from 280FF. It is closed from November to February. Its restaurant offers a tempting *menu du terroir* (country dishes) at 100FF.

The *grocery* across from the tourist office is open daily, except on Sunday afternoon.

Getting There & Away

The train station (☎ 05 53 06 97 22) is 600m north of the tourist office. The ticket windows are open until 9 pm on weekdays (to 7.15 pm on Saturday and to 8.20 pm on Sunday).

Destinations served include Le Buisson (19FF; 15 minutes; two to four services daily); Bordeaux (change at Le Buisson; 109FF, two to three hours; four daily), Périgueux (41FF, 30 minutes; two to four daily), Sarlat-la-Canéda (change at Le Buisson; 46FF; 50 minutes; three daily) and Paris' Gare d'Austerlitz (284FF; 5½ hours; three to five daily, including one direct service).

Getting Around

Classic/mountain bikes can be rented from M Fardet (☎ 05 53 46 70 15), near Font de Gaume, for 60/90FF a day or 300/470FF a week.

PREHISTORIC SITES

The following are the most important sites in the Vézère valley, listed here roughly from south-west to north-east. For details of

THE DORDOGNE

Lascaux, see Montignac later in this chapter. Note that guided tours are obligatory at all the sights.

Le Gouffre de Proumeyssac

This huge cavern (☎ 05 53 07 27 47), 3km south of Le Bugue (off the road to Le Buisson), is nicknamed the Cathédrale de Cristale thanks to its crystallised rock formations and fountains. Guided tours (lasting 45 minutes) take place from 9.30 am to noon and 2 to 5.30 pm daily (except in January) from March to November (9 am to 7 pm in June, July and August) and from 2 to 5 pm during the rest of the year. Admission costs 41FF (five to 12 year-olds 24FF; 12 to 16 year-olds 32FF).

Grotte de Bara-Bahau

Some 2km south-west of Le Bugue, this 100m-long cave displays eerie claw-scratchings made by bears some 150,000 years ago as well as outlines of various animals drawn on the rock around 115,000 years later. It's open from 10 am to noon and 2 to 5 pm from 29 March to 11 November (9 am to 7 pm during July and August). Admission costs 29FF (12 to 16 year-olds and students 24FF; five to 12 year-olds 18FF).

Grotte de Font de Gaume

This cave, just over 1km east of Les Eyzies on the D47, has one of the most astounding collections of prehistoric paintings still open to the public. About two dozen of its 230 remarkably sophisticated polychrome figures of bison, reindeer, horses, bears, mammoths and other creatures, created by Cro-Magnon people 14,000 years ago, can be seen. A number of the animals, engraved and/or painted in red and black, are depicted in movement or in three dimensions.

To protect the cave, discovered in 1901, the number of visitors is limited to 200 a day, and the 40-minute group tours (explanatory sheets in English available) are limited to 20 participants. To make reservations, stop by the cave or call ☎ 05 53 06 90 80. From April to October, reserve a place several days ahead; in July and August do

so at least a week in advance. It is open year-round except on Wednesday and certain public holidays. Tours are held from 9 am to noon and 2 to 6 pm (10 am to noon and 2 to 5 pm from November to the end of February and from 9.30 am to noon and 2 to 5.30 pm from March to October). The last visit is one hour before closing time. Tickets cost 35FF (12 to 25 year-olds 23FF).

Grotte de Combarelles

The long and very narrow Combarelles Cave, 3km north-east of Les Eyzies and 1.6km east of Font de Gaume, averages only 80cm in width. Discovered in 1894, it is renowned for its 600 often superimposed engravings of animals, especially reindeer, bison and horses; there are also some human and half-human figures. The works date from 12,000 to 14,000 years ago.

The number of visitors is limited to 100 a day. To reserve a place in a six-person group (tours last around 40 minutes), stop by the Grotte de Font de Gaume or call ☎ 05 53 06 90 80. It is open year-round except on Wednesday. Hours, admission costs and reservations guidelines are the same as for Font de Gaume.

Abri du Cap Blanc

High- and low-relief figures of horses, reindeer and bison, created 14,000 years ago, decorate this natural shelter, formed by an overhanging rocky outcrop. Situated on a pristine, forested hillside 9km east of Les Eyzies, the privately owned Abri (☎ 05 53 59 21 74) is open from 4 April to 2 November. Guided tours lasting 45 minutes (English explanatory sheets are available) are held from 10 am to noon and 2 to 6 pm daily (9.30 am to 7 pm in July and August, with no midday closure). Admission costs 30FF (seven to 15 year-olds 16FF). It's accessible to the handicapped.

Grotte du Grand Roc

Grand Roc Cave (☎ 05 53 06 92 70), known for its masses of delicate, translucent stalactites and stalagmites, is a few kilometres north-west of Les Eyzies along the D47. It

Rambles Through the Past

The Abri du Cap Blanc, 8km east of Les Eyzies along the beautiful D48, is a fine place to begin a day hike which takes you from prehistoric to medieval sites. When the path – actually the GR6 from Les Eyzies – isn't impassibly muddy, you can walk about 1km south-east from the Abri to the eery ruins of the fortified 12th-century **Château de Commarque** on the other side of the Beune River. Facing it is the **Château de Laussel** (not open to the public), a much-restored 14th-century fairytale of a chateau.

A few kilometres farther south-east on the GR6 you'll reach the **Cabanes du Breuil**, a charming hamlet of traditional dry-stone huts, an historical monument (☎ 05 53 29 67 15) open from 10 am to noon and 2 to 6 pm between Easter and November (10 to 7 pm during July and August) for 15FF (children 8FF). There's a gîte d'étape nearby, at *Ferme Auberge La Taulado* (☎ 05 53 29 67 63) where you can crash for 55FF a night.

is open from 9.30 am to 6 pm daily (to 7 pm during July and August and from 10 am to 5 pm in February, March, November and December; closed in January). It costs 38FF for the 30-minute tour which is given in French with an English translation (six to 12 year-olds 20FF).

Nearby is a still-inhabited troglodytic hamlet and the prehistoric **Abri de Laugerie Basse** (accessible to wheelchairs). Admission costs 28FF (six to 12 year-olds 15FF). The telephone number and opening times are the same as for Grand Roc.

Grotte de Rouffignac

The cave at Rouffignac (☎ 05 53 05 41 71), the largest in the area (it has some 10km of galleries), is 10km north of Les Eyzies along the D47 and the D3. It is known for its 100 engravings and paintings of mammoths (many sadly disfigured by graffiti) which you reach by an electric train. It's open from 10 to 11.30 am and 2 to 5 pm daily from 28 March to 1 November (from 9 to 11.30 am and 2 to 6 pm during July and August). Admission costs 31FF (five to seven year-olds 10FF). It's accessible to the handicapped.

Village Troglodytique de la Madeleine

This cave-dwelling village (☎ 05 53 06 92 49), 8km north of Les Eyzies along the D706, is in the middle of a delightfully lush forest overlooking a hairpin curve in the Vézère River. The site has two levels: 10,000 to 14,000 years ago, prehistoric people lived on the bank of the river in an area now closed to the public; and five to seven centuries ago, medieval French people built a fortified village – now in ruins – halfway up the cliff face. Their chapel, dedicated to Ste-Madeleine, gave its name to the site – and to the entire Magdalenian era. On the plateau above the cliff are the ruins of a 14th-century castle (closed to the public). Many of the artefacts discovered here are in the prehistory museum in Les Eyzies.

The site is open from 9.30 am to 7 pm daily during July, August and September; at other times it's open from 10 am to 6 pm daily. Guided tours (45 minutes) are in French (English brochure available). Admission costs 30FF (five to 12 year-olds 17FF). Several walking trails pass by here.

La Roque St-Christophe

This 900m-long series of terraces and caves (☎ 05 53 50 70 45), on a sheer cliff face 30m above the Vézère River, has had an extraordinary history as a natural bastion, serving Mousterian (Neanderthal) people some 50,000 years ago, enemies of the Normans in the 10th century, the English from 1401 to 1416 and Protestants in the late 16th century.

La Roque St-Christophe is on the D706, overlooking the Vézère River 9km north-east of Les Eyzies, a kilometre south-east from the village of Le Moustier (finds here gave the Mousterian era its name). It's open from 10 am to 7 pm daily from March to October, from 10 am to 6.30 pm from October to 11 November, and from 11 am to

THE DORDOGNE

5 pm during the rest of the year. Tickets cost 34FF (students 26FF; five to 13 year-olds 17FF). The informative brochure in English, which can be borrowed from the ticket kiosk, makes a valiant effort to bring the now empty rooms and caverns alive.

Just 3km south of here (off the road to Les Eyzies) the **Prehisto Parc** theme park is just the kind of thing to make serious anthropologists shiver but it's fun for the kids nonetheless, with its figures of cavemen throwing arrows at hairy mammoths (some with sound effects). It's open from 10 am to 6 pm daily from March to mid-November (from 9.30 am to 7 pm during July and August). Admission costs 30FF (students/children aged under five 21/15FF).

Le Conquil: Parc Naturel Troglodytique

As with La Roque St-Christophe, this riverside collection of rock shelters (some housing extraordinary dovecots) just south-west of St-Léon-sur-Vézère was a popular medieval refuge and even served as an occasional hideout for the Resistance in WWII. Today, it's the 'parc naturel' aspect which is the most delightful, with a route leading through the dense woods to a panoramic viewpoint over the valley. Explanatory signs (including botanical ones) are in French. The site (π 05 53 51 29 03) is open from 10 am to 6 pm daily from March to November (to 7 pm from May to September). Admission costs 28FF (children 17FF).

ST-LÉON-SUR-VÉZÈRE

postcode 24290 • pop 400 • elevation 70m

This atmospheric village, 9km south-west of Montignac, lies in a picturesque loop of the Vézère River. It contains two chateaux (not open to the public) – the squat 14th-century **Château La Salle** and the more refined Renaissance-turreted **Château de Clérans**. More notably, it also has one of Périgord's finest **Romanesque churches**. Once part of a Benedictine priory, it was built on the ruins of a Roman villa, part of whose walls can still be seen between the church and the river.

Meditation on the Côte de Jor

High above the Vézère Valley, on the hilltop ridge of Côte de Jor 1km above Le Moustier, flutter the incongruous prayer flags of a Tibetan Buddhist centre, the **Dhagpo Kagyu-Ling** (π 05 53 50 70 75, fax 05 53 50 80 54, email Dhagpo.Kagyu .Ling@wanadoo.fr).

Established in 1975, this is now one of the largest Tibetan Buddhist centres in France. It holds workshops and courses (around 60FF a day; headphone translations available in English, German and Spanish) under Lama Jigme Rinpoche and others. Accommodation is available but must be booked in advance (100FF redeemable deposit for a weekend, 300FF for longer courses). The temple is open from 7 am to 10 pm daily with meditation sessions taking place several times daily.

Across the bridge is the delightful **Le Conquil: Parc Naturel Troglodytique** (see the previous Prehistoric Sites section).

Places to Stay & Eat

Camping St-Léon's small riverside *Camping Municipal* (π 05 53 50 73 16) is open during July and August only. It costs 9/12FF per person/tent.

Three kilometres to the west, off the Les Eyzies road, the deluxe riverside *Le Paradis* (π 05 53 50 72 64, fax 05 53 50 75 90, email le.paradis@perigord.com) has swimming pools, tennis courts, bike and canoe rental. High season rates are 36/56.50FF per person/site. It's open from late March to late October.

The pleasant lakeside *Camping Le Lac* (π 05 53 50 75 86, fax 05 53 50 58 36), 11km north-west of St-Léon, at Plazac (5km north of Le Moustier), charges 26/25FF per person/site. It's open from Easter to mid-October.

Hotels & Restaurants St-Léon's *L'Auberge du Pont* (π 05 53 50 73 07) runs the *Hôtel le Relais de la Côte de Jor* (π 05 53

50 73 07, fax 05 53 51 16 22), 2.5km above the village. Doubles start at 230FF. *L'Auberge de la Poste* (☎ *05 53 50 73 08*), in the village, serves up excellent local cuisine, with menus from 65FF. It is closed on Monday.

Near the ancient hamlet of Sergeac, across the river, the ridgetop *Auberge de Castel-Merle* (☎ *05 53 50 70 08, fax 05 53 50 76 25)* has four charming rooms from 220FF and a restaurant with *menus* from 69FF (including a 85FF vegetarian *menu*). Its shady outdoor dining area has spectacular views.

In Le Moustier, *Hôtel La Roque St-Christophe* (☎ *05 53 50 70 61, fax 05 53 50 81 29)* has doubles from 170FF (200FF twin). There's a spiffier Logis de France round the corner, the *Auberge du Vimont* (☎ *05 53 50 75 17, fax 05 53 50 46 06)*, where doubles cost from 260FF. Both have decent restaurants.

Getting There & Away
The nearest bus service is to Montignac, 9km north-east of St-Léon (a taxi from Montignac to St-Léon-sur-Vézère will cost around 80FF). Sample bus fares include Brive-la-Gaillarde (28FF, 1¼ hours, one service daily in late afternoon); Sarlat-la-Canéda (23FF, 30 minutes) and Périgueux (34FF, one hour).

There are train stations at Les Eyzies (14km south-west) or Condat-le-Lardin (9km north-east of Montignac). Services to Les Eyzies include Brive-la-Gaillarde and Périgueux (41FF, 30 minutes).

Getting Around
Bikes are available from Le Paradis (see Places to Stay & Eat) at 75/300FF per day/week. Canoes are also available here, or from Aventure Plein Air (APA, ☎ 05 53 50 67 71), by the river in St-Léon.

MONTIGNAC
postcode 24290 • pop 2900 • elevation 300m
The relaxing and very picturesque town of Montignac, on the Vézère River, achieved sudden fame after the discovery of the nearby Grotte de Lascaux.

Montignac's attractive old town and commercial centre is on the river's right bank, but of more use for visitors is the left bank area around place Tourny and along rue du 4 Septembre, which links the D65 with the D704 and the D704E to Lascaux.

Orientation & Information
The tourist office (☎ 05 53 51 82 60), 150m west of place Tourny at 22 rue du 4 Septembre, is next to the 14th-century Église St-Georges le Prieuré. It is open from 9 am to noon and 2 to 6 pm Monday to Saturday (open until 7 pm with no midday closure during July and August). Handy walking guides available here include *Randonnées en Périgord Noir* (20FF) and *Les Sentiers d'Emilie en Périgord Noir* (49FF). IGN maps are sold at the Maison de la Presse across the street. For details about canoe/kayak trips here and nearby, see Activities at the start of this chapter.

There are a couple of banks near the tourist office. The post office on place Tourny (open until 4.45 pm on weekdays and until noon on Saturday) also has currency exchange.

Grotte de Lascaux & Lascaux II
Lascaux Cave, 2.5km south of Montignac off the D704E, has some of the most extraordinary prehistoric paintings in the world.

They were discovered in 1940 by four teenage boys who, it is said, were out searching for their dog, Robot. The cave's main room and a number of steep galleries are decorated with figures of wild oxen, deer, horses, reindeer and other creatures depicted in vivid reds, blacks, yellows and browns. They have been carbon-dated to around 15,000 to 17,000 years old.

The cave – in pristine condition when found – was opened to the public in 1948 but was closed 15 years later when it became clear that human breath and the resulting carbon dioxide and condensation were causing a green fungus and even tiny stalactites to grow over the paintings and their colours to fade.

To respond to massive public curiosity about the prehistoric art, a precise replica of

THE DORDOGNE

the most famous section of the original was meticulously recreated a few hundred metres away. The idea of Lascaux II (☎ 05 53 51 95 03) sounds kitschy, but the reproductions are surprisingly evocative and well worth a look.

The 40m-long Lascaux II, which can handle 2000 visitors a day (in groups of 40), is open from 9 am to 7 pm daily from April to October (closed on Monday in October); 10 am to 12.30 pm and 1.30 to 5.30 pm from November to March (closed on Monday and from 4 to 26 January). Tickets cost 50FF (six to 12 year-olds 25FF). For an extra 7FF (children 5FF) you'll also get admission to Le Thot (see Around Montignac later in this chapter). Tickets are *only* sold in Montignac, on the ground floor of the tourist office (get there early as queues are long; the ticket booth is open from 9 am to 6 pm daily throughout the year). No telephone or written bookings can be made.

Musée Eugène Le Roy

Within the tourist office building (and open the same hours) this small museum shows typical farming implements and local crafts and a wax figure scene representing the 19th-century peasant household of Jacquou le Croquant, hero of Eugène Le Roy's novel (see Literature in the Facts about South-West France chapter for more about this famous Périgordian work).

Special Events

The Festival du Périgord Noir (☎ 05 53 51 95 17, fax 05 53 50 87 00) is the region's premier cultural event of the year with classical concerts by French and international musicians taking place in abbeys (especially Abbaye Ste-Claire in Sarlat) and churches (especially in St-Léon-sur-Vézère) over a month from mid-August. Tickets (from 120 to 190FF; reductions for students) are available at the tourist office here; advance bookings by telephone (for an extra 20FF) can also be made.

Much more flamboyant and fun is the Festival du Folklore de Montignac, held in late July for five days, with groups from all over the world parading in the streets in Montignac and nearby towns and villages.

Paradise

When the late American writer Henry Miller decided to take a pre-WWII holiday in Greece, he stopped for an inspirational detour in the Dordogne. More commonly known for his erotic writings, Miller lavished some memorable prose on this 'country of enchantment which the poets have staked out and which they alone may lay claim to. It is the nearest thing to Paradise this side of Greece', he wrote in *Colossus of Maroussi*:

> I believe that this great peaceful region of France will always be a sacred spot for man and that when the cities have killed off the poets this will be the refuge and the cradle of the poets to come... it gives me hope for the future of the race, for the future of the earth itself. France may one day exist no more, but the Dordogne will live on just as dreams live on and nourish the souls of men.

Places to Stay

The camp site *Camping Municipal Le Bleufond* (☎ 05 53 51 83 95, fax 05 53 50 88 95), 700m down-river (from the tourist office turn left at the bridge), is open from mid-May to October and charges 15/20FF per person/tent.

Hôtel de la Grotte (☎ 05 53 51 80 48, fax 05 53 51 05 96, 63 rue du 4 Septembre), 200m east of the tourist office, has doubles/triples for 165/195FF (225/265FF with shower and toilet). Their restaurant has Périgord-style *menus* from 58/78FF (lunch/dinner).

Some 400m farther down this road (past the gendarmerie), the Logis de France *Auberge Le Lascaux* (☎ 05 53 51 82 81, fax 05 53 50 04 73, route de Sarlat) offers charming doubles/triples from 220/260FF and restaurant *menus* from 88FF.

Le Relais du Soleil d'Or (☎ 05 53 51 80 22, fax 05 53 50 27 54, 16 rue du 4 Septembre), 200m west of the tourist office, has upmarket doubles from 350FF (30FF for your dog!) and a swimming pool. Good-value *menus* here start at 65FF.

Most attractive of all is the *Hostellerie La Roseraie* (☎ 05 53 50 53 92, place d'Armes), across the bridge in a picturesque riverside square; spacious doubles start at 320FF (395FF, minimum three nights, for obligatory half-board in July and August). There's a swimming pool and beautiful rose garden.

Places to Eat

In addition to the hotel-restaurants mentioned above there are several more casual places, including the riverside *Restaurant Pizzeria Les Pilotis* (☎ 05 53 50 88 15, 6 rue Laffitte), on the right bank, which serves salads, pizzas and meat dishes. The restaurant is closed from November to mid-February.

Popular with locals at lunchtime as well as Lascaux-visitors is *Le Bellevue* (☎ 05 53 51 81 29, Le Regourdou) 500m beyond Lascaux, whose restaurant has some great views as well as excellent regional fare, *menus* cost from 55FF.

Self-caterers will find excellent supplies at the Wednesday and Saturday *markets* (on the right bank by the church) and at *Casino supermarket*, on place Tourny next to the post office. It's closed on Sunday afternoon and on Monday.

The adjacent *Bar Le Tourny* (38 rue du 4 Septembre), is open until 2 am daily and sometimes features light music.

Getting There & Away

The nearest train station, 9km to the northeast of Montignac, is at Condat-le-Lardin (between Condat and Le Lardin-St-Lazare) on the Périgueux (40 minutes) to Brive-la-Gaillarde (20 minutes) line with two to three services daily. A taxi (☎ 05 53 50 86 61 or 05 53 51 29 78) to the station will cost around 80FF.

For information on buses to/from Montignac, see Getting There & Away in the Sarlat-la-Canéda, Brive-la-Gaillarde and Périgueux sections. The bus stop is on rue du 4 Septembre (place Tourny). The tourist office has some timetables.

AROUND MONTIGNAC

Le Thot

This museum and animal park, 5km southwest of Montignac (1.5km off the D706), is known as Le Thot – Espace Cro-Magnon (☎ 05 53 50 70 44). Intended as an introduction to the world of prehistoric people, it has models of animals that appear in prehistoric art, live specimens of similar animals and fascinating exhibits on the creation of Lascaux II. Admission costs 30FF (six to 12 year-olds 15FF) but is free with a combined Lascaux II/Le Thot ticket. It is open from 10 am to 12.30 pm and 1.30 to 7 pm (closed on Monday and in January). In July and August, when tickets must be purchased in Montignac near the tourist office, it's open from 10 am to 7 pm daily.

St-Amand de Coly

Ten kilometres east of Montignac, the old slate-tiled houses of St-Amand de Coly are dominated by the village's tall yellow limestone **abbey-church** – a splendid example of the region's fortified churches, with its high defensive walls. At one time there were 400 monks here, but following the Hundred Years' War only two remained.

Hôtel-Restaurant Gardette (☎ 05 53 51 68 50), near the abbey, has charming, simple doubles from 175FF and a reasonable restaurant.

SARLAT-LA-CANÉDA

postcode 24200 • pop 10,000
• elevation 173m

The beautiful, well-restored town of Sarlat, administratively twinned with nearby La Canéda, is the capital of Périgord Noir. Established around a Benedictine abbey founded in the late 8th century, the town became prosperous in the Middle Ages but was ravaged during the Hundred Years' War (when it was on the border between French and English territory) and the Wars of Religion. These days, Sarlat's medieval and Renaissance old town – much of it built of tan sandstone in the 16th and 17th centuries – attracts large numbers of tourists, especially for the year-round Saturday market.

Sarlat is an excellent base for car trips to

THE DORDOGNE

the prehistoric sites of the Vézère valley and the fortresses and chateaux of the Dordogne valley but you'd need to book accommodation way ahead in high season.

Orientation

Sarlat stretches north for 2km from the train station to the Auberge de Jeunesse. The heart-shaped medieval town *(cité médiévale)* is bisected by the ruler-straight rue de la République (locally known as La Traverse), laid out during the last century. The medieval town is centred around place de la Liberté, rue de la Liberté and place du Peer.

Information

Tourist Offices The main tourist office (☎ 05 53 31 45 45, fax 05 53 59 19 44, email ot24.sarlat@perigord.tm.fr) on place de la Liberté occupies the beautiful Hôtel de Maleville, made up of three 15th- and 16th-century Gothic houses. It is open from 9 am to noon and 2 to 6 pm Monday to Saturday (7 pm from June to September, when it's also open from 10 am to noon and 2 to 6 pm on Sunday). There's no midday break during July and August. From June to September the tourist office runs guided walking tours of the old town (usually in French only) at least twice daily (including an evening one at 10 pm) for 25FF (children 15FF). For details of walking/biking circuits in and around town, pick up *Promenades et Randonnées* (8FF for one or 75FF for all 21).

During July and August, the tourist office annexe (☎ 05 53 59 18 87) on ave du Général de Gaulle is open from 9 am to noon and 2 to 6 pm Monday to Saturday. Both offices charge 10FF for hotel bookings.

There's a Bureau d'Information Jeunesse (☎ 05 53 31 56 36, fax 05 53 31 56 34), at the Espace Economie Emploi (place Marc Buisson), where you can get information about temporary jobs. It's open from 8.30 am to 5.30 pm Monday to Friday.

Money There are several banks along rue de la République including Banque Populaire at No 1 and Crédit Lyonnais at No 15. Currency exchange is also available at the main post office.

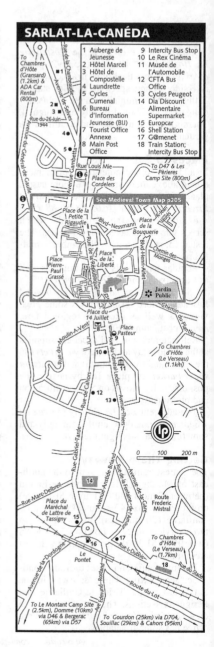

SARLAT-LA-CANÉDA

1	Auberge de Jeunesse
2	Hôtel Marcel
3	Hôtel de Compostelle
4	Laundrette
5	Cycles Cumenal
6	Bureau d'Information Jeunesse (BIJ)
7	Tourist Office Annexe
8	Main Post Office
9	Intercity Bus Stop
10	Le Rex Cinéma
11	Musée de l'Automobile
12	CFTA Bus Office
13	Cycles Peugeot
14	Dia Discount Alimentaire Supermarket
15	Europcar
16	Shell Station
17	G@menet
18	Train Station; Intercity Bus Stop

Post & Communication The main post office on place du 14 Juillet is open until 6 pm on weekdays and until noon on Saturday.

At G@menet (☎ 05 53 21 45 91, mobile ☎ 06 08 93 22 09) at Le Pontet, near the train station, Internet use costs 10FF per 10 minutes. It's open from 11 am to 10 pm Tuesday to Saturday and from 2.30 to 10 pm on Sunday.

Laundry Le Lavandou, at 10 place de la Bouquerie, is open from 6 am to 10 pm daily. The laundrette at 74 ave de Selves is open until 9 pm daily.

Medieval Town

The tourist office's free brochure *Guide Pratique* takes you on a walking tour of Sarlat's historic centre.

Cathédrale St-Sacerdos, once part of Sarlat's Cluniac abbey, is a hotchpotch of styles. The wide, airy nave and its chapels date from the 17th century; the cruciform chevet (at the far end from the entrance) is from the 14th century; and the western entrance and much of the belfry above it are 12th-century Romanesque. The organ dates from 1752.

Behind the cathedral is the **Jardin des Enfeus**, Sarlat's first cemetery, and the 12th-century **Lanterne des Morts** (Lantern of the Dead), which looks like the top of a missile. It may have been built to commemorate St-Bernard, who visited Sarlat in 1147 and whose relics were given to the abbey.

Across the square from the front of the cathedral is the ornate facade of the Renaissance **Maison de la Boétie**, birthplace of the 16th-century writer Étienne de la Boétie (see under Literature in the Facts about South-West France chapter).

The quiet, largely residential area to the west of rue de la République is also worth exploring. Rue Jean-Jacques Rousseau makes a good starting point.

THE DORDOGNE

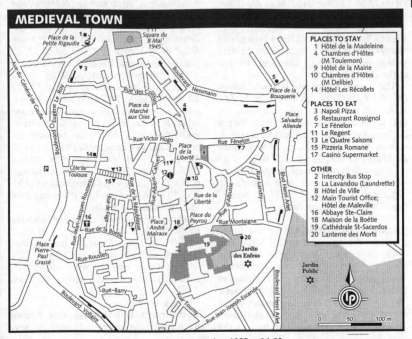

MEDIEVAL TOWN

PLACES TO STAY
1 Hôtel de la Madeleine
4 Chambres d'Hôtes (M Toulemon)
9 Hôtel de la Mairie
10 Chambres d'Hôtes (M Delibie)
14 Hôtel Les Récollets

PLACES TO EAT
3 Napoli Pizza
6 Restaurant Rossignol
7 Le Fénelon
11 Le Regent
13 Le Quatre Saisons
15 Pizzeria Romane
17 Casino Supermarket

OTHER
2 Intercity Bus Stop
5 La Lavandou (Laundrette)
8 Hôtel de Ville
12 Main Tourist Office; Hôtel de Maleville
16 Abbaye Ste-Claire
18 Maison de la Boétie
19 Cathédrale St-Sacerdos
20 Lanterne des Morts

euro currency converter 10FF = €1.52

Musée de l'Automobile

From April to September, the vintage motor vehicles on display in this museum (☎ 05 53 31 62 81) at 17 ave Thiers can be viewed from 2.30 to 6.30 pm daily except Monday (also closed on Tuesday during April); from 10.30 am to 7 pm daily during July and August. Admission costs 35FF (eight to 12 year-olds 15FF).

Special Events

The biggest event on the cultural calendar is the Festival des Jeux du Théâtre (☎ 05 53 31 10 83), with events in churches and on place de la Liberté over a fortnight at the end of July. The Festival du Cinéma, in early November at Le Rex cinema complex (☎ 08 36 68 69 24), ave Thiers, features a week's worth of good French movies.

Places to Stay

Camping & Hostels The most convenient place to camp is the *Auberge de Jeunesse* (☎ 05 53 59 47 59 or 05 53 30 21 27, 77 ave de Selves), open 15 April to 15 November. A bed costs 48FF; tents can be pitched in the tiny back garden for 27FF a person; call ahead to see if there's space. From the train station, you can take an infrequent local bus to the Cimetière stop.

The nearest camp site is *Les Périères* (☎ 05 53 59 05 84, fax 05 53 28 57 51), about 800m north-east of town along the D47 towards Ste-Nathalène, which charges a whopping 144FF forfait for two people. It is open from April to the end of September. *Le Montant* (☎ 05 53 59 18 50 or 05 53 59 37 73), 2.5km south-west on the D57 towards Bergerac, is open from mid-May to September. Charges are 24/31FF per person/tent. There's no bus service.

Chambres d'Hôtes Among the many chambres d'hôte in and around Sarlat, two of the most central are those of *M Delibie* (☎ 05 53 59 35 27, 11 place de la Liberté), where doubles in a typical Périgordian house cost from 250FF, and *M Toulemon* (☎ 05 53 31 26 60, 4 rue Magnanat), where rooms, furnished with antiques, start from 200FF. About 1.2km north of town on the

Colline de Péchauriol, the chambres d'hôte run by *Madame Gransard* (☎ 05 53 59 35 20) are open from April to October. Extremely comfortable doubles/triples cost 200/240FF. To get there, head up the ave de Selves to the northbound D704 past the Intermarché supermarket, turn right just before the entrance to the Mazda garage and follow the 'chambres' signs.

The singles/doubles/quadruple (from 100/130/220FF) at *Le Verseau* (☎ 05 53 31 02 63, 49 route des Pechs) are complemented by a wonderful and huge garden; breakfast costs 25FF. From the train station, it's a 1.7km uphill walk: follow rue de Stade above the station, then take the first left onto route Frédéric Mistral (Les Pechs). There's a shorter (1.1km) route from the town centre to Le Verseau via chemin du Plantier.

Hotels The friendly *Hôtel Les Récollets* (☎ 05 53 31 36 00, fax 05 53 30 32 62, email otelrecol@aol.com, 4 rue Jean-Jacques Rousseau) is up a narrow old alleyway (nearest parking is a block up the hill on blvd Eugène Le Roy). Quiet, comfortable doubles start at 250FF (350FF with bath). *Hôtel de la Mairie* (☎ 05 53 59 05 71, 13 place de la Liberté) has fairly basic doubles/triples with shower from 220/260FF.

The rustic *Hôtel Marcel* (☎ 05 53 59 21 98, fax 05 53 30 27 77, 50 ave de Selves) has doubles from 220FF with shower and toilet. It is closed from mid-November to mid-February. At No 64 on the same avenue, *Hôtel de Compostelle* (☎ 05 53 59 08 53, fax 05 53 30 31 65) has pretty, modern doubles from 290/310FF (with shower/bath). Two-/three-room combinations (400/460FF) would suit families. It's closed from mid-November to Easter.

The more elegant *Hôtel de la Madeleine* (☎ 05 53 59 10 41, fax 05 53 31 03 62, 1 place de la Petite Rigaudie) has spacious doubles with shower from 350FF (425/490FF for doubles/triples with bath; less off-season). It is closed from January to February.

Places to Eat

Restaurants & Bar-Brasseries Among the many tourist-geared restaurants are several decent pizzerias including the rustic, informal ***Napoli Pizza*** (**☎** *05 53 31 26 93, 2 blvd Eugène Le Roy*), closed on Sunday lunchtime; and *Pizzeria Romane* (**☎** *05 53 59 23 88, 3 côte de Toulouse*), closed on Sunday lunchtime and Monday, which also has a Périgordian *menu* (80FF) that includes *confit de canard* (duck preserved in its own fat).

Le Regent brasserie (**☎** *05 53 31 06 36*), at the heart of place de la Liberté, offers a weekday *plat du jour* for 43FF, or a 100FF *menu du terroir* including foie gras, confit de canard and *gateau aux noix* (walnut cake). *Le Fénelon* (**☎** *05 53 29 47 80, 10 rue Fénelon*) is a popular bar-brasserie (its walls are covered with photos of visiting film stars), open from 8 am to 1 am daily from June to September (closing at 3 pm daily at other times). Its *omelette aux cèpes* (wild-mushroom omelette) is a bargain at 55FF including a glass of white wine.

More upmarket establishments offering Périgordian cuisine include ***Restaurant Rossignol*** (**☎** *05 53 31 02 30, 15 rue Fénelon*), closed on Wednesday, which has *menus* from 87FF; the elegant restaurant attached to *Hôtel de la Madeleine* (see Places to Stay), which serves *menus* from 110FF; and the reliable *Le Quatre Saisons* (**☎** *05 53 29 48 59, côte de Toulouse*), which has a good-value 65FF weekday lunchtime *menu* and others from 90FF including foie gras.

Self-Catering Long a driving force in the town's economy, Sarlat's Saturday *market* offers edibles in the morning (on place de la Liberté) and durables (such as clothing and handicrafts) all day long (especially on rue de la République). Depending on the season, Périgord delicacies on offer include truffles, foie gras, mushrooms and geese and their various products. A smaller *fruit and vegetable market* is held on place de la Liberté on Wednesday morning. Many shops around town sell foie gras and other pricey regional specialities.

The ***Casino supermarket*** at 32 rue de la République is open until 7.15 pm daily except Monday and from 8 am to noon on Sunday (open longer during July and August). *Dia Discount Alimentaire*, an inexpensive

supermarket between rue de Gabriel and ave Aristide Briand, is open until 7 pm daily except on Sunday.

Getting There & Away

Bus Bus services are very limited. There's no bus station – departures are from the train station, place Pasteur or place de la Petite Rigaudie, depending on your final destination.

Daily except Sunday, the CFTA bus to Périgueux via Montignac (49.50FF, 1½ hours to Périgueux; 23FF, 30 minutes to Montignac), the town nearest Lascaux II, leaves from place de la Petite Rigaudie at 6 am, plus 12.30 pm on Wednesday (plus 8.30 am and 5.30 pm on Wednesday in July and August); the bus back leaves Montignac at 7.15 pm (plus 1.05 pm on Wednesday and Saturday; 6.05 pm in July and August). Check the timetable at the tourist office or the CFTA office (**☎** 05 53 59 01 48) at 31 rue de Cahors: it's usually open from 9 am to noon and 2 to 6 pm on weekdays.

The SNCF bus to Souillac via the Dordogne valley (28.50FF, 50 minutes, four to seven daily) stops in Sarlat at the train station and on place Pasteur. Brive is served by one non-SNCF bus daily (42FF, 1¾ hours, no service on Sunday or on holidays), which leaves from place Pasteur.

Train The train station (**☎** 05 53 59 00 21), 1.3km south of the old city at the southern end of ave de la Gare, is poorly linked with the rest of the region. The ticket windows are staffed until 7.25 pm daily (closed at lunchtimes).

Destinations served include Bordeaux (118FF, 2½ hours, four or five daily) via Bergerac (59FF); Périgueux (75FF) with a change at Le Buisson (34FF) or Libourne (97FF); and Les Eyzies de Tayac (with a change at Le Buisson; 46FF, 50 minutes, three daily). To get to Paris' Gare d'Austerlitz (295FF) you have to change at Souillac, linked to Sarlat by regular SNCF buses (see Bus earlier in this section).

Car & Taxi Europcar (**☎** 05 53 30 30 40, fax 05 53 31 10 39) has an office near the

THE DORDOGNE

train station. ADA Locations (☎ 05 53 29 97 95, fax 05 53 30 25 38, to the north-west of town on the route de Brive) is cheaper: they'll deliver to the city centre. For a taxi call ☎ 05 53 59 02 43.

Getting Around

Among eight bike-rental outlets in the area, Cycles Cumenal (☎ 05 53 31 28 40) at 8 ave Gambetta has city/mountain bikes for 50/80FF a day (250FF a week). It is open from 9 am to 7 pm Tuesday to Sunday and has branches in Périgueux and Ribérac where you could drop off the bike. Cycles Peugeot (☎ 05 53 28 51 87) at 36 ave Thiers charges 70FF a day (300FF a week).

DOMME

postcode 24250 • pop 1030 • elevation 150m

Set attractively on a dramatically steep promontory high above the Dordogne River, the trapezium-shaped walled village of Domme was fought over and besieged frequently during the Hundred Years' War and Wars of Religion. This is one of the most famous bastides in the region, partly because it's one of the few to have retained most of its 13th-century ramparts, including three fortified gates: porte del Bos, porte des Tours and porte de la Combe.

The very attractive village, which is a bit too perfectly restored and certainly too commercialised, also has some stunning panoramas of the Dordogne River and valley.

Orientation & Information

At the top of the village's main street, Grand Rue, is the central market place, place de la Halle, and the tourist office (☎ 05 53 31 71 00). It opens from 10 am to 6 pm daily (from 10 am to noon and 2 to 6 pm on Saturday; 10 am to 7 pm daily during July and August).

Things to See

The best views are a few steps from place de la Halle, from the cliff-side **esplanade du Belvédère** and the adjacent promenade de la Barre, which stretches west along the forested slope to the Jardin Public. The pre-cipitous bluff below was, amazingly, scaled by Huguenot besiegers during the Wars of Religion, one of the few times the bastide was captured.

Across from the tourist office, the 19th-century reconstruction of the 16th-century covered market (*halle*) houses the entrance to the **grottes**, 450m of stalactite-filled galleries underneath the village which gave the inhabitants a handy refuge during times of attack; a lift whisks you back up at the end of the 30-minute tour. It is open throughout the year except in January. Tours take place at least eight times daily during the season. Admission costs 33FF (children 18FF; students 27FF). Tickets are sold at the tourist office.

On the far side of the square from the tourist office, the **Musée d'Arts et Traditions Populaires** has nine rooms of clothing, toys, tools and other memorabilia from the past (especially the 19th century). It's open from 10 am to 12.30 pm and 2.30 to 6 pm daily except Saturday from Easter to November. Admission costs 17FF (children 12FF).

Places to Stay

The camp site *Camping Municipal* (☎ 05 53 28 31 91), 1.5km down the D46 in Cénac, charges 20/22FF per person/tent. It's open from June to mid-September. *Camping Le Bras* (☎ 05 53 28 34 20), a farm camp site 4km east of Cénac (south of the river) charges 14/14FF per person/tent. Nearby is the more upmarket *Camping Le Bosquet* (☎/fax 05 53 28 37 39), 300m from the river (plus it has a swimming pool); rates are 20/20FF. It's open from April to mid-October. Several other sites are en route to Beynac.

Walkers on the GR64 can find a *gîte d'étape* (hikers' dormitory; ☎ 05 53 28 32 77) 2km south-west of Cénac off the D50, where beds cost 45FF.

Nouvel Hôtel (☎ 05 53 28 38 67, fax 05 53 28 27 13), two buildings down from the tourist office on Grand Rue, has doubles with shower and toilet for 200FF. It is open from Easter to October. Farther down the hill is *Hôtel Lou Cardil* (☎ 05 53 28 38 92) which has doubles with showers from 170FF (230FF twin).

Just outside porte del Bos are the comfortable *chambres d'hôte* (with a swimming pool) of Nadine and Daniel Delpech (☎ 05 53 28 58 55); doubles start at 200FF. The tourist office has details of others nearby.

Getting There & Away
There is no bus service to Domme. Taxis from Sarlat (☎ 05 53 59 39 65 or mobile 060 857 3010), the nearest train station, charge around 100FF one-way.

For information on getting to and from Sarlat see Getting There & Away in that section.

Getting Around
Bicycles can be rented in Cénac at the Élan petrol station (☎ 05 53 28 30 08) for 80/400FF a day/week. It is open from 8 am to noon and 2 to 7 pm daily. For details of canoe/kayak outfits see Activities at the beginning of this chapter.

LA ROQUE GAGEAC
postcode 24250 • pop 360 • elevation 80m
This famously picturesque hamlet of tan stone houses, nestled under a cliff on the right bank of the Dordogne, has a number of cave dwellings known as the **Fort Troglodyte**. There's a tiny tourist office (☎ 05 53 29 17 01) in the car park, open from 10 am to noon and 4 to 6 pm daily (2 to 6 pm from June to September).

Places to Stay & Eat
There's a string of places along the riverside D703: the modest *Bar-Hôtel* (☎ *05 53 29 51 63*), open from Easter to October, has doubles with shower for 180FF. The Logis de France *Hôtel La Belle Étoile* (☎ *05 53 29 51 44, fax 05 53 29 45 63),* has doubles with shower/bath and WC, costing from 200/260FF (310FF twin) and restaurant *menus* from 120FF. It is open from early April to mid-October. *Hôtel-Restaurant Gardette* (☎ *05 53 29 51 58, fax 05 53 31 19 32)* charges similar prices.

Also along the riverside is a small *grocery*

store and *bakery* and *Pizzeria Saladerie* (☎ 05 53 29 20 74) offering pizzas and yummy salads. The nearby *L'Ancre d'Or* (☎ 05 53 29 53 45) has tables overlooking the river and *menus* from 65FF, including a (rare) vegetarian *menu* for 129FF.

Getting There & Away
Sarlat, 10km to the north, has the nearest train and bus stations. For a taxi call ☎ 05 53 59 39 65 or mobile 060 857 3010. For information on getting to and from Sarlat see Getting There & Away in that section.

Getting Around
Bikes can be rented in Cénac (see Getting Around under Domme earlier in this chapter) and from Canoë Vélos (☎ 05 53 29 50 27), 2.3km along the D703 towards Beynac, which charges 90/250FF per day/five days.

Les Caminades (☎ 05 53 29 40 95) and Les Gabares Norbert (☎ 05 53 29 40 44) both offer one-hour river trips (French commentary with some English translation) on board replicas of wine-carrying *gabares* for 45FF (children 25FF). Between April and November they operate regularly from 10 am to 5 pm (every 30 minutes from 10 am to 6 pm in July and August).

BEYNAC-ET-CAZENAC
postcode 24220 • pop 460 • elevation 80m
For centuries Beynac and Cazenac, 3km to the west, were arch enemies; today, ironically, their names remain inextricably linked for administrative convenience. Beynac's dramatic fortress, rising from the cliff face, was once one of the greatest Périgord strongholds, dominating a strategic bend in the Dordogne and rivalling the English-held fortress of Castelnaud on the other bank of the river. Today, it's in the full glare of the tourist traffic while neighbouring Cazenac, still worth a visit for its Gothic church and exceptional views, is little more than a sleepy hamlet.

Orientation & Information
The tourist office (☎ 05 53 29 43 08), in the car park between the river and the D703 (which passes right through the village), is

THE DORDOGNE

Dordogne Chateaux

Périgord isn't in the same league as the Loire Valley, but it does have a number of impressive medieval chateaux (1001, in fact, according to the tourist board). They include the turreted 15th- to 17th-century **Jumilhac-le-Grand** (☎ 05 53 52 42 97) about 50km north-east of Périgueux along the N21 and D78; the Renaissance-influenced **Puyguilhem** (☎ 05 53 54 82 18), some 30km north-east of Périgueux; the imposing neoclassical **Hautefort** (☎ 05 53 50 51 23), 40km east of Périgueux, with its English-style garden and French flower terraces; **Eyrignac** (☎ 05 53 28 99 71), 13km north-east of Sarlat, famed for its exceptional 18th-century French-style gardens; the castle-like **Puymartin** (☎ 05 53 59 29 97), 8km north-west of Sarlat; **Losse** (☎ 05 53 50 80 08), in the Vézère valley, 5km south-west of Montignac, decorated with 16th- and 17th-century tapestries and furniture; and the feudal, hilltop **Beynac-et-Cazenac** (☎ 05 53 29 50 40), 10km south-west of Sarlat on the Dordogne River. Many chateaux are open for only part of the year, so call before dropping by. (More details about Hautefort, Puyguilhem and Beynac can be found in this chapter).

open from 10 am to 12.30 pm and 2 to 6 pm daily (from 9.30 am to 12.30 pm and 2 to 7 pm daily during July and August) and has information on boat trips, fishing, canoe hire and hikes in the area.

Château de Beynac

The heavily fortified chateau (☎ 05 53 29 50 40) has a wild and colourful past: during the Middle Ages it was the seat of one of Périgord's four baronies (the others were at Biron, Mareuil and Bourdeilles); during the Albigensian Crusade it was seized and sacked by Simon de Montfort; and during the Hundred Years' War it was continually tussled over by the French and English. Not surprisingly, it's been rebuilt many times

and retains features from all ages (notably some rare 15th-century frescoes) as well as a timeless view over the river.

It is open from 10 am to 6 pm daily (to 6.30 pm from June to October and to 5 pm from October to December). From December to March it's open from noon to around 5 pm. The excellent one-hour guided visits cost 40FF (children 17FF).

Behind the chateau is an open-air **Parc Archaeologique** (☎ 05 53 29 51 28 or 05 53 04 85 02), containing a series of reconstructed Neolithic dwellings and tools. It is open from 10 am to 7 pm daily except Saturday from July to mid-September. Admission costs 30FF (six to 16 year-olds 20FF).

Places to Stay & Eat

The camp site *Camping Le Capeyrou* (☎ 05 53 29 54 95, fax 05 53 28 36 27), 600m east of Beynac, off the D703, charges 24/33FF per person/site. It's open from mid-May to mid-September. The spacious *Camping La Cabane* (☎ 05 53 29 52 28, fax 05 53 59 09 15) by the river 5km east of Beynac charges 17/17/17FF per person/site/car and also offers *chambre d'hôte* in an old-fashioned farmhouse costing from 120FF (130FF with shower). There's a *gîte d'étape* (☎ 05 53 29 51 29) at Camping Maisonneuve 800m from Castelnaud, which charges 50FF per bed; it's open from April to October.

Hôtel-Restaurant du Château (☎ 05 53 29 50 13, fax 05 53 28 53 05, email Hôtel duChateau@perigord.com), overlooking the river on the main road through Beynac, has comfortable doubles with shower from 230FF (260FF with bath). The restaurant specialises in regional cuisine, with *menus* from 80FF. Some 400m eastwards, *Hôtel-Restaurant Bonnet* (☎ 05 53 29 50 45, fax 05 53 28 29 58) has doubles from 350FF (360FF twin) and *menus* from 85FF.

Getting There & Away

With no public transport, your best bet is to get a taxi from Sarlat (☎ 05 53 59 02 43), 11km to the north-east, or St-Cyprien (☎ 05 53 29 28 74), 10km to the west. For information on getting to and from Sarlat see Getting There & Away in that section.

Getting Around

Bike rental (80FF per day) is available from Canoë Copeyre (☎ 05 53 28 95 01), by the river below the tourist office. See Activities at the beginning of this chapter for details of other local canoe operators.

Gabares de Beynac (☎ 05 53 28 51 15) offer 50-minute riverboat trips for 35FF (under-12s 15FF) between 10 am and 1 pm and 2 to 6 pm from mid-March to November (every 30 minutes during July and August).

CHÂTEAU DE CASTELNAUD

This 12th- to 16th-century chateau (☎ 05 53 31 30 00), about 4km across the river from Beynac (along the D57), has everything you'd expect from a cliff-top castle: walls up to 2m thick (as you can see from peering through the loopholes, some designed for crossbows, others for small cannon); a superb panorama of the meandering Dordogne; and fine views of the fortified chateaux that dot the nearby hilltops.

The interior rooms are occupied by a **museum of medieval warfare**, whose displays range from daggers and spiked halberds to huge catapults. The houses of the medieval village of Castelnaud cling to the steep slopes below the fortress.

The chateau is open from 10 am to 6 pm daily from March to mid-November (until 7 pm in May, June and September; 9 am to 8 pm in July and August). For the remainder of the year, the opening hours are 2 to 5 pm (closed on Saturday). Admission costs 35FF (10 to 17 year-olds 18FF). A comprehensive English-language guidebook can be borrowed at the ticket counter.

BELVÈS

postcode 24170 • pop 1800 • elevation 190m

Perched high above the Nauze River, this lively, ancient market town 22km southwest of Beynac-et-Cazenac has a well-preserved old bastide core with some attractive Gothic and Renaissance houses. Bell towers are the town's speciality (its nickname is the City of Seven Bell Towers) but it nevertheless has a timeless ambience. The GR36 passes close by, via the dense Fôret de la Bessède to the west.

Orientation & Information

The old town is a couple of kilometres above the busy D710 and just off the D53. At its heart is the place d'Armes; overlooking it, in the old Maison des Consuls, is the tourist office (☎/fax 05 53 29 10 20), open

---

The Rainbow Tribe's Home

The claim to fame of the smallish, late 15th-century Château des Milandes (☎ 05 53 07 16 38) is its post-war role as the home of the African-American dancer and music-hall star Josephine Baker (1906–75), who helped bring black American culture to Paris in the 1920s with her *Revue Nègre* and created a sensation by appearing on stage wearing nothing but a skirt of bananas.

Awarded the *Croix de Guerre* (Military Cross) and the *Légion d'Honneur* (Legion of Honour) for her very active work with the French Resistance during WWII, and later participating in the US civil rights movement, Baker established her Rainbow Tribe here in 1949, adopting 12 children from around the world as 'an experiment in brotherhood'. But by 1964 she was broke and had to sell the chateau and retire to Monaco.

The chateau is open year-round. Visits, guided by a laser-disk commentary (English text available), take place from 10 am to noon and 2 to 5 pm (from 2 to 5 pm only in January, February, November, December and from 10 am to 7 pm between May and September). Admission costs 43FF (four to 15 year-olds 33F). When the weather is good, the chateau's courtyard is home to a number of fierce-looking falcons, buzzards and goshawks (the present owner is a falconry fan).

from 10.30 am to 12.30 pm and 3 to 7 pm daily during mid-June to mid-September and from 11 am to 3.30 pm at other times.

Things to See

On place d'Armes there is an attractive 15th-century **covered market** with stone and wooden pillars: spot the pillory chain on one of them, once used for tying up criminals.

From the tourist office you can get tickets (20FF, children 10FF) for the nearby **Abris Troglodytiques**, a cavern showing medieval troglodyte lifestyle; it's open from 10.30 am to 12.30 pm and 3 to 7 pm between mid-June and mid-September. Guided visits are at 11 am, 3 and 5 pm daily except Sunday afternoon.

Places to Stay & Eat

Among several camp sites nearby, *Les Nauves* (☎ 05 53 29 12 64, Le Bos-Rouge) 4km south-west, off the D53, is particularly pleasant, with a pool, tennis courts and horses to ride. Charges are 25/35FF per person/tent.

The gîte d'étape *Relais de St-Paradoux,* on the GR36, 3km south-west of Belvès, charges 50FF a bed; bookings must be made via the tourist office (see Orientation & Information earlier in this section). On the other side of town, 1km east of the D710, the *ferme de séjour* (farm accommodation) *Le Bugou* (☎ 05 53 29 01 08) offers dormitory beds at 50FF; showers for 10FF, breakfast 20FF and evening meals 80FF (and 30FF to feed and water your horse). Rooms are also available at 160/240FF per single/double; horse rides cost 80FF for an hour.

On the D53, on the western edge of town, *Hôtel Le Home* (☎ 05 53 29 01 65, fax 05 53 59 46 99, place de la Croix-des-Frères) has double rooms starting from 135FF (175FF with shower) and *menus* from around 59FF; nearby is the classier Logis de France *Belvédère de Belvès* (☎ 05 53 31 51 41, fax 05 53 31 51 42, 1 ave Paul-Crampel) where doubles cost 280FF and *menus* from 78FF.

For cheaper fare (for example salads, lasagnes and casseroles), head 200m to the

west along the D53 to *Le Midi-Minuit* (☎ 05 53 29 12 74, 12 ave du Lt-Gifault).

Between here and Hôtel Le Home, the *Boulangerie Viennoiserie* bakes fabulous bread.

Getting There & Away

Belvès is on the Agen–Périgueux line. The train station is 2km downhill (east), just off the D710. The ticket and information office (☎ 05 53 29 00 22) is open to 6.30 pm on Monday, to 3.10 pm Tuesday to Saturday and to 11 pm on Sunday.

Two to three trains run to Agen daily (68FF, 1¼ hours); Le Buisson (16FF, 25 minutes); Les Eyzies (31FF, 45 minutes); and Périgueux (62FF, 1¼ hours). Change at Le Buisson for Bergerac (46FF) and at Périgueux for more regular connections to Paris (296FF).

Getting Around

Monsieur Baconnier at the train station rents out mountain bikes for 100FF per day. You can also call ☎ 05 53 31 63 99 in Siorac-en-Périgord (4km north of the train station) for cheaper rates (80/350FF per day/week): the owner may deliver the bike to you.

Périgord Pourpre

'Purple' Périgord, stretching both sides of the Dordogne River, is famous for its vineyards (especially around Bergerac) and its medieval bastides (notably Monpazier).

BERGERAC

postcode 24100 • pop 27,000 • elevation 60m
The less-than-thrilling town of Bergerac, on the right bank of the Dordogne, makes a convenient stopover on the way from Périgueux (47km to the north-east) to Bordeaux (93km to the west). In addition to its vines, Bergerac is also an important tobacco-growing centre and has a fascinating tobacco museum.

The old town and harbour quarter near the museum is well worth exploring; as a Protestant stronghold in the 16th century,

Cyrano de... Where?

You'd be forgiven for thinking that Cyrano de Bergerac – sad, big-nosed romantic hero of Edmond Rostand's 1897 play – was born, bred and died in Bergerac town, so well have the locals adopted him (they've even erected a statue in his honour) and used his name and image in all kinds of promotions (including Bergerac wine and a food festival). But the truth is that the real-life dramatist, swordsman and satirist, Savinien Cyrano de Bergerac (1619–55), on whom Rostand based his play, has an extremely tenuous connection, if any, with his namesake town; it is said that he actually came from another town called Bergerac near Paris, or at most stayed here just a few nights en route elsewhere.

much of the rest of the town sustained heavy damage during the Wars of Religion.

Orientation

The east–west rue de la Résistance is the modern town's main shopping street. The old town is south of here, towards the river, with place du Dr Cayla at its heart, surrounded by museums and restaurants, and place Louis de Labardonnie, 200m to the north, the market centre. On the northern side of rue de la Résistance is place de Lattre de Tassigny, with its landmark Église Notre Dame; place Gambetta, with upmarket hotels, is on its western side. Some 600m to the north-east of the church is the train station and 400m to the east, the spacious place de la République.

Information

Tourist Offices On the southern side of place de la République you'll find the efficient tourist office (☎ 05 53 57 03 11, fax 05 53 61 11 04, email tourisme-bergerac@aquinet.tm .fr) at 97 rue Neuve d'Argenson. It's open from 9.30 am to 12.30 pm and 2 to 6.30 pm (closed on Sunday and holidays). During July and August (opening hours

from 9.30 am to 7 pm and 4 to 7 pm on Sunday) they run guided tours of the old town for 25FF per person.

There's a Centre d'Information de Jeunesse (☎ 05 53 58 11 77, fax 05 53 61 78 88), across place de la República from the tourist office, in Galerie du Tortoni shopping arcade, which provides information on jobs and youth-geared events. It's open from 8.30 am to noon and 1.30 to 6 pm Tuesday to Saturday.

Post & Communications The post office on rue de la Résistance, is open until noon on Saturday as well as on weekdays and offers currency exchange.

You can connect to the Internet (30FF per hour) at Créasciences (☎ 05 53 22 11 21), 45 rue Leconte de Lisle, 1.7km north of the train station. A school for art and technology, its Internet room is officially open from 9 to 11 am and 2.30 to 4.30 pm on Wednesday only, but you may get access at other times if you call ahead.

Laundry The self-service laundrette at 44 place Gambetta is open from 7 am to 10 pm daily.

Medical Services & Emergency Hôpital de Bergerac (☎ 05 53 63 88 88) is at 9 ave de Prof Albert Calmette about 1km to the east of town. The municipal police station (☎ 05 53 74 66 22) is south of the tourist office at 19 rue Neuve d'Argenson.

Musée du Tabac & Musée de la Ville

The Tobacco Museum, housed in the elegant, early 17th-century Maison Peyrarède at 10 rue de l'Ancien Port (100m south-east of place du Dr Cayla), has fascinating details about the origins and uses of tobacco (for example for rituals as well as medicine) and all varieties of smoking utensils including some incredibly ornate 19th-century pipes. Several other rooms in this well-restored old building are devoted to Bergerac's past, with bits and bobs of prehistoric, Neolithic and Gallo-Roman remains.

THE DORDOGNE

It's open from 10 am to noon and 2 to 6 pm Tuesday to Saturday (to 5 pm on Saturday) and from 2.30 to 6.30 pm on Sunday. Admission costs 17FF (students free).

Musée du Vin et de la Batellerie

This little museum (☎ 05 53 57 80 92) in the old quarter, at 5 rue des Conférences (100m west of place du Dr Cayla), is also known as the Musée Régional. It mainly records the traditions and modes of transport along the Dordogne River, with models of the gabares once used to transport wine down to Bordeaux and the *sabliers* for carrying sand. There's also a small display about the traditional methods of making wine-barrels. It's open from 10 am to noon and 2 to 5.30 pm Tuesday to Friday, from 10 am to noon on Saturday and from 2.30 to 6.30 pm on Sunday. Admission costs 6FF (students free).

La Maison des Vins de Bergerac

Housed in a former 17th-century monastery and cloisters (Le Cloître des Récollets) at 2 place du Dr Cayla, this imposing riverside building is now the headquarters of the Conseil Interprofessionel des Vins de la Région de Bergerac (CIVRB – a promotional organisation for Bergerac wines) known as La Maison des Vins (☎ 05 53 63 57 55, fax 05 53 63 01 30, email vin.civrb@wanadoo.fr). You can wander through the former cloisters (free admission), pick up information about the surrounding vineyards and wine chateaux open to the public, or stay for a wine-tasting session (minimum 10 people; 10FF per person). Or, of course, buy some wines.

The cloisters are also used for art exhibitions and, from June to August, free jazz performances at 5 pm every Wednesday.

La Maison des Vins is open from 10 am to noon and 2 to 6 pm daily (closed on Sundays during April). A second entrance is on the riverside quai Salvette.

Places to Stay

The municipal *Camping La Pelouse* (☎ 05 53 57 06 67) on the southern bank of the river is open year-round and charges 16/7FF per person/tent.

Sweet, Mouldy Monbazillac

There's nothing so delicious as a sweet, golden and icy-cold Monbazillac to drink with your foie gras or walnut gateau. Like other sweet, rich wines, this famous *vin liquoreux* from south of Bergerac depends on a particular mould (*Botrytis cinereaor;* 'noble rot') growing on the grape skins to achieve its superb sweetness and fragrance.

You can have a free tasting after a tour of the Monbazillac Cooperative's beautiful headquarters, the **Château de Monbazillac** (☎ 05 53 61 52 52) 6km south of Bergerac. Built in 1550, it's scarcely changed, still displaying its machicolations and round towers, its Renaissance decorations and defensive moat. Inside are 17th-century furnishings and tapestries, old documents and rustic Périgord items.

It's open from 10 am to noon and 2 to 6 pm daily (to 5 pm from November to March when it's also closed on Monday; to 7 pm in May and October; and from 10 am to 7.30 pm daily during July and August). Admission costs 35FF. A taxi from Bergerac (☎ 05 53 57 20 70) will cost around 90FF plus 80FF an hour waiting and drinking time.

The best budget hotels are directly opposite the train station on ave du 108ème RI: *Hôtel-Restaurant L'Ovale* (☎ 05 53 57 78 75), at No 27, has small and gloomy doubles from 140FF (150FF with shower or 210/330FF for a triple/quad). The flashier *Hôtel-Restaurant Le Moderne* (☎ 05 53 57 19 62), at No 19, has considerably nicer rooms from 160FF (without shower but with TV and telephone). Hall showers are free.

The friendly *Hôtel Le Family* (☎ 05 53 57 80 90, 3 rue du Dragon), right beside the covered market near the old town, has rooms with shower, WC and telephone from 170FF (200FF in July and August). You need to book ahead in high season.

Among the upmarket hotels on place Gambetta are *Hôtel de France* (☎ 05 53 57

11 61, fax 05 53 61 25 70), at No 18, where rooms cost from 270FF; and *Hôtel de Bordeaux* (☎ *05 53 57 12 83, fax 05 53 57 72 14)*, at No 38, where rates start at 330FF (380FF from June to August). Both places have swimming pools.

Places to Eat

Restaurants in the old quarter have the most enjoyable ambience, including *Restaurant Pizzeria Chez Marceau* (☎ *05 53 63 07 50, 14 rue St-Clar; closed on Thursday)* with a 58FF midday *menu* or an omelette aux cèpes and salad for 60FF. Bagging the best riverside location at the foot of the old quarter, *La Treille* (☎ *05 53 57 60 11, 12 quai Salvette)* has classy *menus* (with plenty of fish dishes) from 79/105FF (midday/evening).

Among hotel-restaurants (see Places to Stay), *Le Jardin d'Épicure* at Hôtel Le Family has excellent home-made fare and *menus* from 42/82FF midday/evening; and Hôtel-Restaurant Le Moderne has a generous 63FF *menu du jour*, available until 9 pm.

For snacks, drinks and people-watching, the cafe-bars along pedestrianised rue du Colonel de Chadois (south of rue de la Résistance leading into the old town) are fun.

Getting There & Away

Air The Aéroport de Bergerac-Roumanière (☎ 05 53 57 00 09), 4km south of town, hosts three flights daily to/from Paris with Flandre Air-Air Liberté.

Bus Limited bus services leave from outside the train station: SAB (☎ 05 53 40 23 30) goes to Villeneuve-sur-Lot (50.80FF, 1¼ hours, twice daily in term-time, once at other times); and CFTA (☎ 05 53 08 43 13) to Périgueux (43.50FF, 1½ hours, three to four daily).

Eurolines' international services stop on place de la République (opposite the tourist office) but only on request.

Train Bergerac is on the tertiary rail line that links Bordeaux (78FF, 1½ hours, four to six daily) with Sarlat-la-Canéda (59FF, 1¼ hours, two to four daily) via St-Émilion

(48FF, 50 minutes, two daily) and Le Buisson (36FF, 45 minutes, three to four daily). Change at Le Buisson for Agen (97FF) and Libourne or Bordeaux for Paris (309FF). The station's information and ticket office (☎ 05 53 63 53 81) is open until around 7.45 pm daily (to 10.30 pm on Sunday).

Getting Around

For a taxi call ☎ 05 53 57 20 70. A taxi from the airport to the town centre will cost around 80FF.

On ave du 108ème RI near the train station are Europcar (☎ 05 53 58 97 97, fax 05 53 27 13 00) at No 3; Hertz (☎ 05 53 57 19 27, fax 05 53 57 90 49) at No 15 and Budget (☎ 05 53 74 20 00, fax 05 53 74 20 01) at No 14. None are open on Sunday. Périgord Cycles (☎ 05 53 57 07 19) at 11 place Gambetta rents mountain bikes for 100/500FF per day/week. It's open 9 am to noon and 2 to 7 pm daily except on Sunday and Monday.

One-hour trips along the Dordogne in a gabarre take place at least three times daily in summer, from opposite La Maison des Vin on quai Salvette, for 35FF (children 25FF).

MONPAZIER

postcode 24540 • pop 530 • elevation 180m
Of all the bastides in South-West France, Monpazier, 45km south-east of Bergerac, is considered the best model.

Perfectly laid out in rectangular grid-style, most of its buildings date from the 13th century. Over 30 are classified as historic monuments. Of particular note is the main square **place des Cornières** with its covered arcades, the covered market with its set of 15th-century measures and the town's three fortified gateways. For information on the market held here see the boxed text 'Périgord Market Days' earlier in this chapter.

Established in 1285 by King Edward I, Monpazier has had a tough life, assaulted during the Hundred Years' War, taken over by the Huguenots during the Wars of Religion and the hub of peasant uprisings in the 17th century. Today, picturesque and popular

Monpazier is an essential market town that thrives on the region's produce of tobacco, chestnuts, mushrooms and strawberries. If you've got your own transport, the **Château de Biron** or bastide town of **Beaumont** make excellent day-trips from here.

Orientation & Information

The tourist office (☎ 05 53 22 68 59, fax 05 53 74 30 08) in the main square is open from 9 am to 12.30 pm and from 2 to 6.30 pm Monday to Friday and from 10 am to 12.30 pm and 2.30 to 6.30 pm at the weekend (9 am to 6 pm daily in July and August).

The post office is on the northern edge of town, near the Foirail Nord (northern parking lot) and there's a Crédit Agricole bank in the south-western corner.

Organised Tours & Activities

The tourist office runs several tours including 90-minute guided visits of the bastide (in French) at 10.30 am and 3.30 pm daily from June to August. On Tuesday and Friday evenings in July (at 10 pm) and August (9.30 pm) scenes of medieval life are enacted during the tour, amusing even if you don't understand much French. The tours cost 20FF (children 8FF).

Special interest tours include two-hour botanical promenades through the Sentier du Bois Sec (the nearby woods of Capdrot); and the Circuit Gourmand (around 75FF per person) to nearby *fermes auberges* (farm restaurants) to taste the local produce.

Horse-riders can head for the Centre Équestre de Marsalès (☎/fax 05 53 22 63 14), 2km to the north off the D660. Rates are 95/430FF per hour/day; weekend or six-day *randonnées* can also be arranged (4380FF all-inclusive six-day package).

Places to Stay & Eat

At *Le Moulin de David* (☎ 05 53 22 65 25, fax 05 53 23 99 76), a tranquil, shady camp site 3.2km west of Monpazier, off the D104, rates are 20/25FF per person/site. It's open mid-May to mid-September. A *gîte d'étape* (☎ 05 53 63 24 75, Le Bost) near the GR36 is about 9km to the north, in Montferrand. Beds cost 40FF a night (150FF half-board).

Just outside the walls, on the northern edge of town by the Foirail (parking lot) *Hôtel-Restaurant Le Londres (05 53 22 60 64, 05 53 22 61 98, Foirail Nord)* offers pleasant doubles from 220FF. Inside the bastide, *Hôtel-Restaurant de France (☎ 05 53 22 60 06, fax 05 53 22 07 27, 21 rue St-Jacques)* has a couple of rooms at 160FF, the rest from 220FF. Both places offer evening *menus* from 85FF.

As well as several restaurants on place des Cornières, others along rue St-Jacques (the north–south road west of place des Cornières) include *Le Croquant (☎ 05 53 22 62 63)*, at No 28, whose 60FF *menu* includes some tasty Périgord fare; and *La Bastide (☎ 05 53 22 60 59)*, at No 52, whose 80FF *menu* includes 0.25L of wine. It is closed on Monday.

Getting There & Away

The nearest train station is at Belvès, 19km to the north-east (see Getting There & Away under Belvès earlier in this chapter). The closest major bus service (from Villeneuve-sur-Lot) goes to Villeréal, 15km to the west (32FF; one hour; daily during term-time, weekly during the rest of the year).For a taxi, call ☎ 05 53 22 07 15.

Getting Around

Bikes can be rented from Monsieur Mouret (☎ 05 53 22 63 46) at 17 rue St-Jacques for 60/250FF per day/week.

AROUND MONPAZIER
Château de Biron

Eight kilometres south of Monpazier, this grand chateau dominates the peaceful land around it.

It wasn't always so tranquil: first established in the 11th century the chateau was razed by Simon de Montfort and fought over bitterly by English and French during the Hundred Years' War. And all the time, various generations of the Gontaut-Biron family (who owned it for 800 years) rebuilt, altered and fiddled with it. New additions included a Renaissance chapel and colonnaded arcade, a great state hall and a re-designed keep.

Today, owned by the département, many of its rambling basement rooms have been converted to display medieval activities (for example a tannery, pottery, bakery and a particularly gruesome torture chamber) with moody candlelit lighting.

It's open from 10 am to 12.30 pm and 1.30 to 7 pm daily from April to the end of June and September to November (from 10 am to 7 pm daily in July and August); at other times it opens from 10 am to 12.30 pm and 1.30 to 5.30 pm (closed during January). Admission costs 30FF (six to 12 year-olds 15FF). Visits (in French) are sometimes guided; an English text is available.

Beaumont

Another substantial English bastide town, 16km north-west of Monpazier, Beaumont was founded in 1272 in the name of King Edward I. Traffic on the D660 now rushes past its spacious, unguarded square, **place Jean Moulin**, and the only major fortification left is a 13th-century gateway **porte de Luzier** on the western edge of town. But grabbing the limelight still is a huge fortified 13th-century church, **Église de St-Front** overlooking place Jean Moulin with four fortress-like towers and an incongruously ornate western doorway.

Next door is the tourist office (☎ 05 53 22 39 12, fax 05 53 22 05 35), open from 10 am to noon and 2 to 5 pm (closed on Monday; open only Tuesday, Thursday and Friday from November to March) and from 10 am to 7 pm daily from June to November.

Dolmen fans might like to head 3km to the south to see the **Dolmen du Blanc** (just off the D676), a Neolithic burial chamber of three huge stones.

Places to Stay & Eat The very good *Camping Les Remparts* (☎ 05 53 22 40 86), 800m south-west of Beaumont, off the D676, charges 18/22FF per person/site.

By the church, on the main road, the friendly *Hôtel-Restaurant Le Beaumontois* (☎ 05 53 22 30 11, fax 05 53 22 38 99, rue Romieu) has fraying but perfectly adequate doubles from 220FF with bidet and bath. The restaurant is pricier, with *menus* from 95FF but there's an excellent hors d'oeuvres buffet for 70FF, overseen by a stuffed goose wearing a tie.

Getting There & Away

The nearest train station is Lalinde, 10km to the north on the Bordeaux–Sarlat line. Villeréal is the closest bus station. For a taxi call ☎ 05 53 22 98 52.

THE DORDOGNE

Lot & Lot-et-Garonne

South-east of the Dordogne lies the Lot département, a warm, distinctively southern region where many of the residents still speak Occitan. Like the Périgord region (modern département name – Dordogne), the Lot still tends to be known by its pre-Revolution name, Quercy (after the tough Celtic tribe, Cadurcii), which once included most of present-day Tarn-et-Garonne.

Dry limestone plateaus (called *causses*) are a feature of the area. The plateau in the north, known as Haut Quercy, is covered with oak trees and cut by dramatic canyons created by the serpentine Lot River and its tributaries. Here are two of South-West France's most famous and popular destinations – the rock-clinging pilgrims' haven of Rocamadour and the deep cavern of Gouffre de Padirac. South of here, the départemental capital, Cahors, is surrounded by fine vineyards; to its east is one of the prettiest stretches of the Lot River and the dreamy Célé valley, home to some of the finest prehistoric cave paintings in South-West France, at the Grotte du Pech Merle.

To the west of Cahors lies the agricultural and fruit-rich Lot-et-Garonne département, whose southern region still considers itself part of proud Gascony. There are a scattering of impressive *bastides* (fortified villages) and some great boat trips on the Lot, Baïse and Garonne rivers and Canal Latéral.

This chapter lists the towns of the Lot in roughly north to south order before heading west to Lot-et-Garonne.

Information

The Comité Départemental du Tourisme du Lot (see Tourist Offices under Information in the Cahors section for contact details) is notably efficient: among its many useful publications (available at most tourist offices) is *Key to the Lot,* which details transport, sites, activities, accommodation and much more; and *Countryside Sports in the Lot,* with contact details for all kinds of

Highlights

- Follow in pilgrims' footsteps at the famous cliff-hugging site of Rocamadour

- Relax in Cahors, the low-key départemental capital, and enjoy great wines, markets and restaurants

- Meander along the delightful Célé valley with its once-grand hamlets

- Marvel at the mysterious cave paintings at Cougnac and the rare prehistoric footprints at Pech Merle

- Sample Europe's best prunes (unforgettable in chocolate or Armagnac) in Agen, the lively capital of the Lot-et-Garonne

- Explore Grandes Randonnées, trails through fabulous countryside, or pamper your feet and hire a houseboat on the Canal Latéral or the Garonne, Baïse or Lot rivers

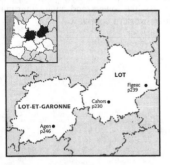

pruneaux d'Agen – prunes from Agen

agneau fermier du Quercy – high quality lamb

cabécou de Rocamadour – small round portions of goat's cheese

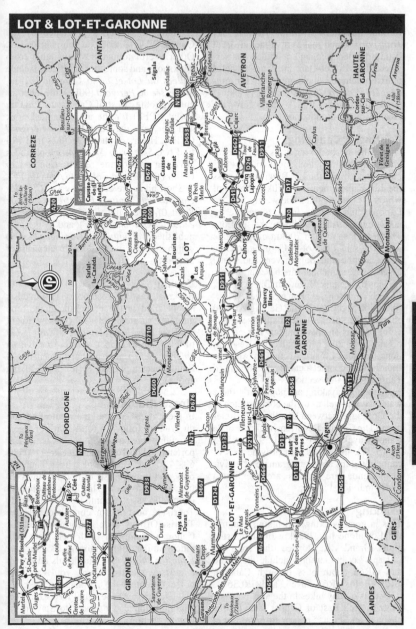

euro currency converter 10FF = €1.52

activities plus suggested walks. Invaluable for bus-travellers is *Guide Horaire des Transports* which makes a valiant effort at listing the département's muddled bus services. The Lot-et-Garonne's most useful tourist brochure is a planning map for *Randonnées Pédestres/Équestres/VTT* (walking/horse-riding/biking trails), which shows the area's Grandes Randonnées.

Boating & Canoeing

One of the most relaxing ways to see the region is by renting a houseboat on one of its many waterways: the Lot River runs across the Lot département for 170km, 65km of which is navigable, between St-Cirq Lapopie and Luzech (and, sometime by 2003, even further to Villeneuve-sur-Lot). There are also around 200km of navigable waterways in the Lot-et-Garonne, on the Lot, Garonne and Baïse rivers and Canal Latéral. The main boat-hire bases are Agen, Le Mas d'Agenais, Buzet-sur-Baïse, Nérac, Luzech and Bouziès. For more general information see Boat in the Getting Around chapter; for specific information see individual towns in this chapter. For an all-organised boating trip, contact the Réservations Services Loisirs Accueil in Agen or Cahors (for contact details see Organised Tours later in this section).

Canoeing/kayaking are popular on these waterways as well as on the 60km-stretch of the Dordogne between Souillac and Bretenoux. The Comité Départemental du Lot de Canoe Kayak (☎ 05 65 35 91 59, fax 05 65 30 15 37), in Cahors, can provide lists of canoeing clubs and a programme of activities. Canoe-hire outlets are mentioned under individual towns.

Walking

This is great walking and biking country: the Lot alone has 2950km of signposted paths. Grandes Randonnées that cross the Lot and Lot-et-Garonne include the GR36 and GR65 (both pass through Cahors), GR6, GR46, GR64, GR652 and GR636.

Details on day hikes in the area between Bouziès (see East of Cahors later in this chapter) and Figeac appear in *Entre Lot et Célé* (39FF), a topoguide in the Promenades et Randonnées series published by the Comité Départemental du Tourisme du Lot. Other useful topoguides (available from bookshops and some tourist offices) include *Vallées du Lot et de la Garonne* (52FF), *Traversée du Périgord* (90FF), the latter including routes west of Cahors; *Le Pays du Dropt* (52FF) for the area around Duras; and *Le Pays du Haut-Agenais Périgord* (52FF). Hikers on the St-Jacques trail will find two *Sentier de St-Jacques* topoguides covering part of the region: *Conques to Cahors* (75FF) and *Cahors to Agen* (90FF).

Short hikes are covered by *Les Chemins Qui Parlent: Sentiers Pédestres – Pays de Saint Cirq Lapopie*; *Les Sentiers d'Émilie en Lot-et-Garonne* (80FF); and by the UK-published *Walking in the Dordogne* (£5.99) which includes over a dozen routes east of Souillac.

Cycling

Backroads and off-road options for cyclists are detailed in the French-language topo guides *Cyclotourisme en Quercy* (about 40FF), *Guide du Cyclotourisme dans le Lot* (40FF) and *VTT 36 Circuits – Le Lot en Quercy* (50FF), and in the Promenades et Randonnées topoguide series (see Walking above).

Horse Riding

In the Lot-et-Garonne, the Route Équestre du Pruneau follows a route north of Agen, through prune country. Agen's Comité Départemental de Tourisme Équestre (☎ 05 53 69 44 65), at 7 rue E Dolet, open Thursday only, can provide lists of horse-riding centres and activities. The Lot's equivalent (same address as Comité Départemental du Tourisme du Lot, for contact details see Tourist Offices under Information in the Cahors section later in this chapter), provides similar information in its *Tourisme Équestre dans le Lot*. For details on *fermes équestres* (farms where you can hire horses), contact the Association Départementale de Tourisme Rural (see Rural Accommodation under Places to Stay in the Cahors section).

Organised Tours

For organised outdoor activities, excursions, cookery courses or special camps for kids, contact the Réservations Services Loisirs Accueil (☎ 05 65 53 20 90, fax 05 65 30 06 11, email loisirs.accueil.lot@wanadoo.fr) at Maison du Tourisme, place François Mitterand, Cahors; or the same outfit in Agen (☎ 05 53 66 14 14, fax 05 53 68 25 42) at 4 rue André Chénier (this office is sometimes promoted under the name ACTOUR 47).

Lot

SOUILLAC

postcode 46200 • pop 3700 • elevation 80m
This small town, squeezed between the Dordogne and Borrèze rivers and the N20, with its traffic hurtling between Brive-la-Gaillarde (34km to the north) and Cahors (69km to the south), isn't worth an overnight stay but does have two good reasons for a few hours' diversion: a superb Romanesque abbey and a fascinating museum.

Orientation & Information

The tourist office (☎ 05 65 37 81 56, fax 05 65 27 11 45, email souillac@wanadoo.fr), on blvd Louis-Jean Malvy (the N20), is open from 10 am to noon and 2 to 6 pm daily except on Sunday (from 9.30 am to 12.30 pm and 2 to 7 pm daily in July and August). The abbey and adjacent museum are five minutes' walk downhill (to the west) from the tourist office.

Abbaye Ste-Marie

The former Benedictine abbey dates from the 12th century but the Hundred Years' War and Wars of Religion, plus fires and over-enthusiastic 'restorers', have given it a hard time. Still outstanding, however, are its three huge Islamic-like domes, its sparsely decorated single nave and the extraordinary carved doorway, replaced facing inside after damage caused during the Wars of Religion. The carvings show how St-Theophilus made a pact with the devil and was rescued by the Virgin Mary. Don't miss the amazingly lifelike low relief of the so-called 'dancing' Isaiah, on the right side. The abbey is open from 9 am to 7 pm daily.

Musée de l'Automate

Around the corner from the abbey, this fascinating museum (☎ 05 65 37 07 07) has a beguiling collection of some 3000 automata, many dating from the late 19th and early 20th centuries. It's open from 10 am to noon and 3 to 6 pm daily except Monday from April to October (from 10 am to 7 pm daily during July and August); at other times it opens from 2 to 5 pm daily except Monday and Tuesday. Admission costs 30FF (students 20FF, children 15FF).

Getting There & Away

Souillac train station is 1.1km north of town. It's on the main Paris–Toulouse line with regular connections to Brive (37FF, 25 minutes) and Cahors (56FF, around 40 minutes). Bus departure points include the train

LOT

Prehistoric Finger Prints & Mysterious Men

The Grottes de Cougnac (☎ 05 65 41 22 25), 32km south of Souillac and 3km north of Gourdon, contain some of the most amazing prehistoric cave paintings in South-West France: 20,000-year-old ochre and black images of mountain goats and hump-backed deer, a flurry of fingerprints and some mysterious half-human, half-animal 'wounded men', with misformed heads and pierced with spears. There's another cave, 200m away, with delicate stalactites and stalagmites. The caves are open from 9.30 to 11 am and 2 to 7 pm daily between Easter and November (from 9.30 am to 6 pm during July and August). Guided visits cost 33FF (children 20FF).

---

euro currency converter 10FF = €1.52

station and ave de Sarlat. Sample fares include Sarlat-la-Canéda (28.50FF, 50 minutes, four to seven buses daily) and Martel (12FF, 20 minutes, twice daily).

EAST OF SOUILLAC

From Souillac you have two choices eastwards: up to Martel or along the Dordogne valley which has a string of attractions all the way to Bretenoux.

Grottes de Lacave

In one of the most picturesque loops of the Dordogne River, 11km south-east of Souillac, the vast caverns of Lacave (☎ 05 65 37 87 03), accessible by train and lift, are famous for their unusual rock formations and fantastic lighting effects, reflected in numerous lakes. They're open from 9 am to noon and 2 to 6 pm daily (closing at 5 pm in low season but open continually from 9 am to 6.30 pm from mid-July to 25 August). They're closed entirely from 11 November to 7 February. Admission costs 42FF (children 32FF).

Martel

postcode 46600 • pop 1470 • elevation 270m

Twelfth-century Martel, the 'Town of the Seven Towers', 24km north of Rocamadour, 15km east of Souillac, is an attractive, historic town which has long been the centre of the regional walnut trade: the ancient weighing measures can still be seen at the wooden marketplace in the square.

The town is reputedly named after the Frankish conqueror, Charles Martel (whose son founded the Carolingian dynasty); he built an abbey here after his victory over the Moors in 732. It later became the capital of the viscounts of Turenne, its strong fortifications bearing witness to its violent past – even the church is comprised of battlements and buttresses.

Orientation & Information The best entrance to the old town is from the N140 which runs along the northern, modern edge of town: the post office is here and banks and cafe-restaurants are on nearby place Gambetta. At the heart of the old town, on

The Gauls' Last Stand

Some say it's at Capdenac, others favour Luzech, but most archaeologists now agree that the Puy d'Issolud, a 311m-high plateau 14km east of Martel, is the site of Uxellodunum, where the Gauls lost their last bastion to the Romans. Heavily defended with earthworks, ditches and dry-stone defences, Uxellodunum fell only after the canny Romans cut off the water supply; the Cadurcii tribe inside believed their gods had deserted them and gave up the fight.

place des Consuls, is the tourist office (☎ 05 65 37 43 44, fax 05 65 37 37 27, email marteltourisme@europost.org), open from 10 am to noon and 3 to 6 pm daily (9 am to 12.30 pm and 3 to 7 pm in July and August).

Things to See & Do The place des Consuls, with its 18th-century covered market, is surrounded by picturesque medieval buildings and decorated towers including the striking 14th-century Hôtel (or Palais) de la Raymondie which houses the town hall, tourist office and a small Musée d'Uxellodunum (☎ 05 65 37 30 03) with a display of Gallo-Roman remains (see the boxed text 'The Gauls' Last Stand'). It's open from 10 am to noon and 3 to 6 pm during July and August only. Admission costs 7FF.

The Maison Fabri, sited in the square's south-eastern corner, is where Henry 'Short Coat' died of fever-ridden guilt in 1183 after ransacking Rocamadour's shrines to pay for his fight against his father, King Henry II. You can follow rue Droite south of here to find more Gothic and Renaissance townhouses.

Offering a charming 90-minute round trip, the Chemin de Fer Touristique de Haut Quercy (☎ 05 65 37 35 81) uses a steam or diesel engine to run 11km from Martel to St-Denis-près-Martel. The steam engine runs at 2.45 and 4.45 pm every Sunday and holiday between April and October (plus on Wednesday from mid-July to mid-August) for 50FF return (children 30FF); the diesel engine runs at 2.45 pm on Wednesday and Friday (daily except Monday during July and August) for 35FF (children 20FF). The station (for this train only) is 500m south-east of town, off the D23 to Creysse.

Places to Stay & Eat The basic *Camping Municipal La Callopie* (☎ 05 65 37 30 03), off the D23, opposite the Hôtel-Restaurant Le Lion D'Or (see below), charges 9/9FF per person/tent. *Camping Les Falaises* (☎ 05 65 37 37 78), by the cliffs overlooking the Dordogne 5km to the south in Gluges, charges 20/20FF per person/site.

Hôtel-Restaurant Le Lion d'Or (☎ 05 65 37 30 16, fax 05 65 37 37 46), 200m north of place Gambetta, has doubles/triples from 180/280FF; the restaurant offers a 65FF *menu* with regional specialities. On the south-western edge of town the Logis de France *Hôtel-Restaurant Le Quercy-Turenne* (☎ 05 65 37 30 30, ave Laveyssière) has similar rates and serves *menus* from 75FF.

La Mère Michèle (☎ 05 65 37 35 66, rue de la Remise), 50m down rue Montpezat opposite Le Quercy-Turenne (follow the cat drawings), has several small rooms facing an inner garden for 220/240FF per double/triple; the cat-loving Michèle also does meals (from 75FF).

There are several *bar-brasseries* around place Gambetta and a couple of *creperies* and *pizzerias* on place des Consuls.

Getting There & Away The nearest train station, St-Denis-près-Martel (☎ 05 65 32 42 08), 8km to the east, has connections to/from Brive about six times daily (28FF, 25 minutes). A bus from the station goes to Martel (and on to Souillac: 12FF, 20 minutes) twice daily.

Carennac

postcode 46110 • pop 370 • elevation 180m
This charming little village tucked beside the Dordogne River, 33km east of Souillac, is famous for its typical Quercy houses and turrets, its finely decorated Romanesque priory-church and its association with the renowned 17th-century bishop, writer and philosopher, François de Salignac de la Mothe-Fénelon who was abbot at the priory for 15 years (see the Arts section in Facts about South-West France for more about Fénelon).

Orientation & Information The village clusters by the river between the D20 and the river-hugging D43. The main sites are inside the former priory, accessible through a fortified gateway. The tourist office (☎/fax 05 65 10 97 01), also here, is open from 10 am to noon and 1.30 to 6 pm daily (from 10 am to 7 pm daily during July and August and from 10 am to noon and 2 to 5 pm on weekdays only between November and April).

Things to See The most notable part that remains of the priory – founded in the 10th century, rebuilt and fortified in the 16th century, and ruined during the Revolution – is the Romanesque **Église St-Pierre**. Its highlight is a magnificent carved tympanum over the porch, with doe-eyed, light-of-foot apostles and a frieze of animals. The **cloisters** (access through the tourist office and open the same hours, for 10FF, children 5FF) boast a fine 15th-century Entombment scene, with expressive, life-size figures.

Beside the church, the **Maison de la Dordogne Quercynoise** (☎ 05 65 32 59 19), housed in a 16th-century chateau, has excellent audio-visual displays on the theme of the People and the Dordogne River. It's open from 10 am to 1 pm and 2 to 7 pm daily between mid-April and November for 25FF (children and students 20FF, entry to the cloister 5FF extra).

Places to Stay & Eat The riverside *Camping L'Eau Vive* (☎ 05 65 10 97 39), open from April to November, is 1.1km to the south-east, off the D30. Rates are 20/11/11FF per person/tent/car.

Hôtel-Restaurant des Touristes (☎ 05 65 10 94 31, fax 05 65 39 79 85), near the D20

LOT

entrance to town, has comfortable (though thin-walled) doubles without shower costing 180FF (230FF with) and generous *menus* from 61FF. There are two Logis de France inns (both with swimming pools): ***Hostellerie Fénelon*** *(☎ 05 65 10 96 46, fax 05 65 10 94 86),* near Hôtel-Restaurant des Touristes, where doubles cost from 270FF (200FF for a basement double without shower) and restaurant *menus* from 86FF; ***Auberge du Vieux Quercy*** *(☎ 05 65 10 96 59, fax 05 65 10 94 05),* on the D20 above town, has doubles from 280FF and *menus* from 88FF.

Getting There & Around The nearest train station is Bétaille (4.5km to the north) but services to/from Brive-la-Gaillarde (28FF, 25 minutes, around six daily) run more frequently to/from St-Denis-près-Martel (14km to the north-west). See Getting There & Away in the earlier Martel section for details.

Cars Quercy Corrèze (☎ 05 65 39 71 90) runs buses via Carennac on their Brive–Gramat line four times weekly during term-time. The bus stop is on the D20 above the village. Auberge du Vieux Quercy rents mountain bikes for 60/80FF per half/full day. In high season, canoes are available from Saga Team (☎ 05 65 10 97 39) at Camping L'Eau Vive.

Château de Castelnau-Bretenoux

This imposing red-stone chateau, 17km east of Carennac, towers over the surrounding countryside. Its amazing medieval fortifications, built during the Hundred Years' War and among the best of its era, include a huge keep and six round towers, fortified curtain walls and ramparts. Restored in the early 20th century, its interior is lavishly furnished and decorated. The chateau (☎ 05 65 10 98 00), by the village of Prudhomat, is open from 9.30 am to 12.15 pm and 2 to 6.15 pm daily between April and October (9.30 am to 6.45 pm between July and September; and from 10 am to 12.15 pm and 2 to 5.15 pm daily except Tuesday between October and April). Admission costs 32FF (children 21FF).

ROCAMADOUR

postcode 46500 • pop 600 • elevation 250m

This famous pilgrimage centre, 59km north of Cahors, is one of the most dramatic sites in France, spectacularly situated on a vertical, 150m-high cliff-face above the Alzou River. It was founded in the 12th century, on the site of a shrine to a Black Virgin (or Madonna) and a hermit's rocky cave (*roc amator* means 'he who likes the rock' in Occitan). The hermit was supposedly the tax-gatherer Zaccheus, disciple of Jesus, who was believed to have fled with his wife Veronica to this remote corner of France. The shrine rapidly became famous for its miraculous powers and hosted tens of thousands of pilgrims and a stream of VIPs.

For 200 years, its expanding village of shrines – called the Cité – was an important stop on the pilgrimage route to Santiago de Compostela but its riches attracted a succession of pillagers. Desecrated during the Wars of Religion and the Revolution,

NICKY CAVEN

Medieval Rocamadour was an important stop on the Santiago de Compostela pilgrimage.

Rocamadour was restored in the 19th century and has once again become a major pilgrimage site. But its popularity has made it a tourists' nightmare, overrun with coaches and filled to overflowing with souvenir shops. Come here off-season or in the early morning if you want a glimmer of its precipitous attractions.

Orientation

Rocamadour is on four levels: the valley below the Cité with its car park and electric tourist train stop (see Getting Around later in this section); the medieval Cité, full of shops, hotels and restaurants; the level above this featuring the chapels; and the plateau, 500m above the valley, with the remains of a 14th-century chateau and ramparts.

Some 900m to the east of the plateau is L'Hospitalet (1.7km via the D32 from the Cité). This busy village (once the site of a 11th-century pilgrims' hospital) is centred round the place de l'Europe crossroads: near here is the main tourist office, a few hotels and restaurants and various non-pilgrimage tourist attractions.

Information

The tourist office (☎ 05 65 33 22 00, fax 05 65 33 22 01; email rocamadour@wanadoo.fr), in a big new glass-fronted building just off L'Hospitalet's place de l'Europe, is open from 10 am to noon and 2 to 6 pm daily (10 am to 8 pm during July and August). There's a smaller office (☎ 05 65 33 62 59) in the Cité's main street, rue de la Couronnerie, open from 10.30 am to 12.30 pm and 1.30 to 7 pm daily from April to June and during September; from 9.30 am to 7.30 pm during July and August; from 10 am to noon and 2 to 6 pm in October; and from 2.30 to 5.30 pm daily except on Tuesday from November to March. They run guided tours of the chapels daily except at the weekend (except on Sunday morning in July and August) for 16FF (children 12FF).

There's a post office in the Cité and banks both here and in L'Hospitalet; currency exchange is also available at the post office and tourist offices.

In The Cité

Coach tourists with glazed eyes obediently plod through a number of over-restored Gothic chapels, notably **Chapelle Notre Dame**, home to the renowned, smoke-blackened Black Virgin. Other sights in the Cité to refresh less pious visitors include the **Musée du Jouet Ancien Automobile** (☎ 05 65 33 60 75), which has over a hundred early 20th-century kiddie cars. It is open from 10 am to noon and 2 to 6 pm daily between mid-March and mid-November and costs 20FF (children 10FF).

The Cité's main street is connected to the chapels and to the plateau above by the **Grand Escalier** (Great Staircase, also called Via Sancta) – the 223 steps were once climbed by the pious on their knees – and a path whose switchbacks are marked with graphic stations of the Cross.

L'Hospitalet

One of the best attractions here is simply the view of the Cité below from the ramparts of the **chateau** (open from 8 am to 8 pm daily, admission costs 13FF). The freshwater **aquarium** (☎ 05 65 33 73 61), on place de l'Europe, is open from 10 am to noon and 2 to 7 pm daily between Easter and October (from 2 to 6 pm at the weekend and during school holidays for the rest of the year). Admission costs 25FF (children 10FF). The **Grotte des Merveilles** (☎ 05 65 33 67 92), a small cave next to the tourist office, has some mediocre stalactites and prehistoric cave paintings and is open from 10 am to noon and 2 to 6 pm daily from April to November (9 am to 7 pm during July and August). Admission costs 30FF (children 15FF). The bizarre **La Feerie du Rail** (☎ 05 65 33 71 06) is an animated and illuminated miniature fantasyland; shows (held three to eight times daily depending on the season) cost 38FF (children 23FF). At the other end of the spectrum, the engrossing natural attraction of **Le Rocher des Aigles** (☎ 05 65 33 65 45), near the chateau, has demonstrations by various birds of prey three to four times daily during the high season for 40FF (children 25FF).

LOT

Places to Stay & Eat

In L'Hospitalet, the grassy camp site *Relais du Campeur* (☎ *05 65 33 73 50*), open from April to October, has a *forfait* (fixed price deal covering two people) of 63FF for two.

Nearby, the gaudy *Comp'Hostel* (☎ *05 65 33 73 50, fax 05 65 33 69 60, place de l'Europe)*, has modern doubles/quads for 200/280FF (220/340FF between July and September). It's open from April to September.

On rue de la Couronnerie, in the Cité (where you'll have to book way ahead in high season), *Hôtel du Globe* (☎ *05 65 33 67 73)* has doubles/triples with shower and toilet from 190/240FF. In December and January it's open at the weekend only. *Hôtel-Restaurant du Lion D'Or* (☎ *05 65 33 62 04, fax 05 65 33 72 54)* has similar doubles/triples for 260/290FF. For more frills, at the Logis de France *Hôtel-Restaurant Le Terminus des Pélerins* (☎ *05 65 33 62 14, fax 05 65 33 72 10)* doubles cost from 250FF.

In addition to the *hotel-restaurants* and the plentiful *creperies* and *cafes* in town, the kid-friendly *Restaurant Chez Anne-Marie* (☎ *05 65 33 65 81)* has midday/evening *menus* from 69/78FF.

Getting There & Away

Rocamadour town is 4km south-west of Rocamadour-Padirac train station (☎ 05 65 33 63 05), which is on the Toulouse to Brive-la-Gaillarde (43FF, 37 minutes) line via Figeac (42FF, around 30 minutes). Services run at least three times daily. Taxis (☎ 05 65 33 72 72) charge around 50FF to/from the station.

Getting Around

Car drivers are advised to park near the chateau and take a lift down to the Cité (see below) or head for the valley parking and take the tourist train (Le Petit Train) up: it runs every 15 minutes from 10 am to 7.30 pm daily between Easter and September for 20FF return (children 15FF).

The Ascenseur Incline Solveroc links the chateau with the shrines for 15/23FF one-way/return. The Ascenseur de Rocamadour lift runs between the Cité and the shrines for

15/11FF. Both run between 8 am and 8 pm daily in the high season (to 10 pm during July and August) but operate fewer hours in the low season.

ST-CÉRÉ

postcode 46400 • pop 3500 • elevation 137m
The old market town of St-Céré, 30km east of Rocamadour in the valley of the Bave River, is a picturesque, prosperous place, renowned for its strawberries and plums and for being the adopted home town of the tapestry designer, Jean Lurçat (see the boxed text 'Tapestries & Cockerels'). It makes a pleasant base for touring the area – traditional Quercy hamlets such as Autoire to the west or the emptier, rye lands of La Ségala to the east.

Orientation & Information

The huge place de la République forms the hub of town. The old town comprises the area on either side of the main shopping street, rue de la República, which runs for 300m north-west of the square; turn right (to the north) off rue de la République to reach place du Mercadial, the old market square.

The tourist office (☎ 05 65 38 11 85, fax 05 65 38 38 71, email saint-cere@wanadoo .fr), on place de la República, is open from 10 am to noon and 2 to 6 pm Monday to Sat-

---

Tapestries & Cockerels

The artist Jean Lurçat (1892–1966), who specialised in bright, inventive paintings, mosaics and ceramics, first won fame for reviving the flagging, 500-year-old tapestry industry of Aubusson where he was appointed chief designer in 1939. During WWII, Lurçat joined the Resistance in the Lot and once the war was over he settled in St-Céré, establishing a studio in the hilltop Tours de St-Laurent. It was here he produced some of his most famous designs, characterised by enormous cockerels – a rallying cry to restore French pride in the post-war days.

urday (9 am to 12.30 pm and 2.30 to 7 pm in July and August, when it is also open on Sunday morning). It has comprehensive information on the surrounding Pays de St-Céré region including the booklet *Randonnées au pays de Saint-Céré* with a choice of trails (15FF to 35FF). In season the office runs guided tours of the town (15FF, 1½ hours). Alternatively, pick up the free leaflet *Saint-Céré – Visite de la Ville* (French only).

The post office is 300m west of place de la République, on rue Faidherbe. Banks can be found on both place and rue de la République.

Place du Mercadial & Old Town

This attractive old heart of town is surrounded by picturesque half-timbered houses; one at the corner of rue Pasteur still has the *taouilé* (stone bench) where fishermen once displayed their catch. Nearby, the glass-fronted **Maison des Consuls** now holds temporary art exhibitions. South-east off place du Mercadial, rue St-Cyr and rue du Mazel have attractive medieval and Renaissance houses. Across the other side of rue de la République is the 17th-century **Église Ste-Spérie** and more turreted houses.

Galerie d'Art du Casino & Atelier-Musée Jean Lurçat

Some 200m north-east of the tourist office, the **Galerie d'Art du Casino** (☎ 05 65 38 19 60), on rue Moussinac (off blvd Jean Lurçat), has a permanent display of some of Lurçat's brilliantly coloured tapestries (as well as temporary exhibitions of other artwork). It's open from 9 am to noon and 2 to 7 pm daily (closed on Tuesday from October to June). Admission is free.

Just behind the gallery, a footpath leads to the medieval **Tours St-Laurent** (☎ 05 65 38 28 21) on a hill overlooking the town, worth the climb for the great views alone. The tower, once Lurçat's studio, is now the **Atelier-Musée Jean-Lurçat** – a museum of his work (☎ 05 65 38 28 21). It is open from 9.30 am to noon and 2.30 to 6.30 pm from mid-July to September and for two weeks around Easter. Admission costs 15FF (children and students 10FF).

Places to Stay

The pleasantly shady *Camping Le Soulhol* (☎/fax 05 65 38 12 37, quai Auguste-Sallesses), 700m south across the Bave River, charges 19/17FF per person/tent; it's open from April to October.

The truckers' favourite eatery, *Hôtel-Restaurant La Taverne de Gargantua* (☎/fax 05 65 38 04 83, 21 ave Anatole de Monzie), on the D673 on the western edge of town, charges 150FF for a basic double and serves big simple meals at reasonable prices.

The old-fashioned *Grand Hôtel Maury* (☎ 05 65 38 29 99, fax 05 65 38 22 75, 9 place de la République) has doubles costing from 230FF (260FF in July/August). Nearby, by the Bave River, the attractive Irish-run *Hôtel-Bar-Restaurant Victor Hugo* (05 65 38 16 15, fax 05 65 38 39 91, 7 ave des Maquis) has doubles (all with shower, WC and TV) from 240FF and restaurant *menus* from 87FF.

Places to Eat

In addition to the hotel-restaurants, other possibilities include *Bar-Restaurant du Centre* (☎ 05 65 38 21 14, 5 rue Centrale), north of the church, which serves *casse-croute* – soup, cheese (or meat) and wine – from 25FF and *menus du jour* (menu of the day) at 59FF. It is closed on Tuesday. *Restaurant Pizzeria du Mercadial* (☎ 05 65 38 35 77, 4 place du Mercadial) serves pizzas and pastas. It is closed Sunday and Monday lunchtime.

Getting There & Away

St-Céré is 8km south of Bretenoux-Biars' train station, which is on the Brive–Aurillac line. There are connections to Brive (42FF, 45 minutes) three to four times daily. A shuttle bus (*navette*) connects the station with St-Céré. The tourist office has the timetable.

There's a bus service (☎ 05 65 38 08 28) to Cahors (45FF, 1¾ hours, three times weekly, twice out of term-time) and Figeac (38FF, one hour, four times weekly or twice out of term-time). The bus stop is on place de la République.

Getting Around

Peugeot Cycles (☎ 05 65 38 03 23), at 43 rue Faidherbe (opposite the post office), rents mountain bikes for 80/450FF per day/week. For a taxi call ☎ 05 65 10 80 80.

AROUND ST-CÉRÉ
Château de Montal

Three kilometres west of St-Céré, off the D673, this delightful chateau (☎ 05 65 38 13 72) was built in 1523 by Jeanne de Balsac for her eldest son, Robert, who was away fighting in Italy. No expense was spared to create the beautiful Renaissance facade with finely sculpted portrait busts and the staircase of golden Carennac stone with individually different carvings. But Robert was killed in battle. His mother had the words *Plus d'espoir* ('no more hope') carved on a stone scroll at one of the windows.

Badly damaged during the Revolution, the chateau was bought in the 19th century by a wheeler-dealer who sold off its treasures. In 1908, a new owner, oil magnate Maurice Fénaille, came to the rescue and spent years (and a small fortune) retrieving almost everything.

The chateau is open from 9.30 am to noon and 2.30 to 6 pm daily except on Saturday between April and September. Admission costs 30FF (children 12FF).

Autoire

postcode 46400 • pop 270 • elevation 300m
No other village in Quercy boasts as many towers and turrets as Autoire, one of the most beautiful villages in France, 7km west of St-Céré in what was once an important wine-growing area. The village has many grand Renaissance manor houses built by wealthy *vignerons* (wine merchants). At the top of the surrounding high cliffs, you can just see the ruins of a folly-like fortress dating from the Hundred Years' War, called the **Château des Anglais**, a name given to many ancient ruins of uncertain history in the region. Further up (5km by road), the **Loubressac** hamlet boasts more noble houses and spectacular views.

There is no tourist office in Autoire, but

you can get some information from the town hall (☎ 05 65 38 05 26).

Places to Stay & Eat The Logis de France *L'Auberge de la Fontaine* (☎ 05 65 10 85 40), at the heart of the village, has double rooms (all with shower) starting at 240FF and restaurant *menus* from 60/75FF midday/evening. Across the road, *La Cascade Crêperie* (☎ 05 65 38 20 02) serves delicious *galettes* (wheat pancakes).

Among several *chambres d'hôtes* (B&Bs) in the area, Madame Gauzin's modest *La Plantade* (☎ 05 65 38 15 61), 1.5km to the north-east, off the D38, has horses, hens and doubles/triples/quads for 180/250/280FF (including breakfast).

Gouffre de Padirac

The truly spectacular Padirac Cave (☎ 05 65 33 64 56), 15km north-east of Rocamadour and 18km west of St-Céré, offers the closest thing to a cruise to Hades across the River Styx. Discovered in 1889, the cave's navigable river – 103m below ground level – is reached through a 75m-deep, 33m-wide chasm (and three lifts and 300 steps!). Boat pilots ferry visitors along a 500m stretch of the subterranean waterway, guiding them up and down a series of stairways to otherworldly pools and vast, floodlit caverns. The whole operation is unashamedly mass-market, but it retains an innocence and style reminiscent of the 1930s, when the first lifts were installed.

It's open from 9 am to noon and 2 to 6 pm between April and 11 October, with 45-minute tours (from 8.30 am to 6.30 pm between 10 and 31 July and 8 am to 7 pm in August). Admission costs 47FF (children 27FF).

CAHORS

postcode 46000 • pop 20,000
• elevation 128m
Cahors, the départemental capital of the Lot (and former capital of the Quercy region), is a low-key city with a relaxed atmosphere. Surrounded on three sides by a bend in the Lot River and circled by a ring of hills, it is endowed with a couple of minor Roman

sites, a famous medieval bridge and a large medieval quarter.

Cahors was founded by the Romans, who called it Divona Cadurcorum and, like their Celtic predecessors, the Cadurcii, worshipped Divona the goddess of a sacred riverside spring, now known as the Fontaine des Chartreux. During the Middle Ages, Cahors became a prosperous commercial and financial centre, thanks to steady rule by powerful Catholic bishops and to the famously usurious Italian Lombard merchants who had fled here from the Albigensian Crusade. Pope John XXII, a native of Cahors and the second of the Avignon popes, established a university here in 1331.

Cahors kept the English at bay during the Hundred Years' War, but the Wars of Religion led the fiercely Catholic city right into the fray: after massacring its Protestants in 1560, it was besieged by the Huguenots 20 years later and thoroughly sacked.

Orientation

The main commercial thoroughfare, blvd Léon Gambetta, is named after Cahors-born Léon Gambetta, one of the founders of the Third Republic (see the boxed text 'Honourable Statesman or Raving Mad Dictator?'). This shady avenue divides Vieux Cahors (Old Cahors), to the east, from the new quarters, to the west. At its northern end is place Général de Gaulle, a giant car park surrounded by busy bar-brasseries catering to students; about 500m to the south is place François Mitterrand, central

Cahors' lively main square. The famous pont Valentré is around 600m to the west.

Information

Tourist Offices The efficient tourist office (☎ 05 65 53 20 65; fax 05 65 53 20 74, email cahors@wanadoo.fr) on place François Mitterrand is open from 9 am to 12.30 pm and 1.30 to 6.30 pm Monday to Saturday (to 6 pm on Saturday). During July and August it's also open from 10 am to noon on Sunday and holidays.

For information on the département contact the Comité Départemental du Tourisme du Lot (☎ 05 65 35 07 09, fax 05 65 23 92 76, email le-lot@wanadoo.fr) at 107 quai Eugène Cavaignac, open from 8 am to 12.30 pm and 1.30 to 5.30 pm Monday to Friday (to 4.30 pm on Friday).

There's a Bureau d'Information Jeunesse (BIJ; ☎ 05 65 23 95 90, fax 05 65 22 60 66) in the same building as the Auberge de Jeunesse (see Places to Stay later in this section) where you can find information on temporary jobs, lodgings and courses. It's open from 9 am to noon and 1 to 6 pm on weekdays and until 5 pm on Saturday.

Money There are a number of banks along blvd Léon Gambetta, including Société Générale at No 85 (open Tuesday to Saturday) and Crédit Agricole at No 22 (open Monday to Friday).

Post & Communications The main post office, at 257 rue Président Wilson, is open

Honourable Statesman or Raving Mad Dictator?

Cahors' most famous son, Léon Gambetta (1838–82), came from humble beginnings (his father was a grocer) to become an outstanding lawyer and politician. After Napoléon's downfall, he was among those who proclaimed the Third Republic in 1870 and became Minister of the Interior. When Paris fell to the Prussians soon afterwards, he escaped to Tours in a hot-air balloon and organised the fight against the enemy with dictatorial skill (though not always with military success).

In 1879 he became head of the Republican Union, promoting liberty of the press, separation of Church and State and other radical ideas (radical enough that even fellow Republicans thought he was raving mad). He became prime minister in November 1881, resigning only three months later when his bill to reform the electoral process was defeated.

CAHORS

PLACES TO STAY

4 Hôtel-Restaurant À L'Escargot
7 Grand Hôtel Terminus;
   Restaurant Le Balandre
12 Foyer des Jeunes en Quercy
16 Hôtel Melchior
18 Hôtel de France
21 Auberge de Jeunesse;
   Bureau d'Information Jeunesse
22 Hôtel Aux Perdreaux
36 Hôtel de la Paix
47 Hôtel-Restaurant La Bourse
57 Camping Municipal St-Georges
58 Hôtel La Chartreuse

PLACES TO EAT

20 Restaurant Le Mandarin
25 Restaurant La Taverne
29 La Baladine Crêperie
31 Le Paseo
34 Restaurant L'Orangerie
35 Covent Market
35 Restaurant Troquet des Halles
43 Marie Colline
46 L'Arapagous
49 Champion Supermarket
54 La Pizzeria

OTHER

1 Intercity Bus Stop
2 Église St-Barthélemy
3 Tour du Pape Jean XXII
5 Musée de la Résistance
6 Arc de Diane
8 Train Station; SNCF Buses
9 Avis
10 Crédit Agricole
11 Cycles 7 Bike Rental
13 Palais de Justice
14 Musée Henri Martin
15 Maison du Vin
17 Haxhi
19 Small Hydroelectric Station
23 Lavarie Laveco
24 Maison de la Presse
26 Préfecture
28 Cathédrale St-Étienne
30 Hôtel des Roaldès
32 Cloister
33 Bisrot "O" Rock
37 Hôtel de Ville
38 Hôtel P Lagarde
39 Hospital
40 Main Post Office
41 Tourist Office; Réservations
   Services Loisirs Accueil;
   Association Départementale
   de Tourisme Rural
42 Société Générale
44 Église St-Urcisse
45 Lavarie GTI
48 Théâtre Municipal
50 Police Station
51 Intercity Bus Stops
52 Espace Valentré
53 Les Bateaux Safaraïd
55 Comité Départemental
   du Tourisme du Lot
   (Regional Tourist Office)
56 Europcar

until 7 pm on weekdays and to noon on Saturday. Exchange services are available.

You can connect to the Internet at the BIJ (see Tourist Offices) for 20FF per hour.

Bookshops Maps and topoguides are available from Librairie P Lagarde at 36 blvd Léon Gambetta (closed on Sunday and Monday) and Maison de la Presse, 73 blvd Léon Gambetta, (closed on Sunday afternoon).

Laundry In Vieux Cahors, Laverie Laveco, on place de la Libération, and Laverie GTI, at 208 rue Georges Clemenceau, are both open from 7 am to 9 pm daily.

Medical Services & Emergency Centre Hospitalier Jean Rougier (☎ 05 65 20 50 50) is opposite 428 rue Président Wilson. The police station (☎ 05 65 35 27 00) is on rue St-Géry.

Pont Valentré

This fortified medieval bridge – one of France's finest – consists of six arches and three tall towers, two of them outfitted with machicolations (projecting parapets equipped with openings that allow defenders to drop missiles on the attackers below). Built in the 14th century (the towers were added later), it was designed as part of the town's defences rather than as a traffic bridge.

Cathédrale St-Étienne

The cavernous nave of this Romanesque-style cathedral, consecrated in 1119, is crowned with two 18m-wide cupolas (the largest in France), an obvious import from the east. The chapels along the nave (repainted in the 19th century) are Gothic, as are the choir and the massive west facade. The wall paintings between the organ and the interior of the west facade are early 14th-century originals.

The **cloister** (cloître), accessible from the choir or through the arched entryway opposite 59 rue de la Chantrerie, is in the Flamboyant Gothic style of the early 16th century. Most of the decoration was muti-

lated during the Wars of Religion and the Revolution.

Old Cahors

Old Cahors, the medieval quarter east of blvd Léon Gambetta, is densely packed with old four-storey houses linked by streets and alleyways so narrow you can almost touch both walls.

In 1580, during the Wars of Religion, the Protestant Henri of Navarre (later to become the Catholic King Henri IV) captured the Catholic stronghold of Cahors and stayed in the **Hôtel des Roaldès** (☎ 05 65 35 04 35), at 271 quai Champollion, for one night. It is open from 10 am to noon and 2 to 6 pm on major holidays and from April to 20 September. Admission costs 20FF (children 5FF).

The 34m-high **Tour du Pape Jean XXII**, a square, crenellated tower at 1–3 blvd Léon Gambetta, was built in the 14th century as part of the home of Jacques Duèse, later Pope John XXII (reigned 1316–34). The interior is closed to the public. Next door is the 14th-century **Église St-Barthélémy**, with its massive brick and stone belfry.

It is possible to walk around three sides of Cahors by following the quays along the town's riverside perimeter.

West of Blvd Léon Gambetta

The **Musée Henri Martin** (☎ 05 65 30 15 13), at 792 rue Émile Zola, also known as the Musée Municipal, has some archaeological artefacts and a collection of works by the Cahors-born pointillist painter Henri Martin (1893–1972). It is open only when there are temporary exhibitions, usually from April to September (closed on Tuesday). Admission costs 20FF.

The small **Musée de la Résistance** (☎ 05 65 22 14 25), on the northern side of place Général de Gaulle, has illustrated exhibits on the Resistance, the concentration camps and the liberation of France. It is open from 2 to 6 pm daily. Admission is free.

The **Arc de Diane**, opposite 24 ave Charles de Freycinet, is a stone archway with red-brick stripes that once formed part of a Gallo-Roman bath-house.

LOT

Mont St-Cyr

The 264m-high, antenna-topped hill, Mont St-Cyr, across the river from Old Cahors affords excellent views of the town and the surrounding countryside. It can easily be climbed on foot – the trail begins near the southern end of the 19th century pont Louis-Philippe.

Boating & Canoeing

To rent a houseboat or motorboat for jaunts along the Lot, contact Baboumarine (☎ 05 65 30 08 99, fax 05 65 23 92 59) at Port St-Mary. Club Canoë-Kayak (☎ 05 65 22 62 62 or ☎ 05 65 20 15 27), at place Chico Mendès, rents canoes/kayaks.

Organised Tours

The tourist office organises guided visits of Cahors on specific themes (such as the old city or pont Valentré) throughout the year, usually at 3 pm on Saturday and/or Monday for 35FF (students 25FF) and at 5 pm daily during July and August (except on Sunday).

Les Bateaux Safaraid (☎ 05 65 35 98 88) leaves from Terrasses Valentré, just south of pont Valentré, for 90-minute river cruises with commentary in French and English, four times daily between April and November (50FF).

An enjoyable day-trip excursion is on the Train Touristique Quercyrail (☎ 05 63 40 11 93), a restored 1950s Micheline train which trundles as far as Cajarc (about 40km). The trip (from 9 am to 6.30 pm) runs on Sunday from May to October (plus on Saturday in July and August) and costs 150FF (children 50FF). Shorter Quercyrail trips include a train ride plus a 4.5km walk around Bouziès on Friday in July and August, this trip costs 100FF (children 50FF).

Places to Stay – Budget

Camping & Hostels The riverside *Camping Municipal St-Georges* (☎ 05 65 35 04 64, ave Anatole de Monzie), hemmed in by heavily trafficked roads, charges 14/14FF per adult/tent. It is open from mid-April to mid-November. The office is generally closed from 11.30 am to 4.30 pm.

The more salubrious *Rivière de Cabessut* (☎ 05 65 30 06 30), 1.5km north-west of town, across the other side of the river, charges 12/50FF per person/site.

Auberge de Jeunesse, in a complex known as Espace Frédéric Suisse (☎ 05 65 35 64 71, fax 05 65 35 95 92, 20 rue Frédéric Suisse), charges 51FF a bed (60FF without a Hostelling International card). The office is closed on Saturday afternoon and on Sunday.

The antiquated but friendly *Foyer des Jeunes en Quercy* (☎ 05 65 35 29 32, 129 rue Fondue Haute), run by nuns, provides accommodation for students during the academic year but welcomes travellers of all religions, sexes and ages from late June to early September. A bed in a very basic single or triple with washbasin costs around 78FF including breakfast; dinner (on weekdays only) costs 32FF. There's no curfew.

Rural Accommodation For information on staying out in the countryside (for example in *gîtes ruraux* – rural cottages – or chambres d'hôtes) contact the Association Départementale de Tourisme Rural (☎ 05 65 53 20 75) on place François Mitterrand, open from 8 am to 12.30 pm and 1.30 to 6 pm Monday to Friday.

Hotels In Old Cahors, the laid-back *Hôtel-Restaurant La Bourse* (☎ 05 65 35 17 78, 7 place Claude Rousseau) has large doubles/quads with washbasin and bidet for 110/185FF (130FF with shower) in a medieval house down a nearby grungy alley. Hall showers are free.

Hôtel de la Paix (☎ 05 65 35 03 40, place des Halles), on the square also known as place St-Maurice, has simple, clean doubles costing from 160FF (200FF with shower). Hall showers cost 10FF.

Hôtel Aux Perdreaux (☎ 05 65 35 03 50, 137 rue du Portail Alban), on place de la Libération, has smallish, nondescript doubles with shower from 160FF (200FF twin). Reception (at the bar) at all three hotels is closed on Sunday (open during July and August).

Places to Stay – Mid-Range

At *Hôtel de France* (☎ 05 65 35 16 76, fax 05 65 22 01 08, 252 ave Jean Jaurès), part of the Inter-Hotel chain, basic but comfortable doubles cost 238FF (350FF with bath). *Hôtel Melchior* (☎ 05 65 35 03 38, fax 05 65 23 92 75) has adequate doubles costing 230FF (250FF twin). Except from July to mid-October, reception (at the bar) is closed on Sunday. Both hotels are near the train station.

The more attractively located *Hôtel-Restaurant À L'Escargot* (☎ 05 65 35 07 66, fax 05 65 53 92 38, 5 blvd Léon Gambetta) has comfortable doubles/triples costing 265/335FF.

Across the Lot River from the southern end of town, the riverside *Hôtel La Chartreuse* (☎ 05 65 35 17 37, fax 05 65 22 30 03, chemin de la Chartreuse) has doubles from 260FF.

Places to Stay – Top End
The elegant 1920s *Grand Hôtel Terminus* (☎ 05 65 35 24 50, fax 05 65 22 06 40, 5 ave Charles de Freycinet) has very comfortable singles/doubles with shower starting at 300/350FF.

About 7km north-west of Cahors in Mercuès, *Le Mas Azemar* (☎/fax 05 65 30 96 85, rue du Mas de Vinssou) is a delightful chambre d'hôte in an 18th-century house. It is open year-round by reservation only, with doubles costing from 360FF.

Places to Eat
Most restaurants are closed on Sunday.

French The friendly and unpretentious *Restaurant Le Troquet des Halles* (☎ 05 65 22 15 81, rue St-Maurice), near place des Halles, has bargain *menus* for 55FF, including wine. In the morning (from 7 to 10 am), the soup (16FF) comes with a glass of wine so you can *faire chabrol* (add some wine to the dregs of the soup and drink it together). Dinner is available only from June to September.

Restaurant La Taverne (☎ 05 65 35 28 66, place Pierre Escorbiac) specialises in French and regional cuisine. *Menus* cost between 75FF and 250FF. It is closed at the weekend except during July and August. Reservations are recommended on Friday and Saturday nights.

The elegant *Restaurant Le Balandre* (☎ 05 65 30 01 97, 5 ave Charles de Freycinet), attached to the Grand Hôtel Terminus (see Places to Stay – Top End), serves creative cuisine based on traditional regional ingredients. *Menus* start at around 150FF. It is closed on Sunday night and all day Monday, though this may alter during peak season.

Less daunting is *L'Arapagous* (☎ 05 65 35 07 66, 134 rue St-Urcisse) which serves tempting midday/evening *menus* from 65/80FF, featuring regional specialities and charcoal-grilled meat dishes.

Vegetarian The attractive *Restaurant L'Orangerie* (☎ 05 65 22 59 06, 41 rue St-James) serves salads from 20FF and *menus* from 68FF. It is closed on Sunday and Monday. *Marie Colline* (☎ 05 65 35 59 96, 173 rue Georges Clémenceau) also serves vegetarian snacks but at lunchtime only, Tuesday to Saturday.

Other The popular *La Pizzeria* (☎ 05 65 35 12 18, 58 blvd Léon Gambetta) serves reasonably priced pizzas, pastas and salads. It is closed Sunday midday and, from November to April, Sunday evening. In a more atmospheric setting near the cathedral are several other pizzerias, creperies and restaurants (all with outdoor seating) including *Le Paseo* (☎ 05 65 53 15 16, 24 place Champollion), which offers tapas, salads and charcoal-grilled dishes; and *La Baladine Crêperie* (☎ 05 65 22 36 52, 57 rue Clément Marot) for galettes, salads and crepes.

The Chinese-Vietnamese *Restaurant Le Mandarin* (☎ 05 65 22 22 93, 216 ave Jean Jaurès) has main courses from around 40FF and a lunch *menu* for 70FF. *Chez Ngo* (☎ 05 65 22 17 30, place des Consuls) on the northern edge of town, also has a wide variety of Oriental dishes from around 36FF.

Self-Catering Regional specialities such as deep-red Cahors wine, foie gras, truffles and *cabécou* (a small, round goat's cheese) – plus the freshest of fruits and vegetables and take-away dishes – can be found in the covered market (*marché couvert*), also known as Les Halles, on place des Halles. It's open Tuesday to Saturday from 8 am to noon and 3 to 7 pm and on Sunday and holidays from 9 am to noon. There's a vibrant *open-air market* around the Marché Couvert and place de la Cathédrale on Wednesday and Saturday morning (or the previous day if it clashes with holidays).

Near the tourist office, the ***Champion supermarket*** across from 109 blvd Léon Gambetta is open daily except on Sunday.

Entertainment
Concerts, plays and other events take place at the Espace Valentré (☎ 05 65 20 37 37) or in the auditorium (☎ 05 65 30 18 16) on place des Consuls. Tickets are available at the tourist office.

For late-night drinks with a rock-music backing, head for ***Biscot 'O' Rock*** (*☎ 05 65 35 99 63, 10 rue St-James*) open till 2 am; or ***Irish Pub*** (*☎ 05 65 53 15 15, place des Consuls*) hidden at the side of a car park, which has regular live music and is open from 6 pm to 2 am. Both are closed on Sunday.

Getting There & Away
Bus In Cahors, SNCF buses for Fumel (46FF, 70 minutes, five times daily) via Puy l'Évêque (45 minutes, eight times daily); Capdenac (43FF, two hours, once daily except Monday) via Bouziès (27FF, 27 minutes), Cajarc (43FF, 50 minutes) and Figeac (62FF, 1¾ hours); and Montauban (75 minutes, once daily) via Montpezat de Quercy (45 minutes, once daily) all leave from the SNCF train station. A few other services start from the unmarked car park on the northern side of place Général de Gaulle or along rue St-Géry, just west of allées Fénelon: these services often stop at the train station too.

Train The train station (☎ 08 36 35 35 35) is on place Jouinot Gambetta (place de la Gare). The information office is open from 6.20 am to 9.30 pm daily (from 7.30 am to 11.20 pm on Sunday).

Cahors is on the main SNCF line that links Paris' Gare d'Austerlitz (310FF, 5½ hours, five daily) with Brive-la-Gaillarde (79FF, around 70 minutes), Souillac (56FF, around 45 minutes), Montauban (54FF, 45 minutes) and Toulouse (86FF, 70 minutes, five to seven times daily). To get to Bordeaux (168FF) change at Montauban. For Sarlat-la-Canéda, take a train to Souillac and an SNCF bus from there.

Car Europcar (☎ 05 65 22 35 55) is at 68 blvd Léon Gambetta; Avis (☎ 05 65 30 13 10) at 512 ave Jean Jaurès and Hertz (☎ 05 65 35 34 69) at 385 rue Anatole France. All are closed on Saturday afternoon and on Sunday.

Getting Around
Cycles 7 (☎ 05 65 22 66 60), at 417 Quai de Regourd, rents mountain bikes for 80/350FF daily/week. It's open from 9 am to noon and 2 to 7 pm Tuesday to Saturday.

EAST OF CAHORS
The limestone hills between Cahors and Figeac are cut by the dramatic, cliff-flanked Lot and Célé rivers. The narrow, winding and supremely scenic D662 (signposted 'Vallée du Lot') follows the Lot River, while the even narrower and more spectacular D41 (signposted 'Vallée du Célé') follows the tortuous route of the Célé as does the GR651.

Bouziès
postcode 46330 • pop 70
• elevation approx 115m
The quiet hamlet of Bouziès, near the confluence of the Lot and Célé, 28km east of Cahors, has an impressive location opposite the **Défilé des Anglais**, the remains of a Hundred Years' War fortress carved into the rockface. It's also the site of several **river activities**: on the riverbank below the Hôtel les Falaises (see Places to Stay & Eat), Safaraid (☎ 05 65 35 98 88) runs 90-minute riverboat trips (with French and English commentary) four times daily from April to November for 50FF per person. Nature & Loisirs (☎ 05 65 30 25 69) rents canoes, kayaks and mountain bikes for 90/100/

100FF per person per day or can arrange trips lasting several days.

For an interesting **walk**, follow the GR36 south-eastwards beside the river for 500m to see a towpath carved from the rockface, part of it sculpted with a contemporary bas-relief.

Places to Stay & Eat At *Hôtel Les Falaises* (☎ 05 65 31 26 83, fax 05 65 30 23 87) doubles start at 262FF. It is closed from 28 November to 27 March. The hotel's *restaurant*, which has a lovely terrace, serves good regional cuisine with *menus* from 80FF.

The remote and beautifully situated *chambres chez l'habitant Pech Larive* (☎ 05 65 30 20 93), in the hills 1.6km to the south, has a fabulous view over the valley and neat doubles in a converted barn for 200FF (240FF with bath) or 340FF including kitchen/dining area. All prices include breakfast. No other meals are available but the young Larive couple make delicious home-made honey.

Getting There & Away The SNCF bus that links Cahors (27FF, 25 minutes, five to seven daily) with Figeac (one hour) stops on the D662 across the narrow suspension bridge from Bouziès.

The hotel will send its minivan to pick up guests at Cahors' train station or drop you off at the starting point of a hike.

Cabrerets
postcode 46330 • pop 200 • elevation 130m
The hamlet of Cabrerets, on the Célé River 5km upriver from Bouziès, is a dozy place en route to the famous Grotte du Pech Merle. It's dramatised only by the restored 14th-century **Château de Gontaut-Biron** on a clifftop overlooking the road, illuminated at night.

There's a tourist office (☎ 05 65 31 27 12, fax 05 65 30 27 17) in what little there is of a village centre, the place de la Mairie (just off the D41, the turning to the grotte), open from 2 to 5 pm Thursday to Sunday. You can rent laser disks here (see Things to See & Do in the St-Cirq Lapopie section

later in this chapter) for details of guided walks in the region.

Things to See & Do The **Musée en Plein Air du Quercy** at Cuzals, 7km to the north-east, off the D41, is a delightful open-air ethnological museum recreating farm life from the 1900s. It's open from 2 to 6 pm daily except Saturday (9.30 am to 6.30 pm during June and 10 am to 7 pm during July and August). Admission costs 50FF (children 25FF; 20% less if you have a ticket to Grotte du Pech Merle).

Les Amis du Célé (☎ 05 65 31 26 73), 5.1km to the east, at the turn-off to the museum, rents **kayaks/canoes** from 110/160FF per day.

Places to Stay & Eat In a shady, grassy area on the right bank of the Célé is *Camping Familial Cantal* (☎ 05 65 31 26 16), 700m north-east of the turn-off to the D13 (which goes to the Grotte). It charges 14/14FF per person/tent.

Opposite the tourist office is the *gîte d'étape* (hikers' dormitory) and *chambre d'hôte* of the accommodating Madame Bessac (☎ 05 65 31 27 04). Camp beds for walkers (50FF, or 70FF with linen) are in the converted loft which also has a kitchen. Comfortable doubles downstairs cost 220FF including breakfast.

Hôtel des Grottes (☎ 05 65 31 27 02, fax 05 65 31 20 15), on the D41 overlooking the river, has doubles from 175FF; doubles/triples/quads with shower and toilet cost 250/370/450FF (20FF more in summer). It's open from mid-May to October. The hotel's *restaurant* serves a hearty *menu* for 75FF. The spiffier *Auberge de la Sagne* (☎ 05 65 31 26 62, fax 05 65 30 27 43), 2km up the road towards the cave, has doubles from 270FF (280FF half-board is obligatory during July and August), a swimming pool and a pleasant garden.

Next to the accommodation run by Madame Bessac, the cosy *O'Louise Restaurant* (☎ 05 65 30 25 56) serves sandwiches, salads and omelettes, a *plat du jour* from around 45FF and an excellent-value 65FF dinner *menu*.

Getting There & Away SNCF buses on the Cahors–Figeac route stop just under 4km south of Cabrerets at the intersection of the D662 and the D41.

Grotte du Pech Merle

This spectacular, 1200m-long cave (☎ 05 65 31 27 05), 30km east of Cahors and 3km from Cabrerets, is not only a natural wonder, with thousands of stalactites and stalagmites of all varieties and shapes but also a prehistoric art gallery with dozens of paintings of mammoths, horses and 'negative' human handprints, drawn by Cro-Magnon people 16,000 to 20,000 years ago. Prehistoric artefacts found in the area are on display in an adjacent museum.

From April to October, one-hour guided tours (English text available) begin every 45 minutes (every 15 minutes in summer) between 9.30 am and noon and 1.30 and 5 pm daily. Tickets cost 44/38FF in the high/low season (children 30/25FF) and are well worth the price. During the high season, get there early as only 700 people daily are allowed to visit. Reservations are accepted.

On foot, the cave is about 3km from Bouziès via the GR651 and 1km from Cabrerets (follow the path behind the tourist office).

Marcilhac-sur-Célé

postcode 46160 • pop 200 • elevation 200m
One of the most striking sights along this languid stretch of the Célé River is the **ruined abbey** of this once-important hamlet, with the towering cliff-face of the limestone plateau opposite. Marcilhac, 16km upstream of Cabrerets, might have been a good deal more important today had the abbots of its 12th-century Benedictine abbey kept their hands on Rocamadour, which it originally controlled (the canny abbots of Tulle took over instead). After bouts of devastation during the Hundred Years' War and the Wars of Religion the abbey gradually sunk into ruin but you can still glimpse its grandeur from the carved lintel and Romanesque chapterhouse.

There's an enthusiastic tourist office

(☎ 05 65 40 68 44) within the grounds of the abbey, open from 10 am to noon and 2 to 5 pm Monday to Saturday and from 2 to 5 pm on Sunday. Guided visits of the abbey's interior are available here for 15FF.

Places to Stay & Eat The *gîte d'étape* (town hall ☎ 05 65 40 61 43), in the abbey grounds, charges 30FF per person, and *Camping Municipal le Pré du Monsieur* (town hall ☎ 05 65 40 61 43, or ☎ 05 65 40 77 88) by the river, is open from June to September (canoes and bikes are also available to hire here during the high season).

There are several *chambres d'hôtes*: contact the tourist office or the *Café des Touristes* on the main road through the village, where you can also get decent meals for around 80FF.

Espagnac Ste-Eulalie

postcode 46320 • pop 70 • elevation 250m
Some 12km upstream of Marcilhac-sur-Célé, on the south bank of the Célé, this handsome hamlet is dominated by an ornately topped 16th-century belltower, once part of a 12th-century convent, Notre Dame du Val Paradis. Walk through the ancient gateway, past an incongruously modern wooden statue of a pilgrim, to find Madame Bonzani (first house on the right) who provides guided tours of the church.

Places to Stay & Eat There's a *gîte d'étape* (☎ 05 65 40 05 24) inside the convent grounds. Under the arches of the convent, *Les Jardins cafe* (☎ 05 65 40 08 34) offers *bio-dynamique* sorbets, fruit juices and crepes, plus a *table paysanne menu* (country menu) for 80FF from 10 am to 1 pm and 4 to 8 pm daily except on Sunday.

Camping du Moulin Vieux (☎ 05 65 40 00 41), 1.7km downstream, charges 24/25FF per person/site and is open from May to October.

Nearby, in Brengues, *Restaurant-Hôtel de la Vallée* (☎ 05 65 40 05 24) charges 210FF for a double (240FF with bath) and has *menus* from 60FF. The nearby *Le Romantic Bar* (☎ 05 65 40 04 00) serves snacks and also rents out kayaks/canoes for 100/160FF per day.

Getting There & Away There are no regular buses to Espagnac Ste-Eulalie or Marcilhac-sur-Célé. Call ☎ 05 65 34 00 70 for information on pre-arranged buses (usually on Wednesday afternoon and Saturday morning) to Figeac. For taxis, call 05 65 31 26 15.

ST-CIRQ LAPOPIE
postcode 46330 • pop 200 • elevation 147m
St-Cirq Lapopie, 25km east of Cahors, is perched on a clifftop 100m above the Lot River. It's named after St Cirq, a child martyred in Asia Minor under Diocletian; his relics, it is believed, later found their way here. Lapopie, a word of Celtic origin that refers to an elevated place, was the family name of the local lords during the Middle Ages.

Although swamped with tourists in summer, the spectacular views and the area's natural beauty make up for the village's overstated charm.

Information
The tourist office (☎/fax 05 65 31 29 06, email saint-cirq-lapopie@wanadoo.fr), in the town hall, is open from 10 am to 6 pm on weekdays and from 10 am to 12.30 pm at the weekend, 2.30 to 6 pm between April and November (10 am to 7 pm daily during July and August).

Things to See & Do
The fortified early 16th-century **Gothic church** is of no special interest except for its stunning location. The ruins of the 13th-century **chateau** at the top of the hill also afford a fine panorama. Below, along the narrow alleyways, the restored stone and half-timbered houses – topped with steep, red-tile roofs – shelter **artisans' studios** offering leather goods, pottery, jewellery and wooden items. The **Musée Rignault** open, from 10.30 am to 12.30 pm and 2.30 to 6 pm daily except Tuesday (until 7 pm daily in July and August), has a delightful garden and an eclectic collection of French furniture and art from Africa and China. Admission costs 15FF (children 10FF).

The tourist office rents laser disks (in French only), from a collection called *Les Chemins qui Parlent,* of 21 different walks around the countryside. Hire costs 40FF for 24 hours, plus a 500FF deposit.

Kalapca (☎ 05 65 30 29 51, fax 05 65 30 26 48), based at Camping de la Plage (see Places to Stay & Eat) arranges canoeing, canyoning, rock-climbing and caving trips; in July and August different activities take place daily for 100FF to 170FF per person. They also rent mountain bikes (70/100FF per half/full day) and canoes/kayaks (115/130FF per person per day).

Places to Stay & Eat
There's a *gîte d'étape (☎/fax 05 65 31 21 51)* in the Maison de la Fourdonne, a restored Renaissance building in the lower part of the village which also serves as a woodworking and cultural centre. Walkers are charged 60FF per bed.

The riverside *Camping de la Plage (☎ 05 65 30 29 51)*, 2km below town on the south bank of the Lot at the bridge (Tour de Faure) linking the D662 with the road up to St-Cirq Lapopie, charges 30/20FF per person/tent. The hilltop *Camping La Truffière (☎ 05 65 30 20 22)*, 2.8km to the south (off the D26 to Concots), has a pool and children's playground; its forfait rate is 32FF per person. The adjacent *Hôtel-Restaurant du Causse (☎ 05 65 31 24 16, fax 05 65 30 26 48)* has quiet doubles/triples for 240/320FF (225FF in low season).

Auberge du Sombral (☎ 05 65 31 26 08, fax 05 65 30 26 37), directly across the square from the tourist office, has rooms that cost from 260FF. It is open from April to mid-November. The *restaurant*, whose *menus* cost 100FF to 200FF, and the hotel's reception are closed on Wednesday, except between July and September.

There are several chic cafes and restaurants including *Café-Restaurant Lou Bolat (☎ 05 65 30 29 04)* just below the post office, which serves galettes and a 60FF midday *menu* and has a pleasant terrace overlooking the village.

LOT

euro currency converter 10FF = €1.52

Getting There & Away

St-Cirq Lapopie is 2km across the river and up the hill from the D662 and Tour de Faure bridge; the SNCF bus shelter is a few hundred metres upriver from the bridge. Buses run to Cahors (28FF, around 35 minutes, five to seven daily) and Figeac (one hour).

CAJARC

postcode 46160 • pop 1100 • elevation 160m
This low-key town, 22km east of St-Cirq Lapopie and about the same south-west of Figeac, boasts no great sights but makes a pleasant midway stop. Its one unusual attraction is the **Maison des Arts Georges Pompidou** (☎ 05 65 40 63 97), a modern art gallery donated by Pompidou who was once a town councillor here. It is situated 100m north of the town's central place du Foirail and open from 10 am to noon and 2 to 6 pm daily except on Tuesday between April and October (admission costs 20FF).

The tourist office (☎ 05 65 40 72 89, fax 05 65 40 39 05), on place du Foirail, is open from 3.30 to 6.30 pm Monday to Saturday and from 10 am to 12.30 pm on Sunday from mid-June to July and during the first two weeks of September (from 10 am to 12.30pm and 3.30 to 7 pm daily during July and August).

Places to Stay & Eat

A *gîte d'étape* (☎ 05 65 40 71 51, *Madame Annie Mignot*), just off place du Fourail, has beds for 32FF. *Camping Municipal du Terriol* (☎ 05 65 40 72 74), open from mid-May to October, is in a pleasant shady spot by the municipal swimming pool 400m south of place du Foirail (on the GR65). Rates are 13/18FF per person/site.

Hôtel-Restaurant La Promenade (☎ 05 65 40 61 21, *fax 05 65 40 79 12*), on place du Foirail, charges 200FF a double and has reasonable *menus* from 80FF (restaurant closed on Sunday). Cheaper fare is available at several *bar-brasseries* around place du Foirail.

Getting There & Away

Cajarc is on the SNCF bus route from Capdenac to Cahors (43FF) via Figeac (29FF)

with about five services daily. See Organised Tours in the Cahors section for details about an excursion here by Micheline train on summer weekends.

Getting Around

Garage Citroen (☎ 05 65 40 66 48), on place du Foirail, rents bikes for 70/300FF per day/week. It's closed on Sunday morning.

FIGEAC

postcode 46100 • pop 9600 • elevation 250m
The riverside town of Figeac, on the Célé 68km north-east of Cahors, has a picturesque old quarter, with many houses dating from the 12th to 18th centuries. Founded in the 9th century by Benedictine monks, it became a prosperous medieval market town, an important stopping place for pilgrims travelling to Santiago de Compostela and, later, a Protestant stronghold (1576–1623). Figeac's most illustrious son is the brilliant linguist and founder of the science of Egyptology, Jean-François Champollion (see the boxed text 'Champollion the Egyptologist').

Champollion the Egyptologist

Jean-François Champollion (1790–1832), a brilliant academic and linguist from Figeac, became a history professor at the age of 19 and went on to unravel the mysteries of Egyptian hieroglyphics – considered until then to be just decorative pictures. The breakthrough came in 1822 when Champollion deciphered the Greek and Egyptian inscriptions on the so-called Rosetta Stone, a basalt tablet discovered in Egypt in 1799. After deciphering many more texts in Egypt to prove his theory worked – that hieroglyphics were 'figurative, symbolic and phonetic' all at the same time – he became the first curator of the Egyptology Museum he founded at the Louvre, working and lecturing on the language of the pharaohs until his early death.

Orientation

The town spreads on either side of the River Célé with the old quarter, on the northern side, characterised by narrow streets and several intimate squares, notably place Vival and place Carnot. The main commercial roadway of the surrounding modern town is blvd Docteur G Juskiewenski. The train station is 600m south of town.

Information

The tourist office (☎ 05 65 34 06 25, fax 05 65 50 04 58, email figeac@wanadoo.fr) is in Hôtel de la Monnaie on place Vival. It opens from 10 am to noon and 2.30 to 6 pm Monday to Saturday and from 10 am to 1 pm on Sunday (it's open from 10 am to 1 pm and 2 to 7 pm daily from July to mid-September and from 11 am to noon and 2.30 to 5.30 pm Monday to Saturday during the winter). It sells a locally produced topoguide, *Figeac et Son Pays* (30FF), which has details of a dozen short hikes. Its free *Ville d'Art et d'Histoire* leaflet has a suggested walking route round the old town.

The office organises guided visits almost every Wednesday and Saturday at 4.30 pm

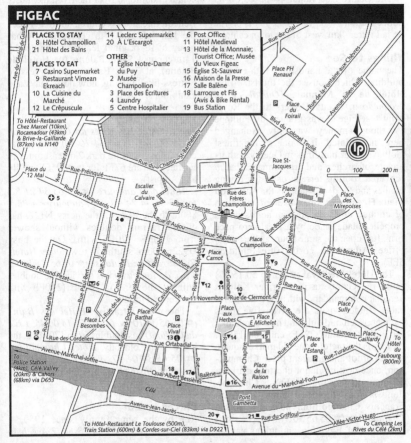

FIGEAC

PLACES TO STAY
8 Hôtel Champollion
21 Hôtel des Bains

PLACES TO EAT
7 Casino Supermarket
9 Restaurant Vimean Ekreach
10 La Cuisine du Marché
12 Le Crépuscule

14 Leclerc Supermarket
20 À L'Escargot

OTHER
1 Église Notre-Dame du Puy
2 Musée Champollion
3 Place des Écritures
4 Laundry
5 Centre Hospitalier

6 Post Office
11 Hôtel Medieval
13 Hôtel de la Monnaie; Tourist Office; Musée du Vieux Figeac
15 Église St-Sauveur
16 Maison de la Presse
17 Salle Balène
18 Larroque et Fils (Avis & Bike Rental)
19 Bus Station

from April to September (at 5 pm daily except on Saturday in July and August) for 25FF (children 10FF).

The post office at 6 ave Fernand Pezet, open until 5.30 pm on weekdays and until noon on Saturday, offers currency exchange. There are a couple of banks along the same street.

Maps and topoguides are available at the Maison de la Presse at 2 rue Gambetta (closed on Sunday afternoon).

There's a laundry at 15 rue des Masquisards, open from 8.30 am to 7.30 pm Monday to Saturday.

The Centre Hospitalier (☎ 05 65 50 65 50) is at 33 rue des Maquisards. The main police station (☎ 05 65 34 17 17) is on rue de la Pintre, 4km west of the town centre.

Things to See

The name of the handsome 13th-century building which houses the tourist office, **Hôtel de la Monnaie** (*Oustal de la Mounédo* in Occitan) refers to the Royal Mint that Figeac was granted by Philippe IV, though money was only exchanged here, not minted. It is one of the finest Gothic secular buildings in Quercy with its arcade of arches and traditional *soleilho* (covered rooftop terrace used for drying clothes and food). Upstairs is the **Musée du Vieux Figeac** which has a varied collection of antique clocks, coins, minerals and a propeller blade made by a local aerospace firm. It is open the same hours as the tourist office. Admission costs 10FF (children 5FF).

The **Hôtel Médiéval** (☎ 05 65 50 15 47) at 41 rue Gambetta is a former Knights Templar commandery with a fine Gothic facade. Guided visits are given five times daily between mid-July and mid-September for 28FF (students 22FF; children 15FF). Nearby is the picturesque old market square **place Carnot** and adjacent **place Champollion**, once hosting major chestnut markets; off here, on tiny rue des Frères Champollion, is the childhood home of Jean-François Champollion, now the **Musée Champollion** (☎ 05 65 50 31 08). The small collection of Egyptian antiquities can be visited from 10 am to noon and 2.30 to 6.30 pm (closed on Monday except in July and August, open from 2 to 6 pm between November and February). Admission costs 20FF (seniors 17FF, children and students 12FF). An enlarged copy of the Rosetta Stone fills the ground of the adjacent ancient courtyard of **place des Écritures**.

North of place Champollion, **rue de Colomb** is lined with centuries-old mansions in sandstone, half-timber and brick. Continue up rue St-Jacques for good views of the town from **Église Notre Dame du Puy**, a Romanesque church with many 17th-century additions. Near the river, the musty **Église St-Sauveur** on rue du Chapitre, a Benedictine abbey church built between the 12th and the 14th centuries, still has many of its original features. The nearby 14th-century **Salle Balène** (or **Hôtel de Balène**), at 7 rue Balène, an impressive fortress-like building, now hosts plays and exhibitions.

Places to Stay

The riverside *Les Rives du Célé* (☎ 05 65 34 59 00, fax 05 65 34 20 80) is at the far end of a huge leisure park 2km east of town. Forfait rates are 67FF for two (95FF in July and August).

Hôtel du Faubourg (☎ 05 65 34 21 82, fax 05 65 34 24 19, 59 Faubourg du Pin), 800m to the east, on the noisy N122, has clean, fragrant doubles without shower from 140FF (170FF with). On the busy D922, 500m south of town, the *Hôtel-Restaurant Le Toulouse* (☎ 05 65 34 22 95, 4 ave de Toulouse) has serviceable doubles without shower for 180FF (210FF with shower and toilet).

The more attractive *Hôtel des Bains* (☎ 05 65 34 10 89, fax 05 65 14 00 45, 1 rue du Griffoul) has doubles from 170FF. In the heart of the old city, *Hôtel Champollion* (☎ 05 65 34 04 37, 3 place Champollion) has double/triples with bathroom for 250/280FF.

Places to Eat

Run by the same family since 1950, *À l'Escargot* (☎ 05 65 34 23 84, 2 Ave Jean

Regional specialities, Sarlat market, Dordogne

The ancient art of basket weaving, Vézère Valley

Historic market town of St-Céré, Lot

St-Céré fair includes a lively cattle market.

Périgourdin truffle hunter and his master

QVIS·VT·DEVS·

South-West France boasts picture-postcard scenery and, encompassing the pilgrim trail to Santiago de Compostela, it is also a region of huge religious significance.

Tumbledown tower in Carennac, Lot

Half-timbered house in St-Cirq Lapopie, Lot

A fortified 16th-century Gothic church overlooks the prettiest village in Lot: St-Cirq Lapopie.

Ruins of the 13th-century Château Tauzia, one of many fortified homes in the Vallée d'Osse, Gers

Western gate of medieval Larressingle, Gers

Pocket-sized but perfect: Labastide d'Armagnac

Jaurès), has *menus* of family-style Quercy cuisine from 100FF and *plats du jour* for 50FF. It is closed on Monday night. One of the town's best restaurants *La Cuisine du Marché* (☎ *05 65 50 18 55, 15 rue de Clermont)*, has midday *menus* from 70FF (230FF *menus* for gourmands). Humbler diners may like *Le Crépuscule* (☎ *05 65 34 28 53, 4 rue de la République)* which serves fresh pasta dishes (from 35FF), salads and galettes (closed Sunday lunchtime).

The Chinese *Restaurant Vimean Ekreach* (☎ *05 65 34 79 65, 10 rue Badue)* offers lunch/dinner *menus* from 58/85FF. It is closed on Monday.

A fine dining excursion, if you've got your own wheels, is to the locally renowned *Hôtel-Restaurant Chez Marcel* (☎ *05 65 40 11 16, fax 05 65 40 49 08)* in Cardaillac, a lovely old village 10km to the north (off the N140); the 100FF *menu* includes a great *côtes d'agneau du causse* (lamb dish).

Self-caterers can find a *Leclerc supermarket* (closed on Sunday) at 32 rue Gambetta and a Saturday morning *food market* and *Casino supermarket* (closed on Sunday afternoon) on place Carnot.

Getting There & Away
The SNCF bus from Cahors (62FF, 1¾ hours, four or five times daily) via Bouziès and Tour de Faure (St-Cirq Lapopie) stops at Figeac's train and bus stations.

The train station (☎ 05 65 80 29 06, staffed from 4 am to midnight), is on two major rail lines: the one that links Toulouse (113FF, 2¼ hours, five daily) with Aurillac (58FF) and Clermont-Ferrand (151FF, four hours, three to four daily); and the one from Paris' Gare d'Austerlitz (304FF, about six hours, five daily, two of them direct) to Rodez via Brive-la-Gaillarde (71FF, 1½ hours, five daily) and Rocamadour-Padirac (42FF, about 30 minutes).

Getting Around
The Larroque et Fils (☎ 05 65 34 10 28) garage at 10 quai Albert Bessières has an Avis car-rental office (☎ 05 65 34 80 26) where you can also rent mountain bikes for 90/450FF daily/week.

WEST OF CAHORS
West of Cahors, the River Lot loops and wriggles all the way to Fumel past rich vineyard estates. A free map with contact details for visiting chateaux and wine-tasting is available from local, or Cahors, tourist offices or the Maison du Vin (☎ 05 65 23 22 24, fax 05 65 23 22 27) at 430 ave Jean Jaurès, Cahors.

Boats and canoes/kayaks can be hired en route at Luzech (Base Nautique de Caix, ☎ 05 65 20 11 30), Albas (Safaraid, ☎ 05 65 30 74 47; open July and August only) and Puy l'Évêque (Base Nautique Le Pigeonnier, ☎ 05 65 21 37 13).

Puy L'Évêque
postcode 46700 • pop 2160 • elevation 86m
One of the most picturesque spots between Cahors and Fumel, tiny Puy l'Évêque clusters high above the River. Cahors bishops (*évêques*) seized the town in the 13th century, building a castle at the top; the **keep** is the only bit left, but the sturdy 14th- to 15th-century **Église St-Sauveur** and various medieval houses are worth a look.

The tourist office (☎ 05 65 21 37 63, fax 05 65 36 40 40), at 8 place du Rampeau, the eastern end of town, just off the D911, is open from 8.30 am to noon and 2 to 6 pm daily (closed on Monday morning and Thursday afternoon).

Places to Stay & Eat Set among vineyards by the river 4km west of town is *Village de Vacances Camping de la Plage* (☎ *05 65 30 81 72)*, open April to October. Rates are 20/22FF per person/site. *Hôtel Restaurant Henry* (☎ *05 65 21 32 24, fax 05 65 30 85 18, 23 rue du Docteur Rouma)*, at a busy crossroads 1km south of town, has doubles costing from 140FF. *Hôtel-Restaurant La Truffière* (☎ *05 65 21 34 54, fax 05 65 30 84 47)*, by the town hall at the top end of town, charges 220FF per double and has a good midday *menu* (60FF).

Getting There & Away The SNCF Cahors (46FF, 45 minutes) to Fumel (20FF, 25 minutes) bus stops by the tourist office around eight times daily.

LOT

Château de Bonaguil

This ruined but still imposing fortress-chateau (☎ 05 53 49 59 76) is set in dreamy countryside on the path of the GR36, about 18km north-west of Puy l'Évêque and 8km north-east of Fumel. Built in the 13th century, in the mid-15th century it fell into the hands of the cruel, megalomaniac Bérenger de Rocquefeuil who transformed it into an impregnable fortress against his many imagined enemies. Even designed to deflect modern cannon fire, it wasn't touched until the Revolution. A vast moat, an enormous barbican, huge towers and a towering, vessel-shaped keep still seem haunted by their owner's paranoia.

It's open from 10.30 am to noon and 2.30 to 5 pm daily (from 10 am to noon and 2 to 5 pm in June). During July and August, when it's open from 10 am to 5.45 pm, there are guided visits three times daily with an English-speaking guide and night-time illuminations until midnight daily. It's closed during December and January. Admission costs 30FF (children 20FF).

Lot-et-Garonne

VILLENEUVE-SUR-LOT
postcode 47300 • pop 23,000
• elevation 150m

Dominated by its red-brick church tower, this old bastide, founded in 1253 and once one of the most powerful in the region, is now surrounded by a busy modern commercial town, with a thriving trade in early vegetables (*primeurs*) and fruit (especially plums). It's a useful base for visiting the hamlets and bastides of the Haut Pays des Serres to the south and several pretty villages along the Lot River to the east.

Orientation & Information

The old town fits snugly between the Lot River to the south and a strip of broad boulevards (with three different names) to the north. Two ancient gateways still stand: porte de Paris in the middle of the boulevards to the north-east and porte de Pujols to the south-west.

The tourist office (☎ 05 53 36 17 30, fax 05 53 49 42 98), in the middle of the boulevards, on blvd Georges Leygues (opposite a grandiose theatre), is open from 9 am to noon and 2 to 6 pm daily except on Sunday (from 8.30 am to 7 pm between mid-June and mid-September). During July and August, if there are enough people, it runs guided tours of the old town (15FF).

The central post office, open until 6.30 pm on weekdays and to noon on Saturday, is south of town, by pont Neuf (also called pont de la Libération). Currency exchange is available.

JLB (☎ 05 53 70 21 41, email jlborgo@aol.com), at 33 rue J Cosse-Manière (near the post office), charges 25FF per hour for Internet access. It's open from 9 am to 5 pm Monday to Friday.

Musée de la Vallée du Lot

This former mill by the river, at 2 rue des Jardins (a block east of the post office), was still undergoing a major transformation at the time of our visit, but if the superbly imaginative temporary exhibition is any indication, the rest – on the history and art of the Lot valley – should definitely be worth a visit. Opening times may change (☎ 05 53 40 48 00 to check) but it's currently open from 2 to 6 pm daily between April and October (from 10 am to 7 pm daily during July and August). Admission costs 15FF (children 10FF).

Pont Vieux & Old Town

The town's central bridge over the Lot, **pont Vieux**, was originally built by the English in the 13th century and is reminiscent of the famous bridge at Cahors (see pont Valentré in the Cahors section earlier in this chapter); it was a major thoroughfare across the Lot on the route to Santiago de Compostela. At the heart of the old town, **place Lafayette** is a busy market square surrounded by attractive arched arcades. Towering over the square is the red-brick **Église Ste-Catherine** built in the 1930s on the site of an earlier Gothic church whose restored 14th- and 15th-century stained glass can still be seen inside.

Places to Stay & Eat

The shady *Camping Municipal Le Rooy* (☎ 05 53 70 24 18) is 1km to the south, off the N21. It's open from mid-April to October and charges 12/13FF per person/tent.

Hôtel des Ramparts (☎ 05 53 70 71 63, fax 05 53 40 52 25, 1 rue Etienne Marcel), 200m west of the tourist office, has gloomy doubles for 125FF without shower (165FF with; hall showers free). *Hôtel les Platanes* (☎ 05 53 40 11 40, fax 05 53 70 71 95, 40 blvd de la Marine), nearer the tourist office, has brighter but noisier rooms from 190/150FF with/without shower (no hall showers available).

In a quieter location by the former train station near port de Pujols, *Hotel Terminus* (☎ 05 53 70 94 36, fax 05 53 70 45 13) has doubles with shower for 280FF.

There are several bar-brasseries with decent *menus* from around 80FF along the boulevards. More atmospheric nooks in the old town include: *Le Parmentier* (☎ 05 53 70 35 02, 13 rue Parmentier) with lunch/dinner *menus* costing 59/89FF; and *L'Intermezzo* (☎ 05 53 70 18 51, 18 rue Parmentier) which serves pizzas and pastas in record speed. Both restaurants have outdoor tables and are closed on Sunday. Bagging the best riverside location, the nearby cosy *Chez Caline* (☎ 05 53 70 42 08, 2 rue Notre Dame) has *menus* from 75FF (10% more to sit on the terrace).

Getting There & Away

SNCF buses run to Agen (31FF, 45 minutes, with TGV connections to Bordeaux 130FF; 10 daily) at least nine times daily. They leave from place du 4 Septembre (near the Musée) with a stop at the former train station where the SNCF ticket office (☎ 05 53 70 00 35) is open from 8.30 am to 6 pm Monday to Friday and from 9.30 am to 5 pm on Saturday.

Also leaving from place du 4 Septembre are SAB (Société des Autocars Brouens, ☎ 05 53 40 23 30) buses to Bergerac (50.80FF, 1¼ hours, twice daily in term-time, once at other times) and Monflanquin (16.80FF, 20 minutes, once daily in term-time). The ticket and information office in

place du 4 September is open from 6.30 am to noon and 2 to 7 pm Monday to Friday (from 6.30 am to noon on Saturday).

Cars Evasion (☎ 05 53 40 88 20) run a twice-daily service to Fumel (25FF) but not in August. The stop is opposite the hospital on blvd Bernard Palissy (just north of place du 4 Septembre).

AROUND VILLENEUVE-SUR-LOT
Pujols

On a hilltop with fabulous views, 2km south-west of Villeneuve-sur-Lot (a pleasant walk from porte de Pujols), this pretty medieval village is a honey-trap for tourists and antique-dealers, with many art and antique shops in its lovingly restored half-timbered houses. Check out the St-Nicholas bell-tower whose archway serves as the main entrance, and faded 15th-century frescoes in Église Ste-Foy-la-Jeune.

Penne d'Agenais

Eight kilometres upriver from Villeneuve-sur-Lot, this is another picturesque and touristy *village perché* (hilltop village), dripping with honeysuckle and roses in summer. It was once the site of a fortress founded by Richard the Lion Heart and a Cathar stronghold, both affiliations attracting savage attacks, repeated during the Wars of Religion. You can see the huge basilica of its church, Notre Dame de Peyragude, from miles around: close up, it's a bit of a disappointment, a 19th-century neo-Byzantine affair to replace its predecessor, once an important pilgrimage stop on the route to Compostela, and destroyed during the Revolution.

The tourist office (☎ 05 53 41 37 80, fax 05 53 49 38 37), at rue du 14 Juillet, is open from 9 am to 12.30 pm and 3 to 7 pm Monday to Saturday and from 3 to 7 pm on Sunday.

Tournon d'Agenais

This imposing 13th-century hilltop bastide, 26km east of Villeneuve-sur-Lot, is better from the outside than in, thanks to its towering white ramparts, now turned into houses. There are grand views from the

LOT-ET-GARONNE

Chemin de Ronde (around the ramparts) of the surrounding Haut Pays des Serres. In the village itself, the most famous thing to try is *tourtière,* a round flaky apple or prune pie (often sold at markets throughout the region). There's even a fete in its honour in mid-August.

The tourist office (☎ 05 53 40 75 82, fax 05 53 40 76 98) right in the village centre, operates from 9.30 to 11 am and 2 to 3.30 pm Monday to Friday (closed on Wednesday).

Places to Stay & Eat Inside Tournon d'Agenais itself, the only option is *Hôtel-Restaurant Le Midi (☎ 05 53 40 70 08)* where doubles cost 300FF. Cheaper digs can be found down at the junction of the D656 and D661: *Hôtel Les Voyageurs (☎ 05 53 40 70 28)* offers doubles with/ without bath for 200/150FF and *menus* start from 65FF.

For accommodation near Penne d'Agenais (there's nothing in the village) contact the tourist office.

Getting There & Away The Villeneuve-sur-Lot to Fumel bus (☎ 05 53 40 88 20) stops at St-Sylvestre, 2km across the river from Penne d'Agenais, once daily. No buses go to Tournon d'Agenais (which is on the GR652) but bikes can be rented in Fumel (9km to the north) from AJF Cycles (☎ 05 53 71 14 57; closed on Sunday and Monday).

MONFLANQUIN
postcode 47150 • pop 2500 • elevation 181m
This beautifully preserved hilltop bastide, 17km north-east of Villeneuve-sur-Lot, is one of the finest of its kind. It was founded in 1256 by the indefatigable brother of King Louis, Alphonse de Poitiers, who strengthened the French hold on the region by also establishing Villeréal, Villeneuve-sur-Lot and a dozen other bastides.

Information
The Maison du Tourisme office (☎ 05 53 36 40 19, fax 05 53 36 42 91, email office .de.tourisme.monflanquin@wanadoo.fr) on place des Arcades is open from 10 am to noon and 2 to 6 pm Monday to Friday (closed on Monday morning), from 10 am to noon and 3 to 5 pm on Saturday and from 3 to 5 pm on Sunday. Its hours are shorter between October and April. In summer, the office organises guided group visits of the bastide (10FF per person).

Things to See & Do
At the heart of Monflanquin is the unspoilt **place des Arcades** surrounded by *cornières* (arched arcades) and dominated by a fortified 15th-century **church**. Upstairs from the tourist office is the excellent **Musée des Bastides**, with interactive displays (listen to troubadour songs or the medieval chants of pilgrims) and explanations (including in English) on all aspects of bastide life. It's open the same hours as the tourist office. Admission costs 20FF (children 12FF).

Places to Stay & Eat
At *Camping de Coulon (☎ 05 53 36 47 35, fax 05 53 36 47 36, route de Cancon),* 2.2km to the west and open from June to October, forfait rates are 50FF for two (62FF from mid-July to mid-September). On the same road, 1km to the west, *Site Touristique de Coulon (☎ 05 53 36 47 35, fax 05 53 36 40 29)* has doubles for 250FF (with bath); for 25FF extra you can use the hotel's Espace Forme facilities (sauna, gym, pool).

Hôtel L'Entrecôte (☎ 05 53 36 40 01, ave de la Libération), 200m to the south, on the D676, has doubles for 140FF; its restaurant offers pizzas or *menus* from 75FF. *Le Bistrot du Prince Noir (☎ 05 53 36 63 00, place des Arcades)* has midday/ evening *menus* for 60/90FF.

Getting There & Away
The once-daily (6.45 pm) Villeneuve-sur-Lot to Monflanquin bus (16.80FF, 20 minutes) stops 400m south of place des Arcades by a car park. The once-daily (more in term-time) Bergerac to Villeneuve service (☎ 05 53 40 23 30; 50.80FF, 1¼ hours) stops in Cancon, 13km to the west. A taxi (☎ 05 53 36 31 08) to Cancon costs around 100FF.

VILLERÉAL

postcode 47210 • pop 1300 • elevation 120m

This untouristy bastide market town is 13km north of Monflanquin by the River Dropt. Its spacious central square, place de la Halle, has a 14th-century timbered **covered market** overlooked by an impressive fortified twin-towered 13th-century **church**. The tourist office (☎ 05 53 36 09 65, fax 05 53 36 00 37), on place de la Halle, is open from 10 am to noon and 3 to 9 pm daily between mid-June and mid-September (except on Sunday and holidays and from 9 am to noon and 2 to 5 pm daily except on Sunday at other times.

Places to Stay & Eat

The *Hôtel-Restaurant de L'Europe* (☎ 05 53 36 00 35, place Jean Moulin), near the church, has decent doubles from 160FF (with shower) and *menus* from 64FF.

Getting There & Away

One bus daily in term-time (once weekly at other times; ☎ 05 53 40 23 30) connects Villeréal with Villeneuve-sur-Lot (32FF, one hour).

Getting Around

Bikes can be rented (☎ 05 53 36 01 21) just north of town on the D207 for 60/250FF per day/week.

AGEN

postcode 47000 • pop 32,000• elevation 50m

To the French, Agen means only one thing: prunes. This lively university capital of the Lot-et-Garonne département, on the banks of the Garonne River and Canal Latéral, is the centre of the famous *pruneaux d'Agen* trade (see the boxed text 'Prunes Galore'), a busy commercial town with horrid outskirts. There's little left of its history as a Roman *oppidum* (defensive town) and Hundred Years' War target (it changed hands between the French and English 11 times), but it's got a good supply of accommodation and restaurants and a renowned rugby team, the Sporting Union Agénais (SUA). It has one big cultural gem: the Musée des Beaux-Arts. If that doesn't interest the kids,

---

Prunes Galore

It won't take you long to realise that prunes are big business in the Lot-et-Garonne, especially around Agen which has given its name to the famous dried *pruneaux d'Agen* – despite the fact that they mostly come from just north of the Lot River, 40km away. Originally introduced from the Middle East by crusaders, the *prunier d'ente* plum trees of the area produce an enormous 30,000 tonnes of plums a year, about 65% of the country's total output.

You can try them served in pancakes (*galette aux pruneaux*), stuffed with almond paste or chocolate (*pruneaux fourrés*), soaked in armagnac, or distilled into an *eau de vie* (brandy). For more prune temptations, trawl the speciality shops in Agen. Several offer free *dégustation* (tasting) including La Confiserie P Boisson, at 20 rue Grande Horloge, which has been making prune delicacies since 1835.

---

try Walibi Parc d'Attractions, the region's biggest amusement park.

Orientation

The main shopping street, blvd de la République, runs for 1.1km from place Jasmin to place du 14 Juillet (also called place du Pin). The Garonne River is crossed by pont de Pierre (600m south of town) while the handsome 23-arched, 19th century Pont Canal aqueduct carries the Canal Latéral over the river 1.5km north-west of place Jasmin. There are pleasant paths (good for biking) beside the river and canal, especially by the peristyle du Gravier and the port de Plaisance (riverboat base).

Information

Tourist Offices The tourist office (☎ 05 53 47 36 09, fax 05 53 47 29 98, email otsi .agen@wanadoo.fr), at 107 blvd du Président Carnot, is open from 9 am to 12.30 pm and 2 to 6.30 pm Monday to Saturday (9 am to 7 pm between July and September) and

LOT-ET-GARONNE

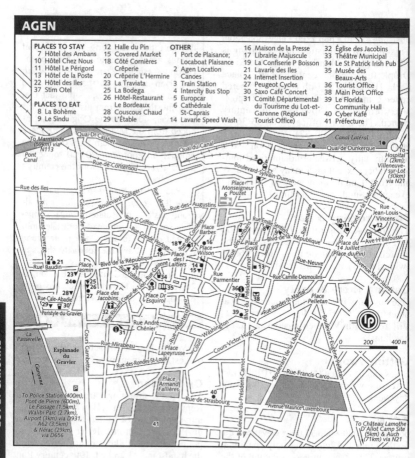

AGEN

PLACES TO STAY
7 Hôtel des Ambans
10 Hôtel Chez Nous
11 Hôtel Le Périgord
13 Hôtel de la Poste
22 Hôtel des Iles
37 Stim Otel

PLACES TO EAT
8 La Bohème
9 Le Sindu

12 Halle du Pin
15 Covered Market
18 Côté Cornières Crêperie
20 Crêperie L'Hermine
23 La Traviata
25 La Bodega
26 Hôtel-Restaurant Le Bordeaux
28 Couscous Chaud
29 L'Étable

OTHER
1 Port de Plaisance; Locaboat Plaisance
2 Agen Location Canoes
3 Train Station
4 Intercity Bus Stop
5 Europcar
6 Cathédrale St-Caprais
14 Lavarie Speed Wash

16 Maison de la Presse
17 Librairie Majuscule
19 La Confiserie P Boisson
21 Lavarie des Iles
24 Internet Insertion
27 Peugeot Cycles
30 Saxo Café Concert
31 Comité Départemental du Tourisme du Lot-et-Garonne (Regional Tourist Office)

32 Église des Jacobins
33 Théâtre Municipal
34 Le St Patrick Irish Pub
35 Musée des Beaux-Arts
36 Tourist Office
38 Main Post Office
39 Le Florida Community Hall
40 Cyber Kafé
41 Préfecture

from 10 am to noon on Sunday. From mid-July to September, it organises free guided tours of the town (one to 1½ hours) at 9 pm on Thursday and at 6 pm on Monday.

The regional Comité Départemental du Tourisme du Lot-et-Garonne (☎ 05 53 66 14 14, fax 05 53 68 25 42), at 4 rue André Chénier, is only useful if you need more detailed information on the département. It's open from 9 am to noon and 2 to 5 pm Monday to Friday.

Post & Communications The main post office on blvd du Président Carnot is open until 7 pm on weekdays and until noon on Saturday.

Le Florida community hall (☎ 05 53 47 59 54), at 167 blvd du Président Carnot, charges 10FF per hour for access to the Internet and is open from noon to 7 pm Tuesday to Saturday. Cyber Kafé (☎ 05 53 48 27 04), at 17 bis rue de Strasbourg, is open from 8 am to 8 pm daily except on Sunday and charges 40FF per hour. Internet Insertion (☎ 05 53 77 88 30, email internet .insertion@3w.fr), a cybercafe at 25 ave du Général de Gaulle, is open from 9 am to noon and 2 to 7 pm on weekdays (to 6 pm on Tuesday) and charges 30FF per hour for access.

Bookshops For maps and guides, head for Maison de la Presse at 65 blvd de la República or Librairie Majuscule at 10 rue des Cornières.

Laundry Lavarie Speed Wash, near the covered market, is open from 7 am to 10 pm daily. Lavarie des Iles, at 25 rue Baudin, is open from 7.30 am to 10 pm daily.

Medical Services & Emergency Centre Hospitalier Agen (hospital; ☎ 05 53 69 70 71), at 21 route Villeneuve, is 3km north-east of the town centre, off the N21. The main police station (☎ 05 53 69 30 00) is 2km to the south at 15 rue Valence.

Musée des Beaux-Arts

Next to the over-the-top Théâtre Municipal on place Dr Esquirol, this is one of the finest provincial museums in the country, housed in 16th- and 17th-century mansions. The collection includes some outstanding Gallo-Roman remains (notably the 1st century BC Vénus de Mas marble statue) and a treasure-trove of 17th- and 18th-century paintings, including five by Goya. Don't miss the upstairs collection of Impressionists including some memorable scenes by Eugène Boudin.

The museum (☎ 05 53 69 47 23) is open from 10 am to 5 pm daily except Tuesday (to 6 pm from May to October). Admission costs 20FF (free to students and those aged under 18).

Activities

Along the Canal Latéral, Agen Location Canoes (☎ 05 53 66 18 49) rents canoes/kayaks daily during July and August (at the weekend only in September) for 60/50FF per hour or 240/140FF per day.

Locaboat Plaisance (☎ 05 53 66 00 74), at port de Plaisance, rents houseboats for weekends or longer.

Ninety-minute trips on the L'Agenais tourist boat also leave from port de Plaisance twice daily at the weekend and on

holidays (plus on Wednesday in June and September and four times daily in July and August) for 35FF (children 20FF).

Walibi Parc d'Attractions This huge amusement park (☎ 05 53 96 58 32), 2.7km south-west of town, has water rides, seal performances, train rides and other entertainments. It's open daily from 10am to 6pm between June and August (at the weekend only during September; at the weekend plus on Wednesday during May). Admission costs 115FF (three to eight year-olds 99FF).

Places to Stay

Near Boé, *Château Lamothe D'Allot* camp site (*☎ 05 53 68 33 11, fax 05 53 68 33 05)*, 5km to the south off the D17, has a pool and sports facilities. Rates are 22.50/22.50FF per person/site; advance reservations are recommended in high season.

Hôtel Chez Nous (☎ 05 53 47 09 06, 41 blvd Sylvain Dumon)* has basic doubles without shower for 100FF (130FF with shower and WC). *Hôtel des Ambans (*☎ 05 53 66 28 60, fax 05 53 87 94 01, 59 rue des Ambans)* has recently renovated doubles from 160/190FF without/with shower. Another cheapie, above a bar-brasserie, is *Hôtel de la Poste (*☎ 05 53 66 37 73, 82 blvd du Président Carnot)* where nothing-special but spacious doubles go for 150FF without shower (200FF twin).

The Logis de France *Hôtel Le Périgord* (*☎ 05 53 77 55 77, fax 05 53 77 55 70, 42 cours du 14 Juillet)* has road-noisy doubles costing from 180FF without shower (from 230FF with). There's free parking nearby. The quieter, welcoming *Hôtel des Iles* (*☎ 05 53 47 11 33, fax 05 53 66 19 25, 25 rue Baudin)* has doubles with shower, TV, WC and telephone from 190FF.

More boringly upmarket is *Stim Otel* (*☎ 05 53 47 31 23, fax 05 53 47 48 70, 105 blvd du Président Carnot)*, where doubles start at 298FF. Other big chain hotels are in the Le Passage district, across the river.

Places to Eat

Along the popular rue Emilie Sentini, chic *La Bohème (*☎ 05 53 68 31 00)*, at No 14, offers a Guyenne *menu* for 85FF and a Gascogne version for 135FF, with a weekday midday *menu* at 69FF. It's closed on Sunday.

L'Étable (☎ 05 53 47 68 79, 41 peristyle du Gravier) has a good choice of salads (from 35FF) and fish dishes as well as interesting specialities such as tagliatelle with foie gras sauce (from 55FF).

On rue Voltaire, *Crêperie l'Hermine* (☎ 05 53 66 14 76), at No 21, has deluxe crepes and galettes from around 35FF. It's closed on Sunday and Monday and packed out on Saturday nights. A cheaper version, with attractive outdoor seating, is *Côté Cornières Crêperie* (☎ 05 53 66 52 37, 5 rue des Cornières). The popular but road-noisy *La Traviata* (☎ 05 53 47 46 79, 39 ave du Général de Gaulle) serves cheap pasta and pizzas.

Among ethnic choices, there's *Le Sindu* (☎ 05 53 66 60 52, 36 rue Emilie Sentini) serving a wide range of Indian dishes; the take-away couscous outfit *Couscous Chaud* (☎ 05 53 87 75 75, rue Cale-Abadie); and *La Bodega* (☎ 05 53 48 26 83, 7 bis place Jasmin) for tapas and other Spanish specialities. The adjacent *Hôtel-Restaurant Le Bordeaux* (☎ 05 53 68 46 46, 8 place Jasmin) serves generous traditional fare at bargain prices (from 60FF for evening *menus*).

The modern *covered market*, just off place Wilson, is the best place to pick up fresh produce daily. There's also a *market* on Wednesday and on Sunday mornings in Halle du Pin (off place du 14 Juillet) and on Saturday morning on the esplanade du Gravier.

Entertainment

The *Saxo Café Concert* (☎ 05 53 48 02 47, 55 peristyle du Gravier) offers good music and cheap beer as well as food. *Le St Patrick Irish Pub* (☎ 05 53 66 60 61, 6 rue Garonne) is open from 3 pm to at least 1 am daily except on Sunday.

Getting There & Away

Air There are three flights to Paris daily with Flandre Air. The tiny airport (☎ 05 53 96 22 50) is 3.5km to the south-west, there are no bus connections and a taxi to the town centre will cost around 50FF.

Bus SNCF bus services (all leaving from the train station) include Auch (60FF, 1½ hours, six daily); Villeneuve-sur-Lot (31FF, 45 minutes, 10 daily) and Nérac (32FF, 40 minutes, four to five daily).

Train Agen is on the Bordeaux (100FF, 1¼ hours) to Toulouse (91FF, one hour 10 minutes) line via Montauban (60FF, 45 minutes) with around a dozen services daily except on Sunday. For Cahors (97FF) change at Montauban. There are two to three services daily to Périgueux (112FF, two hours 20 minutes) via Le Buisson (76FF, one hour 40 minutes). The train (☎ 08 36 35 35 35) information office is open from 9 am to 7.30 pm Monday to Saturday.

Getting Around

Europcar (☎ 05 53 47 37 40, fax 05 53 47 74 98) is at 120 blvd du Président Carnot. Avis (☎ 05 53 47 76 47, fax 05 53 47 74 98) and ADA (☎ 05 53 96 96 40) are both near the train station on blvd Sylvain Dumon. There are some car parks south of esplanade du Gravier and east of place du 14 Juillet.

Peugeot Cycles (☎ 05 53 47 76 76), at 18 ave du Général de Gaulle, is open from 9 am to 7 pm Monday to Saturday and charges 80/345FF per day/six days. They also rent scooters for 210FF per day.

NÉRAC
postcode 47600 • pop 7500
• elevation approx 50m

A pleasant day trip from Agen or a brief stopover, this small town, 27km to the south-west, draws the tourists today mainly for its boat trips along the pretty Baïse River. But its chateau was once the seat of the powerful d'Albret family who turned the tide of French history during the 15th and 16th centuries: Henri d'Albret married the sister of King François I, Marguerite d'Angoulême, who welcomed poets and Protestant preachers to Nérac. Their daughter, the Protestant bigot Jeanne d'Albret, was to fan the flames of the Wars of Religion while her son, Henri of Navarre, the future King Henri IV, finally had the sense to stop the conflict (for more information see England vs

France in the History section of the Facts about South-West France chapter).

Orientation & Information

The wide and busy allées d'Albret (D930) runs above (to the west of) town with hotels, bar-brasseries. But the heart of town, 100m downhill, is place de l'Hôtel de Ville with its jovial modern clocktower. Just below this, at 9 ave Mondenard, is the tourist office (☎ 05 53 65 27 75), open from 9 am to noon and 2 to 6 pm daily except Monday. The chateau is opposite, overlooking the river.

Things to See & Do

The **Château Henri IV** is a shadow of its former self, thanks to 17th-century destruction; only one wing with a loggia of columns is left. Inside, a museum (☎ 05 53 65 21 11) about the town's history is open from 10 am to noon and 2 to 5 pm daily except Monday and Tuesday (to 6 pm between April and June) and from 10 am to noon and 3 to 7 pm daily except Tuesday between July and September.

The loveliest part of the **old town**, called Petit Nérac, is in the lanes across the river where former tanneries have been restored. By the bridge below the chateau, the extensive royal hunting grounds, **La Garenne**, are now a delightful park.

To **cruise along the Baïse** you've got several options, all starting at the quai de la Baïse below the chateau: the Croisière du Prince Henry *gabarre* (flat-bottomed boat; ☎ 05 53 65 66 66) does one-hour trips (with commentary) at least twice daily for 40FF (children 25FF). To rent your own two-to-four-person gabarre it'll cost 400/500FF per half/full day, heading downriver to where the Baïse meets the Canal Latéral at Buzet-sur-Baïse.

Places to Stay & Eat

Situated on the D656, 1.3km east of town, *La Poule au Pot* (☎ 05 53 65 07 92) has basic doubles for 120FF. The Logis de France *Hôtel Le Château* (☎ 05 53 65 09 05, 7 ave Mondenard), next to the tourist office, has more comfortable doubles for

200FF and a decent *restaurant*. The attractive riverside *Les Terraces du Petit Nérac* (☎ 05 53 97 02 91, fax 05 53 65 65 98, 7 rue Séderie) has elegant rooms for 280FF (230FF off-season) and *menus* from 60/ 95FF midday/evening.

Getting There & Away

The SNCF bus to/from Agen runs around four times daily (32FF, 40 minutes); the bus stop is by the clocktower. A bus to Mont de Marsan leaves once or twice daily from a stop east of town, just beyond the bridge.

DURAS

postcode 47120 • pop 1200 • elevation 120m
Set in the drowsy valley of the Dropt, this little hilltop town makes a pleasant base for a couple of days' exploration in the surrounding Pays de Duras – a region famed for its wines, bastides and Romanesque churches. There's nothing much to see and do in the town itself after you've delved into the depths of the Château des Ducs de Duras so try and time your visit for a Monday when at least the market makes the place buzz a bit.

Orientation & Information

The chateau dominates the western edge of town, with the tourist office (☎ 05 53 83 63 06, fax 05 53 83 65 45), on blvd Jean Brisseau, on the northern side (near Hostellerie des Ducs). It's open from 9 am to 12.30 pm and 1.30 to 6 pm Monday to Saturday (daily until 7 pm between mid-June and mid-September). The office promotes the area's fine Côtes de Duras wines with a pamphlet detailing all the *caves particulières* (wineries); it also offers free tastings. Useful publications geared to walkers and bikers includes *Châteaux et Bastides en Haut-Agenais* (40FF).

Château des Ducs de Duras

This imposing chateau (☎ 05 53 83 77 32) dates from the 12th century but was in ruins by the 20th. Taken over and restored by the town, its rambling halls now host exhibitions, musical events and displays (including one on the novelist Marguerite de

Duras). The ethnological museum in the basement is more engaging, with its huge grape presses, threshers, ploughs and prune harvesting implements.

It's open from 10 am to 7 pm daily between June and September; from 10 am to noon and 2 to 6 pm in October (to 7 pm during April and May) and from 2 to 6 pm between November and March. Admission costs 28FF (children 15FF, students 20FF).

Allemans du Dropt

One of the best day-trip or biking excursions from Duras is to this little village 9km to the east, famous for the extraordinary 15th-century frescoes in its church depicting lively devils and gruesome goings-on. If the church is closed, inquire at the tourist office (☎ 05 53 20 25 59), on place de la Mairie, open office hours on weekdays only.

Places to Stay & Eat

The *Camping municipal* (☎ 05 53 20 23 37) camp site, just below the chateau, is open July and August only (on request at other times) for 16/12FF per person/site. The tourist office has a list of *campings à la ferme* in the neighbourhood.

The decent *Auberge du Château* (☎ 05 53 83 70 58, fax 05 53 93 95 64, place Jean Bousquet), opposite the chateau, has doubles at 170FF and restaurant *menus* from 115FF (65FF midday). The posher Logis de France *Hostellerie des Ducs* (☎ 05 53 83 74 58, fax 05 53 83 75 03, blvd Jean Brisseau), near the tourist office, has doubles from 199FF and restaurant *menus* from 128FF (88FF at midday). Cheaper fare is available at *Don Camillo pizzeria* (☎ 05 53 83 76 00, rue Paul Persil), 100m south of the tourist office.

Getting There & Away

Your best bet is a train to Marmande, 23km to the south (and with connections to Agen, around 30 minutes), Toulouse (95 minutes, around four services daily) and Bordeaux (around 45 minutes) and then a taxi (☎ 05 53 83 07 87) which should cost around 160FF. SARL Cars Blew (☎ 05 53 23 81 92) run buses twice-daily between Marmande and Bergerac via Allemans du dropt (30 minutes).

Getting Around

MBK bike shop (☎ 05 53 83 72 05), on rue Paul Persil, rents mountain bikes for 80/350FF per day/week. It's closed on Saturday afternoon and on Sunday.

Toulouse, Tarn-et-Garonne & Tarn

Toulouse, much of Tarn-et-Garonne and Tarn belong to a part of France which for centuries tried to go its own way: politically with the counts of Toulouse, economically on the Canal du Midi and spiritually under the influence of Catharism.

One side of its persona is Toulouse, the high-tech capital of the Midi-Pyrénées région, the south-west's biggest city and a mainstay of Europe's aerospace industry.

The other side is the 'country' side: a generous landscape of oak forests, limestone plateaus, sunny vineyards and the peaks of the Montagne Noir. The Tarn-et-Garonne département alone grows 80% of the région's fruit – melons, greengages, table grapes, peaches, nectarines, kiwi fruit, cherries and apples – making it also one of the best places for temporary summer work. For those with an itch to be outdoors – on foot, bicycle, horse or boat – there's the beautiful Parc Naturel Régional du Haute-Languedoc and the gorges and limestone plateaus of the Aveyron River.

Walking is a burgeoning pastime and the GR36, GR46 and GR653 walking trails – the last following a branch of the pilgrim route to Santiago de Compostela – make it easy. Without strong feet or a bike you'll probably need a car since public transport is limited, with bus connections to smaller villages sometimes petering out to nothing.

Note that some small towns on the western borders of Tarn-et-Garonne belong temperamentally to Gascony and have been included in the Gers chapter.

Toulouse

postcode 31000 • pop 741,100
• elevation 147m

Toulouse – capital of the Midi-Pyrénées région and prefecture (préfecture) of the

Highlights

- Go interplanetary at Cité de l'Espace, Toulouse's amazing space museum and planetarium complex
- Wonder at the Romanesque statuary of Abbaye St-Pierre at Moissac, the finest collection anywhere
- Choose between kayaking, walking or cycling through the limestone landscape of the Averyon Gorges
- Walk round Cordes-sur-Ciel, the 'pearl of the bastides', a hilltop gem with handsome Gothic residences
- Explore Le Sidobre's landscape of fantastic granite shapes and gravestone factories
- Stroll beside, or float upon, Europe's oldest functioning canal system, the Canal du Midi, now a UNESCO World Heritage Site

cassoulet – a rich stew of confit de canard, sausages and haricot beans

sanglier – wild boar from the Forêt de Grésigne

Chasselas – sweet white dessert grape of the Bas-Quercy

TOULOUSE

TOULOUSE, TARN-ET-GARONNE & TARN

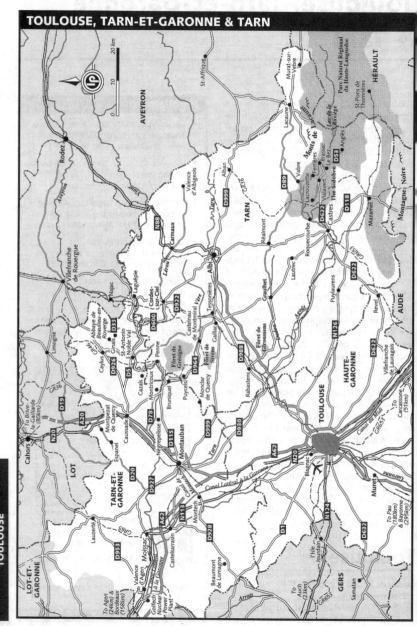

Haute-Garonne département – is the south-west's largest city. It's renowned for its high-tech industries, including some of Europe's most advanced aerospace facilities. Since the anti-Cathar movement of the 13th century this has also been a major centre of higher education, with a student population second in size only to Paris.

This sunny, go-getting city has some of the friendliest people you'll meet in France. The telephone book is full of Spanish names (descendants of refugees from the Spanish Civil War) and Toulousains seem proud of this ingredient in their collective civic personality, along with a large North African community. This, and the huge student population, provides a nice buzz – and an abundance of *bodegas* (Spanish-style wine bars), North African restaurants and laid-back cafes. Nationwide magazine polls identify Toulouse as most people's favourite city.

With no quarries nearby, all the older buildings in the centre were built of red brick. Many were smothered in stucco in the 19th century but it's gradually being stripped away, restoring the city's staid elegance, a certain monotony of colour, and its old nickname, *la ville rose* (the pink city).

History

The city's ancient birthplace is said to be the shallows just downstream of the river's broad left turn, an easy ford in ancient times. Known as Tolosa in Roman times, it was the Visigoth capital from AD 418 until it fell to the Merovingians in 508.

In 778 it became the seat of the counts of Toulouse, southern France's greatest feudal dynasty. Even then this was a tolerant city, but the counts' patronage of the Albigensian or Cathar heresy in the 12th and 13th centuries cost them their power base in the Languedoc (see the boxed text 'The Albigensian Crusade' in the Albi section later in this chapter). The Toulouse *parlement* (local court of law) ruled the Languedoc from 1420 until the 1789 Revolution.

During WWI the French government chose Toulouse as a centre for arms and aircraft manufacture. In the 1920s, Antoine de

Le Pastel

A number of Toulouse merchant families grew rich in the 16th century – as testified by the city's line-up of fine Renaissance *hôtels particuliers* (mansions) – from the trade in dyer's woad *(le pastel)*, a member of the mustard family whose leaves, wetted and fermented, produce a distinctive blue dye. Many of these merchants also rose to positions of power as *capitouls* or town councillors. The woad bubble burst after the Portuguese discovered indigo in India and the Spanish began farming it cheaply, with the help of slave labour, in Venezuela.

St-Exupéry – best known as the author of *Le Petit Prince* (The Little Prince) – and other daring pilots pioneered mail flights from Toulouse to north-western Africa, the south Atlantic and South America. The government built on this aeronautical base by making Toulouse the centre of the country's post-WWII aerospace industry.

Orientation

Toulouse's administrative heart is place du Capitole. Its human heart is probably place du Président Wilson (or just place Wilson), ringed with cafes and shops. Northwards from place du Capitole to the Basilique St-Sernin runs the student haunt of rue du Taur. To the south is the transport hub of place Esquirol.

The main bus station and Gare Matabiau, the train station, are across the Canal du Midi, about 1km north-east of place Wilson via allées Jean Jaurès, and the airport is 7km north-west of the city centre. Beneath the centre runs a one-line metro system. To get from the train station to the city centre, take the metro for two stops (direction Basso Cambo) to Capitole.

Toulouse has few pedestrian zones beyond place du Capitole, but some streets are *semi-piéton* (semi-pedestrian) – meaning that cars can drive through slowly, cannot park and must give way to pedestrians.

TOULOUSE

TOULOUSE

Canal du Midi

To A62
(2.5km)
Albi
(75km)
via A68

To
Cité
de

Espace
(4km) &
Castres
(71km)
via N126

Canal du Midi

Blvd-de-la-Gare

Boulevard d'Monplaisir

Port St-Étienne

Port-St-Sauveur

Avenue de Lyon

Boulevard Pierre Sémard

Boulevard de Bonrepos

Marengo SNCF

Allée Frédéric Mistral

Allées Forain
François-Verdier

Grand Rond

Jardin
des
Plantes

To
Carcassonne
(87km)
via A61

Place
Roquelaine

Rue Matabiau

Rue-St-Jérome

Allées Jean Jaurès

Boulevard de Strasbourg

Boulevard Lazare Carnot

Place
St-Jacques

Rue Ozenne

Allées Jules-Guesde

Rue Alfred
Duméril

To Université Paul CHR
de Rangueil (Hospital), 4km

Place
Occitane

Place
St-Georges

See Central Toulouse Map p256

Rue Matabiau

Boulevard
d'Arcole

Place du
Capitole

Rue-la-Fayette

Place St-
Wilson

Place de
la
Daurade

Place du
Salin

Place du
Parlement

Rue Feral

Rue de
Metz

Rue des Chalets

Boulevard d'Arcole

Place
St-Semin

Rue des Lois

Remparts

Quai-de-Tounis

Ave Honoré-Serres

Place
Anatole
France

Rue-Valade

Université
Sciences
Sociales

Place
St-Pierre

Rue
Pargaminières

Pont
Neuf

Pont de
l'Halle de
la
Tounis

Garonne

Pont
St-Michel

To Le Stadel
Toulousain (1km),
Airport (5km),
Auterive (35km),
Montauban (53km)
& Bordeaux (250km)
via A62

Police Headquarters (350m),
Camping de Rupé (4.5km),
& Agen (110km) via N20

Boulevard-Armand-Duportal

IR-Lascrosses

Rue-des-Amidonniers

Boulevard de la Marquette

R-du-Béarnais

Blvd-Maréchal-Leclerc

Quai-St-Pierre

Place
St-Cyprien

Place
Lafourguette

Pont
St-Pierre

Rue-Viguerie

Place
de la
République

Place
Lagane

Rue-Lascrosses

Rue-du-Pont-St-Cyprien

Rue de la République

Allées Charles-de-Fitte

Cours Dillon

To Barrio
Latino (500m),
Le Mandala (1km),
Stade Municipal (1km)

To CHR Purpan (2.7km),
Polycycles (2.7km) &
Samatan (50km)
via D632

Ave-Étienne Billères

Av-Paul-Séjourné

Pont des
Catalans

Place du
Ravelin

Rue de
Cugnaux

Rue Bonnat

Allées Charles-de-Fitte

To
Université
Le Mirail (3.2km)

To Barrio
Latino

Canal
Latéral
à la
Garonne

Canal du
Midi

Boulevard-de-l'Embouchure

Porte de l'Embouchure

Allées de Barcelone

Allée de Brienne

Allée Emile-Brouardel

Héracès

Garonne

Ramier de la Basacle

Boulevard Richard-Wagner

Boulevard-Jean-Brunhes

Rue-des-Fontaines

Rue-d'Antipoul

Rue-Bourrassol

Avenue de Grande-Bretagne

To Auch (77km)
via N124

To Pau (190km) &
Bayonne (295km)
via A64

PLACES TO STAY		PLACES TO EAT		OTHER
4	Inter Hôtel Icare	9	Why Not Café	2 Main Bus
7	Hôtel Anatole	10	Bar Basque	Station
	France	11	Bar San Pedro	3 Gare Matabiau
		12	Chez Tonton	5 Comité Régional
PLACES TO EAT		14	Galerie Municipale	du Tourisme
1	L'Image d'Afrique		du Château d'Eau	6 Buses for
13	Bistrot Irlandais	15	Semvat Ticket Kiosk	Navette Aéroport
		16	Killarney Bar	8 Laundrette

TOULOUSE

Information

Tourist Offices The city tourist office
(☎ 05 61 11 02 22, fax 05 61 22 03 63) is
in square Charles de Gaulle, in the 16th-
century Donjon du Capitole. It is open from
9 am to 6 pm Monday to Friday, 9 am to
12.30 pm and 2 to 6 pm on Saturday and
from 10 am to 12.30 pm and 2 to 5 pm on
Sunday. The rest of the year it's open from
9 am to 7 pm Monday to Saturday, and
10 am to 1 pm and 2 to 5 pm on Sunday.

If it's general Midi-Pyrénées information
you need, try the Comité Régional du Tourisme (☎ 05 61 13 55 55), 54 blvd de l'Embouchure. It is open from 9 am to 12.30 pm
and 2 to 5.30 pm Monday to Friday.

CRIJ The Centre Régional d'Information
Jeunesse for the Midi-Pyrénées région
(☎ 05 61 21 20 20), at 17 rue de Metz, has
a library full of information on work and
education, and can help you find events,
discounts and accommodation. Internet access is free and there is also a youth travel
agency. It's open from 10 am to 1 pm and 2
to 7 pm Monday to Saturday.

Money There are banks with exchange facilities and ATMs all over the city centre, including on place du Capitole, square Charles
de Gaulle and rue d'Alsace-Lorraine. A
handy one with good terms is Crédit Agricole at 3 place du Capitole, open from
8.15 am to 4.45 pm Monday to Friday. The
post office also exchanges foreign currency.

Post The main post office, opposite the
tourist office at 9 rue La Fayette, is open
from 8 am to 7 pm on weekdays and from
8 am until noon on Saturday.

Email & Internet Access Free Internet
access is available at the CRIJ. The main
post office was expected to have its own access point by early 2000. France Telecom
has several public access points to its own
server (Wanadoo), payable with a telecard,
including a kiosk on allées du Président
Roosevelt (24 hours); at 11 place du Capitole (7 am to 8 pm daily); and in its showroom at the corner of place Esquirol and rue

d'Alsace-Lorraine (10 am to 7 pm Monday
to Saturday). For more information on
Internet access in the region see Post &
Communication in the Facts for the Visitor
chapter.

Online time at Résomania cybercafe
(☎ 05 62 30 25 64, email resomania@
wanadoo.fr), 85 rue Pargaminières, costs
0.75FF per minute. It's open from 10 am to
at least midnight Monday to Saturday.

Travel Agencies A France-based student
travel agency is OTU (☎ 05 61 12 18 88) at
60 rue du Taur, open to 6.30 pm on weekdays. Voyages Wasteels (☎ 05 61 62 67 14),
1 blvd Bonrepos, is open until 7 pm Monday to Saturday. USIT Voyages has a
branch (☎ 05 61 11 52 42) at 5 rue des Lois
and another (☎ 05 61 99 38 47) at 16 rue
Pierre-Paul Riquet, both closed on Sunday.
The CRIJ (see earlier in this section) has its
own youth travel service.

Bookshops Toulouse has scores of bookshops, many concentrated west and north of
place du Capitole. Most are open on weekdays and Saturday. Two good places for
English-language books are The Bookshop
(☎ 05 61 22 99 92), 17 rue Lakanal, and Librairie Étrangère (☎ 05 61 21 67 21), 16 rue
des Lois. Just off place du Capitole at 50 rue
Gambetta, Ombres Blanches (☎ 05 61 21 44
94) specialises in travel guides and maps.

A fine place to sell books or browse second-hand volumes is Books & Mermaides
(☎ 05 61 12 14 29), 3 rue Mirepoix. Librairie Gibert Joseph (☎ 05 61 11 17 77), 3
rue du Taur and 2 bis rue des Lois, also buys
some books. There are other used-book
shops along rue du Taur; one specialising in
Occitania and Catharism is Librairie Occitania (☎ 05 61 21 49 00), 46 rue du Taur.

There are two kiosks selling internation-
al newspapers – on allées du Président
Roosevelt and on the north side of place
Esquirol.

Universities The city's three universities,
14 *grandes écoles* (higher education establishments) and other institutes have some
111,000 students. The Université des

TOULOUSE

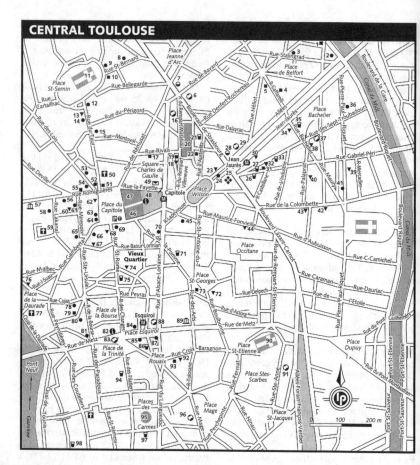

Sciences Sociales, headquartered at place Anatole France, brings a student atmosphere into the city centre. Some 5km away to the south-west is the Université de Toulouse Le Mirail (humanities) and equally far to the south-east is the Université Paul Sabatier (science and technology).

Cultural Centres Two cultural centres near the city centre are the Centre France Grande Bretagne, at La Maison de l'Europe (☎ 05 61 12 34 34), 21 place St-Sernin; and the Goethe Institut (☎ 05 61 23 08 34), 6 bis rue Clémence Isaure.

Laundry Self-service laundrettes near the city centre include those at 10 rue Stalingrad, 29 rue Pargaminières, 7 rue Mirepoix, 20 rue Cujas and 67 rue Pierre-Paul Riquet. All these are open from 7 am to 9 pm daily.

Toilets Public toilets are scarce around the city centre. A handy one is down the stairs to the underground car park, in the south-eastern corner of place du Capitole.

Medical Services Two *centres hospitaliers régionaux* (regional hospitals) are CHR Purpan (☎ 05 61 77 22 33), 4km west of the city

CENTRAL TOULOUSE

PLACES TO STAY
1 Hôtel La Chartreuse
4 Hôtel Beauséjour
5 Hôtel Splendid
10 Hôtel St-Sernin
17 Hôtel Albert 1er
19 Hôtel Majestic
22 Hôtel de France
31 Hôtel Castellane
51 Hôtel du Taur
55 Hôtel du Grand Balcon
73 Hôtel des Arts
79 Hôtel de la Bourse
93 Hôtel Croix-Baragnon

PLACES TO EAT
13 La Salade Gasconne
18 Bar Le Moderne
23 Octave
30 Pizzeria Vecchio
32 Restaurant L'Edelweiss
34 Shun
38 Restaurant L'Indochine
39 L'Alhambra
40 Restaurant Le Tajmahal
42 Restaurant Le Loutania
43 Restaurant Le St-Sylvain
44 Restaurant Saveur Bio
60 Au Gascon
62 Brasserie Le Capitoul
67 Restaurant Benjamin
68 Brasserie St-André
72 Bistrot Le Van Gogh
74 Les Caves de la
      Maréchale
76 Café des Artistes
92 Restaurant La Truffe du
      Quercy
95 Covered Food Market

OTHER
2 Voyages Wasteels
3 Laundrette
6 Canadian Consulate
7 Buses for Navette Aéroport;
      Semuat Kiosk
8 Cinéma ABC
9 Centre France Grande
      Bretagne; La Maison de
      l'Europe
11 Basilique St-Sernin
12 OTU
14 La Cinématheque de
      Toulouse
15 Occitania Bookshop
16 Dutch Consulate
20 Place Victor Hugo;
      Covered Market
21 L'Hugo Club
24 Newsagent; France Telecom
      Internet Kiosk
25 FNAC
26 La Strada
27 Bodega Bodega
28 Buses for Navette Aéroport;
      Air France Office
29 Tunisian Consulate
33 Bar-Restaurant Texxas
35 L'Opus
36 USIT Voyages
37 Algerian Consulate
41 Laundrette
45 Cinéma Utopia
46 Théâtre du Capitole
47 Capitole
48 Tourist Office
49 Main Post Office
50 Église Notre Dame du Taur
52 Gibert Joseph Bookshop

53 Étrangère Bookshop
54 USIT Voyages
56 Résomania
57 Réfectoire des Jacobins
58 The Bookshop
59 Église des Jacobins
61 Laundrette
63 France Telecom Internet
      Kiosk
64 Alliance Française; Octave;
      Semvat Point Contact
65 Books & Mermaides
66 Ombres Blanches
69 Crédit Agricole
70 Monoprix Superstore
71 Shanghai Express
75 L'Ubu
77 Église Notre Dame de la
      Daurade
78 Laundrette
80 Goethe Institut
81 Hôtel d'Assézat
82 Centre Régional
      d'Information Jeunesse
83 German Consulate
84 Newsagent Kiosk
85 Espace Transport Semvat;
      SNCF Information Office
86 Pub Les 2-G
87 France Telecom Showroom &
      Internet Kiosk
88 Italian Consulate
89 Musée des Augustins
90 Cathédrale St-Étienne
91 Spanish Consulate
94 Café-Brasserie Classico
96 Belgian Consulate
97 Pub-Disco B-Machine
98 La Tantina de Burgos

centre at place du Dr Baylac (take westbound bus No 14 from place Esquirol); and CHR Rangueil (☎ 05 61 32 25 33), 5.5km south of the centre on chemin du Vallon (take southbound bus No 2 from place Esquirol).

Emergency The police headquarters (☎ 05 61 12 77 77) are north of the city centre at 23 blvd de l'Embouchure. Toulouse also has a cadre of unarmed young men and women in blue jumpsuits and baseball caps, who walk round the city in twos and threes, apparently to deal with 'social' problems such as domestic arguments and unruly street people.

Place du Capitole

Pedestrianised 'place du Cap' is the city's main plaza, the past symbolised by an inlaid bronze cross of Languedoc and the present by a grid of blue 'runway lights'. On the ceiling of the arcades on the western side are 29 vivid serigraphs illustrating the city's history, by contemporary artist Raymond Moretti. Every Wednesday an open-air second-hand market fills the square, with smaller ones held on Tuesday and Saturday.

Along the entire eastern side runs Toulouse's city hall, the **Capitole**, a name deriving from the ancient city council (*capitol* in Occitan) whose eight councillors or

TOULOUSE

capitouls enjoyed considerable autonomy and prestige in the centuries after the Albigensian Crusade.

Completed in 1760, the brick and marble structure is a focus of civic pride. Under the same roof are the mayor's office and the **Théâtre du Capitole** (☎ 05 61 63 13 13), a prestigious opera venue. The interior, including the over-the-top, gilded **Salle des Illustres** (Hall of the Illustrious; 1898), can be visited on working days. Admission is free.

On the other side of the Capitole is the square's green alter ego, square Charles de Gaulle or Jardin du Capitole.

Vieux Quartier

The Old Quarter, hardly changed since the 18th century, is a web of narrow lanes and pocket-sized plazas – many with cafes spilling onto them and fountains dancing in the centre – south of place du Capitole and place Wilson.

Place Wilson appealingly combines the genteel and the weathered, both architectural and human. With buskers in summer, place St-Georges has some of the feel of a small-town square. Place de la Daurade is the city's 'beach' on the Garonne, peaceful and sun-drenched by day and romantic by night, looking out on the floodlit Pont Neuf.

Basilique St-Sernin

Architecturally speaking, St-Sernin Basilica is Toulouse's finest attraction – and at 115m long it's one of Europe's largest, most complete Romanesque buildings. This was an important stop on the way to Santiago de Compostela (whose own cathedral, begun at about the same time, is almost identical in design).

The chancel was built between 1075 and 1096 and the nave was added in the 12th century. It's topped by a magnificent eight-sided **tower** dating from the early 13th century. No significant changes have been made since then, save the 15th-century spire. Over the Porte Miègeville, the southern entrance to the nave, is a deeply carved tympanum depicting the Ascension, witnessed by 12 cringing disciples. Many of

the church's late 19th-century 'restorations' were de-restored in a complex 1970s effort.

Inside are ambulatory chapels full of gilded 17th-century reliquaries. The two-level **crypt**, rebuilt in the 13th and 14th centuries, contains several medieval tombs; the lower crypt is part of an older church, dating from 402. Directly above the crypt is the sculpted, mid-18th century **tomb of St-Sernin** (see the boxed text). The northern transept bears a **12th-century fresco** of Christ's Resurrection.

The basilica is open, free of charge, from 8.30 to 11.45 am and 2 to 5.45 pm Monday to Friday, and from 8.30 am to 12.30 pm and 2 to 7.30 pm on Saturday; in July and August it's open without a lunch break and from 9 am to 7.30 pm on Sunday.

The ambulatory chapels and crypt are open from 10 to 11.30 am and 2 to 5 pm daily (closed on Sunday morning); and from July to September they are open from 10 am (12.30 pm on Sunday) to 6 pm daily; admission costs 10FF (children aged under 15 free).

Église Notre Dame du Taur

Église Notre Dame du Taur, entered from opposite 21–23 rue du Taur, was built in Southern Gothic style in the 14th century, an additional honour for St Sernin. At the end of the nave are three chapels; the middle one contains a 16th-century Black Madonna known as Notre Dame du Rempart. The church can be visited from 8.30 am to noon and 2.30 to 7 pm daily.

Église des Jacobins

The Dominican or Jacobin order was founded by St Dominic in 1215 to preach Church doc-

St Sernin

Sernin, or Saturninus, was a local evangelist who annoyed the Romans with his teachings. He was martyred in 257 by being dragged behind a *taureau* (wild bull). This is the origin of the name of the Église Notre Dame du Taur, and rue du Taur.

trine to the Cathars. The church of the Jacobins, the order's mother church, was begun soon afterwards and completed in 1385.

Inside the imposing Gothic structure a single row of seven 22m-high columns – topped with fan vaulting that makes them look like gigantic palm trees – runs down the middle of the nave. The remains of **St Thomas Aquinas** (1225–74), the Italian theologian-philosopher and an early leader of the Dominican order, are interred below the modern, grey marble altar on the northern side. All that remains of the ancient monastery are the sacristy, the chapterhouse, a chapel decorated with 14th-century murals and the serene **cloister**.

The church is open from 10 am to 7 pm daily; admission is free to the church but costs 10FF to the cloister, and guided tours at 4.30 pm on Tuesday, Thursday and Friday cost an additional 10FF. After midday the sun through the lovely nave windows fills the place with a fiery light.

At 69 rue Pargaminières, around the corner from the church, is the **Réfectoire des Jacobins**, a 14th-century Dominican refectory which now serves as an art gallery (☎ 05 61 22 21 92). Admission to its changing exhibitions costs 10FF to 20FF.

Hôtel d'Assézat & Toulouse's Hôtels Particuliers

Toulouse boasts about 50 handsome hôtels particuliers – grand private mansions, mostly built in the 16th century by merchants grown rich on the trade in *le pastel* or dyer's woad (see the boxed text earlier in this chapter). Together they form a unique body of fine civil Renaissance architecture. Many have towers, a privilege granted only to *capitouls* (city councillors) of the time.

The Hôtel d'Assézat, 18 rue de Metz, is one of the finest, built in the 1550s for councillor Pierre Assézat, with Greek-style columns on its facade, elaborate doorway decoration and an elegant arcaded portico. It now houses the paintings, bronzes and *objets d'art* of the Fondation Bemberg (☎ 05 61 12 06 89), founded by Georges Bemberg, an Austrian collector. The collection is open from 10 am to 6 pm Tuesday to

Sunday (to 9 pm on Thursday). Admission costs 30FF (students 18FF), with guided tours (48FF) at 3.30 pm on weekdays and 2.30 and 4 pm at the weekend.

Musée des Augustins

The Musée des Augustins displays a rich collection of paintings and stone artefacts dating from Roman times to the late 19th century, including a fine collection of Romanesque sculpture. Among the stone carvings are religious statuary, capitals, sarcophagi, gargoyles, tombstones and inscriptions, some in Hebrew. The museum occupies an Augustinian monastery whose two fine **cloisters** date from the 14th century. The cloisters' medieval-style **gardens** are among the prettiest in southern France.

The museum (☎ 05 61 22 21 82), at 21 rue de Metz, is open from 10 am to 6 pm daily except Tuesday (to 9 pm on Wednesday, and to 10 pm from June to September). Admission costs 12FF (students free), or 20FF when there's a special exhibition.

Cathédrale St-Étienne

One of Toulouse's most striking churches, for its unnerving mishmash of styles (it took five centuries to complete), is the Cathedral of St Étienne. The nave, begun around 1100, is out of line with the vast choir, built in northern French Gothic style as part of an ambitious (and unfinished) late 13th-century plan to enlarge and realign the whole building; note the improvised Gothic vaulting linking the two sections.

The rose window facing the square dates from 1230, the organ case above the nave portal from four centuries later. The belfry itself has Romanesque foundations, a Gothic middle and a 16th-century top. The western portal was added about 1450, the northern portal not until 1929.

The cathedral, on place St-Étienne near the eastern end of rue de Metz, is open from 7.30 am to 7 pm daily.

Galerie Municipale du Château d'Eau

This municipal photography museum (☎ 05 61 77 09 40), founded in 1974, is

Toulouse's most visited museum, offering superb, thought-provoking exhibitions of works by the world's finest photographers, with a new show in one of the three galleries each month. It's in a 19th-century *château d'eau* (water-pumping station) at place Laganne and is open from 1 to 7 pm daily except Tuesday and holidays. Admission costs 15FF (students 10FF, children aged under 12 free). Its shop has a fine collection of postcards and posters.

The museum's documentation centre (photo archive) – the only one of its kind in France – is open from 1.30 to 6 pm on weekdays, and the first Saturday of each month, to anyone who buys a 100FF annual pass (students 60FF).

Cité de l'Espace

The amazing Space Park museum and planetarium complex (☎ 05 62 71 48 71), on ave Jean Gonord on the eastern outskirts, is marked by a full-size Ariane 5 rocket. The museum includes interactive exhibits and fascinating displays on satellites and future life aboard space stations.

It's open from 9.30 am to 7 pm daily from June to September (to 6 pm during the rest of the year) and admission costs 60FF (children 45FF). Take bus No 15 from allées Jean Jaurès to the end of the line, from where it's about 600m; bus Nos 78 and 79 from place Esquirol and southbound bus No 22 from rue d'Alsace-Lorraine pass somewhat further away, around place de l'Ormeau.

Aérospatiale

From Monday to Saturday, Aérospatiale runs 1½ hour tours (55FF, students 45FF, children aged under 8 free) of its huge Clément Ader facility – probably the world's most modern aircraft production unit, where Airbus A330s and A340s are assembled – on ave Jean Monnet in Colomiers, about 10km west of the city centre. For information and reservations, call ☎ 05 61 15 44 00 at least 10 days in advance; in July and August you can book through the tourist office. Bring along a passport or national ID card.

Canals

The city's many canalside paths are peaceful places to walk, run or cycle. Port de l'Embouchure is the juncture of the Canal du Midi (completed in 1681) to the Mediterranean, the Canal de Brienne (1776) which bypasses the river shallows below Pont St-Pierre, and the Canal Latéral à la Garonne (1856) to the Atlantic.

See the later Getting Around section about day trips on the Garonne and the canals. For more on the history of the canals and on self-navigated canal holidays see under Boat in the Getting Around chapter.

Language Courses

Alliance Française (☎ 05 61 23 41 24, fax 05 61 23 05 51, email infos@alliance-toulouse.org), upstairs at 9 place du Capitole, offers an array of French courses for foreigners; for more information refer to Courses in the Facts for the Visitor chapter.

Special Events

Toulouse's big annual events include the following:

June
Festival International de Théâtre d'Enfants
    Kids' theatre – in French, but does it matter?
Garonariége
    Boat races down the Ariége and Garonne to Toulouse.
July
Festival Garonne
    A riverside celebration of music, dance and theatre.
July & August
    Musique d'Été
    A festival of jazz, classical, choral and other music, at 9 pm on Tuesday and Thursday evenings in churches and at many other venues.
October
Jazz sur Son 31
    International jazz festival ('31' refers to the Haute-Garonne département).

Places to Stay

Since many of Toulouse's hotels cater for business people, rooms are easiest to find on Friday, Saturday and Sunday nights, and – surprisingly – throughout most of the July and August holiday period. Many mid-range places offer much better value for money than budget ones.

Places to Stay – Budget

Camping The three-star, year-round *Camping de Rupé* (☎ 05 61 70 07 35, 21 chemin du Pont du Rupé), 6km north-west of the train station, charges a reasonable 70FF *forfait* (fixed price deal covering two people). From place Jeanne d'Arc take bus No 59 to the Rupé stop; the last bus leaves at 7.25 pm.

Hostels Although Toulouse has no official youth hostel, there are several inexpensive *foyers de jeunes* (student dormitories), including at least nine for young women. The Centre International d'Accueil UNESCO (☎ 05 62 13 62 13) also operates five *centres* for foreign workers. Some student accommodation agencies may have spaces in the summer. The best place to ask about all of these is the CRIJ (for contact details see Information earlier in this chapter).

Hotels – Gare Matabiau & Allées Jean Jaurès Most cheap hotels near Gare Matabiau and the red-light district around place de Belfort are dirty, noisy and unpleasant. If you arrive by train, head towards allées Jean Jaurès or take the metro into town.

At *Hôtel Beauséjour* (☎ 05 61 62 77 59, 4 rue Caffarelli), singles/doubles start at 75/100FF and doubles with shower and toilet cost 150FF. Rates at *Hôtel Splendid* (☎ 05 61 62 43 02, fax 05 61 40 52 76, 13 rue Caffarelli) are similar. Hall showers cost about 10FF in both these places.

Hotels – City Centre You can't beat the location of the *Hôtel du Grand Balcon* (☎ 05 61 21 48 08, fax 05 61 21 59 98, 8 rue Romiguières), just off place du Capitole. This faded, genteel place is where aviator-author Antoine de St-Exupéry first stayed (in room No 32) between his 1920s flights, and the lobby is a veritable shrine to him. Spacious doubles are pretty good value at 130/150/185FF with toilet/bath/both; hall showers cost 11FF.

Hôtel des Arts (☎ 05 61 23 36 21, 1 bis rue Cantegril) has adequate doubles (some noisy) without/with shower and toilet for 125/175FF; hall showers cost 10. Doubles at *Hôtel Anatole France* (☎ 05 61 23 19 96, 46 place Anatole France) cost 115FF, or 140FF with shower and 185FF with shower and toilet.

Big, tatty doubles without/with shower and toilet cost 125/150FF at *Hôtel Majestic* (☎ 05 61 23 04 29, 9 bis rue du Rempart Villeneuve). If everything else is full, try the no-star *Hôtel de la Bourse* (☎ 05 61 21 55 86, 11 rue Clémence Isaure), where a room with toilet costs just 90FF and a double/twin with shower is 120/160FF.

Places to Stay – Mid-Range

Hotels – Gare Matabiau & Allées Jean Jaurès At the two-star *Inter Hôtel Icare* (☎ 05 61 63 66 55, fax 05 61 63 00 53, 11 blvd de Bonrepos), spacious, soundproofed singles/doubles start at 190/290FF. The family-run *Hôtel La Chartreuse* (☎ 05 61 62 93 39, fax 05 61 62 58 17, 4 bis blvd de Bonrepos) has small, clean double rooms with shower and toilet from 170FF.

Hôtel Castellane (☎ 05 61 62 18 82, fax 05 61 62 58 04, 17 rue Castellane), which is both friendly and surprisingly quiet for its location, offers doubles/twins with toilet and shower or bath for 280/320FF, family rooms, and 40FF off-street parking. The well-travelled owner speaks English. Breakfast costs 30FF.

Hotels – City Centre For good mid-range value in the city centre, try the peaceful *Hôtel Croix-Baragnon* (☎ 05 61 52 60 10, fax 05 61 52 08 60, 17 rue Croix Baragnon), where clean doubles/quads with toilet and shower cost 180/220FF. Breakfast costs 24FF.

Hôtel du Taur (☎ 05 61 21 17 54, 2 rue du Taur) has quiet, fairly spacious doubles with shower and toilet for 230FF; reception is upstairs. St-Exupéry stayed here too, perhaps to escape the noise at the Hôtel du Grand Balcon. Fully equipped, quiet doubles/triples cost 280/310FF at *Hôtel*

TOULOUSE

St-Sernin (☎ *05 61 21 73 08, fax 05 61 22 49 61, 2 rue St-Bernard*). Parking in the hotel garage is 40FF.

The area around place Victor Hugo abounds in two-star hotels. At the well-run *Hôtel de France* (☎ *05 61 21 88 24, fax 05 61 21 99 77, 5 rue d'Austerlitz and 4 rue Victor Hugo*), spotless, air-conditioned doubles with toilet and shower start at 195FF and quads with shower cost from 390FF. Rooms on the rue Victor Hugo side get disco noise at night. *Hôtel Albert 1er* (☎ *05 61 21 17 91, fax 05 61 21 09 64, 8 rue Rivals*) has comfortable doubles/twins with shower or bath starting at around 270/330FF.

Places to Eat

Toulouse has it all. You can get by on 50FF per meal, or go to town with superb regional cuisine at 200FF and up. Like the Spanish whose blood runs in their veins, Toulousains like to eat late and linger. See Meals of the Day in the Facts for the Visitor chapter for information on standard opening times.

Quick & Cheap Any number of unexceptional eateries around town offer lunch *menus* for 50FF to 60FF. Some of the best value for money can be found at the little lunch-only restaurants on the first floor of the covered market, Les Halles, Victor Hugo, where generous and delicious *plats du jour* cost about 60FF.

Pizzerias, *sandwicheries* and cafe-bars – most closed on Sunday – line the streets radiating north and south from place du Capitole. Try *La Salade Gasconne* (*75 rue du Taur*), serving scores of tasty salads from 40FF to 50FF, plus pasta and grills. The mom 'n' pop *Bar Le Moderne* (*5 rue du Rempart Villeneuve*) has lasagne and other 47FF lunch specials, and pop looks like Jimmy Stewart. *Brasserie Le Capitoul* (☎ *05 61 21 49 52, 11 place du Capitole*) serves unusual salads costing from 65FF, *moules frites* (mussels with chips; 55FF) and quiche (25FF) on a sunny terrace. It's open from 11 am to 10 pm (closed on Saturday).

Almost every square in the Vieux Quartier

has a cafe. When the weather is good, place St-Georges is wall-to-wall with tables and at night it's one of the liveliest outdoor spots in town. Two sun-drenched riverside places are *Café des Artistes* (☎ *05 61 12 06 00, 13 place de la Daurade*) and *Bar San Pedro* (☎ *05 61 12 29 95*) on place St-Pierre, with *menus* from 40FF and first-rate salads.

Octave (☎ *05 62 27 05 21, 11 allées du Président Roosevelt*) is a deluxe ice-cream parlour open until about 2 am daily; there's also an outlet at 9 place du Capitole. Avoid Breathalyzer tests after eating the Armagnac pruneaux or Grand Marnier flavours.

Restaurants – French Specialising in regional cuisine *Les Caves de la Maréchale* (☎ *05 61 23 89 88, 3 rue Jules Chalande*) is in the vaulted brick cellar of a pre-Revolution convent. Try the 56FF lunchtime *formule rapide*; lunch/dinner *menus* start at 85/135FF. It's closed on Sunday and for Monday lunch. Book ahead for dinner.

Restaurant Benjamin (☎ *05 61 22 92 66, 7 rue des Gestes*) serves excellent nouvelle cuisine in a setting that mixes classical with modern. Lunch/dinner *menus* start at 65/135FF. *Bistrot Le Van Gogh* (☎ *05 61 21 03 15, 21 place St-Georges*) offers regional specialities such as *cassoulet* (meat and bean casserole) and *parillade* (eight different kinds of fish), with lunch/dinner *menus* costing 65/120FF. Both places are open daily.

The 75FF and 95FF *menus* and main courses (35FF to 80FF) at the mellow *Brasserie St-André* (☎ *05 61 22 56 37, 39 rue St-Rome*) attract a young clientele, in an arched cellar that feels like being in a brick submarine. It's open from 7.45 pm to 7 or 7.30 am (closed on Sunday).

Restaurant La Truffe du Quercy (☎ *05 61 53 34 24, 17 rue Croix Baragnon*) serves regional specialities, including good lunch/dinner *menus* for 55/78FF; it's closed on Sunday. An excellent place for *canard*, *canard* and more duck is the intimate *Au Gascon* (☎ *05 61 21 67 16, 9 rue des Jacobins*), with generous lunch/dinner *menus* from 45/85FF. It's open daily.

Restaurant Le St-Sylvain (☎ 05 61 62 31 44, *17 rue de la Colombette*) presents imaginative variations on regional specialities (such as moussaka with venison and aubergine). The 58FF dinner *menu* makes a good introduction.

On the pricey side (dinner with wine for 200FF and up), but very good value in this range, is *Restaurant L'Edelweiss* (☎ 05 61 62 34 70, *19 rue Castellane*), with carefully prepared regional specialities and first-rate service. It's open from Tuesday to Saturday for lunch and dinner, and fills up quickly.

Restaurants – Vegetarian Offerings at *Restaurant Saveur Bio* (☎ 05 61 12 15 15, *22 rue Maurice Fonvieille*) include a 40FF lunchtime *assiette* (assorted plate), a 60FF buffet and three 85FF *menus*. It's open for lunch and dinner, except on Saturday evening and Sunday. *Restaurant Le Taj-mahal* (☎ 05 61 99 26 80, *24 rue Palaprat*) is a curry house, with some vegetarian offerings, for example the 80FF Specialité Thali. It's open evenings only.

Restaurants – Other At the elegantly designed Japanese restaurant *Shun* (☎ 05 61 99 39 20, *35 rue Bachelier*), lunch/dinner *menus* start at 80/145FF; it's closed for Sunday lunch and all day Monday. Nearby, *Restaurant L'Indochine* (☎ 05 61 62 17 46, *46 place Bachelier*) is open daily, offering 48FF and 67FF Chinese and Vietnamese *menus*, and unusually big portions.

A Senegalese-run restaurant, *L'Image d'Afrique* (☎ 05 61 58 48 10, *7 ave de Lyon*), is open evenings (closed on Sunday), with main dishes costing from 55FF to 75FF. Two North African restaurants south of allées Jean Jaurès are *L'Alhambra* (☎ 05 61 62 56 49, *58 rue Pierre-Paul Riquet*), open daily with filling lunch/dinner *menus* from 65/100FF that could easily feed two; and couscous specialist *Le Loutania* (☎ 05 61 62 83 24, *29 rue de la Colombette*), with *plats* (plates) costing from 50FF to 100FF and a 70FF lunch *menu*.

Bistrot Irlandais (☎ 05 61 42 12 12, *50 rue de la République*) serves lunch (*menus* from 43FF) and dinner (88FF) on weekdays only. *Pizzeria Vecchio* (☎ 05 61 62 96 26,

22 allées Jean Jaurès) is open daily for lunch and dinner; pizzas and pasta dishes start at around 35FF.

Self-Catering See the boxed text 'The Markets of Toulouse' under Shopping later in this section for a list of covered and open-air food markets; note that only one market operates on Monday. The *Monoprix* superstore at 39 rue d'Alsace-Lorraine is open until 9 pm daily, except Sunday.

Entertainment

For up-to-date information on Toulouse's vibrant cultural life, visit the tourist office or pick up one of the several weekly or monthly, French-language 'what's-on' guides sold at bigger newsagents; try the weekly *Toulouse Hebdo* (6FF).

Bars The city has enough *bars sympas* (bars with a pleasant ambience) to keep you busy for months. Most stay open until 2 am. They're scattered all over, although several cluster around riverside place St-Pierre: *Chez Tonton* (☎ 05 61 21 89 54, *16 place St-Pierre*) and Spanish-flavoured *Bar Basque* (☎ 05 61 21 55 64, *7 place St-Pierre*) are sports bars; around the corner is the *Why Not Café* (☎ 05 61 21 89 08, *5 rue Pargaminières*), with a beautiful terrace.

Two popular bodegas are *La Tantina de Burgos* (☎ 05 61 55 59 29, *27 ave de la Garonnette*) and *Bodega Bodega* (☎ 05 61 63 03 63, *1 rue Gabriel Péri*), both with live music at the weekend. Another place with live Latin music at weekends is *Barrio Latino* (☎ 05 61 59 00 58, *1 rue de la Digue*), south-west of the city centre (take bus No 12 or 52 from place Esquirol to Croix de Pierre). *Bar-Restaurant Texxas* (☎ 05 61 99 14 15, *26 rue Castellane*) serves up Tex-Mex food (chilli, tacos, Mexican and American wines) to south-of-the-border music, nightly from 7 pm.

Killarney Bar (☎ 05 62 26 52 04, *14 rue Alfred Duméril*), about 1.5km south of the city centre, has live Irish music on Saturday night. Take bus No 1 from blvd Lazare Carnot, or bus Nos 52, 53, 54, 56 or 62 from place Esquirol, to St-Michel.

In a more cerebral vein are *Café des Artistes* (☎ 05 61 12 06 00, *13 place de la Daurade*), an art-student hangout, and *Café-Brasserie Classico* (☎ 05 61 53 53 60, *37 rue des Filatiers*), with neoclassical decor, modern art and all kinds of music.

L'Opus (☎ 05 61 62 09 83, *24 rue Bachelier*) offers food until 1.30 am and dancing all night. Another dance-bar is *L'Hugo Club* (☎ 05 61 21 68 05, *18 place Victor Hugo*).

Discos & Clubs Toulouse has dozens of discos. Two hot ones near the centre, open until dawn, are *La Strada* (☎ 05 61 62 56 31, *4 rue Gabriel Péri*), closed on Sunday and Monday, and *L'Ubu* (☎ 05 61 23 26 75, *16 rue St-Rome*), closed on Sunday.

Gay Venues Toulouse is a very gay city – it ain't called *la ville rose* just for those pink bricks – with some of the best clubs this side of the Marais in Paris. Try the popular *Pub Les 2-G* (*rue des Tourneurs*), *Pub-Disco B-Machine* (☎ 05 61 55 57 59, *37 place des Carmes*), or *Shanghai Express* (☎ 05 61 23 37 80, *12 rue de la Pomme*).

Cinemas Two cinemas with nondubbed foreign films are the triplex *Cinéma Utopia* (☎ 05 61 21 22 11, *24 rue Montardy*), where tickets cost 35FF; and *Cinéma ABC* (☎ 05 61 29 81 00, *13 rue St-Bernard*) at 42FF (students 32FF). The ABC is closed for most of August. *La Cinémathèque de Toulouse* (☎ 05 62 30 25 35, *69 rue du Taur*) offers brief special shows (such as a week of Latin-American films) plus noon or 7 pm concerts of folk, jazz or whatever matches the films.

Spectator Sports

Toulouse's rugby league team, frequent national champions, is called Stade Toulousain or 'Le Stade', after the stadium (☎ 05 61 57 05 05) where they usually play, at 114 rue des Troènes, near the airport. Toulouse Football Club or TFC (pronounced *tè-fè-cé*), the city's first-division football team, plays at Stade Municipal (☎ 05 61 55 11 11), on allée Gabriel Biénès in Parc Toulousain, south of the city centre.

There have been no bullfights in Toulouse since 1976, when the city's top bullfight impresario received death threats.

Shopping

Toulouse's main shopping districts are along rue de la Pomme, place St-Georges, rue des Arts and place St-Étienne for fashionable boutiques; rue St-Rome, rue des Changes and rue des Filatiers for small, trendy shops full of clothes and curiosities; and rue d'Alsace-Lorraine for upmarket international brands.

Two giant department stores that close only on Sunday are FNAC (☎ 05 61 11 01

The Markets of Toulouse

The following covered food markets are open from 6 am to 1 pm (closed on Monday) selling meat, deli meats, fish, cheeses, wine and bread:

Place Victor Hugo The city's biggest covered market; on the first floor are several good-value little lunch restaurants (see Places to Eat).

Place des Carmes Includes lots of hawkers in adjacent rue des Filatiers.

Place St-Cyprien Across the river – a small market, but the best place to find fresh cep mushrooms and other seasonal items.

Blvd du Strasbourg The only Monday market, includes lots of pre-prepared food.

Toulouse also has several good open-air markets (but beware of pickpockets):

Place du Capitole A small food market from 6 am to 1 pm (closed on Monday); an organic produce market on Tuesday and Saturday from 6 am to 1 pm; and a huge flea market (including books) on Wednesday from 8 am to 6 pm.

Place St-Sernin A second-hand market from 6 am into the evening, Saturday and Sunday.

Place St-Georges A small affair with fruit, flowers and picnic veggies (closed on Monday).

Place St-Étienne Antiquarian book market, Saturday from 9 am to 6 pm.

01) at 16 allée Président Roosevelt, and Monoprix at 39 rue d'Alsace-Lorraine. FNAC is a good place to go for film, IGN topographic maps and concert tickets (the booking desk is around the corner on blvd Lazare Carnot).

See the boxed text 'The Markets of Toulouse' for a list of good covered and open-air food markets.

Getting There & Away

Air Toulouse's international airport (☎ 05 61 42 44 00) is about 7km north-west of the city centre in the suburb of Blagnac.

Air France and Air Liberté between them have nearly three dozen flights a day to Toulouse from Paris (mainly Orly). There are also daily or almost-daily flights from many other cities in France and Europe; see the Getting There & Away chapter for details.

Bus Toulouse's modern, efficient bus station (☎ 05 61 61 67 67) is near Gare Matabiau on blvd Pierre Sémard, about 1km north-east of the city centre. The information desk is open from 7 am to 8 pm Monday to Saturday.

Among destinations served by various bus lines from here, with multiple daily departures, are Agen (70FF), Albi (60FF, 1½ hours), Auch (60FF, 1½ hours), Castres (60FF, 1½ hours) and Montauban (40FF, 1¼ hours). Semvat's intercity Arc-en-Ciel buses, serving Haute-Garonne and nearby départements, also use this station.

Intercars (☎ 05 61 58 14 53) handles buses to southern and Central Europe. Brussels, Amsterdam, Morocco and parts of Spain are handled by Eurolines (☎ 05 61 26 40 04). For details of connections, see the Getting There & Away chapter.

Train Toulouse's train station, Gare Matabiau (☎ 08 36 35 35 35), is on blvd Pierre Sémard. The information office is open from 5.30 am to 10.30 pm daily (from 6 am to midnight Friday and Sunday). Ticket windows Nos 17 to 19 will exchange enough foreign currency to cover the cost of your ticket.

Regional destinations served by multiple

daily direct trains include Albi (63FF, 1¼ hours), Auch (71FF, 1¼ hours), Bayonne (193FF, 3¾ hours), Bordeaux (163FF, 2½ hours), Brive-la-Gaillarde (141FF, 2¼ hours), Cahors (86FF, 1¼ hours), Carcassonne (73FF, 50 minutes), Castres (72FF, 1¼ hours), Montauban (48FF, 30 minutes) and Pau (143FF, 2½ hours). The fare to Paris is 351FF by Corail (6½ hours, Gare d'Austerlitz) or 433FF by TGV (5½ hours, Gare Montparnasse). Special fares apply if you book at least eight days ahead – for example, Toulouse–Paris costs 275FF.

SNCF has a city centre information and ticketing office, open from 2 to 6 pm Monday to Friday, in Espace Transport Semvat (for details see Bus & Metro under Getting Around later in this section), 7 place Esquirol.

Car Among local or national firms are Century (☎ 05 61 30 03 11), ADA (☎ 05 61 48 55 55) and A2L (☎ 05 61 59 33 99); ADA also has an airport branch (☎ 05 61 30 00 33). Pricier multinational firms, all with airport branches, include Avis (☎ 05 61 63 71 71), Budget (☎ 05 61 63 18 18), Europcar (☎ 05 61 62 52 89) and Hertz (☎ 05 61 62 94 12).

Getting Around

To/From the Airport The Navette Aéroport bus service (☎ 05 34 60 64 00) links the city centre with the airport. Buses run about every 20 minutes from 5.20 am to 9 pm (every 30 minutes from 6 am at the weekend), and take about 20 minutes. Get on at the bus station, or near Jean Jaurès metro station, place Jeanne d'Arc or Compans Caffarelli on blvd Lascrosses. The adult/youth fare is 23/18FF (36/27FF return; tickets are valid for two months). A taxi from the airport will cost about 100FF.

Bus & Metro City buses, and the 15-station metro line, are run by Semvat (☎ 05 61 41 70 70). Most bus lines run until 8 or 9 pm daily. The seven *bus de nuit* (night bus) lines, all terminating at Gare Matabiau, run from 10 pm to just after midnight. Among the central metro stations, Marengo and Esquirol

TOULOUSE

are also major metro-bus interchanges. The metro logo is a white 'M' on a grey background.

The system's magnetic tickets can be used on both bus and metro. For travel in central Toulouse, a single *ticket rouge* (red ticket) costs 7.50FF and a carnet of 10 tickets is 62FF. Tickets are valid for 45 minutes after they've been time-stamped and can be used for up to three transfers. Multiday and multitrip tickets are available but are of marginal value to most visitors.

Single tickets are available from bus drivers. These and carnets are also available from *tabacs* (tobacconists); from machines at each metro station; from the bus stops on place Jeanne d'Arc and place Laganne; from Semvat kiosks at Marengo and Jean Jaurès metro stations and at 9 place du Capitole (6.30 am to 7.30 pm weekdays, 12.30 to 7 pm on Saturday, 4.30 to 10 pm on Sunday); and from the Espace Transport Semvat kiosk (weekdays 8.30 am to 6.30 pm, Saturday until 12.30 pm) at 7 place Esquirol. Route maps are also available from kiosks.

Car Parking is tight in the city centre. There's a huge car park beneath place du Capitole, and a multistorey car park above the covered market at place Victor Hugo. Parking meters cost about 10FF per hour.

Taxi There are 24-hour taxi stands at Gare Matabiau (☎ 05 61 21 00 72), place Wilson (☎ 05 61 21 55 46), place Esquirol (☎ 05 61 80 36 36), place des Carmes (☎ 05 61 52 29 33) and allées Jean Jaurès (☎ 05 61 52 22 22). A typical fare across town is about 50FF.

Bicycle Polycycles (☎ 05 61 49 11 22, 11–13 route de Bayonne) rents *vélos touts terrain* (VTTs; mountain bikes) for 120FF per day or touring bicycles for 180FF per day. It's open until 7.30 pm (closed on Sunday). Take westbound bus No 14 from place Esquirol to the end of the line.

Boat Several Toulouse operators do short passenger trips up and down the canals and/or the Garonne. They run year-round,

but in winter only when there are enough passengers. Baladines (☎ 05 61 32 84 84) does mostly river trips. Cap d'Ambre (☎ 05 61 71 45 95) runs along the Canal de Brienne and through the lock onto the Garonne, and back. Toulouse Crosières (☎ 05 65 30 74 47) concentrates on the Canal du Midi.

Tarn-et-Garonne

MONTAUBAN

postcode 82000 • pop 53,800 • elevation 80m
Montauban, préfecture of the Tarn-et-Garonne département, was founded in 1144 by Count Alphonse Jourdain of Toulouse who, legend says, was so charmed by the gleam of the leaves of its willow trees (*alba* in Occitan) that he named the place Mont Alba. The town (called Montauban-ville-Bourbon on some maps) was the prototype for what came to be known as *bastides* – fortified settlements on a trademark rectangular grid plan around a central arcaded square.

The town took a beating during the Albigensian Crusade, after which the Church put its stamp on the place by making it a bishopric in 1317. The Pont Vieux (old bridge) was built soon afterwards, to better link rebellious Toulouse with the rest of France.

Montauban was a Huguenot (French Protestant) stronghold during the Wars of Religion. It later held out against several sieges by Louis XIII but finally fell, on the heels of the 1628 capture of La Rochelle. After the Edict of Nantes was repealed by Louis XIV in 1685, the town's beleaguered Protestants suffered badly. Montauban's many classical townhouses date from the prosperous decades following the Catholic reconquest.

Orientation

Place Nationale, surrounded by arcaded 17th-century brick buildings, is the town's ancient heart. Today things are spread around outside this historic zone, with no real centre. The bus and train stations are across the Tarn around 1km west of place Nationale.

Information

The tourist office (☎ 05 63 63 60 60) on place Prax-Paris is open from 9 am to noon and 2 to 7 pm Monday to Saturday (also from 10 am to noon and 3 to 6 pm on Sunday in July and August). For general information on the Tarn-et-Garonne département, go to the Comité Départemental du Tourisme (☎ 05 63 66 04 42, fax 05 63 66 80 36) in the Hôtel des Intendants on place du Maréchal Foch.

A Bureau d'Information Jeunesse (BIJ; ☎ 05 63 66 32 12, fax 05 63 66 32 62, email rmontaub@crij.mipnet.fr), at Espace Jeunes on square Piquard, has information on temporary work, plus Internet access for 5FF per 15 minutes. It's open from 9 am to 6 pm on weekdays.

The main post office is at 4 blvd Midi-Pyrénées. The entrance to the Centre Hospitalier (☎ 05 63 92 82 82) is at 100 rue Léon Cladel. The police station (☎ 05 63 21 54 00) is at 50 blvd d'Alsace-Lorraine.

There's a self-service laundrette on rue de l'Hôtel de Ville.

Place Nationale

This not-quite-square square, all in red brick, is the heart of the old bastide. Two sides were destroyed by fire in 1614 and the others by another fire in 1649, although everything was rebuilt to the original plans. In the middle of the north side is a sundial with the inscription *una tibi* ('your time will come' in Occitan). In warm weather the place sprouts cafe tables and a daily market.

Musée Ingres

Many of the detailed, splendidly sensual portraits of the neoclassical painter Jean Auguste Dominique Ingres (1780–1867), a native of Montauban, are exhibited in the Musée Ingres (☎ 05 63 22 12 92), in a former bishop's palace at 19 rue de l'Hôtel de Ville. For more on Ingres, see Arts in the Facts about South-West France chapter.

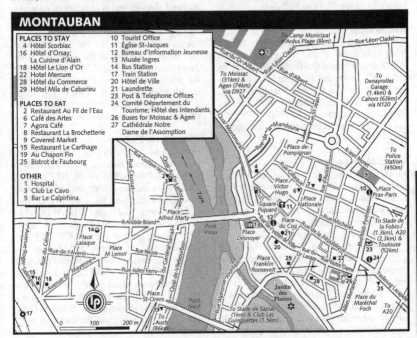

euro currency converter 10FF = €1.52

The museum – also home to many sculptures by another famous Montalbanais, Antoine Bourdelle – is open from 10 am to noon and 2 to 6 pm, (closed on Sunday morning and Monday); and from 9.30 am to noon and 1.30 to 6 pm daily in July and August. Admission costs 20FF (children, students and seniors free).

Churches

The 18th-century **Cathédrale Notre Dame de l'Assomption** on place Franklin Roosevelt contains Ingres' 1824 masterpiece *Le Vœu de Louis XIII*, in which the king pledges France to the Virgin. The building's other attraction is its boastful classical exterior, though this has been swathed in scaffolding for years.

Up the hill from the Pont Vieux is **Église St-Jacques**, begun in 1230 with revenue from, among other things, fines levied on citizens thought to be dressed too finely. Its hexagonal belfry still bears cannonball marks from the Wars of Religion.

Mansions

Among elegant hôtels particuliers dating from after the Catholic resurgence are the **Hôtel des Intendants**, former mansion of the king's *intendant* or governor, and now the préfecture, on place du Maréchal Foch; the **Hôtel Mila de Cabarieu** at 24 rue des Carmes, redecorated in the 1770s by Ingres' father; and the **Hôtel Scorbiac** on square Bourjade.

Special Events

Alors Chante is a festival of local traditional songs, held during the week before Easter. Montauban's biggest annual show is **Jazz à Montauban**, in the second half of July. Tickets, available from the tourist office or BIJ, cost from 100FF to 200FF.

Quatre-cent Coups (400 Blows) is a weekend street festival with parades, rides, music and more. It is held at the end of September, though the date is only decided at the last minute. Local lore says that during a siege in 1621 Louis XIII consulted a Spanish fortune-teller who told him to set up 400 cannons and fire them at the town all at once.

It didn't work, and this is, if you like, a celebration of the town's independent spirit.

Montauban has an ancient royal charter for four annual **fairs**, which take over the town centre on 19 March, 26 July, 13 October and 20 December.

Places to Stay

The nearest camp site is the riverside **Camp Municipal d'Ardus Plage** (☎ 05 63 31 32 29, fax 05 63 31 36 07), 8km to the north at Lamothe-Capdeville, open July and August only.

The old **Hôtel du Commerce** (☎ 05 63 66 31 32, fax 05 63 03 18 46, 9 place Franklin Roosevelt) is central and cheap: 130FF for a double or upwards of 165FF with toilet and shower. It also offers a very generous 30FF buffet breakfast. At **Hôtel Le Lion d'Or** (☎ 05 63 20 04 04, fax 05 63 66 77 39, 22 ave de Mayenne), doubles with shower start at 280FF. Nearby is **Hôtel d'Orsay** (☎ 05 63 66 06 66, fax 05 63 66 19 39, ave Roger Salengro), with comfortable doubles with toilet and shower for 250FF to 350FF, and a good restaurant (see Places to Eat). At the time of research the old Hôtel du Midi was being renovated as the three-star **Hôtel Mercure** (☎ 05 63 63 17 23, fax 05 63 66 43 66, 12 rue Notre Dame), with fully equipped doubles in the 400FF-plus range.

The tourist office can recommend several *chambres d'hôte* (B&Bs) in the area.

Places to Eat

Probably Montauban's best value for money is the 64FF lunch *menu* at smokey **Bistrot de Faubourg** (☎ 05 63 63 49 89, 111 Faubourg Lacapelle), and the dessert list will melt your heart. Another place for good French food is **Restaurant Au Fil de l'Eau** (☎ 05 63 66 11 85, 14 quai du Dr Lafforgue), where lunch/dinner *menus* start at 89/125FF; it's closed on Sunday evening and Monday.

The otherwise pricey Logis de France *Au Chapon Fin* (☎ 05 63 63 12 10, 1 place St-Orens) offers a good 85FF *menu rapide* at lunch. Certainly the best hotel restaurant is **La Cuisine d'Alain** in the Hôtel d'Orsay (see Places to Stay), but the cheapest *menu* costs 180FF.

Place Nationale has several brasseries, including the lunch-only *Café des Artes* (☎ 05 63 20 20 90) at No 4, and the *Agora Café* (☎ 05 63 63 05 74) at No 9, closed on Sunday. The modest *Restaurant La Brochetterie* (☎ 05 63 91 20 14, 12 rue d'Auriol) has grills, salads and a 45FF *plat du jour* (closed on Sunday and Monday).

If you've overdosed on French cuisine, try the Tunisian *Restaurant Le Carthage* (☎ 05 63 20 20 62, 21 ave Roger Salengro), with salads, soups, grilled meats and a 55FF *menu*. If you're self-catering, there's an open-air *farmers market* every Saturday in place Prax-Paris, and a smaller one daily in place Nationale.

Entertainment
Salsa rules at *Bar Le Caïpirhina* (☎ 05 63 91 34 21, 8 quai Montmurat), open until 5 am on Thursday, Friday and Saturday night. The closest disco to the town centre is the rock *Club Le Cavo* (☎ 05 63 63 26 69, 12 quai du Dr Lafforgue). Farther to the south is the retro *Club Les Guinguettes* (☎ 05 63 91 47 46, 993 rue de l'Abbaye, Sapiac).

Spectator Sports
Rugby matches are held at Stade de Sapiac, 1km south of the centre on rue Léo Lagrange; for match information call ☎ 05 63 66 28 18. The main football venue is Stade de la Fobio (☎ 05 63 66 36 90), rue du Général d'Amade.

Getting There & Away
Bus Multiple daily leave daily for Toulouse (40FF), Albi (70FF) and Auch – including on Sunday – from the bus station on place Lalaque, 350m north-east of the train station. Buses to Moissac and Agen (2 hours) buses stop at place Maréchal Foch three times daily except Sunday. Two or three SCNF buses run to Albi (61FF, 1¼ hours) from the train station, daily except Saturday.

Train The information office (☎ 05 63 35 35 35) at the train station is open from 8 am to 8 pm Monday to Saturday. Multiple daily services include Toulouse (48FF, 30 min-

utes), Agen (60FF, 45 minutes) Moissac (30FF, 20 minutes), and Montauban (54FF; 45 minutes).

Getting Around
Bus Local buses of Transports Montalbanais (☎ 05 63 63 52 52) run from about 7 am to 8 pm Monday to Saturday. Tickets, available from the driver, cost 5.50FF. Bus No 3 connects the train and bus stations with blvd Midi-Pyrénées two to four times an hour.

Bicycle Denayrolles Garage (☎ 05 63 03 62 02), north-east of the town centre at 878 ave Jean Moulin, rents bikes, including VTTs.

MOISSAC
postcode 82200 • pop 12,000 • elevation 2m
Moissac was a major stop for pilgrims on the way to Santiago de Compostela, and is today a major stop for connoisseurs of the Romanesque. Here in this quiet artists' colony is France's most beautiful ensemble of Romanesque art and the oldest surviving collection of carved Romanesque capitals anywhere. Here also is a major marketplace for the glorious fruit of the Bas-Quercy, most famously a sweet white dessert grape called Golden Chasselas, with its own *appellation contrôlée* (a system of strict definition and control of quality wines and other spirits).

Day-trip access from Montauban, Agen and Toulouse couldn't be easier, by car, train, bus, canal or even on foot: the GR65, which follows one ancient route to Compostela, runs right through the town.

South-West France's only nuclear power station – at Golfech, about 20km west of Moissac – takes cooling water from the Garonne and produces towers of steam visible for miles. Electricité de France will give you a tour of the place; call ☎ 05 63 29 39 06.

Orientation & Information
Moissac sits on the northern bank of the Tarn a few kilometres from where it empties into the Garonne. The Canal Latéral à la Garonne runs picturesquely alongside.

The tourist office (☎ 05 63 04 01 85,

fax 05 63 04 27 10), place Durand de Bredon, is a three-minute walk from the intercity bus stop (called Tribunal), west through the place des Récollets market and north up rue de la République; or a five-minute walk north-east from the train station along ave Pierre Chabrié. The office is open from 9 am to noon and 2 to 5 pm daily (to 6 pm mid-March to mid-October; to 7 pm in July and August).

Abbaye St-Pierre

A Benedictine monastery here was on the skids when St Odilon, abbot of Cluny, took it under his wing in the early 11th century. Under Durand de Bredon and successive abbots it was reborn – with a new church in 1063 and cloister in 1100 – as one of southern France's most influential monasteries, spiritually and artistically.

It has taken a beating over the centuries – besieged during the Albigensian Crusade, occupied by the English, trashed in the Wars of Religion, nationalised and defaced during the Revolution. In 1856, already designated an historic monument, it was nearly demolished to make way for the Bordeaux–Sète railway. Today TGVs thunder past just beyond the cloister wall and everything rattles; what the railway line didn't wreck initially, it will surely shake to pieces eventually.

The church's **south portal**, completed around 1130, is a panorama of biblical stories carved in stone, with little moral tales enacted around the edges. Above the door is an extraordinary **tympanum** depicting St John's Vision of the Apocalypse, with Christ surrounded by symbols of the four apostles, two angels and 24 awestruck elders. After this the interior is a letdown, a muddle of Romanesque stone and Gothic brick, the latter from its reconstruction after the Hundred Years' War.

What you mustn't miss is the **cloister**, with 116 delicate marble columns topped by robust, deeply carved capitals, every one different and each a little masterpiece of foliage, earthy figures or biblical scenes. The Revolution's toll is sickening, with nearly every face smashed.

The cloister is entered through the tourist office and has the same opening hours. The tourist office will show you a free video (available in English), and a detailed visitor's guide is on sale. A single 30FF ticket admits you to the cloister, a museum of folk art and furnishings in the nearby former abbot's residence, and a picture library containing replicas of the monastery's beautiful illuminated manuscripts.

Moissac Town

Take a 10-minute stroll south past the cafes on rue de la République to the market square, place des Récollets, and via rue Jean Moura to the canal. Head west along the canal to the Pont St-Jacques, one of France's last remaining swivel bridges. A 15-minute walk in the other direction will take you to an aqueduct which vaults the canal right over the river.

Moissac has a large community of artists, and in the lanes south of the abbey are many small workshops. The tourist office can tell you more about them.

Special Events

The **Fête des Arts**, a street festival featuring the work of regional artists, takes over the streets in late April. Moissac's biggest bash is the **Grande Fête de Pentecôte**, on the seventh weekend after Easter, with street and boat parades, music, fairs and food. The **Fête des Fruits et des Légumes** celebrates the region's fine produce, on the third weekend in September of odd-numbered years.

Places to Stay & Eat

The riverside municipal camp site *Île du Bidounet* (☎ 05 63 32 52 52, fax 05 63 04 27 10), 2km south of the town centre on the N113, charges 20/20FF per person/site and has bungalows, canoe rental and kids' activities. It's open from April to September.

Hôtel-Restaurant Luxembourg (☎ 05 63 04 00 27, fax 05 63 04 19 73, ave Pierre Chabrié), on the way to the train station, is good value with doubles costing between 150FF and 230FF and a range of local specialities (*menus* from 60FF). The Logis de

France **Le Chapon Fin** (☎ 05 63 04 04 22, fax 05 63 04 58 44, 3 place des Récollets) has doubles costing from 160FF to 310FF and **menus** from 95FF. The tourist office can recommend nearby **chambres d'hôte** and **gîtes d'étape** (hikers' dormitories).

Place Roger Delthil and rue de la République are full of little **restaurants** and summertime **cafes**. At place des Récollets is a small indoor **market** selling cheese, bread and the region's superb fruit (daily except Monday) and a big outdoor food and clothes market (on Saturday and Sunday mornings).

Getting There & Away

Moissac is right on the Toulouse–Agen N113. There is parking just behind the tourist office and more spaces at place des Récollets.

By train, Moissac station (☎ 05 63 04 01 61) is 20 minutes north-west of Montauban (30FF), with three useful departures by 8.15 am and another after lunch (and return departures at 1 and 6.29 pm). From Agen (41FF) it's 30 minutes, with four departures by midday (return train at 2 pm, with two others after 7 pm). Bikes can be taken on some of these services.

The only useful bus departure to Moissac from Montauban (25FF, one hour) is from place Maréchal Foch at 11.50 am. To get there from Agen (32FF, 1½ hours) you'd have to take the 6.40 am bus leaving from the train station. There are return buses to each at 5 pm.

Getting Around

Moissac Navigation Plaisance (☎ 05 63 04 48 28, fax 05 63 04 26 70), quai Charles de Gaulle, runs two-hour canal cruises for 60FF (kids 35FF), plus longer trips with meals. Another operator is Rosa-Croisières (☎ 05 61 51 03 59).

CAYLUS

postcode 82160 • pop 1300 • elevation 600m

With its Gothic market hall in an arcaded square, Caylus would be a bastide if the streets were more perpendicular. But this town, in a cirque beside the Bonnette, a trib-

utary of the Aveyron, has some of the bastides' appeal and importance. Historically Caylus, and Montpezat de Quercy to the west, belong more to Quercy (see the Lot & Lot-et-Garonne chapter) than to Tarn.

In 1176 the Seigneur de Montpezat acquired Caylus from the count of Toulouse, built a castle and promptly lost it in the Albigensian Crusade. The new overlord, Alphonse de Poitiers, third son of Louis VIII, fortified the town massively; nevertheless it fell to the English in 1362 and was sacked by the Huguenots in 1562. The walls were torn down in the 18th century.

Orientation & Information

The good tourist office (☎/fax 05 63 67 00 28) on rue Droite is open from 10 am to noon and 2 to 4 pm from April to October (9 am to noon and 2 to 7 pm in July and August) but only on Tuesday, Wednesday and Saturday during the rest of the year. West up rue Droite is the market square, place du Marché. Market days are Tuesday (all day, food and second-hand goods) and Saturday morning.

Town Centre

Medieval houses line rue Droite and its extension, rue du Long. Spookiest of the lot is the 13th-century Maison des Loups, opposite the tourist office, bristling with wolf gargoyles and reliefs. Beside the tourist office is the 14th-century **Église St-Jean Baptiste**, with a striking crucifixion carved from an elm tree by the Polish sculptor Zadkine in 1954.

The basin in the ledge around the 14th-century **covered market** was a grain measure – an indication of the importance of this market. Dominating all, on a rise just south of the market, is the **Ancien Château Royal**.

Abbaye de Beaulieu-en-Rouerge

In truth, many people who stop here are on the way to this abbey in a wooded vale at Ginals, about 10km south-east of Caylus via the D19 and D20. Founded in 1144, this rather inaustere Cistercian abbey was trashed in the Wars of Religion, rebuilt in

TARN-ET-GARONNE

the 17th century and converted into barns during the Revolution.

Bought by private owners in 1963, it was restored and donated to the state, and subsequently opened as a centre for contemporary art (☎ 05 63 24 50 10, fax 05 63 24 50 14), open from 10 am to noon and 2 to 6 pm daily except Tuesday (daily in July and August). The serene Gothic church has a fine rose window.

The only way to get here is by car, bicycle or on foot.

Places to Stay

Camping La Bonnette (*☎/fax 05 63 65 70 20*), 750m south of the town centre, charges 17FF per adult and 17/26FF per car plus tent/caravan. It's open from May to September. With the GR46 running through it, Caylus also has its fair share of *chambres d'hôtes* and *gîtes* (the tourist office has details – see Orientation & Information).

The Logis de France *Hôtel-Restaurant La Renaissance* (*☎ 05 63 67 07 26, fax 05 63 24 03 57, ave du Père Huc*) offers comfortable doubles with toilet and shower/bath for 220/240FF, and good Quercy cuisine with *menus* costing from 65FF. South of the town centre on the road to Beaulieu, the *Hôtel-Restaurant de la Vallée* (*☎ 05 63 67 06 80, fax 05 63 24 03 24*) has rooms starting at 150FF.

Getting There & Away

Caylus is 43km north-east of Montauban via the N20 and D926. Three buses leave from Montauban each afternoon except Sunday (one to 1½ hours) and return in the morning, so you'd have to stay the night. There are additional buses from Caussade, where frequent Toulouse–Montauban–Paris trains stop.

The closest bicycle rental is by one Mme Brousses (☎ 05 63 64 92 55) in Puylaroque, 14km west on the D20.

MONTPEZAT DE QUERCY

postcode 82270 • pop 1500 • elevation 265m

This charming village 35km north of Montauban is small enough to see in half an hour. The lanes of the medieval centre, full of half-timbered houses, wind down to the 14th-century Collégiale St-Martin church, with some gorgeous 16th-century tapestries – hung where they were made to hang, behind the altar.

Vignerons du Quercy (☎ 05 63 02 03 50), 300m north-west on the N20, offers a taste of the local Coteaux de Quercy *vin de pays* (country wine) on weekdays. If you're here in mid-May you can join the four-day Ascension Day festivities, culminating in the Fête de la Vigne et du Vin, with music, grilled sausages and free wine tasting.

Orientation & Information

The enthusiastic tourist office (☎ 05 63 02 05 55), on blvd des Fossés outside the gateway to the old town, is open from 10 am to 1 pm and 2 to 7 pm, daily except Monday (and except alternate Saturdays/Sundays in May and alternate Fridays/Saturdays in June and September).

Places to Stay & Eat

The *Parc des Loisirs* (*☎/fax 05 63 02 07 08*), 900m north-east of the village off the D20, has camping for 65FF forfait, gîtes from 550FF per week, plus a pool and sports facilities. The alternatives are two chambres d'hôtes: *Chambres de Monsieur Courpet* (*☎ 05 63 02 06 37*), where singles/doubles start at 130/165FF including breakfast; and *Chambres le Barry* (*☎ 05 63 66 04 42*) charging 270/325FF, with a pool (and meals from 110FF).

The only restaurant is near the N20 junction, 3km north of the village: *Auberge le Pré de Montpezat* (*☎ 05 63 02 07 87*), with good weekday *menus* from 75FF. The *Ferme Auberge de Coutié* (*☎ 05 63 67 73 51*), 9km south-west on the D20 near Espanel, serves a delicious 90FF *menu campagnard* (country meal), but book ahead.

Getting There & Away

Cahors–Montauban trains stop around six times daily at Montpezat station, 5km north-east of the village. If you want a taxi, get off at Caussade, 10km away. A daily Montauban–Cahors SNCF bus stops on the N20, 3km north of Montpezat.

GORGES OF THE AVEYRON

In its lower reaches the Aveyron, tributary to the Tarn, has cut a gorge through the limestone plateau along the boundary between the Tarn and Tarn-et-Garonne départements, snaking back and forth between them. Pretty medieval towns dot the landscape, perched on their own hills or at the edges of the gorge. The GR36 and GR46 run north to south.

By car or bicycle, the area is equally accessible from Montauban (by the D115, running right along the Aveyron) and from Albi (on the D600 via Cordes-sur-Ciel). Few buses reach the area, but the Albi or Montauban tourist office can help you book a mini-bus or taxi.

Activities

This is the kingdom of the walker, cyclist, climber, caver and boater. Floating down the Aveyron costs about 150FF per half-day in a two-person canoe or 100FF in a one-person kayak. You can rent a VTT for around 100FF per day at many places. Following are some major outdoor-adventure outfits:

Association pour l'Animation des Gorges de l'Aveyron et des Causses (AAGAC)
(☎ 05 63 65 83 26) Laguépie. Canoes and kayak trips.
Aventure 82
(☎ 05 63 24 11 58, email r82aven@aol.com) place de la Porte Haute, Montricoux. VTT, canoe and kayak, climbing, caving and hiking trips.
Découverte
(☎ 05 63 68 22 46) 15 blvd des Thermes, St-Antonin-Noble-Val. VTT, canoe, kayak, climbing, caving and hiking trips.
Marc de Baudouin
(☎ 05 63 67 25 00) Étape du Château, promenade du Ravelais, Bruniquel. VTT trips.
Nature et Loisirs
(☎ 05 63 30 66 24) 16 blvd de la Condamine, St-Antonin-Noble-Val. Canoe and kayak trips.
Planète Grimpe
(☎ 05 63 30 66 66) St-Antonin-Noble-Val. Climbing and caving trips.
Variation
(☎ 05 63 68 25 25) La Plage, St-Antonin-Noble-Val. Canoe, kayak, climbing and caving trips.

Almost every tourist office has a list of local places offering horse riding. Topoguides and IGN maps are to be found in even the smallest newsagents.

Montricoux

postcode 82800 • pop 800 • elevation 125m
Here the Aveyron gorge begins in earnest. Montricoux is a small, pretty town with many elegant 15th- and 16th-century **half-timbered houses**, a late 13th-century church with a 16th-century belfry, and fragments of ancient **ramparts**.

In the town's one chateau is the **Musée Marcel Lenoir** (☎ 05 63 67 26 48), dedicated to a local artist (1872–1931) who made good in Paris. There's a fresco by him in the church.

Montricoux's market day is Friday.

Places to Stay & Eat The riverside *Camping Municipal Lalande* (☎ 05 63 67 27 66), about 600m north-west on the D78, charges 10/16FF per adult/tent, and rents VTTs. *Camping Le Midi-Vert* (☎ 05 63 67 20 85) charges 50FF forfait or 25FF for one person with a tent. Both camp sites are open only in July and August.

Aventure 82 (see Activities earlier in this section) has a plain *gîte d'étape* for its groups and – subject to space – anyone else who turns up. Bunk beds cost 54FF and meals are either by arrangement or you can use the kitchen. Call ahead: it fills up in summer. It's 150m north-east of place de la Mairie.

Across the river is *Le Relais du Postillon* (☎ 05 63 67 23 58), with a few rooms for 100/120FF without/with shower, and very good *menus* from 90FF.

Bruniquel

postcode 82800 • pop 450 • elevation 130m
This snug, cobbled village, perched atop a sheer 100m drop to the river, is the stuff of legends. One says it was founded in the 6th century by Brunehaut, queen of the Visigoths, though its chateau dates from the 12th century. It's full of 15th- and 16th-century houses and still has two of its seven medieval gates.

TARN-ET-GARONNE

Orientation & Information Park below the village and walk up. Below the entrance, bear right past the church for the post office and tourist office (☎ 05 63 67 29 84), stocked with topographic maps and pamphlets on regional hiking and biking trails.

Les Châteaux de Bruniquel Why plural? In around 1500 the property was split between two branches of the family and *le château jeune* (the young castle) was built. The place is now a hotchpotch of styles from the 13th to the 19th century. You can snoop around the original keep and the Gothic Salle des Chevaliers (Knight's Room) yourself for 15FF, or take a 20FF tour.

The complex (☎ 05 63 67 27 67) is open from 2 to 6 pm on Saturday and between 10 am to 12.30 pm and 2 to 6 pm on Sunday from Easter to April; 10 am to 12.30 pm and 2 to 6 pm at weekends during May; between 2 and 6 pm daily in June and September (10 am to 12.30 pm and 2 to 6 pm on Sunday); from 10 am to 7 pm daily during July and August; and 10 am to 12.30 pm and 2 to 6 pm October and November. It's closed from December to Easter.

Maison des Comtes Payrol This 13th-century mansion, severe outside and richly Gothic and Renaissance inside (including original murals), houses a museum (☎ 05 63 67 26 42) about Bruniquel and the Aveyron Valley. It's open from 10 am to noon and 2 to 5 pm, and daily from April to October (weekends only in March, to 7 pm in July and August and to 6 pm in September and October). Admission costs 15FF.

Places to Stay Down by the river, *Camping Le Payssel* (☎ 05 63 67 25 95) is open from June to September and charges 14/16/9FF per adult/tent/car.

Marc de Baudouin (see Activities earlier in this section) runs a chambre-d'hôte called *Étape du Château* (☎/fax 05 63 67 26 16), just beyond the tourist office, where a double with breakfast costs 240FF and dinner, by arrangement, costs 90FF.

Penne
This narrow, unrestored village perched on a boat-shaped ridge is topped at one end by the impossible, teetering ruins of a castle dating back to at least to the 13th century. The villagers of that time, loyal to Toulouse, took a thrashing in the Albigensian Crusade.

There is a decidedly dangerous but well-worn path up to the ruins, with sheer drops on both sides and no guard-rails of any sort.

A small tourist office (☎ 05 63 56 14 80) is open from 10 am to noon and 3 to 7 pm during July and August (until 5 pm from Easter to October; closed for the rest of the year).

Bar-Restaurant La Terrasse (☎ 05 63 56 35 03) at the eastern end of the village stumps up a very hearty 65FF *menu du jour*.

Note that Penne actually falls under the administrative powers of the Tarn département.

St-Antonin Noble Val
postcode 82140 • pop 2000 • elevation 130m
This flinty old town boasts France's oldest civic building and a splendidly unrestored medieval centre. A Cathar town, it was captured by Simon de Montfort in 1212, and was occupied by the English in the Hundred Years' War. Louis XIII took it in 1622 after his siege of Montauban flopped (see Special Events under Montauban earlier in this chapter).

Orientation & Information The town sits on the northern bank of the Aveyron, fronted by blvd des Thermes.

The mayor's office and tourist office are in a former convent, two blocks from the bridge, up rue du Pont de l'Aveyron. The tourist office (☎ 05 63 30 63 47, fax 05 63 30 66 33) is open from 9.30 am to 12.30 pm and 2 to 6.30 pm daily in July and August, and afternoons only during the rest of the year.

Banks include Caisse d'Épargne on place de la Mairie and Crédit Agricole on ave Paul Benet. From the tourist office the ancient marketplace, place de la Halle, is one block east and one block north.

North out of place de la Halle, on rue de la Pélisserie, is an English bookshop called... The English Bookshop.

St-Antonin's market day (selling food and second-hand goods) is on Sunday. The town also hosts a district fair on the third Wednesday of each month.

Things to See & Do The handsome early 12th-century **Romanesque mansion** on place de la Halle became the town hall in 1313. The 19th-century architect-restorer Viollet-le-Duc mutilated it with its present curious tower. Today it houses the **Musée du Vieux St-Antonin** (☎ 05 63 30 63 47), an archaeology museum that includes old fragments of the building itself. In the middle of the square is a fine Gothic **market hall**. The surrounding streets are full of old houses testifying to St-Antonin's medieval prosperity.

For the view you can climb 660m **Roc d'Anglars** (English Rock) across the river. About 3km north-east on the D75 is **Grotte du Bosc** (☎ 05 63 30 62 91), a cave formed by an underground river, open from 2 to 6 pm on Sunday and holidays from Easter to September, and 10 am to noon and 2 to 6 pm daily in July and August; take a warm jumper.

Places to Stay & Eat The municipal *Camping Le Ponget* (☎ 05 63 68 21 13), 800m out of town on the D19, costs just 12/18FF per adult/tent. Farther out, *Les Trois Cantons* (☎ 05 63 31 98 57) costs 30/39FF and has a pool and shop. Both camp sites are open from about May to September.

About 1km east on the D115 is *Camping d'Anglars* (☎ 05 63 30 69 76) costing 62FF forfait. Variation (see Activities earlier in this section) has an open-air camp site and small cafe at its *La Plage* site, east of the town centre.

Hôtel des Thermes (☎ 05 63 30 61 08, fax 05 63 68 26 23) by the river has doubles/twins for 190/230FF and a restaurant with lunch/dinner *menus* from 60/98FF. The tourist office has a list of half a dozen *chambres d'hôtes*.

Tarn

ALBI
postcode 81000 • pop 64,500
• elevation 174m

The earliest written references to Albi date back to the 4th century AD, by which time it was a sizeable provincial market town.

This is the 'Albi' of the 12th- and 13th-century Albigensian heresy (see the boxed text below). Albi's massive Gothic cathedral – a symbol of the power of the town's

The Albigensian Crusade

The dualistic doctrine of Catharism was based on the belief that the kingdom of God is locked in battle with an intrinsically evil material world created by Satan. Among other things, Cathars (or Albigenses as they were also known, after the town of Albi) believed that anything concerned with the physical body – materialism, eating, sex, indeed life itself – was ultimately to be renounced, and took inspiration in their struggle (to free the spirit from the flesh) from an ascetic, chaste and vegetarian clergy caste.

Catharism spread from the Balkans to the region around Carcassonne, Toulouse and Albi between the 11th and 13th centuries, partly in response to the materialism of the Church in Rome. Preaching was in the old Occitan tongue (Langue d'Oc). It found wide favour with both common people and aristocrats in the region.

A crusade against the Cathars instigated by Pope Innocent III in 1208 – after a papal representative was murdered by a vassal of the count of Toulouse – provided a perfect opportunity for the French kings, with the help of the cruel Simon de Montfort, to wage a war of conquest against the nobility of the south. After long sieges, the major Cathar centres in Languedoc fell to the crusaders one by one and Cathars in their thousands were slaughtered or burned at the stake. By 1321 Catharism in southern France had been destroyed.

TARN

newly founded bishopric – was begun less than four decades after the Cathar movement was violently crushed.

Heavily influenced by Toulouse and the Languedoc, Albi has a southern feel, laid-back and not overrun with tourists. Most of the inner town, including the cathedral, is built of reddish brick made from the clay of the Tarn River.

One of Albi's most famous natives was Henri de Toulouse-Lautrec (1864–1901), best known for his posters and lithographs of the bars, brothels and music halls of Montmartre in *belle époque* Paris. Although

he spent little time here after an unhappy childhood, the town's Musée Toulouse-Lautrec is the most important collection of his work anywhere.

Orientation

Albi is about 80km north-east of Toulouse, on the Tarn's southern bank. Looming over the city centre – and a landmark from almost anywhere – is Cathédrale Ste-Cécile. A web of narrow streets stretches south-east to place du Vigan, Albi's commercial hub. The train station lies about 1km south-west of the city centre.

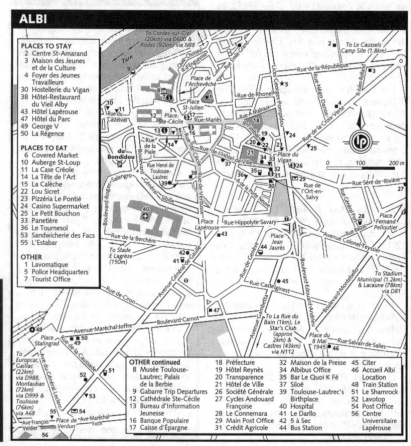

ALBI

PLACES TO STAY
2 Centre St-Amarand
3 Maison des Jeunes et de la Culture
4 Foyer des Jeunes Travailleurs
30 Hostellerie du Vigan
38 Hôtel-Restaurant du Vieil Alby
43 Hôtel Lapérouse
47 Hôtel du Parc
49 George V
50 La Régence

PLACES TO EAT
6 Covered Market
10 Auberge St-Loup
11 La Case Créole
14 La Tête de l'Art
15 La Calèche
22 Lou Sicret
23 Pizzéria Le Pontié
24 Casino Supermarket
25 Le Petit Bouchon
33 Panetière
36 Le Tournesol
53 Sandwicherie des Facs
55 L'Estabar

OTHER
1 Lavomatique
5 Police Headquarters
7 Tourist Office

OTHER continued
8 Musée Toulouse-Lautrec; Palais de la Berbie
9 Gabarre Trip Departures
12 Cathédrale Ste-Cécile
13 Bureau d'Information Jeunesse
16 Banque Populaire
17 Caisse d'Épargne
18 Préfecture
19 Hôtel Reynès
20 Transparence
21 Hôtel de Ville
26 Société Générale
27 Cycles Andouard Françoise
28 Le Connemara
29 Main Post Office
31 Crédit Agricole
32 Maison de la Presse
34 Albibus Office
35 Bar Le Quoi K Fé
37 Siloë
39 Toulouse-Lautrec's Birthplace
40 Hospital
42 5 à Sec
44 Bus Station
45 Citer
46 Accueil Albi Location
48 Train Station
51 Le Shamrock
52 Lavotop
54 Post Office
56 Centre Universitaire Lapérouse

Information

Tourist Offices The tourist office (☎ 05 63 49 48 80, fax 05 63 49 48 98, email otsi albi@wanadoo.fr) on place Ste-Cécile is open from 9 am to 12.30 pm and 2 to 6 pm Monday to Saturday, and from 10.30 am to 12.30 pm and 3.30 to 5.30 pm on Sunday. During July and August the office is open from 9 am to 7.30 pm Monday to Saturday and from 10.30 am to 1 pm and 3.30 to 6.30 pm on Sunday.

Worth asking for is *Tour the Tarn*, a booklet full of things to see and do throughout the département.

Money Because they are open late on Saturday (Albi's market day), banks here close on Monday. Those with exchange desks and ATMs include Banque Populaire and Caisse d'Épargne on place Ste-Cécile, and Crédit Agricole and Société Générale on place du Vigan.

You can exchange money on Sunday at the tourist office and on Monday morning at the main post office.

Post The main post office is on place du Vigan. There's a branch on ave du Général de Gaulle near the university.

Email & Internet Access At the Bureau d'Information Jeunesse (☎/fax 05 63 47 19 15, email bij.albi@wanadoo.fr), 19 place Ste-Cécile, Internet access costs 5FF per 15 minutes. It's open from 10 am to noon and 1.30 to 6 pm on weekdays (with no lunch break on Wednesday).

Bookshops Siloë, on rue de l'Hôtel de Ville, is good for walking and cycling guides and regional history books (in French). It's closed on Sunday and Monday. Transparence, 9 rue Timbal, has a hit-or-miss map selection. Maison de la Presse, place du Vigan, sells lots of international newspapers and some guidebooks; it's open from 7 am to 12.30 pm and 1.30 to 7 pm daily (except on Sunday afternoon).

University The Centre Universitaire Lapérouse, a branch of the Université de Toulouse, is south-west of the city centre near the train station. Some 1800 students are spread out over nine faculties, covering humanities, social sciences and law.

Laundry Two laundrettes, open from 7 am to at least 9 pm daily, are Lavomatique, 10 rue Émile Grand, and Lavotop, ave du Général de Gaulle. If you want someone else to do the washing, go to 5 à Sec, near place Lapérouse.

Medical Services & Emergency The city's Centre Hospitalier (hospital; ☎ 05 63 47 47 47) faces place Lapérouse. The police headquarters (☎ 05 63 49 22 81) are at 6 lices Georges Pompidou.

Dangers & Annoyances The area called du Bondidou, a big car park south-west of Cathédrale Ste-Cécile, is dodgy after dark.

Cathédrale Ste-Cécile

This mighty cathedral – a fine representative of Southern Gothic style – took over a century to build (1282–1392). It's quite outsized – big enough at the time of construction to hold the town's entire population of 5000 to 6000 – and it would be hard to describe it as attractive. Illuminated on a summer night, though, it's impressive.

In contrast to the plain, sunburned exterior, not a single interior surface was left untouched by the Italian artists who painted it in around 1512. Spanning the sanctuary is an intricately carved rood screen from around 1500. The stained-glass windows in the apse date from the 14th to the 16th centuries. Don't miss the *grand chœur* (great choir) with 30 Old Testament figures carved in stone. Below the massive organ is *Le Jugement Dernier* (1475–84), a vivid and Bosch-like Last Judgement.

Opening hours at the time of writing were from 8.45 to 11.45 am and 2 to 5.45 pm daily (8.30 am to 7 pm from June to September). Admission to the nave is free but costs 5FF to the choir and 20FF (students 12FF, kids aged under 12 free) to the treasury. The tourist office runs one-hour, French-language tours of the

TARN

cathedral at 10 am and 2.30 pm daily (except Saturday) from June to September. The tours cost 33FF including the admission fee.

Musée Toulouse-Lautrec

This museum is in the **Palais de la Berbie**, an equally fortress-like archbishop's palace built between the 13th and the 15th centuries. The museum contains the biggest collection of the artist's work anywhere, including his celebrated Parisian brothel scenes. Audio-guides in French, English, German and Spanish, dealing with selected works, are available for hire. Changing exhibits of modern painters take up the top floor.

The museum (☎ 05 63 49 48 70) is open from 10 am to noon and 2 to 5 pm daily

NICKY CAVEN

The diminutive Toulouse-Lautrec is famous for his depictions of Parisian nightlife.

(9 am from June to September; July and August without a lunch break; to 5.30 pm in March and October; to 6 pm in April to September; closed Tuesday from October to March). Admission costs 24FF (student 12FF). Entry to the splendid gardens is free. From June to September, the tourist office has 1½ hour tours (44FF) at 10 am and 2.30 pm on weekdays, and at 11 am and 4 pm on Saturday and Sunday.

A plaque on a private house at 14 rue Henri de Toulouse-Lautrec marks the artist's birthplace. If you haven't had enough already you'll find Toulouse-Lautrec books, photos, postcards, wines, recipes and pastries everywhere you look.

Hôtel Reynès

Albi – and particularly the Reynès merchant family – prospered from the trade in woad even before Toulouse got wind of it (see the boxed text '*Le Pastel*' in the Toulouse section earlier in this chapter). The family mansion, the Hôtel Reynès on rue Timbal, is now occupied by the local chamber of commerce (it is not open to the public). With its ornate window mullions and galleried courtyard, this is a fine example of civil Renaissance architecture.

River Trips

From June to September you can take a 35-minute trip on a flat-bottom sailing barge called a *gabarre*, from just below the Palais de la Berbie. They depart every half-hour from 10 am to 12.30 pm and 2 to 6.30 pm. The trip costs 20FF (students 15FF).

Special Events

The biggest events on Albi's calendar are the **Albi Jazz Festival**, in various squares and cafes in late June; a three-day series of **ancient music concerts** at the end of July; and evenings of **classical music** in Cathédrale Ste-Cécile and other churches at 9 pm every Wednesday, from mid-July to August.

Carnaval (see Public Holidays & Special Events in the Facts for the Visitor chapter) is celebrated with gusto in Albi, with folk music, bands and processions. The date

...out six weeks before Easter – is only de-
ded a few months in advance.

laces to Stay

amping The closest camp site is *Le
aussels* (☎/fax 05 63 60 37 06), off route
e Millau, 2km north-east of place du
igan. It's open from April to mid-October
nd costs 65FF forfait or 18FF for one per-
on with a tent. Take bus No 5 from place
u Vigan to the end of the line.

ostels The *Maison des Jeunes et de la
ulture* (MJC; ☎ 05 63 54 53 65, *13 rue de
 République*) is open year-round with
orm beds costing 30FF and breakfast cost-
g 15FF, and other meals on weekdays cost
0FF. Reception is open from 7 to 9 pm
 to 9 pm at the weekend) but you can
ash your bags if you arrive before 2 pm. If
ot, go round the corner to rue Jules Rol-
nd, where a sign tells you if the hostel is
ll *(complet)*. From the train station, take
us No 1 to the République stop.

Centre St-Amarand (☎ 05 63 48 18 29,
x 05 63 48 18 21, *16 rue de la Répub-
que*) is meant for groups but may have
 monastic room or two for Catholic trav-
llers. The entrance is down the adjacent
npasse du Grand Séminaire. Around the
lock is a *Foyer des Jeunes Travailleurs
ue de la Croix Verte*), where you might
ag a bed if it's not full. It's open on week-
ays only.

otels – Train Station Area Two small
otels on ave Maréchal Joffre near the train
ation are the family-run *George V* (☎ 05
3 54 24 16, fax 05 63 49 90 78) at No 29,
ith large doubles with shower costing
om 216FF (276FF with toilet too); and *La
égence* (☎ 05 63 54 01 42) at No 27,
here doubles with toilet and shower start
t 230FF.

otels – City Centre At *Hôtel du Parc*
☎ 05 63 54 12 80, *3 ave du Parc*), quiet,
lain doubles with toilet and shower start at
58FF. *Hôtel Lapérouse* (☎ 05 63 54 69 22,
x 05 63 38 03 69, *21 place Lapérouse*)
harges from 320FF and has a pool. *Hôtel-*

Restaurant du Vieil Alby (☎ 05 63 54 14
69, fax 05 63 54 96 75, *25 rue Henri de
Toulouse-Lautrec*) charges 326FF and the
food is first-rate (see Places to Eat); it's
closed in late January and from late June to
early July. At the Logis de France *Hostellerie du Vigan* (☎ 05 63 54 01 23, fax 05 63
47 05 42, *16 place du Vigan*) big, modern
doubles start at 320/400FF with toilet and
shower/bath.

Places to Eat

Restaurants – French Ideal for simple
fare at reasonable prices (for example 60FF
for crudités, plat du jour and dessert) is *Le
Petit Bouchon* (☎ 05 63 54 11 75, *77 rue de
la Croix Verte*), closed on Saturday evening
and Sunday. *Hostellerie du Vigan* (see
Places to Stay) has a popular restaurant
where *menus* start at 100FF.

La Tête de l'Art (☎ 05 63 38 44 75, *7 rue
de la Piale*) has a good 75FF four-course
menu. Opposite is *La Calèche* (☎ 05 63 54
15 52, *6 rue de la Piale*), with similar
spreads costing from 85FF. Probably the
best food in the city centre is at *Hôtel-
Restaurant du Vieil Alby* (see Places to
Stay), where lunch/dinner *menus* start at
75/110FF.

Two good restaurants for sampling traditional Albigeoise cuisine are *Lou Sicret*
(☎ 05 63 38 26 40, *1 rue Timbal*) and
Auberge St-Loup (☎ 05 63 54 02 75, *26 rue
du Castelviel*).

Restaurants – Other For seafood dishes
from the Antilles, try *La Case Créole* (☎ 05
63 54 63 39, *rue du Castelviel*) where plats
du jour cost from 60FF; it's closed on
Wednesday. *Pizzéria Le Pontié* (☎ 05 63 49
70 75, *place du Vigan*) serves pizzas from
about 50FF.

Cheerful *L'Estabar* (☎ 05 63 38 29 03,
12 ave François Verdier) serves up Tex-
Mex food, with plats du jour from 37FF.
For those on a genuinely spartan budget,
Sandwicherie des Facs (☎ 05 63 38 70 11,
77 ave du Général de Gaulle) has sandwiches, salads, burgers and crepes until at
least 10 pm daily.

Le Tournesol (☎ 05 63 38 38 14, *11 rue*

TARN

de l'Ort-en-Salvy), Albi's only vegetarian restaurant, would be good value even if it weren't vegetarian. The simple menu includes several fresh vegetable assiettes (platters) plus a hot dish for 47FF, and salad platters from the same price. It's open for lunch on Tuesday to Saturday and for dinner on Friday and Saturday (to 9.30 pm).

Self-Catering Fresh fare can be picked up from the *covered market (place du Marché)*; it is closed on Monday. *Panetière (place du Vigan)* sells bread and other baked goods until 8 pm daily. The *Casino supermarket (lices Georges Pompidou)* is open until 7.30 pm Monday to Saturday.

Entertainment

Bars Three bars near the centre with occasional live music are *Le Darllo* (☎ 05 63 38 93 09, 10 ave du Général de Gaulle), *Le Connemara* (☎ 05 63 54 92 42, 6 rue Balzac) and *Le Shamrock* (☎ 05 63 43 08 50, 57 ave du Général de Gaulle). *L'Estabar* (see Places to Eat) offers up a recorded Latin beat. Music at *Bar Le Quoi K Fé (rue de l'Ort-en-Salvy)* runs mainly to rock and disco.

Most bars in Albi stay open until 2 am and are closed on Monday.

Discos Albi's most popular disco is *Le Star's Club* (☎ 05 63 56 61 11, route des Castres), out on the Castres road (N112). Another hot spot is *La Rue du Bain* (☎ 05 63 54 75 66, rue Lavazière), also south of the centre near the N88. Both are open until dawn on Friday and Saturday nights.

Concerts Ask at the tourist office for details of free jazz, rock and other concerts held around the city centre during July and August. There are free organ concerts in Cathédrale Ste-Cécile at 5 pm on Wednesday and at 4 pm Sunday during July and August.

Spectator Sports

The main rugby venue is the Stadium Municipal, south-east of the city centre on ave Col Teyssier (D81); take southbound bus No 5 from place du Vigan to the Somme

stop. Football matches are also played her and at the smaller Stade E Lagrèze; tak southbound bus No 2 or 4 from place d Vigan to the Lagrèze stop.

Shopping

On Saturday morning an open-air food ma ket spills from place Ste-Cécile into the su rounding streets, with everything fro bulging stalls to farmers with their thre radishes. The covered market at place d Marché booms daily except Monday. clothes market fills place du Vigan ever Tuesday.

Getting There & Away

Bus The bus station is on place Jean Jaurè but there's no real office; for timetable ask at the tourist office. Destinations wi multiple daily departures (except Sunday include Castres (46FF; 50 minutes), Mon auban (61FF) and Toulouse (60FF). Fro the train station SNCF runs two or thre buses daily (except Sunday) to Toulous and two or three to Montauban (excep Saturday).

Train The train station (☎ 05 63 54 50 5(is on place Stalingrad. Albi is on th Toulouse–Rodez line, with services abou hourly during the week and less often o Saturday (no service on Sunday). For Pa or other southern destinations change Toulouse (63FF, 1¼ hours).

Car Two national car rental firms south the bus station are Citer (☎ 05 63 38 45 33 78 ave Gambetta, and Accueil Albi Loca tion (☎ 05 63 47 20 40), 17 blvd du Lude Europcar (☎ 05 63 54 66 56) is two block west of place de Verdun on ave Françoi Verdier.

Other companies include ADA (☎ 05 6 38 96 48), Avis (☎ 05 63 54 76 54) an Hertz (☎ 05 63 54 17 34).

Getting Around

Bus Local buses are run by Albibus (☎ 0 63 38 43 43), with an information office 14 rue de l'Hôtel de Ville. Single ticke cost 5FF from tabacs, drivers or Albibu

Bus No 1 goes from the train station to the bus station and place du Vigan. Buses don't run on Sunday.

Bicycle Cycles Andouard Françoise (☎ 05 63 38 44 47), 7 rue Séré de Rivières, rents VTTs for 80/100/500FF for a half-day/day/ week.

AROUND ALBI
Cordes-sur-Ciel

postcode 81170 • pop 950 • elevation 279m

This proud bastide, chartered in 1222 by Raymond VI, count of Toulouse, lords it over the surrounding countryside. Tourist literature gushes about the 'pearl of the bastides' and indeed it's extraordinarily picturesque, crowned with a cluster of handsome Gothic residences. This is being milked for all it's worth and the town – full of workshops, galleries and antique shops – has an aura of twee artiness. Try to visit early or late in the day to avoid the crowds.

Orientation The town has four layers of walls: two original inner ones, with old gates; another added in the early 14th century and the last in the 16th century as the population grew. The modern town has spread down to the D600 and beyond.

Information The tourist office (☎ 05 63 56 00 52, fax 05 63 56 19 52), on Grand Rue, is open daily from 10.30 am to 12.30 pm and 1.30 to 6 pm. Pick up a free map or an excruciatingly detailed *Walking Guide* for 10FF, or rent an audioguide tape for 30FF.

Things to See The star attractions are four Gothic mansions with filigree windows and extravagantly sculpted sandstone exteriors, built on Grand Rue by wealthy merchants or noble families: **Maison du Grand Fauconnier** (House of the Grand Falconer), the finest of the lot; **Maison du Grand Veneur** (Huntsman), with the most playful decorations; **Maison du Grand Ecuyer** (Equerry); and **Maison Prunet**. All date from the early 14th century. The names are 19th-century inventions.

Stairways and passages climb between the town's layers, past stables, watchtowers, chapels and the workshops of artisans of the past. Near the central **Halle** or marketplace, originally 13th century, is place de la Bride, with fine views north across the land.

Special Events Two big annual events are Les Fêtes du Grand Fauconnier, a medieval festival in mid-July; and Musique sur Ciel, a music festival at the end of July.

Places to Stay Make this a day trip unless you've money to burn.

Two nearby camp sites are *Camp Redon* (☎ 05 63 56 14 64) in Livers-Caselles, 5km east of town, open from April to October and costing 60FF forfait; and *Le Moulin de Julien* (☎ 05 63 56 01 42, fax 05 63 56 11 10, route de Gaillac*), 1.5km south down the D922, open from April to September and costing 80FF forfait.

At *Hôtel Chez Babar* (☎ 05 63 56 02 51), about 2km west on the D600 in Les Cabannes, doubles start at 150FF. The cheapest doubles in Cordes are at *Hotel de la Bride* (☎ 05 63 56 04 02, place de la Bride), at 210FF and 270FF. The tourist office has a list of *chambres d'hôtes* and *ferme auberges* (farm accommodation), typically costing 280FF and up for a double with breakfast; most are open year-round.

Places to Eat Try *La Canaille* in place de la Bride for salads, crepes and snacks. The town has a wide choice of sometimes excellent but very expensive restaurants and cafes. Eat down on the highway instead: try *Restaurant L'Hacienda* (☎ 05 63 56 09 48, route d'Albi) or *Snack Bar Le Menestrel* (☎ 05 63 56 06 67, place de la Bouteillerie), both with *menus* from 65FF.

Getting There & Away On weekdays, buses depart Albi's bus station at 6.10 pm (and during school term at 7.45 am, plus Wednesday and Saturday at 12.15 pm), to Cordes and Vindrac. Return services depart Cordes (on the highway) during school term only, at 6.35 am daily except Sunday, plus 12.50 pm Wednesday and 4.50 pm Monday, Tuesday, Thursday and Friday. The trip

TARN

costs 28FF and takes one hour. For more information call Sudcar at ☎ 05 63 54 11 93.

Cordes' tiny train station at Vindrac, 3km to the west, has one direct connection from Albi daily (about 40FF, 50 minutes), leaving Albi about 9.20 pm or Cordes about 6.45 pm, for about 40FF. Five others, with a change at Tessonnières or Gaillac, take one to 1½ hours.

Parking is heavily regulated, with large free car parks across the D600 and a long slog (or shuttle ride) up – though out of season you can drive right up from the eastern end. From 1 November to 10 March you can park in town.

Getting Around You can rent a VTT or vélo in Les Cabannes for 60/80FF per half/full day; call Joël Guibert (☎ 05 63 56 08 68).

Castelnau de Montmiral
postcode 81140 • pop 1200 • elevation 286m
This pocket-size bastide, founded in 1222 by Raymond VI, remains appealingly unrestored. In the lanes surrounding place des Arcades, the central square, are many cantilevered, **half-timbered houses**.

Within the Castelnau district is the **Forêt de Grésigne**, 35 sq km of deep oak forest laced with footpaths; and alongside it runs the GR46. Closer to the village is **Base de Vère Grésigne** (☎ 05 63 33 16 00), a leisure park offering swimming, sailing, windsurfing and fishing as well as VTT rental. It's open weekends from Easter to June and in September, and from 10.30 am to 8 pm daily in July and August.

Information The tourist office (☎ 05 63 33 15 11, fax 05 63 33 10 18) on place des Arcades is open daily (except Wednesday in September and except Friday from October to April).

Places to Stay & Eat Three-star *Camping Rieutort* (☎ 05 63 33 16 10), 3km west on the D964, is open from June to mid-September and costs 63FF forfait; it also has bungalows. Rooms are available in the centre of town at *Auberge des Arcades* (☎ 05

63 33 20 88) and at a surprising number of *Gîtes de France*. Place des Arcades has one modest *café*.

CASTRES
postcode 81100 • pop 47,000
• elevation 172m
Castres began life as a Roman settlement *castrum*. It grew rapidly when a monastery was founded here in the 9th century and later made its name as a textile centre. The town was trashed during the Wars of Religion. This is the birthplace of Jean Jaurès considered the father of French Socialism.

While it may not warrant a special trip, this cheerful town is worth a detour en route between Albi and Toulouse, and is a natural springboard to the Parc Naturel Régional de Haute-Languedoc.

Orientation
Castres straddles the Agoût, a tributary of the Tarn. The centre of town is place Jean Jaurès, a few blocks north-west of the bus station (on place Soult) and about 1km north-east of the train station (ave Albert 1er). On foot you can cross the town centre in 10 minutes The airport is 8km to the south-east.

Information
The tourist office (☎ 05 63 62 63 62, fax 05 63 62 63 60, email otcastres@mediacastr .com), 3 rue Milhau Ducommun, is open from 8.30 am to 12.30 pm and 1.30 to 6.30 pm Monday to Saturday, and from 2 to 6 pm on Sunday (with Sunday morning hours and no lunch breaks). This is also a good place for information on the Sidobre (see Around Castres later in this chapter).

The Bureau d'Information Jeunesse (☎ 05 63 72 67 40) for the southern Tarn is at 3 rue de la Platé.

Two banks on place Jean Jaurès with ATMs and currency exchanges are Banque Populaire at No 7 and Crédit Agricole at No 17.

The police headquarters (☎ 05 63 35 46 10) are at 2 ave Charles de Gaulle and the hospital (☎ 05 63 71 63 71) is at 20 blvd Maréchal Foch.

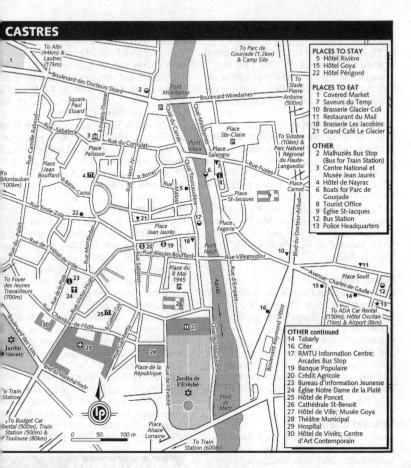

CASTRES

To Albi (44km) & Lautrec (17km)

To Parc de Gourjade (1.2km) & Camp Site

To Stade Pierre Antoine (500m)

Boulevard-des-Docteurs-Sicard

Square Paul Eluard

Rue-Sabaterie

Rue-du-Consulat

Place Pelisson

Place Jean Bouffard

R.Baron-Cachin

Rue-Emile-Zola

Rue-du-Palais

Rue-de-l'Hôtel-de-Ville

Rue-Sabaterie

Place du 8 Mai 1945

Rue-Alquier-Bouffard

Rue-de-la-Platé

Rue-Victor-Hugo

Rue-Chambre-de-l'Edit

R.Gabriel-Guy

Rue-Gambetta

Boulevard-des-Lices

Jardin Frascaty

Blvd-du-Maréchal-Foch

Place de la République

Rue-de-l'Evêché

Jardin de l'Evêché

Place Alsace Lorraine

Pont Mitedames

Boulevard-Miredames

Quai-du-Carras

Quai-Miredames

Pont Vieux

Rue-Henri-IV

R.Borrel

Rue-Malpas

Rue-Tourcaudière

Quai-Tourcaudière

Place Ste-Claire

Place Salengro

Place St-Jacques

Place Jean Jaurès

Place Fagerie

Pont Neuf

Rue-Villegoudou

Rue-d'Empare

Agoüt

Quai-du-Docteur-Aribat

Place Carnot

Place Soult

Avenue-Charles-de-Gaulle

Blvd-du-Docteur-Aribat

Boulevard-Raymond-Vittoz

Quai-du-Moulin

Pont de Metz

Place de la République

To Sidobre (10km) & Parc Naturel Régional du Haute-Languedoc

Rue-Fuzies

To ADA Car Rental (150m), Hôtel Occitan (1km) & Airport (8km)

To Montauban 100km

To Foyer des Jeunes Travailleurs (700m)

To Train Station

To Budget Car Rental (500m), Train Station (500m) & Toulouse (80km)

To Train Station (600m)

0   50   100 m

PLACES TO STAY
5 Hôtel Rivière
15 Hôtel Goya
22 Hôtel Périgord

PLACES TO EAT
1 Covered Market
7 Saveurs du Temp
10 Brasserie Glacier Coll
11 Restaurant du Mail
18 Brasserie Les Jacobins
21 Grand Café Le Glacier

OTHER
2 Malhuziès Bus Stop (Bus for Train Station)
3 Centre National et Musée Jean Jaurès
4 Hôtel de Nayrac
6 Boats for Parc de Gourjade
8 Tourist Office
9 Église St-Jacques
12 Bus Station
13 Police Headquarters

OTHER continued
14 Tabarly
16 Citer
17 RMTU Information Centre; Arcades Bus Stop
19 Banque Populaire
20 Crédit Agricole
23 Bureau d'Information Jeunesse
24 Église Notre Dame de la Platé
25 Hôtel de Poncet
26 Cathédrale St-Benoit
27 Hôtel de Ville; Musée Goya
28 Théâtre Municipal
29 Hospital
30 Hôtel de Viviès; Centre d'Art Contemporain

own Centre

he Tour Romane (Roman Tower) on the 7th-century **Cathédrale St-Benoit** is a remant of the original abbey. Opposite is the **ôtel de Ville** (town hall) in the contemporneous former Bishop's Palace, with the plendid Jardin de l'Evêché stretching out ehind.

Castres' **houses** are a window on its hisry. Old ones along the Agoût, with cellars pening onto the river, began as the homes f 14th-century tanners, dyers and weavers. mong handsome Renaissance **mansions** f late 16th- and 17th-century merchants are

Hôtel de Nayrac on rue Frédéric Thomas, Hôtel de Poncet on rue Gabriel Guy and Hôtel de Viviès, now the Centre d'Art Contemporain, on rue Chambre de l'Edit.

Museums
Musée Goya (☎ 05 63 71 59 27), in the Hôtel de Ville, is France's most important collection of Spanish art from classical to modern, including of course many of Goya's own paintings and engravings. It's open from 9 am to noon and 2 to 5 pm (to 6 pm from April to September), closed on Monday except during July and August.

TARN

Admission costs 15FF (kids aged from 14 to 18 years 8FF).

The important but stuffy **Centre National et Musée Jean Jaurès** (☎ 05 63 72 01 01), 2 place Pelisson, is open the same hours as the Goya; admission costs 10FF (students and children aged between 14 and 18 years 5FF).

Parc de Gourjade

This vast municipal park north of the town centre includes a camp site, outdoor games, a nine-hole golf course, 15km of jogging trails, a first-class riding centre (☎ 05 63 35 02 08) and a water park called L'Archipel (☎ 05 63 62 54 00) with pools, water slides and a winter ice-skating rink. It's on ave de Roquecourbe (D89); take bus No 6 or 7 from the Arcades stop on place Jean Jaurès, or the tourist boat (see the following River Trips section).

River Trips

From the quay in front of the tourist office you can take a 30- to 50-minute journey up-river to Parc de Gourjade in a replica river barge, for 25FF (children aged 14 and 18 years 10FF) one way. It departs at 2, 3.20 and 4.40 pm daily from May to October (plus 6 pm from May to September and 10.30 am in July and August). For more information contact the tourist office or call ☎ 05 63 59 72 30.

Special Events

Festival Goya (☎ 05 63 71 56 58) has nothing to do with Goya but is an annual festival of Latin and North African music, held in the Art-Nouveau Théâtre Municipal from July to mid-August. The city also sponsors numerous open-air events – such as jazz and folk concerts – throughout August.

Places to Stay

The municipal *camp site* (☎ 05 63 59 56 49) at Parc de Gourjade is open from April to September. For two adults with a tent/caravan it costs 26/34FF plus 8.50FF per car; bungalows for four are 255FF. A *Foyer des Jeunes Travailleurs* (☎ 05 63 59 08 46, 7 rue Pasteur Habac) has dorm beds and grub for young workers on weekdays.

Good-value hotels near the town centr include *Hôtel Rivière* (☎ 05 63 59 04 5 fax 05 63 59 61 97, 10 quai Tourcaudière where plain doubles start at 140FF (250F with toilet and shower); and the similarl priced *Hôtel Périgord* (☎ 05 63 59 04 7 22 rue Émile Zola). If these are full try th down-at-heel *Hôtel Goya* (☎ 05 63 35 3 24, 16 place Soult) where basic double cost from 120FF (closed on Sunday). Ou on the airport road is the Logis de Franc *Hôtel Occitan* (☎ 05 63 35 34 20, fax 05 6 35 70 32, 201 ave Charles de Gaulle), wit doubles from 300FF.

Places to Eat

Brasserie Les Jacobins (☎ 05 63 59 01 4 1 place Jean Jaurès) offers good value i the centre of town. It's open daily, servin generous 39FF salads, regional cuisine an fine desserts. *Grand Café le Glacier*, diag onally opposite this on place Jean Jaurè has cheap salads and sandwiches. Two un exceptional places open daily on plac Soult are *Brasserie-Glacier Coll* (☎ 05 6 35 02 54) at No 1, with cheap grills, salad and sandwiches; and *Restaurant du Ma* (☎ 05 63 35 76 09) at No 23, offering 47FF lunch *menu*.

A hotel restaurant worth a mention, wit meaty meals from 75FF, is at the *Hôtel Oc citan* (see Places to Stay); it's closed for Sa urday lunch. For an elegant hit of coffee an pastry, go round the corner from the touris office to *Saveurs du Temp* (☎ 05 63 35 3

Markets of Castres

The covered food market on place de l'Albinque is open from 7 am to 1 pm (to noon on Sunday), daily except Monday. Outside on Tuesday, Thursday and Friday is a clothes market; Saturday features a flea market and, from November to March, a *foie gras* (goose liver) market. You can find food and flowers on place Jean Jaurès on Tuesday, Thursday, Friday and Saturday, and clothes on place Soult on Saturday.

32, 4 rue Fuziès). For do-it-yourself meals, see the boxed text 'Markets of Castres'.

Spectator Sports

Castres' rugby union squad, Olympique, were French champions in 1993 and are the best in the region after Toulouse. Most matches are held at Stade Pierre Antoine, just north-east of the centre.

Getting There & Away

Air France (☎ 08 02 80 28 02) flies six days a week from Paris direct to Castres.

Buses run from the Castres bus station (☎ 05 63 35 37 31) to Albi (46FF, 50 minutes) five to seven times daily, except Sunday; and Toulouse (60FF, 1½ hours) at least seven times a day and twice on Sunday. The only direct train line is from Toulouse (72FF; one to 1½ hours), with eight trains per weekday and three to five on weekends.

A car hire agency near the town centre is Citer (☎ 05 63 51 28 20), 16 blvd Raymond Vittoz. Further away are ADA (☎ 05 63 51 10 26), 32 ave Charles de Gaulle and Budget (☎ 05 63 71 31 28), 98 ave Albert 1er. Several agencies are also represented at the airport.

Getting Around

There is no bus service to/from the airport. From the train station, take bus No 7 to the Arcades stop (once or twice an hour) on place Jean Jaurès; going to the station, catch it at the Malhuziès stop by blvd des Docteurs Sicard. The local bus company, RMTU, has an information centre on place Jean Jaurès.

Tabarly (☎ 05 63 35 38 09), 38 place Soult, rents bikes. In summer there is also a rental kiosk (☎ 05 63 59 22 00) at the train station.

AROUND CASTRES
Lautrec

The region around this pretty, medieval hilltop village, 15km north-west of Castres and 40km south of Albi, produces a tenth of all the garlic consumed in garlic-loving France. The local variety is pink and has its own appellation contrôlée. Buy it at the village market on Friday morning from mid-July to March.

For more information contact the tourist office (☎ 05 63 75 31 40, fax 05 63 75 32 90), on cour de Mairie, open from 9 am to noon and 2 pm to 6 pm daily closed Sunday and Monday the rest of the year (closed from January to mid-February).

But there's more to the place than garlic. The village has a collection of unrestored but well-kept 16th- and 17th-century half-timbered **houses**; fragments of ancient town **walls** and one old gate; and a church from the 15th and 16th centuries, the **Collègiate St-Rémy**.

From behind the church, climb the hill to a shrine and the 17th-century *Moulin à vent* (windmill) **La Salette** – still used to pump water. It's open to the public from 3 to 7 pm daily in July and August and to 6 pm on Sunday during the rest of the year; admission costs 10FF. Here also is your first (or last) look at the sinuous hills of the Sidobre and even the Montagne Noir, to the south-east.

At the edge of the village, the **Aquaval water park** (☎ 05 63 70 52 32) has three pools, water slides and games.

There are direct buses, at least on weekdays, between Castres and Lautrec.

Le Sidobre

The Sidobre is a roughly 100 sq km, 650m-high granite plateau north-east of Castres, a geological oddity in the limestone-dominated south-west. It's an arresting landscape, full of weird extrusions and immense balanced boulders as well as oak forests, cascading streams and tiny villages.

It's also France's main source of granite, and *les granitiers* rule. Some 2500 people in the Sidobre depend directly on the rock for their livelihood, and tourist attractions sit side-by-side with quarries, workshops and rubble heaps. The narrow roads are always clogged with lorries loaded with everything from knick-knacks to gravestones.

Information Six *communes* – Boissezon, Burlats, Ferrières, Lacrouzette, Le Bez and St-Salvy de la Balme – have established the Maison du Sidobre (☎ 05 63 74 63 38,

TARN

fax 05 63 73 04 57), just off the D622 near Vialavert. It's open from 10 am to 6 pm daily from June to September, and from 2 to 5 pm during the rest of the year with as much information on the granite industry as on the landscape.

Things to See & Do The names are at least as dramatic as the **rocks**: Peyro Clabado ('keystone' in Occitan), Rocher Tremblant de Sept Faux (Trembling Rock of the Seven Scythes), Trois Fromages (Three Cheeses). If you've spent time in granite mountains elsewhere, these might not be very dazzling, but it's an agreeable land to walk or cycle through in any case. The GR36 crosses the area and the Maison du Sidobre sells a packet of hiking cards, colour-coded, to over a dozen **trails** from three to 25km long.

Lacrouzette is the centre of the granite works. At **Ferrières** (on the D53 between Brassac and Vabre) is the small Musée du Protestantisme en Haute-Languedoc (☎ 05 63 50 47 93, fax 05 63 50 40 14), open from 11 am to 1 pm and 2 to 7 pm daily during July and August. In **Burlats** is the Pavillon d'Adélaïde, a 13th-century haven for troubadours, and from Burlats you can take a canoe or kayak trip down the Agoût (call ☎ 05 63 35 70 77).

Places to Stay & Eat Camp sites include *Le Plo* (☎ 05 63 74 00 82, Le Bez), open mid-June to September, costing 10/10/5FF per adult/tent/car; *Camping Club de France* (☎ 05 63 74 01 13, Vialavert) at 11/11/11FF; *La Lande* (☎ 05 63 74 09 11, Brassac) at 9/8/4FF; *Siloé* (☎ 05 63 75 80 29, Roquecourbe) at 12FF per adult and 15FF per tent; and *Le Roussy* (☎ 05 63 50 45 92, Vabre). The Sidobre's only *gîte d'étape* (☎ 05 63 50 52 59) is run by the town hall in Boissezon.

The Maison du Sidobre has a *Guide Pratique* with hotel and restaurant listings. All agree that the best food is at the *Auberge de Crémaussel* (☎ 05 63 50 61 33), on the GR36 in Lacrouzette, closed on Sunday evening and Wednesday; accommodation is available too. Also in Lacrouzette is the

English-run *Au Relais du Sidobre* (☎ 05 63 50 60 06, 8 route de Vabre), with rooms and OK food. In a 16th-century house in Burlats, the five-bed *Le Castel du Burlats* (☎ 05 63 35 29 90, 8 place du 8 Mai 1945) has rooms from 300FF and a restaurant (call ahead).

Getting There & Away Vialavert is 15km east of Castres on the D622. Cars Balent (☎ 05 36 35 74 77) runs from Castres bus station at 11.45 am and 4.15 pm to Burlats (10 minutes), Lacrouzette (20 minutes) and Brassac (45 minutes), and returns starting at Brassac at 8.30 am, daily except Sunday, with additional services to Boissezon, St-Salvy and Brassac on certain days.

Parc Naturel Régional du Haut-Languedoc

This park was founded in 1973 with the aim of preserving the natural wealth and economic health of the region – an isolated, 2606 sq km zone straddling the divide between the Tarn and Hérault départements and between southern France's Atlantic and Mediterranean watersheds.

Within the park – jointly administered by the Languedoc-Roussillon and Midi-Pyrénées régions – are 93 communes, 47 of them in Tarn. Major geological features on the Tarn side are the **Monts de Lacaune**, an ancient refuge for Cathars and Protestants, with some of France's best fishing and one of its largest collections of Stone Age menhirs; a section of the oak- and beech-forested **Montagne Noir**, source of the water that feeds the Canal du Midi (see the boxed text 'Les Canaux des Deux Mers' in the Getting Around chapter); and the **Sidobre** (see the preceding section).

Public transport is scarce but if travelling by car doesn't appeal to you, you can walk, cycle or ride (the GR653 spans the park from west to east and the GR36 crosses its western limb), canoe the Agoût River, or sail on Lac de la Raviège or Lac de Sts-Peyres.

For more information on the park in both départements, contact the Maison du Parc (☎ 04 67 97 38 22, fax 04 67 97 38 18), 13 rue du Cloître, 34220 St Pons de Thomières (Hérault département).

Gers

The region historically known as Gascony – roughly speaking, the area west of the Garonne River – first had a separate life under the Romans, as Novempopulana. The Visigoths, after losing it to the Franks in 507, drove a branch of the Celtic tribe called the Vascones across the Pyrénées into the region over the next century.

Gascony was largely English territory from the 1259 Treaty of Paris until the end of the Hundred Years' War, after which it fell into three major domains: Armagnac, Foix-Béarn and Albret. By the 16th century it all belonged to the House of Albret – first to Jeanne d'Albret and then to her son Henri of Navarre, the future Henri IV of France.

In 1789 Gascony ceased to exist politically, shrivelling on the post-Revolutionary map to 'The Gers' (the *s* is pronounced), a sparsely populated agricultural hinterland in the Midi-Pyrénées région.

But don't assume there's nothing to see. Here you'll find a peaceful, undulating landscape of vineyards, orchards and fields of grain, etched by a score of rivers fanning out of the Hautes-Pyrénées. Through here runs the main artery of the medieval pilgrimage route, the *chemin de St-Jacques* to Santiago de Compostela, with five UNESCO World Heritage Sites within the Gers alone. Here too are some fine examples of medieval and Renaissance architecture, including a disproportionate number of 12th- to 14th-century *bastides* (fortified new towns).

And here is the soul of the south-west's hearty cuisine, a land of garlic and goose fat, sausages and beans, chestnuts and plums – and the biggest foie gras market in the country. Many of the Gers' attractions are farm-oriented – tastings and meals, rural accommodation, camping *à la ferme* (on the farm). This has also become the heartland of farmer militancy against the EU's Common Agricultural Policy.

One thing that stands out historically about South-West France is its vigorous

Highlights

- Ponder the esoteric 14th-century frescoes in the little Collégiale St-Pierre church in La Romieu, then gaze across Gascon farmland from its Belvedere Tower

- Catch your breath at the astonishing carved-oak choir stalls and gorgeous Renaissance stained glass of the Cathédrale Ste-Marie in Auch

- Imagine how life was for a 4th-century Gallo-Roman aristocratic family as you wander through the excavated remnants of their, state-of-the-art villa in Séviac

- Soak up the light in the austere Église Notre-Dame in Abbaye de Flaran, a medieval Cistercian monastery

magret de canard – lightly roasted duck breast

pastisse Gascogne – a lightly flambeed tart of armagnac-soaked apples and tissue-thin pastry

floc de Gascogne – a velvety fortified wine made from grape juice and the region's famous Armagnac

self-confidence. In this it owes much to Gascony, a state of mind as much as a patch on the map. The swashbuckling Gascon is indeed a kind of French icon, a defining

GERS

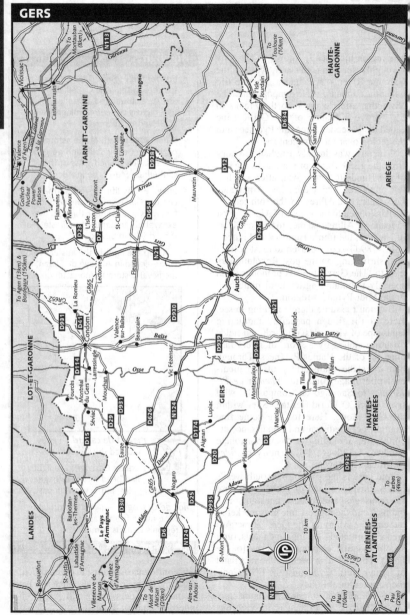

Hôtel d'Assézat, home of the Fondation Bemberg

Taking in the sun, Place de la Daurade, Toulouse

Basilique St-Sernin in Toulouse is one of Europe's largest and most complete Romanesque buildings.

Lining the Agoût River, 14th-century Castres mansions as seen from the Pont Vieux, Tarn

Ornate gardens of the Palais de la Berbie in Albi

Garlic capital of Tarn: Lautrec village, near Albi

component of the national temperament: the French often refer to boastfulness as *gasconnade*. Everything seems to be named D'Artagnan here – after the Gascon hero immortalised by novelist Alexandre Dumas in *Les Trois Mousquetaires* (The Three Musketeers); see the boxed text on page 304 for more information.

Accommodation is top-heavy, with budget places scarce or nonexistent. Without a car or bike, getting around is more of a problem than anywhere else in the south-west: the only useful train service is Toulouse–Auch, and most useful bus connections terminate at Auch.

Auch

**postcode 32000 • pop 25,000
• elevation 166m**

Of all the préfectures in the south-west, Auch (rhymes with gauche) is by far the least dressed-up and self-important, perhaps reflecting the Gers' own unassuming personality. But scratch beneath the surface and you will find a gorgeous cathedral with UNESCO World Heritage status (you'll have to look inside to see why), arguably the south-west's best provincial museum, a unique neighbourhood of medieval stepped streets, and a fine place to enjoy genuine Gascon cuisine. Bang in the middle of the Gers, with roads radiating from it like the spokes of a wheel, Auch is also a sensible base for exploring the département's lovely, underrated countryside.

History

The first known settlers on this big hill by the Gers River were a Celtic tribe called the Auscii. The Romans who conquered them in 56 BC built their town, Augusta Auscorum, on the flats across the river, and it grew into a major trade crossroads. By the 9th century the hill was again the centre – of a busy fortified town jointly run by the counts of Armagnac, the archbishops of Auch and the now-gone Priory of St Orens.

In 1473, after his soldiers had dispatched the last of the Armagnacs at Lectoure, the last of the Armagnacs at Lectoure, Louis XI installed the first in a series of *intendants* or governors here. When Gascony's lord, Henri of Navarre, became Henri IV of France, Auch became the province's administrative centre. Its golden era was the late 18th century, following the building of new roads to Toulouse and the Pyrénées by Intendant Antoine Mégret d'Étigny. A slide into rural obscurity followed the Revolution in 1789.

Orientation

Hilltop Auch, centred around place de la Libération, contains most sights, restaurants, shops and hotels. The medieval town, falling away to the south, is a web of lanes, steps and little courtyards. Pedestrianised rue Dessoles is the main shopping street, and the bus station is about 200m to the north-west. Across the river is 'new' Auch, and the train station.

Information

Tourist Offices The tourist office (☎ 05 62 05 22 89, fax 05 62 05 92 04) is at 1 rue Dessoles in a handsomely restored 15th-century building, the Maison Fedel. It's open from 9 am to noon and 2 to 6 pm Monday to Saturday (from 10 am on Monday), and also from 10.30 am to noon and 3.30 to 6 pm on Sunday from June to August.

For information about the Gers, go to the Comité Départemental du Tourisme du Gers (☎ 05 62 05 95 95, fax 05 62 05 02 16, email cdtdugers@wanadoo.fr) at 7 rue Diderot.

Bureau d'Information Jeunesse Auch's BIJ (☎ 05 62 60 21 21, email bijauch@ caramail.com), at 17 rue Rouget de Lisle, is open from 1 to 6 pm Monday, Tuesday, Thursday and Friday, and from 9 am to 1 pm and 2 to 5.30 pm Wednesday and Saturday. Internet access costs 20FF per hour.

Money Most banks stay open on Saturday (market day) and close on Monday. Crédit Agricole has branches at 7 bis rue Gambetta and ave d'Alsace, Caisse d'Épargne is on place de la Libération, and Banque Courtois is opposite Cathédrale Ste-Marie.

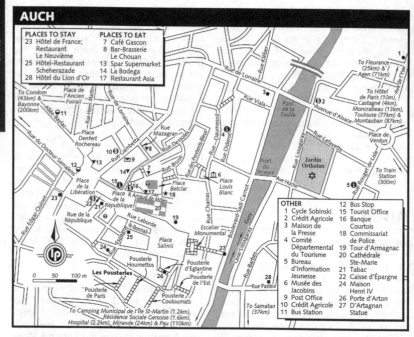

AUCH

PLACES TO STAY
23 Hôtel de France;
Restaurant
Le Neuvième
25 Hôtel-Restaurant
Scheherazade
28 Hôtel du Lion d'Or

PLACES TO EAT
7 Café Gascon
8 Bar-Brasserie
Le Chouan
13 Spar Supermarket
14 La Bodega
17 Restaurant Asia

OTHER
1 Cycle Sobinski
2 Crédit Agricole
3 Maison de
la Presse
4 Comité
Départemental
du Tourisme
5 Bureau
d'Information
Jeunesse
6 Musée des
Jacobins
9 Post Office
10 Crédit Agricole
11 Bus Station
12 Bus Stop
15 Tourist Office
16 Banque
Courtois
18 Commissariat
de Police
19 Tour d'Armagnac
20 Cathédrale
Ste-Marie
21 Tabac
22 Caisse d'Épargne
24 Maison
Henri IV
26 Porte d'Arton
27 D'Artagnan
Statue

Bookshops Maison de la Presse on rue de Lorraine stocks guidebooks, maps and many foreign newspapers. A tabac on rue de la République sells a few maps and newspapers.

Medical Services & Emergency The Centre Hospitalier (hospital; ☎ 05 62 61 32 32) is south of the town centre. The Commissariat de Police (☎ 05 62 61 70 00) is in the 18th-century episcopal palace, by Cathédrale Ste-Marie.

Cathédrale Ste-Marie

This splendid church, built by the counts of Armagnac between 1489 and 1680, moved Napoleon III to say, 'A cathedral like this should be put in a museum!' Gothic in plan but largely Italian Renaissance in execution, it was one of the last cathedrals to be completed in France.

Though the heavy western face looks rather grand illuminated at night, what people come to see is inside: 18 vivid Renaissance **stained-glass windows**, created between 1507 and 1513 by the celebrated Arnaud de Môles; and the astonishing **Grand Chœur** (Great Choir), completed in the 1550s by Dominic Bertin of Toulouse and others, featuring over 1500 individual carvings of biblical scenes and mythological creatures in 113 choir stalls.

In December 1998 the cathedral was made a UNESCO World Heritage Site. A good thing too, for its exterior is now getting a well-deserved cleaning.

The cathedral is open from 9.30 am to noon and 2 to 5 pm daily. It costs 8FF to see the Grand Chœur – if you can find someone to let you in. A French-language audioguide about the windows can be hired for 10FF.

The 14th-century, 40m-high Tour d'Armagnac behind the cathedral served the medieval archbishops of Auch (and later Revolutionaries) as a prison. It's closed to the public.

Musée des Jacobins

This eclectic art and archaeology collection, founded in 1793, is one of France's best provincial museums, and would be reason enough to visit Auch. Highlights include frescoes and other artefacts from a 1st- or 2nd-century Gallo-Roman villa near Auch (including an epitaph for a pet dog); landscapes by locally born painter Jean-Louis Rouméguère (1863–1925), who was clearly fascinated with sunsets; and one of the country's finest collections on the ethnography of the Americas, from pre-Colombian pottery to 18th-century religious art.

The museum (☎ 05 62 05 74 79), in a 15th-century Dominican monastery at 4 place Louis Blanc, is open from 10 am to noon and 2 to 5 pm Tuesday to Sunday (to 6 pm from May to September); admission costs 15FF (students and children 7.50FF).

Escalier Monumental

Descending to the river from place Salinis is the 370-step Monumental Stairway, completed in 1863. Bronze letters embedded in the first landing, telling the story of the Biblical flood in Latin, are the work of a Catalan artist, Jaume Plensa, inspired by a flood here in 1977. Near the bottom is a **statue of D'Artagnan**, the Gascon hero immortalised by novelist Alexandre Dumas in *Les Trois Mousquetaires* (see the boxed text 'D'Artagnan & the Three Musketeers' in the Bas-Armagnac section later in this chapter).

Les Pousterles

Plunging to the river from south of place Salinis is a series of narrow, stepped alleyways, collectively called Les Pousterles. Though unrestored, and in places dank and graffiti-stained, this is the face of old Auch. The layout allowed medieval citizens to reach the river without leaving the town's fortifications. One town gate, the **Porte d'Arton**, is on Pousterle d'Eglantine.

In 1578 the future Henri IV stayed in the fine house at 22 rue Espagne (now called Maison Henri IV), with a narrow, lofty courtyard and a handsome wood and stone stairway.

Places to Stay

Camping The spartan, riverside *Camping Municipal de l'Île St-Martin* (☎ 05 62 05 00 22), 1.2km south of the town centre, is open from mid-April to mid-November and costs 15/7.50/2FF per adult/tent/car. Take bus No 5 from place de la Libération to the Mouzon stop. A quiet camping à la ferme site called *Castagné* (☎ 05 62 05 28 32) is about 4km to the east on the N124.

Hostels At *Résidence Sociale Gersoise* (☎ 05 62 05 34 80, fax 05 62 60 00 44, 36 rue des Canaris), a youth and workers' hostel in a residential complex south of the centre, a bed costs 74FF and there's a small cafeteria. The office is open from 10.30 am to 6 pm Monday to Friday, with a guard on duty at other times. There's no curfew. Take bus No 1 or 2 from place de la Libération to the Grand Carros stop.

Hotels The pokey *Hôtel-Restaurant Scheherazade* (☎ 05 62 05 13 25, 7 rue Espagne) – also called Les 3 Mousquetaires – is a block south of the cathedral. Doubles cost 150/210FF without/with shower and toilet. At *Hôtel de France* (☎ 05 62 61 71 71, fax 05 62 61 71 81, 2 place de la Libération) singles/doubles start at 295/365FF, and buffet breakfast costs 60FF.

Two places across the river are pretty good value. *Hôtel du Lion d'Or* (☎/fax 05 62 63 66 00, 7 rue Pasteur) has comfortably furnished old rooms with toilet and shower or bath from 200FF to 300FF. Doubles at *Hôtel de Paris* (☎ 05 62 63 26 22, fax 05 62 60 04 27, 38 ave de la Marne) cost 170FF (210FF with shower, 250FF with shower and toilet). It's closed in November.

Places to Eat

The bar at *Bar-Brasserie Le Chouan* (☎ 05 62 05 08 47, rue Mazagran) offers a good 45FF *buffet des entrées* – a glorified salad bar with crudités, salmon and other goodies. In the brasserie upstairs salads, omelettes and Gascon *plats* start at 70FF. Both are open for lunch and dinner, except on Sunday. Another modest introduction to regional fare is the 75FF *menu* at *Café*

GERS

Gascon (☎ 05 62 61 88 08, 5 rue Lamartine), closed Tuesday and Sunday.

If you're serious about Gascon food, go to *Restaurant Le Neuvième (☎ 05 62 61 71 99)* in the Hôtel de France (see Places to Stay), whose owner-chef, André Daguin, is an acknowledged specialist. Even budgeters will like the 55FF buffet des entrées in the hotel brasserie. It's closed on Sunday.

Hôtel-Restaurant Scheherazade (see Places to Stay) offers inexpensive Moroccan specialities and even Moroccan wines. *Restaurant Asia (☎ 05 62 05 93 17, 3 rue Arnaud de Môles)* is open daily except Monday with better-than-average Chinese and Vietnamese dishes from 30FF to 60FF. *La Bodega (☎ 05 62 05 69 17, 7 rue Dessoles)* is open for lunch and dinner (except Sunday lunch), with tapas or full meals and occasional live Latin/Spanish music.

For self-caterers, a *Spar supermarket* at 4 place Denfert Rochereau is open from 8.30 am to 8 pm on weekdays and from 9 am to 1 pm at the weekend. Auch's weekly markets are held on Thursday around Jardin Ortholan and on Saturday in front of the cathedral.

Getting There & Away
Except as noted, buses stop at both the bus station (☎ 05 62 05 76 37) and the train station (☎ 05 62 60 62 12). Useful long-distance connections include Condom (33FF, 40 minutes, one to four daily), Mont de Marsan (65FF, 1¾ hours, one daily), Toulouse (60FF, 1½ hours, one or two daily), Montauban (52FF, 1¾ hours, two on Monday, Wednesday and Friday) and Agen (60FF, 1½ hours, up to eight daily, train station only). Sunday services are limited.

The only useful direct trains serve Toulouse (71FF, 1¼ hours, three to six daily).

Getting Around
Drivers note: old right-of-way rules still apply at the place du Libération roundabout (ie entering drivers have priority).

Cycle Sobinski (☎ 05 62 63 60 56), 35 ave de l'Yser, touring street bikes and *vélos tout-terrains* (VTTs; mountain bikes).

The Lomagne

Between the Gers and Garonne rivers, reaching east into the Tarn-et-Garonne département, stretches the Lomagne, a postcard-pretty landscape of rolling green hills and aimless rivers, punctuated by limestone farmsteads, chateaux and ruined towers. This is the Gers' best farmland, and if the air has a certain tang it's because a good third of France's garlic is grown here.

LECTOURE
postcode 32700 • pop 4500 • elevation 180m
Lectoure, old capital of the Lomagne, is a handsome, stoic place, with a turbulent past that seems to have left it enervated behind its neoclassical facades. It sits on a boat-shaped rock above the Gers River that was already occupied by a tribe called the Lactoratii when the Romans moved in. The Romans built in the valley below, leaving the rock for temples to Jupiter and to Cybele, the ancient mother-goddess of Asia Minor.

Over time the high ground was reoccupied and the counts of Armagnac made this their capital. In 1472 Louis XI's army, admitted to the town on the strength of false promises, trashed it and murdered the last count. Protestant Lectoure was occupied by Catholic troops during the Wars of Religion. When Auch was made the Gers' capital after the Revolution, Lectoure faded away.

Orientation & Information
From the bus stand on rue Alsace-Lorraine, walk three blocks west to the tourist office (☎ 05 62 68 76 98, fax 05 62 68 79 30), on rue Nationale just beyond Cathédrale St-Gervais et St-Protais. The office is open from 9 am to noon and 2 to 6 pm daily, except Saturday afternoon and Sunday, and from 9 am to 12.30 pm and 2.30 to 7 pm daily in July and August. Most items of interest are clustered here at the eastern end of the old town. Three blocks west down rue Nationale are Caisse d'Épargne and Crédit Agricole banks.

Cathédrale St-Gervais et St-Protais

Most of this big cathedral dates from a 15th-century rebuild after its predecessor was wrecked by Louis XI's soldiers. With its curious, ornate tower, it's more interesting outside than in, though there's a collection of religious art in the baptistery. The tower is closed, though you might be able to persuade the caretaker to let you up for a view right out to the Pyrénées on a clear day.

Musée Lapidaire

Lectoure has an excellent museum of stonework in the cellars of the 17th-century episcopal palace (now the town hall), beside the cathedral. In pride of place are 20 Gallo-Roman altars decorated with bulls' or rams' heads (sacrificial animals used during ceremonies to Cybele). Other highlights include huge wine amphorae, early Christian funeral monuments and an ominous mosaic portrait of the god Oceanus.

Nominally the museum (☎ 05 62 68 70 22) is open from 10 am to noon and 2 to 6 pm daily (closed on Tuesday from October to February), but it is often closed early. Admission costs 15FF.

Other Things to See

The 14th-century **Tour du Bourreau** was once a defensive tower and the town executioner's home; from the cathedral walk two blocks north on rue Subervie and turn right. The **Tour d'Albinhoc**, 1½ blocks west of the tourist office down rue Nationale, was part of a 16th-century fortified house. The two towers are closed to the public. **Fontaine Diane** is a spring covered by a little Gothic vault, two blocks south of the tourist office on rue Fontélie.

Among several 18th-century private mansions are the **Hôtel de Trois Boules**, across rue Nationale from the cathedral, and the **Hôtel de Castaing** (now the Hôtel-Restaurant de Bastard), north of the tourist office off rue St-Gervais.

Places to Stay & Eat

Cheap accommodation and food are scarce. The nearest camp site, *Lac des Trois Vallées*

(☎ 05 62 68 82 33), charges 45FF per walker or cyclist with a tent, but otherwise 168FF *forfait* (a fixed price deal covering two people). It's part of a leisure complex with a pool, open-air cinema, windsurfing and boating, 4km south of town by the Gers River, and is open from Easter to mid-September.

Hôtel-Restaurant de Bastard (☎ 05 62 68 82 44, fax 05 62 68 76 81, rue Lagrange) offers simple, elegant doubles from 250FF, set *menus* from 90FF in a vaulted dining room, and a pool. The tourist office has a list of nearby *chambres d'hôtes* (B&Bs).

On rue Nationale and rue Alsace-Lorraine, east of the town centre, are a *cafe* and several *pizzerias*.

Getting There & Away

Lectoure is 36km north of Auch. SNCF's (☎ 08 36 35 35 35) Auch–Agen buses stop here eight times daily Monday to Friday, less often at the weekend (Auch 35FF, 40 minutes; Agen 36FF, 50 minutes).

EAST OF LECTOURE
L'Isle Bouzon

This photogenic hilltop village is 9km east of Lectoure on the D7. Up close it's a picturesquely run-down hamlet in the early stages of restoration, with traces of ancient walls, a diminutive 16th-century chateau and a charming *pigeonnier* (dovecote) of the same age.

St-Clar

A fortified chateau and a Benedictine priory founded here in the 10th century formed the nucleus of a little *castelnau* (literally a small village that grew up around the chateau of a local lord) run by the viscount of Lomagne and the bishop of Lectoure. A separate English bastide was founded in 1274 by agreement between the then bishop of Lectoure and Edward I, duke of Aquitaine.

Orientation & Information St-Clar is 6km south-east of L'Isle Bouzon. Its clearest landmark is the big parish church. Just to the south is ancient St-Clar, a tangle of alleys around place Dastros. Facing this little square is the crumbling, 12th-century

Vieille Église (old church), now ignominiously boarded up. Eastwards is the not-very-square **place de la République**, arcaded on three sides. The heart of 'English' St-Clar is two blocks north of the parish church in **place de la Mairie** (or place de la Halle), with the town hall, the tourist office (☎ 05 62 66 34 45, fax 05 62 66 32 17), a Crédit Agricole bank (with ATM) and a 13th-century wooden market hall.

St-Clar is the Lomagne's main centre for the processing of *l'ail blanc* (white garlic), with a *marché de l'ail* (garlic market) every Thursday morning from July to December, and a garlic festival on the second Thursday of August. The garlic market is 300m west of place de la République.

Places to Stay & Eat A three-room *chambre d'hôte* (☎ 05 62 66 47 31, fax 05 62 66 47 70) on place de la Mairie offers doubles from 280FF to 320FF, and dinner by arrangement for 90FF. *Restaurant Le Rison* (☎ 05 62 66 40 21, place de la Lomagne), with a rear entrance on place Dastros, serves garlicky regional *menus* from 95FF and offers a good-value 65FF lunch *menu*. It's closed on Monday evening and Wednesday.

Gramont

Tiny (population 107) Gramont, 3km east of L'Isle Bouzon on the Arrats River, is barely more than a church and a chateau.

The staid **Château de Gramont** (☎ 05 63 94 05 26, fax 05 63 94 14 63) has been carefully restored and donated to the state. At the front is the original 14th-century Gothic mansion. The immense wing at the back, begun in 1530 and chock-full of period furnishings and Aubusson tapestries, may represent the earliest appearance of the Italian Renaissance style in France. It's open daily for tours from 9 am to noon and 2 to 7 pm from May to October, and from 2 to 6 pm during the rest of the year (closed in December and January). Admission costs 32FF. This is also the venue for art exhibits and a small festival of classical music from July to mid-August.

For something more down to earth, visit the village's **Musée du Miel** (☎ 05 63 94 00 20), a small museum of honey production with, of course, a shop. Opposite the church and chateau is the twee *Auberge le Petit Feuillant* (☎ *05 63 94 00 08*), whose restaurant offers traditional dishes in *menus* costing from 90FF (closed Sunday evening and Wednesday).

Flamarens

The 13th- to 15th-century hilltop **chateau** (☎/fax 05 62 28 68 25) in this hamlet in the north-eastern corner of the Gers has a fine round tower-keep with a grand view over the countryside. Its single wing and adjacent ruined church are undergoing a slow private restoration, but they're open for tours in July and August, from 10 am to noon and 2 to 7 pm daily (except Tuesday). West of the village is the simple **Ecomusée de la Lomagne** (☎ 05 62 68 76 98), a museum about life in the Lomagne in the 19th century.

Flamarens is about 20km north-east of Lectoure on the D23.

FLEURANCE
postcode 32500 • pop 6500 • elevation 92m
A handsome bastide, sturdy and ungentrified, Fleurance was founded on the Gers River in 1274 by Eustache de Beaumarchais, royal governor or *sénéchal* of Toulouse, who established several other Gascon bastides too, naming many for famous cities of Italy and Spain. Though this one is no match for Florence, it's a cheaper and more agreeable base than Lectoure for exploring the Lomagne.

Orientation & Information
From the bus stand on allées Aristide Briand (the N21), walk north about four blocks to the central square, place de la République. The tourist office (☎ 05 62 64 00 00, fax 05 62 06 27 80), a block south of the square on rue de la République, is open from 9 am to 6.30 pm daily (closed from noon on Sunday and from noon to 2 pm on Monday) in July and August, and from 9 am to 6 pm Monday to Saturday during the rest of the year.

Things to See

The ancient bastide grid is now populated with 18th-century buildings. At the centre of place de la République stands a handsome **market hall** (and town hall) completed in 1837, with statues at each corner representing the seasons. Don't miss the vast Gothic **Église St-Laurent**, started soon after the bastide's founding and 2½ centuries in construction, with three fine stained-glass windows by Arnaud de Môles.

Places to Stay & Eat

The basic *Camp Municipal* (☎ 05 62 06 10 01) is three blocks east of the bus stand, by the river and a small leisure centre. It's open from mid-June to mid-September and costs 8/5/5FF per adult/tent/car.

Two modest hotels a few blocks south of place de la République are *Hôtel de France* (☎ 05 62 64 03 28, fax 05 62 06 07 13, 69 rue de la République) which has doubles with toilet and shower costing 260FF, and *Hôtel Capelli* (☎ 05 62 06 11 88, 72 rue Gambetta) with doubles that cost from 110FF to 190FF. Up a notch is the two star *Hôtel Le Relais* (☎ 05 62 06 05 08, fax 05 62 06 03 84, 32 ave Général de Gaulle), south on the N21 with doubles with toilet and toilet costing around 250FF. The tourist office has the details of nearby *chambres d'hôtes*.

Le Chantpie (☎ 05 62 64 04 85, 24 place de la République) is an adequate and fairly cheap brasserie.

Getting There & Away

Fleurance is 24km north of Auch on the N21, the road to Lectoure. SNCF's Auch–Agen buses (☎ 08 36 35 35 35) stop here eight times daily Monday to Friday, less often at the weekend (Auch 30 minutes; Agen 50 minutes).

Pays d'Armagnac

North-west Gers is the land of Armagnac, the south-west's answer to cognac (see the boxed text 'Armagnac'). Its gentle hills are a patchwork of vineyards, plum orchards and wheat fields. This is also, more or less, the historical domain of the counts of Armagnac, Gascony's godfathers until Louis XI brought the line to an end in 1472 (see Lectoure in the earlier Lomagne section).

CONDOM

postcode 3210 • pop 8070 • elevation 80m

Poor Condom, whose resonant name (see the boxed text 'Put It This Way, How Did the Condom Get *Its* Name?') has made it the butt of endless English jokes. Some tourists only stop to be photographed beside

---

Put It This Way, How Did the Condom Get *Its* Name?

You would think from all the sniggering that the town was named for the contraceptive sheath. Condoms have been used since the 18th century as a means to control the spread of syphilis and, although a 'Dr Condom' is often identified as its inventor, no physician by that name has been traced. The word carries no overtones for French speakers, who refer to the little latex device as a *préservatif*.

Nobody is sure where Condom-the-town got its name either, though it probably derives from a Roman-era name – perhaps from the Latin *condominium*, for shared ownership or rule, as was the case with the Vascone people who first settled here.

At any rate the town is not about to let itself become an international joke. In true Gascon style, it has taken the offensive, hosting exhibitions and a conference on *le préservatif*. In the works is the Musée Condom, a museum on sexuality and contraception, and an international centre for research on sexually transmitted diseases and family planning, to open around 2002. For more information contact the *mairie* (town hall; ☎ 05 62 28 24 88, fax 05 62 28 48 32, email condom1@cie.fr) or visit their Web site at www.condom.org.

GERS

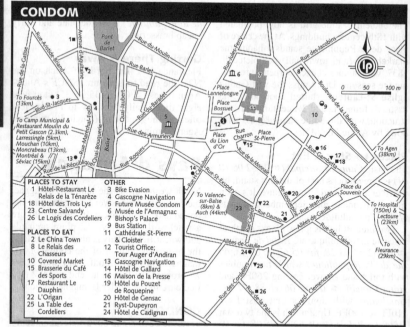

CONDOM

0 50 100 m

PLACES TO STAY		OTHER	
1	Hôtel-Restaurant Le Relais de la Ténarèze	3	Bike Evasion
18	Hôtel des Trois Lys	4	Gascogne Navigation
23	Centre Salvandy	5	Future Musée Condom
26	Le Logis des Cordeliers	6	Musée de l'Armagnac
		7	Bishop's Palace
PLACES TO EAT		9	Bus Station
2	Le China Town	11	Cathédrale St-Pierre
8	Le Relais des Chasseurs		& Cloister
10	Covered Market	12	Tourist Office;
15	Brasserie du Café des Sports		Tour Auger d'Andiran
17	Restaurant Le Dauphin	13	Gascogne Navigation
22	L'Origan	14	Hôtel de Gallard
25	La Table des Cordeliers	16	Maison de la Presse
		19	Hôtel du Pouzet de Roquepine
		20	Hôtel de Gensac
		21	Ryst-Dupeyron
		24	Hôtel de Cadignan

the sign *Bienvenue à Condom, Ville Propre* (Welcome to Condom, the Clean Town). But this pretty – and indeed very clean – town beside the Baïse River is worth a visit for its cathedral and a clutch of sober neoclassical mansions, and for its access to the surrounding Ténarèze region.

History

The Vascone people – forebears of both the Gascons and the Basques (see History in the Facts about South-West France chapter) – settled here in the early 8th century. One of Condom's nicknames is 'the town of 100 towers', which may refer to the fortified homes of the families who shared control of the settlement's affairs.

A proper town grew around the 11th-century Benedictine Abbey of St Pierre. Condom suffered repeatedly during the Albigensian Crusade (following which it was made a bishopric), the Hundred Years' War and the Wars of Religion. Much of the

'old' town dates from Condom's economic revival in the 17th and 18th centuries.

Orientation & Information

The tourist office (☎ 05 62 28 00 80, fax 05 62 28 45 46, email otsi.condom.org.etotsi@wanadoo.fr) is on place Bossuet, in the 13th-century Tour Auger d'Andiran. The office is open from 10 am to 1 pm and 2.30 to 7.30 pm daily in July and August; from 9 am to 12.30 pm and 2 to 6.30 pm (closed Sunday) in May, June, September and October; and from 9 am to noon and 2 to 6 pm (closed Sunday) during the rest of the year.

Place St-Pierre is the town's centre. Several banks here have ATMs, including Caisse d'Épargne and Crédit Agricole, open on weekdays only. The Centre Hospitalier (hospital; ☎ 05 62 28 20 77) is at 21 ave Maréchal Joffre. A small Maison de la Presse at 26 rue Gambetta sells guidebooks, maps and French-language books on the region, plus a few foreign newspapers.

Cathédrale St-Pierre & Around

Built in less than three decades at the start of
the 16th century, Condom's cathedral immediately took a severe beating in the Wars
of Religion. Its finest portal faces place St-
Pierre in an otherwise sombre Gothic-
Renaissance facade. The Flamboyant Gothic
interior has a few original stained-glass windows and many from the 19th century. The
Chapelle Ste-Marie at the eastern end was
there two centuries before the cathedral.

North of the cathedral is the **cloister**, now
occupied by the town hall. Nearby, on place
Lannelongue, is the sub-prefecture, in the
18th-century **bishop's palace**, with one fine
Renaissance portal.

Armagnac

The **Musée de l'Armagnac** (☎ 05 62 28 31
41), in the former episcopal stables at 2 rue
Jules Ferry, offers a look at the traditional
production of Armagnac (see the boxed text
'Armagnac' later in this section). It's open
from 10 am to noon and 3 to 5 pm daily except Tuesday, from March to October (to
6 pm in September and to 7 pm in July and
August); admission costs 14FF.

Family-run **Ryst-Dupeyron** (☎ 05 62 28
08 08, fax 05 62 28 16 42) is one of several
Armagnac producers offering free tastings
and tours, from 10 am to noon and 2 to 5 pm
Monday to Friday (to 6 pm, plus from 3.30
to 6.30 pm at the weekend in July and August). It's in an 18th-century mansion, the
Hôtel de Cugnac, at 36 rue Jean Jaurès.

Mansions

Condom is graced with many 18th-century
hôtels particuliers (mansions), quite unlike
the Renaissance confections of Toulouse
and Montauban. Handsomer ones include
the Hôtel de Gallard (rue H Cazaubon),
Hôtel de Gensac (rue de Roquepine), Hôtel
du Pouzet de Roquepine (rue Jean Jaurès,
along the line of the old town walls) and
Hôtel de Cadignan (allées de Gaulle). None
is open to the public.

River Cruises

A 20km stretch of the Baïse between Mon-
crabeau and Valence-sur-Baïse is open to

navigation, with six bypass locks open from
late March to November. Gascogne Navigation (☎ 05 62 28 46 46, fax 05 62 28 37
28), on quai Bouquerie and at 4 rue
Maréchal Foch, rents small boats by the day
and bigger ones by the week and – in July
and August – runs 1½ hour cruises (45FF;
children aged four to 12 years 35FF) every
afternoon except Sunday.

Special Events

On the second weekend in May, Bandas à
Condom (☎/fax 05 62 68 31 38) brings
marching bands from all over Europe for 48
hours of singing, dancing, competitions and
hi-jinks. The town has recently started its
own rock festival, Rockin' Condom, for a
week in mid-June.

Places to Stay

The tourist office keeps a list of *chambres
d'hôtes* around Condom, and can tell you
about several *camping à la ferme* within
5km.

The well-equipped *Camp Municipal*
(☎ 05 62 28 17 32, fax 05 62 28 48 32),
south-west on the D931, is open from April
to mid-September, and charges 18FF per
adult and 19FF per site plus car. There are
also bungalows that sleep up to six people
costing 2570FF per week. Nearby is a
sports centre with tennis, swimming and
horse riding. There's no public transport.

Centre Salvandy (☎ 05 62 28 23 80, 20
rue Jean Jaurès) has a *gîte d'étape* (hikers'
accommodation) where dorm beds cost
41FF (46FF in winter).

*Hôtel-Restaurant Le Relais de la Téna-
rèze* (☎ 05 62 28 02 54, fax 05 62 28 46 96,
22 ave d'Aquitaine) has doubles with
shower for 210FF, and with toilet and
shower/bath for 245/285FF. The restaurant
is closed on Saturday evening and Sunday.

Peaceful *Le Logis des Cordeliers* (☎ 05
62 28 03 68, fax 05 62 68 29 03, rue de la
Paix) offers quiet doubles from 260FF
(closed in January).

Indulge yourself at the first-rate, family-
run *Hôtel des Trois Lys* (☎ 05 62 28 33 33,
fax 05 62 28 41 85, email hoteltroislys@
minitel.net, 38 rue Gambetta), sited in an

GERS

18th-century townhouse, where doubles start at 380FF. Both these hotels have swimming pools.

Places to Eat

If your budget's tight, **Brasserie du Café des Sports** (☎ 05 62 28 15 26, 11 rue Charron) serves grills and big salads from noon to 7.30 pm daily. Les Routiers restaurants are always good value; Condom's is **Le Relais des Chasseurs** (☎ 05 62 28 20 14, 3 blvd de la Libération), where menus start at 55FF. It's closed Sunday and Monday evenings. For a change from French food try **Le China Town** (☎ 05 62 68 25 10, 9 ave d'Aquitaine), closed on Monday.

Recommended is the 48FF plat du jour (meal of the day) at **Restaurant Le Dauphin** (☎ 05 62 28 44 67, 38 rue Gambetta), closed Sunday evening and on Monday. Another top choice is **L'Origan** (☎ 05 62 68 24 84, 4 rue Cadéot), a popular, good-value place with a robust choice of Italian dishes. It's closed on Sunday and for lunch on Monday.

Popular **La Table des Cordeliers** (☎ 05 62 68 28 36, 1 rue des Cordeliers) offers fine Gascon cuisine daily (except Friday from mid-September to mid-May) for lunch and dinner, in a 14th-century chapel. On the river by Camp Municipal, **Restaurant Moulin du Petit Gascon** (☎ 05 62 28 28 42) is open daily with sandwiches, snacks and a 95FF three-course menu.

Condom's **covered market**, behind the bus station, comes to life all day Wednesday.

Getting There & Away

ATR (☎ 05 62 05 46 24) has one to four daily buses to Auch (33FF, 50 minutes), including one that continues to Toulouse (81FF, 2½ hours); and one daily to Bordeaux (101FF, 3 hours). Citram Pyrénées runs once daily from Pau (128FF, 2¼ hours); the same service continues to Agen (46FF, 45 minutes).

Getting Around

Bike Evasion (☎ 05 62 28 00 47), 14 blvd St Jacques, rents bikes for 70/120FF per day/weekend (for children 50/90FF). It's open Tuesday to Saturday. Camp Municipal (see Places to Stay) also rents bikes.

AROUND CONDOM

Condom is within reach of a spectrum of sights in the Ténarèze, from a Gallo-Roman villa to UNESCO-protected waystations on the road to Santiago de Compostela.

La Romieu

postcode 32480 • pop 550 • elevation 185m

Tradition holds that two monks returning from a pilgrimage to Rome founded a monastery here in 1062. They named the place La Romieu, from the Latin romaeus or Occitan roumieu (pilgrim). A village grew up around the monastery.

Arnaud d'Aux was born into a noble family here in about 1265. When his cousin became Pope Clement V and moved the papacy to Avignon, Arnaud was made a cardinal. With the wealth that soon came his way he bought the monastery, enlarged it and built himself a collegiate church and palace, completed in 1318. Though the palace has mostly disappeared, the church and monastery have probably changed little since then, with Arnaud's towers rising above folds of Gascon farmland.

In 1999 the church was, along with other French landmarks on the road to Compostela, granted UNESCO World Heritage protection. The GR65 arcs north around the village.

Orientation & Information The tourist office (☎ 05 62 28 86 33), opposite the cloister at the eastern end of the central square, place Bonet, is open from 10 am to noon and 2 to 6 pm daily (to 7 pm in June and September, 7.30 pm in July and August). It's closed in January.

Monastery & Church Tourist office staff will let you into the 14th-century complex; admission costs 20FF. Through the Gothic cloister – originally three storeys tall – is the luminous little Collégiale St-Pierre church. Along the side walls are the tombs of Arnaud d'Aux and several of his nephews. The stained glass dates from the

1860s except for a small 16th-century head of Christ at the centre of the rose window.

Left of the altar is the **sacristy**, whose original frescoes include biblical characters, family portraits and esoteric symbols. From there, climb the double-helix stairway into the octagonal **Belvedere Tower**, with views over the countryside. The church also has a square belfry, and just to the west is the **Cardinal's Tower**, all that remains of Arnaud's palace.

Arboretum Coursiana This six-hectare arboretum at the western end of the village, with over 600 trees and rare plants, was the personal project of a local agricultural engineer. It's open daily; admission costs 25FF. Nearby is the village's own, smaller arboretum.

Places to Stay & Eat About 300m east of the town centre the four star *Camp de Florence* (☎ 05 62 28 15 58, fax 05 62 28 20 04), open from April to October, charges 112FF forfait. It also has bungalows, a swimming pool and a pricey restaurant.

Two eateries on place Bonet have a few doubles: *Restaurant Le Cardinal* (☎ 05 62 28 80 08) from 180FF, and *Crêperie Bretonne* (☎ 05 62 28 84 35) from 300FF. The tourist office has a list of local *rooms*, *gîtes* (cottages), *chambres d'hôtes* and *camping à la ferme*.

Getting There & Away No buses come here, but it's an undemanding drive or cycle ride from Condom (go north-east on the D931 for 2.5km, then turn right on the D41 for 8.5km).

Fourcès

Fourcès (pronounce the *s*), 13km northwest of Condom beside the Auzoue River, is a heavily restored, unbearably cute bastide, founded by the English in the 13th century. What makes it interesting is that it's circular, with sturdy, arcaded medieval houses ringing the shady central 'square,' plus a 15th - or 16th-century bell tower and fragments of a surrounding wall.

The population swells from 350 to thousands during the village's *Marché aux Fleurs* (Flower Market) on the last weekend of April.

At *L'Auberge* (☎ 05 62 29 49 53) on the main square, enjoy a drink and a snack with the other foreign tourists. Lunch/dinner *menus* start at 85FF/105FF, though the delicately prepared dishes won't fill you up. It's open daily, except Wednesday evening.

Larressingle & the Pont d'Artigue

Larressingle, about 5km west of Condom on the D15, may be France's cutest fortified village. Armies of Compostela pilgrims and breathless tourists seem to have put its tiny community on the defensive. Locals, presumably with tongues deep in their cheeks, refer to it as 'the Carcassonne of the Gers'.

But it's pretty amazing, a textbook bastion bearing witness to the troubled times of medieval Gascony, driven by the Hundred Years' War. From its 12th-century founding it belonged jointly to the abbeys of Agen and Condom, and was later an official residence of the bishops of Condom.

The original walls are largely intact, surrounded by a moat once spanned by a drawbridge. Inside are the remains of a castle-keep, the sturdy Romanesque Église St-Sigismond, an unconvincing museum of medieval life, plus a small creperie and a couple of craft shops. You can see the whole place in half an hour.

About 1.5km south of the village is the **Pont d'Artigue**, a simple stone bridge with asymmetrical arches, across the Osse River. Built for Compostela pilgrims in the Middle Ages, it's part of the inventory of pilgrim sites with a joint UNESCO World Heritage designation.

Montréal du Gers & Séviac

postcode 32250 • pop 1400 • elevation 165m

Montréal du Gers was one of Gascony's first bastides, begun in 1255 by Alphonse de Poitiers, although the English moved in before he had finished it. The once-fortified site, above the gorge of the River Auzoue, is all the more attractive for being largely unrestored. Its chunky Gothic church squats at the edge of the main square, thumbing its nose at the bastide's precision by aligning itself instead with the town walls. The arcaded square is the scene of a bustling Friday market The town's trump card, however, is the excavated remains of a Gallo-Roman country house, 1½km south-west of the centre, at Séviac.

Orientation & Information The tourist office (☎ 05 62 29 42 85, fax 05 62 29 45 45) and an attached museum of Séviac artefacts are on the main square, place Hôtel de Ville. Both are open from 10 am to noon and 2 to 7 pm daily, from June to October; and from 3 to 5 pm daily except Sunday during the rest of the year (closed in January).

Séviac This site came to light in 1866, when the curate of nearby Labarrère found a patch of mosaic tiles. Further work came in 1909, but most excavation was done between 1959 and 1992.

What archaeologists found were the remnants of a luxurious villa on the agricultural estate of a 4th-century Roman aristocrat, along with other buildings dating from the 2nd to the 7th centuries. Large areas of the villa's spectacular mosaic floors – in some 30 detailed patterns – had survived intact. An attached bathing complex was equipped with a forced-air heating system – state-of-the-art for its time and the grandest ever found in a private house.

Admission to the two-hectare site costs 20FF (the ticket also permits you to visit the museum attached to Montréal's tourist office). The site is open from 10 am to noon and 2 to 6 pm daily from March to November (to 7 pm with no lunch break in July and August), and a detailed multilingual text is available to borrow. From Montréal, take the D29 to Eauze for 500m, turn right (west) for 1km and turn right again.

Places to Stay Camp sites include *La Rose d'Armagnac* (☎/fax 05 62 29 47 70), just north of Montréal on the D29, open from April to October (10/18/25FF per adult/tent/car); and *Camp Municipal* (☎ 05 62 29 20 21, fax 05 62 29 23 73)*, 8km south on the D29, open June to September (8/6/6FF).

The *Hôtel de la Gare* (☎ 05 62 29 43 37), 3km south on the D29, was once the local train station. It's now open from Easter to October, with basic singles/doubles from 180/250FF, with breakfast. For walkers there's a *gîte d'étape* (☎ 05 62 29 48 57) at Séviac. The tourist office has a list of nearby *chambre d'hôtes* with doubles from 170FF to 210FF (some also do meals by arrangement), and *camping à la ferme*.

Places to Eat Just off the main square, *Restaurant Chez Simone* (☎ 05 62 29 44 40, place des Champions de France de Rugby)* has a 70FF menu du jour. If that sounds too much, there's an *épicerie* (grocery) on the main square.

Château de Cassaigne

You can enjoy a free visit to this 13th-century chateau, ancient country-house of the bishops of Condom, and sample the Armagnac produced in its 18th-century distillery. Also worth a look is the 16th-century kitchen. The chateau (☎ 05 62 28 04 02, fax 05 62 28 41 43), 6.5km south-west of Condom, just off the D931 to Eauze, is open from 9 am to noon and 2 to 7 pm, year-round.

Mouchan

Mouchan's main attraction is a humble, pretty **Romanesque church**, the 13th-century Église St-Austrégésille (or Austrigile). The base of the square belfry dates from its 10th-century predecessor, a Benedictine priory. Around the choir are several stone **capitals** carved with foliage, abstract designs and tiny biblical scenes. The church is open to the public from 10 am to noon and 3 to 7 pm, daily (except Monday morning) from May to mid-October.

Two blocks south-west is what's left of a protective **ditch**, contemporaneous with the priory. Just west of the ditch by the Osse River are the remains of a **Roman bridge**. In the neighbourhood east of the church are several 16th-century **stone houses**.

Getting There & Away Mouchan is 10km south-west of Condom on the D931. Citram Pyrénées' Agen–Pau bus stops in Condom at 11.15 am Monday to Friday and at 9.10 am on Saturday, and in Mouchan 15 minutes later, with a return stop in Mouchan at 7.35 pm. The trip costs 9FF. ATR's Toulouse–Barbotan buses leave Condom at 12.20 pm and return through Mouchan at 3.35 pm, daily except Sunday.

Abbaye de Flaran

Flaran Abbey was founded on the banks of the Baïse in 1151, part of the Cistercian movement for a return to back-to-basics monasticism. Despite severe damage in the Hundred Years' War, desecration by Protestant troops in 1569 during the Wars of Religion, and layers of Baroque plaster applied in the 17th and 18th centuries, you can still sense its founding spirit, particularly in the beautiful church. This is the Gers' best-preserved Cistercian site, feasible as a day trip from Auch or Condom.

You enter through lavish **guest quarters** dating from the 18th century (by which time the monks were spending little time in the monastery). Turn right into the **cloister**. One gallery dates from the 14th century, with capitals carved with foliage and faces, and traces of its Romanesque predecessor. The other three, trashed by the Protestants, are now supported by simple bevelled columns. Off the cloister are kitchen, refectory, a fine vaulted chapter house, and above it a dormitory with some Romanesque windows. The best part is the early 13th-century **church** – the Église Notre Dame – startlingly austere but full of light, with a transept longer than the nave.

The complex (☎ 05 62 28 50 19) is open from 9.30 am to noon and 2 to 6 pm (to 7 pm with no lunch break in July and August). Privately owned since the Revolution, it's now being transferred to the state. During the transition, admission has been free, though an entry charge is in the offing.

Places to Stay Flaran is 1km west across the river from Valence-sur-Baïse, which has

a *gîte-d'étape* (☎ 05 62 28 59 19). The Logis de France *Ferme de Flaran (☎ 05 62 28 58 22, fax 05 62 28 56 89)*, in Maignaut-Tauzia, 2km north-east of Valence, offers comfortable doubles from 200FF.

Getting There & Away The nearest bus stop is in Valence-sur-Baïse. Useful ATR bus departures from Condom (9FF; 15 minutes) are at 10 am and 4 pm, with return departures from Valence at 12.10 and 7 pm, daily except Sunday.

Chateaux of the Hundred Years' War

The Osse River was an important natural boundary between French and English holdings during the Hundred Years' War, making its valley a pretty nerve-wracking place to live. Many rich Gascon landowners built fortified homes, and today their 13th- and 14th-century ruins dot the hilltops. None is open to the public but you can see them from the road. One photogenic ruin that's not hard to find is **Château Tauzia**, about 2km north-east of Valence.

BAS-ARMAGNAC

The north-western corner of the Gers – with some overlap into Lot-et-Garonne and the Landes – is called Bas-Armagnac. This is the heart of Armagnac brandy country, the zone of its best-known *appellation contrôlée*. Here too is the boyhood home of the prototype Gascon, Alexandre Dumas' larger-than-life hero, D'Artagnan.

Labastide d'Armagnac

postcode 40240 • pop 730 • elevation 94m
This pocket-sized bastide – vine-covered, cobbled and unassuming – was founded in 1291 by Comte Bernard VI d'Armagnac. Though marooned since the Revolution in the Landes, it's decidedly Gascon. Most villagers today are involved in one way or another with the production of Armagnac and floc de Gascogne at nearby Château Garreau.

Information The tourist office (☎ 05 58 44 67 56, fax 05 58 44 84 15) is on the

Armagnac

> O Lord, give me good health, for a long time; love, from time to time; work, not much of the time; and Armagnac, all the time.
>
> **Village prayer, Fourcès**

Armagnac is probably France's original brandy (distilled wine), first produced as a medicine in the 15th century.

White-wine grapes of 10 approved varieties are harvested in October, made into wine, and single-distilled over the winter into a potent, colourless *eau de vie*. This is matured in 400L oak casks – traditionally made from trees grown on the same soil as the grapes – for 10 to 40 years or more, taking from the wood its amber colour and an array of subtle aromas.

Then it's blended and bottled. Armagnac's high alcohol content (at least 40%) means that it doesn't mature further in the bottle. It can be drunk immediately and will keep indefinitely. Its 'age' is the time spent in the cask: a Trois Étoiles brandy is aged at least two years; VO, VSOP and Réserve at least five; Extra, Napoléon, XO and Vieille Réserve at least six; and Hors d'Age at least 10. Vintage brandies, like vintage wines, are blended only from grapes harvested in specific years.

A gentler fortified wine called Floc de Gascogne (Flower of Gascony), with the strength of sherry or port, is made by blending young Armagnac and the juice of a single grape variety from the same vineyard, and ageing it in casks for at least 10 months. This may be *floc blanc* or *floc rosé*, according to whether the juice grape is white or red.

The Armagnac area covers some 150 sq km in north-west Gers, plus a few parishes of the Landes and Lot-et-Garonne. There are three *appellations d'origine contrôlée*. From the sandy, acidic soil of the **Bas-Armagnac** come the finest brandies, delicate and fruity. The chalky clay of the **Ténarèze** produces full-bodied brandies that age well. The **Haut-Armagnac** is a 19th-century expansion with only a small fraction of the total output.

You can stop for a free taste at any number of small producers (bigger tourist offices keep lists of them). A good place for a guided walk through the process is the Domaine Départemental d'Ognoas (see that section on the following page). Condom also has an Armagnac museum.

---

central square, place Royale. It's open from 10.30 am to 12.30 pm and 2.30 to 6.30 pm (but closed Sunday morning) from April to October, and from 10 am to noon and 2 to 6 pm on weekdays during the rest of the year (closed in December and January).

Musée des Bastides Labastide takes aim at the tourist market with this earnest museum of bastides. An audioguide (French only) walks you through a pocket history of bastides and through the construction and occupation of one, complete with 'medieval street' soundtrack. The museum (☎ 05 58 44 81 42) is open from 10.30 am to 12.30 pm and 2.30 to 4.30 pm daily from April to September. Admission costs 20FF (children aged under 12 years 8FF).

The museum is in a restored Protestant church *(temple)*, built outside the walls after the one inside was burned following the 1685 revocation of the Edict of Nantes.

Ecomusée de l'Armagnac At Château Garreau (☎ 05 58 44 88 38), 3km south-east of Labastide d'Armagnac, is a collection of old Armagnac stills and other apparatus, along with vineyards, woods and a small bird refuge, open from 9 am to noon and 2 to 6 pm daily (only from 3 pm on Sunday from April to October); admission costs 20FF. Free tastings of their own floc and Armagnac are also available.

Places to Stay & Eat The three-star *Camping Le Pin (☎/fax 05 58 44 88 91)*, 4km north-west at St-Justin, costs 90FF for-fait. Simpler options within 15km of Labastide include *Camp Municipal de Nauton (☎ 05 58 45 50 45)* at Roquefort (12.50FF per adult, 14.50FF per tent) and *Le Relais Landais (☎ 05 58 45 36 23)* at Villeneuve de Marsan (15/25/5FF per adult/tent/car).

There are four *chambres d'hôtes* in or near the village; ask at the tourist office. There are no hotels, and the only place to eat is the small *Crêperie Sucre-Paille (☎ 05 58 44 81 43, place Royale)*, open from May to October. In St-Justin is the two-star *Hôtel de France (☎ 05 58 44 83 61, fax 05 58 44 83 89, place des Tilleuls)*.

Getting There & Away The Mont de Marsan–Agen bus stops here (see Mont de Marsan in the Bordeaux, the Atlantic Coast & the Landes chapter), daily except Saturday. The fare is 37FF from Mont de Marsan and 80FF from Agen.

Domaine Départemental d'Ognoas

This is Gascony's oldest distillery, founded in 1486, and the only one in France owned

by the state. In 1847 the heirless family left the *domaine* (estate) to the church. After the formal separation of church and state in 1905 it went to the Landes département, which now runs it like a private operation, with a quality product and all profits re-invested, but also as a showplace for Armagnac production.

The 540-hectare estate includes 25 hectares of vineyards and 300 hectares of dedicated forests. Armagnac is produced using a single 1804 copper still. Casks – from oak trees at least 80 years old, dried for seven years – are made in the traditional way by the only cooper in the region who still knows the art.

The estate (☎ 05 58 45 22 11, fax 05 58 45 38 21) is 4km east of Villeneuve de Marsan and 21km east of Mont de Marsan on the D1. It's open for free tours and tast-ing from 9 am to noon and 2 to 5.30 pm Monday to Friday, and from May to Sep-tember from 2 to 6 pm at the weekend and on holidays – but call first, preferably several days ahead. Non-French-speaking guides are available in high season.

Centre d'Artagnan (Lupiac)

Tiny Lupiac's sole claim to fame is that Charles de Batz-Castelmore, better known as D'Artagnan (see the boxed text 'D'Ar-tagnan & the Three Musketeers'), was born and raised at Château Castelmore, 4km to the north. The chateau is closed to the public, but a small museum, the Centre D'Artagnan, has been grafted onto the Chapelle St-Jacques, built in 1605 by D'Artagnan's uncle Charles for pilgrims on the way to Santiago de Compostela.

For 20FF (children aged 10 to 18 years 15FF) you rent an audioguide cassette, with narratives triggered electronically by each exhibit. There's also a short video. Though jumbled and vaguely corny, they provide a good introduction to the times D'Artagnan lived in, and dispel a few of the myths pro-mulgated by Alexandre Dumas.

The museum (☎ 05 62 09 24 09, fax 05 62 09 22 68), a stone's throw from the arcaded centre of Lupiac, is open from 10.30 am to 7 pm daily in July and August

GERS

D'Artagnan & the Three Musketeers

Many people think the reckless heroes of Alexandre Dumas' romantic novel, *Les Trois Mousquetaires* (The Three Musketeers), are pure invention. In fact they really existed, though not as Dumas portrayed them.

D'Artagnan, whose real name was Charles de Batz-Castelmore, was born around 1611 in Castelmore. At the age of 19 – and borrowing the name D'Artagnan from his mother's side of the family for its aristocratic ring – he left for Paris, enrolling as a cadet in the royal guards.

Little is known of his early years there but he gained a reputation – partly via Paris' salon society – as a brave soldier and a gallant gentleman. This brought him to the attention of Cardinal Mazarin, Louis XIV's chief minister, and before long he had become a friend and confidant of the King himself. Eventually D'Artagnan was given command of the musket-armed elite of the royal guards, the *mousquetaires*. Arrogant, quarrelsome, rowdy but brave and disciplined, the mousquetaires were always at the head of royal corteges.

Soon he had become Maréchal

NICKY CAVEN

Charles de Batz-Castelmore (c1611-73) was Dumas' inspiration for the musketeer D'Artagnan.

D'Artagnan, taking part in military campaigns all over Europe. He was rewarded in 1672 with the governorship of Lille, but soon grew restless for the soldier's life. He died a hero's death, of a musket-shot to the neck, in the siege of Maastricht in 1673.

Fake D'Artagnan 'memoirs', anonymously ghost-written 27 years after his death, were discovered by Dumas in a Marseille library, and served as background for the latter's now-famous novel. D'Artagnan (who apparently did have three close friends in the musketeers) had come back to life in swashbuckling, highly fictionalised form. But, as Dumas wrote, history is just 'the nail upon which I hang my stories'.

Never mind: the novel was received with enthusiasm, and over the years some 50 films have been made about the imaginary adventures of D'Artagnan and his companions Athos, Porthos and Aramis.

and from 2 to 6 pm daily (except Monday and 1-15 January) the rest of the year.

Lupiac is 9km east of Aignan on the D174; Aignan is 22km south of Eauze on the D20. There's no public transport.

Southern Gers

This is about as out-of-the-way as you can get in this out-of-the-way département. Most of the Gers' major rivers seem to fan out from a single imaginary point in the High Pyrénées, and south of Auch they carve the landscape into corduroy.

MARCIAC
postcode 32230 • pop 1200 • elevation 155m
Marciac's annual jazz festival, now one of the biggest in France, has put it on the map. But this is also an emblematic bastide of South-West France, founded in 1298 for Philippe IV, and now under unhurried renovation. The town's tall steeple rises above the countryside like the spire of a wayward cathedral. A nearby lake and water-sports complex make this a good place to stop with kids.

Orientation & Information
On the spacious, arcaded central square, place de l'Hôtel-de-Ville, are the town hall, post office, bank and – on Wednesday mornings – a big produce market. The tourist office (☎ 05 62 09 30 55, fax 05 62 09 31 88, email marciac@wanadoo.fr), at nearby place du Chevalier d'Antras, is open from 9 am to noon and 2 to 6 pm (from 9.30 am on Sunday) daily from April to September, and daily except Saturday during the rest of the year.

Église Notre-Dame de Marciac
Marciac's fine 14th-century Gothic church has portals and interior capitals carved in an appealing, almost Romanesque style. The 85m steeple is the highest tower in the Gers.

Les Territoires du Jazz
Les Territoires du Jazz (☎ 05 62 09 30 18, fax 05 62 09 31 88) is a multi-media 'museum' of jazz from its African roots to the present. Visitors don headsets and jive through a dozen musical settings from Dixieland to the Blues. It shares space with the tourist office in a 15th-century abbey on place du Chevalier d'Antras, and is open from 9.30 am to 12.30 pm and 2.30 to 6.30 pm, daily from early April to September and daily except Saturday and holidays during the rest of the year. Admission costs 30FF (students and children aged under 18 years 20FF).

Base Nautique
About 1km north of the town centre on the D3 is a big water-sports complex (☎ 05 62 09 34 65) on a 30 hectare lake with windsurfing, sailing, boats of every sort, waterskiing and fishing.

Special Events
Jazz in Marciac is the grandfather of the Midi-Pyrénées' many jazz festivals, with big-name concerts, jam sessions and masterclasses, as well as special markets and exhibitions, for 10 days in August. It's gradually expanding across the calendar, with guest artists throughout the year. Festival tickets cost from 60FF to 250FF; for information and bookings check out the Web site at www.marciac.com or contact them direct on ☎ 05 62 09 33 33/08 03 02 00 40, fax 05 62 09 38 67.

Places to Stay & Eat
The year-round *Camping du Lac* (☎/fax 05 62 08 21 19), at the Base Nautique, charges 29FF per adult plus 22/32FF per site with tent/caravan, during most of August. Lower rates apply for the rest of the year. On the same site is the floating *Restaurant La Péniche* (☎ 05 62 09 38 46), where *menus* start at 85FF (closed on Monday).

Right in the town centre is the two-star *Hôtel Comte de Pardiac* (☎ 05 62 08 20 00, 28 place de l'Hôtel de Ville), where doubles cost from 200FF to 260FF. An alternative is *Hôtel-Restaurant Les Promenades* (☎ 05 62 09 38 13, 21 rue Henri Laignoux), the restaurant is closed on Saturday. The tourist office has lists of nearby *chambres d'hôtes* and can arrange *homestays* during the jazz festival.

Brasserie Le Festival (☎ *05 62 08 25 00, 23 rue St-Justin*) has menus du jour from 60FF, plus theme *menus* at the weekend; it's closed on Tuesday evening. Opposite the town hall is similarly priced *Restaurant La Petite Auberge* (☎ *05 62 09 31 33, 16 place de l'Hôtel de Ville*), closed on Thursday in low season.

Getting There & Away

Surprisingly, there are no bus services. The nearest useful bus stop is in Laas, 16km south-east on the Auch–Tarbes route (N21), with three SNCF buses daily (only one service on Sunday, in the evening). By bus, Auch–Laas takes an hour, Tarbes–Laas 1¼ hours. The nearest useful train stations are at Tarbes (40km) and Auch (45km).

For a taxi, call ☎ 05 62 09 38 05 or 05 62 08 20 36 (a taxi to Laas will take 1 hour and to Laas 1¼ hours).

MIRANDE

postcode 32300 • pop 4200 • elevation 175m
Another of Eustache de Beaumarchais' orderly bastides, founded on the river Baïse in 1281, cheerful Mirande served as the capital of the medieval province of Astarac. Most visitors come to see its arresting parish church and perfect checkerboard grid, or in mid-July for, of all things, a five-day festival of country music.

Orientation & Information

Buses stop in the arcaded main square, place d'Astarac. The main landmark is the pointed church tower, two blocks north. Across rue de l'Évêché from the church is the tourist office (☎ 05 62 66 68 10), open from 9 am to noon and 2 to 6 pm daily (from 10 am at the weekend, and morning only on Sunday). A block east on rue de Rohan is a Crédit Agricole bank with an ATM. Mirande's weekly market, in place d'Astarac, is on Monday.

Église Ste-Marie de Mirande

There's no other church like it, a stocky Gothic thing far too big for the space, with buttresses flying right across the road, and a remarkable belfry-cum-lookout tower with pointy hats.

For a time in the 15th century there were three popes, including one in Avignon. One of the many things on which they didn't agree was where to put a new bishopric for the region; one said Mirande, so for its early years (1410–13) this was a 'cathedral' (Auch eventually took the title). It was used as a barn for almost a century after the Revolution.

The austere interior is warmed by luminous 19th-century stained glass high above the altar. One chapel on the northern side has its original window, depicting St-Michael with a dragon. The church is open from 9 am to noon and 2 to 5 pm (only from 9.30 am to noon on Sunday).

Other Things to See

Arcaded **place d'Astarac** presides over one of the most perfectly regular bastide grids you'll see – the central blocks are all precise 50m squares – dotted with medieval half-timbered houses, the finest of them along **rue de l'Évêché**. A block north is the **Tour de Rohan**, a medieval watchtower. Four blocks north-east are 500m of old **town walls**.

Beside the tourist office is the municipal **Musée des Beaux-Arts et des Arts Decoratifs**, with 15th- to 19th-century fine art and china. It's open from 10 am to noon and 3 to 6 pm daily except Sunday; admission costs 12FF (children aged under 16 years 7FF).

Places to Stay & Eat

Within the riverside leisure centre a few hundred metres east of the town centre is the well-equipped *Camping L'Ile du Pont* (☎ *05 62 66 64 11, fax 05 62 66 69 86*), open from April to September, costing 60FF to 70FF forfait; bungalows and chalets are also available.

Of the town's three hotel-restaurants, the best choice looks like the Logis de France *Métropole* (☎ *05 62 66 50 25, fax 05 62 66 77 63, 31 rue Victor Hugo*), three blocks south of the square, with doubles from

240FF and *menus* from 60FF. Three blocks east of the square are the *Maupas* (☎ 05 62 66 51 42, ave d'Étigny), where rooms start at 250FF; and the Logis de France *Les Pyrénées* (☎ 05 62 66 51 16, fax 05 62 66 79 96, 5 ave d'Étigny), where doubles cost 200FF to 500FF and there is a pool. For details about *chambres d'hôtes* near Mirande, ask at the tourist office.

Good value for a weekday lunch is *Le Coup d'Envoi,* on the eastern side of the square, with a 40FF plat du jour. Also on the square are the *Grand Café* and *La Squadra* pizzeria. For a change, try the Vietnamese *Restaurant Sông Huöng*, two blocks south down rue Victor Hugo.

Getting There & Away
From Auch, SNCF (☎ 08 36 35 35 35) has three or four buses daily (one service only on Sunday, in the evening), and Voyages Labriffe (☎ 05 62 66 51 20) one or two daily (except Sunday).

AROUND MIRANDE
This gently folded landscape conceals dozens more villages with medieval cores, some restored and some not.

The petite, one-street *castelnau* of Tillac seems to harbour more pigeons than people, but its twin gate-towers suggest that it was once important. Stop by early or late, sit down at the pricey *Relais de la Tour* (☎ 05 62 70 00 81) by the western gate, and have coffee in another century (Tillac was founded in the 13th century, the church was built in the 14th, and its prettily restored houses date from the 17th). If golf's your game, there's a nine-hole course at nearby Château de Pallane (☎ 05 62 70 00 06).

Sleepy Miélan (population 1300) was founded in 1284 by Eustache de Beaumarchais, the royal sénéchal with a penchant for naming bastides after southern European cities, this one for Milan. Leaning, half-timbered houses surround its central square, place Jean Sènac, with the town hall in the middle. About 2km north on the N21 is a small lake and leisure complex. SNCF buses serving Mirande also stop here.

One of the finest mountain views anywhere in the south-west – weather permitting – is from the highest point in the Gers, a nondescript 315m rise called Puntous de Laguian, 6km west of Miélan on the N21. Pull over for a stunning view of some 150km of the Hautes-Pyrénées. On the way there is *Auberge de la Vallée* (☎ 05 62 67 50 24), where hearty game, poultry and other regional dishes are served daily at modest prices (*menus* from 50FF).

SAMATAN
postcode 32130 • pop 2000 • elevation 165m
This easygoing market town in the south-eastern corner of the Gers has little of historical interest to offer but, with probably the biggest foie gras market in France, it's pretty important to foodies and restaurant owners. For more on foie gras – the enlarged, fatty liver of a force-fed goose or duck, an essential ingredient in the south-west's renowned gastronomy – see the special section 'Food & Wine of the South-West'. On the subject of force-feeding, refer to Treatment of Animals under Society & Conduct in the Facts about South-West France chapter.

Orientation & Information
The town centre is, predictably, the market square, place des Halles. The cheerful tourist office (☎ 05 62 62 55 40, fax 05 62 62 50 26), at 3 rue Chanoine Dieuzaide, two blocks to the east, is open from 10 am to noon and 4 to 6 pm daily (except Sunday afternoon) in July and August, and from 10 am to noon and 3 to 5 pm except Tuesday and Sunday during the rest of year.

Two banks with ATMs are Crédit Agricole on place des Halles and Caisse d'Épargne a block east on rue du Pradel. The post office is a block north on blvd des Castres.

Markets
Every Monday an open-air **produce market** fills place des Halles. On the same day the big **foie gras market** cranks up at the Halle au Gras, a few hundred metres south on allée du 14 Juillet, across the canal and past the Shopi supermarket.

Buyers mill outside while sellers arrange

their tables; a whistle sounds, and in they go. The professionals – probably including many of the south-west's best chefs or their agents – are finished in 20 minutes. During peak foie gras season, from October to December, 45 tonnes of carcasses and 4 tonnes of livers are sold every Monday morning. Most sellers are from the Gers, Haute-Garonne or Hautes-Pyrénées, while buyers come from all over the Midi-Pyrénées region and beyond.

From October to April, carcasses are sold at 9.30 am, livers at 10.30 am and live birds at 11.30 am. The rest of the year, it's carcasses and livers at 9.30 am and live birds at 10.30 am. A smaller foie gras market takes place on Sundays from November to March at Gimont, 19km north on the D4.

Foie Gras Museum

At the back of the tourist office is a miscellany of farmer mannequins, old gadgets for grinding maize, and more alarming ones – manual and electric – for cramming it into geese. Entry is free, and it's open the same hours as the tourist office.

Foie Gras Farms

If you'd like to see how the geese and ducks are raised, and possibly watch the *gavage* (force-feeding), ask at the tourist office for a list of farms that welcome visitors. One

near the centre is Conserverie Bernard Duplan (☎ 05 62 62 31 33); turn right about 1.2km west down the Lombez road (D39).

Places to Stay

The two star *Camp Municipal* (☎ 05 62 62 02 98), part of a lakeside leisure complex to the west behind the foie gras market, is open from June to September. It charges 12/7/8FF per adult/tent/car.

Places to Eat

Restaurant Le Castre (☎ 05 62 62 39 15, 9 blvd des Castres), a short distance north of place des Halles, has everything a restaurant should: delicious, uncomplicated regional fare, cheerful service and a 60FF lunch *menu*. On market day, get there by noon. On the lake (approach from the Lombez road) is *Restaurant Les Rivages de Samatan* (☎ 05 62 62 35 64), which serves a 65FF plat du jour. Both are closed on Sunday.

Getting There & Around

There are no buses to Samatan from Auch, though Semvat's (☎ 05 61 61 67 67) Nos 65, 66 or 67 makes the 1¼ hour trip to Toulouse five times daily (more on Monday, fewer on Sunday).

You can rent a VTT at the Camp Municipal leisure complex (see Places to Stay).

The French Basque Country & Béarn

Like California, the Pyrénées-Atlantiques département is too big for itself and should have been split at the (post-Revolutionary) beginning. Mitterrand promised to do it, but couldn't. So for now Bayonne goes on taking orders from the préfecture in Pau.

But tourism officials did it, sensibly splitting themselves into two equal *Agences du Tourisme* – and a good thing too, for this immense département probably has more to see and do than any other in South-West France.

The French Basque Country

The French Basque country (Pays Basque; *Euskal Herria* in Basque) is a land apart, stubbornly independent and different from either of the nation-states which have adopted it. The part of it on the French side of the Pyrénées – *Iparralde* in Basque, *Le Pays Basque* in French – occupies about a third of the Pyrénées-Atlantiques département. The three provinces on this side – Labourd, Basse-Navarre and Soule – no longer have any administrative function. They comprise about 20% of Euskal Herria and are less populous and less industrialised than the Spanish Basque provinces, collectively called *Hegoalde* in Basque or *País Vasco* in Spanish.

Bayonne, administrative capital of the French Basque country, is the best springboard for seeing the region, with an agreeable mix of the French and the Basque, and essential transport links. The balance tips to Basque just down the coast at St-Jean de Luz. But to take the pulse of this region you must head for inland towns such as Sare, Aïnhoa or Bidarray, or up the valley of the Nive into the western Pyrénées.

Highlights

- Delight yourself in Bayonne with southern Europe's finest chocolate
- Ride a cog-wheel railway to the hallowed mountaintop of La Rhune in the Basque country
- Climb the battlements or follow in pilgrims' footsteps in the centuries-old Pyrénéan staging-post of St-Jean Pied de Port
- Admit that you cannot capture the Cirque de Lescun on film and just enjoy one of the most stupendously photogenic spots in South-West France
- Get quietly lost in the 13th century in the gentle fortified town of Sauveterre de Béarn

axoa – a spicy veal stew of onions, garlic, tomatoes and Espelette pimentos

ttoro – the classic Basque fish chowder

piperade – a piquant mush of red and green peppers, tomatoes, garlic and whipped eggs

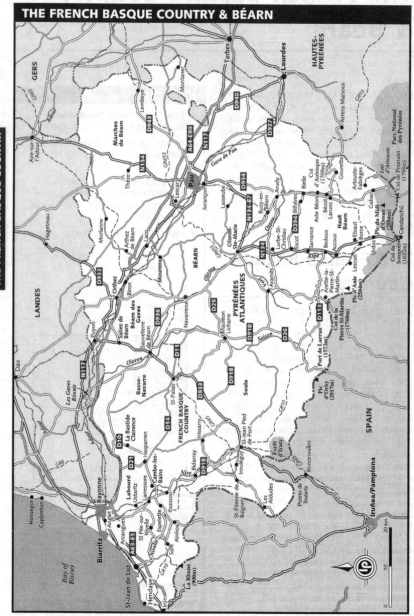

THE FRENCH BASQUE COUNTRY & BÉARN

The Basque Language

Basque (Euskara) is the only language in south-western Europe to have withstood the onslaught of Latin and its derivatives, and is probably unrelated to any other tongue on earth. It's now spoken by about a million people in Spain and France, most of them bilingual. Two television stations in Spain and one in France broadcast in Basque. You'll occasionally see *Hemen Euskara emaiten dugu* on shop doors, which means 'Basque spoken here'.

Good morning	Egun on
Good afternoon	Arratsalde on
Good evening	Gau on
How are you?	Norazira?
Fine/well	Ongi
Not well	Gaizki
Goodbye	Agur or Ikus arte
Thank you	Milesker
Pardon me	Barkatu
Please	Otoi or Plazer baduzu
Yes	Baï
No	Ez

History

Basques are thought to be descended from a Celtic tribe called the Vascones, driven south across the Pyrénées by the Romans in the 1st century AD and north again by Visigoths in the 9th century. Basques on both sides of the Pyrénées emerged from the turbulent Middle Ages with a fair degree of autonomy. As part of the duchy of Aquitaine, the French Basque country was under English rule from the 12th to 15th centuries.

French Basque autonomy came to an end during the 1789 Revolution. After the Spanish Basque provinces (except Navarra) were stripped of autonomy in 1876, Basque nationalism gathered strength. Several provinces threw in their lot with republicans in the Spanish Civil War, and Franco came down hard on them afterwards. Until Franco's death in 1975, many Spanish Basque nationalists sheltered in France.

In 1961 a group of nationalists called ETA (*Euskadi ta Askatasuna*, 'Basque Nation and Liberty') carried out its first terrorist attack, starting a cycle of violence and repression that continues today in Spain.

Converted to Christianity in the 10th century, Basques are still known for their devotion to Catholicism.

Basque Symbols

The Basque flag looks like a false-colour UK flag, with a red field, white vertical cross and green diagonal cross. Another common Basque symbol, a kind of rounded swastika with arms pointing clockwise, is said to represent the sun. On gravestones the arms always seem to point anticlockwise.

Basque Games

Force Basque *Euskal indar-jokotak* is a male Basque tournament of muscle-power, with its origins in rural work: chopping through massive logs, running with 80kg sacks, lifting immense weights. One event that Basques probably gave to the rest of the world is *soka tira*, tug-of-war. The biggest annual Force Basque festival is held in mid-August in St-Palais, 70km south-east of Bayonne, with smaller festivals somewhere just about every weekend between May and September.

Pelote Basque Called pelota in Basque and English, *pelote basque* is the generic name for over 20 different games played with a hard, rubber-cored ball. Most use either bare hands, a wooden paddle called a *pala*, a lighter one called a *paleta*, or a wicker scoop called a *chistera*, strapped to the wrist. Play is usually on an outdoor, one-walled court called a *fronton* or a three-walled indoor one called a *trinquet*, with all players facing the same wall. The three essential ingredients of every Basque village are the church, the *herriko-etxea* (town hall) and the fronton!

The most common games are *eskuz huska* (French *main nue*) using bare hands, *joko garbi (petit-gant)* using a small chistera, *chistera (grand-gant)* using a bigger

NICKY CAVEN

Pelota is an essential part of Basque life.

chistera, *pala*, *paleta* and lightning-fast *cesta punta*, using a big chistera on a long, three-sided indoor court called a *jaï alaï*.

Whaling-Boat Races Popular in the Spanish Basque country, whaling-boat races are catching on here too. Fixtures include the Régates de Trainières at St-Jean de Luz on the first weekend in July, and Hendaye's Fêtes de la Mer in mid-July.

Bullfighting

Corrida, Spanish-style bullfighting, has unapologetic fans all over the French Basque country, with several tournaments each summer. Tickets cost from 80FF to 450FF and advance reservations are usually necessary; ask at tourist offices in the area. The corrida season is from July to early September.

Shopping

Calling a *makhila* a 'Basque cane' is like calling a Lamborghini a 'car'. Made from the wood of the medlar tree, engraved with runes and mottoes and fixed with a steel tip, they're elegant instruments of status and self-defence. Only three families in the

French Basque country have maintained the art: Ainciart Bergara in Larressore, Gérard Léoncini in Bayonne and Pierre Harispuru in Ibarolle. Expect to pay between 1000FF and 5000FF and wait six months or more.

Some worthy edibles are *jambon de bayonne* (cured Bayonne ham) and chocolate; see Shopping in the Bayonne section. Ossau-Iraty is a federation of *fromageurs* producing modestly priced Pyrénées sheep's cheese (French *fromage de brebis*, Basque *ardi gasna*), among others. Their outlets are on main roads all over the French Basque country and Béarn.

BAYONNE

postcode 64100 • pop 40,000 • elevation 5m

If Pau weren't préfecture of the Pyrénées-Atlantiques département, agreeable Bayonne (Baïona in Basque) would deserve the title. Unlike the upmarket beach resort of Biarritz, a short bus ride away, Bayonne retains plenty of Basque-ness: its timber-framed, red and green-shuttered buildings are typical of the region. You can hear almost as much Basque as French in certain quarters, and every male over the age of 40, it seems, wears a beret.

History

Bayonne, founded by the Romans at the strategic confluence of the Nive and Adour rivers, enjoyed particular favour and prosperity under English rule and was one of the last English-held towns to give in to the French, in 1451.

Anxiety about the Spanish led to heavy fortification, and Bayonne mutated into a military centre. The city gave its name to the *baïonnette* (bayonet), developed here in the early 17th century. That period's hallmark is the magnificent fortifications by Sébastien de Vauban, Louis XIV's famous chief military engineer.

Bayonne again went into high gear after being declared a free port in 1759. Trade with Holland and Spain was brisk and Basque *corsaires* (pirates; see the boxed text 'The Basque Corsairs' under St-Jean de Luz later in this chapter) landed richer cargoes than Basque cod fisherman did. A second crash came when the free-port status was abolished after the 1789 Revolution.

En route from Spain in 1813 to battle Napoleon, Wellington twice laid siege to Bayonne. With Napoleon's defeat, the city's military career came to an end and commerce returned to the fore.

Orientation

Bayonne is now part of a vast conurbation with Anglet and Biarritz, abbreviated BAB, sharing a public transport system (STAB; see Getting Around later in this section) and airport. The best maps of the whole area are Éditions Grafocarte's 1:13,500 *Bayonne Anglet Biarritz*, available from bigger bookshops, and STAB's bus map, from the tourist office.

Trisected by the Nive and Adour rivers, Bayonne has no clear centre. The three central *quartiers* (districts) are St-Esprit north of the Adour River; the Petit Bayonne on the Nive's east bank; and Grand Bayonne on the west bank. Each has a riverside plaza; Grand Bayonne's is place de la Liberté, beside the town hall (Hôtel de Ville). A lively shopping district centres on pedestrianised rue Port Neuf, rue Lormand and rue Victor Hugo.

BAB's airport is 5km south-west of the city centre. Bayonne's train and bus stations are both in St-Esprit.

Information

Tourist Offices The tourist office (☎ 05 59 46 01 46, fax 05 59 59 37 55, email bayonne.tourisme@wanadoo.fr), place des Basques, is open 9 am to 6.30 pm on weekdays and 10 am to 6 pm on Saturday (from 9 am to 7 pm Monday to Saturday and from 10 am to 1 pm on Sunday during July and August). An annexe (☎ 05 59 55 20 45) at the train station is open from 9.40 am to 12.30 pm and 2 to 6.30 pm daily during July and August. A branch is open at the airport from mid-May to mid-September.

Among useful brochures are *Fêtes*, listing French Basque country cultural and sporting events, and *Guide Loisirs*, for walking, biking and other activities. In July and August the office runs 30FF city tours

at 3 pm on Tuesday and 10 am on Wednesday, Friday and Saturday.

Bureau d'Information Jeunesse The city's Bureau d'Information Jeunesse (BIJ; ☎ 05 59 59 35 29, fax 05 59 59 35 34), 16 rue Pontrique in Petit Bayonne, is open from 10 am to 7 pm Monday to Saturday.

Money Most banks in Bayonne open from Monday to Friday only. Useful ones with exchange facilities and ATMs are around place de la République in St-Esprit (Crédit Mutuel, 7 blvd Alsace-Lorraine, opens Tuesday to Saturday), and in Grand Bayonne near the Town hall and on rue Thiers. The Crédit Agricole ATM at 23 rue Thiers dispenses francs and Spanish pesetas. The post office at 11 rue Jules Labat also has exchange services.

Post The post office at 11 rue Jules Labat is open from 8 am to 6 pm on weekdays and to noon on Saturday. Poste restante items addressed to '64100 Bayonne-Labat' come here; all other poste restante mail goes to the main post office (rue de la Nouvelle Poste), about 1km north-west of the city centre, off ave blvd du BAB. A smaller post office is at 21 blvd Alsace-Lorraine in St-Esprit.

Travel Agencies Pascal Voyages (☎ 05 59 25 48 48), 8 allées Boufflers, is Bayonne's only travel agent serving incoming visitors. It's open until 6.30 pm on weekdays and, except in August, to noon on Saturday.

Bookshops Librairie Zabal Elkar (☎ 05 59 25 43 90), 52 rue Pannecau, is Bayonne's best source of books on Basque history and culture, walking in the Basque Country and Basque music. It's closed on Sunday and on Monday morning. Librairie Celhay, 12 rue de la Salie, stocks a modest selection of guidebooks. For foreign newspapers and general maps, go to Maison de la Presse, 15 rue de la Salie.

Universities Bayonne has a branch of the Universitaire de Pau et de Pays de l'Adour,

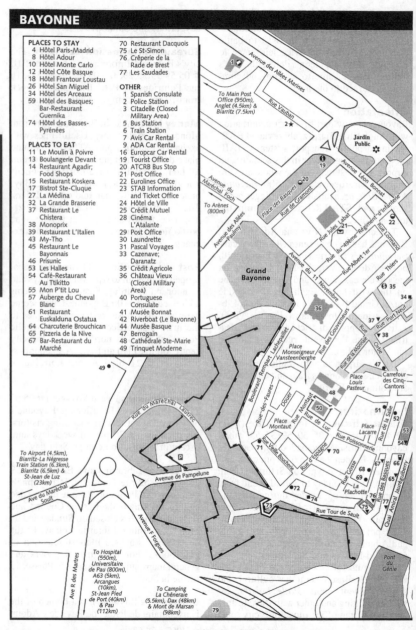

BAYONNE

PLACES TO STAY
4 Hôtel Paris-Madrid
8 Hôtel Adour
10 Hôtel Monte Carlo
12 Hôtel Côte Basque
18 Hôtel Frantour Loustau
26 Hôtel San Miguel
34 Hôtel des Arceaux
59 Hôtel des Basques;
   Bar-Restaurant
   Guernika
74 Hôtel des Basses-
   Pyrénées

PLACES TO EAT
11 Le Moulin à Poivre
13 Boulangerie Devant
14 Restaurant Agadir;
   Food Shops
15 Restaurant Koskera
17 Bistrot Ste-Cluque
27 La Médina
32 La Grande Brasserie
37 Restaurant Le
   Chistera
38 Monoprix
39 Restaurant L'Italien
43 My-Tho
45 Restaurant Le
   Bayonnais
51 Prisunic
53 Les Halles
54 Café-Restaurant
   Au Ttikitto
55 Mon P'tit Lou
57 Auberge du Cheval
   Blanc
61 Restaurant
   Euskalduna Ostatua
64 Charcuterie Brouchican
65 Pizzeria de la Nive
67 Bar-Restaurant du
   Marché

70 Restaurant Dacquois
75 Le St-Simon
76 Crêperie de la
   Rade de Brest
77 Les Saudades

OTHER
1 Spanish Consulate
2 Police Station
3 Citadelle (Closed
   Military Area)
5 Bus Station
6 Train Station
7 Avis Car Rental
9 ADA Car Rental
16 Europcar Car Rental
19 Tourist Office
20 ATCRB Bus Stop
21 Post Office
22 Eurolines Office
23 STAB Information
   and Ticket Office
24 Hôtel de Ville
25 Crédit Mutuel
28 Cinéma
   L'Atalante
29 Post Office
30 Laundrette
31 Pascal Voyages
33 Cazenave;
   Daranatz
35 Crédit Agricole
36 Château Vieux
   (Closed Military
   Area)
40 Portuguese
   Consulate
41 Musée Bonnat
42 Riverboat (Le Bayonne)
44 Musée Basque
47 Berrogain
48 Cathédrale Ste-Marie
49 Trinquet Moderne

To Main Post
Office (950m),
Anglet (4.5km) &
Biarritz (7.5km)

To Arènes
(800m)

Jardin
Public

Grand
Bayonne

To Airport (4.5km),
Biarritz-La Négresse
Train Station (6.3km),
Biarritz (6.5km) &
St-Jean de Luz
(23km)

To Hospital
(550m),
Universitaire
de Pau (800m),
A63 (5km),
Arcangues
(10km),
St-Jean Pied
de Port (40km)
& Pau
(112km)

To Camping
La Chêneraie
(5.5km), Dax (48km)
& Mont de Marsan
(98km)

Avenue des Allées Marines

Rue Vauban

Avenue Léon Bonnat

Place des Basques

Rue de Gramont

Rue Jules Labat

Rue du 49ème Régiment d'Infanterie

Rue Lormand

Rue Albert-1er

Rue Thiers

Rue Port Neuf

Rue de la Monnaie

Orbe

Carrefour
des Cinq-
Cantons

Place
Louis
Pasteur

Place
Monseigneur
Vansteenberghe

Rue des Gouverneurs

Boulevard Rempart Lachepaillet

Douer

Rue-des-Faures

Rue Montaut

Rue de Luc

Place
Montaut

Rue Poissonnerie

Place
Lacarre

Rue de la Salle

Rue Vieille Boucherie

Rue Espagne

Rue Crosse

Rue des Basques

Quai Amiral Jauréguiberry

La
Plachotte

Rue Tour de Sault

Pont
du
Génie

Rue du Maréchal Lautrec

Avenue de Pampelune

Ave du Maréchal Soult

Ave R des Martres

Avenue Forgues

Avenue du Maréchal Foch

Avenue des Allées Paulmy

Avenue du 11 Novembre

THE FRENCH BASQUE COUNTRY

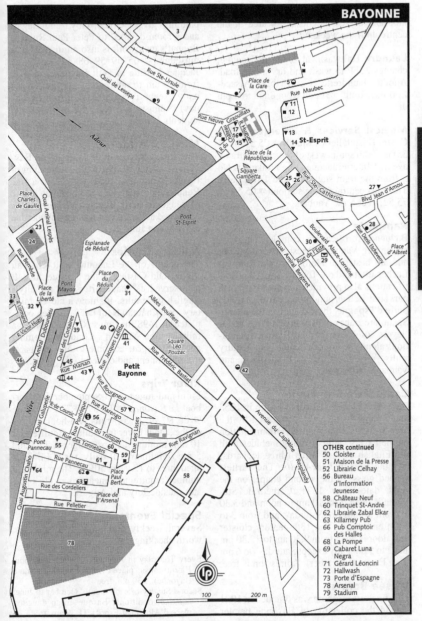

BAYONNE

OTHER continued
50 Cloister
51 Maison de la Presse
52 Librairie Celhay
56 Bureau
   d'Information
   Jeunesse
58 Château Neuf
60 Trinquet St-André
62 Librairie Zabal Elkar
63 Killarney Pub
66 Pub Comptoir
   des Halles
68 La Pompe
69 Cabaret Luna
   Negra
71 Gérard Léoncini
72 Hallwash
73 Porte d'Espagne
78 Arsenal
79 Stadium

0   100   200 m

euro currency converter 10FF = €1.52

south-west of the city centre, though its thousand or so students are scarce in the centre until the weekend.

Laundry Hallwash, at 6 rue d'Espagne, charges 22FF to wash and dry a 6kg load. Another laundrette is at 16 blvd Alsace-Lorraine. Both are open from 8 am to 8 pm daily.

Medical Services & Emergency The Centre Hospitalier (hospital; ☎ 05 59 44 35 35) is 500m south-west of the city centre on ave de l'Interne Jacques Loeb (take bus No 3 from the train station or the Town hall). The most central police station (☎ 05 59 59 75 52) is at 5 rue Vauban.

Ramparts

Bayonne's fortifications, completed in 1679, are among Vauban's finest surviving work and are best seen along blvd du Rempart Lachepaillet and rue Tour de Sault. The fortifications also provide an excuse for a lush parkland belt around the centre. Around **porte d'Espagne**, the old gate on the road to Spain, are traces of Bayonne's three major 'layers' of fortifications: Roman foundations along rue Tour de Sault, 16th-century walls from the time of François I, and Vauban's outer walls.

Cathédrale Ste-Marie

Bayonne's Gothic cathedral, begun in 1258 under English rule, was completed by the French in the 16th century. Ornamentation on the nave's vaulted ceiling includes both the English coat of arms (three leopards) and the French *fleur-de-lis*. The earliest stained glass, in the second chapel on the right, dates from 1531. Cathédrale Ste-Marie is open from 10 am to noon and 3.30 to 6 pm Monday to Saturday, and from 3 to 6 pm on Sunday. The 13th-century **cloister** next door is open from 9.30 am to 12.30 pm and 2 to 5 pm daily except Saturday (to 6 pm from Easter to October). Admission is free.

Musée Bonnat

This fine-arts museum was founded in 1901 around the collection of Bayonne painter Léon Bonnat (1833–1922). Works include paintings by El Greco, Goya and Degas, and a room devoted to Peter Paul Rubens. Bonnat's own work is also on display. The museum (☎ 05 59 59 08 52), at 5 rue Jacques Laffitte in Petit Bayonne, is open from 10 am to noon and 2.30 to 6.30 pm daily except Tuesday (to 8.30 pm on Friday). Admission costs 20FF (children and students 10FF).

Musée Basque

The Musée Basque et de la Tradition Bayonnaise (☎ 05 59 59 08 98), a museum of Basque culture, opened in 1924 in a fine Renaissance merchant's house at 1 rue Marengo in Petit Bayonne. It was being renovated at the time of writing but was due to reopen in June 2000.

Military Castles

The counts of the Labourd built **Château Vieux** (Old Castle) in the 11th century. It also served as headquarters for the city's English governors. It's now a closed military area. **Château Neuf** (New Castle), completed in 1498 for Louis XI, is no longer a military area. Vauban's **Citadelle**, looming above St-Esprit, is home to an elite paratroop regiment and closed to the public.

River Trips

From mid-June to mid-September the riverboat *Le Bayonne* (☎ 05 59 47 77 17, mobile ☎ 06 80 74 21 51) runs two-hour cruises on the Adour River from allées Boufflers, at 10 am (minimum 15 passengers), 2.45 and 5 pm (minimum 10) daily, for 80FF (kids aged three to 12 years 50FF). The minimum number requirement means it rarely operates outside July and August.

Special Events

Several weekly and monthly events are worth checking out:

Every Thursday in July and August: traditional Basque music, place Charles de Gaulle (Grand Bayonne), 9.30 pm, free

Second Sunday of each month, October to June: *mutxiko*, traditional Basque group dancing, place d'Albret (St-Esprit), 11.30 am, free

Fourth Saturday of each month, October to June: *Baïona kantus*, a kind of public Basque singalong, place Lacarre (Grand Bayonne), 11 am, free

Festivals Bayonne's most important festival is the annual **Fêtes de Bayonne**, from the first Wednesday in August to the following Sunday, with fireworks, Basque music, a float parade, *courses landaises* (see Spectator Sports in the Facts for the Visitor chapter), corridas, rugby and lots of jollity.

Two prestigious summer fairs with daily corridas are the **Feria de l'Assomption** in mid-August and the **Feria de l'Atlantique** in early September.

Jazz on the Ramparts features six days of 24-hour jazz and blues in mid-July. During Easter week the city hosts a **Ham Fair** with its origins in the 15th century; see Shopping in this section for more about the famous hams of Bayonne.

Places to Stay – Budget

Camping The four-star *Camping la Chêneraie* (☎ 05 59 55 01 31, fax 05 59 55 11 17, *chemin de Cazenave*) is open from April to September and costs 26/58FF per adult/site; bungalows are also available. Facilities include a swimming pool. The camp site is on the N117 about 5.5km east of the city centre in the St-Étienne *zone industrielle*. By public transport it's easier to reach camp sites in Biarritz and Anglet (see the following sections on those towns).

Hotels Good value in St-Esprit, and popular with travellers, is *Hôtel Paris-Madrid* (☎ 05 59 55 13 98, fax 05 59 55 07 22, *place de la Gare*). Big, pleasant doubles without/with shower start at 125/170FF. Rooms at *Hôtel Monte Carlo* (☎ 05 59 55 02 68, 1 rue Ste-Ursule) start at 90FF (150FF with shower). At *Hôtel San Miguel* (☎ 05 59 55 17 82, fax 05 59 50 15 22, 8 rue Ste-Catherine), generous doubles without/with shower cost 140/170FF and doubles/twins with shower and toilet cost 190/220FF.

In Petit Bayonne, doubles/twins at *Hôtel des Basques* (☎ 05 59 59 08 02, 5 rue des Lisses) start at 135/170FF (150/210FF with shower, toilet and a view over the square).

In Grand Bayonne, *Hôtel des Arceaux* (☎ 05 59 59 15 53, 26 rue du Port Neuf) offers large, bare doubles/triples from 130/170FF and doubles with bath and toilet for 230FF.

Places to Stay – Mid-Range

In St-Esprit, *Hôtel Adour* (☎ 05 59 55 11 31, fax 05 59 55 86 40, 13 rue Ste-Ursule) offers comfortable doubles/triples with shower for 240/290FF. *Hôtel Côte Basque* (☎ 05 59 55 10 21, fax 05 59 55 39 85, 2 rue Maubec) has doubles for 200FF (320FF with shower and toilet), and twins/quads for 310/360FF.

In Grand Bayonne, at the well-run *Hôtel des Basses-Pyrénées* (☎ 05 59 59 00 29, fax 05 59 59 42 02, 12 rue Tour de Sault) basic rooms cost from 170FF, doubles/triples with shower and toilet from 280/350FF and private parking costs 30FF.

Places to Stay – Top End

St-Esprit's best hotel is the three-star *Hôtel Frantour Loustau* (☎ 05 59 55 08 08, fax 05 59 55 69 36, rue de la Chateau), facing the Adour River. Standard doubles/triples with shower and toilet are 430/475FF and off-street parking costs 50FF.

Places to Eat

Restaurants – French The service is manic but French and Basque dishes at *La Grande Brasserie* (place de la Liberté) are good, with *menus* from 89FF and a 40FF *plat du jour* (meal of the day); it's open daily, for lunch only. *Crêperie de la Rade de Brest* (☎ 05 59 59 13 62, 7 rue des Basques) offers traditional Breton specialities for lunch and dinner, plus crepes and *galettes* (wholemeal or buckwheat pancake) costing from 10FF to 36FF; it's closed on Sunday (and also on Monday from October to April). The award-winning chef at *Le St-Simon* (☎ 05 59 59 27 71, 1 rue des Basques) creates some superb dishes; *menus* start at 99FF; it's closed on Sunday evening and Monday. Unpretentious *Restaurant Dacquois* (☎ 05 59 59 29 61, 48 rue d'Espagne), open from 8 am to 8.30 pm (except on Sunday), offers a 65FF *menu*.

In Petit Bayonne, smoky *Bar-Restaurant*

THE FRENCH BASQUE COUNTRY

Guernika (☎ 05 59 59 28 69, *5 rue des Lisses*) is a popular, lunch-only place with a 52FF *menu*. *Auberge du Cheval Blanc* ☎ 05 59 59 01 33, 68 rue Bourgneuf) boasts a Michelin star, with 118/185/260FF *menus*. It's open daily (closed Sunday evening and Monday from September to June).

Restaurants – Basque The tiny *Café-Restaurant Au Ttikitto*, at the corner of the covered market, offers snacks, sandwiches and a 40FF Basque lunch; is open for breakfast. One of Bayonne's most appealing eateries is lunch-only *Bar-Restaurant du Marché* (☎ 05 59 59 22 66, *39 rue des Basques*), with home-style cooking and a madly cheerful atmosphere; try the 42FF *piperade* (see the boxed text in the Food & Wine section for the recipe) and Bayonne ham. It's closed on Sunday. Up the scale Basque-owned *Restaurant Le Chistera* (☎ 05 59 59 25 93, *42 rue du Port Neuf*), open daily for lunch and Thursday to Sunday for dinner, with excellent Basque and French dishes.

In St-Esprit, *Restaurant Koskera* (☎ 05 59 55 20 79, *2 rue Hugues*) serves inexpensive plats du jour and *menus* from 70FF; it's open for lunch (and from mid-June to September for dinner), daily except Sunday. Homy *Le Moulin à Poivre* (☎ 05 59 50 19 10, *4 rue Maubec*) offers Basque, French and Moroccan dishes in the 45FF to 70FF range, daily for lunch and daily except Sunday and Wednesday for dinner.

In Petit Bayonne, *Restaurant Euskalduna Ostatua* (☎ 05 59 59 28 02, *61 rue Pannecau*) has a Basque *menu* for 60FF, main dishes from 35FF to 50FF, has a loyal clientele. It's open for lunch daily except Sunday.

Restaurants – Other In Grand Bayonne, *Les Saudades* (☎ 05 59 25 60 13, *15 quai Amiral Jauréguiberry*) serves Portuguese meals from 72FF and good fish dishes from 25FF to 80FF; it's closed on Sunday. *Pizzeria de la Nive* (*39 quai Amiral Jauréguiberry*) is unexceptional but open on Sunday.

Good value in Petit Bayonne is modest

Restaurant Le Bayonnais (☎ 05 59 25 61 19, *38 quai des Corsaires*), offering regional and Spanish *plats* from 65FF to 80FF and a 98FF *menu*, daily except Sunday evening and Monday lunch. The Vietnamese-Chinese restaurant *My-Tho* (☎ 05 59 59 15 07, *40 rue Bourgneuf*) has excellent value lunch and dinner *menus* from 70FF (including wine); it's closed at lunchtime on Tuesday and Wednesday. *Mon P'tit Lou* (☎ 05 59 25 59 03, *16 rue des Tonneliers*) serves 30FF to 45FF pizza and pasta dishes in the evening (and for lunch during July and August). Also good for pasta freaks is bright *Restaurant L'Italien* (☎ 05 59 59 48 31, *56 quai des Corsaires*), closed on Sunday.

In St-Esprit, *Restaurant Agadir* (☎ 05 59 55 66 56, *3 rue Ste-Catherine*) offers Moroccan couscous from 60FF to 80FF and *menus* from 80FF; it's open for lunch and dinner, daily except Monday lunch. The Tunisian restaurant *La Médina* (☎ 05 59 55 85 17, *13 blvd Jean d'Amou*) serves salads from 26FF and couscous and grills from 65FF. *Bistrot Ste-Cluque* (☎ 05 59 55 82 43, *9 rue Hugues*) specialises in paella (60FF) and offers *menus* from 55FF. It's open daily.

Self-Catering Grand Bayonne's central *covered market* is open every morning (except Sunday) and all day Friday and Saturday. There's a Friday morning market on place de la République and another on Sunday morning along rue Ste-Catherine.

Near the train station, *Boulangerie Devant* (*36 place de la République*) is open from 7 am to 1 pm and 3 to 7.30 pm Monday to Saturday and from 7 am to 1 pm and 4 to 7.30 pm on Sunday. Other *food shops* are along rue Ste-Catherine. *Prisunic* (*27 rue Victor Hugo, 1–3 quai Amiral Dubourdieu*) and *Monoprix* (*8 rue Orbe*) have food sections and are open from 8.30 am until 7.30 pm Monday to Saturday.

Entertainment

Pubs & Bars Students converge in Petit Bayonne at the weekend, lots of them to *Killarney Pub* (☎ 05 59 25 75 51, *33 rue* *des Cordeliers)*, with frequent live music and a huge choice of beers. An alternative across the Nive is *Pub Comptoir des Halles* (☎ 05 59 25 72 52, 47 quai Jauréguiberry).

Bayonne's only discotheque is *La Pompe* (☎ 05 59 25 48 12, 7 rue des Augustins), open 10 pm to dawn from Thursday to Sunday. *Cabaret Luna Negra* (☎ 05 59 25 78 05, rue des Augustins) is a cafe-theatre with a kaleidoscope of offerings, from jazz to improvisational theatre, bluegrass to marionettes, plus food.

Cinemas Nondubbed films are shown at *Cinéma L'Atalante* (☎ 05 59 55 76 63, 7 rue Denis Etcheverry), but it's closed during July and August. A ticket costs 37FF (students 25FF).

Spectator Sports

Pelote Basque Weekly *main nue* (see under Pelote Basque earlier in this chapter) matches take place at **Trinquet St-André** (☎ 05 59 59 18 69), at the eastern end of rue des Tonneliers, at 4.10 pm every Thursday afternoon, from October to June. Tickets cost 50FF.

Rugby Bayonne's rugby club, Aviron Bayonnais, plays in the stadium just south of the centre in the Parc des Sports. Ask at the tourist office for details about upcoming matches.

Bullfights From July to early September, corridas are held at the *arènes* (arena), 1km west of the city centre on ave du Maréchal Foch. The tourist office will know of upcoming corridas and can sell you a ticket (80FF to 450FF).

Shopping

Bayonne is famous throughout France for its ham. The best prices are found at the covered market (see Self-Catering under Places to Eat); or you can go to a specialist shop such as Charcuterie Brouchican (☎ 05 59 59 27 18), 20 quai Augustin Chaho.

Bayonne's other famous edible produce is chocolate (see the boxed text). Two of its finest *chocolatiers* are on rue du Port Neuf: Cazenave at No 19 and Daranatz at No 15. At Cazenave, treat yourself to the best *chocolat chaud* (hot chocolate) you've ever had, served with toast or a croissant.

A master makhila maker (see Shopping in the French Basque Country section) is Gérard Léoncini, whose workshop (☎ 05 59 59 18 20) at 37 rue Vieille Boucherie is open from 10 am to noon and 4 to 6.30 pm daily except Saturday afternoon and Sunday.

For fine Basque linen and cotton, visit

Chocolate

Christopher Columbus brought cocoa beans back from the New World in 1502. A drink made from them, sweetened with sugar and vanilla and spiced with cinnamon, took the Spanish court by storm for its stimulant, tonic and, some said, aphrodisiac properties.

Several Sephardic Jewish families who had learned the art of brewing chocolate fled to Bayonne during the Spanish Inquisition (or arrived later via Portugal). The drink remained an upper-class privilege until the 17th century, when these *chocolatiers* began pitching it to the masses. Before long, *salons de chocolat* were sprouting all over Europe, though the Church regarded the development with suspicion.

Only in the 19th century was a way found to solidify chocolate. In the 1850s Bayonne had no fewer than 32 chocolate workshops (today there are seven). Surprisingly, the city's last genuine chocolate-maker closed its doors in the 1960s: confectioners now begin with ingots of basic chocolate from a few national firms (but for one that starts from the bean, see Espelette later in this chapter).

The French like their chocolate *noir* – dark and strong, with 60–70% cocoa content.

Berrogain (☎ 05 59 59 16 18) at the carrefour des Cinq-Cantons.

Getting There & Away

Air The small Aeroport de Parme (☎ 05 59 43 83 83) – usually identified in timetables as Biarritz airport – is 5km south-west of central Bayonne. Air France flies directly to/from Paris Orly about eight times daily; a one-way youth or student fare costs around 300FF. Ryanair (☎ 03 44 11 41 41) flies from London Stansted, daily in July and August and daily except Sunday during the rest of the year.

Bus From place des Basques, ATCRB's (☎ 05 59 26 06 99) regional services follow the coast to the Spanish border, including six to 10 services daily to St-Jean de Luz (22FF, 35 minutes) and Hendaye (35FF, one hour). Summer beach traffic can make some trips twice as long as scheduled.

From the small bus station in front of the train station, RDTL (☎ 05 59 55 17 59) runs services into the Landes – to Capbreton (20FF, 30 minutes), Hossegor (35 minutes), Dax (46FF, 2½ hours) and Mont de Marsan (90FF). RDTL also has a daily-except-Sunday coastal service that stops at Capbreton and Hossegor every one to 1½ hours. TPR (☎ 05 59 27 45 98) has three buses daily to Pau (85FF, 2¼ hours).

Bayonne is one of three hubs in South-West France for Eurolines (see the Getting There & Away chapter). The Eurolines office (☎ 05 59 59 19 33) at 3 place Charles de Gaulle is open from 9 am to noon and 2 to 6 pm on weekdays (from 10 am to noon and 2 to 6 pm daily except Sunday during July and August). This is also where Eurolines' buses stop.

Train The information office at the train station is open from 9 am to noon and 2 to 6.30 pm Monday to Saturday (from 9 am to 7.30 pm daily in July and August). TGVs to/from Paris' Gare Montparnasse (413FF) take five hours. Two daily non-TGV trains go overnight to Paris' Gare d'Austerlitz (375FF) in about eight hours. There are multiple daily services to Dax (48FF, 40

minutes) and Bordeaux (133FF, 2¼ hours); to St-Jean de Luz (26FF, 25 minutes), Hendaye (36FF, 40 minutes) and Irún (45 minutes); to St-Jean Pied de Port (50FF, one hour), Pau (82FF, 1¼ hours) and Toulouse (193FF, around 3¾ hours).

Car Three rental agencies are near the train station: the French discount chain ADA (☎ 05 59 50 37 10) is at 11 quai de Lesseps, Europcar (☎ 05 59 55 38 20) at 5 rue Hugues and Avis (☎ 05 59 55 06 56) at 1 rue Ste-Ursule. All are open daily except Sunday.

Getting Around

To/From the Airport There's no useful bus connection to the airport. A taxi from the city centre costs about 60FF.

Bus The bus network linking BAB is called STAB. Individual tickets cost 7.50FF and a carnet of 10 costs 62FF. Tickets remain valid (for an onward or return trip) for an hour after they've been time-stamped. STAB's information and ticket office (☎ 05 59 59 04 61), at the Town hall, is open from 8 am to noon and 1.30 to 6 pm Monday to Friday. Tickets can be bought here or on board.

Taxi To order a taxi, call ☎ 05 59 59 48 48. There's a large rank in front of the train station.

BIARRITZ

postcode 64200 • pop 30,000 • elevation 45m

The high-toned coastal town of Biarritz, 8km west of Bayonne, got its start as a resort in the mid-19th century when Napoleon III and his Spanish-born wife, Eugénie, began coming here. In later decades Biarritz was popular with wealthy Britons and was visited by Queen Victoria and King Edward VII.

These days it's best known for its fine beaches and some of Europe's best surfing. Architecturally the town is a muddle. It's easy to see everything of interest in a day trip from Bayonne. This also saves money, since Biarritz can be a budget-buster. If you're here to surf, stay on a camp site or at

St-Jean de Luz, in the French Basque country, combines a picturesque harbour and busy fishing port.

JOHN KING

An unusual way to appreciate the scenery: parasailing at Accous, vallée d'Aspe, Haute Béarn

JOHN KING

Engrossed spectators at the pelote Basque match: the week's highlight in Trinquet St-André, Bayonne.

The Basque flag is proudly displayed on the half-timbered facades of rue Argenterie, Bayonne.

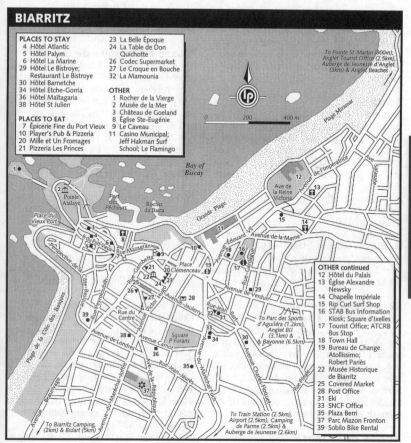

BIARRITZ

PLACES TO STAY
4 Hôtel Atlantic
5 Hôtel Palym
6 Hôtel La Marine
29 Hôtel Le Bistroye;
   Restaurant Le Bistroye
30 Hôtel Barnetche
34 Hôtel Etche-Gorria
36 Hôtel Maïtagaria
38 Hôtel St Julien

PLACES TO EAT
7 Épicerie Fine du Port Vieux
10 Player's Pub & Pizzeria
20 Mille et Un Fromages
21 Pizzeria Les Princes

23 La Belle Époque
24 La Table de Don
   Quichotte
26 Codec Supermarket
27 Le Croque en Bouche
32 La Mamounia

OTHER
1 Rocher de la Vierge
2 Musée de la Mer
3 Château de Goeland
8 Église Ste-Eugénie
9 Le Caveau
11 Casino Municipal;
   Jeff Hakman Surf
   School; Le Flamingo

OTHER continued
12 Hôtel du Palais
13 Église Alexandre
   Newsky
14 Chapelle Impériale
15 Rip Curl Surf Shop
16 STAB Bus Information
   Kiosk; Square d'Ixelles
17 Tourist Office; ATCRB
   Bus Stop
18 Town Hall
19 Bureau de Change
   Atollissimo;
   Robert Pariès
22 Musée Historique
   de Biarritz
25 Covered Market
28 Post Office
31 Eki
33 SNCF Office
35 Plaza Berri
37 Parc Mazon Fronton
39 Sobilo Bike Rental

THE FRENCH BASQUE COUNTRY

one of the two excellent youth hostels – in Biarritz and in Anglet – within easy reach of the beaches.

Orientation

Long-distance buses stop in front of the tourist office on square d'Ixelles, from where it's a 250m walk to place Clémenceau, the town centre. Some 200m north of this square is the beach, running north to a headland called Pointe St-Martin. West of place Clémenceau, rue Mazagran rollercoasters through the old town to Biarritz's own headland, Pointe Atalaye. The train station and airport are both about 3km south-east of the town centre.

Information

The tourist office (☎ 05 59 22 37 10, fax 05 59 24 97 80), 1 square d'Ixelles, is open from 9 am to 6.45 pm daily (from 8 am to 8 pm in July and August), and has a summer annexe at the train station. If you're into surfing, go straight to one of the hostels (see Places to Stay later in this section and in the Anglet section) for everything you need to know.

Place Clémenceau is surrounded by

euro currency converter 10FF = €1.52

banks equipped for foreign exchange. The Bureau de Change Atolíssimo (☎ 05 59 22 27 27) at No 27 offers very good rates. The main post office on rue de la Poste is open from 8.30 am to 7 pm on weekdays and to noon on Saturday.

Beaches

In summer **Grande Plage** and **plage Miramar**, Biarritz's main beaches, are wall-to-wall with people and lined with striped bathing tents. At low tide there's nude bathing beyond the boulders at the northern end of plage Miramar. Beyond Pointe St-Martin the fine surfing beaches of **Anglet** stretch northwards for over 4km (get there on eastbound bus No 9 from place Clémenceau).

Southwards are the long, exposed **plage de la Côte des Basques**, **plage de Marbella** and, 2km away, **plage de la Milady** (take westbound bus No 9 from place Clémenceau to the Madrid Milady or Thermes Marins stop).

Rocher de la Vierge

The mauve cliffs of Pointe Atalaye come to a head at the Rocher de la Vierge (Rock of the Virgin), a splendid outcrop topped by a statue of the Virgin Mary and accessible only by a long footbridge (designed by Gustave Eiffel) that whistles in the wind. From here, on a clear day you can see north to the Landes and south to the mountains of the Spanish Basque country.

Musée de la Mer

If you're here with children, don't miss the four-storey Musée de la Mer (Sea Museum), facing the Rocher de la Vierge. The aquarium is full of beasties from the Bay of Biscay. Upstairs are exhibits on commercial fishing and whaling (Biarritz was once a whaling port). Seals are fed in their pool at 10.30 am and 5 pm daily; a nearby pool holds sharks.

The museum (☎ 05 59 22 75 40, fax 05 59 22 75 30) is open from 9.30 am to 12.30 pm and 2 to 6 pm daily (to 7 pm from mid-June to September and to midnight in July and August). Admission costs 45FF (students and kids aged five to 16 years

30FF), with 5FF off if you buy your ticket from the tourist office.

Musée Historique de Biarritz

The Musée du Vieux Biarritz (Biarritz History Museum; ☎ 05 59 24 86 28), in a former Anglican church opposite 10 rue Broquedis, has exhibits on the town's history. It's open from 10 am to noon and 2.30 to 6.30 pm daily, except Thursday and Sunday. Admission costs 15FF for adults (children 5FF).

Other Things to See

A promenade follows the coast above the **Port des Pêcheurs**, an old fishing port now filled with pleasure craft. Standing above the port is the striking Byzantine and Moorish-style **Église Ste-Eugénie**, built for Empress Eugénie in 1864.

The most imposing landmark along the Grande Plage is the stately **Hôtel du Palais**, a villa built for Eugénie in 1854 and now a luxury hotel.

Across ave de l'Impératrice at No 8 is **Église Alexandre Newsky**, a Russian Orthodox church built by and for Russian aristocrats before the Revolution of 1917. Nowadays Russians are again in evidence.

The **Chapelle Impériale** on ave de la Marne was built for Empress Eugénie in 1864. It's open from 3 to 7 pm on Tuesday, Thursday and Saturday from mid-April to mid-October (daily except Sunday from mid-July to mid-September).

To the north on Pointe St-Martin are gardens and the **Phare de Biarritz**, the town's 73m-high lighthouse, erected in 1834. It's open from 10 am to noon and 3 to 7 pm daily in July and August, and on weekends from 3 to 7 pm from mid-April to June.

Surfing

For board rental at 50/80FF per half/full day, go to the Rip Curl Surf Shop (☎ 05 59 24 38 40, fax 05 59 24 28 25), 2 ave de la Reine Victoria, open to at least 7 pm Tuesday to Saturday (also Monday from April to October). One/three/seven two-hour lessons cost about 200/500/ 1000FF. The Jeff Hakman Surf School (☎ 05 59 22 03 12, fax 05

59 24 32 44) is open to 7.30 pm daily in the Casino Municipal.

Special Events
The Festival International de Folklore, an international gathering of traditional singers and dancers, takes place every year in early July. Around mid-July Biarritz hosts a Force Basque festival in Parc Mazon.

In July and August the tourist office sponsors free Friday-night concerts in front of Église Ste-Eugénie and elsewhere (check with the tourist office). The Jardin Public is the venue for frequent folklore performances on Sunday night and other nights in summer; ask for details at the tourist office.

Places to Stay
Camping Open from April to late September, *Biarritz Camping* (☎ 05 59 23 00 12, fax 05 59 43 74 67, 28 rue d'Harcet), 3km south-west of the town centre, costs 105FF *forfait* (fixed price deal for two people). Take westbound bus No 9 from place Clémenceau to the Biarritz Camping stop.

Hostels Biarritz's *Auberge de Jeunesse* (☎ 05 59 41 76 00, fax 05 59 41 76 07, 8 rue Chiquito de Cambo) is 800m west of the train station. Dorm beds cost 76/85FF in winter/summer, including breakfast, for Hostelling International (HI) card-holders. It's open mid-January to mid-December. Reception hours are 8.30 to 10 am and 6 to 10 pm (all day during July and August); get there early in summer. It's run by the same people as the Auberge de Jeunesse d'Anglet (see Anglet later in this chapter) and offers a similar range of facilities and activities.

The otherwise expensive *Hôtel Barnetche* (☎ 05 59 24 22 25, fax 05 59 24 98 71, 5 ave Charles Floquet) has dorm beds costing 100FF.

Hotels Inexpensive hotels are scarce in Biarritz, and beds at any price are hard to find in July and August, but space multiplies and prices drop by as much as 30% at other times of the year. The following are open year-round except as noted.

Hôtel Etche-Gorria (☎ 05 59 24 00 74, fax 05 59 22 13 12, 21 ave du Maréchal Foch), in a converted villa with garden and terrace, has doubles from 180FF (290FF with shower and toilet).

Two newish hotels close to the sea are *La Marine* (☎ 05 59 24 34 09, 1 rue des Goélands), where doubles with shower and toilet cost from 150FF and the *Palym* (☎ 05 59 24 16 56, fax 05 59 24 96 12, 7 rue du Port Vieux) where similar rooms cost from 180FF. *Hôtel Maïtagaria* (☎ 05 59 24 26 65, fax 05 59 24 27 37, 34 ave Carnot) has big, spotless doubles/triples with shower and toilet for 260/300FF, plus a garden and terrace at the back.

Hôtel St Julien (☎ 05 59 24 20 39, fax 05 59 22 19 80, 20 ave Carnot), open from mid-March to November, offers doubles with shower and toilet for 360FF. Rooms at *Hôtel Le Bistroye* (☎ 05 59 22 01 02, fax 05 59 31 05 43, 6 rue Jean Bart) cost 240FF. *Hôtel Atlantic* (☎ 05 59 24 34 08, 10 rue du Port Vieux) has singles/doubles with washbasin for 170/200FF and doubles/triples/quads with shower and toilet for 275/310/ 330FF.

Places to Eat
Restaurants Around the covered market are several decent restaurants. *Le Croque en Bouche* (☎ 05 59 22 06 57, 5 rue du Centre) serves quality regional dishes from 75FF and *menus* from 90FF. It's closed on Sunday evening and Monday. *La Belle Époque* (☎ 05 59 24 66 06, 10 ave Victor Hugo) offers regional dishes plus some from Spain and the Antilles, *belle époque* decor and 1930s jazz on the box. Fish and meat dishes cost from 60FF to 100FF, or there is a 68FF *menu*.

The restaurant at *Hôtel Le Bistroye* (see Places to Stay) serves delicious hot dishes from 48FF; it's closed on Wednesday evening and Sunday. An excellent place for lunch is *La Mamounia* (☎ 05 59 24 76 08, 4 rue Jean Bart), with couscous from 75FF to 105FF and other Moroccan specialities from 90FF.

Pizzeria Les Princes (☎ 05 59 24 21 78, 13 rue Gambetta) serves 40FF to 50FF pizzas and pasta and is open daily except Sunday. Touristy but convenient, with a sea view and a good 45FF *salade Basquaise*, is

THE FRENCH BASQUE COUNTRY

Player's Pub & Pizzeria, opposite the Casino Municipal.

Self-Catering Biarritz's *covered market*, two blocks south-west of place Clémenceau, is open from 7 am to 1.30 pm daily. Nearby are many *food shops*, including a *Codec supermarket* at 2 rue du Centre (closed on Sunday). *La Table de Don Quichotte* (12 ave Victor Hugo) sells Spanish hams, sausages and wines. Further down at No 8 is a tempting array of cheeses at *Mille et Un Fromages*. In the Port Vieux area, *Épicerie Fine du Port Vieux* (41 bis rue Mazagran) is a convenient if pricey place to assemble a gourmet picnic.

Entertainment
You'll find a scattering of cheerful bars in the streets either side of rue du Port Vieux, in the neighbourhood of the covered market and around place Clémenceau. Two discotheques near the town centre are *Le Caveau* (☎ 05 59 24 16 17, 4 rue Gambetta) and *Le Flamingo* (☎ 05 59 22 77 59) in the Casino Municipal.

Spectator Sports
Pelote Basque (see under Basque games in the earlier French Basque Country section matches are held at the fronton at Plaza Berri (☎ 05 59 22 15 72), 42 ave du Maréchal Foch, at 9.15 pm every Tuesday and Friday from June to early September. Tickets cost about 40FF.

From July to mid-September, the fronton at Parc Mazon has *grand chistera* matches at 9 pm on Monday; take bus No 9 from place Clémenceau to the Paul Bert stop.

From mid-June to mid-September, Euskal-Jaï Parc des Sports d'Aguiléra (☎ 05 59 23 91 09), 2km east of the town centre on ave Henri Haget, has professional *cesta punta* matches at 9 pm every Wednesday and Saturday evening. Tickets cost from 40FF to 50FF. Take bus No 1 from the Town hall to the Aguiléra stop.

Shopping
Basque music, crafts and guidebooks are available from Eki (☎ 05 59 24 79 64), 21 ave de Verdun, open Tuesday to Saturday. For fine chocolate and Basque sweets go to Robert Pariès (☎ 05 59 22 07 52), 27 place Clémenceau.

Getting There & Away
Air See Air under Getting There & Away in the Bayonne section about flights to/from the Aéroport de Parme (☎ 05 59 43 83 83).

Bus ATCRB buses to St-Jean de Luz, Hendaye and other southern coastal points – nine daily (six on Sunday) – stop outside the tourist office. For connections to southern Landes, you're better off going from Bayonne.

Train SNCF has an office (☎ 05 59 24 00 94) at 13 ave du Maréchal Foch, open from 9 am to noon and 2 to 6 pm on weekdays. The Biarritz La Négresse train station is served by three TGVs daily to/from Paris' Gare Montparnasse and one direct non-TGV train to/from Paris' Gare d'Austerlitz. Other multiple daily services include Dax, Bordeaux, St-Jean de Luz, Hendaye, Pau and Toulouse. Fares and travel times are similar to those listed under Getting There & Away in the Bayonne section.

Getting Around
To/From the Airport Bus No 6 runs between the Town hall and the airport once or twice per hour (on Sunday, line C goes once in the morning and every 40 minutes in the afternoon), until about 7 pm.

Bus For information on the STAB bus system, see Getting Around in the Bayonne section. Biarritz has a STAB information kiosk (☎ 05 59 52 59 52) across square d'Ixelles from the tourist office, open from 8 am to noon and 1.30 to 6 pm Monday to Saturday. Useful lines include No 1 (town hall via Anglet to Bayonne's town hall and train station), No 2 (train station and town hall via Anglet tourist office to Bayonne's town hall and train station), No 6 (town hall to the airport) and No 9 (train station and town hall to Anglet youth hostel and beaches).

Motorcycle & Bicycle Sobilo (☎ 05 59 24 94 47), 24 rue Peyroloubilh, rents mountain bikes for 50FF a day and scooters from 100FF. It's open from 9 am to 1 pm and 3 to 7 pm daily in July and August (from 10 am, and closed on Sunday from March to November).

ANGLET

Anglet (the final 't' is pronounced) seems little more than a suburb wedged between Biarritz and Bayonne, but this is the place to be if you're here to surf.

Orientation & Information

Anglet hasn't much of a centre. The tourist office (☎ 05 59 03 77 01, fax 05 59 03 55 91) is at 1 ave de la Chambre d'Amour (take bus No 7/2 from Bayonne's town hall or No 2 from Biarritz's town hall, to the Cinq-Cantons stop). It is open from 9 am to 12.15 pm and 1.45 to 6 pm on weekdays and Saturday morning (9 am to 7 pm daily except Sunday during July and August). An annexe is open during the summer at plage de Marinella.

Anglet's Bureau d'Information Jeunesse (☎ 05 59 58 35 30, fax 05 59 58 35 32) is in the town hall, at 4 rue Amédée Dufourge, a few steps off the Bayonne–Biarritz road (bus No 1, Anglet Centre stop). It's open from 8.30 am to 12.30 pm and 2 to 6 pm on weekdays (to 5 pm on Friday). Internet access is available here, and at Media Copy (☎ 05 59 52 07 74), 1 ave Minerva, two blocks to the east.

Beaches

The tourist office publishes the excellent French-English *Anglet Surf Guide*, with jargon, safety tips, tournament dates, surf shops and schools, places to stay and eat, and details of the 10 best spots along Anglet's 4km of championship-quality beaches.

The centre of all activity is plage de Marinella, offering low-risk surfing and big crowds; there's also a summer tourist office annexe here. Bus Nos 7/1 and 7/2 come here from Bayonne's town hall. Bus No 9, from place Clémenceau or the

youth hostel in Biarritz, stops at all the beaches.

Activities

The Auberge de Jeunesse d'Anglet (see Places to Stay) offers popular one-week courses (Sunday evening to Saturday afternoon) throughout the year in surfing, sailing, bodyboarding, mountain biking, pelota, scuba diving and horse riding. They're in French, though instructors usually speak some English. Fees start at 2400FF, including accommodation, meals and equipment. Hostel guests can rent surfboards from 60FF to 100FF per day.

Places to Stay

Camping BAB's only year-round camp site, the three-star *Camping de Parme* (☎ 05 59 23 03 00, route de l'Aviation), by a lake just south of the airport, charges 35/38FF per adult/site.

You can also pitch a tent at the *Auberge de Jeunesse d'Anglet* (see under Hostels) for about 45FF per person. For details of other BAB camp sites see Places to Stay in the Biarritz and Bayonne sections.

Hostels The lively *Auberge de Jeunesse d'Anglet* (☎ 05 59 58 70 00, fax 05 59 58 70 07, 19 route des Vignes) is open from mid-January to mid-December. Reception hours are 8.30 to 10 am and 6 to 10 pm (no break in July and August); in summer, get here early as it's very popular. Dorm beds are 76/85FF in winter/summer, including breakfast, for HI card-holders. See the earlier Activities section for details of the hostel's sports courses. Take STAB bus No 9 from Biarritz's train station or place Clémenceau to the Auberge de Jeunesse stop (on Sunday take line C from the town hall).

Getting There & Away

Refer to Getting There & Away in the earlier Biarritz and Bayonne sections.

Getting Around

Bus No 6 links southern Anglet with Aéroport de Parme. From elsewhere in Anglet you must change to the No 6 at Biarritz Town hall.

THE FRENCH BASQUE COUNTRY

ST-JEAN DE LUZ

postcode 64500 • pop 13,200 • elevation 6m

St-Jean de Luz, 24km south-west of Bayonne at the mouth of the Nivelle River, is gathered round a small harbour, its long beach facing a sheltered, perfectly oval bay. Add to this its strong Basque and seafaring roots and you've got a winner. So it's no surprise that St-Jean de Luz (Basque name Donibane Lohizune) and Ciboure (Basque name Ziburu), its twin town across the harbour, are packed to the gunwales in summer. They're expensive too, and you'll save a fair bit by making this a day trip from Bayonne. That's about what you'll need for a good look.

St-Jean de Luz is still an active fishing port, known for its large catches of sardines, anchovies and tuna.

History

There isn't much to see that's ancient: only one building survived a 1558 sacking by the Spanish, and another great bite was taken by massive storms in 1749. But traditions go back at least as far, including a colourful history of fishing and whaling, and of piracy (see the boxed text 'The Basque Corsairs').

St-Jean de Luz's single moment of glory was Louis XIV's lavish, geopolitically important marriage held here on 9 June 1660. He was married to the Spanish *infanta* Maria Teresa (Marie Thérèse), daughter of King Philip IV of Spain, as specified in the 1659 Treaty of the Pyrénées ending 24 years of war. Everywhere that the royal feet trod became hallowed ground, and 3½ centuries later people still talk about it as if it happened last year.

Orientation

St-Jean de Luz and its long beach occupy the eastern side – and Ciboure the western side – of the Baie de St-Jean de Luz, protected from the sea by three 19th-century breakwaters between the headlands of Socoa and Pointe Ste-Barbe. Before emptying into the bay the Nivelle pools in a small fishing harbour between the two towns.

The axis of St-Jean de Luz is its pedestrianised shopping precinct, rue Gambetta, 200m inland from the beach, with place Louis XIV at the south-western end. The train station is a further 200m inland from place Louis XIV; the bus station, the Halte Routière, is 150m along blvd du Commandant Passicou from the train station.

Information

The good tourist office (☎ 05 59 26 03 16, fax 05 59 26 21 47) on place Maréchal Foch is open from 9 am to 12.30 pm and 2 to 6 pm Monday to Saturday (to 7 pm from April to October). It's open all day until 8 pm, plus from 10 am to 1 pm and 3 to 7 pm on Sunday, in July and August.

The town centre is full of banks with ATMs and exchange facilities, including no fewer than six along blvd Victor Hugo, open to at least 5 pm on weekdays and to noon on Saturday. The Change Plus exchange bureau at 32 rue Gambetta is open to 7 pm daily except Sunday (to 8 pm, plus on Sunday to 7 pm, in July and August). Socoa Voyages (☎ 05 59 26 06 27, fax 05 59 51 09 27), 31 blvd Thiers – the only American Express office between Bordeaux and the Spanish border – is open to 6.30 pm daily except Sunday.

The post office at 44 blvd Victor Hugo is open to 5.30 pm on weekdays (to 6 pm in July and August) and until noon on Saturday. Ciboure's post office is at 3 quai Maurice Ravel. Librairie Louis XIV, facing

The Basque Corsairs

From the time of Louis XIV, many Basque shipowners supplemented their whaling or fishing income with piracy, and with gusto after the 1713 Treaty of Utrecht deprived France of the cod-rich waters off Newfoundland. These were no eyepatched scoundrels of the sea, but privateers, their ships fitted out for battle by royal consent, their spoils shared with the crown or with the wealthy citizens who commissioned them, and their families looked after if they should die on the high seas.

ST-JEAN DE LUZ

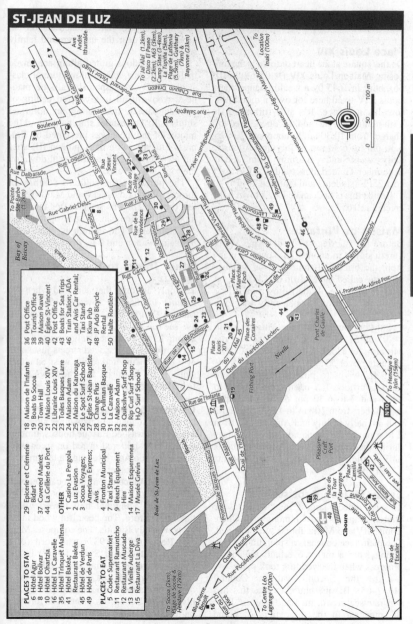

PLACES TO STAY
6 Hôtel Agur
8 Hôtel Bolívar
10 Hôtel Ohartzia
16 Hôtel La Caravelle
35 Hôtel Trinquet Maïtena
41 Hôtel Bakéa;
   Restaurant Bakéa
45 Hôtel de Verdun
49 Hôtel de Paris

PLACES TO EAT
5 Codec Supermarket
11 Restaurant Ramuntcho
12 Restaurant Muscade
13 La Vieille Auberge
15 Restaurant La Diva

29 Epicerie et Crémerie
   Bidart
37 Covered Market
44 La Grillerie du Port

OTHER
1 Casino La Pergola
3 Luz Evasion
3 Socoa Voyages;
   American Express;
   Avis
4 Fronton Municipal
7 Taxi Stand
9 Beach Equipment
   Hire
14 Maison Esquerrenea
17 Musée Grévin

18 Maison de l'Infante
19 Boats to Socoa
20 Town Hall
21 Maison Louis XIV
22 Librairie Louis XIV
23 Toiles Basques Larre
24 Maison Adam
25 Maison du Kanouga
26 Le Spot Surf School
27 Église St-Jean Baptiste
28 Change Plus
30 Le Pullman Basque
31 La Caravelle
32 Maison Adam
33 Quiksilver Surf Shop
34 Rip Curl Surf Shop;
   H₂O Surf School

36 Post Office
38 Tourist Office
39 Maison Ravel
40 Église St-Vincent
42 Post Office
43 Boats for Sea Trips
46 Train Station; ADA
   and Avis Car Rental;
   Taxi Stand
47 Kixu Pub
48 JP Ado Bicycle
   Rental
50 Halte Routière

euro currency converter 10FF = €1.52

place Louis XIV, sells maps and foreign newspapers.

Place Louis XIV

On this square at the heart of town is the imposing **Maison Louis XIV** (☎ 05 59 26 01 56), built in 1643 by a wealthy shipowner. Louis XIV lived here for over a month before his marriage. It's still furnished in 17th-century style and is open, free of charge, from 10.30 am to noon and 2.30 to 5.30 pm (to 6.30 pm in July and August), daily except Sunday morning, from June to September. Guided tours (with English text) cost 25FF (students and children 20FF).

Beside this is St-Jean de Luz's **town hall**, erected in 1657.

Maison de l'Infante

Before her marriage to Louis XIV, Maria Teresa stayed in another shipowner's mansion, the brick-and-stone Maison Joanoenia, now called the Maison de l'Infante, on quai de l'Infante. Aside from ground-floor shops the interior is open only to group tours.

But you can pop into the **Musée Grévin** (☎ 05 59 51 24 88), in an annexe at 3 rue Mazarin, for a look at the historical context, including over 50 wax figures of everyone from fishwives to pirates, musketeers to Paris courtiers. It's open from 10 am to noon and 2 to 6.30 pm daily from April to October; from 10 am to 12.30 pm and 2 to 8 pm daily in July and August; and from 2 to 6 pm at the weekend and on holidays during the rest of the year. Admission costs 34FF (children aged under 13 and students 17FF).

Église St-Jean Baptiste

This is France's largest and finest Basque church – and its most famous one, where Louis XIV and Maria Teresa were married. The plain face conceals a splendid interior, dating from a major overhaul already in progress when the wedding took place.

Until the Second Vatican Council (1962–65), Basque churches like this had separate seating for men and women. Here the men sat in the three tiers of grand oak galleries (five tiers at the rear) and sang as a chorus. The women sat on the ground floor near the underground family sepulchres.

The stupendous gilded **altarpiece**, made in 1665–70, is a delightful mixture of classical severity and Spanish baroque madness. Above it all is a **vaulted ceiling** of painted panels, resembling an upturned ship's hull. The **model ship** hanging in the middle of the nave was presented by Empress Eugénie (wife of Napoleon III) after her own ship *L'Aigle* nearly went down on the rocks off Ciboure.

The **portal** on the church's south side, through which Louis XIV and Maria Teresa left the church, was sealed after the ceremony; its outline can be seen opposite 20 rue Gambetta. The church is open from 8.30 am to noon and 2 to 7 pm daily.

Other Things to See in St-Jean de Luz

The only building that survived when the Spanish torched the town in 1558 is the **Maison Esquerrenea**, the stone building at 17 rue de la République, conspicuous among its whitewashed neighbours.

Narrow, closely spaced streets just south of rue Gambetta, and to the west on either side of rue Mazarin, are the town's old **fisherfolk neighbourhoods**.

Ciboure & Socoa

Ciboure is St-Jean de Luz's quiet alter ego. Many whitewashed Basque houses, timber-framed and shuttered in red or green, survive along **rue Agorette, rue de la Fontaine** and **rue de l'Escalier**.

Église St-Vincent, on rue Pocalette, built in the 16th and 17th centuries, is topped by an unusual octagonal bell tower with a three-tiered roof. The beautiful wood interior is typically Basque. The composer Maurice Ravel (1875–1937) was born (of a Basque mother and Swiss father) in the **Maison Ravel** at 27 quai Maurice Ravel.

The village of **Socoa** is 2.5km north-west of Ciboure along quai Maurice Ravel and blvd Pierre Benoît. Its prominent **fort** was built in 1627 under Henri IV. You can walk out to the **Digue de Socoa** breakwater, or climb to the **lighthouse** via rue du Phare, then out along rue du Sémaphore for fabulous **coastal views**.

Pointe Ste-Barbe

This promontory at the northern end of the Baie de St-Jean de Luz is a fine place for panoramas of the town and the wind-tossed sea. It's 1km north-east St-Jean de Luz's beach, via blvd Thiers and the seaside promenade des Rochers.

Beaches & Surfing

St-Jean de Luz's family-friendly beach sprouts bathing tents from June to September. You can rent your own, at the kiosk by the northern end of rue Tourasse, for 40FF a day. Ciboure has its own modest beach below blvd Pierre Benoît.

Plage de Socoa, 2km west of Socoa on the coastal road called the Corniche (D912), is served by ATCRB buses (see Getting There & Away later in this section) on this route to Hendaye (7FF, Socoa Centre stop) – and in high season by boats (see Getting Around later in this section).

For prime surfing, head 4.5km north-east from the centre of St-Jean de Luz to **plage de Lafitenia**; ATCRB's Biarritz and Bayonne buses pass within 1km of the beach on the N10 (Martienia or Bubonnet stop, 9FF). Surf schools based in the Rip Curl Surf Shop at 72 rue Gambetta and the Quiksilver Surf Shop at 68 rue Gambetta run their own shuttle buses. Another surf school on rue Gambetta is Le Spot.

Other Activities

From Easter to September, École de Voile International (☎ 05 59 47 06 32), near the Socoa parking lot (Bordagain stop on ATCRB's Corniche route to Hendaye), offers windsurfing lessons costing 60/100/150FF for one/two/three hours, plus private instruction.

Tech Ocean (☎ 05 59 47 96 75), 45 ave du Commandant Passicot below Socoa Fort (Socoa stop), is a year-round diving school with introductory dives at 280FF all-in, plus longer courses.

Sea Trips From quai du Maréchal Leclerc, the *Marie Rose* (☎ 05 59 26 25 87) and *Nivelle III* (mobile ☎ 06 09 73 61 81) take visitors for 150FF deep-sea fishing trips in the morning or 70FF ocean cruises in the afternoon, from May to mid-September.

Special Events

Kantuaren Eguna is a Basque singing competition held on the last Sunday in March. **Festival Andalou** brings dancing troupes from Andalusia on Pentecost weekend, and they come from all over the Spanish and French Basque country for **Danses des 7 Provinces Basque** in late May or early June.

St John the Baptist's day is 24 June, celebrated as the **Fêtes de la St-Jean** on the preceding or following weekend, with a choral concert at the Église St-Jean Baptiste, plus bonfires, music and dancing. **La Fête du Thon** (Tuna Festival), on the first Saturday after 1 July, brings buskers to place des Corsaires, quai du Maréchal Leclerc and Ciboure, Basque music and rock to place Maréchal Foch, and midnight fireworks. **Régates de Traînières** is a weekend of whale-boat races on the first weekend in July.

On the first Saturday in September the **Fête du Ttoro** pits chef against chef in the preparation of this classic Basque fish soup. Église St-Jean Baptiste and other churches in St-Jean de Luz and Ciboure resound with **classical French and Basque music** during the first two weeks of September.

For tourists, the city lays on a pop concert, a confetti battle and fireworks on place Louis XIV every Wednesday and Sunday evening from June to August.

Places to Stay – Budget

Camping Between St-Jean de Luz and Guéthary, 7km up the coast, are no fewer than 16 camp sites, clustered behind plage d'Erromardie in quartier Erromardie, and behind plage de Mayarkoenia in quartier Acotz. ATCRB's Biarritz and Bayonne buses (see Getting There & Away later in this section) stop within 1km of them all – get off at the Trikaldi stop for Erromardie camp sites and Martienia for Acotz camp sites. Acotz has the best access to the surfing beaches of Lafitenia and Senix.

Among cheaper sites in Erromardie are *Elgar* (☎ 05 59 26 85 85), open mid-April to September, which charges 60/70FF for two people with tent/car; and the municipal camp site *Chibaou-Berria* (☎ 05 59 26 11 94), open June to mid-September and costing 28/28FF per adult/site. In the same price range in Acotz are *Luz Europ* (☎ 05 59 26 51 90), open Easter to October at 27/40FF; and *Le Maya* (☎ 05 59 26 54 91), open mid-June to September at 26/20/9FF per adult/tent/car.

Two camp sites within 5km south-west of Ciboure are the year-round *Larrouleta* (☎ 05 59 47 37 84), which charges 24/17/10FF per adult/tent/car; and *Suhiberry* (☎ 05 59 47 06 23), open May to September at 24/20/8FF.

Hostels The *Centre Léo Lagrange* (☎/fax 05 59 47 04 79, 8 rue Simone Menez) in Ciboure has dorm beds for about 50FF.

Places to Stay – Mid-Range
Many hotels get the same clients year after year, so it can be very hard to find a room in July and August. Rates soar and some hotels require that you take half-board. At other times of the year prices may drop by a third or more. We give peak prices.

St-Jean de Luz At the *Hôtel Trinquet Maïtena* (☎ 05 59 26 05 13, fax 05 59 26 09 90, 42 rue du Midi), basic doubles with shower/bath cost from 220/240FF and triples/quads start at 320FF. Near the train station is *Hôtel de Verdun* (☎ 05 59 26 02 55, 13 ave de Verdun), where big, plain doubles cost 200FF (230FF with shower, 295FF with bath and toilet); half-board (170FF extra per person) is obligatory in July and August.

Hôtel Bolivar (☎/fax 05 59 26 02 00, 18 rue Sopite) is open from May to September with doubles for 195FF (295FF with bath and toilet). *Hôtel de Paris* (☎ 05 59 26 00 62, fax 05 59 26 90 02, 1 blvd du Commandant Passicot) has nondescript doubles/triples with shower and toilet for 300/390FF.

Ciboure The friendly *Hôtel Bakéa* (☎ 05 59 47 34 40, fax 05 59 47 48 87, 9 place Camille Julian), open from March to December, has rooms with shower and toilet from 200FF to 250FF. At *Hôtel La Caravelle* (☎ 05 59 47 18 05, blvd Pierre Benoît), doubles/quads with shower and toilet cost 260/360FF. ATCRB buses (see Getting There & Away) pass by all day.

Places to Stay – Top End
Functional doubles/triples at the Scots-run *Hôtel Agur* (☎ 05 59 51 91 11, fax 05 59 51 91 21, 96 rue Gambetta), open from mid-March to mid-November, start at 395/495FF; self-catering flats for two cost 3500FF per week in summer or 1500FF in the low season. Pleasant rooms at *Hôtel Ohartzia* (☎ 05 59 26 00 06, fax 05 59 26 74 75, 28 rue Garat) cost 400/450FF with shower/bath, including breakfast.

Places to Eat
Just *look* at all the posh restaurants lined up waiting for you along rue de la République! There are more, plus lots of cafes, around place Louis XIV. Most seem to shut down for a few days a week outside July and August, and for a few months outside summer.

Restaurants – St-Jean de Luz For good value and a great buzz, stuff yourself full of freshly cooked sardines, tuna and omelettes for under 100FF at the hugely popular, harbourside *La Grillerie du Port* (☎ 05 59 51 18 29, quai Maréchal Leclerc), open from 11.30 am to 2.30 pm and 6 to 10 pm daily from mid-June to mid-September.

The Basque fish chowder called *ttoro* (say 'tyoro') is touted all along rue de la République, usually as an entrée for about 90FF. It's part of a good 85FF lunch *menu* at *Restaurant La Diva* (☎ 05 59 51 14 01, 7 rue de la République), open from March to October.

Restaurant Muscade (☎ 05 59 26 96 73, 20 rue Garat) specialises in big mixed salads (50FF to 100FF) and lovely *tartes* (30FF to 60FF), both savoury and sweet. It's open to 9 or 10 pm daily.

La Vieille Auberge (☎ 05 59 26 19 61, 22

rue Tourasse) serves generous portions of traditional French and Basque cuisine, including *moules marinières* (mussels marinated in their own juices) for 50FF. *Menus* start at 75FF.

Restaurant Ramuntcho (☎ 05 59 26 03 89, 24 rue Garat) has a unique mix of regional dishes. The *patron* is from Normandy so sauces are rich with fresh cream. Specialities include duck and fish, with *menus* from 90FF.

Restaurants – Ciboure With spectacularly good seafood, the restaurant in **Hôtel Bakéa** (see Places to Stay) is a great place for a splurge. See if you can get through their 150FF *plateau de fruits de mer* (seafood platter). *Menus* start at 90FF.

Self-Catering Tuesday and Friday (plus Saturday during July and August) are market days at the *covered market* on blvd Victor Hugo. Ciboure's market is on Sunday morning on place Camille Julian.

Épicure et Crémerie Bidart (29 rue Gambetta) offers a kaleidoscope of cold meats and cheeses daily except Sunday, and there is a good *fruit and vegetable shop* opposite (also open Sunday morning in summer). Other *food shops* line rue Gambetta. The *Codec supermarket* at 87 rue Gambetta is open to at least 7 pm (closed on Sunday).

Entertainment
Bars & Discos The cheerful **Kixu Pub** (5 ave Labrouche) has Guinness on tap. St-Jean de Luz has two discos: **El Paseo** (☎ 05 59 26 38 60, 48 ave André Ithurralde), 2km east of the bus station (Halte Routière) and **La Tupiña** (☎ 05 59 54 73 23), 5km east on the N10.

Casinos The beachside *Casino La Pergola* is open until 3 am, with slot machines from 11 pm daily and gaming from 9 pm daily except Monday.

Spectator Sports
Cesta punta matches take place at 9 pm every Tuesday and Friday at the Jaï Alaï Campos Berri (☎ 05 59 51 65 30), opposite

43 ave André Ithurralde. Tickets cost 50FF to 120FF. Look out for daytime matches on Monday and Thursday at the Fronton Municipal, at the eastern end of rue St-Jacques.

Shopping
Bust your budget with *mouchous* (almond biscuits), *kanouga* (chewy chocolate or coffee candy) or *gâteau Basque* at Maison du Kanouga, 9 rue Gambetta (open to midnight in July and August), or the venerable Maison Adam (founded 1660) at 49 rue Gambetta (closed on Monday) and 6 rue de la République.

This is also a good place to buy Basque linen, for example at La Caravelle, 64 rue Gambetta, or Toiles Basques Larre, 4 rue de la République.

Getting There & Away
Bus From the Halte Routière, ATCRB's buses (☎ 05 59 08 00 33) run up the coast to Biarritz (18FF, 30 minutes, nine daily) and Bayonne (22FF, 35 minutes, six to 10 daily). ATCRB also goes down to Hendaye (17FF, 20 minutes) 10 to 12 times daily (four on Sunday), with three weekday departures taking the Corniche coastal route.

Train At the train station (information ☎ 08 36 35 35 35), ticket windows are open until 7.30 pm daily, the information office to 7 pm and luggage lockers from 6 am to 11 pm. There are at least 20 trains daily to Biarritz (17FF, 12 minutes) and Bayonne (26FF, 25 minutes), and to Hendaye (17FF, 12 minutes), from where shuttle trains continue to San Sebastián in Spain (see Hendaye later in this chapter). A non-TGV ticket to Bordeaux costs 148FF.

Car The French budget-rate agency ADA (☎ 05 59 26 26 22) is open daily at the train station. International agencies include Europcar (☎ 05 59 26 82 40), open only in July and August at 3 blvd du Commandant Passicot; and Avis, with an office (☎ 05 59 26 76 66) at the train station, closed on Monday, and one (☎ 05 59 26 17 43) at Socoa Voyages, 31 blvd Thiers.

THE FRENCH BASQUE COUNTRY

Getting Around

Bus ATCRB goes via Ciboure to Socoa (7FF, 10 minutes) five times daily (except Sunday), from the Halte Routière.

Boat The *Lixto* (mobile ☎ 06 81 20 84 98) sails between quai de l'Infante and Socoa every 30 minutes during the day, for 12FF one way – daily from June to September, at the weekend and on holidays in May and October, and on holidays only in April.

Bicycle & Motorcycle JP Ado (☎ 05 59 26 14 95), 7 ave Labrouche, rents bicycles (*vélos*) for 60/294FF and up per day/week, VTTs (*vélos tout terrains*, mountain bikes) for 80/365FF, and 50cc motorbikes for 430FF to 535FF a week. The shop is open Tuesday to Saturday (plus Sunday morning in July and August). Other outlets are Luz Evasion (☎ 05 59 26 43 88), 4 rue Dalbarade, and Location Inaki (☎ 05 59 26 32 26), 12 ave de Habas. In summer, Sobilo (☎ 05 59 26 75 76) rents VTTs, scooters, motorbikes and rollerblades from a kiosk at the train station.

HENDAYE

postcode 64700 • pop 11,200 • elevation 25m
Hendaye's main claim to fame is as South-West France's main border crossing point and rail link into Spain (to Irún on the other side), although it is also a pleasant, if unexceptional, beach resort. If you've come this far, don't miss a walk around the clifftop Domaine d'Abbadia.

Orientation

Hendaye sits beside the Bidassoa River – the frontier – across which is the twin Spanish resort of Fuenterrabía and, just upstream, the Spanish border post and rail terminus of Irún. The Bidassoa River has silted up enough to form a natural harbour, the Baie de Txingudi, just before it empties into the Atlantic.

There are three distinct Hendayes – the train station and border area, the town centre, and the beach – too far apart for easy walking but linked by local bus services. ATCRB buses from up the coast also stop in all three areas.

Information

The tourist office (☎ 05 59 20 00 34, fax 05 59 20 79 17, email tourisme.hendaye@ wanadoo.fr) is at 12 rue des Aubépines, 400m from the beach. It's open from 9 am to 8 pm daily (10 am to 1 pm on Sunday) in July and August, and from 9 am to 12.30 pm and 2 to 6.30 pm daily except Saturday afternoon and Sunday during the rest of the year. The post office is next door.

Château d'Abbadie & Domaine d'Abbadia

East of town on a rugged plateau above the sea stands a neo-Gothic castle built in the 1860s for an Irish-Basque explorer named Antoine d'Abbadie d'Arrast. The chateau (☎ 05 59 20 04 51), with an observatory and the eclectic furnishings of a wealthy traveller to the Orient, can be visited on guided tours daily except Sunday at 11 am, 3, 4 and 5 pm from June to September and at 3 and 4 pm on weekdays in March, April, May and October. Admission costs 35FF (children 18FF).

Domaine d'Abbadia, the windswept estate, is a protected area, owned since 1979 by the Conservatoire du Littoral. Its lawns, moors and cliffs are open, via the Maison de la Lande visitor centre (☎ 05 59 20 37 20), from 9.30 am to 12.30 pm and 2.30 to 6.30 pm daily in July and August, and from 9 am to noon and 2 to 6 pm daily except Sunday during the rest of the year. The centre also has an exhibit on the estate's rich flora and fauna. Admission is free.

Activities

The swells along Hendaye's 3km beach will please novice surfers, and there are at least two surf schools in town, Fluide Système (☎ 05 59 20 67 47) at 4 rue des Orangers and Vent d'Est (☎ 05 59 48 14 08, email vendest@aol.com) at 69 blvd du Général Leclerc.

Moby Dick (☎/fax 05 59 20 45 33), also on rue des Orangers, is a dive shop (introductory dives cost 180FF) and rents out motorboats by the day and sailboats by the week. Across the road is another dive shop, Club Urpean (☎ 05 59 20 55 55).

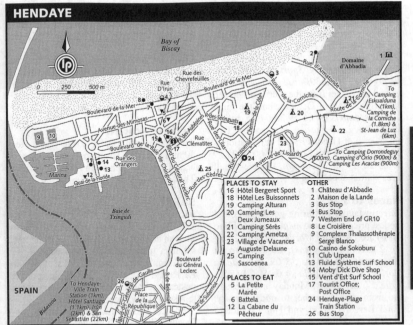

HENDAYE

THE FRENCH BASQUE COUNTRY

PLACES TO STAY
16 Hôtel Bergeret Sport
18 Hôtel Les Buissonnets
19 Camping Alturan
20 Camping Les
   Deux Jumeaux
21 Camping Sérès
22 Camping Ametza
23 Village de Vacances
   Auguste Delaune
25 Camping
   Sascoenea

PLACES TO EAT
5 La Petite
   Marée
6 Battela
12 La Cabane du
   Pêcheur

OTHER
1 Château d'Abbadie
2 Maison de la Lande
3 Bus Stop
4 Bus Stop
7 Western End of GR10
8 Le Croisière
9 Complexe Thalassothérapie
   Serge Blanco
10 Casino de Sokoburu
11 Club Urpean
13 Fluide Système Surf School
14 Moby Dick Dive Shop
15 Vent d'Est Surf School
17 Tourist Office;
   Post Office
24 Hendaye-Plage
   Train Station
26 Bus Stop

From the marina, the *Arguia* (mobile ☎ 06 86 32 16 33) will take you deep-sea fishing all morning for 150FF, or on a one/two-hour afternoon ocean cruise for 35/60FF.

The GR10 trail, which runs the length of the Pyrénées, starts at the beach at Hendaye.

Thalassotherapy
One of the Basque coast's bigger centres for thalassotherapy (see Activities in the Facts for the Visitor chapter) is the Complexe Thalassothérapie Serge Blanco (☎ 05 59 51 35 35, fax 05 59 51 36 00), beside the marina.

Le Croisière
The prominent, Moorish-style building sticking out onto the beach started out in 1884 as a casino. Today it includes a shopping centre, an apartment complex and a restaurant.

Fuenterrabía
The pretty Spanish resort of Fuenterrabía (Fontarrabie to the French) has a charming old centre full of timber-frame houses, a castle and baroque church, its own beach, modest accommodation and good food. Behind it rises the 500m peak of Jaizkibel. Several boats shuttle to and from Hendaye's marina every 15 to 30 minutes into the evening, for about 10FF one way.

Places to Stay
Hendaye has at least 10 camp sites (see the map). At the lower end (with season and peak forfait rates shown) are *D'Orio* (☎ 05 59 20 30 30), July and August at 80FF; *Dorrondeguy* (☎ 05 59 20 26 16, rte de Glacière), April to September at 80FF; and *Les Acacias* (☎ 05 59 20 78 76), April to September from 82FF.

The plain bungalows at *Village de Vacances Auguste Delaune* (☎ 05 59 20 07 07, fax 05 59 48 02 52) are for groups in July and

August but at other times may be available to all; a four-bed bungalow with kitchen costs 200FF per weekday or 475FF for the weekend. It's open from April to October.

Two good-value hotels within 400m of the beach are the *Bergeret Sport* (☎ 05 59 20 00 78, fax 05 59 20 67 30, 4 rue des Clématites), around the corner from the tourist office and open from May to October; and the quiet *Les Buissonnets* (☎ 05 59 20 04 75, fax 05 59 20 79 72, 29 rue des Seringuats). Two blocks east of Hendaye-Ville train station is the *Santiago* (☎ 05 59 20 00 94, fax 05 59 20 83 26, 29 rue Santiago). Doubles at all three start at about 220FF.

Places to Eat
Three restaurants offering good seafood at modest prices (evening *menus* from 60FF to 75FF) are *La Petite Marée* (☎ 05 59 20 77 96, 2 ave des Mimosas), *La Cabane du Pêcheur* (☎ 05 59 20 38 09, quai de la Floride) and the *Battela* (☎ 05 59 20 15 70, 5 rue d'Irún), closed Monday and Tuesday and from mid-December to mid-February. Hôtel Bergeret Sport and Hôtel Santiago (see Places to Stay) also have restaurants.

Getting There & Away
Bus ATCRB uses the same beach, centre and train station stops as local buses (see Getting Around later in this section). Services to St-Jean de Luz (17FF, 20 minutes) operate at least 10 times daily (four on Sunday), including three weekday runs via the Corniche (see Car later in this section). Most continue to Bayonne (35FF, one hour).

Train Six to nine trains daily (except Sunday) link Hendaye-Ville station to St-Jean de Luz (17FF, 10 minutes), Biarritz (27FF, 25 minutes) and Bayonne (36FF, 35 minutes). About half of these also serve Hendaye-Plage station, near the beach. Daily Paris–Bordeaux–Irún TGVs also stop at Hendaye-Ville.

From Hendaye-Ville station, two private, Spanish-gauge shuttle trains cross the border: El Topo to San Sebastián (10FF return, 30 minutes) every 30 minutes from 7 am to 9 pm; and EuskoTren via San Sebastián to

Bilbao (84FF return, 2½ hours) at 7.50 am and 3.50 pm, and departing on the return trip from Bilbao at 11.50 am and 7.50 pm.

Car Treat yourself to the slow but spectacular drive from St-Jean de Luz (D912) atop the seaside cliffs called the Corniche, where the Pyrénées tumble into the sea. The views along the Basque coast are superb.

Getting Around
An unnumbered local bus runs daily, every 30 minutes from 10 am to 7 pm, linking the beach, the town centre and the train station. The fare is 5FF.

SARE
postcode 64310 • pop 2000 • elevation 70m
Sare (Sara in Basque), 14km south-east of St-Jean de Luz, is a handsome Basque town set in a lush Labourde landscape dotted with farmhouses, on the flanks of solitary La Rhune mountain. The whole, picture-postcard scene has earned town and mountain some heavy tourist traffic.

Sare's centre is dominated, as in most Basque villages, by its severe church – with five gilded altars and typical gallery seating – and a tall fronton that serves as the focus of most social events. The entrance to the tiny town hall is squashed between a pharmacy and a bar on the central square. The GR10 passes through the middle of town.

Half of La Rhune is in the Spanish Basque Country. The Basques have never paid much attention to the border, and the people of Sare have a history of cheerful, matter-of-fact smuggling here, over a network of remote tracks.

Information
The tourist office (☎ 05 59 54 20 14, fax 05 59 54 29 15), in the town hall, is open from 9 am to 12.30 pm and 2 to 6 pm on weekdays from May to October (plus 9 am to noon on Saturday in June), and from 1.30 to 5.30 pm on weekdays during the rest of the year.

La Rhune
Antenna-topped, 905m La Rhune (Larrun in Basque) is something of a Basque sym-

bol. Indeed it was sacred as early as the Stone Age, as witnessed by the many stone circles, dolmens, barrows and tumuli in its middle reaches. Ever since Empress Eugénie visited in 1859, it has been a Basque Country must-see.

There are stunning views of the Basses-Pyrénées, the Spanish Basque province of Navarra and the Bay of Biscay from the summit, which can be reached on foot or via a *train à crémaillère* (cog-wheel railway; ☎ 05 59 54 20 26). The train, built in 1924, runs from the Col de St-Ignace, 3km northwest of Sare on the D4 (the St-Jean de Luz road), from Easter to mid-November, with departures roughly every 35 minutes from 9 am (from 8.30 am in July and August). The 4km trip takes 30 minutes each way, for 60FF return (children 35FF). Waits of an hour or more are common in July and August.

En route, watch for the shaggy, shy feral ponies called *pottok* (say 'potyok'), once used in local mines and crossbred for drayage, now mainly sought after for pony trekking. There's a brisk local trade in them (see Espelette later in this chapter), as well as a private nature reserve for them (see Bidarray later in this chapter). For more on efforts to protect this unique animal, see Endangered Species in the Facts About South-West France chapter.

Les Grottes de Sare
Through a yawning cave mouth 6km south of Sare via the D306 is a network of underground passages, galleries and a huge central chamber. Bones and tools found here show that these limestone caves had longterm occupants in the late Palaeolithic period, about 20,000 years ago. Local lore says the underground river that formed them emerges in Spain and that smugglers used to pass *under* the border here!

The caves (☎ 05 59 54 21 88) are open from 10 am to 6 pm daily from Easter to October (from 9.30 am to 8 pm in July and August); from 11 am to 5 pm from October to early November; and from 2 to at least 4 pm during the rest of the year. Hours are a bit longer at the weekend. A 900m multi-

lingual guided tour and French-language *son et lumière* cost 30FF (kids aged under 14 years 15FF).

Special Events
Everything in Sare happens at the fronton. Weekly events include pelote Basque at 9 pm on Monday in July and August, and Basque dancing at 9.30 pm on Wednesday all summer. Seasonal events include a Sunday handicrafts and Basque food fair in mid-July, and another in late August, preceded on the Saturday by a Fête de la Pelote.

Places to Stay & Eat
Camp sites around Sare include *Goyenetche* (☎ 05 59 54 21 71, rte des Grottes), 3km south of Sare on the road to the grottoes, open from July to mid-September for 13/12/7FF per adult/tent/car; and *La Petite Rhune* (☎ 05 59 54 20 91, fax 05 59 54 23 42, quartier Lehenbiscaye), 1km south of town, open from May to September for 17/17/10FF or 65FF forfait.

Hôtel Lastiry (☎ 05 59 54 20 07, place du Fronton) offers plain doubles for 170FF to 270FF. Tops in Sare, and with the best food (and famous gâteau Basque), is the three-star *Hôtel Arraya* (☎ 05 59 54 20 46, fax 05 59 54 27 04, place du Village), open from April to mid-November with doubles from 400FF.

Getting There & Away
Le Basque Bondissant (☎ 05 59 26 30 74) has regular buses from St-Jean de Luz to Col de St-Ignace (10FF, 20 minutes), Sare (15FF, 30 minutes) and the Grottes de Sare (15FF, 45 minutes). Departures are at 9.30 am on Wednesday from April to June and September to October (change at Col de St-Ignace or Sare for the caves) and at 2 pm on Tuesday and Thursday, with return buses starting from the caves at 3.15 and 5.45 pm, respectively. Departures in July and August are at 10.30 am and 2 pm on weekdays, with return buses from the caves at 2.45 and 5.45 pm (plus a run to Sare at 7 pm, and a return at 1.15 pm).

Two St-Jean de Luz agencies with halfday tours to La Rhune are Bruno Francisco

(☎ 05 59 51 23 40), 5 ave Georges Clémenceau, 9 and 10.30 am and 1.30 pm on Tuesday and Friday from April to October, for 50FF (minimum two people); and Le Pullman Basque (☎ 05 59 26 03 37), 33 rue Gambetta, 9 am on Tuesday from June to September, for 90FF (minimum 15).

AÏNHOA
postcode 64250 • pop 550 • elevation 120m
Aïnhoa (Ainhoa in Basque) is France's most south-westerly bastide, jointly founded around 1230 by Premonstratensian monks, keen to make a buck from Compostela pilgrims, and Juan Pérez de Baztan, a Navarre signeur worried about the English. The Spanish trashed it in 1629 so almost everything dates from the late 17th and 18th centuries, with hardly a younger building to be seen.

This is the place to come for a look at classic Labourd Basque village architecture. The single main street is lined on both sides with stout, half-timbered, brightly painted houses of the 17th and 18th centuries, some with unnerving outward tilts. Facades on the western side are noticeably finer than those opposite: the latter are actually backsides, according to a tradition that houses should face away from the sea, source of stormy weather.

Many bear stone lintels engraved in Latin or French with the essentials of their founding. One of the most detailed of these, on the so-called Maison Gorritia, notes that the house was paid for with money earned overseas. The confidence implicit in these permanent declarations arises from another Basque tradition (now overruled by French law), that houses cannot be sold out of the family after the second generation.

The paint and whitewash are renewed annually. The overall effect is dignified and harmonious: this must be one of the southwest's most photogenic villages. Of course everybody from everywhere wants to see it, so it's wall-to-wall with visitors all summer.

Things to See & Do
Aïnhoa's fortified church, parts of which date from the 14th century, contains two tiers of wooden galleries and a grand, gilded altarpiece. It shares an outer wall with the village fronton and has a little cemetery full of Basque grave markers.

The GR10 passes through town: Sare is a 3½ hour walk to the west, Bidarray seven hours to the east. For a shorter (45-minute) walk – or rather a climb – that will reward you with lofty views as far as Navarra and St-Jean de Luz, follow signs east from the main street to a pilgrims' chapel called Vierge d'Ainhoa (the Aïnhoa Virgin).

Places to Stay & Eat
Camping The basic *Air Naturelle Harazpy* (☎ 05 59 29 89 38, fax 05 59 29 73 82), just north-west of the town centre, is open from mid-June to mid-September and costs 17/20/9FF per adult/tent/car. At Dancharia, 3km to the south at the Spanish border, year-round *Camping Xokoan* (☎ 05 59 29 90 26, fax 05 59 29 73 82) costs the same and also has rooms.

Hotels Across the main street from the church is the Logis de France *Hôtel Oppoca* (☎ 05 59 29 90 72, fax 05 59 29 81 03), with doubles with toilet and shower or bath from 250FF (about 20FF more in July and August) and a restaurant (closed on Sunday evening and Monday) with *menus* from 95FF.

ESPELETTE
postcode 64250 • pop 1700 • elevation 72m
The dark red peppers called pimentos, which arrived from Spain and Mexico in the 17th century, are now an essential part of Basque cuisine. The best known variety is grown around Espelette (Ezpeleta in Basque), and for weeks after the September harvest, chains of *le piment d'Espelette* are hung out to sun-dry on the village's many traditional Basque facades, trimmed in the same blood-red colour.

Rising above them are a little stone chateau, dating originally from the 11th century, and a boxy 17th-century church with some of the most exuberant interior woodwork in the French Basque country. The church graveyard is full of disk-shaped

Basque markers. Beside the village runs the Laxia or Laxa, a tributary of the Nive.

Orientation & Information

Sundered by the D918, Espelette has no real centre. Just off place du Jeu de Paume on rue Nagusia is the tourist office (☎ 05 59 93 91 44, fax 05 59 93 89 71), open from 8.30 am to 12.30 pm and 1.30 to 6 pm on weekdays. The town hall, in the old chateau, has a free exhibition on pimentos around the world, open the same hours as the tourist office, but only from April to October.

Chocolate

Among the few chocolatiers who still begin with the bean – and offer free tastings – is Chocolats Anton (☎ 05 59 93 80 58) on place du Marché. For more on the region's most famous confection, see the boxed text 'Chocolate' under Bayonne earlier in this chapter.

Special Events

Espelette's weekly market of local products is held on place du Marché on Wednesday, and also on Saturday in July and August.

The French Basque country's last big festival of the year is the **Fête du Piment**, held here on the last weekend in October, with a blessing of the peppers, processions and the selection of a *chevalier du piment* (knight of the pimento).

Pottoks, the shaggy ponies of the Basque high country, are bought and sold at Espelette's **Foire aux Pottoks**, on the last Tuesday and Wednesday in January.

Places to Stay & Eat

Hôtel Chilhar (☎ 05 59 93 90 01, fax 05 59 93 93 25, rue Principale) has adequate rooms with toilet and shower from 195FF for two. Up a notch is the nearby *Hôtel Euzkadi* (☎ 05 59 93 91 88, fax 05 59 93 90 19, rue Principale), with doubles for 270FF, a pool and a good restaurant.

Another famous local speciality is *axoa* (French *hachoa*), a spicy veal stew with onions, garlic, tomatoes and, of course, pimentos. A good-value place to find it is on the 95FF *menu* at *Restaurant Pottoka* (☎ 05 59 93 90 92, place du Jeu de Paume), closed on Sunday evening and Monday. Between the Pottoka and the tourist office is *Restaurant Extemendi* (rue Nagusia), open for weekday lunch with a 55FF axoa *plat*.

Getting There & Away

Espelette is 30 minutes by bus from St-Jean de Luz. Hasparren-bound buses of Lata (☎ 05 59 54 11 37) depart St-Jean de Luz at 11 am on Tuesday and Friday and at 7 pm daily except Sunday (daily except Wednesday and Saturday in winter), and from Espelette at 7.20 am daily except Sunday (weekdays only in winter) and at 1.55 pm on Tuesday and Friday.

BIDARRAY

postcode 64780 • pop 650 • elevation 480m
Now you're over into the Basse-Navarre and its main artery, the valley of the Nive. Typical of rural Basque settlements, little Bidarray (Bidarrai in Basque) is not so much a village as a scattering of farmsteads and hamlets, perched on its own plateau where the river Bastan joins the Nive.

Orientation & Information

From the D918, bus stop or train station, cross the bridge over the railway tracks and river (noticing, upstream, the graceful 14th-century Pont Noblia, the Nive's first bridge). Turn right for 700m, then left for a steep 800m up to the centre, place de l'Église – little more than the customary town hall/church/fronton plus a small hotel and a restaurant. The tourist office (☎/fax 05 59 37 74 60), in the town hall, is open from 9 am to 8 pm daily in July and August, and from 12.30 to 2 pm and 5 to 8 pm on weekdays and 9 am to 8 pm Saturday during the rest of the year.

La Maison du Pottok

This private nature reserve in the hills above Bidarray was opened in 1993 to preserve traditional breeds of the shaggy wild pony of the Basque Country, the pottok (see also La Rhune in this chapter, and Endangered Species in the Facts About South-West

THE FRENCH BASQUE COUNTRY

France chapter). La Maison du Pottok (☎ 05 59 52 21 14, email pottok@aol.com) offers film presentations, exhibits, guided visits from 11 am to 6 pm daily from June to September, and fine views across the Basque Country. Admission and a year's membership is 40FF (kids from six to 13 years 30FF). The reserve is on a signposted road about 5km from the D918 and the train station.

Activities

A year-round youth activity centre called Auñamendi (☎/fax 05 59 37 71 34), west of the square beyond the town hall, organises hikes (40/80FF per half/full day), VTT trips (60/90FF rental plus 40/70FF), climbing (70/120FF), horse-riding (70FF per hour), canyonning (170/300FF), rafting the Nive (90FF per half day), caving (90FF per half day), pelota (50FF per half day) and more. If your French is good enough you can also hear talks on Basque culture and agriculture.

Ur Bizia (☎/fax 05 59 37 72 37), down on the D918 just south of the train station, organises rafting, hydrospeed and other white-water activities for about 240FF per person per day.

Bidarray Village

The nice thing is that there's little to do, except snoop around Bidarray's tiny Romanesque church (built in 1132 as the chapel of a long-gone priory and now fronted by an outsize, 17th-century belfrywall), soak up the silence and the view over deliciously rolling, fertile countryside, or set out on the GR10, which runs past.

Places to Stay & Eat

Auñamendi (see Things to See & Do) runs two year-round *gîtes d'étape* (dormitory accommodation for hikers) near the centre, for 51FF per bed.

Three hotels down by the river, with doubles from about 170FF, are *Chez Anny* (☎ 05 59 37 70 88, fax 05 59 37 76 60); *Erremundeya* (☎/fax 05 59 37 71 21), open from March to November; and *Noblia* (☎ 05 59 37 70 89), open closed mid-December to mid-January.

Opposite the church, *Hôtel Barberaenea* (☎ 05 59 37 74 86, fax 05 59 37 77 55) has a few comfortable rooms, most with eye-popping views, for 180FF (320FF with twin beds, toilet and shower), and a big 35FF breakfast. Book it well ahead. Opposite the town hall, *Auberge Iparla* (☎ 05 59 37 77 21) serves Basque *menus* from 100FF.

Getting There & Around

SNCF has at least three daily trains (two on Sunday) from Bayonne to Pont-Noblia station (40 minutes).

VTTs can be hired from the shop opposite Hôtel Barberaenea, from April to September.

ST-JEAN PIED DE PORT
postcode 64220 • pop 1800 • elevation 170m

You can't arrive in St-Jean Pied de Port (Basque name Donibane Garazi) without feeling a little surprised. Here at the head of the rustically beautiful valley of the Nive River, 6km from the Spanish border, is a handsome, stoutly fortified town with an important look to it.

Indeed it has been very important. The French name means 'St John at the Foot of the Pass,' and this is the northern gateway to Puerto de Ibañeta, the pass of Roncesvalles (Roncevaux), a funnel for history for centuries. The many French pilgrim routes to Santiago de Compostela coalesced here at the final stop before Spain. And through here passed Visigoths, Muslim raiders, Charlemagne, and Basque refugees from the Spanish Civil War.

The town was founded in the 13th century by the last great Basque king, Sancho VII (The Strong) of Navarre, after its predecessor (at present-day St-Jean le Vieux, 5km to the east) was razed by Richard the Lionheart (see the boxed text in the History section of the Facts about South-West France chapter). Jeanne d'Albret's Protestant troops desecrated the town in 1569.

The capital and main market town of the Basse-Navarre has now bitten the golden apple of tourism. In summer it's choked with day-trippers, and residents have a besieged look. Although it's a straightforward day trip from Bayonne, consider staying the night and exploring before breakfast, or come in the low-season. Half the reason for coming is the journey itself, by train or car up the dreamy valley of the Nive. If you want more, rent a bike and head off into the hills.

Orientation

The town centre nowadays is place Charles de Gaulle, a 500m walk south from the train station via place du Trinquet, where buses stop. Enter the walled town from place Charles de Gaulle through the old porte de

Navarre, or from place du Trinquet through the porte de France, to the medieval main street, rue de la Citadelle. To the left this climbs steeply through the prettiest part of town to the Citadelle. From 2 to 7 pm in summer it's pedestrians-only here.

Information

The tourist office (☎ 05 59 37 03 57, fax 05 59 37 34 91), 14 place Charles de Gaulle, is open from 9 am to noon and 2 to 7 pm on weekdays and to 6 pm on Saturday (from 10.30 am to 12.30 pm and 3 to 6 pm daily from mid-June to mid-September).

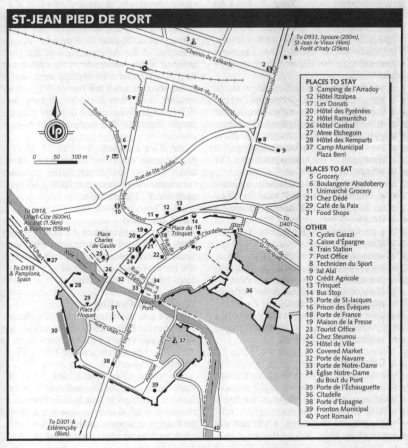

ST-JEAN PIED DE PORT

To D933, Ispoure (200m),
St-Jean le Vieux (4km)
& Forêt d'Iraty (25km)

Chemin-de-Zalikarte

Rue-du-11-Novembre

Avenue-du-Jaï-Alaï

Rue-de-la-Poste

Avenue-Renaud

Rue-de-Ste-Eulalie

Avenue-Renaud

To D918,
Uhart-Cize (600m),
Ascarat (1.5km)
& Bayonne (55km)

Route-d'Uhart

Place
Charles
de Gaulle

Nive

To D933
& Pamplona,
Spain

Place du
Trinquet

Rue-de-France

Rue-de-la-Citadelle

To
D401

Chemin-de-
St-Jacques

Place
Floquet

Rue de
l'Église

Vieux
Pont

Rue-d'Uhart

Rue-d'Espagne

Avenue-du-Fronton

To D301 &
Estérençuby
(8km)

PLACES TO STAY
3 Camping de l'Arradoy
12 Hôtel Itzalpea
17 Les Donats
20 Hôtel des Pyrénées
26 Hôtel Ramuntcho
26 Hôtel Central
27 Mme Etchegoin
28 Hôtel des Remparts
37 Camp Municipal
   Plaza Berri

PLACES TO EAT
5 Grocery
6 Boulangerie Ahadoberry
11 Unimarché Grocery
24 Chez Dédé
29 Café de la Paix
31 Food Shops

OTHER
1 Cycles Garazi
2 Caisse d'Épargne
4 Train Station
7 Post Office
8 Technicien du Sport
9 Jaï Alaï
10 Crédit Agricole
13 Trinquet
14 Bus Stop
15 Porte de St-Jacques
16 Prison des Évêques
18 Porte de France
19 Maison de la Presse
23 Tourist Office
24 Chez Steunou
25 Hôtel de Ville
30 Covered Market
32 Porte de Navarre
33 Porte de Notre-Dame
34 Église Notre-Dame
   du Bout du Pont
35 Porte de l'Échauguette
36 Citadelle
38 Porte d'Espagne
39 Fronton Municipal
40 Pont Romain

0   50   100 m

At least five banks have currency exchanges and/or ATMs, including Crédit Agricole, just up ave Renaud from place du Trinquet, and Caisse d'Épargne, near Camping d'Arradoy, both open weekdays to 5 pm. The post office, just off the road from the station, is open to 5 pm on weekdays and noon on Saturday.

Old Town

The town's ancient heart is at the bottom of rue de la Citadelle by the river. The church leaning heavily against the restored **porte de Notre Dame** gate-tower is the single-galleried **Église Notre Dame du Bout du Pont** – Our Lady at the End of the Bridge – with foundations as old as the town but thoroughly rebuilt in the 17th century. That's John the Baptist, the town's original patron saint, in the niche on the inner side of the belfry.

From the **Vieux Pont** (Old Bridge) check out the excruciatingly photogenic white-washed houses with balconies leaning out above the water. Fishing is forbidden where the crystal-clear Nive passes through town, and the fat trout here seem to know it. On the other side is the commercial artery of **Rue d'Espagne**.

Now climb **rue de la Citadelle**, a gauntlet of bright, well-tended 16th- to 18th-century houses trimmed in red or brown, on foundations of pink granite. The lintels of many are carved with the date of construction (the oldest is 1510).

A common motif is the scallop shell, symbol of the pilgrims of Compostela, perhaps an ancient sign of welcome. Pilgrims would enter the town through the **porte de St-Jacques** at the top, and some days later leave for Spain – refreshed and probably a little poorer – through the **porte d'Espagne** on the other side of the river.

La Citadelle

From the top of rue de la Citadelle a rough cobblestone path climbs up to the massive Citadelle, offering fine views of the town, the Nive River and the surrounding hills. Often attributed to Vauban, it was actually completed in 1628, before the great man

was even born, although his military engineers beefed it up around 1680. Under renovation for years, it presently serves as a high school.

A more interesting route up is from the riverside just behind the church, through the Gothic **porte de l'Échauguette** (Watchtower Gate) and up a narrow staircase clinging to moss-covered ramparts that predate the Citadelle.

Prison des Évêques

The so-called Bishops' Prison, a vaulted cellar at 41 rue de la Citadelle, is a bit of Gothic hyperbole. It certainly feels like a dungeon, with damp walls and one tiny, barred window, and dates from the 13th century when St-Jean Pied de Port was a bishopric of the Avignon papacy. But the building above it dates from the 16th century, by which time the bishops were gone. It did serve as town jail from 1795, and a military brig from the 19th century. In WWII the Germans used it to intern people caught trying to flee to Spain and North Africa.

But it's a museum (☎ 05 59 37 03 57) just the same, open from 10 am to 12.30 pm and 2 to 6 pm daily from Easter to mid-November. Admission costs 10FF (children aged under 12 years 5FF).

Pont Romain

This pretty stone bridge on the pastoral outskirts of the town, 500m upriver from the Vieux Pont, is a perfect picnic spot, though it's probably not Roman (what you see dates from the 17th century).

Walking & Cycling

This is a fine place from which to walk or cycle into the Pyrenean foothills, where the loudest sounds you'll hear are cowbells and the wind. The GR10 and the GR65 pass right through town.

The tourist office sells a 10FF folder of rudimentary maps for five backroad loops of 2km to 16km from St-Jean Pied de Port; free photocopies of *petites randonnées* around the villages of Ispoure and Estérençuby; and a brochure on six hikes through the beeches of the **Forêt d'Iraty**, 25km south-east on the Spanish border. The Maison de la Presse at 23 place Charles de Gaulle, open to 7.30 pm daily (to 12.30 pm on Sunday) is a good source of walking maps.

You can bring bicycles free of charge on certain trains (such as the 9.10 am train from Bayonne) and then cycle back down, or you can hire a bike locally (see Getting Around later in this section).

Guided Tours
The tourist office conducts tours of the old town for individuals at 10 am on Monday, Thursday and Saturday in July and August, for 30FF (students 15FF, kids aged under 12 free).

Special Events
Three summer **handicraft and food fairs** take place in the covered market: 15–22 July, 5–19 August and 16 September. The fronton municipal hosts a festival of **force Basque** – traditional games of brute strength – on the third Sunday in July, and a competition on the second Sunday in August.

In July and August, **Basque music and dancing** feature at the jaï alaï at 9.30 pm on Thursday.

Places to Stay
Camping Right within the old walls is shady, riverside *Camp Municipal Plaza Berri* (☎ 05 59 37 11 19, ave du Fronton), open from May to September and charging 15/8/8FF per adult/tent/car.

Camping de l'Arradoy (☎ 05 59 37 11 75, 4 chemin de Zalikarte), near the train station, is open from April to September and costs about 10FF per adult and 8FF per site.

In the adjacent village of Uhart-Cize, plain *Camping Bidegainia* (☎ 05 59 37 03 75) is open from April to September for 7/7/5FF per adult/tent/car. About 2km down the D918 at Ascarat are *Camping La Truite* (☎ 05 59 37 06 55), open mid-June to October at 30FF forfait or 7/8/6FF, and *Camping Narbaïtz* (☎ 05 59 37 10 13), open mid-March to September for 72FF forfait.

Gîtes d'Étape & Chambres d'Hôtes
There's a heavy emphasis here on hostel and B&B accommodation, for both walkers and pilgrims, and the tourist office maintains a long list of non-hotel accommodation. Two good gîtes d'étape for walkers, open from at least May to October for about 50FF per bed (breakfast extra) are *Les Donats* (☎ 05 59 37 15 64, 40 rue de la Citadelle) and *Mme Etchegoin* (☎ 05 59 37 12 08, 9 route d'Uhart).

Hotels St-Jean has lots of hotels, whose high rates increase in July and August. The two cheapest, where doubles with shower start at about 200FF, are *Hôtel des Remparts* (☎ 05 59 37 13 79, fax 05 59 37 33 44, 16 place Floquet)*, closed on Saturday and Sunday nights from October to March; and *Hôtel Itzalpea* (☎ 05 59 37 03 66, fax 05 59 37 33 18, 5 place du Trinquet).

The only hotel within the old walls is the Logis de France *Hôtel Ramuntcho* (☎ 05 59 37 03 91, fax 05 59 37 35 17, 1 rue de France)*, where doubles with shower and toilet start at 265FF (closed from mid-November to December). Doubles at the venerable *Hôtel Central* (☎ 05 59 37 00 22, fax 05 59 37 27 79, 1 place Charles de Gaulle) start at 390FF, and the back rooms look out on the Nive (closed Christmas to mid-February).

Top of the line is *Hôtel des Pyrénées* (☎ 05 59 37 01 01, fax 05 59 37 18 97, 19 place Charles de Gaulle)*, with a much acclaimed restaurant (see Places to Eat) and doubles from 700FF.

Places to Eat
Restaurants *Chez Dédé* (☎ 05 59 37 16 40, 3 rue de France)*, just inside the porte de France, serves lots of simple, cheap, tasty *menus*, from 50FF up (closed on Wednesday evening and Thursday, and for 10 days during June). Budgeteers will also like *Café de la Paix* (☎ 05 59 37 00 99, 4 place Floquet)*, with salads and pizzas from 35FF, paella for 60FF and *menus* from 62FF (closed the last two weeks in June).

The restaurant in *Hôtel Itzalpea* (see Places to Stay) serves family-style regional

THE FRENCH BASQUE COUNTRY

cuisine, with *menus* from 60FF (closed on Saturday outside July and August). The one at *Hôtel Ramuntcho* serves first-rate *menus* from 78FF (closed Wednesday outside July and August).

Top of the line again is the restaurant at *Hôtel des Pyrénées*, with two Michelin stars, where *menus* of classical French and Basque cuisine start at 240FF (open daily except Tuesday from November to June and except Monday evening from November to March; closed mid-November to mid-December and most of January).

Self-Catering St-Jean Pied de Port's *weekly market* is held on Monday at place Charles de Gaulle. A small *grocery (35 ave Renaud)* near the station is open until at least 7.30 pm (to 12.30 pm on Sunday) and *Boulangerie Ahadoberry (2 rue de la Poste)* until 8 pm (to 1 pm on Sunday). A *Unimarché grocery* on place du Trinquet is open until 7.30 pm (to 12.30 pm at the weekend). Food shops on rue d'Espagne include a *grocery* at No 12 and a *boulangerie* at No 38.

Spectator Sports

Weekly **pelote Basque** (see under Basque Games in The French Basque Country section earlier in this chapter) matches in July and August include main nue at the Trinquet at 5 pm on Monday; joko garbi at the fronton municipal at 9.30 pm on Wednesday; grand chistera at the fronton municipal at 5 pm on Friday; and cesta punta at the jaï alaï at 9 pm on Saturday. Tickets cost about 50FF.

A two-hour **course landaise** (see the boxed text under Spectator Sports in the Facts for the Visitor chapter) takes place at the jaï alaï at 9 pm on Monday from mid-July to early September.

Getting There & Away

Bus Buses to/from Bayonne (around 50FF, 1½ hours, three or four daily except on Sunday) run by Transports Basques (☎ 05 59 65 73 11 in St-Palais) stop opposite the trinquet on place du Trinquet.

Train This is the best way to get here, a lovely trip from Bayonne, up the Nive Val-

ley to the end of the line (46FF, one hour), with at least two daily trains and another Monday to Saturday in July and August. The tiny station (☎ 05 59 37 02 00) is open from 6.20 am to 7.40 pm (to 9.40 pm on Friday, Saturday and Sunday). For a day trip, take the 9.10 am from Bayonne; the last train back leaves St-Jean Pied de Port at 4.33 pm (times vary from season to season).

Getting Around

VTTs can be hired from Cycles Garazi (☎ 05 59 37 21 79), at 1 place St-Laurent, for 50/80FF per half/full day. It's open from mid-May to September, daily from 9 am to noon and 2 to 7 pm. Another place to find VTTs is Technicien du Sport (☎ 05 59 37 15 98), 18 ave du Jaï Alaï. A souvenir shop called Chez Steunou (☎ 05 59 37 25 45), at 12 place Charles de Gaulle by the tourist office, rents bikes for about 40/60FF.

Béarn

The history and culture of the ancient province of Béarn are as un-French as those of the French Basque country, but Béarnais – being landlocked, generally modest and not prone to terrorism – are less well known in the wider world. They dislike it when you confuse Béarn with the French Basque country, or lump them together. The language of their ancestors is a cousin of Occitan, not of Basque. Béarn had Catholicism imposed upon it, while Basques embraced it.

But it's no accident that Béarn is lumped in the same département with the French Basque country. Had the viscounts of Béarn not got their act together early on, this might well be Basque Country too. Béarnais, like Basques, have historical links south of the border, and their traditions have been shaped by the mountains. They certainly have a distrust of outside authority equal to the Basques. And at their festivals the men wear berets as comfortably as the Basques do (indeed most 'Basque' berets are made in the Béarn!).

Béarn's biggest attraction for tourists is

the Basses-Pyrénées and the activities available in them; river sports, cycling, trekking, horse riding, fishing and skiing.

Orientation

Béarn has three traditional parts: the Marches de Béarn, hilly and dotted with castles, like the Gers; Béarn des Gaves, the lowlands along its main rivers, the Gave de Pau and Gave d'Oloron (*gave* is a Béarnaise word for river); and the mountainous Haut-Béarn.

History

Béarn first appears in history in 820, with the conquest of the region by Charlemagne and the founding of a viscountcy, with its capital at Lescar. Before long the title had become hereditary. Many of its holders seem to have been named Gaston, making it hard to keep track of them.

When Lescar was sacked by the Moors in 841 the capital was moved to Morlaás. The first important Gaston was Gaston IV, who in the early 11th century signed a charter called the *For de Morlaás*, setting forth the limitations of the law and setting the tone for centuries of Béarnais distrust of central authority. Gaston VII de Moncade moved the capital to Orthez in the late 13th century.

In 1290 the House of Foix (in the Ariège) absorbed the viscountcy through marriage. The best known Gaston was Gaston the Hunter (1331–91), known as Gaston Fébus, 'The Golden', for his long blonde locks. This was the Gaston who moved the capital to Pau.

By the 16th century, judicious marriages had given a minor Gascon family named d'Albret control of the lands and titles of Foix, Basse-Navarre and Béarn. Henri d'Albret and Marguerite d'Angoulême were the parents of Jeanne d'Albret, who as the staunchly Calvinist queen of Navarre was to have a major hand in prolonging France's Wars of Religion.

Jeanne's son was Henri of Navarre, the future Henri IV of France, who even on the throne would regard Béarn as a separate kingdom. But his son, Louis XIII, finally seized it in the name of France in 1620 and filled it with Catholic settlers and monasteries.

After the 1789 Revolution, the British under the future Duke of Wellington handed Napoleon a major defeat near Orthez in 1814. The English were welcomed throughout Béarn, perhaps out of hope for the return of the monarchy.

PAU

postcode 64000 • pop 90,000
• elevation 207m

Pau (say 'Po'), capital of Béarn and préfecture of the Pyrénées-Atlantiques département, is famed for its mild climate, flower-filled public parks and magnificent views of the Pyrénées. In the 19th century it was a favourite wintering spot for wealthy English and Americans, and is proud of its Anglophone heritage.

The city owes its present prosperity to a high-tech industrial base, the huge natural gas field at Lacq, 20km to the north-west, and an abundance of Spanish tourists and shoppers. If French highway planners have their way (see Vallée d'Aspe later in this chapter), it looks set to grow into an important gateway city from Spain.

Though it has some of the roughness of a city twice its size, Pau is still an agreeable place to visit, well supplied with cheap hotels, and an obvious base for forays into the Basses-Pyrénées.

History

For centuries a feature of life here has been transhumance: seasonal migration between summer pastures in the Pyrénées and lowlands north of the Pau River (Gave de Pau). Pau began as a stockade at an easy ford of the river. This also lay on an important east-west trade route, and by the 11th century the town was important enough that the comte de (count of) Foix built a castle overlooking the river.

Strategic marriages gradually transformed the family into an important dynasty in southern France, giving Pau considerable stature. In the 14th century Gaston Fébus enlarged the castle and fortified the town

Anglophone Pau

The first British to 'discover' Pau were Wellington's soldiers, fresh from thrashing Napoleon at Orthez in 1814. Many soon returned as tourists and some retired here. After falling ill with typhus, a Scots physician named Alexander Taylor came here, kicked it in three weeks and in 1842 wrote enthusiastically of Pau's curative climate.

Upper-class Britons flooded in and by the 1850s were numerous enough to dominate local society. They built the blvd des Pyrénées promenade and scores of grand villas. They gave Pau a taste for fine gardens and for sports – steeplechase, polo, fox hunting, angling, tennis – and in 1856 founded the continent's first golf club. They gave France its first gas-lamps and its first sewer system.

Americans arrived soon afterwards and by the 1860s formed a substantial community. At its peak the foreign population was perhaps 10,000.

When Queen Victoria's attention turned to Biarritz and the seaside, off went the English, leaving Anglophone Pau to the Scots, Welsh and especially the Americans. Two Americans whose careers took off here were the Wright brothers, attracted by Pau's almost windless climate. In 1908 they founded the world's first flying school and an aeroplane factory here – perhaps sowing the seeds for the region's prominence in aeronautics.

The entire expatriate community fled in the Great Depression. But to this day a segment of upper-class Béarnaise society still hunts foxes and plays golf at exclusive clubs, and Pau has a high percentage of English speakers. The Pau Golf Club (at Billère, about 3.5km to the west of the city centre) is straight out of upper-class England, right down to the cravats and cashmere.

and eventually made it the capital of Béarn. By 1484 it presided over the entire kingdom of Navarre – and then in 1512 lost everything south of the Pyrénées to Ferdinand of Aragon. Pau was the birthplace in 1553 of Henri of Navarre, the future Henri IV of France.

After the Revolution of 1789, the English handed Napoleon a major defeat near Orthez in 1814, and discovered the charms of Pau (see the boxed text 'Anglophone Pau'). Over the next 75 years the town grew into an international winter resort. The Great Depression put an end to the fun and by WWII Pau was lost in obscurity.

A surge in wartime and postwar industrial development gave Pau a new lease of life, and its population quadrupled in 20 years. Its greatest expansion dates from the 1960s, since when the population has again quadrupled. But thanks to a legacy of gardens – monastic and English – it boasts an extraordinarily high per capita endowment of green space.

Orientation

Pau's ancient heart is the *Vieille Ville* (old town) beside Gaston Fébus' chateau. Its axis is the thoroughfare of rue Maréchal Joffre, rue Maréchal Foch and cours Bosquet. The 'English' centre is the promenade along blvd des Pyrénées, with its Cinemascope views of the mountains. Long-distance and local buses converge on place Clémenceau, the train station is just below the promenade by the river, and the airport is 10km north-west of the centre.

Information

Tourist Offices The tourist office (☎ 05 59 27 27 08, fax 05 59 27 03 21) on place Royale is open from 9 am to 12.30 pm and 1.30 to 6 pm Monday to Saturday (to 5.30 pm on Saturday) and 9 am to 6 pm daily in July and August. Good free resources here are the *Béarn Guide des Loisirs*, a detailed summary of almost everything there is to do in the area, and *Pau – Ville Authentique*, with practical information on the city.

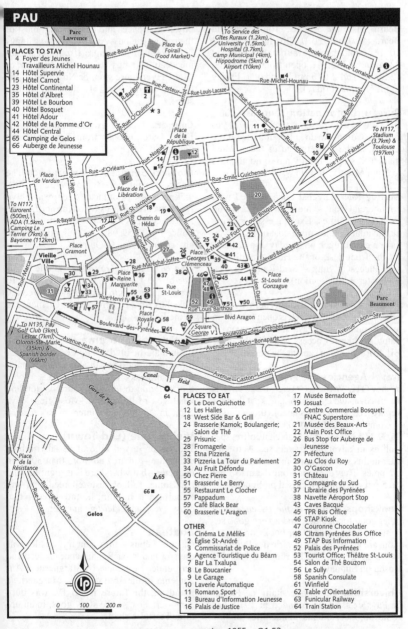

PAU

PLACES TO STAY
- 4 Foyer des Jeunes Travailleurs Michel Hounau
- 14 Hôtel Supervie
- 15 Hôtel Carnot
- 23 Hôtel Continental
- 35 Hôtel d'Albret
- 39 Hôtel Le Bourbon
- 40 Hôtel Bosquet
- 41 Hôtel Adour
- 42 Hôtel de la Pomme d'Or
- 44 Hôtel Central
- 65 Camping de Gelos
- 66 Auberge de Jeunesse

PLACES TO EAT
- 6 Le Don Quichotte
- 12 Les Halles
- 18 West Side Bar & Grill
- 24 Brasserie Kamok; Boulangerie; Salon de Thé
- 25 Prisunic
- 28 Fromagerie
- 32 Etna Pizzeria
- 33 Pizzeria La Tour du Parlement
- 34 Au Fruit Défondu
- 50 Chez Pierre
- 51 Brasserie Le Berry
- 55 Restaurant Le Clocher
- 57 Pappadum
- 59 Café Black Bear
- 60 Brasserie L'Aragon

OTHER
- 1 Cinéma Le Méliès
- 2 Église St-André
- 3 Commissariat de Police
- 5 Agence Touristique du Béarn
- 7 Bar La Txalupa
- 8 Le Boucanier
- 9 Le Garage
- 10 Laverie Automatique
- 11 Romano Sport
- 13 Bureau d'Information Jeunesse
- 16 Palais de Justice
- 17 Musée Bernadotte
- 19 Josuat
- 20 Centre Commercial Bosquet; FNAC Superstore
- 21 Musée des Beaux-Arts
- 22 Main Post Office
- 26 Bus Stop for Auberge de Jeunesse
- 27 Préfecture
- 29 Au Clos du Roy
- 30 O'Gascon
- 31 Château
- 36 Compagnie du Sud
- 37 Librairie des Pyrénées
- 38 Navette Aéroport Stop
- 43 Caves Bacqué
- 45 TPR Bus Office
- 46 STAP Kiosk
- 47 Couronne Chocolatier
- 48 Citram Pyrénées Bus Office
- 49 STAP Bus Information
- 52 Palais des Pyrénées
- 53 Tourist Office; Théâtre St-Louis
- 54 Salon de Thé Bouzom
- 56 Le Sully
- 58 Spanish Consulate
- 61 Winfield
- 62 Table d'Orientation
- 63 Funicular Railway
- 64 Train Station

0 100 200 m

euro currency converter 10FF = €1.52

For further general information about the Béarn, visit the Agence Touristique du Béarn (☎ 05 59 30 01 30, fax 05 59 84 10 13, email bearn@tourisme64.com) at 22ter rue de Monaix, open from 8.30 am to 12.30 pm and 2 to 6 pm Monday to Friday (until 5 pm on Friday).

Bureau d'Information Jeunesse Pau's BIJ (☎ 05 59 27 89 49, fax 05 59 83 78 96) is in the Complexe de la République on rue Carnot, at the western end of the covered market. It's open from 9 am to noon and 2 to 5 pm Monday to Friday.

Money Rue Maréchal Foch is lined with commercial banks, most have ATMs and exchange facilities. Exchange services are also available at the main post office. If you have a cash crunch on Sunday or a holiday, try the front desk of the Hôtel Continental (see Places to Stay – Mid-Range & Top End, later in this section).

Post & Communications The main post office, at 21 cours Bosquet, is open from 8 am to 6.30 pm on weekdays and until noon on Saturday. Internet access is available at the BIJ (20FF per hour) and at the post office.

Travel Agencies The French youth-travel agency OTU Voyages (☎ 05 59 02 26 98) has an office on ave Doyen Poplawski at the university (see Universities later in this section).

Compagnie du Sud (☎ 05 59 27 04 24, fax 05 59 27 63 25), 27 rue Maréchal Joffre, specialises in adventure travel; see Activities later in this section for more about their programmes. They are open from 10 am to 7 pm (to 5 pm on Saturday, closed on Sunday).

Bookshops *Walking in the Pyrénées* and other good topoguides, and a very good selection of maps and other books on the region, are available at Librairie des Pyrénées (☎ 05 59 27 78 75), 14 rue St-Louis. It's closed on Sunday.

Universities The Universitaire de Pau et de Pays de l'Adour, founded in 1970, has some 50,000 students in faculties of law and economic science, social sciences, physical sciences and engineering, most of them at a spacious, American-style campus 2km north of the centre (from place Clémenceau, take bus No 4 to the Facultés or Cité Universitaire stop, or No 2 or 6 to the Commune de Paris, Leclerc or Monge stop).

Laundry Laverie Automatique, 66 rue Émile Garet, is open from 7 am to 10 pm daily.

Medical Services & Emergency The Centre Hospitalier (☎ 05 59 92 48 48), 4.5km north-east of the city centre at 4 blvd Hauterive, is the last stop on the northbound Nos 3 and 6 bus lines. The Commissariat de Police (☎ 05 59 98 22 22) is north of the city centre on rue O'Quinn.

Gay & Lesbian Travellers The local office of Act Up (☎ 05 59 02 35 07) is at 10 rue d'Eauze, 3.5km north-east of the centre (take bus No 3 or 5 from place Clémenceau to the Eauze stop.

Pyrénées Panorama

From majestic blvd des Pyrénées on a clear day you can see a breathtaking panorama of Pyrenean peaks. Opposite No 20 is a *table d'orientation* to tell you your position and what you're looking at. Most clear days come in autumn and winter.

Vieille Ville (Old Town)

Pau has preserved little of its labyrinthine old centre – an area no more than 300m in diameter – but what there is is dignified and handsome, full of restored medieval and Renaissance buildings, and streets that cross over and under one another.

Chateau

Gaston Fébus' 14th-century castle was transformed into a Renaissance chateau and surrounded by gardens by Marguerite d'Angoulême in the 16th century. Marguerite's grandson, the future Henri IV, was born here – cradled, so the story goes, in an upturned tortoise shell.

Neglected in the 18th century and used as a barracks after the Revolution, the chateau was a mess by 1838, when King Louis-Philippe ordered a complete interior renovation, completed by Napoleon III. The result is a chilly, unconvincing imitation of medieval and Renaissance architecture.

Most of the furniture, including an oak dining table big enough to seat 100, dates from this time. The chateau's pride and joy is one of Europe's finest collections of 16th- to 18th-century **Gobelins tapestries**. In the room where Henry IV was born is what's claimed to be his tortoise-shell **cradle**.

Musée Béarnais (☎ 05 59 27 07 36) on the third floor features, among other things, traditional Béarnaise architecture, handicrafts, furnishings and clothing, and an exhibit on how berets are made. The museum is open from 9.30 am to noon and 2 to 5.30 pm daily. Admission to the museum costs 10FF (accompanied children aged under 18 free).

On the river side of the chateau are a 33m-high brick tower erected by Gaston Fébus and the medieval, brick-and-stone Tour de la Monnaie.

The chateau (☎ 05 59 82 38 00) is open from 9.30 to 11.45 am and 2 to 5.15 pm daily. It's owned by the Ministry of Culture & Communication, whose main aim is to preserve it, not to show it off. The 27FF entrance fee (those aged 18 to 26 years 18FF, under-18s free) includes an obligatory, often tedious, one- to two-hour guided tour in rapid-fire French or Spanish (though a printed narrative in English is available).

Musée Bernadotte

The Bernadotte Museum (☎ 05 59 27 48 42), 8 rue Tran, tells the curious story of how a French general, born in this building, became king of Sweden and Norway (see the boxed text 'France's Swedish King'). The museum is open from 10 am to noon and 2 to 6 pm Tuesday to Sunday. Admission costs 10FF (children and students 5FF).

Musée des Beaux-Arts

Pau's Fine Arts Museum is one of the south-west's better provincial museums.

France's Swedish King

Jean-Baptiste Bernadotte, born in Pau in 1763, enlisted in the French army at the age of 17 and went on to a distinguished career as a general and diplomat, serving both the Revolutionary government and Napoleon.

Sweden at the time was in the throes of a political and dynastic crisis, and the Swedish Riksdag concluded that the only way out was to install a foreigner on the throne. Full of respect for French military prowess, they turned to Bernadotte, electing him crown prince in 1810.

Against Napoleon's expectations, Bernadotte did not follow a pro-French foreign policy. Indeed Swedish troops under his command at the 1813 Battle of Leipzig helped the allied army deal Napoleon his first major defeat. Bernadotte's 1814 defeat of Denmark gave him control of Norway. In 1818 he became King Charles XIV John of Sweden and Norway, dying in office in 1844. The present king of Sweden is the seventh ruler in the Bernadotte dynasty.

Among works on display are 17th- to 20th-century European paintings, including some by Rubens, El Greco and Degas. The museum (☎ 05 59 27 33 02), entered opposite 15 rue Mathieu Lalanne, is open from 10 am to noon and from 2 to 6 pm (closed on Tuesday). Admission costs 10FF (children and students 5FF).

Activities

Compagnie du Sud (see Travel Agencies earlier in this section earlier in this section) offers guided, small-group treks with English-speaking guides in the French and Spanish Pyrénées, from May to October (June to September at higher elevations). Accommodation is in mountain huts. The company can also arrange food, lodging or other support for unaccompanied hikes and biking trips, for 1500FF to 2200FF per person for four to seven days.

BÉARN

Romano Sport (☎ 05 59 98 48 56), 1 rue Jean Réveil, rents walking, skiing, caving and mountaineering gear. It's open from 9 am to noon and 3 to 7 pm Monday to Saturday (daily from December to March).

Special Events

The **Festival de Pau** is a three-week extravaganza of dance, music and theatre, held from mid-June to early July at the Théâtre St-Louis and the Cour du Château. The **Festival de Dance** (modern dance) runs from mid-March to mid-April and the **Festival de Flamenco** for 15 days in early April. Pentecost weekend sees the **Formula 3000 Grand Prix** in the city's streets.

Places to Stay

Pau's hotels offer some of the best value for money in France. Peak season is April to October – except, curiously, July and August – but you can always find a room if you arrive in the morning.

Places to Stay – Budget

Camping At the Base de Plein Air recreational area in the suburb of Gelos, *Camping de Gelos* (☎ 05 59 06 57 37, fax 05 59 06 38 39) is open from mid-May to September and costs 15/23/5FF per adult/tent/car. Take bus No 1 from place Clémenceau to the Mairie de Gelos stop.

The city-run *Camp Municipal de la Plaine des Sports et des Loisirs* (☎ 05 59 02 30 49), 4km north of the city centre, charges 17/33FF per adult/tent and is open from April to October. Take bus No 4 to the end of the line.

The three-star, year-round *Camping Le Terrier* (☎ 05 59 81 01 82, fax 05 59 81 26 83, ave du Vert Galant), 7km away in Lescar, costs 23FF per adult plus 32FF per site. Take bus No 8 to the Laou stop and walk 1.5km to the Pau River.

Hostels At the year-round *Auberge de Jeunesse* (☎ 05 59 06 69 35) at the Base de Plein Air in Gelos (see Camping), beds cost 53FF and sheets rented for 18FF. Lunch is served only on weekdays, but there's a self-serve restaurant and the kitchen is available

(bring your own utensils). Doors close from midnight to 6 am and the maximum stay is five nights. Reception is open after 5 pm.

The *Foyer des Jeunes Travailleurs Michel Hounau* (☎ 05 59 72 61 00, 30 rue Michel Hounau) usually has a few beds for travellers, and reception is staffed 24 hours. Singles with washbasin cost 52FF for HI card-holders; sheets cost 18FF. Kitchen facilities are available and there's a cafeteria.

In summer, one *university dormitory* in the complex at the north-west corner of the campus (the modern-looking one at the east end of the row) is open to non-French students with student ID.

Rural Accommodation The tourist office keeps a list of nearby *chambres d'hôte* (B&Bs), *gîtes d'étape* and *campings à la ferme* (camping on a farm). For more information on rural accommodation and help with reservations, contact Service des Gîtes Ruraux (☎ 05 59 80 19 13, fax 05 59 30 60 65) in the Maison de l'Agriculture, 124 blvd Tourasse, 1.2km north of the centre. It's open from 9 am to 12.30 pm and 2 to 5 pm on weekdays.

Hotels The family-run *Hôtel d'Albret* (☎ 05 59 27 81 58, 11 rue Jeanne d'Albret) offers clean doubles for 90FF (120FF with shower, 145FF with shower and toilet). At *Hôtel de la Pomme d'Or* (☎ 05 59 27 78 48, fax 05 59 98 09 71, 11 rue Maréchal Foch), twins/doubles cost 100/120FF (125/150FF with shower, 140/160FF with shower and toilet. Credit cards are not accepted.

Large rooms with washbasin and bidet at the friendly *Hôtel Carnot* (☎ 05 59 27 88 70, 13 rue Carnot) are good value at 108FF. *Hôtel Supervie* (☎ 05 59 27 83 32, 1 rue Nogué) has simple doubles for 130FF (165FF with shower); it's closed on Sunday night and for the first two weeks of August.

Places to Stay – Mid-Range & Top End

Two clean, characterless places offering doubles with shower for about 200FF (260/270FF with toilet and shower/bath) face one another across rue Valéry Meunier: *Hôtel*

Adour (☎ 05 59 27 47 41) at No 10 and *Hôtel Bosquet* (☎ 05 59 27 76 38) at No 11.

A good bet in this range is *Hôtel Central* (☎ 05 59 27 72 75, fax 05 59 27 33 28, 15 rue Léon Daran), where big doubles with soundproofed windows cost 235FF (260FF with toilet and shower, 300FF and up with twin beds). The central *Hôtel Le Bourbon* (☎ 05 59 27 53 12, fax 05 59 82 90 99, 12 place Clémenceau) offers very comfortable doubles/triples with shower and toilet from 310/360FF, some with air-conditioning.

Pau's landmark hotel is the three-star *Hôtel Continental* (☎ 05 59 27 69 31, fax 05 59 27 99 84, 2 rue Maréchal Foch). Singles/doubles cost 230/270FF with toilet or shower, or 400/500FF with all the trimmings.

Places to Eat

Pau may have lots of cheap accommodation, but not much cheap food.

Brasseries Brasseries are open all afternoon and tend to have a wider choice than restaurants. Top value is *Brasserie Le Berry* (☎ 05 59 27 42 95, 4 rue Gachet), with Béarnaise specialities for under 100FF, lots of fish dishes under 80FF, some half-servings and an immense dessert menu. Go early.

Brasserie Kamok (☎ 05 59 27 59 43, 20 rue Maréchal Foch), upstairs from the boulangerie of the same name, is open from 11 am to 8 pm daily except Sunday, with pâtés and pasta dishes for 30FF to 40FF, and quick service.

Blvd des Pyrénées, west from blvd Aragon, is lined with sun-washed bar-cafebrasseries. Popular *Brasserie L'Aragon* (☎ 05 59 27 12 43, blvd des Pyrénées) has friendly service and very good French and international dishes, a 50FF plat du jour and menus from 90FF. *Café Black Bear* (☎ 05 59 27 52 67, blvd Aragon) is a cavernous sports bar/cafe, nothing special except for its 92FF Sunday brunch.

Restaurants – French Spanish influence may account for unnervingly late dinnertimes here: most restaurants are deserted until after 8 pm. *Restaurant Le Clocher*

(☎ 05 59 27 72 83, 8 rue de Foix) offers Béarnaise and Landaise lunch/dinner *menus* from 60/80FF (closed Sunday).

For a change, try cheese, fish or chocolate fondue or grill-it-yourself *pierrades* (80FF to 100FF) at *Restaurant Au Fruit Défondu* (☎ 05 59 27 26 05, 3 rue Sully), open for dinner daily. If you're in the mood to treat yourself, try lobster and saffron *cassoulet* (duck casserole) at *Chez Pierre* (☎ 05 59 27 76 86, 16 rue Louis Barthou), or go for the 185FF *menu*. It's closed on Saturday at lunchtime and on Sunday.

Restaurants – International The *West Side Bar & Grill* (☎ 05 59 82 90 78, 3 rue St-Jacques) has On-The-Road decor and serves an all-American menu from 40FF clam chowder to steaks, fried chicken and ribs from 70FF. The 75FF, three-course *menu* is good value and portions are big. It's closed on Sunday.

Pappadum (☎ 05 59 27 51 67, 9 impasse Honset) offers Indian biryanis from 60FF and lunch *menus* from 50FF. *Pizzeria La Tour du Parlement* (☎ 05 59 27 38 29, 36 rue du Moulin) is open daily, and popular with *paloises* as well as visitors. Pizza and pasta at *Etna Pizzeria* (☎ 05 59 27 77 94, 16 rue du Château) start at 40FF. It's open until midnight daily.

Le Don Quichotte (☎ 05 59 27 63 08, 30 rue Castetnau) serves up tapas from 15FF and Spanish and Basque main dishes from 50FF, until 1 am (closed Saturday and Monday lunchtime and all day on Sunday).

Self-Catering The big covered market, *Les Halles*, on place de la République, is open Monday to Saturday (closed 1 to 3.30 pm except Saturday). On Wednesday and Saturday mornings there's a *food market* on place du Foirail.

Prisunic (22 rue Maréchal Foch), open to 8 pm Monday to Saturday, has a supermarket section. Another supermarket is *Champion*, in the Centre Commercial Bosquet at 14 cours Bosquet. Several *food shops* cluster around place Reine Marguerite in the Vieille Ville, and there's a *fromagerie* at 24 rue Maréchal Joffre.

BÉARN

Entertainment

Pubs & Bars The centre of student nightlife is the laid-back zone known as *le Triangle*, bounded by rue Henri Faisans, rue Émile Garet and rue Castelnau. Several bars offer live music at the weekend. Being student bars, they have a sizeable concentration of English speakers, so striking up a conversation is not hard. Good bets are the Irish-owned *Le Garage* (☎ 05 59 83 75 17, 49 rue Émile Garet), the bodega *Bar La Txalupa* (☎ 05 59 98 06 73, 34 rue Émile Garet) and *Le Boucanier (64 rue Émile Garet)*.

The Vieille Ville is full of upmarket pubs including *O'Gascon* (☎ 05 59 27 64 74, 13 rue du Château)* and popular *Le Sully* (☎ 05 59 82 86 56, 13 rue Henri IV)*. The bar of *West Side Bar & Grill* (see Places to Eat) is open to 2 am daily except Sunday. The *Winfield* (☎ 05 59 27 80 60, 20 blvd des Pyrénées)* calls itself an Australian bar.

Classical Music & Dance The main venue is the Théâtre St-Louis, around the corner from the tourist office on rue St-Louis (tickets can be bought at the box office or the tourist office).

Cinema Pau's only cinema with non-dubbed English films is *Cinéma Le Méliès* (☎ 05 59 27 60 52, 6 rue Bargoin)*. Tickets cost 35FF (students 28FF, children 20FF, and 22FF for everyone after 10 pm). It's closed from mid-July to mid-August.

Spectator Sports

Pau has France's second biggest horse-training centre after Chantilly in Paris, and horse racing and steeplechase are big here. The Hippodrome du Pont Long (☎ 05 59 32 07 93) is 5km north of the city centre on blvd du Cami-Salié; take bus No 3 (direction Perlic) to the Hippodrome stop. The racing season is from late autumn to March.

Rugby union is popular here, and matches are played at a stadium about 4km north-east of the city centre; ask the tourist office about upcoming matches. Tickets are available at the FNAC superstore at the Centre Commercial Bosquet, 14 cours Bosquet.

Shopping

Pau's trendiest shops are along rue des Cordeliers and rue Serviez. Another place for general shopping is the big Centre Commercial Bosquet at 14 cours Bosquet.

Two *caves* (cellars) where you can taste and buy the area's best-known **wine**, Jurançon, are Au Clos du Roy, 50 rue Maréchal Joffre, and Caves Bacqué, 1 place St-Louis de Gonzague.

Pau, like Bayonne, has a serious sweet-tooth. Two of the city's best **chocolatiers** – with closely guarded recipes – are Couronne, in the Palais des Pyrénées facing place Clémenceau, and Josuat, at 23 rue Serviez, but plenty more modest patisseries and *confiseries* (confectioners) have good chocolate too. Treat yourself to sublime *chocolat chaud* (hot chocolate) at Salon de Thé Bouzom, 6 rue Henri IV.

Getting There & Away

Air The Pau-Pyrénées airport (also known as Uzein; ☎ 05 59 33 33 00) is 10km north-west of central Pau. Air France flies directly to Paris, at least four times daily to Orly and twice daily to Charles de Gaulle. The airport is due for major expansion starting in 2000.

Bus TPR, with an information and ticket office (☎ 05 59 27 45 98) and bus stand on rue Gachet, goes to Bayonne (85FF, 2¼ hours) three times daily (once on Sunday, mid-June to August only), via Orthez (36FF) and Salies de Béarn (51FF). TPR also goes to Navarrenx (51FF) once daily except on Sunday.

The main operator into the Vallée d'Ossau is Citram Pyrénées (☎ 05 59 27 22 22), with an office, closed on Saturday afternoon, Sunday and Monday, in the Palais des Pyrénées, across rue Gachet from TPR. Most of its buses go as far as Laruns (46FF, one hour), two to three times daily except Sunday (three to four daily including Sunday in July and August and from mid-December to April).

The main operator into the Vallée d'Aspe is SNCF, with trains and buses to Oloron-Ste-Marie and buses onwards from there; see Train.

Citram also goes to Mont de Marsan (83FF, two hours) at 7pm daily except Sunday.

Train The information office at the train station (☎ 05 59 98 71 26, national ☎ 08 36 35 35 35) is open from 9 am to 6 pm daily. SNCF has four to five trains and three to five buses daily (fewer on Sunday) via Arudy to Oloron-Ste-Marie (36FF, 40 minutes) – with onward bus connections from Arudy into the Vallée d'Ossau and from Oloron-Ste-Marie into the Vallée d'Aspe (see Basses-Pyrénées later in this chapter). Some Vallée d'Aspe buses continue to the big Spanish railhead of Canfranc-Estación, from where there are trains to Saragossa and elsewhere in Spain.

Long-haul destinations served by direct trains from Pau include Bayonne (82FF, 1¼ hours, nine daily), Bordeaux (151FF, 2¼ hours, 11 daily) and Toulouse (143FF, 2¾ hours, eight daily).

Car Eurorent (☎ 05 59 27 44 41) is at 15 rue d'Étigny. ADA (☎ 05 59 72 94 40) is at 3 bis route de Bayonne in Billère, but if you call ahead they'll deliver a car to you in town; they're open from 8 am to noon and 2 to 7 pm Monday to Saturday. Citer (☎ 05 59 33 25 00) is at the airport.

Getting Around
To/From the Airport The Navette Aéroport shuttle bus (☎ 05 59 02 45 45) departs from 5 place Clémenceau (in front of Floriste Interflora) for the airport at 10 am on weekdays and at 2 and 6 pm daily; and leaves the airport at 10.30 am on weekdays and at 2.40, 6.50 and 10.50 pm daily. The fare is 30FF each way (pay on board).

A taxi to the airport costs about 120FF (150FF on Sunday).

Bus The local bus company, STAP (☎ 05 59 27 69 78), has an office in the Palais des Pyrénées on rue Gachet and a kiosk at the south-eastern corner of place Clémenceau (information and tickets available at both), open from 9 am to 12.15 pm and 1.45 to 5.30 pm on weekdays. Bus maps are avail-

able here and from the tourist office. Bus No 7 links the train station with place Clémenceau, though it's easier to take the funicular (see Funicular Railway).

All nine local lines run from about 6 am to 7 or 7.30 pm daily, except on Sunday and holidays, and each stops somewhere on place Clémenceau (see the map at the kiosk). Single tickets, sold on board, cost 6FF. A carnet of four tickets (good for eight rides) costs 32FF and is available from many *tabacs* (tobacconists) and at STAP kiosks. For example those on place Clémenceau and at Centre Commercial Bosquet. Tickets are valid for one hour after they've been time-stamped.

Funicular Railway The train station is linked to blvd des Pyrénées by a free *funiculaire*, a funny little contraption that saves you about four minutes of easy uphill walking. It was built in 1908 by the hotels along blvd des Pyrénées. Cars leave about every five minutes between 7 am and 9 pm Monday to Saturday, and between 1.30 and 9 pm on Sunday. It's handy if you're getting a train with baggage.

Taxi There's a taxi stand (☎ 05 59 27 14 14) on place Clémenceau.

Bicycle Romano Sport (☎ 05 59 98 48 56), 1 rue Jean Réveil, rents bikes. It's open from 9 am to noon and 3 to 7 pm Monday to Saturday (daily from December to March).

AROUND PAU
Lescar
postcode 64230 • pop 6000 • elevation 183m
Lescar is today a somnolent suburb of Pau, reached via a sea of factories and discount furniture warehouses. But in its day this was the heart of Béarn, and its first capital. Its Roman predecessor, Beneharnum, was obliterated by the Vikings but bequeathed its name to Béarn. On a hill adjacent to the ruins a new town grew from the 10th century.

At the top is a quiet ensemble of old buildings, centred around the Romanesque **Cathédrale Notre Dame**, completed in

BÉARN

1140. The exterior is of little interest, having been smashed up during the Wars of Religion. But inside capitals brim with carved foliage, mythical animals and Biblical scenes. The apse is tiled in original mosaics – only uncovered in the 19th century – with curiously secular subjects like boar-hunting (note the archer with a peg-leg).

Behind the altar, a bronze plaque installed in 1984 marks the resting place of many of the princes of Foix-Béarn and kings and queens of Navarre, including Henri II d'Albret and the saintly Marguerite d'Angoulême, and their daughter Jeanne d'Albret, sword of Calvinism and mother of the future Henri IV of France. The church is open from 8.30 am to noon and 2 to 7 pm daily (to 5 pm in winter).

Opposite the north-west entrance, two towers of the 13th and 14th centuries mark the extremities of the bishop's palace, wholly rebuilt in the early 18th century and almost destroyed during the Revolution. Here also is a little archaeological museum. Just south of the cathedral is the 16th-century **Tour du Presbytère**, now occupied by the **tourist office** (☎ 05 59 81 15 98, fax 05 59 81 12 54). Surrounding the whole ensemble are remnants of Lescar's medieval fortifications.

Getting There & Away Lescar is 8km north-west of Pau. From place Clémenceau, STAP's No 9 bus goes there all day (Mariotte stop) and TPR's Biarritz buses call at Lescar three times daily (once on Sunday, mid-June to August only), tickets cost 6FF.

OLORON-STE-MARIE
postcode 64400 • pop 12,000
• elevation 225m

Poor Oloron-Ste-Marie, everybody hurries through, bound for the Pyrénées. But this attractive town at the confluence of the Basses-Pyrénées' two main rivers, the Aspe River (Gave d'Aspe) and Ossau River (Gave d'Ossau), has something to offer. At least give it a few hours while you wait for your bus into the mountains.

Oloron-Ste-Marie's best known export is the beret. In fact most *chapeaux Basques* are made here.

History
Before the mid-19th century this was two separate towns. Oloron was probably founded by the Romans. Its important position led the viscounts of Béarn to fortify it at the end of the 11th century, about the time Ste-Marie was created on the ruins of another Roman settlement.

Orientation
The oldest part of town is the quartier Ste-Croix, on a hill like a ship's prow above the point where the two rivers unite as the Oloron River (Gave d'Oloron). The centre of quartier Notre-Dame, on the Oloron side, is place de la Résistance, where long-distance buses stop. The heart of quartier Ste-Marie is the cathedral of the same name, and 800m north of this is the train station. The train station and bus stop are about 700m apart via ave Sadi Carnot and the two bridges.

Information
The keen tourist office (☎ 05 59 39 98 00, fax 05 59 39 43 97), in the middle of place de la Résistance, is open from 9 am to noon and 2 to 7 pm daily except Sunday (from 9 am to 7 pm except Sunday afternoon in July and August). A Parc National des Pyrénées office (☎ 05 59 39 75 55) is at 14 rue Adoue.

Quartier Ste-Croix
At the heart of the tiny medieval quarter is the 11th- to 12th-century **Église Ste-Croix** – Romanesque but with a great ribbed dome, perhaps an inspiration from Moorish Spain.

Down rue Dalmais, the ancient main street, are several handsome Renaissance houses and the 13th- or 14th-century **Tour de la Grède**. Beside this, in a 17th-century mansion at No 52, is the **Maison du Patrimoine** (☎ 05 59 39 10 63), a very modest museum of the archaeology, ethnography and geology of Oloron-Ste-Marie and Béarn. The collection includes artefacts from the ruins of a Roman villa recently unearthed at Goes, 2km to the north-east. The museum is open from 10 am to noon and 3 to 7 pm, daily except Monday, from July to

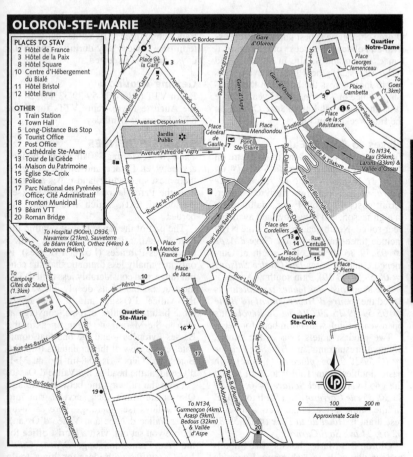

OLORON-STE-MARIE

PLACES TO STAY
2 Hôtel de France
3 Hôtel de la Paix
8 Hôtel Square
10 Centre d'Hébergement
   du Bialé
11 Hôtel Bristol
12 Hôtel Brun

OTHER
1 Train Station
4 Town Hall
5 Long-Distance Bus Stop
6 Tourist Office
7 Post Office
9 Cathédrale Ste-Marie
14 Tour de la Grède
14 Maison du Patrimoine
15 Église Ste-Croix
16 Police
17 Parc National des Pyrénées
   Office; Cité Administratif
18 Fronton Municipal
19 Béarn VTT
20 Roman Bridge

September. Admission costs 10FF (kids free).

The nearby promenade offers fine views down to quartier Ste-Marie and up the Vallée d'Aspe into the mountains.

Quartier Ste-Marie

Quartier Ste-Marie feels less ancient, though not by much. The town's centrepiece, **Cathédrale Ste-Marie**, is mainly Gothic (14th century), but it too has a Romanesque pedigree, evident at the western end. The best part is the delightful 12th-century **portal** under the belfry porch – a

rival for the portal in Abbaye St-Pierre, Moissac (see the Moissac section in the Toulouse, Tarn-et-Garonne & Tarn chapter) for sheer exuberant imagination. Beneath St John's vision of the Apocalypse are visions of a life of happy industry down on earth (hunting, fishing, cheese-making, goose-plucking); a man-eating monster to remind us of the Day of Judgement; a mounted Emperor Constantine (or perhaps Gaston IV of Béarn, who founded the church when he returned triumphant from the First Crusade); and Saracens or Moors in chains.

euro currency converter 10FF = €1.52

Special Events

Oloron-Ste-Marie is best known for its **Festival du Folklore**, 1½ weeks of international dance, music and theatre in late July and early August. It's held here in even years and in Jaca, across the border in the Spanish province of Aragón, in odd years. Since 1995 the town has hosted **Jazz Oloron** on the first weekend in July.

Places to Stay & Eat

Two kilometres west of the town centre on the D919, *Camping Gîtes du Stade* (☎ 05 59 39 11 26, fax 05 59 36 12 01, chemin de Lagravette), is open from April to October; forfait costs 45/57/60FF per adult/tent/car in high season; and bungalows are available year-round. Nearby camp sites on the N134 include three-star *Le Val du Gave d'Aspe* (☎ 05 59 36 05 07), 4km south at Gurmençon, and two-star *Les Quatre Saisons* (☎ 05 59 34 43 10), 9km south at Asasp.

The local *foyer des jeunes travailleurs* is called the *Centre d'Hébergement du Bialé* (☎ 05 59 39 15 29, 10 rue de Révol). It's open year-round, with dorm beds for 52FF.

Two modest hotels near in the centre, both with restaurants, are *Hôtel de France* (☎ 05 59 39 01 63, place de la Gare) with basic doubles from 130FF to 200FF, and the good-value *Hôtel Square* (☎ 05 59 39 13 30, 55 rue Carrérot), at 160FF to 220FF. In the same price range but without a restaurant is *Hôtel de la Paix* (☎ 05 59 39 02 63, 24 ave Sadi Carnot).

Oloron-Ste-Marie boasts two hotel-restaurants with two-chimney Logis de France ratings: the *Bristol* (☎ 05 59 39 43 78, fax 05 59 39 08 19, rue Carrérot) with doubles from 210FF and *menus* from 65FF, and the *Brun* (☎ 05 59 39 64 90, fax 05 59 39 12 28, 5 place de Jaca), where rooms cost 260FF and *menus* 60FF and 85FF.

Getting There & Away

SNCF (☎ 05 59 39 00 61) has four to five trains and three to five buses daily (fewer on Sunday) from Pau (36FF, 40 minutes), plus daily onward connections into the Vallée d'Aspe (see the following Basses-Pyrénées section). Citram Pyrénées buses from Pau (37FF, 50 minutes) come to the train station three to five times daily during term time (twice daily during school holidays), Sundays excepted.

Getting Around

Béarn VTT (☎/fax 05 59 39 33 43), 24 bis rue Auguste Peyre, rents VTTs for about 65/90FF per half/full day.

BASSES-PYRÉNÉES

The Pyrénées form a 430km natural boundary between France and Spain. Some of their most spectacular landscapes are in or near the Parc National des Pyrénées (see the boxed text), which runs along the border.

The part of the range that lies within the Pyrénées-Atlantiques département, called the Basses-Pyrénées (Lower Pyrénées), is only marginally less dramatic than the central range, and considerably less tamed. The most accessible of its deeply cut valleys, the Vallée d'Ossau, and the decidedly more beautiful Vallée d'Aspe, converge at Oloron-Ste-Marie. The highest peak in the Basses-Pyrénées – and the one that dominates every view of the mountains from the Béarn and Gers – is 2884m Pic du Midi d'Ossau, at the head of the Vallée d'Ossau.

From the railway line between Pau and Oloron-Ste-Marie, bus services run into both valleys (see Getting There & Away under Vallée d'Aspe and Vallée d'Ossau). Before you set out, visit a tourist office for the free French-language *Béarn: Guide Loisirs*, stuffed with ideas for things to do and, with contacts for people to help you do them. The possibilities for walking, cycling, climbing, caving and whitewater sports (and winter skiing) will make your head spin. For the names of qualified local guides, contact the Bedous or Laruns tourist office.

Walking The two valleys are laced with hundreds of kilometres of walking trails – including the GR10 and GR653 – some of which link up with trails in Spain.

The upper valleys are dotted with *refuges* (basic accommodation for hikers), open in

Parc National des Pyrénées

The Parc National des Pyrénées, created in 1967, comprises about 45,000 hectares, of which some 40% is within the Pyrénées-Atlantiques département. It runs in a strip – never more than about 15km wide – along the Spanish border, eastwards from the Vallée d'Aspe for about 100km, sharing part of that border with a Spanish national park, the Parque Nacional Ordesa y Monte Perdido. A buffer zone taking in most of the Aspe and Ossau valleys is also managed by the national park but is not fully protected.

Important animal species under the park's protection include chamois (a kind of mountain goat), large birds of prey including the royal eagle and, most urgently, some of the very last brown bears in southern Europe (see the boxed text, 'L'Ours Brun,' later in this section). Among protected plants are the park's extensive beech forests (about 12% of the park is forested).

National park offices with visitor centres in the Béarn are at Arudy, Etsaut and Gabas, though they're not especially useful. Park headquarters (☎ 05 62 44 36 60, fax 05 62 44 36 70) are at 59 route de Pau, 65000 Tarbes. There is also a park office (☎ 05 59 39 75 55) at 14 rue Adoue, Oloron-Ste-Marie. There are plans for a big office at Laruns (vallée d'Ossau).

Among park regulations worth noting are:

VTTs (vélos tout terrains; mountain bikes) are forbidden except on designated tracks; these include cross-country ski routes at Brousset in the vallée d'Ossau and Somport in the Vallée d'Aspe.

Camping is prohibited – except for a small tent, pitched during the hours of darkness, at least an hour's walk from any road, for a maximum of one night.

Dogs may not be brought into the park, even on a lead.

---

summer (roughly July to September), with dorm beds from 50FF to 90FF (and sizeable discounts for children) and meals for 80FF to 100FF. Some refuges are run by the National Park but most by Club Alpin Français. Individuals can't book ahead, though they'll usually fit you in somewhere. In winter they're open on a limited basis (parts left open for hikers and skiers to camp but no warden to cook meals). A useful listing of refuges is in *Hébergement en Montagne*, published by Éditions Randonnées and available in many bookshops.

Pau's Librairie des Pyrénées bookshop is full of maps and detailed topoguides. The best general walking map for the two valleys is IGN's 1:50,000 *Béarn*; a more detailed option is the 1:25,000 Série Bleue *Ossau/ Vallée d'Aspe. Promenades dans le Parc National des Pyrénées – Vallée d'Aspe* (40FF) has French-language information on 12 hikes around the Vallée d'Aspe.

For weather information in the Pyrénées-Atlantiques département, call the *météo* (weather bureau) on ☎ 08 36 68 02 64, or Pau weather station on ☎ 05 36 68 02 64.

White-Water Rafting One outfit that runs white-water and canyoning trips in the Vallée d'Aspe and Vallée d'Ossau is Maison pour Tous Léo Lagrange (☎ 05 59 06 66 89, fax 05 59 06 28 58), 41 rue du Colonel Gloxin, 64000 Pau. A half/full day rafting will cost around 150/250FF per person (children 150FF).

Skiing The Basses-Pyrénées' biggest downhill ski resort is at Gourette (Vallée d'Ossau). Others are at Artouste-Fabrèges (Vallée d'Ossau) and family-friendly Arette-la-Pierre-St-Martin (Vallée d'Aspe). Le Somport (Vallée d'Aspe) is good for cross-country skiing. For a general look at skiing in the Pyrénées, see Activities in the Facts for the Visitor chapter.

Vallée d'Aspe

The Aspe River (Gave d'Aspe) flows for some 60km from the Col du Somport down

BÉARN

to Oloron-Ste-Marie. The lush, exceedingly lovely valley has always been one of the remotest corners of the Pyrénées range. Fewer than 3000 souls live in its 13 villages, and away from the valley bottom it still seems untouched by the 20th century.

But this has been a trans-Pyrenean transport route since the legionaries of Julius Caesar marched through, and this may be its undoing. The Col du Somport is the central Pyrénées' only all-weather pass. From it the N134 runs the length of the valley. European Union (EU) planners have designated it the E7 and want to see it become a major road link between Spain and France. Not everybody is happy about this (see the boxed text 'You Want to Build a *What* Here?').

Meanwhile public transport may be limited, but accommodation is inexpensive and food is downright cheap. The tourist office in Bedous (see Bedous later in this section) is the valley's best and is the place to ask about camp sites, refuges and gîtes d'étape, as well as walking itineraries, equipment rental and local events.

Getting There & Away SNCF goes from Pau to Oloron-Ste-Marie (four to five trains and three to five buses daily, fewer on Sunday; see those sections for details), and from there has onward bus connections into the valley, via Bedous (two to four daily, fewer on Sunday; 53FF and 70 minutes from Pau) all the way to the Spanish railhead of Canfranc (one to three daily; 78FF and 2¼ hours from Pau). There are no direct buses into the valley from Pau.

Escot Escot (pop 122, elevation 330m), 15km above Oloron-Ste-Marie, was the valley's first village. From here the D294 twists and turns over the 1035m Col de Marie-Blanque for 20km to Bielle in the Vallée d'Ossau.

You Want to Build a *What* Here?

The Vallée d'Aspe once had its own railway: a marvel of bridges, viaducts and an extraordinary spiral tunnel, completed in 1928, that worked its way up below the Col du Somport – and then tunnelled for 8km beneath it to the Spanish railhead at Canfranc. What nobody had thought of was the need for a reliable link from the bottom of the valley to the south-west's existing network of roads and railroads.

Then one day in 1970, a bridge at l'Estanguet, just south of Accous, collapsed under the weight of an overloaded train. Everybody got cold feet and the railway line was abandoned.

Since then, as part of a European Union (EU) initiative to improve road links between France and Spain, a road tunnel has been driven under the Col du Somport, parallel to the old rail tunnel, and the N134 (now called the E7) is to be widened. But the project has generated lots of local anxiety about the effects of a multilane highway on this narrow, fragile valley (not to mention the impact on its vanishing brown bears).

Now that heavy construction lorries are starting to use it, the present narrow road is clearly dangerous. There have been numerous accidents. One alternative to widening it is to leave it as it is and shift cargo onto a revitalised rail link. Either option would shatter the valley's calm and mar its beauty, but the latter has the advantage that the railway is already part of the scenery.

So far the French response has been political gridlock, and the EU has shown little interest in studying the rail option.

Grassroots resistance is taking shape. A symbol of it is the train station at Cette-Eygun, 2km south of the ill-fated bridge at l'Estanguet, which has been converted by eco-activist Eric Petetin into *La Goutte d'Eau* (☎ 05 59 34 78 83), a brightly painted cafe, gîte d'étape and meeting place for road opponents.

Sarrance At Sarrance (pop 228, elevation 400m), 7km south of Escot, is a 17th-century cloister. From here the D241 climbs for 10km to Lourdios-Ichère (population 175, elevation 450m) and what must be the south-west's most remote *auberge de jeunesse* (☎ 05 59 34 46 39).

Bedous The valley's biggest village (postcode 64490, pop 554, elevation 416m), 25km south of Oloron-Ste-Marie, sits commandingly in a wide basin. This is the place to get your bearings, the starting point for some good lower-elevation hikes and a good place to stock up on food.

Orientation & Information Buses stop at the car park near Le Choucas Blanc and in front of the police station. The N134 is called rue Gambetta within the town.

The tourist office (☎ 05 59 34 71 48), in the arcaded town hall on place François Sarrail, opposite the church, is open from 9 am to noon and 2 to 6 pm daily except Sunday (from 10 am to 7 pm and to 1 pm on Sunday in July and August).

Exchange money at Caisse d'Épargne, on the western side of the town hall, or Crédit Agricole on rue Pierre Portes; they're open to 5 pm Tuesday to Saturday and to 3.30 pm on Saturday.

The post office, out on the N134, is open to 4.45 pm on weekdays and until noon on Saturday. The newsagent near the tourist office has trekking maps.

Walking & Cycling The prettiest short walk from here is eastwards along the tumbling Gabarret River up to Aydius (pop 74, elevation 780m), 7km to the east. Follow the signs to Plateau d'Ourdinse, with its excellent views up and down the valley. Aydius also has a gîte d'étape and a good restaurant (see Places to Stay & Eat).

VTT Nature (☎ 05 59 34 75 25, fax 05 59 34 75 77), on the N134 just south of town, rents VTTs for about 70/110FF a half-day/day and can direct you to some good routes in the area. Guided trips with/without your own bike cost 180/250FF per day, including transport.

Arette-la-Pierre-St-Martin Fifteen tortu-ous kilometres west of Bedous is the ski re-sort of Arette-la-Pierre-St-Martin (☎ 05 59 66 20 09 from December to April), good for novice and intermediate skiers. The Maison des Jeunes et de la Culture in Bedous (see Places to Stay & Eat) has skis, boots, snow-boards and even snowshoes for hire.

Places to Stay & Eat About 300m off the N134, *Camp Municipal de Carolle* (☎ 05 59 34 59 19), open from March to November, charges 14/5/5FF per adult/tent/car.

The friendly gîte d'étape *Le Choucas Blanc* (☎ 05 59 34 53 71, fax 05 59 87 19 88, 4 rue Gambetta, Bedous), has beds for 48FF (but you must buy a three-month membership card for 5FF) or half-board at 140FF. You can use the kitchen for 5FF and they're generous with good advice. Another on the main square in Bedous is *Le Mandragot* (☎ 05 59 34 59 33), at 50FF per bed or 140FF half-board. Both are open year-round. Up in Aydius, *Gîte Prieur* (☎ 05 59 34 58 07) has dorm beds for 47FF.

The best choice for good Béarnaise specialities at very modest prices is *Restaurant des Cols* (☎ 05 59 34 70 25) in Aydius. Food shops in Bedous include two groceries: *Casino* at 5 rue Gambetta (closed on Sunday afternoon) and *Guyenne et Gascognén*, two doors down. Bedous' weekly market is on Thursday morning.

Accous Accous (postcode 64490, pop 400, elevation 460m), 2.5km south of Bedous and 800m to the east of the highway, sits at the yawning mouth of the Vallée Berthe with a splendid backdrop of 2000m-plus peaks. North of Accous the valley is almost Swiss, prim and pretty. South of here it closes in dramatically.

Activities Look up: this is the home of École de Parapente Ascendance (☎ 05 59 34 52 07, fax 05 59 34 53 33), a parasailing school offering accompanied introductory flights for 350FF and five-day introduction courses for about 2500FF plus board and lodging. From October to June the school is open only at the weekend. Nearby is

BEARN

9 34 50 30), a hang-gliding f-day, accompanied intro

December you can hire a ... at the Auberge Cavalière (see the following Places to Stay & Eat) for 75FF an hour or 250/395FF per half/full-day. Advance reservations are necessary.

Places to Stay & Eat The camp site, *Camping Despourrins* (☎ 05 59 34 71 16), by the highway turning to the village, is open from March to October and costs 15FF per adult and 17FF per site. The gîte d'étape *Maison Despourrins* (☎ 05 59 34 53 50), open year-round, offers beds for 60FF and half-board for 160FF.

Also just off the highway, *Hôtel Le Permayou* (☎ 05 59 34 72 15, fax 05 59 34 72 68) offers fully-equipped doubles from 230FF and serves good 50FF lunch *plats* and *menus* from 70FF. About 3km south of Accous is *Auberge Cavalière* (☎ 05 59 34 72 30, fax 05 59 34 51 97), open year-round with doubles with shower for 240FF, and Pyrenean specialities cooked over a wood fire, such as *poule au pot* (chicken stuffed with vegetables and prepared with tomato sauce. *Menus* start at about 100FF.

If you've never had Pyrénées sheep's cheese (*fromage de brebis*), the big Ossau-Iraty fromagerie on the N134 is the place to try it.

Lescun About 6km south of Bedous is the bridge at l'Estanguet whose collapse in 1970 brought an end to train traffic in the valley. Here also is the turning for a steep and twisting 5.5km ride up to Lescun (postcode 64490, pop 198, elevation 900m), whose slate roofs once sheltered a leper colony. In a valley already too beautiful for its own good, here's a view to take your breath away and blow your film budget: the **Cirque de Lescun**, an amphitheatre of jagged limestone mountains, rising at the back to 2504m Pic d'Anie, one of Basses-Pyrénées' highest.

Walks The GR10 passes through Lescun, and perhaps the best of many fine walks

here is to take it west up the valley of the River Lauga, over the Pas d'Azuns to Arette-la-Pierre-St-Martin, a strenuous half to full-day trek.

Places to Stay You might want to soak this up for a day or two; certainly the right time to be here is for sunrise on those peaks. *Camping Municipal du Lauzart* (☎/fax 05 59 34 51 77), 1.5km south-west of the village, is open mid-April to mid-September, forfait for 57FF. A few kilometres to the north-west (on the trek to Arette) is the *Refuge de l'Labérouat* (☎ 05 59 34 50 43), with beds for 60FF and half-board for 150FF.

Hôtel du Pic d'Anie (☎ 05 59 34 71 54, fax 05 59 34 53 22), right in the village, has obligatory half-board for 245FF for two. It's only open from May to September.

Etsaut About 12km south of Bedous is Etsaut (postcode 64490, pop 92, elevation 590m), the last substantial village in the valley. This and nearby Borce (pop 195, elevation 700m) are obvious bases for higher-elevation hikes.

Orientation & Information The bus stop is in the main square, which doubles as a car park. You can exchange money at the post office, beside the church in the village centre. It is open to 4.30 pm on weekdays and to 11.30 am on Saturday.

You may be able to squeeze some information from staff at the Maison du Parc National des Pyrénées (☎ 05 59 34 88 30 or 05 59 34 70 87), in the old train station at the northern end of town. It's open from 9.30 am to 12.30 pm and 1.30 to 6.30 pm daily from May to September, and has a free exhibit on the park's rapidly disappearing brown bears.

A 15-minute walk to the north-west brings you to another bear centre, the Clos aux Ours (☎ 05 59 34 88 88; see the boxed text 'L'Ours Brun'), open from 10 am till noon and 2 to 8 pm from June to September and 2 to 7 pm on Wednesday, Saturday and Sunday during the rest of the year. Admission costs 20FF (children aged under 16 years 15FF).

L'Ours Brun

The upper Vallée d'Aspe and Vallée d'Ossau are the last Pyrenean home of the brown bear (Ursos arctos). But tourism, roadbuilding and forest management, plus a long (two-year) breeding cycle, has driven the numbers relentlessly down. From 2000 in 1967, there are now an estimated *six* adult bears left in the National Park, including just one female.

The Institution Patrimonial du Haut-Béarn (IPHB), a heritage agency which gets some 40% of its support from the European Union (EU), has proposed stocking the region with more females, but the project is gridlocked by politics and tradition. The French Environment Ministry has agreed to the plan, provided local organisations agree to participate in the EU's 'Réseau Natura 2000' programme which includes Europe-wide scientific surveys. But Béarn's historical hostility to centralised authority has predisposed local farmers and politicians to say no to this. Without their agreement, the IPHB doesn't get its 40%, and there it stands.

Walks About 3km south of Etsaut is the privately owned **Fort du Portalet**, an early 19th-century fortress overlooking a particularly narrow and defensible bit of the valley. From 1941 to 1945 the Germans and the Vichy government used it as a prison.

From Etsaut you can walk south and then east along part of the GR10 known as the **Chemin de la Mâture**, partly hacked out of solid rock and used in the 18th century to harvest timber for the Bayonne shipyards. With unprotected sheer drops, this is not for the faint hearted. A strenuous segment of the trail continues south-eastwards to the **Lacs d'Ayous**, at the foot of Pic du Midi d'Ossau. The National Park *Refuge d'Ayous* (☎ 05 59 05 37 00) has beds for 48FF.

Places to Stay & Eat About 1.5km uphill from Borce along the D739, *Camping du Parc National* (☎ 05 59 34 87 29 in July and August, ☎ 05 59 34 86 15 at other times of the year) is open from June to mid-September at 14FF per site and 15FF per adult. This camp site is on the GR10.

Etsaut's *Maison des Jeunes et de la Culture* (MJC; ☎ 05 59 34 88 98, fax 05 59 34 86 91) has 50FF dorm beds, 18FF sheet rental and 20FF to 50FF meals. Kitchen facilities are available and there's a washing machine. From the village centre, it's a few minutes walk down the alleyway next to the church. In Borce is the National Park *Refuge d'Arlet* (☎ 05 59 36 00 99), with beds for 50FF and half-board for 150FF.

The year-round gîte d'étape *Maison de l'Ours* (☎ 05 59 34 86 38), also known as the Centre d'Hébergement Léo Lagrange, is beside the car park in the village centre. A place in a two- to four-bed room with breakfast costs 75FF. The centre organises bike trips and other activities for guests.

The year-round *Hôtel des Pyrénées* (☎ 05 59 34 88 62, fax 05 59 34 86 96), the only hotel in the village, has doubles without/with shower and toilet for 150/260FF, and a restaurant with *menus* from 70FF. The *alimentation* (grocery) on the corner of the main square, open daily, is ideal for picnic supplies.

Getting Around VTTs can be hired at the MJC (see the preceding Places to Stay & Eat) for 50/90FF a half-day/day.

Vallée d'Ossau

In its 60km journey from the 1794m Col du Pourtalet to its confluence with the Aspe River at Oloron-Ste-Marie, the Ossau River cuts a more stately figure than its sibling. The valley is broader, the peaks rounder, the villages less rough-cut. The tourist office with the most to tell you about the Vallée d'Ossau is at Laruns.

Getting There & Away SNCF goes to Buzy-en-Béarn on the Oloron-Ste-Marie line (four to five trains and three to five buses daily, fewer on Sunday), and from there has onward bus connections into the valley, mainly as far as Laruns (three to four daily, fewer on Sunday). Citram Pyrénées

BÉARN

has buses directly from Pau as far as Laruns, two to four times daily (with Sunday services in July and August and from mid-December to April only).

In July and August, and in the ski season (mid-December to April), SNCF has one morning and one afternoon bus each on Saturday and Sunday from Pau to Artouste-Fabrège, and Canonge (Laruns ☎ 05 59 05 30 31) runs two buses each weekday from Laruns to Artouste-Fabrège.

Aste-Béon There's just one reason to stop off at Aste-Béon (postcode 64260, pop 231, elevation 480m): to be a vulture voyeur (see the boxed text 'La Falaise aux Vautours').

Places to Stay & Eat Just to the south in the Aste part of the village is a primitive camp site, *Aire Naturelle Toussaü* (☎ 05 59 34 91 01), open from June to September, for 15FF per adult and 20FF per site. Close by in Béon is a good restaurant-bar, *L'Étape du Berger* (☎ 05 59 82 65 58), open daily with good-value *menus* of Béarnaise specialities from 56FF.

Getting There & Away Citram Pyrénées buses from Pau (40FF, 50 minutes) to

---

La Falaise aux Vautours

The griffon vulture *(Gyps folvus)* is one of France's largest birds of prey. The huge bird – with an adult wingspan of almost 3m – is a familiar sight over the Pyrénées, with its stately gliding flight. It is unique in feeding exclusively on carrion, which nowadays means mainly livestock killed by predators, disease or age – thus acting as a kind of 'alpine dustman'.

In 1974, on the initiative of National Park officer Charles Gerbet, the villages of Aste-Béon, Bielle, Bilhères and Castet established a 92-hectare reserve for the protection of seven to 10 griffon vulture pairs nesting in the limestone cliffs above the villages, and threatened by egg poachers and careless photographers. A measure of its success is that there are now about 120 nesting pairs, along with various other raptors and five pairs of migratory Egyptian vultures. This is not a park operation but a private one, under the control of the mayor

NICKY CAVEN

The huge griffon vulture

of Aste-Béon, and all the more amazing for succeeding without government 'help'.

In 1993 a public information and education centre called La Falaise aux Vautours (Cliff of the Vultures) was opened at Aste-Béon, centred on a video theatre showing live images of 10 griffon vulture nests from a remote-controlled camera installed on the cliffs just 30m away, and from a fixed camera right beside one of the nests. Visitors can thus look in on nesting, hatching and feeding in real time, an extraordinary achievement. Also here is a child-friendly interactive museum about vultures, including English captions.

The museum is free and the 'vulture show' costs 37FF (kids aged from five to 12 years 23FF). The centre (☎ 05 59 82 65 49, fax 05 59 82 65 65) is open from 10 am to 1 pm and 2 to 7 pm daily from June to August, but keeps more limited hours at other times (check with the Pau tourist office). It's closed to the public for much of the winter.

Laruns stop here (on the main D934 road) two or three times daily, except Sunday, leaving Pau at around 10 am, 1 pm and 6 pm and calling at about the same times on their return (but get current times from the Pau tourist office).

Laruns Though it has little else to offer, Laruns (postcode 64440, pop 1500, elevation 536m), 19km south of Buzy-en-Béarn, is the best place to stop for information or supplies.

Orientation & Information The valley tourist office, La Maison de la Vallée d'Ossau (☎ 05 59 05 31 41, fax 05 59 05 35 49), is on place de La Mairie, the little main square with the fountain just off the D934. It's open from 9 am to 12.30 pm and 4 to 6.30 pm daily from June to September, and from 9 am to noon and 2 to 5 pm daily during the rest of the year. Check out their 15FF booklet on VTT circuits and the 30FF book of local *petites randonnées* (short family walks). Within sight of the office are two banks and a Maison de la Presse which sells maps.

Places to Stay & Eat About 1.8km to the north by the river, *Camping Geteu* (☎ 05 59 05 37 15), open from May to mid-September and on winter holidays, charges 14/22FF per adult/site. The year-round *Camping Pont Lauguère* (☎ 05 59 05 35 99), 1km south on the riverside, charges 16/30FF. Not far from the latter is the three-star, year-round *Camping des Gaves* (☎ 05 59 05 32 37, fax 05 59 05 47 14), charging 21/52/52FF per adult/tent/car.

The refuge *Auberge L'Embaradère* (☎ 05 59 05 41 88, ave de la Gare) has 60FF beds, 60FF dinner and 20FF breakfast; it's closed on Monday except in school holidays. *Hôtel d'Ossau* (☎ 05 59 05 30 14, fax 05 59 05 47 00, place de la Mairie) has rooms for 160FF to 275FF. At least three adequate restaurants surround place de la Mairie.

Getting There & Away Citram's direct buses from Pau (46FF; one hour) stop two to four times daily (but with Sunday ser-

vices only in July and August and during the ski season). SNCF buses from Pau (39FF), with a change at Buzy-en-Béarn, stop three to four times daily (less often on Sunday).

Gabas Tiny Gabas (postcode 64440, pop 36, elevation 1027m), 13km south of Laruns, is mainly a trekking base, though its little modern chapel actually dates from the 12th century. A National Park visitor centre (☎ 05 59 05 32 13, fax 05 59 05 43 09) is open from 10 am to 1 pm and 2 to 7 pm daily from mid-June to mid-September.

A trekkers' *refuge* (☎ 05 59 05 33 14) here has 48FF beds, and meals by request. Rooms at *Hôtel Vignau* (☎ 05 59 05 34 06, fax 05 59 05 46 12) start at 145FF for a double, or half-board for 150FF per person; restaurant *menus* start at 50FF. A good bet for a modest meal is the *Restaurant Le Pic du Midi* (☎ 05 59 05 33 00).

From Gabas, a sharp 5km climb to the **Lac de Bious-Artigues** reservoir (1420m) will reward you with superb views, south-east to Pic du Midi d'Ossau from the western shore, and south-west to 2288m Pic d'Ayous. Nearby, *Camping de Bious Oumettes* (☎ 05 59 05 38 76), open from mid-June to mid-September, charges 13/12FF per adult/site; and *Refuge Pyrénéa-Sport* (☎ 05 59 05 32 12), open from mid-June to September, charges 55FF per bed.

Le Petit Train d'Artouste About 1.5km east of Gabas on the D934 is the settlement of Artouste-Fabrèges (postcode 64440, elevation 1250m), devoted to maintaining the **Lac de Fabrège** reservoir or to feeding tourists and sending them in a cable car up the flanks of 2032m Pic de la Sagette. From there they ride for 10km to another reservoir, **Lac d'Artouste** (1991m), in an open-topped train, built for dam workers in the 1920s. It's touristy, popular and crowded, but great for kids, and the ride is gorgeous.

The whole thing is open from the last week in May to the first week in October, with a diabolical price structure that depends on your age and the season, from 46FF for kids aged from four to 10 in the

BÉARN

lowest season, to 95FF for adults in the highest season (August). Kids under four years old, or under 1m tall, go for free.

Give yourself four hours to get up and back, and dress warmly. In July and August you're only allowed to stay 1½ hours at the upper lake. If you'd like to stay longer, consider walking up – a two-hour trip from the lower to the upper lake. Beside Lac d'Artouste is *Refuge d'Arrémoulif* (☎ 05 59 05 31 79), open from mid-June to September.

For current information on the train, call ☎ 05 59 05 36 99. There's a tourist office at Artouste-Fabrèges (☎ 05 59 05 34 00, fax 05 59 05 37 55). Overpriced snack bars are at both ends of the cable car and train rides.

Up the D934 from Artouste-Fabrèges is 1794m **Col du Pourtalet** into Spain, normally clear of snow only from July to October.

Getting There & Away The bus from Pau via Buzy-en-Béarn to Artouste-Fabrèges costs 55FF.

ORTHEZ
postcode 64300 • pop 11,500 • elevation 60m
Viscount Gaston VII of Béarn made Orthez his capital in the late 13th century, though even when Gaston Fébus moved it to Pau he often held court here. The town's two claims to fame are Gaston VII's striking fortified bridge over the Pau River, and an earnest Museum of Protestantism. Surprisingly, one of the town's big exports is Bayonne ham!

Orientation & Information
Buses stop in rue Jeanne d'Albret, two blocks north of the modern bridge. Walk two blocks west on rue Pierre Lasserre and a block north on rue Bourg-Vieux to the tourist office (☎ 05 59 69 02 75, fax 05 59 69 12 00), in a 16th-century town house called Maison Jeanne d'Albret (though it's unlikely she ever stayed here). The office is open from 9 am to noon and 2 to 6 pm daily except Sunday (also on Sunday morning in July and August). From the train station it's an 800m walk west to the tourist office.

The Bureau d'Information Jeunesse (BIJ; ☎ 05 59 69 31 30, fax 05 59 69 31 12), at 10 place Brossers, two blocks north of the bus stop, is open from 8 am to 1 pm and 2 to 6 pm on weekdays. The post office is a block before the BIJ.

Gaston VII's Town
The axis of the old town is rue Bourg-Vieux and its northward extension, rue de l'Horloge and rue Moncade. Little remains of Gaston's fortress but a tower, the **Tour Moncade**, 500m north of the tourist office. Townsfolk knocked off the top for building materials before the town council blew the whistle in the 19th century. The tower is open from 10 am to noon and 2 to 6 pm daily from April to October (to 7 pm in July and August, to 5 pm in April and afternoons only in October). Admission costs 12FF.

A one-block walk west down rue des Jacobins from the tourist office brings you into the big market plaza, around the 13th-century **Église St-Pierre**, once part of the town walls. Inside this otherwise boxy and uninspiring church are some Gothic capitals carved with mermaids and mythical beasts.

Gaston's fortified bridge – and Orthez's trademark – the **Pont Vieux**, crosses the Bayonne–Pau TGV line and a churning river, three blocks south and a block west of the tourist office. Once it had a second tower and guarded the entrance to the town, stopping Wellington himself in 1814. Across the river is one of the town's prettiest streets, rue du Pont Vieux.

The only decent photos will be taken from the riverside, but beware the dangerously unprotected TGV line!

Musée du Protestantisme Béarnais
If you grew up Protestant, or among Protestants, you may find it hard to take this staid museum seriously, but most French people – 98% of whom have never seen the inside of a Protestant *temple* – will probably find it pretty interesting. Aside from a few remote villages in the Basses-Pyrénées where Protestants number as much as 50%, Orthez has an unusually large Protestant community (about 10%) for France.

The museum consists of a reconstructed 19th-century Protestant church, an exhibit of tiny chalices, hymnals and other concealable paraphernalia of worship, and a few too many exhibits on the tolerant years after the Revolution. Some staff speak English and are keen to tell visitors all about Protestantism in France and Europe.

The museum (☎ 05 59 69 14 03) is upstairs from the tourist office and is open from 10 am to noon and 2 to 6 pm, daily except Sunday. Admission costs 10FF.

Places to Stay & Eat

Hôtel Moulia (☎ *05 59 69 02 82, 18 rue Pierre Lasserre*), near the bus stop, has doubles from 120FF to 180FF and serves *menus* from 53FF in its plain restaurant (closed on Sunday and mid-August to mid-September). A stone's throw from the tourist office is the Logis de France *Hôtel La Reine Jeanne* (☎ *05 59 67 00 76, fax 05 59 69 09 63, 44 rue Bourg-Vieux*), with comfortable rooms from 310FF and *menus* from 85FF.

Getting There & Away

TPR buses stop here en route from Pau (36FF; 45 minutes) to Bayonne, three times daily, and SNCF runs one or two daily buses. Trains from Pau stop here about 10 times daily, taking 25 minutes.

SALIES DE BÉARN

postcode 64270 • pop 5000 • elevation 53m
This is one of the most picture-postcard villages in Béarn, its half-timbered, brightly painted, hygienically whitewashed houses festooned with flowerboxes and washing, and its compact, well-marked centre a network of serene, sun-washed lanes, all nestled in an arc of the channelised River Saleys. Wooden balconies lean picturesquely out over the water. Here you may refresh yourself, or you may perish from boredom.

Hyper-saline, 50°C springs gave Salies its name and its vocation. Back in the mists of time, says a legend, an injured wild boar stumbled into a swamp and died, only to be discovered the following year, encrusted with salt and perfectly preserved. For centuries Salisiens made their living from this salt. Curing with it is deemed essential to

the taste of famous Bayonne hams. When the competition from sea-salt got tough, Salies reinvented itself as a thermal spa.

Orientation & Information

From the bus stop on place du Général de Gaulle, walk south over the bridge, to the end of rue Loumé. Then turn right and cross the Pont d'Andioque to the tourist office, or turn left into place de la Trompe and place du Bayaá, the heart of town, complete with a little saline fountain in the shape of a boar's head and a Béarnaise motto that says, 'If I hadn't died here, nobody would live here'.

The well-organised tourist office (☎ 05 59 38 00 33, fax 05 59 38 02 95), on rue des Bains, is open from 9.30 am to noon and 3 to 6 pm daily except Sunday (from 9.30 am to 12.30 pm and 2 to 6.30 pm, plus Sunday morning, from July to mid-September).

Things to See & Do

The station thermale is just north of the tourist office. Hot, super-salty pools are for spa patients, but visitors can soak in cooler (34°C), diluted pools for 50FF per hour. It's open from 10.30 am to noon and 2 to 8 pm daily (to 7 pm on Saturday, from 9.30 am to 12.30 pm and 2.30 to 7.30 pm on Sunday).

Up rue des Puits Salants from place de la Trompe is a 17th-century house with a little Musée du Sel, with a reconstruction of a traditional salt workshop. Near the boar's-head fountain is a folklore museum, the Musée des Arts et Traditions. Both are open from 3 to 6 pm, Tuesday to Saturday from April to September (only on Thursday and Saturday from April to mid-May). Admission costs 15FF.

Places to Stay

Salies has a small, year-round *Auberge de Jeunesse* (☎ *05 59 65 06 96, stade Al Cartero, chemin du Padu*) where beds cost 40FF, guests can use the kitchen and there is space to pitch a tent. To get there walk south and south-west out of place du Bayaá on rue du Canal, continuing on rue Félix Pécaut, for 600m.

Camp Municipal de Mosqueros (☎ *05 59 38 12 94, ave Al Cartero*), 1.2km west

BÉARN

on the Bayonne road (D17), is open from April to mid-October for 16FF per adult and 33F per site.

The good-value *Hôtel Hélios* (☎ 05 59 38 37 59, fax 05 59 38 16 41), 1km east on the road to Pau (D933), is open from July to September with doubles for 110FF. A free shuttle bus to and from town is available for guests.

Places to Eat

Keep it cheap at *Pizzeria Il Capitello* (☎ 05 59 65 04 17, place du Bayaá), with pizza and pasta *menus* from 30FF. For something a little more traditional, *Restaurant La Terrasse* (☎ 05 59 38 09 83, rue Loumé) offers *menus* from 40FF and a riverside terrace. Place du Bayaá comes alive every Thursday morning for its *weekly market*.

Getting There & Away

Salies is midway between Pau and Bayonne, just over an hour to either by bus (50FF); TPR's Pau–Bayonne bus stops here three times daily. The nearest train station is 7km to the north at Puyoô, on the Pau–Bayonne line (about 35 minutes and 50FF either way), with about five services daily (fewer at the weekend).

SAUVETERRE DE BÉARN

postcode 64390 • pop 1600 • elevation 70m

Here's a town good for strolling, and letting your imagination go – fortified in stone and cloaked in greenery, with plenty of well-preserved and interesting architecture, set on a cliff above a peaceful, sighing river. Like Orthez, Sauveterre has a fortified bridge, but only half of one, full of mystery. The longer you wander, the more you find: vine-covered stairways and landings, little courtyards, old fountains.

History

Viscount Centule IV of Béarn chartered the town in 1090 as a *sauveterre*, a free zone from the miseries of war, and – just to make sure – fortified it to the hilt, perhaps because of its position on routes between Béarn and its tumultuous neighbours, Navarre and Aquitaine. Much of what you

see now are 12th- to 14th-century improvements by his descendants, Gaston VII and Gaston Fébus.

Orientation & Information

The old town sits beside the Oloron River. The tourist office (☎ 05 59 38 58 65, fax 05 59 38 94 82) is on place Royale, the town's administrative heart. Here you'll find a good, 20FF English-language *Guided Tour of Sauveterre* that will show you around without sounding like an advert for the place. The office is open from 10 am to 12.30 pm and 3 to 7 pm during July and August (closed Sunday), and from 10 am to 12.30 pm and 2 to 6 pm during the rest of the year (closed all day Sunday and Monday morning).

Also on place Royale are the post office and a Crédit Agricole bank, both open weekdays and Saturday morning.

Pont de la Légende

It's thought that this bridge was built by Gaston VII in the 13th century and fixed with a drawbridge by Gaston Fébus. Once upon a time it presumably crossed the river via the little island. Nobody seems to know when the other part collapsed.

Of course the bridge has a legend attached to it – literally, on a plaque by the tower door. Sancie, wife of Gaston V, gave birth to a dead child while her husband was away on a campaign. Rumours of witchcraft spread. Sancie's brother Sanche, king of Navarre, had her put to trial by water: tie her up, throw her in the river (from this bridge, goes the story) and see if God saves her. Of course He does and the story ends happily. The only problem is that the bridge was built decades after Sancie and Gaston lived here.

Église St-André

The St Andrew Church, consecrated in the 12th century, is Romanesque outside – including a simple, inventive tympanum over the door – and plain, more or less Gothic inside. But look for Romanesque columns framing both little side-chapels; a scattering of charming carved capitals; and, just to the right of the main door as you

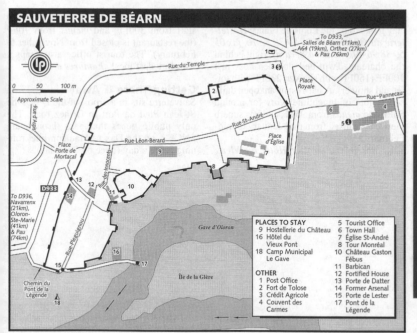

SAUVETERRE DE BÉARN

Approximate Scale
0   50   100 m

To D933,
Salies de Béarn (11km),
A64 (19km), Orthez (27km)
& Pau (76km)

Place Royale

Rue-du-Temple

Rue-Pannecau

Rue-St-André

Place d'Église

Place Porte de Mortacal

Rue-Léon-Berard

Rue d'Aspis

D933

To D936,
Navarrenx (21km),
Oloron-Ste-Marie (41km)
& Pau (74km)

Rue Pleugnegrou

Gave d'Oloron

Île de la Glère

Chemin du Pont de la Légende

PLACES TO STAY	5 Tourist Office
9 Hostellerie du Château	6 Town Hall
16 Hôtel du Vieux Pont	7 Église St-André
18 Camp Municipal Le Gave	8 Tour Monréal
	10 Château Gaston Fébus
OTHER	11 Barbican
1 Post Office	12 Fortified House
2 Fort de Tolose	13 Porte de Datter
3 Crédit Agricole	14 Former Arsenal
4 Couvent des Carmes	15 Porte de Lester
	17 Pont de la Légende

BÉARN

enter, a little door for the use of *les cagots*, a curious medieval 'untouchable' caste – possibly ostracised for deformity, illness or ancestry, nobody knows today – about which bits of evidence appear in the older towns throughout the region. Behind the church is a fine view down to the river.

Other Things to See
The so-called **Château Gaston Fébus** was almost certainly built by Gaston VII. Originally it was entered through a barbican (a covered outer gate) and drawbridge on the western side. It's closed to the public, though if you ask at the Hostellerie du Château (see Places to Stay) you might get a closer look from that side.

The stark 12th-century **Tour Monréal** – named after a 19th-century family who saved it from demolition – was probably the ancient keep, with metre-thick walls and slit windows. It's closed to the public. Beside it is one of several stairways leading

down to the riverside, from where you get a good look at the **ramparts**, some of the sturdiest of any town in the Béarn des Gaves.

Inside the ancient **porte de Datter** on the western side are the heavy walls of the old **armoury**, and across the lane is a **fortified house** that may once have been a guardhouse. Up an alley by a shop on rue Léon Berard is the **Fort de Tolose**, a 16th-century addition to strengthen the northern ramparts, which run through the middle of the block here.

East of the tourist office is a former **Couvent des Carmes** or Carmelite convent, built at the request of Gaston Fébus. The interior is visible through a gate on rue Pannecau.

Places to Stay & Eat
The plain, perfectly sited *Camp Municipal Le Gave* (☎ 05 59 38 53 30) is open from June to September and costs 10/7/14FF per adult/tent/car.

euro currency converter 10FF = €1.52

Sauveterre's most interesting place to stay looks to be the Logis de France *Hostellerie du Château* (☎ 05 59 38 52 10, fax 05 59 38 96 49, rue Léon Berard), right behind the chateau. Twin-bed doubles cost just 100FF (160FF with shower, 230FF with toilet and shower). A bar-restaurant open daily serves lots of lunchtime *plats* for around 50FF and *menus* from 95FF, and has superb views. It's closed from mid-January to mid-February.

Rooms in the smaller *Hôtel du Vieux Pont* (☎ 05 59 38 95 11, fax 05 59 38 99 10) start from 300FF, and *menus* from 70FF (the restaurant is closed from November to February). The tourist office also keeps a list of modest local *chambres d'hôte*.

Getting There & Away

Sauveterre sits in a crook of the D933, the St-Jean Pied de Port to Orthez road. The only public buses that pass through are SNCF's, on the Dax to Mauléon line, running twice a day (once on Saturday).

Language

Modern French developed from the *langue d'oïl*, a group of dialects spoken north of the Loire River that grew out of the vernacular Latin used during the late Gallo-Roman period. The langue d'oïl – particularly the Francien dialect spoken in the Île de France – eventually displaced the *langue d'oc*, the dialects spoken in the south of the country and from which the Mediterranean region of Languedoc got its name.

Standard French is taught and spoken in France, but its various accents and sub-dialects are an important source of identity in certain regions. In addition, some of the peoples subjected to French rule many centuries ago have preserved their traditional languages. These include Flemish in the far north; Alsatian in Alsace; Breton (a Celtic tongue similar to Cornish and Welsh) in Brittany; Basque (a language unrelated to any other) in the Basque Country; Catalan in Roussillon (Catalan is the official language of nearby Andorra and the first language of many in the Spanish province of Catalonia); Provençal in Provence; and Corsican on the island of Corsica.

Around 122 million people worldwide speak French as their first language; it is an official language in Belgium, Switzerland, Luxembourg, the Canadian province of Quebec and over two dozen other countries, most of them former French colonies in Africa. It is also spoken in the Val d'Aosta region of north-western Italy. Various forms of Creole are used in Haiti, French Guiana and parts of Louisiana. France has a special government ministry (Ministère de la Francophonie) to deal with the country's relations with the French-speaking world.

While the French rightly or wrongly have a reputation for assuming that all human beings should speak French – until WWI it was *the* international language of culture and diplomacy – you'll find that any attempt to communicate in French will be much appreciated. Probably your best bet is always to approach people politely in French, even if the only sentence you know is *Pardon, madame/monsieur/mademoiselle, parlez-vous anglais?* (Excuse me, madam/sir/miss, do you speak English?).

For a more comprehensive guide to the French language get hold of Lonely Planet's *French phrasebook*.

Grammar

An important distinction is made in French between *tu* and *vous*, which both mean 'you'. *Tu* is only used when addressing people you know well, children or animals. When addressing an adult who is not a personal friend, *vous* should be used unless the person invites you to use *tu*. In general, younger people insist less on this distinction and they may use *tu* from the beginning of an acquaintance.

All nouns in French are either masculine or feminine and adjectives reflect the gender of the noun they modify. The feminine form of many nouns and adjectives is indicated by a silent *e* added to the masculine form, as in *étudiant* and *étudiante*, the masculine and feminine for 'student'. In the following phrases we have indicated both masculine and feminine forms where necessary. The masculine form comes first, separated from the feminine by a slash. The gender of a noun is often indicated by a preceding article: 'the/a/some', *le/un/du* (m), *la/une/de la* (f); or a possessive adjective, 'my/your/his/her', *mon/ton/son* (m), *ma/ta/sa* (f). With French, unlike English, the possessive adjective agrees in number and gender with the thing possessed: 'his/her mother', *sa mère*.

Pronunciation

Most letters in French are pronounced more or less the same as their English equivalents. A few which may cause confusion are:

j   as the 's' in 'leisure', eg *jour* (day)

c before **e** and **i**, as the 's' in 'sit';
before **a**, **o** and **u** it's pronounced as
English 'k'. When undescored with a
'cedilla' (ç) it's always pronounced
as the 's' in 'sit'.

French has a number of sounds that are difficult for Anglophones to produce. These
include:

• The distinction between the 'u' sound (as
in *tu*) and 'oo' sound (as in *tout*). For both
sounds, the lips are rounded and projected
forwards, but for the 'u' the tongue is
towards the front of the mouth, its tip
against the lower front teeth, whereas for
the 'oo' the tongue is towards the back of
the mouth, its tip behind the gums of the
lower front teeth.

• The nasal vowels. With nasal vowels the
breath escapes partly through the nose and
partly through the mouth. There are no
nasal vowels in English; in French there
are three, as in *bon vin blanc* (good white
wine). These sounds occur where a sylla-
ble ends in a single **n** or **m**; the **n** or **m** is
silent but indicates the nasalisation of the
preceding vowel.

• The **r**. The standard **r** of Parisian French is
produced by moving the bulk of the tongue
backwards to constrict the air flow in the
pharynx while the tip of the tongue rests
behind the lower front teeth. It's similar to
the noise made by some people before spit-
ting, but with much less friction.

Basics

Yes.	*Oui.*
No.	*Non.*
Maybe.	*Peut-être.*
Please.	*S'il vous plaît.*
Thank you.	*Merci.*
You're welcome.	*Je vous en prie.*
Excuse me.	*Excusez-moi.*
Sorry/Forgive me.	*Pardon.*

Greetings

Hello/Good morning.	*Bonjour.*
Good evening.	*Bonsoir.*
Good night.	*Bonne nuit.*
Goodbye.	*Au revoir.*

Small Talk

How are you?	*Comment allez-vous?* (polite)
	Comment vas-tu?/ *Comment ça va?* (informal)
Fine, thanks.	*Bien, merci.*
What's your name?	*Comment vous appelez-vous?*
My name is ...	*Je m'appelle ...*
I'm pleased to meet you.	*Enchanté/ Enchantée.* (m/f)
How old are you?	*Quel âge avez-vous?*
I'm ... years old.	*J'ai ... ans.*
Do you like ...?	*Aimez-vous ...?*
Where are you from?	*De quel pays êtes-vous?*
I'm from ...	*Je viens ...*
Australia	*d'Australie*
Canada	*du Canada*
England	*d'Angleterre*
Germany	*d'Allemagne*
Ireland	*d'Irlande*
New Zealand	*de Nouvelle Zélande*
Scotland	*d'Écosse*
Wales	*du Pays de Galle*
the USA	*des États-Unis*

Language Difficulties

I understand.	*Je comprends.*
I don't understand.	*Je ne comprends pas.*
Do you speak English?	*Parlez-vous anglais?*
Could you please write it down?	*Est-ce que vous pouvez l'écrire?*

Getting Around

I want to go to ...	*Je voudrais aller à ...*
I'd like to book a seat to ...	*Je voudrais réserver une place pour ...*
What time does the ... leave/arrive?	*À quelle heure part/arrive ...?*
aeroplane	*l'avion*
bus (city)	*l'autobus*
bus (intercity)	*l'autocar*
ferry	*le ferry(-boat)*
train	*le train*
tram	*le tramway*

Signs

ENTRÉE	ENTRANCE
SORTIE	EXIT
COMPLET	NO VACANCIES
RENSEIGNEMENTS	INFORMATION
OUVERT/FERMÉ	OPEN/CLOSED
INTERDIT	PROHIBITED
(COMMISSARIAT DE) POLICE	POLICE STATION
CHAMBRES LIBRES	ROOMS AVAILABLE
TOILETTES, WC	TOILETS
HOMMES	MEN
FEMMES	WOMEN

Where is (the) ...?	*Où est ...?*
bus stop	*l'arrêt d'autobus*
metro station	*la station de métro*
train station	*la gare*
tram stop	*l'arrêt de tramway*
ticket office	*le guichet*

I'd like a ... ticket.	*Je voudrais un billet ...*
one-way	*aller-simple*
return	*aller-retour*
1st class	*première classe*
2nd class	*deuxième classe*

How long does the trip take?	*Combien de temps dure le trajet?*

The train is ...	*Le train est ...*
delayed	*en retard*
on time	*à l'heure*
early	*en avance*

Do I need to ...?	*Est-ce que je dois ...?*
change trains	*changer de train*
change platform	*changer de quai*

left-luggage locker	*consigne automatique*
platform	*quai*
timetable	*horaire*

I'd like to hire ...	*Je voudrais louer ...*
a bicycle	*un vélo*
a car	*une voiture*
a guide	*un guide*

Around Town

I'm looking for ...	*Je cherche ...*
a bank	*une banque/*
an exchange office	*un bureau de change*
the city centre	*le centre-ville*
the ... embassy	*l'ambassade de ...*
the hospital	*l'hôpital*
my hotel	*mon hôtel*
the market	*le marché*
the police	*la police*
the post office	*le bureau de poste/ la poste*
a public phone	*une cabine téléphonique*
a public toilet	*les toilettes*
the tourist office	*l'office de tourisme*

Where is (the) ...?	*Où est ...?*
beach	*la plage*
bridge	*le pont*
castle/mansion	*le château*
cathedral	*la cathédrale*
church	*l'église*
island	*l'île*
lake	*le lac*
main square	*la place centrale*
mosque	*la mosquée*
old city/town	*la vieille ville*
the palace	*le palais*
quay/bank	*le quai/la rive*
ruins	*les ruines*
sea	*la mer*
square	*la place*
tower	*la tour*

What time does it open/close?	*Quelle est l'heure d'ouverture/ de fermeture?*
I'd like to make a telephone call.	*Je voudrais téléphoner.*

I'd like to exchange ...	*Je voudrais changer*
... some money	*de l'argent*
travellers cheques	*chèques de voyage*

Directions

How do I get to ...?	*Comment dois-je faire pour arriver à ...?*
Is it near/far?	*Est-ce près/loin?*

Can you show me on the map/ city map?	*Est-ce que vous pouvez me le montrer sur la carte/le plan?*
Go straight ahead.	*Continuez tout droit.*
Turn left.	*Tournez à gauche.*
Turn right.	*Tournez à droite.*
at the traffic lights	*aux feux*
at the next corner	*au prochain coin*
behind	*derrière*
in front of	*devant*
opposite	*en face de*
north	*nord*
south	*sud*
east	*est*
west	*ouest*

Accommodation

I'm looking for ...	*Je cherche ...*
the youth hostel	*l'auberge de jeunesse*
the campground	*le camping*
a hotel	*un hôtel*
Where can I find a cheap hotel?	*Où est-ce que je peux trouver un hôtel bon marché?*
What's the address?	*Quelle est l'adresse?*
Could you write it down, please?	*Est-ce que vous pourriez l'écrire, s'il vous plaît?*
Do you have any rooms available?	*Est-ce que vous avez des chambres libres?*
I'd like to book ...	*Je voudrais réserver ...*
a bed	*un lit*
a single room	*une chambre pour une personne*
a double room	*une chambre double*
a room with a shower and toilet	*une chambre avec douche et WC*
I'd like to stay in a dormitory.	*Je voudrais coucher dans un dortoir.*
How much is it ...?	*Quel est le prix ...?*
per night	*par nuit*
per person	*par personne*

Is breakfast included?	*Est-ce que le petit dé-jeuner est compris?*
Can I see the room?	*Est-ce que je peux voir la chambre?*
Where is ...?	*Où est ...?*
the bathroom	*la salle de bains*
the shower	*la douche*
Where is the toilet?	*Où sont les toilettes?*
I'm going to stay ...	*Je resterai ...*
one day	*un jour*
a week	*une semaine*

Shopping

How much is it?	*C'est combien?*
It's too expensive for me.	*C'est trop cher pour moi.*
Can I look at it?	*Est-ce que je peux le/la voir? (m/f)*
I'm just looking.	*Je ne fais que regarder.*
Can I pay by credit cards?	*Est-ce que je peux payer avec ma carte de crédit?*
Can I pay by travellers cheques?	*Est-ce que je peux payer avec des chèques de voyage?*
It's too big/small.	*C'est trop grand/petit.*
more/less	*plus/moins*
cheap	*bon marché*
cheaper	*moins cher*
bookshop	*la librairie*
chemist/pharmacy	*la pharmacie*
laundry/laundrette	*la laverie*
market	*le marché*
newsagency	*l'agence de presse*
stationers	*la papeterie*
supermarket	*le supermarché*

Time & Dates

What time is it?	*Quelle heure est-il?*
It's (two) o'clock.	*Il est (deux) heures.*
When?	*Quand?*
today	*aujourd'hui*
tonight	*ce soir*

tomorrow	*demain*
day after tomorrow	*après-demain*
yesterday	*hier*
all day	*toute la journée*
in the morning	*du matin*
in the afternoon	*de l'après-midi*
in the evening	*du soir*
Monday	*lundi*
Tuesday	*mardi*
Wednesday	*mercredi*
Thursday	*jeudi*
Friday	*vendredi*
Saturday	*samedi*
Sunday	*dimanche*
January	*janvier*
February	*février*
March	*mars*
April	*avril*
May	*mai*
June	*juin*
July	*juillet*
August	*août*
September	*septembre*
October	*octobre*
November	*novembre*
December	*décembre*

Numbers

1	*un*
2	*deux*
3	*trois*
4	*quatre*
5	*cinq*
6	*six*
7	*sept*
8	*huit*
9	*neuf*
10	*dix*
11	*onze*
12	*douze*
13	*treize*
14	*quatorze*
15	*quinze*
16	*seize*
17	*dix-sept*
18	*dix-huit*
19	*dix-neuf*
20	*vingt*
100	*cent*
1000	*mille*
one million	*un million*

Health

I'm sick.	*Je suis malade.*
I need a doctor.	*Il me faut un médecin.*
Where is the hospital?	*Où est l'hôpital?*
I have diarrhoea.	*J'ai la diarrhée.*
I'm pregnant.	*Je suis enceinte.*
I'm ...	*Je suis ...*
diabetic	*diabétique*
epileptic	*épileptique*
asthmatic	*asthmatique*
anaemic	*anémique*
I'm allergic ...	*Je suis allergique ...*
to antibiotics	*aux antibiotiques*
to penicillin	*à la pénicilline*
to bees	*aux abeilles*
antiseptic	*antiseptique*
aspirin	*aspirine*
condoms	*préservatifs*
contraceptive	*contraceptif*
medicine	*médicament*
nausea	*nausée*
sunblock cream	*crème solaire haute protection*
tampons	*tampons hygiéniques*

FOOD

breakfast	*le petit déjeuner*
lunch	*le déjeuner*
dinner	*le dîner*

Emergencies

Help!	*Au secours!*
Call a doctor!	*Appelez un médecin!*
Call the police!	*Appelez la police!*
Leave me alone!	*Fichez-moi la paix!*
I've been robbed.	*On m'a volé.*
I've been raped.	*On m'a violée.*
I'm lost.	*Je me suis égaré/ égarée. (m/f)*

grocery store	l'épicerie
I'd like the set menu.	Je prends le menu.
I'm a vegetarian.	Je suis végétarien/ végétarienne.
I don't eat meat.	Je ne mange pas de viande.

Basics

beurre	butter
chocolat	chocolate
confiture	jam
crème fraîche	cream
farine	flour
huile	oil
lait	milk
miel	honey
œufs	eggs
poivre	pepper
sel	salt
sucre	sugar
vinaigre	vinegar

Utensils

bouteille	bottle
carafe	carafe
pichet	jug
verre	glass
couteau	knife
cuillère	spoon
fourchette	fork
serviette	serviette (napkin)

Meat, Chicken & Poultry

agneau	lamb
aiguillette	thin slice of duck fillet
andouille or andouillette	sausage made from pork or veal tripe
bifteck	steak
bœuf	beef
bœuf haché	minced beef
boudin noir	blood sausage (black pudding)
brochette	kebab
canard	duck
caneton	duckling
cervelle	brains
charcuterie	cooked or prepared meats (usually pork)

cheval	horse meat
chèvre	goat
chevreau	kid (goat)
chevreuil	venison
côte	chop of pork, lamb or mutton
côtelette	cutlet
cuisses de grenouilles	frogs' legs
entrecôte	rib steak
dinde	turkey
épaule d'agneau	shoulder of lamb
escargot	snail
faisan	pheasant
faux-filet	sirloin steak
filet	tenderloin
foie	liver
foie gras de canard	duck liver pâté
gibier	game
gigot d'agneau	leg of lamb
jambon	ham
langue	tongue
lapin	rabbit
lard	bacon
lardon	pieces of chopped bacon
lièvre	hare
mouton	mutton
oie	goose
pieds de porc	pigs' trotters
pigeonneau	squab (young pigeon)
pintade	guinea fowl
porc	pork
poulet	chicken
rognons	kidneys
sanglier	wild boar
saucisson	large sausage
saucisson fumé	smoked sausage
steak	steak
tournedos	thick slices of fillet
tripes	tripe
veau	veal
venaison	venison
viande	meat
volaille	poultry

Fish & Seafood

| anchois | anchovy |
| anguille | eel |

brème	bream	*betterave*	beetroot
brochet	pike	*cannelle*	cinnamon
cabillaud	cod	*carotte*	carrot
calmar	squid	*céleri*	celery
carrelet	plaice	*cèpe*	cepe (boletus mushroom)
chaudrée	fish stew		
colin	hake	*champignon*	mushroom
coquille Saint-Jacques	scallop	*champignon de Paris*	button mushroom
crabe	crab	*chou*	cabbage
crevette grise	shrimp	*citrouille*	pumpkin
crevette rose	prawn	*concombre*	cucumber
écrevisse	small, freshwater crayfish	*cornichon*	gherkin (pickle)
		courgette	courgette (zucchini)
fruits de mer	seafood	*crudités*	small pieces of raw vegetables
gambas	king prawns		
goujon	gudgeon (small fresh water fish)	*échalotte*	shallot
		épice	spice
hareng	herring	*épinards*	spinach
homard	lobster	*estragon*	tarragon
huître	oyster	*fenouil*	fennel
langouste	crayfish	*fève*	broad bean
langoustine	very small saltwater 'lobster'; (Dublin Bay prawn)	*genièvre*	juniper
		gingembre	ginger
		haricots	beans
maquereau	mackerel	*haricots blancs*	white beans
merlan	whiting	*haricots rouge*	kidney beans
morue	cod	*haricots verts*	French (string) beans
moules	mussels	*herbe*	herb
oursin	sea urchin	*laitue*	lettuce
palourde	clam	*légume*	vegetable
poisson	fish	*lentilles*	lentils
raie	ray	*maïs*	sweet corn
rouget	mullet	*menthe*	mint
sardine	sardine	*navet*	turnip
saumon	salmon	*oignon*	onion
sole	sole	*olive*	olive
thon	tuna	*origan*	oregano
truite	trout	*panais*	parsnip
		persil	parsley
		petit pois	pea

Vegetables, Herbs & Spices

ail	garlic	*poireau*	leek
aïoli or *ailloli*	garlic mayonnaise	*poivron*	green pepper
aneth	dill	*pomme de terre*	potato
anis	aniseed	*ratatouille*	casserole of aubergines, tomatoes, peppers and garlic
artichaut	artichoke		
asperge	asparagus		
aubergine	aubergine (eggplant)	*riz*	rice
avocat	avocado	*salade*	salad or lettuce
basilic	basil	*sarrasin*	buckwheat

seigle	rye
tomate	tomato
truffe	truffle

Fruit & Nuts

abricot	apricot
amande	almond
ananas	pineapple
arachide	peanut
banane	banana
cacahuète	peanut
cassis	blackcurrant
cerise	cherry
citron	lemon
datte	date
figue	fig
fraise	strawberry
framboise	raspberry
grenade	pomegranate
groseille	red currant/gooseberry
mangue	mango
marron	chestnut
melon	melon
mirabelle	type of plum
myrtille	bilberry (blueberry)
noisette	hazelnut
noix de cajou	cashew
orange	orange
pamplemousse	grapefruit
pastèque	watermelon
pêche	peach
pistache	pistachio
poire	pear
pomme	apple
prune	plum
pruneau	prune
raisin	grape

Cooking Methods

à la broche	spit-roasted
à la vapeur	steamed
au feu de bois	cooked over a wood-burning stove
au four	baked
en croûte	in pastry
farci	stuffed
fumé	smoked
gratiné	browned on top with cheese
grillé	grilled

pané	coated in breadcrumbs
rôti	roasted
sauté	sautéed (shallow fried)

Starters (Appetisers)

assiette anglaise – plate of cold mixed meats and sausages

assiette de crudités – plate of raw vegetables with dressings

entrée – starter

fromage de tête – pâté made with pig's head set in jelly

soufflé – a light, fluffy dish made with egg yolks, stiffly beaten egg whites, flour and cheese or other ingredients

Soup

bouillabaisse – Mediterranean-style fish soup, originally from Marseille, made with several kinds of fish, including *rascasse* (spiny scorpion fish); often eaten as a main course

bouillon – broth or stock

bourride – fish stew; often eaten as a main course

croûtons – fried or roasted bread cubes, often added to soups

potage – thick soup made with puréed vegetables

soupe au pistou – vegetable soup made with a basil and garlic paste

soupe de poisson – fish soup

soupe du jour – soup of the day

Common Meat & Poultry Dishes

blanquette de veau or *d'agneau* – veal or lamb stew with white sauce

bœuf bourguignon – beef and vegetable stew cooked in a red wine (usually burgundy)

cassoulet – Languedoc stew made with goose, duck, pork or lamb fillets and haricot beans

chapon – capon

chou farci – stuffed cabbage

choucroute – sauerkraut with sausage and other prepared meats

confit de canard or *d'oie* – duck or goose preserved and cooked in its own fat

coq au vin – chicken cooked in wine

civet – game stew

fricassée – stew with meat that has first been fried

grillade – grilled meats

marcassin – young wild boar

quenelles – dumplings made of a finely sieved mixture of cooked fish or (rarely) meat

steak tartare – raw ground meat mixed with onion, raw egg yolk and herbs

Ordering a Steak

bleu – nearly raw

saignant – very rare (literally, 'bleeding')

à point – medium rare but still pink

bien cuit – literally, 'well cooked', but usually like medium rare

Sauces & Accompaniments

béchamel – basic white sauce

huile d'olive – olive oil

mornay – cheese sauce

moutarde – mustard

pistou – pesto (pounded mix of basil, hard cheese, olive oil and garlic)

provençale – tomato, garlic, herb and olive oil dressing or sauce

tartare – mayonnaise with herbs

vinaigrette – salad dressing made with oil, vinegar, mustard and garlic

Desserts & Sweets

crêpe – thin pancake

crêpes suzettes – orange-flavoured crêpes flambéed in liqueur

bergamotes – orange-flavoured confectionary

dragée – sugared almond

éclair – pastry filled with cream

far – flan with prunes (a Breton speciality)

flan – egg-custard dessert

frangipane – pastry filled with cream and flavoured with almonds or a cake mixture containing ground almonds

galette – wholemeal or buckwheat pancake; also a type of biscuit

gâteau – cake

gaufre – waffle

gelée – jelly

glace – ice cream

glace au chocolat – chocolate ice cream

île flottante – literally 'floating island'; beaten egg white lightly cooked, floating on a creamy sauce

macarons – macaroons (sweet biscuit made from ground almonds, sugar and egg whites)

sablé – shortbread biscuit

farine de semoule – semolina flour

tarte – tart (pie)

tarte aux pommes – apple tart

yaourt – yoghurt

Snacks

croque-monsieur – a grilled ham and cheese sandwich

croque-madame – a croque-monsieur with a fried egg

frites – chips (French fries)

quiche – quiche; savoury egg, bacon and cream tart

Glossary

Refer to the boxed text 'The Basque Language' in The French Basque Country & Béarn chapter for some Basque words and phrases.

(m) indicates masculine gender, (f) feminine gender and (pl) plural

accueil (m) – reception; welcome
alimentation (f) – grocery shop
aller-retour – round trip (return)
aller-simple or **aller** – one way (single)
AOC (f) – *appellation d'origine contrôlée*; a system of strict definition and control of quality wines and spirits
appellation – wine-producing area
arrondissement (m) – administrative division of a *département*
auberge (f) – inn (generally family-run)
auberge de jeunesse (f) – youth hostel

barrage (m) – dam
base/parc de loisirs (m) – leisure centre with outdoor activities
bastide (f) – fortified 'new town' built between the 13th and 14th centuries, usually on a grid surrounding an arcaded square
billet (m) – ticket
billeterie (f) – ticket office or counter
bodega (f) – literally 'cellar'; a Spanish-style bar serving wine from the barrel
boisson (f) – drink
bordereau de détaxe (m) – export sales invoice
boulangerie (f) – bakery, bread shop
boules (f pl) – a game, not unlike lawn bowls, played with heavy metal balls on a sandy pitch; also called *pétanque*
bourse (f) – stock exchange
BP (f) – *boîte postale*; post office box
brasserie (f) – a restaurant, usually serving food all day
brocante (f) – second-hand item or bric-a-brac

camping à la ferme (m) – camping on the farm

canton (m) – parish
carnet (m) – a book of bus, tram or metro tickets sold at a reduced rate
carrefour (m) – crossroads
carte (f) – card; menu; map
causse (m) – limestone plateau
cave (f) or **chai** (m) – wine cellar or above-ground storage area for fermentation casks
CDT (m) – *comité départemental du tourisme;* départemental tourism bureau
centre (de) hospitalier (m) – hospital
chambre (f) – room
chambre d'hôte (f) – B&B
charcuterie (f) – pork butcher's shop and delicatessen
col (m) – mountain pass
commissariat (m) – police station
commune (f) – district, parish
composteur (m) – ticket-punching machine
conseil général (m) – local council
conseil régional (m) – regional council
consigne (f) – left-luggage office
consigne automatique (f) – left-luggage locker
couchette (f) – sleeping berth on a train or ferry
courses landaises (m pl) – 'running of the bulls', during which cows are taunted, chased and dodged in an arena
cuisine du terroir (f) – country cooking

DAB – *distributeurs automatiques de billets*; automated teller machine (ATM)
dégustation (f) – tasting
demi-pension (f) – half-board (B&B with either lunch or dinner)
demi-tarif (m) – half-price
département (m) – department of a région, with its own local council
domaine (m) – estate, property
douane (f) – Customs

église (f) – church
enveloppe prétimbrée (f) – aerogramme
épicerie (f) – small grocery shop
équitation (f) – horse riding

escalade (f) – rock-climbing

fermes auberges – farm restaurants that offer home-cooked local cuisine
fête (f) – festival
fête patronale (f) – saint's day
forêt (f) – forest
forfait (m) – package camping rate for two people plus car and tent/caravan
formule or **formule rapide** (f) – like a *menu*, but with a choice of two out of three courses (eg starter and main course or main course and dessert)
foyer (m) – workers' or students' hostel
fromagerie (f) – cheese shop
fronton (m) – a one-walled court used for pelote basque, usually outdoors

gabarre (f) – flat-bottomed river boat used to transport wine
gare or **gare SNCF** (f) – railway station
gare routière (f) – bus station
gave (f) – river (Béarnaise)
gendarmerie (f) – police station; police force
gîte (m) – cottage
gîte d'étape (m) – simple accommodation for hikers or pilgrims
gîte rural (m) – country cottage
GR (f) – *grande randonnée*; long-distance hiking trail

halles (f pl) – covered food market
halte routière (f) – bus stop
hébergement chez l'habitant (m) or **hôtes payants** (m pl) – homestay
horaire (m) – timetable
hôtes payants (m pl) home-stay
hôtel de ville (m) – city or town hall
hôtel particulier (m) – town house, typically of a wealthy merchant

jardin (m) – garden, park
jour férié (m pl) – public holiday

lac (m) – lake
Langue d'Oc (f) – the medieval language of southern France, also called Occitan
laverie (f) or **lavomatique** (m) – laundrette
lits jumeaux (m pl) – twin beds

location (f) – rental
maire (m) – mayor
mairie (f) – town or village hall
maison de la presse (f) – newsagent
marché (m) – market
marché couvert (m) – covered market
menu (m) – fixed-price meal with two or more courses
menu campagnard (m) – country meal
menu du pêcheur (m) – fisherman's menu
meublé (m) – furnished accommodation
musée (m) – museum

navette (f) – shuttle bus, train or boat
nom de famille (m) – surname, family name
numéro vert (m pl) – toll-free telephone number

Occitan – see *Langue d'Oc*
office de tourisme – tourist office run by local government

parapente (f) – parasailing
parc (m) – park
parlement (m) – parliament or local court of law
pâtisserie (f) – pastry shop
pelote basque (f) – generic name for Basque court games using racquets and a hard, rubber-core ball (*pilota* in Basque)
pétanque (f) – see *boules*
piste cyclable (f) – bicycle path
place (f) – square
plage (f) – beach
plan (m) – city map
planche à voile (f) – windsurfing
plat du jour (m) – daily special in a restaurant
plat principal (m) – main course
plongée (f) – diving
point d'argent – automated teller machine (ATM)
pont (m) – bridge
port de plaisance (m) – marina or harbour for pleasure-boats
porte (f) – gate in a city wall
pourboire (m) – tip

préfecture (f) – prefecture, capital of a
département
prénom (m) – first name
pression (f) – draught beer
produce du terroir (m) – local produce

quai (m) – quay; railway platform
quartier (m) – quarter, district

randonnées pédestres (f pl) – hikes;
hiking
refuge (m) – mountain hut, basic shelter
for hikers
région (f) – the largest French administrative division
riverain (m) – local resident
routier (m) – trucker; truckers' restaurant

sentier (m) – trail, footpath
SNCF – Société Nationale des Chemins de
Fer; state-owned railway company
sortie (f) – exit
sous-préfecture (f pl) – sub-prefecture
spéléologie (f) – caving
supplément (m) – supplement, additional
cost
syndicat d'initiative (m) – tourist office
founded by local merchants

tabac (m) – tobacconist (also sells bus
tickets, phonecards etc)

table d'hôte (f) – meals in a private house
tapas (f pl) – Spanish-style snacks, traditionally served at a *bodega* or other bar
tarif réduit (m) – reduced price
taxe de séjour (f) – municipal tourist tax
télécarte (f) – phonecard
téléférique (m) – cable car
temple (m) – protestant church
terroir (m) – land, soil, earth (eg see
cuisine du terroir)
TGV (m) – *train à grande vitesse*; high-
speed train
timbre (m pl) – stamp
tour (f) – tower
tour d'horloge (f) – clock tower
troubadour (m) – medieval poet-musician

ULM (m) – *ultraléger motorisé;* microlight
aircraft

vente en détaxe (f) – duty-free sales
v.f. (f) – *version française;* refers to a film
dubbed in French
vieille ville (f) – old town/city
vin de pays – local wine
v.o. (f) – *version originale;* refers to a nondubbed film with French subtitles
voile (f) – sail; sailing
vol (m) – theft; flight
vol à voile (m) – gliding
VTT (m pl) – *vélo touts terrain;* mountain
bike

LONELY PLANET

Phrasebooks

Lonely Planet phrasebooks are packed with essential words and phrases to help travellers communicate with the locals. With colour tabs for quick reference, an extensive vocabulary and use of script, these handy pocket-sized language guides cover day-to-day travel situations.

- handy pocket-sized books
- easy to understand Pronunciation chapter
- clear & comprehensive Grammar chapter
- romanisation alongside script to allow ease of pronunciation
- script throughout so users can point to phrases for every situation
- full of cultural information and tips for the traveller

'...vital for a real DIY spirit and attitude in language learning'
– Backpacker

'the phrasebooks have good cultural backgrounders and offer solid advice for challenging situations in remote locations'
– San Francisco Examiner

Arabic (Egyptian) • Arabic (Moroccan) • Australian *(Australian English, Aboriginal and Torres Strait languages)* • Baltic States *(Estonian, Latvian, Lithuanian)* • Bengali • Brazilian • British • Burmese • Cantonese • Central Asia • Central Europe *(Czech, French, German, Hungarian, Italian, Slovak)* • Eastern Europe *(Bulgarian, Czech, Hungarian, Polish, Romanian, Slovak)* • Ethiopian (Amharic) • Fijian • French • German • Greek • Hebrew phrasebook • Hill Tribes • Hindi/Urdu • Indonesian • Italian • Japanese • Korean • Lao • Latin American Spanish • Malay • Mandarin • Mediterranean Europe *(Albanian, Croatian, Greek, Italian, Macedonian, Maltese, Serbian, Slovene)* • Mongolian • Nepali • Pidgin • Pilipino (Tagalog) • Quechua • Russian • Scandinavian Europe *(Danish, Finnish, Icelandic, Norwegian, Swedish)* • South-East Asia *(Burmese, Indonesian, Khmer, Lao, Malay, Tagalog Pilipino, Thai, Vietnamese)* • South Pacific Languages • Spanish (Castilian) *(also includes Catalan, Galician and Basque)* • Sri Lanka • Swahili • Thai • Tibetan • Turkish • Ukrainian • USA *(US English, Vernacular, Native American languages, Hawaiian)* • Vietnamese • Western Europe *(Basque, Catalan, Dutch, French, German, Greek, Irish)*

Lonely Planet Journeys

JOURNEYS is a unique collection of travel writing – published by the company that understands travel better than anyone else. It is a series for anyone who has ever experienced – or dreamed of – the magical moment when they encountered a strange culture or saw a place for the first time. They are tales to read while you're planning a trip, while you're on the road or while you're in an armchair, in front of a fire.

These outstanding titles explore our planet through the eyes of a diverse group of international writers. JOURNEYS books catch the spirit of a place, illuminate a culture, recount a crazy adventure, or introduce a fascinating way of life. They always entertain, and always enrich the experience of travel.

MALI BLUES
Traveling to an African Beat
Lieve Joris (translated by Sam Garrett)

Drought, rebel uprisings, ethnic conflict: these are the predominant images of West Africa. But as Lieve Joris travels in Senegal, Mauritania and Mali, she meets survivors, fascinating individuals charting new ways of living between tradition and modernity. With her remarkable gift for drawing out people's stories, Joris brilliantly captures the rhythms of a world that refuses to give in.

THE GATES OF DAMASCUS
Lieve Joris (translated by Sam Garrett)

This best-selling book is a beautifully drawn portrait of day-to-day life in modern Syria. Through her intimate contact with local people, Lieve Joris draws us into the fascinating world that lies behind the gates of Damascus. Hala's husband is a political prisoner, jailed for his opposition to the Assad regime; through the author's friendship with Hala we see how Syrian politics impacts on the lives of ordinary people.

THE OLIVE GROVE
Travels in Greece
Katherine Kizilos

Katherine Kizilos travels to fabled islands, troubled border zones and her family's village deep in the mountains. She vividly evokes breathtaking landscapes, generous people and passionate politics, capturing the complexities of a country she loves.

'beautifully captures the real tensions of Greece' – *Sunday Times*

KINGDOM OF THE FILM STARS
Journey into Jordan
Annie Caulfield

Kingdom of the Film Stars is a travel book and a love story. With honesty and humour, Annie Caulfield writes of travelling in Jordan and falling in love with a Bedouin with film-star looks.

She offers fascinating insights into the country – from the tent life of traditional women to the hustle of downtown Amman – and unpicks tight-woven Western myths about the Arab world.

LONELY PLANET

Lonely Planet Travel Atlases

L onely Planet has long been famous for the number and quality of its guidebook maps. Now we've gone one step further and produced a handy companion series: Lonely Planet travel atlases – maps of a country produced in book form.

Unlike other maps, which look good but lead travellers astray, our travel atlases have been researched on the road by Lonely Planet's experienced team of writers. All details are carefully checked to ensure the atlas corresponds with the equivalent Lonely Planet guidebook.

- full-colour throughout
- maps researched and checked by Lonely Planet authors
- place names correspond with Lonely Planet guidebooks
- no confusing spelling differences
- legend and travelling information in English, French, German, Japanese and Spanish
- size: 230 x 160 mm

Available now: Chile & Easter Island • Egypt • India & Bangladesh • Israel & the Palestinian Territories • Jordan, Syria & Lebanon • Kenya • Laos • Portugal • South Africa, Lesotho & Swaziland • Thailand • Turkey • Vietnam • Zimbabwe, Botswana & Namibia

Lonely Planet TV Series & Videos

L onely Planet travel guides have been brought to life on television screens around the world. Like our guides, the programs are based on the joy of independent travel, and look honestly at some of the most exciting, picturesque and frustrating places in the world. Each show is presented by one of three travellers from Australia, England or the USA and combines an innovative mixture of video, Super-8 film, atmospheric soundscapes and original music.

Videos of each episode – containing additional footage not shown on television – are available from good book and video shops, but the availability of individual videos varies with regional screening schedules.

Video destinations include: Alaska • American Rockies • Argentina • Australia – The South-East • Baja California & the Copper Canyon • Brazil • Central Asia • Chile & Easter Island • Corsica, Sicily & Sardinia – The Mediterranean Islands • East Africa (Tanzania & Zanzibar) • Cuba • Ecuador & the Galapagos Islands • Ethiopia • Greenland & Iceland • Hungary & Romania • Indonesia • Israel & the Sinai Desert • Jamaica • Japan • La Ruta Maya • The Middle East (Syria, Jordan & Lebanon • Morocco • New York • Northern Spain • North India • Outback Australia • Pacific Islands (Fiji, Solomon Islands & Vanuatu) • Pakistan • Peru • The Philippines • South Africa & Lesotho • South India • South West China • South West USA • Trekking in Uganda • Turkey • Vietnam • West Africa • Zimbabwe, Botswana & Namibia

The Lonely Planet TV series is produced by: Pilot Productions
The Old Studio
18 Middle Row
London W10 5AT, UK

LONELY PLANET

Lonely Planet On-line

Whether you've just begun planning your next trip, or you're chasing down specific info on currency regulations or visa requirements, check out Lonely Planet On-line for up-to-the minute travel information.

As well as mini guides to more than 250 destinations, you'll find maps, photos, travel news, health and visa updates, travel advisories, and discussion of the ecological and political issues you need to be aware of as you travel. You'll also find timely upgrades to popular guidebooks which you can print out and stick in the back of your book.

There's also an on-line travellers' forum where you can share your experience of life on the road, meet travel companions and ask other travellers for their recommendations and advice.

And of course we have a complete and up-to-date list of all Lonely Planet travel products including travel guides, diving and snorkeling guides, phrasebooks, atlases, travel literature and videos, and a simple on-line ordering facility if you can't find the book you want elsewhere.

Lonely Planet Diving & Snorkeling Guides

Beautifully illustrated with full-colour photos throughout, Lonely Planet's Pisces Books explore the world's best diving and snorkelling areas and prepare divers for what to expect when they get there, both topside and underwater.

Dive sites are described in detail with specifics on depths, visibility, level of difficulty, special conditions, underwater photography tips, and common and unusual marine life present. You'll also find practical logistical information and coverage on topside activities and attractions, sections on diving health and safety, plus listings for diving services, live-aboards, dive resorts and tourist offices.

LONELY PLANET

Guides by Region

L onely Planet is known worldwide for publishing practical, reliable and no-nonsense travel information in our guides and on our Web site. The Lonely Planet list covers just about every accessible part of the world. Currently there are thirteen series: travel guides, shoestring guides, walking guides, city guides, phrasebooks, audio packs, city maps, travel atlases, diving and snorkeling guides, restaurant guides, first-time travel guides, healthy travel and travel literature.

AFRICA Africa – the South ● Africa on a shoestring ● Arabic (Egyptian) phrasebook ● Arabic (Moroccan) phrasebook ● Cairo ● Cape Town ● Cape Town city map ● Central Africa ● East Africa ● Egypt ● Egypt travel atlas ● Ethiopian (Amharic) phrasebook ● The Gambia & Senegal ● Healthy Travel Africa ● Kenya ● Kenya travel atlas ● Malawi, Mozambique & Zambia ● Morocco ● North Africa ● South Africa, Lesotho & Swaziland ● South Africa, Lesotho & Swaziland travel atlas ● Swahili phrasebook ● Tanzania, Zanzibar & Pemba ● Trekking in East Africa ● Tunisia ● West Africa ● Zimbabwe, Botswana & Namibia ● Zimbabwe, Botswana & Namibia travel atlas
Travel Literature: The Rainbird: A Central African Journey ● Songs to an African Sunset: A Zimbabwean Story ● Mali Blues: Traveling to an African Beat

AUSTRALIA & THE PACIFIC Auckland ● Australia ● Australian phrasebook ● Bushwalking in Australia ● Bushwalking in Papua New Guinea ● Fiji ● Fijian phrasebook ● Islands of Australia's Great Barrier Reef ● Melbourne ● Melbourne city map ● Micronesia ● New Caledonia ● New South Wales & the ACT ● New Zealand ● Northern Territory ● Outback Australia ● Out To Eat – Melbourne ● Papua New Guinea ● Papua New Guinea (Pidgin) phrasebook ● Queensland ● Rarotonga & the Cook Islands ● Samoa ● Solomon Islands ● South Australia ● South Pacific Languages phrasebook ● Sydney ● Sydney city map ● Tahiti & French Polynesia ● Tasmania ● Tonga ● Tramping in New Zealand ● Vanuatu ● Victoria ● Western Australia
Travel Literature: Islands in the Clouds ● Kiwi Tracks ● Sean & David's Long Drive

CENTRAL AMERICA & THE CARIBBEAN Bahamas, Turks & Caicos ● Bermuda ● Central America on a shoestring ● Costa Rica ● Cuba ● Dominican Republic & Haiti ● Eastern Caribbean ● Guatemala, Belize & Yucatán: La Ruta Maya ● Jamaica ● Mexico ● Mexico City ● Panama ● Puerto Rico
Travel Literature: Green Dreams: Travels in Central America

EUROPE Amsterdam ● Amsterdam city map ● Andalucía ● Austria ● Baltic States phrasebook ● Barcelona ● Berlin ● Berlin city map ● Britain ● British phrasebook ● Brussels, Bruges & Antwerp ● Budapest city map ● Canary Islands ● Central Europe ● Central Europe phrasebook ● Corsica ● Croatia ● Czech & Slovak Republics ● Denmark ● Dublin ● Eastern Europe ● Eastern Europe phrasebook ● Edinburgh ● Estonia, Latvia & Lithuania ● Europe ● Finland ● France ● French phrasebook ● Germany ● German phrasebook ● Greece ● Greek phrasebook ● Hungary ● Iceland, Greenland & the Faroe Islands ● Ireland ● Italian phrasebook ● Italy ● Lisbon ● London ● London city map ● Mediterranean Europe ● Mediterranean Europe phrasebook ● Norway ● Paris ● Paris city map ● Poland ● Portugal ● Portugal travel atlas ● Prague ● Prague city map ● Provence & the Côte d'Azur ● Romania & Moldova ● Rome ● Russia, Ukraine & Belarus ● Russian phrasebook ● Scandinavian & Baltic Europe ● Scandinavian Europe phrasebook ● Scotland ● Slovenia ● Spain ● Spanish phrasebook ● St Petersburg ● Switzerland ● Trekking in Spain ● Ukrainian phrasebook ● Vienna ● Walking in Britain ● Walking in Ireland ● Walking in Italy ● Walking in Switzerland ● Western Europe ● Western Europe phrasebook
Travel Literature: The Olive Grove: Travels in Greece

INDIAN SUBCONTINENT Bangladesh ● Bengali phrasebook ● Bhutan ● Delhi ● Goa ● Hindi/Urdu phrasebook ● India ● India & Bangladesh travel atlas ● Indian Himalaya ● Karakoram Highway ● Kerala ● Mumbai ● Nepal ● Nepali phrasebook ● Pakistan ● Rajasthan ● Read This First: Asia & India ● South India ● Sri Lanka ● Sri Lanka phrasebook ● Trekking in the Indian Himalaya ● Trekking in the Karakoram & Hindukush ● Trekking in the Nepal Himalaya
Travel Literature: In Rajasthan ● Shopping for Buddhas

LONELY PLANET

Mail Order

onely Planet products are distributed worldwide. They are also available by mail order from Lonely Planet, so if you have difficulty finding a title please write to us. North and South American residents should write to 150 Linden St, Oakland, CA 94607, USA; European and African residents should write to 10a Spring Place, London NW5 3BH, UK; and residents of other countries to PO Box 617, Hawthorn, Victoria 3122, Australia.

ISLANDS OF THE INDIAN OCEAN Madagascar & Comoros • Maldives • Mauritius, Réunion & Seychelles

MIDDLE EAST & CENTRAL ASIA Arab Gulf States • Central Asia • Central Asia phrasebook • Hebrew phrasebook • Iran • Israel & the Palestinian Territories • Israel & the Palestinian Territories travel atlas • Istanbul • Istanbul to Cairo • Jerusalem • Jordan & Syria • Jordan, Syria & Lebanon travel atlas • Lebanon • Middle East on a shoestring • Syria • Turkey • Turkish phrasebook • Turkey travel atlas • Yemen
Travel Literature: The Gates of Damascus • Kingdom of the Film Stars: Journey into Jordan

NORTH AMERICA Alaska • Backpacking in Alaska • Baja California • California & Nevada • Canada • Chicago • Chicago city map • Deep South • Florida • Hawaii • Honolulu • Las Vegas • Los Angeles • Miami • New England • New Orleans • New York City • New York city map • New York, New Jersey & Pennsylvania • Pacific Northwest USA • Puerto Rico • Rocky Mountain States • San Francisco • San Francisco city map • Seattle • Southwest USA • Texas • USA • USA phrasebook • Vancouver • Washington, DC & the Capital Region • Washington DC city map
Travel Literature: Drive Thru America

NORTH-EAST ASIA Beijing • Cantonese phrasebook • China • Hong Kong • Hong Kong city map • Hong Kong, Macau & Guangzhou • Japan • Japanese phrasebook • Japanese audio pack • Korea • Korean phrasebook • Kyoto • Mandarin phrasebook • Mongolia • Mongolian phrasebook • North-East Asia on a shoestring • Seoul • South-West China • Taiwan • Tibet • Tibetan phrasebook • Tokyo
Travel Literature: Lost Japan

SOUTH AMERICA Argentina, Uruguay & Paraguay • Bolivia • Brazil • Brazilian phrasebook • Buenos Aires • Chile & Easter Island • Chile & Easter Island travel atlas • Colombia • Ecuador & the Galapagos Islands • Latin American Spanish phrasebook • Peru • Quechua phrasebook • Rio de Janeiro • Rio de Janeiro city map • South America on a shoestring • Trekking in the Patagonian Andes • Venezuela
Travel Literature: Full Circle: A South American Journey

SOUTH-EAST ASIA Bali & Lombok • Bangkok • Bangkok city map • Burmese phrasebook • Cambodia • Hanoi • Healthy Travel Asia & India • Hill Tribes phrasebook • Ho Chi Minh City • Indonesia • Indonesia's Eastern Islands • Indonesian phrasebook • Indonesian audio pack • Jakarta • Java • Laos • Lao phrasebook • Laos travel atlas • Malay phrasebook • Malaysia, Singapore & Brunei • Myanmar (Burma) • Philippines • Pilipino (Tagalog) phrasebook • Singapore • South-East Asia on a shoestring • South-East Asia phrasebook • Thailand • Thailand's Islands & Beaches • Thailand travel atlas • Thai phrasebook • Thai audio pack • Vietnam • Vietnamese phrasebook • Vietnam travel atlas

ALSO AVAILABLE: Antarctica • The Arctic • Brief Encounters: Stories of Love, Sex & Travel • Chasing Rickshaws • Lonely Planet Unpacked • Not the Only Planet: Travel Stories from Science Fiction • Sacred India • Travel with Children • Traveller's Tales

LONELY PLANET

FREE Lonely Planet Newsletters

We love hearing from you and think you'd like to hear from us.

Planet Talk

Our FREE quarterly printed newsletter is full of tips from travellers and anecdotes from Lonely Planet guidebook authors. Every issue is packed with up-to-date travel news and advice, and includes:

- a postcard from Lonely Planet co-founder Tony Wheeler
- a swag of mail from travellers
- a look at life on the road through the eyes of a Lonely Planet author
- topical health advice
- prizes for the best travel yarn
- news about forthcoming Lonely Planet events
- a complete list of Lonely Planet books and other titles

To join our mailing list, residents of the UK, Europe and Africa can email us at go@lonelyplanet.co.uk; residents of North and South America can email us at info@lonelyplanet.com; the rest of the world can email us at talk2us@lonelyplanet.com.au, or contact any Lonely Planet office.

Comet

Our FREE monthly email newsletter brings you all the latest travel news, features, interviews, competitions, destination ideas, travellers' tips & tales, Q&As, raging debates and related links. Find out what's new on the Lonely Planet Web site and which books are about to hit the shelves.

Subscribe from your desktop: www.lonelyplanet.com/comet

Index

Text

Carennac 223–4

Bold indicates maps.

Boxed Text

MAP LEGEND

BOUNDARIES

............International
............State
............Disputed

HYDROGRAPHY

............Coastline
............River, Creek
............Lake
............Intermittent Lake
............Salt Lake
............Canal
⊚ ⇢⟶ ....Spring, Rapids
⇥⟶ ....Waterfalls
............Swamp

ROUTES & TRANSPORT

............Freeway
............Highway
............Major Road
............Minor Road
============Unsealed Road
............City Freeway
............City Highway
............City Road
............City Street, Lane

AREA FEATURES

............Building
❄ ....Park, Gardens
............Cemetery

............Pedestrian Mall
⇥⟶====:............Tunnel
├─┼─┼─●─┼─...Train Route & Station
━━Ⓜ━━............Metro & Station
............Tramway
╫─╫─╫─╫─╫...Cable Car or Chairlift
── ── ── ──............Walking Track
. . . .Walking Tour
── ── ── ──............Ferry Route

............Market
............Beach, Desert
............Urban Area

MAP SYMBOLS

✪	**CAPITAL**	National Capital	✈		............Airport
⊚	**CAPITAL**	State Capital	∿		...Ancient or City Wall
●	**CITY**	City	∴		......Archaeological Site
●	**Town**	Town	❸		............Bank
•	**Village**	Village	🀫		............Beach
○		Point of Interest	⍦		............Bird Sanctuary
			⌒		............Cave
■		Place to Stay	🏥 🛉		............Church
⛺		Camping Ground	⌒⌒⌒		Cliff or Escarpment
⚏		Caravan Park	◐		............Embassy
⌂		Hut or Chalet	⊕		............Hospital
			🏮		............Lighthouse
▼		Place to Eat	▲		............Monument
♟		Pub or Bar	▲ ∿		......Mountain or Range

............Museum
🅿 ....Parking
)(............Pass
★ ....Police Station
✉ ....Post Office
← ....One Way Street
🅿 ....Petrol Station
🏛 ....Stately Home
🏄 ....Surf Beach
🏊 ....Swimming Pool
☪ ....Synagogue
🚻 ....Toilet
❶ ....Tourist Information
◒ ....Transport

Note: not all symbols displayed above appear in this book

LONELY PLANET OFFICES

Australia
PO Box 617, Hawthorn, Victoria 3122
☎ 03 9819 1877 fax 03 9819 6459
email: talk2us@lonelyplanet.com.au

UK
10a Spring Place, London NW5 3BH
☎ 020 7428 4800 fax 020 7428 4828
email: go@lonelyplanet.co.uk

USA
150 Linden St, Oakland, CA 94607
☎ 510 893 8555 TOLL FREE: 800 275 8555
fax 510 893 8572
email: info@lonelyplanet.com

France
1 rue du Dahomey, 75011 Paris
☎ 01 55 25 33 00 fax 01 55 25 33 01
email: bip@lonelyplanet.fr
www.lonelyplanet.fr

World Wide Web: www.lonelyplanet.com *or* AOL keyword: lp
Lonely Planet Images: lpi@lonelyplanet.com.au